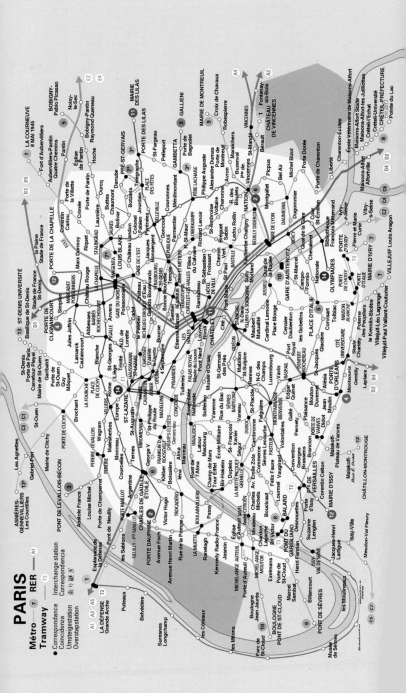

PARIS

Métro — 7 — RER — A1

Tramway — T3

● Correspondance
  Coincidenza
  Umsteigestation
  乗り継ぎ駅

◯ Interchange station
  Correspondencia

THEGREENGUIDE
Northern France
and the Paris Region

Cathédrale at Chartres/© Raga Jose Fuste/age fotostock

THEGREENGUIDE **NORTHERN FRANCE AND THE PARIS REGION**

Editorial Director	Cynthia Clayton Ochterbeck
Produced & Edited by	Jonathan P. Gilbert, Azalay Media
Principal Writers	Steven Durose
Production Manager	Natasha G. George
Cartography	Peter Wrenn
Photo Researcher	Sean Sachon
Interior Design	Chris Bell
Layout	Natasha G. George, Jonathan P. Gilbert
Cover Design	Chris Bell, Christelle Le Déan
Cover Layout	Michelin Travel Partner, Natasha G. George

Contact Us	Michelin Travel and Lifestyle North America
	One Parkway South
	Greenville, SC 29615
	USA
	travel.lifestyle@us.michelin.com
	www.michelintravel.com
	Michelin Travel Partner
	Hannay House
	39 Clarendon Road
	Watford, Herts WD17 1JA
	UK
	℘01923 205240
	travelpubsales@uk.michelin.com
	www.ViaMichelin.com
Special Sales	For information regarding bulk sales,
	customized editions and premium sales,
	please contact us at:
	travel.lifestyle@us.michelin.com
	www.michelintravel.com

HOW TO USE THIS GUIDE

PLANNING YOUR TRIP

The blue-tabbed PLANNING YOUR TRIP section at the front of the guide gives you **ideas for your trip** and **practical information** to help you organise it. You'll find tours, practical information, a host of outdoor activities, a calendar of events, information on shopping, sightseeing, kids' activities and more.

INTRODUCTION

The orange-tabbed INTRODUCTION section explores the **Nature** and geology of the Northern France and Paris region. The **History** section spans the Celts through to today. The **Art and Culture** section covers architecture, art, literature and music, while **The Region Today** delves into contemporary culture, population and the economy of the area.

DISCOVERING

The green-tabbed DISCOVERING section features Principal Sights by region, featuring the most interesting local **Sights**, **Walking Tours**, nearby **Excursions** and detailed **Driving Tours**. Admission prices shown are normally for a single adult.

ADDRESSES

We've selected the best hotels, restaurants, cafés, shops, nightlife and entertainment to fit all budgets. See the Legend on the cover flap for an explanation of the price categories. See the back of the guide for an index of where to find hotels and restaurants.

Sidebars

Throughout the guide you will find blue, orange and green-coloured text boxes with lively anecdotes, detailed history and background information.

😊 A Bit of Advice 😊

Green advice boxes found in this guide contain practical tips and handy information relevant to your visit or to a sight in the Discovering section.

STAR RATINGS★★★

Michelin has given star ratings for more than 100 years. If you're pressed for time, we recommend you visit the ★★★, or ★★ sights first:

★★★   **Highly recommended**
★★   **Recommended**
★   **Interesting**

MAPS

  Principal Sights map
  Region maps
  Maps for major cities and villages
  Local tour maps

All maps in this guide are oriented north, unless otherwise indicated by a directional arrow. The term "Local Map" refers to a map within the chapter or Tourism Region. A complete list of the maps found in the guide appears at the back of this book.

© Lourmel-Chicurel/Château de Vaux-le-Vicomte

PLANNING YOUR TRIP

© Jesús Nicolás Sánchez/agefotostock

INTRODUCTION TO NORTHERN FRANCE AND PARIS

DISCOVERING PARIS AND ÎLE-DE-FRANCE

CONTENTS

Welcome to Northern France and the Paris Region

Whether you prefer the urban villages of Paris or the rural hamlets of Picardy, the variety of this region is hard to beat, from the estuaries, beaches and dunes of the north and the forests and marshland of its leafy heartland, to the valleys, castles and cities of the south and west.

Paris: Pont Alexandre III over the River Seine

PARIS (pp108–141)

Set on the banks of the River Seine and its myriad bridges, Paris grew from an ordinary Gallo-Roman oppidum into a major centre of political, cultural and artistic life. Busy day and night, the French capital is a great place to soak up the urban buzz, while enjoying a café crème with a fresh croissant at a lively café. Other must-dos include getting lost in the narrow streets of the trendy Marais neighbourhood; exploring the Louvre, one of the most impressive art museums in the world and its impressionist neighbour the Musée D'Orsay; and tracing the history of the city from the outstanding Notre-Dame Cathedral to Saint-Denis Basilica, burial site of French Kings.

HALF-DAY TRIPS FROM PARIS
(pp142–169)

Visitors often reserve time for the Château de Versailles but there are countless other fascinating places to visit in the "Petite Couronne" (little crown). Comprising three *départements* that circle the outskirts of the city – Seine-St-Denis, Hauts-de-Seine and Val-de-Marne – this area also boasts sophisticated artistic and cultural facilities and world-renowned architecture.

DAY TRIPS FROM PARIS
(pp170–334)

If you want to escape the crowded metropolis, the peaceful landscape, beautiful forests and family outdoor activities of Île de France are for you. To the north, Picardie is home to several historical towns including the regional capital Amiens, with its World Heritage Cathedral. Picardie also keeps a faithful watch over the memories of the fallen, as the scene of some of the bloodiest battlefields of World War I.

LILLE MÉTROPOLE
(pp336–355)

Capital of culture, Lille is home to dozens of museums, art galleries, contemporary dance and performance spaces, designer stores, factory outlets, restaurants and trendy bars linked by a fast and efficient metro system.

Lille: Grand'Place

FLANDRE (pp356–375)

From the seafront promenades of its northern ports to southern meadows dotted with mills, belfries, gabled farmsteads and welcoming villages, Flandre enjoys a reputation as the carnival capital of France.

HAINAUT TO L'AVESNOIS (pp376–399)

A favourite spot for bird-watching, fishing and boating, this region is home to a vast nature park stretching from the clay soils and shady lakes of Hainault in the east to the oak forests of Avenois in the west.

THE COTE D'OPALE AND SAINT-OMER REGION (pp400–427)

Dominated by the plunging chalk cliffs and endless sandy beaches of the Opal coast, the valleys and rivers of the Boulonnais, and the canals and marshland of St-Omer, this region is for anyone who prefers their countryside wild and unspoiled.

ARRAS AND L'ARTOIS (pp428–443)

A landscape of memory and courage, the World War I battlefields and the former Lens coalfields explore the heroism, hope and comradeship of two titanic 20C struggles for social progress and change.

LA CÔTE PICARDE AND ABBEVILLE (pp444–459)

The lazy Somme River idles through a myriad of canals and tributaries, rock pools, fishing lakes, castle moats and game-filled forests before washing round the sand dunes and pony tracks of Picardie's tidal estuary.

L'AMIÉNOIS AND LA HAUTE SOMME (pp460–479)

First settled by the Gauls, the cradle of Gothic architecture has over a thousand years of history to explore, from archaeological parks, castles, citadels and priories to the battlefields of World War I.

FROM SAINT-QUENTINOIS TO LA THIÉRACHE (pp480–489)

Ideal for walkers and hikers, the open fields of Picardie, the Avenois nature reserve, the dense woodland of the Massif Ardennais and Serre and Oise valleys with its fortified churches are tailormade for nature lovers.

LAONNOIS AND SOISSONNAIS (pp490–507)

Twin capitals of the early Frankish state, Laon and Soissons stand at the centre of a network of medieval castles and keeps, fortresses and châteaux, soaring cathedrals and troglodytic caves.

L'OISE (pp508–533)

The former playground of France's royal elite, this landscape of oak and beech forests, knolls and headlands, is dotted with rambling palaces, fairytale castles and hunting lodges.

L'Oise: near the village of Chérence

©Gilles Rigoulet/hemis.fr

Château de Vaux-le-Vicomte
© Lourmel-Chicurel/Château de Vaux-le-Vicomte

PLANNING YOUR TRIP

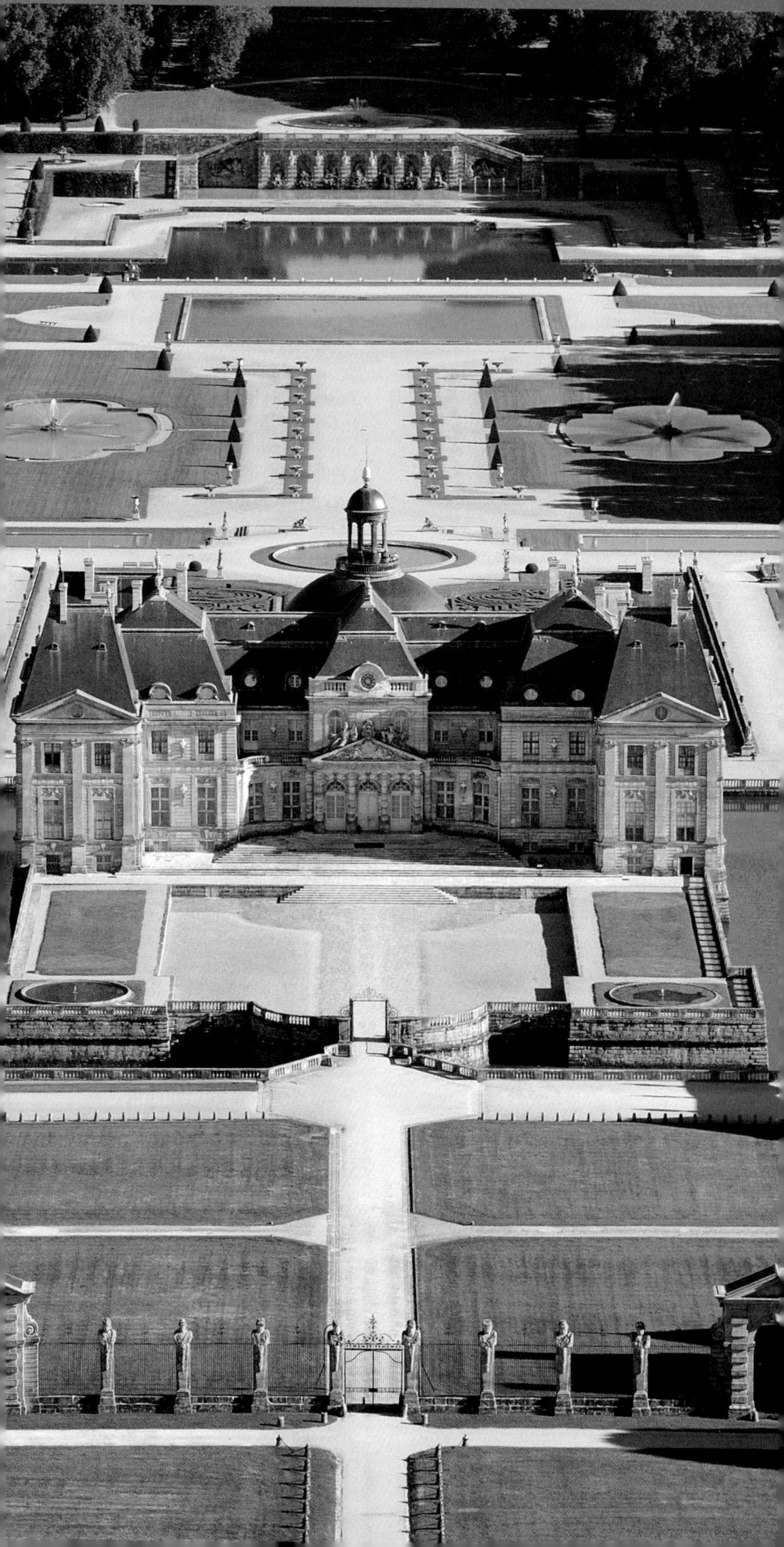

Michelin Driving Tours

PARIS AND ÎLE-DE-FRANCE

Paris to Chartres

An 8hr driving tour from Paris to Chartres. 100km/62mi.

This long excursion allows you to explore the many facets of the Île-de-France region, and winds through verdant river and forest landscapes including the Vallée de la Bievre and the Vallée de Chevreuse, all the way to Chartres.

The Battlefields and the Ourcq Valley

See Vallée de l'OURQ. A 4hr tour stretching 96km/58mi.

This driving tour gives you an overview of the monuments commemorating battles fought here in W W I, including the Memorial de Villeroy and the Chambry Military Cemetery.

Forest and Loing River

See MORET-SUR-LOING. A 2hr circuit 40km/25mi from Moret.

This route takes you along the lovely canal de Loing, through picturesque fields and woods and past a 16C château.

Route des Crêtes

See La ROCHE GUYON. A 1–2hr driving tour along the route de Gasny and its troglodyte caves. 4km/2.5mi round-trip.

Explore the oddly carved man-made caves of La Roche Guyon, then enjoy a splendid view over the loop in the Seine and the old town keep.

From Forest to Town

See Brunoy. Allow 1 day.

Explore the lovely Foret de Senart stretching between the Seine River and the N 6, populated with oaks, chestnuts and the many animals traditionally hunted here.

NORD-PAS-DE-CALAIS AND PICARDY

Pévèle and Le Mélantois

See SECLIN. A 90min tour around Le Pévèle and Le Mélantois. 52km/32mi.

Explore pivot mills, battlefields and traditional roof-tiled Flemish houses.

Towards Belgium

See DUNKERQUE. A 3hr tour of the Flemish coast. 62km/39mi.

Visit an Art Nouveau resort, a nature reserve and miles of breezy dunes.

Northern Heights

See BAILLEUL. A 1hr tour over the hills of Flandre. 36km/22mi.

A journey through the Flemish countryside into Belgium.

Avenois Region

See AVNES-SUR-HELPE. A 2hr30min drive south of Meubeuge. 100km/62mi.

Explore the region's medieval crafts tucked away in the valleys and forests of the Avesnois region.

La Côte d'Opale

See La Côte d'OPALE. A 2hr30min drive along the Opal coast. 50km/31mi.

Vast sandy beaches, chalk cliffs, military ports and military museums.

Le Boulonnais

See BOULOGNE-SUR-MER. A 3hr tour of the Boulonnais region. 75km/46mi.

Visit traditional villages and manor houses as you wind through leafy valleys planted with cider orchards.

Vallée de la Course: Montreuil to Samer

See MONTREUIL. A 1hr tour through the Course valley. 38km/24mi.

Discover meadowland, farmsteads, and the Desvres faience museum.

Vallée de la Canche: Montreuil to Hesdin

See MONTREUIL. A 1hr tour the Canche valley. 25km/16mi.

Wind your way through a valley dotted with whitewashed houses and waterside manors.

Vallée de la Canche: Hesdin to Frévent

See MONTREUIL. A 1hr tour through a gently sloping valley. 38km/24mi.

Follow the "villages in bloom" route through medieval hamlets and discover a 17C château and a Cistercian monastery.

Ternoise and Planquette

See HESDIN. A 1hr drive through a lush green landscape. 44km/27mi.

Experience the drama of the Battle of Agincourt on this tour through the historic Ternoise valley.

Haute Vallée de l'Aa to Dennlys Parc

🚗*See AIRE-SUR-LA-LYS. A 1hr15min tour of the Aa valley. 50km/31mi.*

Explore one of France's earliest Gothic buildings, fortified churches, an ancient mill and an adventure park.

Lesgueulles Noires

🚗*See LENS AND LE BASSIN MINIER. A one day tour to the southwest of Lens. 115km/71mi.*

Explore developments in workers' housing throughout the 19C and 20C.

Around the Baie de Somme

🚗*See BAIE DE SOMME. A 1hr drive from Marquenterre to Cayeux-sur-Mer. 42km/26mi.*

Explore the region's largest bird sanctuary before heading to a museum dedicated to fauna and flora.

Crécy Forest

🚗*See CRÉCY-EN-PONTHIEU. A 1hr forest tour. 29km/18mi.*

Discover the famous battlefield of Crécy, before visiting a hermitage, a historic inn and the deep Maye valley.

Auxi-le-Château to Fort-Mahon-Plage

🚗*See Vallée de l'AUTHIE. A 1hr tour through the lush Authie valley. 55km/34mi.*

Discover Gothic churches, an 18C château and a whimsical garden before a walk along the dunes.

Vallée de la Somme: Abbeville to Amiens

🚗*See ABBEVILLE. A 3hr tour through the moats, marshes and lakes of the Somme valley. 58km/36mi.*

Wind your way through the island castles of the Somme valley to a fascinating archaeology park.

Vallée de la Somme: Amiens to Péronne

🚗*See AMIENS. A 1hr30min tour affording stunning views over this wooded valley. 63km/38mi.*

A host of churches and abbeys, canals and lakes to explore at your leisure.

The Poppy Route

🚗*See ALBERT. A 1hr tour of the battlefields to the north of Albert. 34km/21mi.*

Battlefields, trenches, memorials and museums devoted to the Somme.

Fortified churches

🚗*See La THIÉRACHE. A 3hr tour of the region's fortified churches. 63km/49mi.*

Explore dozens of churches fortified during the Hundred Years War in the 16C and 17C.

LAONNOIS, SOISSONNAIS AND L'OISE

Le Laonnois

🚗*See LAON. A 2hr tour through the Laon plain and up into the "montagne de Laon". 31km/19mi.*

Explore the Gothic and Romanesque churches of the Laonnois region.

Soissons to Berry

🚗*See CHEMIN DES DAMES. A 3hr30min battlefield tour. 63km/49mi.*

Eight sites exploring the sacrifices of the French army during World War I.

Saint-Gobain Route

🚗*See FORÊT DE SAINT-GOBAIN. A 2hr tour of the abbeys around Saint-Gobin. 23km/14mi.*

Explore the roots of the Premonstratensian order.

East of Tardenois

🚗*See FÈRE-EN-TARDENOIS. A 2hr drive around the castles and châteaux of the Tardenois region. 16km/10mi.*

Discover a Renaissance bridge, a medieval stronghold and an eight-towered bastion.

Clairière de L'Armistice

🚗*See COMPIÈGNE. A 2hr tour of the forests around Compiègne 6km/3.5mi.*

Visit the clearing and a reconstruction of the railcar where the German army surrendered to the Allies in 1918.

When and Where to Go

WHEN TO GO
SEASONS

Inland, the winters are chilly and darkness comes early in the northern latitudes. As spring turns to summer, the days become long and warm, and by June the sun lingers until after 10pm. Spring and autumn provide a chance to explore the valleys of the Aa, Canche, Authie and Somme, and the different regional nature parks.

Spring in Île-de-France offers a glorious contrast between the vivid yellow of rapeseed fields against the green background of the copses and forests, while autumn in the oak and beech woods of Compiègne, Rambouillet, Sénart or St-Germain is accompanied by the warm colours of changing leaves.

CLIMATE

While the beaches of the Opal Coast are spectacular, stretching out for 1km/0.6mi at low tide, the relatively cool weather and the chilly waters of the Channel are generally more appealing for shell-seekers, horse riders, landsailers and kite-flyers than for swimmers. In the winter months,

---

What to Pack

As little as possible! Cleaning and laundry services are available everywhere. Most personal items can be replaced at reasonable cost. Try to pack everything into one suitcase and a small bag. Porter help is limited or non-existent in rural France, and new purchases simply add to the original weight. If you think it may be necessary, take an extra bag for packing new purchases, shopping at the open-air market, carrying a picnic, etc. Be sure luggage is clearly labelled and old travel tags removed. Do not pack medication in checked luggage; keep it with you.

---

the coast is often buffeted by strong winds. Statistically, June is the sunniest month on the coast and August the warmest. The highest period of rainfall is in November, and the lowest in April (for a total of 170 days per year). Peak summer temperatures usually hover around 25°C/77°F.

WEATHER FORECAST

National forecast: ✆32 50
Local forecast: ✆08 92 68 02 XX, where XX is the number of the *département* (e.g. for the Nord – ✆08 92 68 02 59).
This information is also available on www.meteofrance.com.

WHERE TO GO
CITY BREAKS
Paris

If you have a long weekend in Paris, begin with a Seine River Cruise followed by one of the hop-on, hop-off coach tours to get an overview of the major sights. You'll want to explore the charming, history-packed streets of the Marais, St-Germain-des-Prés and Montmartre on foot, where you'll find plenty of boutiques, cafés and sights worth a closer look. Reserve a table in advance at one really great restaurant, and possibly an opera, dance or cabaret show. Pick one or two museums that fit your interests, or if the weather is right join the locals in one of the small but beautiful city parks.

Lille

Discover the unique charm of French Flanders with a long weekend in Lille. Start with a walk through the historic Old Town to get acquainted with the distinct Flemish architectural style of the 17C and 18C buildings. Shop for luxury goods, antiques and second-hand books in the Vieille Bourse before popping into the history museum of the Hospice Comtesse. Art lovers should reserve the better part of a day for the world-class Palais des Beaux Arts, while fans of military fortifications can visit the Citadelle by

Château de Dampierre, Chevreuse Valley

© Kevin O'Hara/age fotostock

reserving in advance. In the evening enjoy the regional cuisine and locally brewed beers, or a show at the Folies de Paris.

ONE WEEK

Using Paris as a base, explore the Île-de-France on day trips starting with Fontainebleau-Vaux-le-Vicomte and Barbizon. A morning in Chartres can be complemented by visits to Breteuil or Dampierre and the Abbaye de Port Royal des Champs. Spend a full day at Versailles, Disneyland or, to appeal to all ages, the medieval town of Provins. For a more relaxed day, visit the riverside village of Auvers-sur-Oise and L'Isle-Adam, followed by a tour of Napoléon's Malmaison. A day enjoying the artworks at the Château of Chantilly and an equestrian show at the living horse museum can be finished with a stroll through the romantic medieval streets of Senlis. If the weather is agreeable you can spend the final day hiking in the beautiful forests in Compiègne.

TWO WEEKS

A second week will give you time to visit the cathedral at Amiens, followed by an afternoon in the gardens of the Abbaye de Valloires. Spend a day exploring the Opal Coast, with an afternoon at the beach or the Nausicaä aquarium. Visits to St-Omer and Bergues can be combined with stops at World War II military sites like La Coupole in Helfaut-Wizernes. A day in Lilles will reveal French Flanders at its best, while Arras shows off the finest aspects of the Artoise region. Enjoy the natural sights on your last day with a drive through the Avesnois Regional Nature Park and its charming villages.

THEMED TOURS
HISTORY TOURS

These itineraries mostly explore the region's architectural heritage and its historical context.

There are several historical routes in the area covered in this guide:

♦ **Route du Camp du Drap d'Or:** the 'Cloth of Gold' route from Calais to Arras. Contact the Office de Tourisme des Trois-Pays in Guînes, ℘03 21 35 73 73, www.tourisme-3pays.fr.

♦ **Route des Archers:** explore the battle of Agincourt, when French knights were defeated by English archers during the Hundred Years War. Contact the Office de Tourisme d'Azincourt, ℘03 21 47 27 53.

♦ **Route des Valois:** the Valois dynasty in the heart of the forests of Retz and Compiègne. Contact M. de Montesquiou, abbaye de Longpont, 02600 Longpont, ✆03 23 96 01 53.

- **Route du Lys de France et de la Rose de Picardie:** 'Lily of France and Rose of Picardie' route from St-Denis to Boulogne-sur-Mer, via Écouen, Royaumont, l'Isle-Adam, Gerberoy, Poix-en-Picardie, St-Riquier, Rue and Montreuil. Apply to the Château de Troissereux, 60112 Troissereux, ✆03 44 79 00 00.
- **Le Circuit du Souvenir:** 92km/57mi tour of the main Somme battlefields, www.somme-battlefields.com

Brochures on these and other routes are available in local tourist offices.

CULTURAL HERITAGE

- **Route des Villes Fortifiées:** This itinerary covers 16 **walled towns** in the Nord-Pas-de-Calais region: Ambleteuse, Arras, Avesnes-sur-Helpe, Bergues, Bouchain, Boulogne-sur-Mer, Calais, Cambrai, Condé-sur-l'Escaut, Gravelines, Le Quesnoy, Lille, Maubeuge, Montreuil-sur-Mer, St-Omer and Watten. The route is 500km/311mi in length, subdivided into shorter sections, with lots of possibilities for excursions and tours. Each town has a *Route des Villes Fortifiées* signpost at its entrance, accompanied by a logo. Visit www.espaces-fortifies.com or contact the **Comité Régional de Tourisme du Nord-Pas-de-Calais** (see *Tourist Offices in France, p35*).
- **Route François 1e:** This itinerary explores four châteaux either built by François I (Fontainebleau, his favourite residence and Saint-Germain-en-Laye, rebuilt from scratch by the king) or leading members of his court (Rambouillet, where he died, and

Ecouen, now home to the national museum of the Renaissance).

- **Chemins des Retables:** several tours enable visitors to discover the rich interior of churches in the Flanders region. Contact the Association des Retables de Flandre, ✆03 28 68 69 78, www.retablesdeflandre.fr
- **Route des Maisons d'Écrivains:** visit the residences of famous authors in the Île-de-France, including Zola and Dumas. Info: 125 r. de Longchamp, 75116 Paris, www.routecrivains.fr
- **Route Normandie-Vexin:** discover French Vexin, in the Oise and Val d'Oise regions, its castles and landscapes as depicted in the works of Impressionist painters. Information: www.route-normandie-vexin.fr
- **Route des Impressionnistes en Val d'Oise:** Impressionist painters in the Val d'Oise region, Auvers-sur-Oise, Pontoise, L'Isle-Adam, Vétheuil, La Roche-Guyon, Argenteuil… in the footsteps of Manet, Daubigny, Pissarro, Renoir and Van Gogh. Information: ✆01 30 29 51 00, www.val-doise-tourisme.com
- **Balades au Pays des Impressionnistes:** Nine municipalities situated along the River Seine form what is known as Impressionist country, including Carrières-sur-Seine, Bougival, Louveciennes, Marly-le Roi, le Port-Marly, Le Pecq-sur-Seine and Noisy-le-Roi. ✆01 30 61 61 35, www.pays-des-impressionistes.fr

TRADITIONS

Windmills – Once a common sight in the region, surviving examples of windmills have gradually been restored by a local organisation. The **Musée des Moulins** (*59650 Villeneuve-d'Ascq,* ✆03 20 05 49 34, *www.aram-nord.asso.fr*), can provide brochures, maps and books on the subject. Most of the windmills cited in this guide are open to visitors.

On the plains of the Beauce and Brie, a few sails still catch the wind from time to time and sell freshly ground flour. Listed below are a few operating windmills where visitors are welcome, at least for a look around the outside of the mill.

In the Beauce *(located off the A 10 "Allainville" exit or, from Orléans, the "Allaines-Chartres" exit)*:

- **Ouarville:** Open Sundays, Apr to Oct, 2–6pm. ℘02 37 22 13 87.
- **Levesville-la-Chenard:** Sunday 2.30-6.30pm, Jun–Sept, or by reservation. For more information call: ℘02 37 22 11 40.
- **Bouville:** Sat and Sun, mid-Mar–mid-Oct 2.30–6.30pm. ℘02 37 96 31 08.

The following windmills are described in the *Discovering* section of this guide:

- Musée des Moulins (☾*see VILLENEUVE D'ASCQ*).
- Moulins de CASSEL, Steenmeulen (at Terdeghem), Drievemeulen, Noordmeulen near Steenvoorde, Moulin Deschodt at Wormhout (☾*see CASSEL*).
- Oudankmeulen at Boeschepe (☾*see BAILLEUL*).

The association's annual regional windmill festival is held in June.

Carillons – Chiming bells are part of everyday life in many towns in northern France and particularly in Flanders. A carillon consists of several bells hung in a bell-tower or belfry. The bells ring out different refrains to indicate the hour, the quarter and the half hour. The word comes from a medieval term 'quadrillon''', a peal of four bells ringing in harmony. In the Middle Ages, clocks were mechanical; they included small bells that the bell-ringer struck using a mallet or hammer.

After a gradual increase in the number of bells, the mallet was replaced by a keyboard. The automatic system with cylinders is progressively being replaced by an electrical system that is easier to maintain.

The main carillons in the Nord-Pas-de-Calais area are as follows:

- **Tourcoing** – Eglise St-Christophe: 61 bells
- **Douai** – Town hall: 62 bells
- **Bergues** – Belfry: 50 bells
- **Avesnes-sur-Helpe** – Collégiale St-Nicolas: 48 bells
- **Capelle-la-Grande** – Belfry: 49 bells
- **Dunkerque** – Tour St-Eloi: 48 bells
- **Le Quesnoy** – Town hall: 48 bells
- **St-Amand-les-Eaux** – Tower on the abbey church: 48 bells
- **Seclin** – Collégiale St-Piat: 42 bells
- **Orchies** – Church: 48 bells

Carillon concerts are held regularly in certain towns *(for information, contact the local tourist office)*.

LOCAL CRAFTS AND INDUSTRY

Below are a few suggestions for visits; it is usually necessary to make an appointment.

- **Usine élévatoire de Tribardou** – Rte. de Charmentray, 77450 Tribardou, ℘01 60 09 95 00. *Guided tours year round, on request.* This factory, situated a few miles from Meaux, uses a waterwheel to pump water from the River Marne and supply the Ourcq canal; an insight into 19C technology.
- **Météo-France** – Centre départemental des Yvelines, 3 r. Teisserenc-de-Bort, 78190 Trappes, ℘01 30 66 47 80, www.tourisme. yvelines.fr. This regional weather station is open year round for guided tours by reservation only.
- **Verrerie d'art de Soisy-sur-École** – Le Moulin de Noues, BP 2, 91840 Soisy-sur-École, ℘01 64 98 00 03, www.verrerie-soisy.com. Visit the glassworks, exhibition centre and shop.
- **Coca Cola Entreprise** – 1–3 r. J.J.-Rousseau, ZAC Les Radars, 91350 Grigny, ℘01 69 02 20 00; Monday to Friday 10am–5pm.

What to See and Do

OUTDOOR FUN
WALKING

There is an extensive network of well-marked footpaths in France which make rambling *(la randonnée pédestre)* a breeze. **Grande Randonnée (GR)** trails, recognisable by red and white horizontal marks on trees, rocks and in town on walls, signposts, etc, can be found across the region. Along with the GR, there are also **Petite Randonnée (PR)** paths, which are usually blazed with blue (2hr walk), yellow (2hr15min–3hr45min) or green (4–6hr) marks. Of course, with appropriate maps, you can combine walks to suit your needs.

To use these trails, obtain the *topo-guide* for the area published by the **Fédération Française de la Randonnée Pédestre**. Their information centre is at 64 r. du Dessous-des-Berges, 75013, Paris, ℘01 44 89 93 93, www.ffrandonnee. fr. Some English-language editions are available. Another source of maps and guides for excursions on foot is the **Institut National Géographique (IGN)**, which has a boutique in Paris at 50 r. de la Verrerie, 75004; to order from abroad, visit the website *(www. ign.fr)* for addresses of wholesalers in your country.

Among their publications, France 1M903 is a map showing all of the GR in France *(7€)*; the *Série Bleue* and *Top 25* maps, at a scale of 1:25 000 (1cm = 250m), show all paths, whether waymarked or not, as well as refuges, camp sites, beaches, etc *(from 10.50€)*. The **Conseil général du Nord** publishes, jointly with the **Association Départementale de la Randonnée**, itineraries covering various distances, with maps and information. Visit www. tourisme-nord. fr or contact the **Comité Départemental de Tourisme du Nord** *(for address, ᕀsee Tourist Offices in France, p35)*.

A guide *(Guide des Sentiers de Promenade dans le Massif Forestier de Fontainebleau, 12€)* to the famous forest southeast of Paris – a popular spot for ramblers, climbers, mushroom hunters and cyclists on day trips – and local guided tours, is also available. For a programme, visit the bilingual website **Association des Amis de la Forêt de Fontainebleau** *(26 r. de la Cloche, BP 14, 77301 Fontainebleau Cedex, ℘01 64 23 46 45, www.aaff.fr).* Join up with fellow ramblers via the **Randonneurs d'Île-de-France club** *(92 r. du Moulin-Vert, 75014 Paris, ℘01 45 42 24 72, www.rifrando.asso.fr)*, which organises walks in the region *(small membership fee)*.

Walking, Cote d'Opale, Audinghen, Cap Gris-Nez

© Nicolas Thibaut/Photononstop

Horse Racing

The Paris region has the largest number of race tracks anywhere in France, hosting all types of horse races. **France Galop** specialises in improving breeds of horses in France and manages the flat racing tracks in the Paris area: 46 place Abel-Gance, 92655 Boulogne Cedex, ℘01 49 10 20 30; www.france-galop.com.

Track	Trotting	Flat course	Steeplechase	Main races
Chantilly (June)	–	●	–	Prix du Jockey-Club
(June)				Prix de Diane-Hermès
Enghien (April)	●	–	●	Prix de l'Atlantique
				Prix d'Europe (July) Grand Steeple-Chase (October)
Longchamp (June)	–	●	–	Grand Prix de Paris
				Arc de Triomphe (October)
Maisons-Laffitte	–	●	Cross-country	Prix Robert Papin (July)
St-Cloud (July)	–	●	–	Grand Prix de St-Cloud Critérium de St-Cloud (October)

The region also includes the Parisian race tracks of Auteuil (steeplechases) and Vincennes (trotting races).

CYCLING

The network of country roads is ideal for cycling. Lists of cycle hire shops are available from local tourist offices. Bikes are carried free of charge on many regional trains and on the Paris-Amiens-Boulogne line. Cycle tours are easy to organise as cycle hire companies are often located near or in train stations close to the main forests.

The **Fédération française de Cyclotourisme** (8 r. Jean-Marie-Jégo, 75013 Paris, ℘01 44 16 88 99, www.ffct. org) supplies itineraries covering most of France, outlining mileage, the level of difficulty of routes and sights to see. Mountain biking (VTT), or off-road cycling, has become very popular in France. There are many tracks laid out in the region, suitable for both new and experienced riders.

The **Office National des Forêts** publishes waymarked paths for mountain bike enthusiasts on their website. The itineraries cover between 15km/9mi and 30km/18.6mi. www.onf.fr.

The **Fédération Française de Cyclisme** (5 r. de Rome, 93561 Rosny-sous-Bois Cedex, ℘01 49 35 69 24) also publishes a guide with over 62 000km/38 500mi of marked mountain biking tracks, available on their website: www.ffc.fr.

GOLF

Golfers can enjoy their favourite sport and take part in competitions in the region. Courses abound in the Nord-Pas-de-Calais region, in pleasantly rustic settings, taking players up hill and over dale, around the edge of forests, or overlooking the sea (for address, see Tourist Offices in France, p35). There are several golf courses in Picardy, including Fort-Mahon, Quend-Plage, Grand-Laviers, Nampont-Saint-Martin, Salouel

Landsailing, Berck-sur-Mer, Pas-de-Calais

© Marc Marin/Fotolia.com

(3km/2mi from Amiens) and Querrieu *(7km/4.3mi from Amiens)*. For more information:
Ligue de Golf du Nord-Pas-de-Calais, 5 r. Jean-Jaurès, 59650, Villeneuve-d'Ascq ℰ03 20 98 96 58, www.liguegolf-npc.com.
Fédération Française de Golf, 68 r. Anatole-France, 92300 Levallois-Perret, ℰ01 41 49 77 00, www.ffgolf.org.

HORSE RIDING

The Nord-Pas-de-Calais and Île-de-France regions have hundreds of miles of bridle paths running through forest and along the coast.
The **Comité National de Tourisme équestre**, 9 bd. Mac-Donald, 75019 Paris, ℰ01 53 26 15 50, www.cnte.fr, publishes an annual review called *Cheval Nature, l'officiel du tourisme équestre en France*. It lists all the possibilities for riding by *région* and *département*.
Addresses of riding stables and information on bridle paths are available from:

♦ **Comité Régionale de Tourisme équestre du Nord-Pas-de-Calais**, L19 r. Blanquy, 59135, Wallers, ℰ03 27 31 35 68, www.cre59-62.com

♦ **Association des cavaliers randonneurs Flandre Artois**, 19 r. Blanqui, 59135, Wallers,

ℰ03 27 20 55 85. Gatherings of riders and teams, trekking. Calendar and itineraries on request.

♦ **Comité nationale de tourisme équestre**, Parc équestre, 41600, Lamotte, ℰ02 54 94 46 80, www.ffe.com/tourisme. This organisation produces an annual brochure *Cheval nature, l'officiel du tourisme équestre* listing useful addresses and accommodation for riders and horses.

Horse farm

It is possible to visit the Haras national de Bréviaires, a few miles north of Rambouillet. ☛*Guided tours (1hr30min) on first Saturdays of the month at 2.30pm.* ⊗*Closed Aug and Dec.* ⊛8€. ℰ01 34 57 85 34. www.haras-nationaux.fr.

LANDSAILING

Landsailing, or sand yachting, uses a strange combination of a three-wheeled go-kart and a sail-boat. Powered solely by the wind, they can exceed 100kph/62mph on the vast stretches of fine, hard sand along the coasts of northern France. In addition to landsailers, there are also speedsail boards which resemble windsurfing boards on wheels.
For information, contact the **Fédération française de char à voile,**

17 r. Henri-Bocquillon, 75015, Paris, 𝒫01 45 58 75 75, www.ffcv.org.

KITE FLYING

This is another popular activity in northern France, particularly on beaches. To obtain a good kite and learn how to fly it, it is advisable to join a club or an association *(addresses are available from local tourist offices)*. For general information, contact the **Fédération française de vol libre** (hang-gliding, paragliding and kite-flying), 4 r. de Suisse, 06000 Nice, 𝒫04 97 03 82 82; federation.ffvl.fr.

ROCK CLIMBING

The Île-de-France area offers beginners and seasoned climbers numerous possibilities at a number of natural sites; the sites best equipped for bouldering are in and around **Fontainebleau Forest**, while the highest rocks are to be found in Larchant and the Dame Jouanne. The Massif des Trois-Pignons offers remarkable scenery and many different levels of difficulty. Bouldering may look easy, but requires excellent technical knowledge and an awareness of safety procedures, and is best practised as part of a club or with professional climbers.

Fédération Française de la Montagne et de l'Escalade, 8–10 quai de la Marne, 75019 Paris, 𝒫01 40 18 75 50, www.ffme.fr.

Club alpin Île-de-France, 12 r. Boissonade, 75014 Paris, 𝒫01 42 18 00 00, www.clubalpin-idf.com.

Mur Mur, 55 r. Cartier-Bresson, 93500 Pantin, 𝒫01 48 46 11 00, www.murmur.fr.

GO-KARTING

There are several go-karting tracks in the Paris region, including:

Karting Buffo, RN 19, BP3, 77390 Les Étards (35km/22mi from Paris), 𝒫01 64 07 61 66, www.karting-buffo. com. Kart rental available from age 7 upwards.

Aérodrome de Pontoise-Cormeilles, 95650 Boissy-l'Aillerie, 𝒫01 30 73 28 00; www.rkc.fr. Three tracks including one for kids.

SKIING

In the north, Noeux-les-Mines has been converted into a ski resort without snow! But that doesn't make it any less enjoyable.

Loisinord, r. Léon-Blum, 62290 Noeux-les-Mines, 𝒫03 21 26 84 84. France's first artificial ski resort (320m), Loisinord has one main run and one learning slope. Skiing instructors from the French skiing school are available.

Rock climbing in Fontainebleau Forest

© Ph. Gajic/MICHELIN

WATER SPORTS
SWIMMING

Bathing conditions are indicated by flags on beaches monitored by lifeguards (no flags means no lifeguards): green indicates it is safe to bathe and lifeguards are on duty; yellow warns that conditions are not that good, but lifeguards are still in attendance; red means bathing is forbidden as conditions are too dangerous. Quality control tests are regularly conducted from June onwards.

Well-equipped beaches offer facilities such as swimming pools, water-skiing, diving, jet-skiing, landsailing, kite-flying, rowing, etc. Information available from local tourist offices.

SAILING AND WINDSURFING

The Paris region boasts around 15 lakes and half a dozen locations on the River Seine and River Marne where sailing facilities are available. There are a number of sports and recreation parks (*bases de loisirs*), where windsurfing and dinghy or catamaran sailing are possible, occasionally combined with other activities such as tennis, swimming, horse riding, golf or water-skiing. They include **St-Quentin-en-Yvelines** (*Centre de voile de la base de loisir, ℰ01 30 58 91 74*); **Moisson-Mousseaux** (*78840 Moisson, ℰ01 30 33 97 80*); **Jablines/Annet** (*77450 Jablines, ℰ01 60 26 04 31*) and **Cergy-Neuville** (*r. des Étangs, 95001 Cergy-Neuville, ℰ01 30 30 21 55*).

There are sailing schools all along the coast of northern France from Bray-Dunes to Auly-Onival. Some of the inland lakes are also ideal for these sports, for example the Val-Joly water park in the Avesnois region (*☞see map p393, AVESNES-SUR-HELPE*), the Étangs de la Sensée and Escaut, and the Lac de Monampteuil near Soissons. For information, contact the:

♦ **Fédération française de voile**, 17 r. Henri-Bocquillon, 75015, Paris, ℰ01 40 60 37 00. www.ffvoile.org

♦ **France Stations Nautique**, 17 r. Henri-Bocquillon, 75015, Paris. ℰ01 44 05 96 55, www.france-nautisme.com.

CANOEING AND KAYAKING

Canoes, propelled by a single-bladed paddle, are ideal for a day out on a lake or along a river. **Kayaks**, propelled by a double-bladed paddle, are more suitable for exploring large lakes and the lower part of rivers. **Sea-kayaks** are narrower and longer and beginners are advised to start out in the company of an experienced guide. **Fédération française de canoe-kayak**, 87 quai de la Marne, 94344, Joinville-le-Pont, ℰ01 45 11 08 50, www.ffck.org. This organisation, in conjunction with the IGN, publishes a map, *Rivières de France*, featuring all of France's navigable rivers.

FRESHWATER FISHING

This region is ideal for fishing, which is particularly popular along the Somme, Course, Lys, Aisne, Oise and Aa rivers, as well as the Sept Vallées area (Canche, Authie, Ternoise, etc).

For more information, contact your local tourist office or angling union.
Nord *7–9 chemin des Croix BP 50019, Le Quesnoy, ℰ03 20 54 52 51, www. peche59.com.*

Obligatory fishing permits (*cartes de pêche*) are often sold on-site in cafés or sports shops near popular spots. Between June and September, it is possible, in certain places, to obtain a special holiday fishing permit (*permis de pêche 'vacances'*), valid for a fortnight. Day permits are available for fishing in some of the region's lakes.

SEA FISHING

Day or half-day fishing trips are organised along the coast of northern France, with equipment supplied by the organisers. Advance reservation is recommended.
Fédération française des pêcheurs en mer, Résidence Alliance, centre Jorlis, 64600 Anglet. ℰ05 59 31 00 73, www.ffpm-national.com.

Le Chemin de Fer de la Baie de Somme

© SommeTourisme–AB

SIGHTSEEING
TOURIST TRAINS

Le p'tit train de la Haute-Somme – This narrow-gauge railway runs from Froissy to Dompierre via the Cappy Tunnel *(300m/328yd)*, south of Albert, 3km/2mi from Bray-sur-Somme. The round trip covers a distance of 14km/8.7mi and takes about 1hr30min. Round off your trip with a visit to the railway museum. ✆03 22 83 11 89, http://appeva. perso.neuf.fr.

Le Chemin de Fer de la Baie de Somme – Made up of vintage carriages, wooden platforms and a steam engine, this train runs through the fields and salt marshes from Noyelles to Le Crotoy, St-Valéry-sur-Mer and Cayeux-sur-Mer. ✆03 22 26 96 96, www.cfbs.eu.

Chemin de Fer Touristique du Vermandois – This classic steam train runs from St-Quentin to Origny-Ste-Benoîte *(44km/27mi round trip)* via Ribemont. For information and bookings visit www.cftv.fr.

Chemin de Fer Touristique de la vallée de l'Aa – This railway journey takes you on a 15km/9mi trip from Arques to Lumbres along the old St-Omer to Boulogne-sur-Mer branch line. Perfect for visits to the Fontinettes barge lift or a stop at the Coupole d'Helfaut-Wizernes Second World War rocket-launch pad. Learn more by calling ✆03 21 12 19 19 or visit www.cftva62.com.

Tramway Touristique de la vallée de la Deûle – Trips by tram along a metre-gauge track over 3km/2mi between Marquette and Wambrechies in the suburbs of Lille. For information, contact the Val de Deûle tourist office, ✆09 72 34 57 87 or visit www.amitram.asso.fr.

COACH TOURS

Paris Vision – Day trips to many Île-de-France destinations: Thoiry, Provins, Fontainebleau, Vaux-le-Vicomte, Chantilly in minivans for up to 12 passengers, and coach tours to Versailles, Disneyland, Parc Asterix, Chartres and Giverny. 214 r. de Rivoli, 75001 Paris. ✆01 44 55 61 00. www.parisvision.com.

Viatours – Coach trips (1–3 days) to World War I battlefields in northern France and Belgium (Somme, Ypres Salient, Vimy Ridge) Lille, Giverny and Versailles. ✆+1 (702) 648-5873 (International). www.viator.com.

BIRD'S-EYE VIEWS
Tourist flights
A 35min plane flight is just one of the highlights of a weekend break (2 days and nights) in the Oise *département*: contact Loisirs Accueil at the **Comité Départementale du tourisme de l'Oise** (✆03 64 60 60 60, www.

oisetourisme.com). Other tourist flights are organised by:

Aéroclub de St-Omer *(Plateau des Bruyères, BP 7, 62967 Longuenesse, ℰ03 21 38 25 42, http://acsto.free.fr)* – flights over the Helfaut-Wizernes rocket launch pad area and the Marais audomarois.

ULM flights are available from Dreux or Viabon daily from April to October, depending on weather conditions; contact **Loisirs Accueil Eure-et-Loir** *(10 r. du Dr-Maunoury, BP 67, 28002 Chartres Cedex, ℰ02 37 84 01 00, www. tourisme28.com)*; also from Abbeville: contact **Ludair** *(Abbeville airport, 80132 Buigny-St-Maclou, ℰ03 22 24 36 59, www.ludair.com)* – flights over the Baie de Somme.

Hot-air ballooning

Take off from Moret-sur-Loing with professional bilingual pilots for a bird's eye view of the landscapes that inspired the Impressionists, or the hunting grounds of the French kings: from April to October, mornings and evenings, depending on the weather: **France Montgolfières** *(ℰ03 80 97 38 61, www.franceballoons.com)*. This company is certified by the civil aviation authority. Flights also available in other areas of France, including from La Roche-Guyon with **Airshow** *(6 r. du Faubourg-Poissonnière, ℰ01 53 24 95 47, www. airshow.fr)*; and from Hazebrouck with **Club Montgolfière Passion** *(253 r. d'Aire, 59190 Hazebrouck, ℰ03 28 41 65 59)*. Two flights a day (morning and evening) to discover the Flanders landscape.

Tethered balloon rides

Tethered rides are organised outside the Parc préhistorique de Samara, near Amiens: **Samara**, 80310 La Chaussée-Tirancourt, ℰ03 22 51 82 83, www.samara.fr.

CRUISING THE WATERWAYS

Once plied by heavily-laden barges, northern France is crossed by a network of rivers and canals extending over 1 609km/1 000mi, the largest of which are the Deûle, Scape,, Lys, Aa, Sensée and Escaut, while major river ports are located in Halluin, Wambrechies and Saint-Amand. The website of the **Comité Régional de Tourisme d'Île-de-France** features a list of major resorts and ports with marina facilities. For information on ports and marinas in northern France: **France Stations Nautiques** – *17 r. Henri-Bocquillon, 75015, Paris, ℰ01 44 05 96 55, www.france-nautisme.com.*

Cruises and boat rentals:

◆ **Les Canalous** –
ℰ03 85 53 76 74,
www.canalous-plaisance.fr.
Live-onboard boat rentals (no permit required) for 2–12 people.

◆ **Nogent-sur-Marne Marina** –
Quai du Port, 94130 Nogent-sur-Marne, ℰ01 48 71 41 65.
Pedal boats and small motor boats for hire.

◆ **Arques Plaisance** –
Base nautique, rue d'Alsace, 62510 Arques, ℰ03 21 98 35 97.
River launches to hire for a day,

☺ Tourist Passes ☺

The **Paris Museum Pass** allows free direct entry to the permanent collections of 60 museums and monuments **in and around Paris**. Valid for 2 days *(39€)*, 4 consecutive days *(54€)* or 6 consecutive days *(69€)*, it can be purchased in participating museums and monuments, at major metro stations, the tourist bureau at the Carrousel du Louvre, and at the National Tourist Bureau in the Champs Elysées. Information: www.parisinfo.com.

Visit www.parismuseumpass.com for participating museums and hyperlinks. Other towns in Île-de-France, Nord and Pas-de-Calais have their own Passport offers. Be sure to ask at the local tourist offices.

weekend or week; river permit or pilot on board.

- **Locaboat Plaisance** – Small barges for hire on the River Somme (departure from Cappy); reservations: Port au Bois, BP 150, 89303 Joigny Cedex, *℘03 86 91 72 72*, www.locaboat.com.
- **Somme Plaisance** – 27 r. Georges-Clemenceau, 80110 Moreuil, *℘03 22 09 75 50*. Boat rental (4–10 people), departure from Corbie.

Maps of waterways can be obtained from:
- **Navicarte**, 175 r. Jean-Jacques-Rousseau, 92138, Issy-les-Moulineaux, www.navicarte.com *℘04 72 01 58 68*.
- **Éditions du Plaisancier**, 43 porte du Grand-Lyon, 01700 Neyron, *℘04 72 01 58 68*.

Boat trips
- In the Audomarois region (℘see ST-OMER).
- Around the market garden district of Amiens (℘see AMIENS: Hortillonnages).
- **Paris Canal** – Bassin de La Villette, 9–21 quai de la Loire, 75019 Paris, *℘01 42 40 96 97*, www.pariscanal.com. On the canals of Paris and along the meanders of the Marne (Paris-Chennevières-Paris).
- **Un canal, deux canaux** – BP 69, 77440 Lizy-sur-Ourcq, *℘03 23 96 41 25*.

NATURE PARKS AND RESERVES
Regional nature parks are protected natural environments where traditional lifestyles, crafts and trades are still carried out. Information can be obtained from individual *Maisons du Parc*.

South of Paris, the Château de Dampierre, the Château de Breteuil and the Abbaye de Port-Royal-des-Champs (℘see ABBAYE DE PORT-ROYAL-DES-CHAMPS) are within the

Parc naturel régional de la Haute Vallée de Chevreuse, created in 1985 (*Maison du Parc, Château de la Madeleine, BP 73, 78460 Chevreuse, ℘01 30 52 09 09, www.parc-naturel-chevreuse.fr*). Woodland and farmland share the plateau with lush green valleys. The park offers over 200km/125mi of sign-posted hiking trails.

The **Parc naturel régional du Vexin français**, created in 1995 just north of Paris (*Maison du Parc, Château de Théméricourt, ℘01 34 48 66 10, www.pnr-vexin-francais.fr*), offers 500km/310mi of marked footpaths as well as cycling tracks and bridle paths.

The **northern area** covered in this guide is filled with dunes, forests, bays and wetlands that are ideal for anyone who loves exploring the landscape on foot, horseback or bike. The region's nature parks include the **Parc naturel régional de l'Avesnois** (*Maison du Parc, Grange Dîmière, 4 cour de l'Abbaye, 59550 Maroilles, ℘03 27 77 51 60, www.parc-naturel-avesnois. fr*); the **Parc naturel regional des Caps et Marais d'Opale** (*Maison du Parc, le Grand Vannage, 62510 Arques, ℘03 21 87 90 90, www.parc-opale.fr*); the **Parc naturel regional Scarpe-Escaut** (*Maison du Parc, Le Luron, 357 r. Notre-Dame-d'Amour, 59230*

Parc naturel régional du Vexin français

Excursions to the UK

Many visitors to Northern France take advantage of the close proximity to the UK by taking a quick trip over the Channel to Kent or even London (passport required):

From Calais – 75min by ferry to Dover (☙*see Getting There: By Ship*).

The **Eurotunnel** is situated at Coquelles *(3km/2mi from the coast)*. For those travelling by car, the **Shuttle** links Calais with Folkestone in Kent, 24hr 7 days a week. The journey

Ferries crossing the Channel

© F. Bocquet/MICHELIN

lasts 35min, 28 of which are spent in the tunnel. ℘09 90 35 35 35, www.eurotunnel.com.

From Paris or Lille – For those travelling by train, **Eurostar** takes around 2.5hr for the journey from Paris-Gare du Nord to London St Pancras, or around 1.5hr from Lille-Europe (www.eurostar.com).

To obtain tourist information in Paris, contact the **Office du tourisme de la Grande Bretagne**, BP 154-08, 75363 Paris Cedex 08, ℘01 58 36 50 50, www.visitbritain.com/fr/FR.

St-Amand-les-Eaux, ℘03 27 19 19 70, www.pnr-scarpe-escaut.fr).

CONSERVATION AREAS

The **Conservatoire du Littoral** *(Corderie Royale, rue Jean-Baptiste Audebert, 17300 Rochefort, ℘05 46 84 72 50, www.conservatoire-du-littoral.fr)* was set up in 1975 to protect France's coastal areas and to safeguard its ecological balance.

The Conservatoire and its partners protect 152 602 hectares of coastline, including 339 protected sites, such as the dunes at Garennes-de-Lornel in Pas-de-Calais, the first to be covered by conservation measures.

Various other organisations and centres are tasked with safeguarding the ecological balance of sites across northern France:

- ◆ **Centre Permanent d'Initiatives pour l'Environnement Vallée de Somme**, 32 rte. d'Amiens, 80480 Dury, ℘03 22 33 24 24, www.cpie80.com *(guided walks, guided tours of the Samara marshland).*

- ◆ **Conservatoire des Sites Naturels de Picardie**, 1 pl. Ginkgo, Village Oasis, 80044 Amiens Cedex 1, ℘03 22 89 63 96, www.conservatoirepicardie.org.

- ◆ **Conservatoire des Sites Naturels du Nord-Pas-de-Calais**, 4 allée Saint-Éloi, ZA La Becquerelle, 59118 Wambrechies, ℘03 21 54 75 00, www.cen-npdc.org

- ◆ **Centre Ornithologique Île-de-France** (CORIF), ℘01 48 51 92 00, www.corif.net. Birdwatching in the Paris region.

- ◆ **Ferme pédagogique de Versailles**, In the Hameau de la Reine, www.chateauversailles.fr

WILDLIFE RESERVES

These areas provide a haven for rare or remarkable flora and fauna, and exceptional geological features, or act as a way station for migratory species. Some reserves are vast while others are quite modest. Waymarked footpaths allow visitors to observe these natural habitats.

- **Le Marais d'Isle**, Aisne (&see SAINT-QUENTIN); Maison de la Nature, &03 23 05 06 50. Walk round the marsh, a sanctuary for migratory birds, on a specially designed footpath.

- **La Baie de Somme** is the largest reserve in the region. (&see BAIE DU SOMME). Information from the Parc Ornithologique du Marquenterre, &03 22 25 68 99, www.marquenterrenature.com

SPAS
SPECIALISED CENTRES

Enghien-les-Bains has the only spa centre in Île-de-France. It specialises in throat ailments, skin conditions and rheumatism, but there are also programmes purely for relaxation.
Les Thermes, 87 r. du Général-de-Gaulle, 95880, &01 39 34 12 00, www.ot-enghienlesbains.fr.
In the northern part of the region, **St-Amand-les-Eaux** specialises in respiratory complaints and rheumatism.
Les Thermes, 1303 rte. Fontaine-Bouillon, &03 27 48 25 00, www.saint-amand-les-eaux.fr
Chaîne thermale du Soleil/Maison du Thermalisme, 32 av. de l'Opéra, 75002 Paris, &0 800 05 05 32, www.chainethermale.fr.

SEA-WATER THERAPY

Le Touquet is a well-known seaside resort with a sea-water therapy (thalassothérapie) centre offering a wide range of treatments (health, fitness, post-natal, dietetics, personalised programmes, etc.).
Institut Thalassa, sea front, &03 21 09 86 00, www.thalassa.com;
Centre Thalgo, Park Plaza hotel, 4 bd. de la Canche, &03 21 06 88 84.
France Thalasso, &06 66 85 64 50, www.france-thalasso.com

ACTIVITIES FOR KIDS 👫

The region abounds in parks, sites and leisure activities for children. The reader's attention is drawn to these features by the symbol 👫. Below is a selection from this guide.

NORTHERN FRANCE

Parc d'Olhain (&see Colline de NOTRE-DAME-DE-LORETTE).
Prés du Hem, 7 av. Marc-Sangnier, 59280 Armentières, 15km/9mi north-west of Lille, &03 20 63 11 27 (&see BAILLEUL, Excursion to Armentières).
Val Joly, Parc départemental, 59132 Eppe-Sauvage, &03 27 61 83 76 (&see AVESNES-SUR-HELPE).
Loisinord, 62290 Nœux-les-Mines, &03 21 26 89 89, www.noeux-les-mines.fr (&see LENS AND LE BASSIN MINIER). Water sports and downhill skiing on an artificial slope.

ÎLE-DE-FRANCE

Parc Astérix, 60128 Plailly, &08 92 68 30 10; www.parcasterix.fr (&see Parc ASTÉRIX).
Disneyland Resort Paris, 77777 Marne-la-Vallée, &0 825 300 500. Advance booking, schedules and prices at www.disneylandparis.com (&see DISNEYLAND PARIS).
Mer de Sable, 60950 Ermenonville, &03 44 54 18 48, www.merdesable.fr (&see Abbaye de CHAALIS).
Thoiry, 78770 Thoiry, &01 34 87 40 67, www.thoiry.net (&see THOIRY).

Puppets

The north is an area traditionally known for its puppets (marionnettes) and several theatres continue to put on shows to the great delight of children and adults alike:
Théâtre Le Grand Bleu, 36 av. Max-Dormoy, Lille, &03 20 09 88 44, www.legrandbleu.com.
Théâtre Louis Richard, 26 r. du Château, Roubaix, &03 20 73 10 10, www.theatre-louis-richard.com
Théâtre du Broutteux, 11 bis pl. Ch.-Roussel, Tourcoing, &03 20 76 09 24.
Musée Itinérant des Marionnettes du monde, &05 55 64 34 28, marionnettes-du-monde.com

Théâtre "Chès Cabotans d'Amiens", r. E.-David, Amiens, ☎03 22 22 30 90, www.ches-cabotans-damiens.com.

SHOPPING
OPENING HOURS

Most large shops are open Monday to Saturday from 9am to 6.30 or 7.30pm. Smaller shops may close during the lunch hour. Food shops (grocers, wine merchants and bakeries) are generally open from 8am to 6.30 or 7.30pm; some open on Sunday mornings. Many food shops close between noon and 2pm and on Mondays. Hypermarkets usually stay open non-stop until 9pm or later.

Plant products or fresh food, including fruit, cheeses and nuts cannot be brought into the USA.

VALUE ADDED TAX (VAT)

There is a **Value Added Tax** (VAT) in France of 19.6% on almost every purchase. VAT **refunds** are available to visitors from outside the EU only if purchases exceed 175€ on one day in one store; the VAT cannot be refunded for shipped items. This service is mainly offered in large stores catering to tourists, luxury stores and shops with a Duty Free sign. Show your passport and the store will complete a form that needs to be stamped by a customs agent at whatever point you are leaving the EU. You may need to show the agent your purchases; don't pack them in checked luggage. www. douane.gouv.fr.

Galeries Lafayette, Paris
© PhotoTalk/iStockphoto

Booze Cruise

The English associate Northern France with a dash across the channel to stock up on wine and beer bargains. The streets of Calais around the port are lined with discount shops, but these are a good place to start:

Calais Vins (Zone Curie, r. Gutenbert, ☎03 21 36 40 40, www.calais-vins.com)

Franglais (CD 215 Frethun, ☎03 21 85 29 39, www.franglais-wine.com)

Majestic Wine & Beer World (r. de Judee, ZA Marcel Doret, ☎+1923 298 297, www.majesticinfrance.co.uk)

Check your limits with customs regulations; you will need to prove that any amount you are carrying is for personal use only.

LOCAL SPECIALITIES
Food and drink

Brie cheese comes from Meaux, east of Paris, but also from Coulommiers and Melun further south. Meaux also produces a gourmet **mustard** made according to a traditional recipe. Northern France's cheeses include the mild **Mont-des-Cats** and the stronger-flavoured **Maroilles**, first produced by monks in the 10C, and often used in regional dishes. **Beer** is Northern France's traditional drink and there are many varieties to be enjoyed along the "route des Brasseurs" (the brewers' trail).

Liqueurs

Liqueurs from Île-de-France include the **Noyau de Poissy**, made from brandy flavoured with apricot stones, and the famous **Grand Marnier** produced in Neauphle-le-Château, west of Versailles.

Handicrafts

This region offers a wide choice of beautiful objects to take home: **porcelain** manufactured in Sèvres and Arras; **earthenware** from

Desvres; **pottery** from Sars-Poteries; **glassware** and **crystal** from Arques; **lace** from Calais; **puppets** from Amiens.

BOOKS
THE MONARCHY

Memoirs Duc De Saint-Simon: 1710–1715 (Lost Treasures) - Lucy Norton, Editor (Prion Books)

The Duc de Saint-Simon was at the very centre of Louis XIV's court at Versailles.

Marie Antoinette: The Journey - Antonia Fraser (Anchor Books, 2002)

The Queen was much-maligned by rumours in her own time, but this book reveals her terrible dilemma.

Versailles: A Novel by Kathryn Davis - (Houghton Mifflin Co, 2002)

Queen Marie Antoinette arrives in France at age 14 to marry Louis, a distracted young man who was to take his wife to the guillotine…

The Many Lives & Secret Sorrows of Josephine B. (Sandra Gulland - Scribner, 1999)

The first historic novel in a trilogy about the life of Napoléon I's first wife, Joséphine de Beauharnais.

THE WORLD WARS

Good-Bye to All That: An Autobiography - Robert Graves (Anchor, 1958)

This book serves as a memoir for an entire generation of Englishmen who suffered in WW I.

Battle of the Somme - Gerald Gliddon (Sutton Publishing, 2000)

Gerald Gliddon is an author specialising in WW I.

A Storm in Flanders: The Ypres Salient, 1914-1918: Tragedy and Triumph on the Western Front - Winston Groom (Grove Press, 2003)

The author describes the terrors of the Ypres salient.

Suite Française - Irène Némirovsky (Vintage Books, 2007)

The author of this novel set in the year France fell to Germany died in Auschwitz before the book was published.

GENERAL INTEREST

More More France Please - Helena Frith Powell (Gibson Square, 2007).

What do you do when your well dries up? Real life stories of Brits in France.

Calais, An English Town in France - Susan Rose (Boydell Press, 2008)

The story of Calais from its capture by the English in 1347 until its surrender to the French in 1558.

Universe of Stone: A Biography of Chartres Cathedral - Philippe Ball (Harper, 2008).

The story of one of the world's greatest Gothic cathedrals.

FILMS

Dangerous Liaisons, 1988. Starring Glenn Close, John Malkovitch, Michelle Pfeiffer.

Bored aristocrats playing a high-stakes games of passion and betrayal.

Germinal, 1993. Starring Gérard Depardieu. After the book by Émile Zola.

A realistic depiction of the living conditions of the miners of northern France in the 1860s.

Vatel, 2000. Starring Gérard Depardieu, Uma Thurman.

This lush period piece tells the story of a doomed head steward in love with a lady in waiting.

Bienvenue Chez les Ch'tis (Welcome to the Sticks), 2008. Starring Dany Boon and Kad Merad.

A hapless French postal worker from the South of France gets transferred to the northern French town of Bergues. After his initial difficulties with the local accent, he gradually warms to the region.

Calendar of Events

JANUARY

Massy– International circus festival, www.cirque-massy.com

FEBRUARY

Le Touquet – Enduropale quad and moto beach race, www.enduropaledutouquet.fr

Mardi gras

Dunkerque – Carnival (Sun before Mardi gras)

Equihen Plage – Carnival (Mardi gras week)

Bailleul – Carnival with giant Gargantua (week after Mardi gras).

Malo-les-Bains – Carnival (Sun after Mardi gras)

Cassel – Winter carnival (Sun before Mardi gras)

MARCH

Créteil – Women's Film Festival, www.filmsdefemmes.com

Béthune – Carnival (Sun during March)

Valenciennes – Festival 2 Cinéma annual film festival attracting directors and actors from around the world. 𝄞03 27 26 78 82, www.festival2valenciennes.com

Coulommiers – Cheese and wine fair, 𝄞01 64 03 22 92, www.foire-fromages-et-vins.com

APRIL

Seine-Saint-Denis – Banlieues Bleues jazz festival, 𝄞01 49 22 10 10, www.banlieuesbleues.org

Berck – International Kite Festival, www.cerf-volant-berck.com

Abbeville et baie de Somme – Bird Film Festival (screenings, exhibits, nature walks, lectures), www.festival-oiseau-nature.com

Vaux-le-Vicomte – Easter egg hunt, www.vaux-le-vicomte.com

Marly-le-Roi – Carnival, www.marlyleroi.fr

Chartres – *Les samedis musicaux de Chartres* (classical music, jazz, folk music), 𝄞06 26 07 66 13, www.samedismusicaux.fr

Journées Eurorégionales des Villes Fortifiées – Regional fortified towns festival in Northern France and Belgium, 𝄞03 28 82 05 43, www.nordmag.fr

Cassel – Carnival with the giants Reuze-Papa and Reuze-Maman (Easter Sun and Mon), www.ot-cassel.fr

Denain – Carnival (Easter Mon), www.ville-denain.fr

Fontainebleau – Foulée impériale: half-marathon across the park, www.lafouleeimperiale-fontainebleau.fr

Foire du Trône – Hundreds of funfair attractions. Until early May, www.foiredutrone.com

APRIL-OCTOBER

Provins – Aux temps des ramparts, medieval festival.

Vaux-le-Vicomte – Water displays in the gardens (2nd and last Sat afternoon)

Versailles – Fountain shows.

MAY

Fivestival – Street theatre, sound installations, contemporary circus and evening concerts across Lille, www.fivestival.org

St-Quentin – Fêtes du Bouffon, www.les-fetes-du-bouffon.com

Lille – Montgolfiades balloon festival, 𝄞03 20 05 40 62, montgolfiades.ec-lille.fr

Tourcoing – Medieval market, European knights tournament, 𝄞03 20 28 13 20, www.tourcoing-tourisme.com

Dunkerque – Cycle race, www.4joursdedunkerque.org

Maubeuge – Jean Mabuse festival: giants and floats, www.ville-maubeuge.fr

Rambouillet - Lily festival. Floats, crowning of the queen. Château park, www.rambouillet.fr

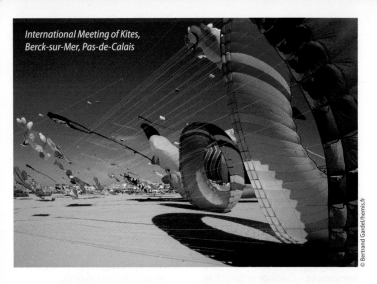

International Meeting of Kites, Berck-sur-Mer, Pas-de-Calais

© Bertrand Gardel/hemis.fr

Nogent-sur-Marne - Medieval festival, www.nogentsurmarne.fr

Seine-Saint-Denis -Rencontres Choréographiques dance festival, rencontreschoreographiques.com

Val-de-Marne – Festival de l'Oh. Water sports and boat rides. festival-oh.cg94.fr

Aérodrome de Cerny –Air show for vintage aircraft, www.ajbs.fr

MAY-JUNE

Chantilly – Polo championships, ✆03 44 64 04 30, www.poloclubchantilly.com

Montereau – Confluences: blues & rock music festival, ✆01 64 70 44 14, www.festivalmontereau.fr.

Oise – Parks and gardens festival (mid-May to mid-Sep.), ✆03 44 06 60 60, www.oise.fr.

St-Denis – Festival de St-Denis classical music concerts, ✆01 48 13 06 07, www.festival-saint-denis.com.

Vaux-le-Vicomte – The Age of Louis XIV festival: picnics in 17C and 18C costume, ✆01 64 14 41 90, www.vaux-le-vicomte.com.

JUNE

Auvers-sur-Oise – International Music Festival, www.festival-auvers.com.

Bièvres – Photo fair, ✆01 43 22 11 72, www.foirephoto-bievre.com.

Bourbourg – Festival of the giants Gédéon, Arthurine and Florentine (Sun closest to St. Jean).

Maubeuge – Les Folies. Music and street theatre festival, ✆03 27 65 65 40, www.lemanege.com

Laon – Les Euromédiévales. Medieval tournaments and costumed events, ✆03 23 20 28 62, www.tourisme-paysdelaon.com

Aérodrome du Bourget – International Air and Space Show (odd-numbered years), ✆01 53 23 33 33, www.paris-air-show.com.

Lille– Fêtes de Lille: various events around the city, www.mairie-lille.fr

Provins– Medieval festival, www.provins-medieval.fr

Samer– Strawberry festival.

Journée nationale des moulins – National Windmill Day (3rd Sun). ✆03 20 05 49 34, www.moulinsdefrance.org

La Défense – Jazz festival. Free.✆01 47 29 30 48, ladefensejazzfestival.hauts-de-seine.net

Fontainebleau – Hunting and nature festival: falcony demonstrations, ✆01 64 31 87 89.

Samois-sur-Seine – Django Reinhardt jazz festival (end Jun), ☎0 811 74 77 73, www.festivaldjangoreinhardt.com

Seine-et-Marne – Open garden festival, ☎01 64 03 30 62, www.77couleurjardin.com

JUNE-JULY

Saint-Denis – Festival of classical music, ☎01 48 13 06 07, www.festival-saint-denis.com

Calais – Festival of folk music, street parades, musical events (last weekend Jun, first weekend Jul), ☎03 21 96 62 40.

St-Germain-en-Laye – Fête des Loges fun fair, www.fetesdes loges.org

Royaumont – Concerts at the abbey, ☎01 34 68 05 50, www.royaumont.com

JUNE-AUGUST

Chartres – Chartres estivales, www.chartrestivales.com

JUNE-SEPTEMBER

Vincennes – Paris Jazz Festival and Festival Classique au Vert – every Sun and Sat eve.

JULY

Côte d'Opale – Music Festival (end Jun–early Jul), ☎03 21 30 40 33, www.festival-cotedopale.fr

St-Riquier – Classical music festival, ☎03 22 71 82 20.

Desvres – Fête de la faïence (earthenware festival), www.ville-desvres.fr

Hazebrouck – Summer carnival: parade of giants Roland, Tisje, Tasje, Toria and Babe Tisje (1st weekend).

Douai – Gayant giants parade (Sun after 5 Jul), ☎03 27 88 26 79.

Arras – Water jousting, ☎03 21 51 26 95.

Loison-sur-Créquoise – Gooseberry festival (w.-end after 14).

Wimereux – Mussel festival (last weekend).

Buire-le-Sec – Craft festival (last Sun).

Saint-Omer – Sea parade (last Sun).

Saint-Valéry-sur-Somme – William the Conqueror Festival, www.visit-somme.com

Noyon – Red fruit market, www.noyon-tourisme.com

Bray-Dunes – World Folklore Festival, www.bray-dunes.fr

Medieval festival, Provins

© Godong/age fotostock

JULY–AUGUST

Montreuil-sur-Mer – "Les Misérables" sound and light show (end Jul–early Aug). ☎03 21 06 72 45, www.les miserables-montreuil.com

Hardelot – Classical Music Festival. ☎03 21 83 51 02, www.festival-hardelot.fr

Chartres – *Soirées Estivales* (summer nights music, theatre and entertainment festival), www.chartrestivals.com

Sceaux – Festival de l'Orangerie. Music concerts. www.festival-orangerie.fr

St-Cloud – Festival Rock en Seine rock festival in St-Cloud park, www.rockenseine.com

AUGUST

Le Touquet – Les pianos folies, www.lespianosfolies.com

Le Quesnoy – Fête du Bimberlot

Versailles – Baroque music concert series, www.cmbv.fr

SEPTEMBER

Île-de-France concert festival. ☎01 58 71 01 01, www.festival-idf.fr

Arleux Garlic Fair (1st Sun), www.arleux.com.

Lille Grande braderie: largest regional flea market (1st weekend)

Armentières Fête des Nieulles, small biscuits (2nd weekend)

Amiens International jazz festival, ☎03 22 97 79 79, www.amiensjazzfestival.com.

Chatou Ham and antiques fair, chatou.sncao-syndicat.com.

La Courneuve – Communist party annual festival: concerts, shows for kids, tastings and debates, ☎01 49 22 73 86, fete.humanite.fr.

SEPTEMBER-OCTOBER

Versailles – Autumn baroque music festival at the château de Versailles, ☎01 39 20 78 10, www.cmbv.fr.

OCTOBER

Steenvoorde Hops festival (1st weekend), ☎03 28 48 19 90.

Tourcoing Jazz Festival, ☎03 59 63 43 63, www.tourcoing-jazz-festival.com

Suresnes Grape harvest festival (1st weekend), ☎01 42 04 96 75.

Sains-du-Nord Cider festival (3rd Sun), ☎03 27 59 82 24.

Meaux – National brie de Meaux competition: tastings, ☎01 64 33 02 26.

St-Ouen – Mondial de l'antiquité aux Puces: European antiques festival, ☎01 40 1177 36, www.marcheauxpucessaintouen.com

NOVEMBER

Etaples– Herring festival (weekend around 11), ☎01 60 66 40 24.

Nogent-sur-Marne – New wine festival (3rd Thu in Nov.): pl. de l'Ancien-Marché, Confrérie du Petit Vin Blanc de Nogent, ☎01 43 94 39 37, www.petitvinblanc-nogent.confreries.org

DECEMBER

Licques Turkey festival, www.tourisme-3pays.fr

Boulogne-sur-Mer *Fête des Guénels* (a *guénel* resembles a jack-o'-lantern, carved out of a beetroot!).

Seine-St-Denis – Africolor Festival (concerts in 15 towns in the *département*): festival of music from Sub-Saharan and Northern Africa and the Indian Ocean. ☎01 47 97 69 99, www.africolor.com

Vaux-le-Vicomte – Christmas festival. Festive indoor and outdoor decorations. Children's events.

Know Before You Go

USEFUL WEBSITES

www.ambafrance-uk.org
The French Embassy's website offers basic information (geography, demographics, history), a news digest and business-related information. It also features special pages for children, and pages devoted to culture, language study and travel, as well as links to other selected sites (regions, cities and ministries).

atout-france.fr
Atout France is France's official tourism development agency. It provides visitors with information on holidaying in France, plus practical information and advice. It also operates online under the name Rendez-Vous En France.

rendezvousenfrance.com
The official website for tourism in France.

www.visiteurope.com
The European Travel Commission provides useful information on travelling to and around 27 European countries, and includes links to some commercial booking services.

www.fngic.fr
Federation of Licenced Tour Guides. Membership of over 700 guides working in 32 languages.

www.franceguide.com
The French Government Tourist Office site is packed with practical information and tips for those travelling to France. Links to more specific guidance for American or Canadian travellers, and to the FGTO's London pages.

www.franceway.com
An online magazine focusing on culture and heritage, including suggested activities for each region and practical information on where to stay and how to get there.

www.northernfrance-tourism.com
The regional tourism office website for the Pas de Calais and Nord *départements* in English. Accommodation, dining, sightseeing and events, with an excellent photo album showing the diversity of the northern France landscape.

www.pas-de-calais.com
The website of the regional tourist office for the Pas de Calais, featuring maps, useful addresses, scheduled events, and information on booking *gîtes*, other furnished accommodation and B&Bs.

www.picardietourisme.com
Accommodation, where to eat, history, culture and leisure in Picardy.

TOURIST OFFICES
FRENCH TOURIST OFFICES ABROAD

For information, brochures, maps and assistance in planning a trip to France, travellers should apply to the official French tourist office in their own country. For more addresses visit atout-france.fr

Australia – New Zealand
- **Sydney** – Level 13, 25 Bligh Street, Sydney, New South Wales 2000
  ℘(02) 9 231 52 44.
  Fax (02) 9 221 86 82.

Canada
- **Montreal** – 1800 McGill College Avenue, Bureau 1010, Montreal, H3A 3J6.
  ℘(514) 288-2026.
  Fax (514) 845 4868.

United Kingdom
- **London** – Lincoln House, 300 High Holborn,London WCIV 7JH.
  ℘(09068) 244 123.
  Fax (020) 7061 6466.

United States
- **New York** –
  Atout France, 825, 3rd Avenue,

New York, NY 10022.
☎ 212-745-0952.
- **Los Angeles** – 9454 Wilshire Bld, Suite 210, Beverly Hills, CA 90212. ☎ +1 310 271 26 93. Fax +1 310 276 28 35.
- **Chicago** – 205 N. Michigan Ave, Suite 3770, Chicago, IL 6060. ☎ +1 312 327 02 90.

TOURIST OFFICES IN FRANCE

Visitors may also contact local tourist offices for more detailed information, and to receive brochures and maps. The addresses, telephone numbers, and websites of tourist offices in individual towns are listed in that town's listing after the symbol 🄸 .

Below are addresses for the regional tourist offices of the *départements* and *régions* covered in this guide.

Regional Tourist Offices
- **Paris Île-de-France** – Comité Régional du Tourisme, 11 r. du Faubourg-Poissonnière – 75009 Paris. ☎ 01 73 00 77 00.
www.new-paris-ile-de-france.co.uk
- **Nord-Pas-de-Calais** – Comité Régional du Tourisme, 6 pl. Mendès-France, 59028 Lille. ☎ 03 20 14 57 57. www.createursdhorizons.com
- **Picardie** – Comité Régional du Tourisme, 3 r. Vincent Auriol, 80011 Amiens 1. ☎ 03 22 22 33 63. www.picardietourisme.com

Departmental Tourist Offices
PICARDIE
- **Aisne** – 24-28 av. Charles-de-Gaulle, 02007 Laon. ☎ 03 23 27 76 76. www.evasion-aisne.com
- **Oise** – Espace Galilée, r. du Pont de Paris, 60003 Beauvais. ☎ 03 64 60 60 60. www.oisetourisme.com
- **Somme** – 21 r. Ernest-Cauvin, 80000 Amiens. ☎ 03 22 71 22 71. www.somme-tourisme.com

NORD-PAS-DE-CALAIS
- **Nord** – 6 r. Gauthier-de-Châtillon, BP 1232, 59013 Lille. ☎ 03 20 57 59 59. www.cdt-nord.fr

EMBASSIES AND CONSULATES IN FRANCE		
Australia	Embassy	4 r. Jean-Rey, 75015 Paris ☎ 01 40 59 33 00. www.france.embassy.gov.au
Canada	Embassy	35 av. Montaigne, 75008 Paris ☎ 01 44 43 29 00. www.international.gc.ca
Ireland	Embassy	4 r. Rude, 75016 Paris ☎ 01 44 17 67 00. www.embassyofireland.fr
New Zealand	Embassy	7 r. Léonard-de-Vinci, 75016 Paris ☎ 01 45 01 43 41. www.nzembassy.com/france
South Africa	Embassy	59 quai d'Orsay, 75007 Paris ☎ 01 53 59 23 23. www.afriquesud.net
UK	Embassy	35 r. du Faubourg St-Honoré, 75383 Paris ☎ 01 44 51 31 00. www.gov.uk/government/world
	Consulate	16 bis r. d'Anjou, 75008 Paris ☎ 01 44 51 31 00
	Consulate	353 bd. du Président Wilson, 33073 Bordeaux ☎ 05 57 22 21 10
USA	Embassy	2 av. Gabriel, 75008 Paris ☎ 01 43 12 22 22. france.usembassy.gov
	Consulate	2 r. St-Florentin, 75001 Paris. ☎ 01 43 12 22 22

- **Pas-de-Calais** – rte. La Trésorerie, BP 79, 62126 Wimille. ℰ03 21 10 34 60. www.pas-de-calais.com

ÎLE-DE-FRANCE

- **Essonne** – 19 r. Mazières, 91000 Evry. ℰ01 64 97 35 13. www.tourisme-essonne.com
- **Eure-et-Loir** – 10 r. du Docteur Maunoury, BP 67, 28002 Chartres. ℰ02 37 84 01 00. www.tourisme28.com
- **Hauts-de-Seine** – 14 avenue François Arago, 92000 Nanterre. ℰ01 46 93 92 92. www.tourisme92.com
- **Seine-et-Marne** – 11 r. Royale, 77300 Fontainebleau. ℰ01 60 39 60 39. www.tourisme77.net.
- **Seine-St-Denis** – 140 av. Jean-Lolive, 93695 Pantin. ℰ01 49 15 98 98. www.tourisme93.com.
- **Val de Marne** – 38 quai Victor-Hugo, 94500 Champigny-sur-Marne. ℰ01 55 09 16 20. www.tourisme-valdemarne.com.
- **Val-d'Oise** – 5 avenue de la Palette, 95000, Cergy-Pontoise. ℰ01 30 73 39 20. www.val-doise-tourisme.com
- **Yvelines** – 2 pl. André-Mignot, 78012 Versailles. ℰ01 39 07 78 78. www.tourisme.yvelines.fr

Tourist Information Centres

There are several official tourist information centres or "points information tourisme" near major tourist sites and attractions.

Aéroport Paris Charles de Gaulle – Terminals 2C, 2D, 2E, 2F and T1. Check information panels for directions.

Aéroport Paris Orly – Terminals Sud Porte L and Ouest Arrivals Porte A. Check information panels for directions.

Versailles – 2 bis avenue de Paris, 78000 Versailles. ℰ01 39 24 88 88

Disneyland Paris – Espace du tourisme d'Île-de-France et Seine-et-Marne, pl. François Truffaut, 77705 Marne-la-Vallée ℰ01 60 43 33 33.

Plan Your Itinerary

Local tourist offices *(Syndicats d'Initiative)* provide information on craft courses and itineraries with special themes – wine tours, history tours, artistic tours. Nineteen towns and areas, labelled **Villes et Pays d'Art et d'Histoire** by the Ministry of Culture, are mentioned in this guide (Amiens, Arras, Beauvais, Boulogne-sur-Mer, Cambrai, Compiègne, Douai, Laon, Lille, Meaux, Noyon, Pontoise, Provins, St-Denis, St Germain-en-Laye, St-Omer, St Quentin, Senlis and Soissons). They are particularly active in promoting their architectural and cultural heritage and offer guided tours by qualified guides as well as activities for children. More information is available from www.vpah.culture.fr *(French only)*.

INTERNATIONAL VISITORS
ENTRY REQUIREMENTS

Passport – Nationals of countries within the European Union entering France need only a national identity card; in the case of British citizens, this means your passport. Nationals of other countries must be in possession of a valid national **passport**. Report the loss or theft of your passport to your embassy or consulate and the local police.

Visa – No **entry visa** is required for Canadian, US or Australian citizens travelling as tourists and staying less than 90 days, except for students planning to study in France. If you think you may need a visa, apply to your local French consulate.

US citizens should consult the government website travel.state.gov, which provides useful information on visa requirements, customs regulations, medical care, etc. for international travellers. General passport information is available on usa.gov and by calling the Federal Information office toll-free ℰ1-800-FED-INFO.

DUTY-FREE ALLOWANCES	
Spirits (whisky, gin, vodka, etc.)	10l/2.6gal
Fortified wines (vermouth, port, etc.)	20l/5.2gal
Wine (not more than 60l sparkling)	90l/23.7gal
Beer	110l/29gal
Cigarettes	800
Cigarillos	400
Cigars	200
Smoking Tobacco	1kg/2.2lb

CUSTOMS REGULATIONS

Apply to the Customs Office (UK) for a leaflet on customs regulations and the full range of duty-free allowances; available from HM Customs and Excise, ℘0300 0200 3700, www.hmrc.gov. uk. The US Customs Service offers a publication *Know Before You Go* for US citizens online at www.cbp.gov. There are no customs formalities for holidaymakers bringing their caravans into France for a stay of less than six months. No customs documents are necessary for pleasure boats and outboard motors for a stay of less than six months, but the registration certificate should be kept on board. Americans can take home, tax-free, up to US$ 800 worth of goods (limited quantities of alcohol and tobacco products); Canadians up to CND$ 750; Australians up to AUS$ 900 and New Zealanders up to NZ$ 700. Residents from a member state of the European Union are not restricted with regard to purchasing duty-paid goods for private use or personal consumption.

HEALTH

First aid, medical advice and chemists' night service rotas are available from chemists *(pharmacie)* identified by a green cross sign. All prescription drugs should be clearly labelled; it is recommended that you carry a copy of the prescription. It is advisable to take out comprehensive travel insurance which also covers medical expenses as medical treatment in French hospitals or clinics is not free.

Nationals of non-EU countries should check with their insurance companies about policy limitations. Reimbursement can then be negotiated with the insurance company. **British and Irish citizens**, if they are not already in possession of an **EHIC** (European Health Insurance Card) should apply for one before travelling. Apply at UK post offices or visit www.europeanhealthcard. org.uk. You pay upfront but you can reclaim most of the money.

Americans concerned about travel and health can contact the International Association for Medical Assistance to Travelers, which can also provide details of English-speaking doctors in different parts of France: ℘(716) 754-4883, www.iamat.org

✚ **The American Hospital of Paris** for 24hr emergencies and consultations, with English-speaking staff, at 63 Blvd. Victor Hugo, 92200 Neuilly-sur-Seine, ℘01 46 41 25 25;

✚ **The British Hospital** is just outside Paris in Levallois-Perret, 3 r. Barbès, ℘01 46 39 22 22, www. british-hospital.org. This facility is registered as a charity in the UK and provides English-speaking medical staff to the British community in France.

ACCESSIBILITY

The sights described in this guide that are easily accessible to people with reduced mobility are indicated by the ♿ symbol.

Useful information on transport, tourism and sports associations for the disabled is available on the French-language website www.handicap.fr. In the UK, www.radar.org.uk is a good source of information, while US citizens can find useful tips on www. access-able.com. **The Michelin Guide France** and the **Michelin Camping France** indicate hotels and campsites with facilities suitable for travellers with physical disabilities.

Getting There

BY AIR

Various international and other independent airlines operate services to Paris (**Charles-de-Gaulle/Roissy** located 25km/15.5mi north of Paris, **Orly** located 16km/10mi south, and Beauvais-Tillé). The **RER-B regional rail network** links both airports to central Paris. There are also regular flights from major UK cities to **Paris Beauvais Airport** (☏0 892 682 066, www.aeroportbeauvais.com), located 3.5km from Beauvais in Picardie. Beavais airport is linked to Paris - Porte Maillot by a regular shuttle service (16 €) leaving every 20 mn, with journey times lasting around 1h 15mn. Contact airlines and travel agents for information on package tour flights with rail or **coach link-ups** or fly-drive schemes.

Aéroports de Paris
☏08 36 681 515 from France
www.adp.fr
Air France
☏0 820 820 820 from France
www.airfrance.com
British Airways
☏0825 825 040 from France
☏0870 8509 850 from UK
www.britishairways.com

PRACTICAL ADVICE

Practical advice for travelling by plane, specifically as regards carrying liquids, gels, creams, aerosols, medicines and food for babies is provided on www.franceguide.com. Some countries impose restrictions on liquids bought in duty-free shops when transferring to a connecting flight. Visit www.aeroportsdeparis.fr for more information.

BY SEA
FROM THE UK OR IRELAND

There are numerous **cross-Channel services** (passenger and car ferries, hovercraft) from the United Kingdom and Ireland. To choose the most suitable route between your port of

P&O Ferries	In the UK: ☏08716 645 645 In France: ☏0825 120 156 www.poferries.com
Norfolkline	In the UK: ☏0871 547 7235 Outside the UK: ☏+44 208 127 8303 www.norfolkline-ferries.co.uk
Brittany Ferries	In the UK: ☏0871 244 0744 In France: ☏0825 828 828 In Ireland: ☏021 427 7801 www.brittany-ferries.com
Irish Ferries	In the UK: ☏08717 300 400 In Ireland: ☏0818 300 400 In France: ☏01 70 72 03 26 In the US: visit the website www.irishferries.com
My Ferry Link	In the UK: ☏0844 2482 100 In France: ☏0845 313 3380 www.myferrylink.com

departure and your destination use the **Michelin Tourist and Motoring Atlas France, Michelin map 726** (which gives travel times and mileage) or **Michelin Local Maps** from 1:200 000 series.

BY TRAIN/RAIL

All rail services throughout France can be arranged through **Rail Europe** in the UK, ☏08708 304 862, www.raileurope.co.uk.
Eurostar runs from **London** (St-Pancras) to **Paris** (Gare du Nord) in under 3hr (up to 20 times daily), or **Lille** (Europe) in 2hr (up to 10 times daily). There is a once-daily service (every day of the year) running directly from the UK to **Marne La Vallée Disneyland**, taking 3hr.
Bookings and information:
☏08432 186 186 in the UK or (0)1233 617 575 from outside the UK, www.eurostar.com. In Paris it links to the high-speed rail network (**TGV**) (☏08 36 67 68 69, www.tgv.fr). The main towns served by the TGV network are Lyon, Avignon, Valence, Montpellier, Aix-en-Provence, Marseille and Nice.
ⓘ*Tickets must be validated (composter)*

Gare du Nord, Paris

© Eurostar / Lydia Shalet

using the orange automatic date-stamping machines at the platform entrance.

Eurotunnel (Le Shuttle-Eurotunnel, ☏+44 (0)8443 35 35 35 from UK, +33 (0) 810 63 03 04, www.eurotunnel.com). This train service for cars and foot passengers links Folkestone to Calais via the Channel Tunnel in 35mn, 24 hours a day, 7 days a week.

Eurailpass, **Flexipass** and **Saverpass** are three of the travel passes which may be purchased by residents of countries outside the European Union. In the US, contact your travel agent or Rail Europe *(44 South Broadway, White Plains, NY 10610; ☏1-800-622-8600)* or **Europrail International** *(☏1 888 667 9731, www.europrail.net)*. If you are a European resident, you can buy an individual country pass, if you are not a resident of the country you are buying it for. In the UK, contact Europrail *(179 Piccadilly London W1V OBA, ☏0990 848 848)*. Information on schedules can be obtained on websites for these agencies and the **SNCF**, respectively: www.raileurope.com, www.voyages-sncf.com. On the SNCF site, you can book ahead, pay with a credit card, and receive your ticket in the mail at home free of charge (seven days minimum

before leaving in the case of foreign countries, four days for France). The French railway company, SNCF, operates a website and telephone information, reservation and prepayment service in English. From outside France call ☏+33 8 92 35 35 35 (from 7am to 10pm, French time) or visit www.sncf.com/en.

BY COACH/BUS

Eurolines (UK), 4 Cardiff Rd. Luton, Bedfordshire, LU1 1PP. ☏08705 143219, Fax 01582 400694.
Eurolines (Paris), 22 r. Malmaison, 93177 Bagnolet. ☏01 49 72 57 80, Fax 01 49 72 57 99.
www.eurolines.com is the international website with information about travelling all over Europe by coach (bus).

Getting Around

BY PUBLIC TRANSPORT

Metro lines are identified by a number. For **RER** lines A, B, C, D, E, which extend into the outer suburbs, cost depends on distance travelled. Six Parisian railway stations (Austerlitz, Est, Lyon, Montparnasse, Nord, St-Lazare) link the capital to the Île-de-France region. For information on the *SNCF* Île-de-France regional network and **TGV** high-speed trains serving towns across france call ✆08 36 35 35 35 or visit www.sncf.fr or www.tgv.fr.

BY CAR

The area covered in this guide is easily reached by motorways and national roads. **Michelin map 726** indicates the main itineraries as well as alternate routes for avoiding heavy traffic during busy holiday periods, and gives estimated travel times. **Michelin map 723** is a detailed atlas of French motorways, indicating tolls, rest areas and services along the route; it includes a table for calculating distances and times.

The latest Michelin route-planning service is available on **www.Via Michelin.com**. Travellers can calculate a precise route using such options as shortest route, route avoiding toll roads or a Michelin-recommended route and gain access to tourist information. Over the busy holiday period (particularly weekends in July and August), follow secondary routes (signposted as *Bison Futé – itinéraires bis*).

☺ Travel Passes ☺

The **Paris Visite** pass allows unlimited travel on the entire RATP network in the Paris and Île-de-France area and includes the metro, RER, bus, tram and suburban trains, depending on the geographical zone (1–3 for the inner zone and 1–5, 6, 7 or 8 for the outer suburbs of Île-de-France). Valid for 1, 2, 3 or 5 consecutive days, it can be purchased in main metro and all RER stations, or abroad. Information: ✆08 36 68 77 14, www.ratp.fr.

Other passes are also available on the RATP network, including the *carte navigo découverte* for travel from daily in zones 1–8, or the **Mobilis** card, issued with a voucher, and valid for one day.

DOCUMENTS

Driving licence

EU and US/Can travellers can drive in France with a national or home-state driving licence.

Always carry your passport, driving licence, motor insurance and vehicle registration documents. An **international driving licence** is available from the AA or RAC (UK) or the NAC (USA) ✆650-294-7000 or www.nationalautoclub.com.

INSURANCE

Many motoring organisations offer accident insurance and breakdown services. Check with your insurance company regarding cover abroad.

© Patricia Grube/MICHELIN

RENTAL CARS – RESERVATIONS IN FRANCE		
Avis France:	☎0820 05 05 05 (UK)	www.avis.fr
Europcar:	☎0825 35 83 58 (UK)	www.europcar.com
Budget France:	☎0825 00 35 64 (UK)	www.budget.com
Hertz France:	☎0825 861 861 (UK)	www.hertz.com
SIXT:	☎0820 00 74 98 (UK)	www.e-sixt.com
CITER:	☎0825 16 12 20 (UK)	www.citer.fr
Thrifty:	☎01494 751 500 (UK)	www.thrifty.com
Nova Car Hire:	☎0800 018 6682 (UK)	www.novacarhire.com

ROAD REGULATIONS

The minimum driving age is 18. Traffic drives on the right. All passengers must wear **seat belts**. Children under the age of 10 must ride in the back seat. In the case of a **breakdown**, a red warning triangle or hazard warning lights are obligatory. In the absence of stop signs at intersections, cars must **yield to the right**. Traffic on main roads outside built-up areas (priority indicated by a yellow diamond sign) and on roundabouts has right of way. At **roundabouts**, yield to the cars in the circle. Stop at red lights at road junctions; filter to the right only when indicated by an amber arrow. The regulations on **drinking and driving** (limited to 0.50g/l) and **speeding** are strictly enforced.

Speed Limits

- Toll motorways (*autoroutes*) 130kph/80mph (110kph/68mph when raining).
- Dual carriageways and motorways without tolls 110kph/68mph (100kph/62mph when raining).
- Other roads 90kph/56mph (80kph/50mph when raining) and in towns 50kph/31mph.
- Outside lane on motorways during daylight, on level ground and with good visibility – minimum speed 80kph/50mph.

Parking Regulations

Parking restrictions or fees often apply in urban areas; use a ticket machine (*horodateur*) to buy a ticket to display inside the windscreen.

Tolls

In France, most motorways are subject to a toll (*péage*). You can pay in cash or with a credit card.

CAR RENTAL

Drivers must be over 21. All of the firms listed opposite have websites for reservations and information.

MOTORHOME RENTAL

Worldwide Motorhome Rentals
Equipped campervans for rent.
☎315-849-2596 in the *US*
☎0208 816 7246 in the UK
www.worldwide-motorhome-hire.com

PETROL/GASOLINE

- *sans plomb 98* (super unleaded 98)
- *sans plomb 95* (super unleaded 95)
- *diesel/gazole including high grade diesel* (diesel)
- *GPL* (LPG).

For US citizens: gasoline is more expensive in France that in the USA; it is usually cheaper to fill up after leaving the highway.

Where to Stay and Eat

Hotels and restaurants are listed under each region. See the cover flap for an explanation of the coin symbols.

WHERE TO STAY
FINDING A HOTEL

Turn to the **Addresses** within individual sight listings for descriptions and prices of typical places to stay **(Stay)** with local flair. The key on the front cover flap of the guide explains the symbols and abbreviations used in these sections. We have reported the prices and conditions as we observed them, but of course changes in management and other factors may mean that you will find some discrepancies.

Use the listings to identify recommended places for overnight stops. For an even greater selection, use the **Michelin Guide France**, with its famously reliable star-rating system and hundreds of establishments all over France.

Book ahead to ensure that you get the accommodation you want, not only in tourist season but year round, as many towns fill up during trade fairs, arts festivals, etc. Some places require an advance deposit or a reconfirmation. Reconfirming is especially important if you plan to arrive after 6pm.

For further assistance, **Loisirs Accueil** is a booking service that has offices in some French *départements* – for further information, contact local tourist offices.

A guide to good-value, family-run hotels, **Logis et Auberges de France**, is available from the French Tourist Office, as are lists of other kinds of accommodation such as hotel-châteaux, bed and breakfasts, etc.

Relais et châteaux provides information on booking in luxury hotels with character: ℘08 825 825 108, www.relaischateaux.com; likewise **Chateaux and Hotels de France**, ℘01 72 72 92 02, www.chateaushotels.com.

Economy Chain Hotels

If you need a place to stop en route, these can be useful, as they are inexpensive (around 45€ for a double room) and generally located near the main road. While breakfast is available, there may not be a restaurant; rooms are small, with a television and bathroom. Central reservation numbers:

- **Akena** ℘01 69 84 85 17 www.hotels-akena.com
- **B&B** ℘02 98 33 75 29 www.hotel-bb.com
- **Ibis** www.ibis.com
- **Hotel F1** ℘0892 685 685 www.hotelf1.com
- **Accor Hotels** ℘0825 88 00 00 www.accorhotels.com/fr

The chain hotels listed below are slightly more expensive (from 58€) and offer a few more amenities and services. Central reservation numbers:

- **Campanile** ℘0207 519 50 45 www.campanile.com
- **Ibis** www.ibis.com

COTTAGES, BED & BREAKFASTS

The **Maison des Gîtes de France** provides information on self-catering accommodation in the Northern France region (and the rest of France). *Gîtes* usually take the form of a cottage or apartment decorated in the local style where visitors can make themselves at home, or bed and breakfast accommodation (*chambres d'hôtes*) which consists of a room and breakfast at a reasonable price. Contact the **Gîtes de France office** in Paris (℘01 49 70 75 75, www.gites-de-france.com) or their representative in the UK, **Brittany Ferries**. You can also contact the local tourist office, which may have lists of available properties and local bed and breakfast establishments.

The **Fédération nationale Clévacances** (54 bd. de l'Embouchure, BP 2166, 31022 Toulouse Cedex 09, ℘05 32 10 82 30, www.clevacances.com) offers a wide choice of accommodation (rooms, flats, chalets and villas) throughout France.

The **Fédération des stations vertes de vacances et villages de neige** (*6 r. Ranfer-de-Bretenières, BP 71698, 21016 Dijon Cedex, ℘03 80 54 10 50, www.stationsvertes.com*) is a non-profit organisation that promotes almost 600 rural locations throughout France, selected for the quality of their environment, accommodation and available leisure activities.

Farm Holidays

The *Bienvenue à la Ferme* website (www.bienvenue-a-la-ferme.com) lists the addresses of farms renting out rooms or other types of accommodation to tourists, or which offer fresh farm produce, lunch or dinner, and other activities. Local tourist offices also keep lists of farm accommodation.

HOSTELS, CAMPING

To obtain an **International Youth Hostel Federation card** (there is no age requirement; a senior card is available too), you should contact the IYHF in your own country for information and membership applications (US ℘1 301 495 1240; UK ℘01629 592 700; Australia ℘61 2 9283 7195). There is a booking service online (*www.hihostels.com*), which you may use to reserve rooms as far as six months in advance.

There are two main youth hostel (*auberges de jeunesse*) associations in France, the **Ligue Française pour les Auberges de Jeunesse** (*67 r. Vergniaud, 75013 Paris; ℘01 44 16 78 78; www.auberges-de-jeunesse. com*) and the **Fédération Unie des Auberges de Jeunesse** (*27 r. Pajol, 75018 Paris; ℘01 44 89 87 27; www.fuaj.org*).

The Fédération's informative website has an online booking service.

There are numerous officially graded **campsites** with varying standards of facilities in Northern France.

The **Michelin Camping France** guide lists a selection of campsites. This region is very popular with campers in the summer months, so it is wise to book in advance.

WHERE TO EAT

A selection of places to eat in the different locations covered in this guide can be found in the **Addresses** appearing in the *Discovering* section of this guide. The key at the front of this guide explains the symbols and abbreviations used in these sections. Use the red-cover **Michelin Guide France**, with its well-known star-rating system and hundreds of establishments throughout France, for an even greater choice. If you would like to enjoy a meal in a highly rated restaurant from the **Michelin Guide**, be sure to book ahead! For information on local specialities, see the section on food and drink in the *Introduction*.

In French restaurants and cafés, a service charge is included. Tipping is not necessary, but French people often leave the small change from their bill on their table or about 5 percent for the waiter in an upmarket restaurant.

A number of organisations promote good-quality, local and often independent businesses throughout France. **Sites remarquables du goût** (www.sitesremarquablesdugout. com) organise activities such as walks and cookery courses and their logo will help you identify a restaurant that contributes to the preservation of local or artisan products and customs. **Bistrot des Pays** (www. bistrotdepays.com) are open year round and located in villages of fewer than 2 000 inhabitants, making a vital contribution to local economies and the social life of rural communities. In the countryside, restaurants usually serve lunch between noon and 2pm and dinner between 7.30 and 10pm. It is not always easy to find something in between those two meal times, as the non-stop restaurant is still a rarity in rural France. However, a hungry traveller can usually get a sandwich in a café, and ordinary hot dishes may be available in a *brasserie*. Throughout France, the culture leans more towards sitting and eating than grabbing a sandwich on the go, so plan ahead.

"GUINGUETTES" IN ÎLE-DE-FRANCE

After the golden age of Impressionism in the late 19C, dance halls located along canals and rivers in the countryside around Paris, known as *guingettes*, gradually disappeared from Île-de-France. These dance halls, serving drinks and meals, with music provided by a band, were reintroduced as part of regional policy and as a result of the enthusiasm of the Culture Guingette association (see below). They are now springing up again on the banks of the Marne and Seine, bringing back to life the picturesque atmosphere of the turn of the century.

You may prefer to be a casual spectator, enjoying simple fare at a riverside table. But if you have your dancing shoes on, dress with flair, just like the regulars (men may need a tie to enter the ballroom). Brush up on your paso doble, tango and cha-cha-cha, and they'll be sure to take you for a native.

Association Culture Guinguette
📱 ✆01 45 16 37 51, *www.culture-guinguette.com.* This association promotes traditional *guingettes* and provides information on special events. Dance styles ranging from athletic rock to energetic polka by way of the classic waltz are practised in members' clubs:

- **Domaine Ste-Catherine** 22-24 allée Centrale, Pont de Créteil, Île de Brise-Pain, 94000 Créteil. ✆01 42 07 19 18, www.domaine-ste-catherine.com
- **L'Île du Martin-Pêcheur** 41 quai Victor-Hugo, 94500 Champigny-sur-Marne. ✆01 49 83 03 02, www.guinguette.fr

Chez Gégène

- **Le Moulin Vert** 103 ch. du Contre-Halage, 94500 Champigny-sur-Marne. ✆01 47 06 00 91, www.moulin-vert.com
- **Quai 38** 8 quai du Viaduc, 94500 Champigny-sur-Marne. ✆01 47 06 24 69, www.quai38.com
- **La Goulue** 17 quai Gabriel-Péri, 94340 Joinville-le-Pont. ✆01 48 83 21 77.
- **Le Petit Robinson** 164 quai de Polangis, 94340 Joinville-le-Pont. ✆01 48 89 04 39.
- **Chez Gégène** 162 quai de Polangis, 94340 Joinville-le-Pont. ✆01 48 83 29 43, www.chez-gegene.fr
- **La Grenouillère** 68 av. du 11-Novembre, St-Maur-des-Fossés, 94210 La Varenne-St-Hilaire. ✆01 48 89 23 32.
- **Le Canotier** 2 r. du Bac, 77410, Précy-sur-Marne. ✆01 60 01 62 12, www.lecanotier.fr
- **L'Auberge Charmante** 20 quai de la Rive-Charmante, 93160 Noisy-le-Grand. ✆01 45 92 94 31.

- **Guinguette Auvergnate**
  19 avenue de Choisy, 94190, Villeneuve-Saint-Georges-Triage. ✆01 43 89 04 64, www.guinguette-auvergnate.fr
- **Guinguette de la Plage d'Isle**
  Avenue Léo Lagrange, 02 100, Saint Quentin. ✆03 23 05 30 30, laguinguettedestquentin.com

BRASSERIES IN NORTHERN FRANCE

If you are interested in exploring the culinary heritage of Northern France visit one of its many **brasseries** (the name derives from the French for 'brewery'; hot and cold dishes are usually available all day). This is also the best place to taste inexpensive traditional dishes like *moules et frites*, or a brown-sugar tart, washed down with a glass of beer. The ambience is often lively well into the night.

ESTAMINETS

Food and drink are also served in small, relaxed cafés known locally as *estaminets*. The warm, unpretentious atmosphere is typical of the region. A list of addresses is available at www.leguidedesestaminets.fr and www.estaminets.fr.

- **De Vierpot**
  125 Complexe Joseph-Decanter, 59299 Boeschepe (*see BAILLEUL*).
- **Au Roi du Potje Vleesch**
  31 r. du Mont des Cats, 59270 Godewaersvelde (*see CASSEL*).
- **La Taverne Flamande**
  34 Grand'Place (*see CASSEL*).
- **Le Baron**
  2 rue du Piémont, 59570 Gussignies. ✆03 27 66 88 61.
- **L'auberge du Snouk**
  15 route de la Colme, 59630 Broukerque. ✆03 28 29 88 88.
- **L'estaminet Flamande**
  6 rue des Fusillers-Marins, 59140 Dunkerque. ✆03 28 66 98 35, www.estaminetflamand-dk.fr

GASTRONOMY IN NORTHERN FRANCE

The Coast

Boulogne is France's leading fresh fish port. In addition to its gourmet restaurants serving fish soup, turbot with cream sauce, *sole meunière*, and a fish platter known as *la gainée* consisting of three different types of fish with a shrimp sauce, the port is also home to fishmongers' stalls selling cod, herring and fresh eels.

Picardy

Soup enjoys pride of place in this region and one of the best-known is the *soupe des hortillons*, made with fresh vegetables. Water fowl is used in many different ways, such as duck or snipe pâté. The *ficelle picarde* is a ham pancake rolled up and filled with mushrooms then smothered in béchamel sauce and baked in the oven until the top is crisp and golden. Leek quiche also makes a simple but delicious meal.

Gourmet Guide

Among the towns awarded the **Site remarquable du goût** (www.sitesremarquablesdugout.com) distinction in Picardy are Houille, Loos and Wanbrechies, on the outskirts of Lille, known for *genièvre* (a juniper-flavoured eau-de-vie similar to gin); the port of Boulogne, famous for its fish; the market gardens of the Marais Audomarois in St-Omer; and the *Hortillonnages* marshland in Amiens, for fruit and vegetables (traditional floating market on the 3rd Sunday in June, canal festival in September). You can obtain detailed information on local gastronomy by contacting:

- **Comité de Promotion Nord-Pas-de-Calais** 5 av. Roger-Salengro, BP 39, 62051, St-Laurent-Blangy Cedex, ✆03 21 60 57 86, www.saveurs-npdc.com
- **Terroirs de Picardie**
  www.terroirsdepicardie.com

Basic Information

BUSINESS HOURS

National museums and art galleries are closed on Tuesdays; municipal museums are generally closed on Mondays. Shops hours are usually Monday to Saturday 10am to 6pm. In smaller towns, shops may also close for lunch and off-season. Churches, especially in secluded areas or small villages, are often only opened for services or on request.

DISCOUNTS

Significant discounts are available for senior citizens, students, young people under the age of 25, teachers, and groups for public transportation, museums and monuments and for some leisure activities such as the cinema (at certain times of day). Bring student or senior cards with you, and bring along some extra passport-size photos for discount travel cards. The **International Student Travel Confederation** (www.isic.org), global administrator of the International Student and Teacher Identity Cards, is an association of student travel organisations around the world. ISTC members collectively negotiate benefits with airlines, governments, and providers of other goods and services for the student and teacher community, both in their own country and around the world. The non-profit association sells international ID cards for students, people under the age of 25 and teachers (who may get discounts on museum entrances). The ISTC is also active in a network of international education and work exchange programmes.

ELECTRICITY

The electric current is 220 Volts/50Hz. Circular two-pin plugs are the rule. Adapters and converters (for hairdryers, for example) are best bought before you leave home. If you have a rechargeable device, read the instructions carefully. Sometimes these items only require a plug adapter, in other cases you must use a voltage converter.

EMERGENCIES

Police (Gendarme): 🖉**17**
Fire (Pompiers): 🖉**18**
Ambulance (SAMU): 🖉**15**

INTERNET ACCESS

Internet access is often easiest to find in hotels in larger towns, where Wi-Fi is becoming standard (often free) and dial-up access is virtually nonexistent. Most towns have many wireless hotspots in cafés, bars and libraries, as well as a few internet cafés for those travelling without a computer. Visit **www.easyinternetcafe.com** to find your nearest internet café.

MAIL/POST

Main post offices open Monday to Friday 8am to 7pm, Saturday 8am to noon. Smaller branch post offices generally close at lunchtime between noon and 2pm and at 4pm.

Postage via airmail:
- ♦ **UK:** letter (20g) 0.80€
- ♦ **North America:** letter (20g) 0.95€
- ♦ **Australia, NZ:** letter (20g) 0.95€

Stamps are also available from newsagents and *bureaux de tabac*. Stamp collectors should ask for *timbres de collection* in any post office.

MONEY
CURRENCY

There are no restrictions on the amount of currency visitors can take into France. Visitors carrying a lot of cash are advised to complete a currency declaration form on arrival, because there are restrictions on currency export.

Notes and coins
Since January 2002, the euro has been the official currency of France and other participating EU Member States.

BANKS

Banks are open from 9am to noon and 2pm to 4pm and branches are closed either on Monday or Saturday. Banks close early on the day before a bank holiday. A passport is necessary as identification when cashing traveller's cheques in banks. Commission charges vary and hotels usually charge more than banks for cashing cheques. One of the most economical ways to use your money in France is by using **ATM/cash machines** to get cash directly from your bank account or to use your credit cards to get cash advances. Before you leave home, check with the bank that issued your card about emergency replacement procedures, and ask them to note that your credit card is likely to be used abroad for a while.

Be sure to remember your 4-digit PIN, you will need it to use cash dispensers and to pay with your card in most shops, restaurants, etc. ATM code pads are numeric; use a telephone pad to translate a letter code into numbers. Visa is the most widely accepted credit card, followed by MasterCard; other cards (Diners Club, Plus, Cirrus) are also accepted in most cash machines. Most places post signs indicating the cards they accept; if you don't see such a sign, and want to pay with a card, ask before ordering or making a selection.

Cards are widely accepted in shops, hypermarkets, hotels and restaurants, at tollbooths and in petrol stations. If your card is lost or stolen in France, call one of the following 24-hour hotlines (*see box, below*).

You must report any loss or theft of credit cards or traveller's cheques to the local police who will issue you with a certificate (useful proof to show the issuing company).

American Express	✆01 47 77 70 00
Visa	✆08 36 69 08 80
MasterCard/Eurocard	✆01 45 67 84 84
Diners Club	✆01 49 06 17 50

PUBLIC HOLIDAYS

There are 11 public holidays in France. In addition, there are other religious and national festivals days. Museums and monuments may vary their hours of admission on these days. In addition to the Christmas, spring and summer holidays there are long mid-term breaks (ten days to two weeks) in February and early November.

1 January	**New Year's Day** (*Jour de l'An*)
April (no fixed dates)	**Easter Day and Easter Monday** (*Pâques*)
1 May	**May Day** (*Fête du Travail*)
8 May	**VE Day** (*Fête de la Libération*)
Thurs 40 days after Easter	**Ascension Day** (*Ascension*)
7th Sun-Mon after Easter	**Whit Sunday and Monday** (*Pentecôte*)
14 July	**France's National Day** (*Fête de la Bastille*)
15 August	**Assumption** (*Assomption*)
1 November	**All Saint's Day** (*Toussaint*)
11 November	**Armistice Day** (*Fête de la Victoire*)
25 December	**Christmas Day** (*Noël*)

SMOKING

Smoking has been banned inside all public spaces, including hotel rooms, bars and clubs since January 2008. It is still permitted on outdoor café terraces and in specially-built fumoirs.

TELEPHONES
PUBLIC TELEPHONES

Most public phones in France use pre-paid phone cards (*télécartes*), rather than coins. Some telephone booths accept credit cards (Visa, MasterCard/Eurocard). *Télécartes* (50 or 120 units) can be bought in post offices, branches of France Télécom, *bureaux de tabac* (cafés that sell cigarettes) and newsagents and can be used to make calls in France and abroad.

TO USE YOUR PERSONAL CALLING CARD	
AT&T	☎0-800 99 00 11
Sprint	☎0-800 99 00 87
MCI	☎0-800 99 00 19
Canada Direct	☎0-800 99 00 16

INTERNATIONAL CALLS

To call France from abroad, dial the country code (33) + 9-digit number (omit the initial 0). When calling abroad from France dial 00, then dial the country code followed by the area code and number of your correspondent.
International information:
US/Canada: 00 33 12 11
International operator:
00 33 12 + country code
Local directory assistance: 12

NATIONAL CALLS

French telephone numbers have 10 digits. Paris and Paris region numbers begin with 01; 02 in northwest France; 03 in northeast France; 04 in southeast France and Corsica; 05 in southwest France.

MOBILE/CELL PHONES

In France these have numbers that begin with 06 and 07. Two-watt (lighter, shorter reach) and eight-watt models are on the market, using the Orange (www.orange.fr), Bouygtel (www.bouyguestelecom.fr) or SFR (www.sfr.fr) networks. *Mobicartes* are prepaid phone cards that fit into mobile units. Mobile phone rentals (delivery or airport pickup provided):
World Cellular Rentals:
www.worldcr.com

INTERNATIONAL DIALLING CODES (00 + code)			
Australia	☎61	New Zealand	☎64
Canada	☎1	United Kingdom	☎44
Ireland	☎353	United States	☎1

TIME

WHEN IT IS NOON IN FRANCE, IT IS	
3am	in Los Angeles
6am	in New York
11am	in Dublin
11am	in London
7pm	in Perth
9pm	in Sydney
11pm	in Auckland

In France "am" and "pm" are not used but the 24-hour clock is widely applied.

TIPPING

Since a service charge is automatically included in the price of meals and accommodation in France, any additional tipping is up to the visitor, usually small change, and generally not more than 5%. Hairdressers are usually tipped 10–15%.

As a rule, prices for hotels and restaurants as well as for other goods and services are significantly less expensive in the French regions than in Paris.

Restaurants usually charge for meals in two ways: a *forfait* or *menu*, that is, a fixed price menu with two to three courses, sometimes a small pitcher of wine, all for a set price, or *à la carte*, the more expensive way, with each course ordered separately. It is important to tell the waiting staff that you are ordering from the fixed price menu, otherwise they may charge you separately for each dish.

Cafés have very different prices, depending on where they are located. The price of a drink or a coffee is cheaper if you stand at the counter (*comptoir*) than if you sit down (*salle*) and sometimes it is even more expensive if you sit outdoors (*terrace*). In some big cities, prices go up after 10pm in the evening.

CONVERSION TABLES

Weights and Measures

1 kilogram (kg) 6.35 kilograms 0.45 kilograms	2.2 pounds (lb) 14 pounds 16 ounces (oz)	2.2 pounds 1 stone (st) 16 ounces	*To convert kilograms to pounds, multiply by 2.2*
1 metric ton (tn)	1.1 tons	1.1 tons	
1 litre (l) 3.79 litres 4.55 litres	2.11 pints (pt) 1 gallon (gal) 1.20 gallon	1.76 pints 0.83 gallon 1 gallon	*To convert litres to gallons, multiply by 0.26 (US) or 0.22 (UK)*
1 hectare (ha) 1 sq kilometre (km²)	2.47 acres 0.38 sq. miles (sq mi)	2.47 acres 0.38 sq. miles	*To convert hectares to acres, multiply by 2.4*
1 centimetre (cm) 1 metre (m)	0.39 inches (in) 3.28 feet (ft) or 39.37 inches or 1.09 yards (yd)	0.39 inches	*To convert metres to feet, multiply by 3.28; for kilometres to miles, multiply by 0.6*
1 kilometre (km)	0.62 miles (mi)	0.62 miles	

Clothing

Women			
	35	4	2½
	36	5	3½
	37	6	4½
Shoes	38	7	5½
	39	8	6½
	40	9	7½
	41	10	8½
	36	6	8
	38	8	10
Dresses	40	10	12
& suits	42	12	14
	44	14	16
	46	16	18
	36	6	30
	38	8	32
Blouses &	40	10	34
sweaters	42	12	36
	44	14	38
	46	16	40

Men			
	40	7½	7
	41	8½	8
	42	9½	9
Shoes	43	10½	10
	44	11½	11
	45	12½	12
	46	13½	13
	46	36	36
	48	38	38
Suits	50	40	40
	52	42	42
	54	44	44
	56	46	48
	37	14½	14½
	38	15	15
Shirts	39	15½	15½
	40	15¾	15¾
	41	16	16
	42	16½	16½

Sizes often vary depending on the designer. These equivalents are given for guidance only.

Speed

KPH	10	30	50	70	80	90	100	110	120	130
MPH	6	19	31	43	50	56	62	68	75	81

Temperature

Celsius (°C)	0°	5°	10°	15°	20°	25°	30°	40°	60°	80°	100°
Fahrenheit (°F)	32°	41°	50°	59°	68°	77°	86°	104°	140°	176°	212°

To convert Celsius into Fahrenheit, multiply °C by 9, divide by 5, and add 32.
To convert Fahrenheit into Celsius, subtract 32 from °F, multiply by 5, and divide by 9.

NB: Conversion factors on this page are approximate.

"Couteau" and "Fourchette"

© Andrew Johnson/iStockphoto.com

Useful Words and Phrases

ARCHITECTURAL TERMS
See Introduction: Architecture.

SIGHTS

	Translation
Abbaye	Abbey
Beffroi	Belfry
Chapelle	Chapel
Château	Castle
Cimetière	Cemetery
Cloître	Cloisters
Colombage	Half-timbering
Cour	Courtyard
Couvent	Convent
Écluse	Lock (Canal)
Église	Church
Fontaine	Fountain
Gothique	Gothic
Halle	Covered market
Jardin	Garden
Mairie	Town Hall
Maison	House
Marché	Market
Monastère	Monastery
Moulin	Windmill
Musée	Museum
Pan de Bois (En)	Timber-framed
Parc	Park
Place	Square
Pont	Bridge
Port	Port/harbour
Porte	Gateway
Quai	Quay
Remparts	Ramparts
Romain	Roman
Roman	Romanesque
Rue	Street
Statue	Statue
Tour	Tower

Natural Sites

	Translation
Abîme	Chasm
Aven	Swallow-hole
Barrage	Dam
Belvédère	Viewpoint
Cascade	Waterfall
Col	Pass
Corniche	Ledge
Côte	Coast, Hillside
Forêt	Forest
Grotte	Cave
Lac	Lake
Plage	Beach
Rivière	River
Ruisseau	Stream
Signal	Beacon
Source	Spring
Vallée	Valley

On the Road

	Translation
Parking	Car Park
Diesel/gazole	Diesel

Permis de conduire	Driving licence
Est	East
Garage	Garage (For Repairs)
Gauche	Left
Gpl	Lpg
Autoroute	Motorway
Nord	North
Horodateur	Parking meter
Essence	Petrol/gas
Station d'essence	Petrol/gas station
Droite	Right
Sud	South
Toll	Péage
Feu tricolore	Traffic lights
Pneu	Tyre
Sans Plomb	Unleaded
Ouest	West
Sabot	Wheel Clamp
Passage clouté	Pedestrian Crossing

Time

	Translation
Aujourd'hui	Today
Demain	Tomorrow
Hier	Yesterday
Hiver	Winter
Printemps	Spring
Été	Summer
Automne	Autumn/fall
Semaine	Week
Lundi	Monday
Mardi	Tuesday
Mercredi	Wednesday
Jeudi	Thursday
Vendredi	Friday
Samedi	Saturday
Dimanche	Sunday

Numbers

	Translation
zéro	0
un	1
deux	2
trois	3
quatre	4
cinq	5
six	6
sept	7
huit	8
neuf	9
dix	10
onze	11
douze	12
treize	13
quatorze	14
quinze	15
seize	16
dix-sept	17
dix-huit	18
dix-neuf	19
vingt	20
trente	30
quarante	40
cinquante	50
soixante	60
soixante-dix	70
quatre-vingt	80
quatre-vingt-dix	90
cent	100
mille	1000

Shopping

	Translation
Antiseptique	Antiseptic
Banque	Bank
Boulangerie	Bakery
Grand	Big
Librairie	Bookshop
Boucherie	Butcher's
Pharmacie	Chemist's
Fermé	Closed
Sirop pour la toux	Cough mixture
Cachets pour la gorge	Cough sweets
Entrée	Entrance
Sorite	Exit
Poissonnerie	Fishmonger's
Épicerie	Grocer's
Maison de la Presse, Marchat de Journaux	Newsagent's
Ouvert	Open
Analgésique	Painkiller
Pansement Adhésif	Plaster (Adhesive)
Poste	Post office
Livre	Pound (Weight)
Pousser	Push
Tirer	Pull
Magasin	Shop
Petit	Small
Timbres	Stamps

Food and Drink

	Translation
Bœuf	Beef
Bière	Beer
Beurre	Butter

Pain	Bread
Petit-déjeuner	Breakfast
Fromage	Cheese
Poulet	Chicken
Dessert	Dessert
Dîner	Dinner
Canard	Duck
Poisson	Fish
Fourchette	Fork
Fruits	Fruit
Verre	Glass
Raisin	Grape
Salade verte	Green salad
Jambon	Ham
Glace	Ice cream
Carafe d'eau	Jug of water
Pichet de vin	Jug of wine
Couteau	Knife
Agneau	Lamb
Déjeuner	Lunch
Viande	Meat
Eau minérale	Mineral water
Salade composée	Mixed salad
Jus d'orange	Orange juice
Assiette	Plate
Porc	Pork
Vin rouge	Red wine
Sel	Salt
Eau gazeuse	Sparkling water
Cuillère	Spoon
Eau plat	Still water
Sucre	Sugar
Eau du robinet	Tap water
Dinde	Turkey
Légumes	Vegetables
De l'eau	Water
Vin blanc	White Wine
Yaourt	Yoghurt

Personal Documents and Travel

	Translation
Aéroport	Airport
Carte de crédit	Credit Card
Douane	Customs
Passeport	Passport
Voie, Quai	Platform
Gare	Railway Station
Navette	Shuttl
Valise	Suitcase
Billet de train/d'avion	Train/plane ticket
Portefeuille	Wallet

Clothing

	Translation
Manteau	Coat
Pull	Jumper
Imperméable	Raincoat
Chemise	Shirt
Chaussures	Shoes
Chaussettes	Socks
Bas	Stockings
Costume/tailleur	Suit
Collant	Tights
Pantalon	Trousers

USEFUL PHRASES

	Translation
Au Revoir	Goodbye
Bonjour	Hello/Good Morning
Comment	How
Excusez-moi	Excuse me
Merci	Thank You
Oui/non	Yes/no
Pardon	I Am Sorry
Pourquoi	Why
Quand	When
S'il vous plaît	Please

Do you speak English?
Parlez-vous anglais?

I don't understand
Je ne comprends pas

Talk slowly
Parlez lentement

Where's...?
Où est...?

When does the ... leave?
À quelle heure part...?

When does the ... arrive?
À quelle heure arrive...?

When does the museum open?
À quelle heure ouvre le musée?

When is the show?
À quelle heure est la représentation?

When is breakfast served?
À quelle heure sert-on le petit-déjeuner?

What does it cost?
Ça coûte combien?

Where can I buy a newspaper in English?
Où puis-je acheter un journal en anglais?

Where is the nearest petrol/ gas station?
Où se trouve la station essence la plus proche?

Where can I change travellers' cheques?
Où puis-je échanger des traveller's cheques?

Where are the toilets?
Où sont les toilettes?

Do you accept credit cards?
Acceptez-vous les cartes de crédit?

I need a receipt
Je voudrais une facture, s'il vous plaît.

The Region Today

21ST CENTURY

Northern France and the Paris Region sport an interesting array of similarities and differences.

Culturally speaking, Picardy has much more in common with Nord-Pas-de-Calais than with its southern neighbour, Île-de-France. Its traditional language, 'Picard', so closely resembles its northern counterpart, 'Chtimi', that they are nearly indistinguishable. Its geography, however, closely links it with the Paris Basin, its agricultural flatlands and forests. Many Parisians seek to escape the capital for peaceful weekend hideways in nearby Oise, while many Picards are attracted by the Paris employment *eldorado*.

On the other hand, the culture of Nord-Pas-de-Calais has some unique features of its own, like the still widespread use of Flemish. Its rich privateering past has given birth to some wild festive Carnival celebrations, not to mention a tradition of hospitality that is proverbially unequalled in France, as well as the famous football rivalry between the 'Blood-Red and Golden' of Lens and Lille's 'Mastiffs'.

But be reassured: a narrow seam of nearly impassable muddy cobblestone exists between the three regions: the Paris-Roubaix, one of France's oldest and most popular cycling races, which has been held almost every year since 1896.

POPULATION

NORD-PAS-DE-CALAIS

Nord-Pas-de-Calais is one of France's most populated regions. With a birth rate significantly higher than the rest of the country, its demography is one of the youngest and most dynamic. Its dense population is mostly urban: 9 out of 10 inhabitants live in one of its many towns and cities, including Lille and its metropolis, which attracts workers from no less than fifteen medium-sized neighbouring towns.

Many Belgian migrants moved to the region in the first decade of the 20C, followed by a huge wave of Italian and Polish coal workers in the 1920s. With the decline of the mining industry, the migrationary trend has slackened, but the region still attracts many North African migrants.

PICARDY

A vivid contrast with its northern neighbour, Picardy has one of the weakest demographic growth rates in France which, in contrast, has one of the highest birth rates in Europe. Located between two major industrial basins, the region is steadily losing its inhabitants. Only the southern *département* of Oise is growing, with many former inhabitants

Paris-Roubaix – bicycle race on cobblestones

© Jean-luc Barbat/MICHELIN

The Villages of Paris: An Urban Exception

Take advantage of a nice, sunny day to step out of the hustle and bustle of the city and its tourist landmarks, to discover a more intimate side of the capital. Paris harbours a wealth of small-sized neighbourhoods, sometimes no bigger than a couple of buildings tucked away in a forgotten alley. These are remnants of long-absorbed villages which miraculously escaped Haussmann's urban renovation of Paris. As a sampler, walk half a mile from busy Porte de Bagnolet, and you'll come across the village of **Charonne**, complete with its church and cemetery. Alternatively, stroll along the calm streets and villas of the **Mouzaïa** district, once home to hundreds of craftsmen near the Parc des Buttes-Chaumont, or visit the secluded and libertarian **Butte aux Cailles**, Montmartre's southern sister hidden on a hill in the 13th arrondissement. Finally, discover the former hamlet of **Grenelle**, near the popular rue du Commerce, a hunting ground until the 19C, or the lively ambience of the **village d'Auteuil**, largely unchanged since the 19C.

of Île-de-France and Paris settling there to escape rising property prices, while still working in their original region.

PARIS AND ÎLE-DE-FRANCE

Although Île-de-France covers only 2.2 percent of the surface area of France, over 18 percent of the French population resides in this region. This huge concentration of around 12 million inhabitants is focused around the natural junctions of the Seine, Marne and Oise river basins. These large, slow rivers separate vast plateaus known for their fertile countryside, including the Brie and Beauce regions, and the large forests of Fontainebleau, Halatte, Rambouillet, Marly and St-Germain. These natural areas have somehow managed to escape the urban sprawl which, today, tends to concentrate around the new towns of Cerg, Pontoise, Créteil, Évry, St-Quentin-en-Yvelines, Marne-la-Vallée and Melun-Sénart.

LOCAL GOVERNMENT

Metropolitan France is divided into 22 **administrative regions** (including Nord-Pas-de-Calais, Picardy and Île-de-France) which are further divided into **départements**. The regions are governed by regional assemblies with extensive budgetary powers. They were created in the 1980s in an effort by the state to counterbalance the otherwise overwhelming power of the capital city. Paris is a département city with **20 local**

mayors and an assembly, the Conseil de Paris. The **mayor of Paris** is directly elected by the city's residents. The Police Commissioner, a high ranking civil servant, still takes precedence over the mayor in public order matters. This situation originated in the aftermath of the Commune de Paris in the 19C, when Paris rebelled against the state and elected its own parliament. Horrified by the ensuing bloodshed, the Third Republic's conservative legislators decided to reduce the freedom of action of the Conseil de Paris. They also decided that the Paris budget should be approved by the state, effectively making the city a penniless beggar. Laws introduced in the early 1980s radically changed this situation.

ECONOMY
NORD-PAS-DE-CALAIS

A long-standing trading region, with ports located on several major northern European maritime trade routes, Nord-Pas-de-Calais has been a prosperous textile and trading region since the Middle Ages, providing it with a great deal of autonomy throughout its history. Although fewer and fewer people are employed in heavy industry, the area's small and medium-size enterprises have modernised their practices to take full advantage of the export market and the proximity of vast European markets and the ease of access afforded by the Nord-Europe high-speed train, the Channel

Coal Mines

Mining in the coal fields of Nord-Pas-de-Calais started in the 18C. The deposit lay at the western end of a large coal depression, which extended into Belgium and Germany. The pits employed up to 220 000 people in 1947, although production began to decline from then onwards. In 1959, when productivity reached 29 million tonnes, a gradual closure plan was implemented which led to the shutting of the last pit on 21 December 1990.

A number of different industries have developed around the former mines: the production of oval coal briquettes, foundry and special coke; the manufacture of facing bricks; the sale of mine gas; the production of electricity in power stations, which run largely on fuel products gathered from the slag heaps; the use of shale, also from slag heaps, for road foundations and as ballast for railway lines. About 70 slag heaps can be exploited in this way.

Tunnel and the dense road network. This ideal location has attracted a great deal of foreign investments, including Coca-Cola, MacCain and Rank Xerox.

Established in the Middle Ages, its textile and clothing industries now find it hard to cope with massive low cost imports from low-wage countries such as China. Despite these difficulties, the Nord-Pas-de-Calais area is still France's largest producer of linen (Lys Valley) and high-quality products such as Calais and Caudry lace.

Its glassware and crystal industries include the internationally renowned Arques works.

Coal extraction in Nord-Pas-de-Calais started in the 18C. Following a rise in demand during the Industrial Revolution in the 19C, the coal mining industry became a key element of the region's economy. The conical black **slag heaps** (terrils), of which 300 now remain, became a distinctive feature of the landscape, along with mining communities built using distinctive local bricks. Competition from emerging countries and a drop in productivity in the post WW II era led to the decline of the northern mines. The last pit closed down in 1990. Closely connected to the coal industry, the region's iron and steel sectors also suffered from competitive imports of raw materials with a higher mineral content. The local government is actively looking for alternative solutions to make up for the job losses and to transform the mining landscapes

(*see box, above*). Successes include the steelworks in Dunkerque and the ultra-modern Pechiney aluminium plant in Gravelines.

French rail equipment is produced mainly in the Valenciennes and Douai areas. The threatened automotive industry has plants in Douai (Renault), Maubeuge (MCA), Douvrain (Française de Mécanique) and Hourdain (Peugeot-Fiat). Services such as logistics, distribution and tourism account for more than half of total jobs. Mail order is also an important sector of employment, with half of the ten largest French companies, including La Redoute and Trois Suisses, operating from the area.

The food-processing industry is now the region's leading industrial sector. Regional produce supplies flour mills and biscuit factories in the Lille area. The sugar beet industry has shaped the industrial landscape on the plains near Cambrai and Thumeries. Canning factories produce 30 percent of the total national production of tinned vegetables and ready made meals and 50 percent of canned fish, the latter specifically around Boulogne, France's leading fishing port.

PICARDY

Agriculture is still the best known aspect of the economy of Picardy. A mainly rural area, with over two-thirds of its rich soil occupied by open plains, Picardy is still, as one might expect, France's leading producer of sugar beet and plays a prominent role in the production of other staples, such as potatoes, peas and grain.

Food processing is a crucial part of the economy in many areas: canning factories, based in the Santerre area at Estrée, Rosières and Péronne, are major employers as are the Saint-Louis sugar refineries in Roye and Eppeville.

But Picardy has powerful and long-standing, if less obvious, industrial roots in many other domains: over 300 small and medium-sized plants employing about 20 000 people operate in the **plastic** transformation, **rubber** and **composite materials** industries. **Metallurgy** accounts for one half of the region's industrial workforce and more than 1 700 companies. Five internationally-recognised and government-aided industrial groupings exist in the region: **light metallurgy** in Vimeu; **glass transformation** in the Bresle Valley; **machine-tooling** in Albert; **industrial boilers** in Ham and **car components** in Thiérache.

One of the region's most remarkable features is the strength of its **craft industry**, especially in the domain of tapestry, stained-glass windows, etc.

Finally, new sectors like **logistics** or **call-centres** have recently appeared in Picardy. Located in one of the best connected areas of Europe, they are expected to have a major impact on local jobs in the years to come.

PARIS AND ÎLE-DE-FRANCE

France's economic heavyweight champion, Île-de-France has a Gross Regional Product that accounts for one third of the country's GNP, exceeding those of Sweden or Belgium. The region provides more than five million jobs (over 15 percent of the national labour force), of which four million are in the private sector. Its **education system** welcomes 600 000 students at university level each year. Nearly 75 000 new companies are registered yearly; to assist them in their development, government-sponsored agencies called *pépinières d'entreprises* have been created in the region.

Covering more than 50 percent of the region's territory, highly mechanised agriculture only accounts for 0.5 percent of the local workforce, which says something about the size of the average farmstead. The western plains of **Brie** and the seemingly endless plateau of **Beauce**, southwest of Paris, are nicknamed the granary of France, and for good reason: their silt soils are among France's best for the mass production of wheat and colza, a non-drying oil. Other regional produce includes beetroots and similar fresh vegetables, decorative plants and flowers, especially Brie roses. Meat and dairy production is negligible, with the exception of Seine-et-Marne's famous Brie cheeses.

Over 500 food-processing companies operate in the area.

France's leading industrial area, accounting for more than 650 000 jobs, Île-de-France is paradoxically one of the country's least industrialised regions, with a scant 14 percent of the workforce and only 6 percent of companies engaged in industrial activity. The sector has been steadily losing plants in the region since the 1980s.

The automotive industry is a leading player in the local economy, with French carmakers Renault and PSA, along with their vast network of suppliers, generating one regional industrial job out of four.

The aerospace and defence industry also plays a prominent role, with companies like EADS, Dassault Aviation, Arianespace and the Safran plants and research centres recruiting students from 17 regional universities and numerous high-level specialised engineering schools.

Energy companies like Total or EDF, the French national electricity producer, are also major employers.

Business and services make up for the overwhelming majority (more than 80 percent) of jobs and companies in the Paris region. Education and social welfare employs 1.5 million regional civil servants. Private enterprise includes electricity, phone and water companies as well as a host of consulting companies, the latter a fast-growing player in the region's economy, accounting for nearly 500 000 jobs. Banking and other financial activities account for little more than one half of that job tally (270 000 jobs), telling us much about the region's lack of specialisation.

One of the most visited cities in the world, the capital's economy is dominated by tourism. Paris attracts 31 percent of Île-de-France's jobs in the private sector, with average wages slightly higher than in the rest of the region but well above the national average. Geographic inequalities are also reflected within the city: wages offered in the 8th *arrondissement* are 82 percent higher than in the more working class 20th *arrondissement*.

FOOD AND DRINK
THE CUISINE OF PICARDY

Soups are probably Picardy's best known specialities, particularly tripe, pumpkin (*potiron*) or frog soup (*grenouilles*), as well as the famous vegetable soup *soupe des hortillons* and stuffed pancakes in a creamy mushroom sauce (*ficelle Picarde*). The people of Picardy and Artois love their vegetables: beans from Soissons, Laon artichokes, St. Valery carrots, peas from the Vermandois and leeks, which are used in a delicious pie, the *tarte aux poireaux*.

Starters include duck pâté in a pastry case (*pâté de canard en croûte*) – prepared in Amiens since the 17C –

snipe pâté (*pâté de bécassines*) from Abbeville and Montreuil, and eel pâté (*pâté d'anguilles*) from Péronne.

Duck, snipe and plover, eel, carp and pike from the River Somme are often on the menu. Seafood (shrimps known as *sauterelles* and cockles called *hemons*) is common, as are sole, turbot, fresh herring and cod, often cooked with cream.

FLEMISH CUISINE

Best enjoyed with beer, and often followed by a glass of gin or a *bistouille* (coffee with a dash of alcohol), the most typical Flemish dishes include:

- rabbit with prunes or raisins and pigeon with cherries;
- home-made potted meat made from veal, pork fat, rabbit and sometimes chicken (*potjevleesch*);
- mixed stew of veal, mutton, pork offals, pork fat and vegetables (*hochepot*);
- braised beef in a beer sauce flavoured with onions and spices (*carbonade*);
- eel sautéed in butter and stewed in a wine sauce with herbs (*anguille au vert*);
- small, smoked herrings, a speciality of Dunkerque (*craquelots*).

Among the other specialities of northern France are chitterling sausages (*andouillettes*) from Arras and Cambrai, trout from the River Canche and River Course, and cauliflowers from St-Omer.

CHEESES OF THE NORTH

Local cheeses, except for **Mont des Cats**, are strong. Most come from the Thiérache and Avesnois regions rich in pastureland. The tastiest is **Maroilles**, created in the 10C by monks from Maroilles Abbey: it has a soft centre with a crust soaked in beer, similar to cheese from Munster. The other cheeses in the region are derived from it: **Vieux Lille**, also called Maroilles Gris (grey Maroilles); **Dauphin** (Maroilles with herbs and spices); **Cœur d'Avesnes** or Rollot; and the delicious **Boulette d'Avesnes** (Maroilles with spices, rolled

Mont-des-Cats cheese

© S. Sauvignier/MICHELIN

in paprika). **Flamiche au Maroilles**, a creamy, highly flavoured quiche, is one of the most famous dishes from the northern region of France.

BRIE

The Brie region in Île-de-France is famous for its soft cow's milk cheeses with surface mould. There are two types, Brie and double- or triple-cream cheeses (**Lucullus**, **Grand Vatel**, **Gratte-Paille**, etc.) often made from the fat left over from the production of Brie, a legendary cheese that has enjoyed a reputation for excellence since the 13C. Brie was as popular with the commoners of Paris as with royalty, and it was the outright winner of a competition organised during the Congress of Vienna in 1815 bringing together all the best cheeses from throughout Europe.

There are certain characteristics common to all Brie cheeses: they are made from partially skimmed raw cow's milk; the rind is white with reddish marks; the cheese is soft in texture and pale yellow in colour; the fat content is approximately 45 percent; and the maturing period does not exceed seven weeks. Setting these features aside,

Moule-frites
© S. Sauvignier/MICHELIN

several varieties of Brie have developed and they differ depending on the area of production. The best-known are Brie de Meaux and Brie de Melun.

CAKES

The local pancakes (*crêpes*), waffles and sweet breads (*tartines* and *brioches*) are meals in themselves; brioches with bulging centres are called *coquilles*. Tarts, such as the delicious *tartes au sucre* sprinkled with brown sugar, are often served for dessert. Sweets are accompanied by a light, chicory coffee which people from the region drink at any time of the day.

The Brewing Process

Beer is obtained by the mashing and fermentation of a mixture of water and malt, flavoured with hops. Barley grains are soaked in water (malting) until they germinate. The malted barley, dried and roasted in a kiln, becomes **malt**. This is powdered and then mixed with pure water and hops and cooked, according to each manufacturer's secret procedure. This operation, called brewing, transforms the starch in the malt into sugar and makes it possible to obtain the **wort**. With the addition of a raising agent, the wort begins to ferment.

Beer brewing was formerly undertaken simply by a brewer, with his boy handling a sort of pointed shovel (*fourquet*), but is now a large and sophisticated industry.

Much French beer and lager (paler, 'aged' beer containing more bubbles and often less alcohol) is produced in the Pas-de-Calais region, which is rich in water, barley and hops. The hops grown in Flanders have a particularly strong flavour. The largest breweries are in the areas around Lille-Roubaix and Armentières, and the Scarpe and Escaut (Scheldt) river valleys. Today, there are only 17 left, although many small breweries are now operating locally. Different beers have their own characteristics: the slightly bitter lager (*bière blonde*) of the north; the relatively sweet and fruity dark beer (*bière brune*) or the richly flavoured, amber-red beer (*bière rousse*).

BEER

Gambrinus, the king of beer, is greatly revered in the north of France, as is St Arnould, the patron saint of brewers. Beer *(la bière)* was already known in Antiquity. In Gaul it was called *cervoise*. During the Middle Ages brewing beer was a privilege of the monasteries.
It expanded into Flandre under John the Fearless, Duc de Bourgogne and Comte de Flandre, who developed the use of hops.

GIN

Gin is still produced in Houlle, Wambrechies and Loos. Another drink produced in Loos is an apéritif called *chuche-mourette*, consisting of *crème de cassis* and gin.

WINE

A rather demanding plant in terms of sun exposure and soil quality, grapes never made it to the plains of Picardy or Nord-Pas-de-Calais. However, in the early 19C, the vineyards of Île-de-France were among the country's largest. West of Paris, beyond the skyscrapers of La Défense, is a suburb called Argenteuil, which produced a wine known as **Piccolo**. Massively consumed by Parisians in the guinguettes off the banks of the Seine River in the 19C, the beverage gave its name to the French word for 'boozing': *picoler*. By the end of the Second World War, the vineyards of Île-de-France had almost completely disappeared, victims of phylloxera and unable to compete with increasingly popular southern French wines. Only a few patches remain today, the largest being the **Clos Montmartre**, grown on the slopes of Paris Butte Montmartre, on a little plot beneath the famous Sacré-Coeur Basilica. The small annual production (roughly 850 half-bottles) is sold at the Grape Harvest Festival held in October.

NORTHERN FOLKLORE AND TRADITIONS

For dates of festivals and other events,
see the Calendar of Events in
Planning Your Trip.

The people of Picardy and the north of France belong to the 'Picardy nation' that once spread from Beauvais to Lille and from Calais to Laon, extending as far as Tournai and Mons. The common language of this 'nation' formed a bond between its inhabitants, who are known for being hard workers with a taste for good food and merrymaking. The natives of Flandre, Artois, Lille and Picardy are all fond of get-togethers which is reflected in their many group activities: carnivals, celebrations, patron saint's days, village fairs and associations (each village has its own band).

THE DUCASSE OR KERMESSE

The words *ducasse* (from *dédicace*, meaning a Catholic holiday) and *kermesse* ('church fair' in Flemish) now both designate a town or village patron saint's day. This holiday has preserved aspects of its religious origins (Mass and procession) but today also includes stalls, competitions, traditional games, jumble sales, etc.

CARNIVALS

Carnival time is an occasion to dress up in costume and watch parades of floats and giant figures. It traditionally takes place on Shrove Tuesday *(Mardi Gras)* – as in Dunkerque, where it lasts for three days – but in reality, carnival parades take place throughout the year in the North of France.

FAMOUS GIANTS

Giants originate from various myths, legends and stories, and include:
- **legendary founders**, such as Lydéric and Phinaert in Lille
- **famous warriors** like the Reuzes from Dunkerque and Cassel, said to originate from Scandinavia
- **historic figures**, such as Jeanne Maillotte in Lille, the inn-keeper who fought off the 'Howlers'; the beautiful Roze in Ardres, who saved the town from dragonnades; the Elector of Bergues, portraying Lamartine; Roland in Hazebrouck, one of Baudouin of Flandre's Crusaders,

Yan den Houtkapper *Steenvoorde*

Martin and Martine *Cambrai*

Gayant and his wife *Douai*

The sailor's wife *Grand-Fort Philippe*

Mother Reuze *Cassel*

R. Corbel/ MICHELIN

Carnival in Dunkerque

© Pierre Cheuva/Photononstop

who distinguished himself at the taking of Constantinople

- **famous couples**, like Martin and Martine, the two 'Jack o' the Clocks' of Cambrai; Colas and Jacqueline, the gardeners of Arras; Arlequin and Colombine in Bruay; Manon and Des Grieux in Hesdin

- **popular figures**, like Gédéon, the bell ringer of Bourbourg, who saved the belfry chimes from being stolen; the pedlar Tisje Tasje of Hazebrouck, symbol of the Flemish spirit, with his wife Toria and his daughter Babe Tisje; Pierrot Bimberlot in Le Quesnoy; and Ko Pierre, a drum major, in Aniche

- **legendary heroes**: Gargantua in Bailleul; Gambrinus, the king of beer, in Armentières; Yan den Houtkapper, the woodcutter who made a pair of wooden boots for Charlemagne, in Steenvoorde; Gayant of Douai, said to have delivered the town from brigands

- **representatives of trades**, like the vegetable gardener Baptistin in St-Omer; the miner Cafougnette in Denain; and the fisherman Batisse in Boulogne

- or simply a **child**, like the famous Binbin in Valenciennes.

Giants are often accompanied by their families – they do marry and have large families – and are surrounded by skirted horses, devils, bodyguards and wheels of fortune. Sometimes they have their own hymn, such as the Reuzelieds in Dunkerque and Cassel.

Materials – Traditionally the giants' bodies are made from a willow frame on which a painted papier-mâché head is placed. Once dressed in their costumes, the giants are then carried by one or more people, who make them dance in the procession. The tallest is Gayant in Douai, who is 8.4m/28ft tall.

As giants are often now made of heavier materials (steel tubing, cane, plastic), they are frequently pulled along in carts or on wheels, rather than being carried.

TOWN CARILLONS

Carillons in town belfries, which regularly sound out their melodic tunes, lend rhythm to life in northern French towns. Since the Middle Ages, when four bells were tapped by hand with a hammer, a number of innovations have been introduced, including mechanisms, a manual keyboard and pedals, all of which have made it possible to increase the number of bells (62 in Douai) and the variety of their sounds.

Carillon concerts are held in Douai, St-Amand-les-Eaux and Maubeuge (east of Valenciennes).

TRADITIONAL GAMES AND SPORTS

Traditional entertainment remains popular and includes marionette puppets, ball games, real tennis, ninepins, darts, lacrosse (an ancestor of golf), archery (also a traditional sport in the Valois region), pigeon-breeding, etc. A popular bar game is the *billard Nicolas*, where players squeeze a bulb to blow a marble across a round playing area.

Archery – In the Middle Ages archers were already the pride of the counts of Flandre, who would have the archers accompany them on all their expeditions. As soon as individual towns were founded, the archers formed associations or guilds.

They appeared at all public ceremonies, dressed in brightly coloured costumes, brandishing the great standard of their association.

Today archery is practised in several ways. A method particular to the north is vertical or 'perch' shooting, which consists of firing arrows upwards to hit dummy birds attached to gratings suspended from a pole. At the top of this pole, about 30m/98ft off the ground, is the hardest target of all, the **poppinjay** (*papegai*). Archers must hit this bird with a long, ball-tipped arrow and the winner is proclaimed 'King of the Perch'.

In winter the sport is practised indoors: arrows are shot horizontally at a slightly tilted grating.

Still grouped into brotherhoods, the archers gather every year to honour their patron, St Sebastian.

Crossbow – The art of the crossbow, which also dates from the Middle Ages, has its own brotherhoods. Their gatherings, colourful events featuring these curious weapons from another time, are often given evocative names such as the King's Crossbow Shoot.

Javelin – This feathered arrow measuring 50–60cm/20–24in is thrown into a tightly tied bundle of straw which serves as a target. It is based on the same principle as the game of darts, which is played in many cafés.

Chimes of the belfry in Douai
© S. Sauvignier/MICHELIN

The Game of 'Billons' – A *billon* is a tapering wooden club about 1m/3ft long, weighing about 2–3kg/4–7lb. Two teams throw their *billons* in turn towards a post 9m/29.5ft away. The aim is to land the narrower end of the club nearest to the post and this may be achieved by dislodging the *billons* of the opposing team.

Bouchon – Teams face each other in cafés, and knock down the cork and wood 'targets' with their metal paddles. The best players participate in competitions at local festivals.

Pigeon-Breeding – Pigeon fanciers (*coulonneux*) raise their birds to fly back to the nest as quickly as possible. For pigeon-racing competitions, which are very popular, the birds are carried in special baskets to a distance of up to 500km/310mi and must then return to their dovecote at record speed. A pigeon can fly over 100km/62mph on average.

Singing Finch Competitions – Finches have also become part of folklore in northern France, where they participate in trilling contests. Some can trill as many as 800 times an hour.

History

TIME LINE
CELTS AND ROMANS

C. 300 BC The north of Gaul occupied by a Celto-Germanic tribe, the Belgae.

153 BC First Roman soldiers enter Gaul.

57 BC Belgian Gaul conquered by Caesar. Bavay, Boulogne and Amiens become important Roman centres.

AD 1C–3C Roman peace. Northern France becomes part of the province of Second Belgium (capital at Reims).

406 German tribes invade Gaul.

MEROVINGIANS AND CAROLINGIANS

486 Territory from the Somme to the Loire rivers occupied by Clovis following the defeat of the Roman army at Soissons: his kingdom was called Francia in Latin.

534–36 Franks conquer Burgundy and acquire Provence.

6C and 7C Creation of bishoprics and founding of many abbeys.

751 Pepin crowned first Carolingian King of the Franks.

800 Charlemagne crowned Holy Roman Emperor.

Gallo-Roman ruins in Champlieu near Morienval

© S. Sauvignier/MICHELIN

9C and 10C Norman and Hungarian invasions. Withdrawal of the abbeys into the towns.

911 The Duchy of Normandy created after the Treaty of St Clair-sur-Epte, ending the Normans' ambitions in Île-de-France.

987 Hugh Capet, duke and suzerain of the land extending from the Somme to the Loire rivers, crowned the first King of France, in Senlis.

THE MIDDLE AGES

11C and 12C Period of prosperity. Development of the clothmaking industry in Flanders, Artois and Picardy. Towns obtain charters and build belfries.

1066 William, Duke of Normandy, conquers England.

1095 Pope Urban II preaches the first crusade at Clermont.

1154 Henry II becomes King of England and establishes the Angevin Empire of Britain and western and southern France.

1214 Battle of Bouvines: victory for Philippe Auguste over the Count of Flanders and his allies King John of England, the Holy Roman Emperor Otto IV and the counts of Boulogne and Hainault.

1272 Ponthieu under the authority of the kings of England.

1314 Flandre annexed by Philip the Fair.

1337 Beginning of the Hundred Years War (1337–1453). The death of Philip the Fair and his three sons ('the accursed kings') results in a succession crisis: Philip the Fair's nephew, Philip de Valois, is preferred by the French barons over his grandson, Edward III, King of England. The following century is marked by battles between the French and the English who lay claim to the French Crown, as well as between the Armagnacs, supporters of the family of Orléans, and the Burgundians, supporters of the dukes of Burgundy.

1346 Battle of Crécy: victory of Edward III of England.

1347 Calais surrenders to the English with the famous episode of the Burghers of Calais.

1348 The Black Death.

1369 Marriage of Philip the Bold, Duke of Burgundy, with Marguerite, daughter of the Count of Flanders: Flanders under Burgundian authority.

1415 Battle of Agincourt: victory for Henry V of England.

1420 The Treaty of Troyes signed by Isabeau of Bavaria, wife of the mad King Charles VI, depriving the Dauphin of his rights of succession and designating her son-in-law, Henry V of England, heir to the French throne.

1422 Death of Charles VI. France divided between the English, the Burgundians and the Armagnacs. Charles VII, the legitimate heir, resident in Bourges.

1430 Joan of Arc taken prisoner at Compiègne, and burned at the stake in 1431, in Rouen.

1435 Reconciliation of France and Burgundy in the Treaty of Arras.

1441 English supremacy over Île-de-France ends with the liberation of Pontoise.

1477 Invasion of Picardy, Artois, Boulonnais and Hainault by Louis XI following the death of Charles the Bold; only Picardy subsequently held. Marriage of Marie of Burgundy, daughter of Charles the Bold, to Maximilian of Austria: Flanders brought under Hapsburg control.

FROM THE BOURBONS TO THE REVOLUTION

16C Through the House of Hapsburg, Flanders forms part of the empire of Charles V of Spain.

1520 Meeting between Henry VIII of England and François I at the Field of the Cloth of Gold, Guînes.

1529 Peace of Dames signed at Cambrai: claims to Artois and Flanders renounced by François I.

1557 St-Quentin taken by the Spanish.

1558 Calais taken from the English by the Duke of Guise.

1562 Beginning of the Wars of Religion (1562–98).

1585 Philip II of Spain allied with the Catholic League (Treaty of Joinville).

1593 Henry of Navarre converts to Catholicism after capturing most of Île-de-France; crowned King Henri IV of France.

1598 Edict of Nantes grants religious tolerance to the Hugeunots.

1659 Following the Treaty of the Pyrenees, marriage agreed between Louis XIV and Maria-Theresa of Spain; Artois brought under French sovereignty.

1661 The construction of a huge palace at Versailles commissioned by Louis XIV.

1663 Marriage of Louis XIV with Maria-Theresa, who according to local custom was to inherit all of the Brabant region from her mother. When the inheritance passes to another heir, Louis

XIV declares the war of 'Devolution' on the Spanish Low Countries.

1668 Walloon Flanders given to Louis XIV by the Treaty of Aix-la-Chapelle.

1678 Louis XIV allowed to annex the other northern towns by the Treaty of Nimegen.

1713 The borders of northern France established definitively (Treaty of Utrecht).

1789 The French Revolution. Declaration of the Rights of Man, Storming of the Bastille and formation of the National Assembly.

FROM THE FIRST TO THE SECOND EMPIRE

1802 Treaty of Amiens: peace with Britain.

1803 Napoléon's army mustered at the Boulogne Camp for a possible invasion of England.

1804 Napoléon crowns himself Emperor of France.

1814 France invaded. Unconditional abdication by Napoléon at Fontainebleau. Louis XVIII, returned from exile in England, is enthroned in 1815.

1840 Attempted uprising against King Louis-Philippe organised by Louis-Napoléon in Boulogne.

1848 Louis-Napoléon elected President of the Republic; crowned Emperor (Napoléon III) in 1852.

1870–71 Franco-Prussian War. End of the Second Empire signalled by the defeat at Sedan: the Third Republic proclaimed. Paris besieged by Prussians: Alsace and part of Lorraine given up under the Treaty of Frankfurt.

20TH CENTURY

1914 Outbreak of the First World War. France attacked by German armies through neutral Belgium; four years of bloody trench warfare follow.

1915–18 Battles throughout northern France and Flanders: in Artois (Neuville-St-Vaast, Vimy), in Picardy (Somme Valley, Chemin des Dames in the Aisne Valley, St Quentin) and in Île-de-France (Ourcq Valley, Battle of the Marne).

1918 11 November: armistice signed in Compiègne Forest.

1919 End of the war with the Treaty of Versailles.

1939 Outbreak of the Second World War. In June 1940

German troops in the wrecked streets of St Quentin before the German offensive in Picardy During World War I

France overrun by the German army; occupation of much of the country. The 'French State', established at Vichy, collaborates closely with the Germans, who retain control over northern France. France's honour saved by General de Gaulle's Free French forces and the courage of the men and women of the Resistance. By 1942 all France occupied; the French fleet scuttled at Toulon. Allied landing in Normandy in June 1944, and in the south of France in August: Paris liberated. The 'Dunkirk pocket' retaken by the Allies. The German surrender signed at Reims on 7 May 1945.

1976 Creation of the 'Île-de-France' administrative region.

1987 Start of building works for the Channel Tunnel linking France and England.

1994 6 May: official opening of the Channel Tunnel.

1996 Inauguration of Evry Cathedral.

1998 Inauguration of the Stade de France in St-Denis.

21ST CENTURY

2004 Lille is designated a European Capital of Culture.

2007 Nicolas Sarkozy elected President of France.

2008 Launch of "Grand Paris", a scheme to strengthen the link between the capital and its suburbs via a transport network.

2009 Construction starts on the Louvre Lens.

2010 The LaM modern and contemporary art gallery in Villeneuve d'Ascq near Lille reopens its doors. Paris hosts a record 959 congresses and conferences.

2011 Map of the Paris "super metro" unveiled, featuring five lines and 82 stations.

2012 Belfries of Belgium and France listed as UNESCO World Heritage sites. Opening of Louvre Lens museum. François Hollande elected 7th President of the French Fifth Republic.

2013 Bassin Minier awarded UNESCO World Heritage status.

A short history of walls

When Clovis I (465-511), King of the Franks, defeated the Romans at Soissons in 486, he strengthened the city's walls against his southern enemy, the King of Burgundy. Six hundred years later, it was England to the north that prompted Philippe Auguste to build an impregnable fortress with 4m-/12ft-thick walls on a site called the Louvre. Lacking such lavish means, the inhabitants of La Thiérache, desperate to fend off the outlaws who were invading the region from every direction during the Hundred Years War (1337–1453) came up with the novel idea of fortifying their churches instead! Taking the wall to an entirely new level, Louis XIV ordered his military architect, Vauban, to build 28 citadels and forts across the region to stare down the threat from his Habsburg neighbours in the east during the Spanish War of Succession (1707–1714). These forts turned out to be of little use against the Germans in 1914, however, when earth walls proved to be the most effective form of defence. When the Germans smashed through the Maginot Line in 1940, they built the region's last wall, the "Atlantic Wall", a chain of 10 000 coastal bunkers stretching deep into Nord-Pas-de-Calais. It was joined three years later by "La Coupole", a 5m-/16ft-thick concrete V2 rocket bunker near Saint-Omer, which rendered even the tallest wall obsolete.

INTERIOR DECORATION

Fontainebleau – Galerie François I, fresco by Primaticcio

Renaissance: First Fontainebleau School – Ornate decoration in a free interpretation of the Italian masters. The frescoes framed by stuccowork are above the wainscoting. Coffered ceilings and rafters.

Fontainebleau – Salon Louis XIII

Louis XIII style – The decorative features are more restrained. Above the wainscoting are huge tapestries or frescoes. The ceiling rafters are visible but in most instances the coffering has disappeared.

Versailles – Salon de Vénus

Louis XIV style – The decoration is luxurious in the materials used but understated in design. Marble panels decorate the walls. The ceiling is divided into painted compartments separated by gilded stuccowork.

©2009, White Images/Scala, Florence

Champs – Mme de Pompadour's bedchamber

Louis XV style – Right angles have been banished. Curves, scrolls and arabesques soften straight lines. Light-coloured wainscoting has replaced the marble panels. Mouldings with plant and floral motifs, volutes, cartouches and shells.

© DEA/G DAGLI ORTI/agefotostock

Versailles – Louis XVI's gaming room

Louis XVI style – The decoration is still elegant and light in colour, but straight lines have come back into fashion. The severity of the rectangular panels is relieved by reeds and ribbons or garlands.

Ph. Gajic/MICHELIN

Compiègne – Napoleon's bedchamber

Empire style – Antique green or crimson-red hangings have replaced the wainscoting. Straight lines and semicircular arches predominate. Heavy mouldings and motifs stand out against the dark woodwork.

71

Art and Culture

LIVING LIKE KINGS

After the 15C, medieval castles were converted from fortresses into residential châteaux. Windows were enlarged, and doors and openings were richly adorned. Towers, once strategic elements of the defensive structure, became decorative features, along with crenellated battlements and moats. By the second half of the 16C, such characteristics had become superfluous. Façades were embellished with statues and rows of superimposed columns. Roofs were high and presented a single slope.

The Château d'Écouen is a fine example of the French Renaissance style, as is the Richelieu Pavillon of the Louvre (1546–1654), in Paris. The style, which succeeded Gothic as the style dominant in Europe after the mid-16C, first developed in Italy. The name describes the 'rebirth' of interest in Roman and Greek art and learning. By the early 17C, the Classical style of architecture had emerged, as expressed in the magnificence of royal palaces.

FRANÇOIS I (R. 1515–47)

The early phase of the French Renaissance culminated in the François I style (℃ see FONTAINEBLEAU). The decorative aspects mingle Gothic embellishments with elements inspired by Italian art, and the design features round arches and symmetrical composition. Many of the elegant buildings erected by the monarch bear his distinctive emblem: a crowned salamander.

HENRI IV (R. 1589–1610) – LOUIS XIII (R. 1610–43)

Louis XIII was strongly influenced by the Henri IV style (Place des Vosges, Paris), which marked the beginnings of the Classical period of French architecture. The principal characteristics of this style, which prevailed during the first half of the 17C, are the exact symmetry of the main building and the use of brick panels set into white stonework. Carved ornamentation is limited and sober. Most often, the design is a central block flanked by two end pavilions (℃ see Château de COURANCES). Louis XIII built the first palace in Versailles in this style, in brick, stone and slate.

Galerie des Glaces, Château de Versailles

© Bertrand Rieger/hemis.fr

LOUIS XIV (R. 1643–1715)

Under the skilful hand of François Mansart, civil architecture gave up its straightforward character and acquired a less domestic, nobler appearance. The early period shows columns and pilasters that stand the height of a single floor of the château. Triangular and arched pediments top doorways and windows. Numerous chimneys sprout from the high roofs (*see Château de MAISONS-LAFITTE*).

Châteaux built during the second period are characterised by a high ground floor, a very high first floor and a relatively low second floor. A balustrade conceals the roof. The horizontal lines of the building are broken by rows of sturdy columns and tall windows. Ornamental sculpture is limited to the rooftop and the summit of the front pavilions, and inspired by classical models. Versailles represents the culmination of the high Classical period.

LOUIS XV (R. 1715–74)

After 1700, the Louis XIV style and its harsh angles were mellowed by soft, rounded contours. Under Louis XV, oval spaces and curved surfaces were favoured. Windows and pediments display intricate ornamentation, while the rest of the façade remains austere, without columns; the roof is formed by two sloping planes (*see CHANTILLY: Grandes écuries*). Over time, Classical yielded more and more to Rococo (also known as Baroque classicism in France), which is distinguished by profuse, often semi-abstract ornamentation, and lightness of colour and weight.

LOUIS XVI (R. 1774–92)

The influence of the elegant Louis XV style is still apparent in works of this period, but over-abundant curves are replaced by right angles. Columns make a conspicuous comeback, placed on unadorned façades. This phase is known as 'Classicist', for many of the decorative motifs are inspired by Antiquity, a trend that introduced the so-called Pompeian and Empire styles that followed (*see VERSAILLES: Petit Trianon*). The French Revolution brought an abrupt end to building in this style.

RELIGIOUS AND CIVIL ARCHITECTURE

Île-de-France and the regions north of Paris offer a rich variety of architectural styles: Gallo-Roman at Bavay; Romanesque at Morienval, Rhuis and Chartres; Gothic architecture throughout Île-de-France, where it was born, and the later Flamboyant Gothic mainly in Picardy; Renaissance influence at Amiens and Cassel; Classical architecture in and around Paris; and Baroque in Flanders.

Many of the earliest buildings of note were constructed for religious purposes, and the development of architectural styles is best understood through them. A church consisted basically of a chancel reserved for members of the clergy, where the high altar and the reliquaries were located, and of a nave for the congregation. This simple layout characterised the early churches, built on a basilical plan. During the Romanesque period the plan of the church developed into the shape of a cross. The vestibule (narthex) at the entrance received those who had not been baptised, and the nave was enlarged with aisles. In places of pilgrimage, an ambulatory and side aisles were added to the chancel to facilitate processions. Architects followed this layout as it was convenient for celebrating Mass and easy to build.

ROMANESQUE (11C–12C)

Architects in Romanesque times knew how to build huge, lofty churches, but as the heavy stone vaulting often caused the walls to settle or cave in, they made the windows as small as possible and added aisles surmounted by galleries to support the sombre nave.

One of the main types of roofing in Romanesque churches is groined vaulting, in which two identical barrels meet at right angles. The barrel, in line with the nave, is supported by the transverse arch, while the one set at a right angle is supported by the main arch or by a recess in the wall. Rhuis

ARCHITECTURAL DRAWINGS

Religious architecture

MANTES-LA-JOLIE – Ground plan of Notre-Dame (12C-14C)

Basilical plan without transept: the sacristy was added in the 13C, the radiating chapels and the Chapelle de Navarre in the 14C.

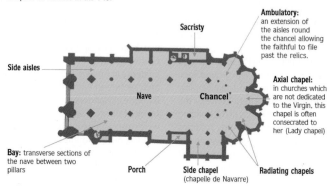

Sacristy

Ambulatory: an extension of the aisles round the chancel allowing the faithful to file past the relics.

Side aisles

Axial chapel: in churches which are not dedicated to the Virgin, this chapel is often consecrated to her (Lady chapel)

Nave

Chancel

Bay: transverse sections of the nave between two pillars

Porch

Side chapel (chapelle de Navarre)

Radiating chapels

CHARTRES – Notre-Dame Cathedral

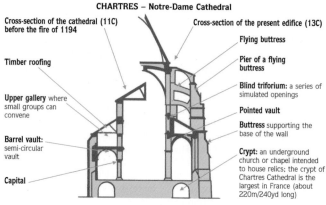

Cross-section of the cathedral (11C) before the fire of 1194

Cross-section of the present edifice (13C)

Flying buttress

Timber roofing

Pier of a flying buttress

Blind triforium: a series of simulated openings

Upper gallery where small groups can convene

Pointed vault

Buttress supporting the base of the wall

Barrel vault: semi-circular vault

Crypt: an underground church or chapel intended to house relics; the crypt of Chartres Cathedral is the largest in France (about 220m/240yd long)

Capital

RAMPILLON – Main doorway of the church (13C)

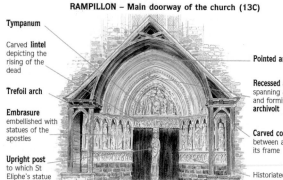

Tympanum

Carved **lintel** depicting the rising of the dead

Pointed archivolt

Trefoil arch

Recessed arches spanning an opening and forming the **archivolt**

Embrasure embellished with statues of the apostles

Carved cornerpiece between an arch and its frame

Upright post to which St Eliphe's statue is bonded

Historiated base

R. Corbel/MICHELIN

AMIENS – West front of the cathedral (13C)

The vast cathedral is the edifice which best reflects the blossoming of Rayonnant Gothic architecture.

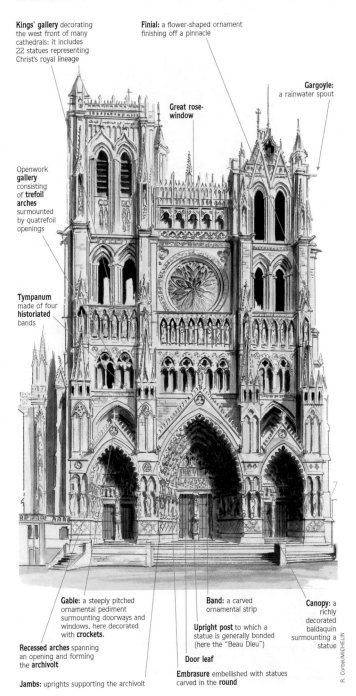

Kings' gallery decorating the west front of many cathedrals: it includes 22 statues representing Christ's royal lineage

Finial: a flower-shaped ornament finishing off a pinnacle

Gargoyle: a rainwater spout

Great rose-window

Openwork **gallery** consisting of **trefoil arches** surmounted by quatrefoil openings

Tympanum made of four **historiated** bands

Gable: a steeply pitched ornamental pediment surmounting doorways and windows, here decorated with **crockets**.

Recessed arches spanning an opening and forming the **archivolt**

Jambs: uprights supporting the archivolt

Band: a carved ornamental strip

Upright post to which a statue is generally bonded (here the "Beau Dieu")

Door leaf

Embrasure embellished with statues carved in the **round**

Canopy: a richly decorated baldaquin surmounting a statue

R. Corbel/MICHELIN

75

BEAUVAIS – East end of the cathedral (13C)

In spite of the missing spire (which collapsed in 1573) and nave (never built owing to lack of funds), the cathedral has a magnificent chancel representing the apogee of Gothic building techniques with vaulting soaring to a height of 48m/157ft.

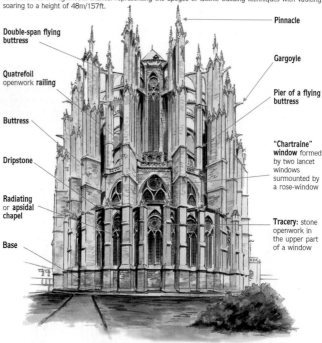

Pinnacle

Double-span flying buttress

Quatrefoil openwork **railing**

Buttress

Dripstone

Radiating or **apsidal** chapel

Base

Gargoyle

Pier of a flying buttress

"Chartraine" window formed by two lancet windows surmounted by a rose-window

Tracery: stone openwork in the upper part of a window

SENLIS – Notre-Dame Cathedral (12C-13C)

Cell or **quarter:** a segment of vaulting defined by intersecting ribs

Intersecting ribs

Lunette: part of the ribbed vaulting which does not extend to the keystone

Pendant keystone

Transverse arch: a reinforcing arch under a vault

Tierceron: an intermediate rib

Tracery: delicate stone openwork in the upper part of a window

Clerestory window

Equilateral arch: a pointed arch whose radii are equal to its span

Gallery

Openwork railing

Composite pillar formed by several bonded columns

Pointed **main arcade**

R. Corbel/MICHELIN

AIRE-SUR-LA-LYS – Organ of the collegiate church (1653)

This richly carved organ comes from the former Cistercian abbey of Clairmarais near Aire-sur-la-Lys.

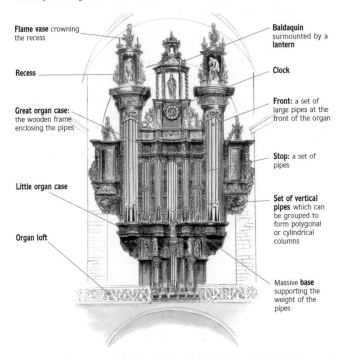

Flame vase crowning the recess

Recess

Great organ case: the wooden frame enclosing the pipes

Little organ case

Organ loft

Baldaquin surmounted by a **lantern**

Clock

Front: a set of large pipes at the front of the organ

Stop: a set of pipes

Set of vertical pipes which can be grouped to form polygonal or cylindrical columns

Massive **base** supporting the weight of the pipes

QUAËDYPRE – High altar and altarpiece of the church (late 17C)

In the 17C and 18C, altarpieces were architectural compositions towering above the altar and intended to channel the congregation's religious fervour.

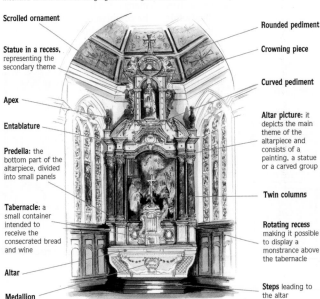

Scrolled ornament

Statue in a recess, representing the secondary theme

Apex

Entablature

Predella: the bottom part of the altarpiece, divided into small panels

Tabernacle: a small container intended to receive the consecrated bread and wine

Altar

Medallion

Rounded pediment

Crowning piece

Curved pediment

Altar picture: it depicts the main theme of the altarpiece and consists of a painting, a statue or a carved group

Twin columns

Rotating recess making it possible to display a monstrance above the tabernacle

Steps leading to the altar

R. Corbel/MICHELIN

and Morienval churches and the Royal Doorway of Chartres Cathedral are splendid examples of Romanesque art and well worth seeing.

GOTHIC (12C–15C)

The transition from Romanesque to Gothic architecture – which originated in Île-de-France – was a slow, natural process that developed in response to the demand for wider, higher and lighter churches. Gothic art, typified by quadripartite vaulting and the use of pointed arches, evolved from sombre 12C Romanesque sanctuaries into light 13C churches and the extravagantly ornate buildings of the 15C. It is rare to find a church with entirely unified features reflecting a given period in history. Building a church was a costly and lengthy operation subject to changes in public taste and building methods as the work progressed. Towards the late 13C, famous personalities and guilds were granted the privilege of having a chapel built in their honour in one of the side aisles. In exchange they were expected to make a generous contribution towards the building or its maintenance.

Architects – The names of the architects of great religious edifices are known to us only from the Gothic period onwards, through texts or through inscriptions carved around the 'labyrinths' outlined on cathedral floors. That is how Robert de Luzarches was revealed as responsible for the plans of Amiens Cathedral.

The most outstanding master builder in the north of France, however, was undoubtedly **Villard de Honnecourt**, born near Cambrai. The towers of Laon Cathedral, Vaucelles Abbey *(south of Cambrai)*, and the chancels at St-Quentin and Cambrai *(no longer extant)* have all been attributed to him.

West fronts – Most main façades were set facing west. Nave and aisles had their own doorway flanked by buttresses that were bare in the 12C and 13C, ornate in the 15C. The tympanum featured ornamentation, and in the 14C its gable was elaborately carved. In the 13C, rose windows were fairly small; in the 14C they were enlarged across the west front to provide light for the nave. As windows grew larger, façades became more delicate. A gallery was built at the base of the towers to break the rigid vertical perspective created by the buttresses and bell towers; in the 15C this was reduced to a balustrade and the gables further embellished.

Ideally, west fronts were to be richly decorated with stone carvings, but in many cases they were the last part to be completed. Architects were often obliged to forego ornamentation, and even towers, owing to insufficient

Transitional (12C)

Early Gothic (early 13C)

High Gothic (late 13C-early 14C)

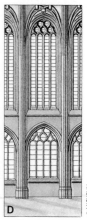
Flamboyant (15C and 16C)

© MICHELIN

funds. In other cases, even the transepts were given remarkable façades (⌕ see CHARTRES).

Spires – After lightening the façades of Gothic churches, architects turned to the spires. By the Flamboyant period the open-work masonry was markedly ornate. In the 19C many bell towers in the region were given a spire by followers of Viollet-le-Duc.

Flying buttresses – In Early Gothic churches the pillars in the nave were supported by masonry concealed in the galleries. During the 12C these walls were reduced to arches supported by sturdy piers. Soon afterwards the galleries themselves were replaced with a row of flying buttresses outside. A number of high openings could therefore be incorporated into the church interior, producing a far more luminous nave.

From then on, tall churches can be schematically described as stone frames consisting of columns supporting diagonal arches and resting on two or three levels of flying buttresses. The buttresses were in turn supported by a series of tall pillars bearing pinnacles.

Diagonal arches – Towards the end of the 11C, groined vaulting was extremely common; but, as it was difficult to build and liable to crack, a group of architects from England, Milan and Île-de-France decided to reinforce the groins.

They found that by building the diagonal arches first and by consolidating them with a small amount of rubble, vaulting that was both sturdy and light was achieved.

By supporting this vaulting on a series of arches, so that the weight of the masonry would have to be borne at the springing, the architects could dispense with the walls in between the arches and replace them with stained-glass windows; this in turn greatly enhanced the luminosity of the interiors.

This significant development heralded the age of quadripartite vaulting.

Vaulting – Quadripartite vaulting, in which the thrust is supported by four main arches, is easy to install in a square-shaped bay. In the 12C bays were enlarged and it was no longer possible to build them square, as the pillars propping up the walls would have been too far apart. The problem was initially resolved by covering the bays two by two, thus forming a square again. An extra transverse arch was then added and made to rest on slim pillars alternating with stout piers.

This type of vaulting – upheld by three diagonal arches – is known as sexpartite vaulting because of the number of its divisions.

When more sophisticated diagonal arches were made to support the vaulting above rectangular bays, the intermediary resting points were eventually discarded.

After the 15C, Flamboyant architects put in additional, decorative ribbing of complex design that formed purely decorative arches (called liernes and tiercerons) and subsequently stars and intricate networks. The main supporting arches were flanked by ornamental arches of no practical use. The keystones – usually pendant – grew thinner and longer.

Elevations (⌕ see illustrations) – Gothic elevations reflect the continual search for higher and lighter buildings.

Transitional Gothic (A) – The term Transitional Gothic covers the birth and early stages of Gothic architecture, from about 1125 to 1190. The first use of diagonal vaulting in France appeared over the ambulatory in the Romanesque abbey church at Morienval.

Though some Romanesque details – such as semicircular arches – can still be observed in early Gothic buildings, there were several significant changes. The new interiors presented four-storey elevations consisting of high clerestory windows at the top lighting the nave directly, a triforium (a narrow, arcaded passageway below the clerestory), a gallery – instrumental in supporting the walls as high up as possible – and arcading at ground level. There were often openings behind the gallery but never behind the triforium.

The pillars of the main arches initially consisted of a thick column; this was

Civil architecture

Château de COURANCES (16C-17C)

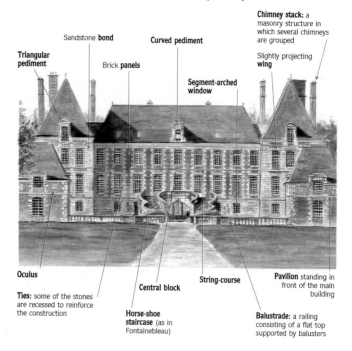

Triangular pediment

Sandstone **bond**

Brick **panels**

Curved pediment

Segment-arched window

Chimney stack: a masonry structure in which several chimneys are grouped

Slightly projecting **wing**

Oculus

Central block

String-course

Horse-shoe staircase (as in Fontainebleau)

Pavilion standing in front of the main building

Ties: some of the stones are recessed to reinforce the construction

Balustrade: a railing consisting of a flat top supported by balusters

Château de CHANTILLY stables – Dome (1721-1740)

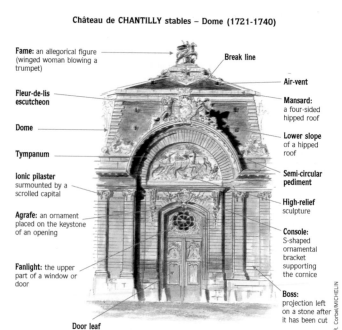

Fame: an allegorical figure (winged woman blowing a trumpet)

Break line

Air-vent

Fleur-de-lis escutcheon

Mansard: a four-sided hipped roof

Dome

Lower slope of a hipped roof

Tympanum

Ionic pilaster surmounted by a scrolled capital

Semi-circular pediment

Agrafe: an ornament placed on the keystone of an opening

High-relief sculpture

Console: S-shaped ornamental bracket supporting the cornice

Fanlight: the upper part of a window or door

Boss: projection left on a stone after it has been cut

Door leaf

R. Corbel/MICHELIN

RUE – Belfry (15C)

Symbolising the power of the city, the belfry was used as a watchtower as well as the aldermen's meeting place.

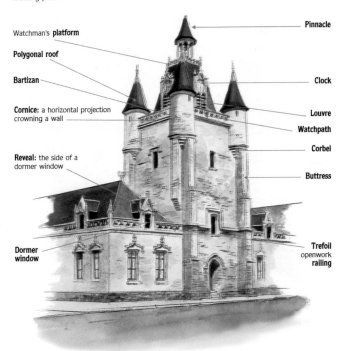

Watchman's **platform**

Polygonal roof

Bartizan

Cornice: a horizontal projection crowning a wall

Reveal: the side of a dormer window

Dormer window

Pinnacle

Clock

Louvre

Watchpath

Corbel

Buttress

Trefoil openwork **railing**

ARRAS – Façades overlooking the Grand'Place (15C-17C)

Left is the Hôtel des Trois Luppars (1467), the oldest house lining the square, right is a house dating from 1684.

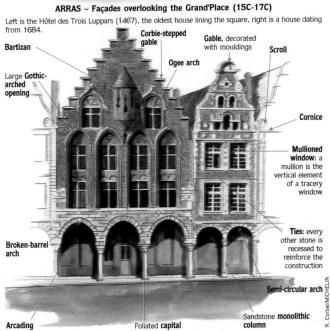

Bartizan

Large **Gothic-arched opening**

Broken-barrel arch

Arcading

Corbie-stepped gable

Ogee arch

Gable, decorated with mouldings

Scroll

Cornice

Mullioned window: a mullion is the vertical element of a tracery window

Ties: every other stone is recessed to reinforce the construction

Semi-circular arch

Sandstone **monolithic column**

Foliated **capital**

R. Corbel/MICHELIN

CHATOU – 19C pavilion

This type of pavilion, built of course-grained limestone, is characteristic of suburban domestic architecture.

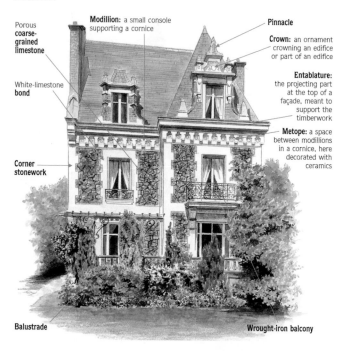

Modillion: a small console supporting a cornice

Porous coarse-grained limestone

Pinnacle

Crown: an ornament crowning an edifice or part of an edifice

White-limestone bond

Entablature: the projecting part at the top of a façade, meant to support the timberwork

Metope: a space between modillions in a cornice, here decorated with ceramics

Corner stonework

Balustrade

Wrought-iron balcony

later replaced by twinned columns supporting the arches and the colonnettes above. Laon Cathedral is a good example of Early Gothic architecture. Semicircular transept endings like the famous south arm at Soissons Cathedral were also a feature.

Early Gothic (B) – This great period (c. 1180–1250), when Gothic architecture was in its ascendancy, produced some of France's finest masterpieces, among them Chartres Cathedral (see illustration). Characteristics include: arches and windows pointed and shaped like a lancet; clerestory windows surmounted by a round opening; the gallery replaced by external flying buttresses. The numerous colonnettes originating from the vaulting rested on the shaft that bore the weight of all the main arches. This pier was generally a large round column flanked by four colonnettes.

High Gothic (C) – This was the golden age of the great cathedrals in France, lasting from about 1250 and the reign

of St Louis to around 1375 when the Hundred Years' War blocked the progress made by medieval architects.

At this time High Gothic, known as 'Rayonnant' in French, reached its peak: the three-storey elevation (large arcades, triforium – the wall at the back now pierced with stained glass – and tall clerestory windows) lightened the nave and formed one huge single stained-glass window in the chancels of churches with no ambulatory; the wall area was reduced to a minimum and the springers supporting the vaulting were doubled by another series of arches. In many cases the colonnettes started from the ground, at the point where they surround the pillar of the main arches. Two slight mouldings – level with the main arches and the springers – were the only features to break the vertiginous ascent. Beauvais Cathedral is the most outstanding example of High Gothic (see illustration).

Versailles Classicism

During the reign of Louis XIV (1643–1715) the centralisation of authority and the all-powerful Royal Academy gave rise to an official art that reflected the taste and wishes of the sovereign. The Louis XIV style evolved in Versailles and spread throughout France, where it was imitated to a lesser degree by the aristocracy in the late 17C.

The style was characterised by references to Antiquity and a concern for order and grandeur, whether in architecture, painting or sculpture. French resistance to Baroque, which had but a superficial effect on French architecture, was symbolised by the rejection of Bernini's projects for the Louvre. One of the rare examples of the style is Le Vau's College of Four Nations (today's Institute of France), which consists of a former chapel with a cupola and semicircular flanking buildings.

In Versailles **Louis le Vau** and later **Jules Hardouin-Mansart** (1646–1708) favoured a majestic type of architecture: rectangular buildings set off by projecting central sections with twin pillars, flat roofs and sculptural decoration inspired by Antiquity. **Charles le Brun** (1619–90), the leading King's Painter, supervised all the interior decoration (paintings, tapestries, furniture and *objets d'art*), giving the palace remarkable homogeneity. There were dark fabrics and panelling, gilded stuccowork, painted coffered ceilings, and copies of Greco-Roman statues. The decoration became less abundant towards the end of the century.

In 1662, the founding of the **Gobelins**, the Royal Manufactory for Crown Furniture, stimulated the decorative arts. A team of painters, sculptors, goldsmiths, warp-weavers, marble-cutters and cabinet-makers worked under Charles le Brun, achieving a high degree of technical perfection. Carpets were made at the Savonnerie factory in Chaillot. The massive furniture of the period was often carved and sometimes gilded. Boulle marquetry, a combination of brass, tortoiseshell and gilded bronze, was one of the most sumptuous of the decorative arts produced at the time.

Versailles park, laid out by **Le Nôtre** (1613–1700), fulfilled all the requirements of French landscape gardening with its emphasis on rigour and clarity. Its geometrically tailored greenery, long axial perspectives, fountains, carefully designed spinneys and allegorical sculptures reflect the ideal of perfect order and control over nature.

Sculptures were placed throughout the gardens. Many of the works were by the two major sculptors of the time, **François Girardon** (1628–1715) and **Antoine Coysevox** (1640–1720) who drew upon mythology from Antiquity. The work of **Pierre Puget** (1620–94), another important sculptor, was far more tortured and Baroque – an unusual style for the late 17C.

Flamboyant Gothic (D) – This last stage in Gothic architecture, which could develop no further, succumbed to ornamental excess, aided by the fine, easily worked Picardy stone.

The style owes its name to the flame shapes in the tracery of the bays and rose windows, and to the exuberant carved and sculpted decoration which tended to obscure the structural lines of the buildings: doorways were crowned with open-work gables, balustrades were surmounted by pinnacles, vaulting featured complex designs with liernes and tiercerons converging on ornately worked keystones. The triforium disappeared, replaced by larger clerestory windows. Arches came to rest on columns or were continued by ribbing level with the pillars. The latter were no longer flanked by colonnettes. In some churches, the ribs formed a spiral around the column.

Flemish civil architecture – From the late 13C the particular nature of Flemish Gothic architecture manifested itself in the civic buildings, belfries and town halls erected by the cities that had obtained charters.

Belfries – A symbol of the town's power, the belfry was either an isolated building (Bergues, Béthune) or part of the town hall (Douai, Arras, Calais). It was built like a keep with watchtowers and machicolations. The rooms above the foundations – which housed the prison – had various functions, such as guard room. At the top, the bell room enclosed the **chimes**. Originally, these consisted of only four bells. Today they often number at least 30 bells which play every quarter-hour, half-hour and hour. The bell room is surrounded by watchtowers from which the sentry looked out for enemies and fires. At the very top is a weather vane symbolising the city: thus the lion of Flanders stands at Arras, Bergues and Douai.

Town halls – Town halls are often imposing with striking, richly embellished façades: niches, statues, gables and pinnacles might adorn the exterior. Inside, the large council chamber or function room had walls decorated with frescoes illustrating the history of the town.

The most beautiful town halls (Douai, Arras, St-Quentin, Hondschoote, Compiègne) were built in the 15C and 16C. Many suffered damage and modification over the centuries and some were completely rebuilt in their original style, as at Arras.

RENAISSANCE (16C)

Renaissance architecture, under the influence of Italian culture, favoured a return to classical themes: columns with capitals imitating the Ionic and Corinthian orders; façades decorated with niches, statues and roundels; pilasters flanking the windows. Quadripartite vaulting was replaced by coffered ceilings and barrel vaulting.

Architects introduced basket-handled arches and semicircular or rectangular openings. Inverted brackets replaced flying buttresses. West fronts, and sometimes the north and south façades too, kept their heavy ornamentation. Spires were replaced by small domes and lantern towers.

Isolated examples of Renaissance art – not widely adopted in the north of France – are the Maison du Sagittaire in Amiens and the Hôtel de la Noble Cour in Cassel.

BAROQUE AND CLASSICAL (17C–18C)

Architecture – Through the 17C and 18C, architecture presented two different faces. One was Baroque, dominated by irregular contours, an abundance of exuberant shapes, generous carving and much ornamentation. The other was Classical, a model of stateliness and restraint, adhering strictly to the rules of Antiquity with rows of Greek columns (Doric, Ionic and Corinthian), pedimented doorways, imposing domes and scrolled architraves.

The Baroque style flourished in Flanders, Hainault and Artois which fell under Spanish influence, while the Classical style found favour in Picardy and Île-de-France.

The Baroque Chapelle du Grand Séminaire in Cambrai is one of many religious buildings erected in the 17C following the influence of the Counter Reformation and its main engineers, the Jesuits. Civil buildings include the House of Gilles de la Boé in Lille and the Mont-de-Piété in Bergues. The Mint in Lille, with its bosses and richly carved ornamentation, exemplifies **Flemish Baroque**.

The Petit Trianon at Versailles is a famous example of Classical architecture.

In Arras, Baroque and Classical elements were combined for the town's splendid main squares framed by houses with arcades and volutes. Combined elements can also be seen at the abbeys in Valloires and Prémontré and at the Château de Long.

Sculpture – The finely grained and easily worked chalky stone found in

Aerial view of Bergues

Picardy was used for much decorative work. By the 13C the 'picture carvers' in Amiens and Arras were already displaying the specific Picardy traits discernible throughout later centuries: lively, finely detailed figures going about their everyday life. The calendar at Amiens is a good example of this engaging art. In the late 15C and early 16C the Picardy wood carvers *(huchiers)* became renowned through their work on the stalls in Amiens Cathedral; the door panels in St Wulfram's in Abbeville; and the finely worked frames of the 'Puy-Notre-Dame' paintings.

Baroque art favoured abundant decorative sculpture. Buildings were covered with a profusion of ornamental fruit, flowers, cornucopias, putti, niches, statues, vases, etc.

MONASTERIES IN ÎLE-DE-FRANCE

A considerable number of priory, convent and abbey ruins are to be found in Île-de-France, and numerous districts and street names recall the many religious communities that have not survived.

Abbeys in the history of Île-de-France – Abbeys would not exist if people didn't feel a strong calling to take up ecclesiastical duties. At the same time, there would be no abbeys if the clergy

had not been given any land. After the 5C, when the victorious Franks divided up the Gallo-Roman territory, it would have been impossible for any religious community to survive without the help of donations. There were many aspiring monks in France up to the 18C, and the different communities were almost entirely dependent on the generosity of benefactors. As the suzerain of Île-de-France was none other than the supreme ruler of France, the king, this region was graced with an abundance of local monasteries.

In the early days of Christianity, during the late 4C, Île-de-France was covered with forests; but the land was also fertile and the area attracted monks who wanted to live in peace and escape the terrible famine ravaging the country. Soon afterwards the Merovingian monarchs, who had been strongly backed by the clergy, encouraged the creation of religious foundations, to which they made considerable contributions. The wealthy Carolingians continued to endow these abbeys, and the practice was kept up by the Capetians and their vassals for over 800 years (Chaalis and Royaumont).

French kings favoured monasteries because the monks used to reclaim uncultivated land and because the monasteries were constantly praying for their patrons. Religious faith was strong from the 10C to the 17C, and kings made donations to abbeys for a variety of reasons: to thank God for a victory, to seek expiation for an offence committed against the Church, to express their own personal belief or to offer a dowry to dowager queens or royal princesses about to take the veil.

Religious Orders – The term abbey does not apply to just any Christian community whose members lead a frugal, secluded life. In fact, it designates a group of men or women placed under the authority of an abbot or an abbess, who live according to a rule approved by the Pope. The monks' day is usually divided into chores related to community life, and spiritual and liturgical duties, which are the main purpose of the association.

All abbeys have an abbot or abbess, who generally enjoys the same rank as a bishop. He or she is elected by fellow companions and incarnates the spiritual and temporal leader of the abbey. After the 16C, the Pope gave the King of France the right to appoint abbots and abbesses. These prelates were called commendatory abbots and usually lived in the king's entourage.

Sometimes, to administer new domains or to fulfil the wish of a patron who wanted to receive monks on his land, the abbots would build a priory. This small community was supervised by a prior who was answerable to the abbey. The Cistercians set up many granges, farming colonies run by lay brothers.

Monastic rules – The Benedictine Order – created by St Benedict in the 6C – was undoubtedly the order which flourished the most in France. Its members founded over 1 000 abbeys throughout the country. The Benedictine rule was subsequently reformed, leading to the creation of two additional orders.

The first originated in the late 10C from Cluny in Burgundy, but unfortunately all the Cluniac houses died out during the Revolution. The second – the Cistercian Order – was, and still is, extremely powerful. It was St Bernard of Cîteaux,

also a native of Burgundy, who founded the order in the 11C. A firm believer in asceticism, he introduced a number of new rules: elaborate ceremonies and the decoration of churches were condemned; monks could no longer be paid tithes, nor receive or acquire land; strict rules were laid down on diet, rest was limited to seven hours and monks had to sleep in their clothes in a common dormitory. They shared their time between liturgical worship (6–7 hours a day), manual labour, study and contemplation. In the 17C, Abbot de Rancé added further austerities to the Cistercian rule (silence, diet). This new rule was named after La Trappe, the monastery near Perseigne where it originated. It is presently enforced in abbeys of strict observance. The other two main orders that founded abbeys in France were the Augustinian friars and the Premonstratensian canons, both dating from the 12C.

Other communities include the Carmelite Order, the Order of St Francis (Franciscans and Capuchins), the Order of Preachers and the Society of Jesus (Jesuits). They do not follow monastic rules, nor do they found abbeys. Their activities (missionary work, caring for the sick) bring them into contact with the lay world. They live in convents or houses under the authority of the prior, the Mother Superior, etc.

A collegiate church is occupied by a community of canons accountable to their bishop.

Monastic buildings – The cloisters are the centre of an abbey; the four galleries allow the nuns or the monks to take their walks under cover. One of the cloister walls adjoins the abbey church, while another gives onto the chapter house, where monks meet to discuss community problems under the chairmanship of the abbot. The third gallery opens onto the refectory and the fourth onto the calefactory, the only room with heating, where the monks study or do manual labour.

The dormitory is generally placed above the chapter house. There is a direct staircase down to the church, so that

Windmill in Hondschoote

© Y. Tierny/ MICHELIN

Steenmeulen at Terdeghem near Steenvoorde

© Y. Tierny/ MICHELIN

the monks could more readily attend early morning and nighttime Mass.

Lay brothers – These are believers who cannot or choose not to take holy orders and therefore have a different status. They spend most of their time in the fields and the workshops, and have their own dormitory and refectory. They may not enter the chapter house or the chancel of the church. Since the Vatican II Council (1962–65), lay brothers have become more and more involved in the life of the community.

Visitors are not allowed to enter the 'enclosure' and are lodged in the guest house. The poor are housed in the almshouse.

Monasteries also include an infirmary, a noviciate, sometimes a school, and the buildings needed to run the abbey: barns, cellars, winepress, stables and cowsheds.

RURAL HOUSING IN THE NORTH

The Coast, Inland Flanders and Artois – Whether in Picardy, Artois or Flandre, the same type of houses can be found along the coast: long and low to form a defence against the west winds, which often bring rain. They are capped by high-pitched roofs covered with Flemish S-shaped tiles called *pannes*. Their whitewashed walls are cheered by brightly coloured doors and shutters;

the bases of the buildings are tarred against the damp.

Behind this apparent uniformity lie very different construction techniques.

In Picardy the walls consist of daubing on wood laths; in certain areas the surface is left plain, as in Ponthieu, but it is usually whitewashed, giving a spruce look to the flower-bedecked villages along the River Canche and River Authie. In Flandre the usual building material is more generally brick, sandy coloured in maritime areas and ranging from red to purplish farther inland. The great Lille and Artois regional farms, known as **censes**, are built around a courtyard with access through a carriage gateway often surmounted by a dovecote.

Some large, partly stone-built farms in the Boulonnais hills are actually old seigniorial homes with a turret or fortifications, giving the impression of a manor house.

Hainaut, Avesnois, Thiérache and Soissonnais – In the Hainaut and Avesnois regions houses are massively built, usually consisting of one-storey brick buildings with facings and foundations in regional blue stone. Their slate roofs are reminiscent of the nearby Ardennes region.

Construction in the Thiérache region, the land of clay and wood, consists of daubing and brick with slate roofs. There are many old dovecotes in the

Military architecture

LE QUESNOY – Fortifications (12C and 17C-19C)

These well-preserved fortifications, remodelled by Vauban from 1667 onwards, are set in green surroundings.

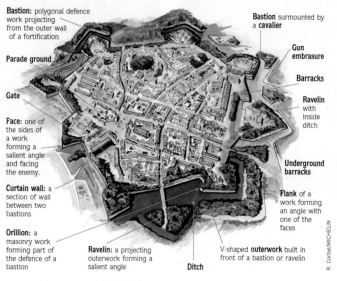

Bastion: polygonal defence work projecting from the outer wall of a fortification

Bastion surmounted by a **cavalier**

Gun embrasure

Parade ground

Barracks

Gate

Ravelin with inside ditch

Face: one of the sides of a work forming a salient angle and facing the enemy.

Underground barracks

Curtain wall: a section of wall between two bastions

Flank of a work forming an angle with one of the faces

Orillion: a masonry work forming part of the defence of a bastion

Ravelin: a projecting outerwork forming a salient angle

V-shaped **outerwork** built in front of a bastion or ravelin

Ditch

R. Corbel/MICHELIN

region, either over carriage gates or free-standing in courtyards. Villages in close proximity to one another huddle around their fortified churches (*see La THIÉRACHE*).

The houses in the Soissonnais region are similar to those of Île-de-France. Beautiful white freestone is used for walls and crow-stepped gables, contrasting with flat, red roof tiles which take on a patina with the years.

Windmills – In the early 19C there were nearly 3 000 windmills in northern France. No more than a few dozen still exist, registered, protected and restored by the Association Régionale des Amis des Moulins du Nord-Pas-de-Calais (ARAM).

Post mills – Built of wood, these mills are the most common in Flanders. The main body of the structure and the sails turn around a vertical post. On the exterior – the side opposite the sails – a beam known as the 'tail' is linked to a wheel which is turned to position the entire mill according to the wind direction. Some fourteen of this type remain in northern France, including those at Boeschepe, Cassel,

Hondschoote, Steenvoorde, Villeneuve d'Ascq and St-Maxent.

On a **tower mill** (or smock mill when made of wood) only the roof, to which the sails are attached, turns. This type of mill is more massive and is usually built of brick or stone; the Steenmeulen at Terdeghem near Steenvoorde is the only one still in working order, but there are other fine specimens at Templeuve and Watten (Nord) as well as Achicourt, Beuvry, Guemps (Pas-de-Calais), and Louvencourt (Somme).

Water mills – Water mills can also be seen throughout the region, particularly in the Avesnois, Ternois, Thiérache and Valenciennes areas. The shape and size of the wheel, which is the essential part of the mill, depends on the rate of flow of the river and on the specific features of the site. Some of these mills are open to the public: Felleries, Sars-Poteries, Marly (Nord), Esquerdes, Maintenay, Wimille and Wissant (Pas-de-Calais).

MILITARY ARCHITECTURE

Of the defensive systems in the north of France, relatively few date from the Middle Ages: the town walls of Boulogne and Laon, and the castles at Coucy, Rambures, Picquigny, Lucheux, Septmonts and Pierrefonds. In contrast, numerous 17C star fortifications along the northeastern border have been preserved, some in their entirety, as at Bergues and Le Quesnoy, others only partially: Avesnes, Maubeuge, Cambrai, Douai, St-Omer and Péronne.

Before Vauban – It was under the last of the Valois kings that military engineers, who had studied Italian examples, adopted a system of curtain walls defended at the corners by bastions. Bastions in the shape of an ace of spades with projections were introduced to protect the men defending the curtain wall. This feature can be seen at Le Quesnoy. Bastions and curtain walls, usually with stone bonding, were crowned with platforms bearing cannon. Raised towers allowed the moats or ditches and surrounding areato be watched. In the 17C Henri IV employed an engineer, **Jean Errard** (1554–1610) nicknamed the Father of French Fortification, who specialised in castrametation. In the north Errard fortified Ham and Montreuil and built the citadels at Calais, Laon, Doullens and Amiens which still stand today. In 1600 he published an authoritative *Treatise on Fortification* which served until Vauban's time.

The Age of Vauban – Inspired by his predecessors, **Sébastien le Prestre de Vauban** (1633–1707) established a system of his own characterised by bastions with half-moons surrounded by deep moats. Making the most of the natural obstacles and using local materials (brick in the north), he also tried to give an aesthetic quality to his works by adorning them with carved monumental stone gateways as at Bergues, Lille and Maubeuge.

On the coast and along the border of Flanders and Hainaut, Vauban established a long line of double defences, known as the **pré carré**. These two close lines of fortresses and citadels were designed to prevent the enemy's passage, and to ensure mutual backup in case of attack.

The first line consists of 15 sites from Dunkerque and Bergues to Maubeuge, Philippeville and Dinant. The second runs a little way behind and includes 13 towns extending from Gravelines and St-Omer to Avesnes, Marienbourg, Rocroi and Mézières. Some of these strongpoints were Vauban's own creations such as the citadel at Lille, which he himself called the 'Queen of Citadels'; others existed already and were remodelled. For over a century this group of fortifications succeeded in defending the north of France, until the invasions of 1814 and 1815.

During the French campaign in 1940 Le Quesnoy, Lille, Bergues, Dunkerque, Gravelines and Calais all formed solid strongholds protecting the retreat of the Franco-British armies.

Atlantic Wall – The concrete bunkers of the Atlantic Wall that stretch along the coastline were erected by the **Todt Organisation**, which from 1940 used prisoners of war for the task. The Nord-Pas-de-Calais region was considered a war zone against England, and in 1944 about 10 000 constructions were counted on the French coast. In the deep forests of Eperlecques and Clairmarais enormous concrete installations were built for launching the V1 and V2 rockets on London. The Eperlecques Bunker (*see ST-OMER*), today designated a historic monument, is one of the most impressive examples of this type of monumental concrete architecture, along with the fort at Mimoyecques (*see CALAIS: Excursion to Guînes*).

FAÏENCE AND PORCELAIN IN ÎLE-DE-FRANCE
FAÏENCE

This term is commonly applied to all ceramics made of porous clay and glazed with waterproof enamel. The enamel was initially transparent but, in the 9C, it became opaque thanks to the discovery in the Middle East of tin glaze. The Arabic influence throughout

12C Notre-Dame-de-la-Belle-Verrière stained-glass window, Cathédrale de Chartres

© Ch. Lepetit/hemis.fr

Stained Glass

Since the early Middle Ages, church windows have been adorned with coloured glass. Unfortunately, none of these very early works has survived.

During the Gothic period, master glassmakers played an important role in the completion and ornamentation of churches. Thanks to them, both the clergy and the congregation could appreciate the shimmering light that came streaming through the roundels. Stained glass is not purely decorative, however. To the Church it is an invaluable teaching aid, permanently communicating catechism, sacred history and the lives of the saints.

The art of making stained glass

Stained-glass windows consist of juxtaposed pieces of coloured glass held together by strips of lead. The window is divided into panels to ensure perfect solidity. When the various coloured pieces have been selected and cut to shape, the glassmaker completes the shading and details of the figures with touches of **grisaille**, a brownish pigment containing silica that is painted on and blends with the glass in the melt. The glass panels are then reassembled and fixed in place in the window. Patches of lichen may develop on stained-glass windows; it starts to attack the lead after 100 years and has been known to break through the glass after 300 to 400 years. However, it is man rather than erosion who is to blame for the disappearance of numerous early stained-glass windows: in the 18C many were dismantled and replaced by plain glass, which afforded a better view of the aisles.

The development of stained glass

Technical developments in glass-making were prompted by artistic trends but also by the search for greater economy and the wish to produce lighter tones.

the Mediterranean Basin led to the development of faïence in Moorish Spain and Italy from the 15C onwards. The Spanish island of Majorca gave its name to 'Majolica ware', the term describing Italian Renaissance ceramics. The name 'faïence' may derive from Faenza, the Italian town.

Faïence developed in France in the 16C and 17C with leading pottery centres such as Nevers and Rouen. The latter influenced the early producers of faïence in Île-de-France such as Pierre Chicaneau who settled in St-Cloud in 1674. In the 18C, as porcelain became more popular, the number of potteries increased in the region and the first pieces of porcelain were produced. The famous ceramist Jacques Chapelle set up the works in **Sceaux** in 1748 and circumvented the Vincennes-Sèvres mono-poly on faïence by creating 'Japanese-style faïence'.

The Rococo style, vivid colours, and original decorations, many of them in relief, brought success to Sceaux until the end of the 18C. This period was marked by the discovery in England

12C – Stained-glass windows were small, with fairly heavy borders. The ornamentation around the main figures was extremely limited.

13C – To ensure perfect cohesion between the panels and the leading, the iron armatures were fastened to the walls.

The clerestory windows presented tall, isolated figures. The lower windows, which could be observed more closely, had medallions depicting scenes from the lives of the saints. This genre is known as historiated stained glass. Panels included architectural features and embellishments. Borders were heavy and the scenes show a marked attempt at realism. Historiated roundels were set in a *grisaille* framework enhanced by brightly painted rose-windows. The daily lives of craftsmen were evoked in lively anecdotal scenes. The lower windows were generally divided into panels composing geometric motifs (stars, diamonds, clover-leaves).

14C – The loss of wealth led to a considerable increase in window space. For reasons of economy, more and more grisaille was produced, its starkness softened by delicate shading and graceful foliage motifs. Angels and rosy cherubs adorned the barer parts of the windows. Borders became smaller and lettering made an appearance. In the second half of the 14C glassmakers discovered that silver staining could be used to accentuate a variety of bright colours: yellow on a white background, light green on blue, amber on red, etc.

15C – The leading was no longer produced using a plane, but instead stretched on a wire-drawing bench: the lead strips were thinner, therefore more flexible and able to hold together larger and thinner panes of glass than previously. Glassmakers worked with a lighter type of glass, and the colours used in the decoration were less vivid. In some churches, two thirds of the window was taken up by grisaille. These panels featured Gothic canopies with high gables and openwork pinnacles. The craftsmanship was of a remarkable quality, and master glassmakers began to sign their own work, introducing original themes.

16C – Stained glass drew inspiration from the works of the great painters and contemporary engravings. Glassmakers had become masters at cutting glass from large sheets – using a diamond and no longer a red-hot iron – and they also excelled at painting with enamels. Stained-glass windows developed into large, transparent paintings in which minute attention was given to detail, perspective and design. In some buildings religious themes were replaced by classical scenes taken from Antiquity.

17C and 18C – The use of coloured glass decreased. Stained glass was painted and decorated with enamels.

of 'fine faïence or white lead-glazed earthenware.

Its reasonable cost and elegance, along with the exceptionally liberal conditions laid down in the Treaty of Vergennes (1786), ensured its popularity and it was massively imported into France. This know-how was gradually taken over in Île-de-France by the works in **Montereau**, **Creil** and **Choisy-le-Roi**. However, the end of the 19C confirmed the preference for porcelain, and faïence went into a decline.

PORCELAIN

Porcelain was discovered in China in the 12C. It is a thin, white ceramic ware that is slightly translucent. Body and glaze are fired together. In the 16C, the popularity of porcelain from the Far East led to numerous experiments in Europe to try and achieve a product that would rival it. The high level of imports by the French East India Company is indicative of European interest in this mysterious technique. Craftsmen did not know the exact nature of the paste used by the Chinese and they progressed by trial and error, using processes similar to the ones used for faïence. A very fine marl used on its own was vitrified by the introduction of a sort of glass called frit. The resulting ceramic was 'soft-paste' porcelain that could be scratched by steel.

In the early 18C, the basic ingredient of porcelain, white china clay, was discovered in Saxony. The secrets of the production process were jealously kept in Meissen, near Dresden.

In France, it was not until 1769 that the output from a white china clay quarry near St-Yriex in the Limousin area enabled craftsmen to produce 'hard-paste' porcelain. Sèvres produced porcelain exclusively from the beginning of the 19C onwards. This new product, in which body and glaze were fired together at a very high temperature (1 400°C/2 500°F), was very strong but more difficult to decorate.

Only five colours are suitable for high-temperature firing – blue, green, yellow, purplish brown and reddish orange.

The introduction of low-firing techniques revolutionised the production of faïence and porcelain. The enamel was fired in succession at low temperatures, enabling the use of fresh, vivid colours.

The porcelain works in **St-Cloud** (1697–1766) were the first to master the techniques required to produce 'soft-paste' porcelain. It was famous for its 'white' ware and applied gilding that differed greatly from the technique used by Sèvres. Numerous porcelain works opened in quick succession in the 18C, with the backing of princes or the royal family. The works in **Chantilly** (1725–1800), for example, were set up by Cirquaire Cirou with the support of Louis-Henri de Bourbon, Prince de Condé. In **Mennecy**, it was the Duke de Villeroy who provided the necessary patronage in the face of ever-increasing privileges granted to some of the works. The one with the highest level of support was in **Vincennes**. Madame de Pompadour and Louis XV both took a keen interest in the company that set up works in **Sèvres** in 1756. The earliest designs were 'natural' flowers and the works gradually specialised in the production of dinner services, statuettes and even veritable pictures in porcelain. Because of the processes used, the decoration and enamel combined perfectly, giving an incomparable blending. In its early days, the Sèvres porcelain works enjoyed exclusive rights to the use of gold on all its products. Even now, unless there is some technical reason against it, all its products must include some gold. 'Biscuit-ware', another speciality of these works, is the term used to describe a production method in which the body of the paste is left unglazed so that the gracefulness of the statuettes is not altered.

LANDSCAPE PAINTING

Although many painters were employed in the internal decoration of châteaux and abbeys around Paris, it was not until the 19C that painters began to show an interest in the landscapes.

Until the 18C, French masters had used landscapes merely as a background to their work, either as a decorative element or to enhance the atmosphere through composition and colour. It was so poorly regarded that often a major artist painting a portrait or other subject would leave the background landscape to be painted by a studio assistant. The two most celebrated French landscape painters were the 17C classicists Nicolas Poussin and Claude Lorrain. Poussin gave his views the heroic qualities of his subject and Lorrain painted scenes of a lost, idyllic Antiquity.

CAMILLE COROT (1796–1875)

Corot was the pioneer of contemporary landscape painting in France. He lived in Barbizon from 1830 to 1835 and worked outdoors in Fontainebleau Forest and all over Île-de-France, studying the contrasts and soft hues of light in the undergrowth, along shaded paths and on the edge of the plain. He later took up painting lakes in a search for more delicate variations; the ponds at Ville-d'Avray *(south of St-Cloud)*, with their subtle reflections, were his favourites.

PAINTERS OF THE OISE

The group was founded in 1845 by two of Corot's followers, **Charles-François Daubigny** and **Jules Dupré**. Daubigny (1817–78) liked to paint the rippling waters of the River Oise and the greenery and blossoms of the orchards and groves. He led a peaceful life: his work paid well and received universal acclaim. He could often be found working on the Île de Vaux near Auvers, or in a small rowing boat he had converted into a studio. Jules Dupré (1811–89), a close friend of Théodore Rousseau, used darker colours and belonged to the Barbizon School.

In 1865 the lithographer and satirical cartoonist Honoré Daumier (1808–79) moved from the capital to Valmondois in Île-de-France, when he met with serious financial difficulties.

In 1866 **Camille Pissarro** (1830–1903) initially settled in Pontoise for two years. Uninterested in the nearby streams and rivers, he concentrated on meadows, grassy slopes, country villages and street scenes featuring peasant women, which he portrayed in a deliberately poetic manner. His gift for expressing light, his qualities as a teacher and his kindness made him the father figure of the Impressionist movement.

THE BARBIZON SCHOOL

This school drew inspiration from the landscapes of Fontainebleau Forest and the nearby Bière plain. The founder of the movement was **Théodore Rousseau** (1812–67) who settled in a modest country cottage in 1847 and stayed there until his death. Diaz and Charles Jacque were among his close friends. They remained cheerful and humorous despite the lack of success of their paintings and their consequent penury. It was only towards the end of the Second Empire that their talent was acknowledged. Troyon (1810–65) specialised in rural scenes representing cattle. Barye, the highly respected animal sculptor, also took up landscape painting because of his love of nature. The charms and hardships of country life were portrayed particularly well in the work of **Jean-François Millet** (1814–75), who lived in Barbizon from 1849 until his death.

The artists of this school generally favoured the dark colours of tree bark and undergrowth, and their preferred subjects included dusk, soft lighting and stormy skies. These sombre tones were criticised by their detractors, who claimed they painted with 'prune juice'.

In around 1865 a group of artists fell under the spell of these magical woodlands and Pierre-Auguste Renoir, Alfred Sisley and Claude Monet settled in Chailly. Though they did not associate themselves with the Barbizon community, they did accept advice from the elders. Diaz encouraged the young Renoir to work with light tones. Impressionism were taking form.

IMPRESSIONISM

The second-generation artists wanted their work to capture the essence of light itself and to reflect the vibrant quality of colour. The term 'Impressionist' was actually coined by a sarcastic journalist in 1874, but was adopted by the group as they felt it conveyed the double revolution they had brought about in the field of painting.

The Impressionist Revolution – The Impressionist movement revolutionised artistic conventions on two counts: it paid little attention to form and it invented a new technique. Until then, the representation of reality was fundamentally important, and no artist would have dared to neglect the lines and shapes of his subject, whether a portrait, still-life painting or landscape. Painters showed little concern for light and its effects, considered a minor component, and priority was given to subject matter. For the Impressionists, light and the analysis of its effects became the principal subject; all the rest – contours, scenes, people – was simply an excuse to paint light.

The Impressionists' favourite subjects were those that played with light, such as water, snow, fabrics, flesh, flowers, leaves or fruit.

Landscape at Pontoise, France, by Camille Pissarro

They wished to capture the infinite depths of the skies, the shimmering of light on water, a dress or a human face. When depicting the undergrowth, they wanted to show how the russet tones glitter in sunlight, how colours sparkle. Such fleeting and indefinite concepts were no longer attainable using traditional techniques. As priority was given to the vibration of light around the edges of objects, the process that applied paint along contours was banished. Traditionally, the layers of paint were applied slowly and acquired their definite colour after the oil had solidified. They were then coated with varnish to produce a transparent effect and to give depth to the colours. Naturally this technique was far too lengthy to capture the ephemeral quality of light. As a consequence, the Impressionists developed a technique more suited to their purpose that involved very little oil and dispensed with varnish. Their art consisted in applying quick, small dabs of colour. The exact shade was conveyed by the juxtaposition of touches of pure colour, the final effect being assessed by the eye of the viewer.

The Impressionists were harshly criticised, and it was only after a 20-year struggle that their work was fully acknowledged. Île-de-France – with its rivers, lakes, gardens, orchards, showers of rain, mists, elegant ladies and regattas – provided them with countless sources of inspiration.

The Painters

The Impressionist School was founded in Honfleur where **Claude Monet** (1840–1926), a painter from Le Havre, was encouraged by the seascape specialist Eugène Boudin to paint landscapes. **Boudin** (1824–98), a friend of Corot's, was also a precursor of Impressionism: his paintings are full of air and light. Following his example, Monet and later the Dutch artist Jongkind worked on the luminosity of the landscapes around the Seine estuary.

They were joined by Bazille and **Sisley**, whom they had befriended in Gleyre's studio, and began to paint around Fontainebleau Forest too, though they remained separate from the Barbizon School. Pissarro, Cézanne and Guillaumin, who met at the Swiss

Academy, were called 'The Famous Three' *(Le Groupe des Trois)*.

The painters were strongly supported by **Édouard Manet** (1832–83), one of their elders who was upsetting artistic conventions and scandalising the public with his bold colours and compositions. It was Manet who encouraged the Impressionists to pursue their efforts at painting light. In 1863, following clashes between the artists and the official salons that refused to show these new works, a now-famous independent exhibition of the rejected works (Salon des Refusés) was set up on the orders of Napoléon III. It gave birth to the Impressionist movement.

In 1871 small groups of amateur painters, pupils and friends, including **Paul Cézanne**, joined Pissarro at Pontoise and Docteur Gachet in Auvers. Another group based in Argenteuil and Louveciennes included **Renoir**, Monet, Sisley and Edgar Degas, who had originally studied under Ingres. Monet's innovative technique put him at the head of the movement and inspired both Manet and later Berthe Morisot.

In the 1880s, Renoir moved to Chatou just west of Paris, where he frequented the Maison Tomaise, a restaurant first opened in 1815 and now restored. After 1880 the group broke up, but its members remained faithful to painting with light colours. Sisley moved to Moret, drawn to the River Loing, while Monet settled in Giverny on the banks of the Epte *(see The Green Guide Normandy)*. For practical reasons, Pissarro left the Oise Valley to live in Eragny, near Gisors.

Georges Seurat (1859–91) remained in Paris but concentrated on the landscapes around the capital and along the Channel coast. His technique amounted to breaking down the subject matter into small dabs of colour, each consisting of a series of dots *(points)*. Maximilien Luce (1858–1941) also experimented with this method – known as Pointillism or Divisionism – in the vicinity of Mantes. Cézanne later returned to Aix-en-Provence where, through the use of colour, tone and accentuated outlines, he developed stylised masses that laid the foundations for the Cubist movement.

Renoir travelled to Algeria and Venice, which inspired him to paint some of his finest works. Degas and Toulouse-Lautrec (1846–1901) lived in Paris. They were fascinated by circuses and theatres where swirling dancers and performers were bathed in complex illuminations created by artificial lighting.

THE DAWN OF THE 20C

The followers of the **Nabis** and **Fauve** movements, which preceded Cubism and the new art forms born in the wake of the First World War, also set up their easels – and sometimes even their studios – in the picturesque outskirts of Paris. On his return from a stay in Pont-Aven, where Paul Gauguin had shown him the magic of composing in flat, bold colours, Paul Sérusier converted his friends from the Académie Julian to the same style and formed the Nabis movement (a Hebrew word meaning prophet). **Maurice Denis** (1870–1943) became the leader of the group, which included Bonnard, Roussel, Vuillard, Maillol, Vallotton and others.

The early Fauves (meaning 'wild beasts') included extremely diverse artists – Matisse, Dufy, Braque, Derain, Vlaminck, Rouault, Marquet. Their paintings of bright, even violent colour created an uproar when they were first shown. The painters, never a coherent group, were influenced by the paintings of **Van Gogh**, who had died in 1890 leaving a collection of brilliant canvases composed of vigorous brushstrokes of pure colour.

The coasts and countryside of the north of France and the region around Paris continue to attract many artists.

Nature

Artois, Picardy and the Île-de-France (the region around Paris) all lie within a vast geological area known as the Paris Basin, which borders Flandre and the great plain of Northern Europe. The landscapes of the Basin comprise forests, lush alluvial valleys with slow-flowing rivers, and limestone plateaux providing rich arable land. The climate is mild in summer and temperate in winter, with damp springs and autumns.

PICARDY

This region, to the north of Île-de-France, comprises three separate *départements*: **Somme**, **Aisne** and **Oise**.

SOMME

Somme really is a land of contrasts, from the towering chalk cliffs of Mers-les-Bains and Ault to the leafy valleys of the Thiérache. It is a region with the best reserves of game-filled ancient forest in Northern Europe, it has the biggest tidal estuary, and the largest expanse of sand dunes. Wide skies, secretive marshland, cosy villages nestling among rolling farmland and orchards, and the open country of the Haute Somme characterise the area.

AISNE

To the east, Aisne is characterised by large farms, often complemented by a sugar refinery or a distillery. St-Quentin, the administrative and industrial centre of the *département*, is the region's main town. The lush, green landscape of Aisne is carpeted with crops and bocage for dairy cattle, rolling green hills and fields of gold that ripple away to the horizon. Nestled within its vales, tiny communities, mostly of less than 100 souls, gather around a series of Middle Age fortified churches, built as a quick and temporary defence against the passage of plundering neighbours.

OISE

To the south, marking the transition to the Île-de-France, the Valois region of **Oise** has a mantle of forests and miles of wheat fields, which in spring are invariably covered with bright poppies and other wildflowers. The Oise may be close to Paris, but it doesn't live in its shadow. In the **Vimeu** region, the chalk has decomposed into flinty clay, and the cold, damp ground has created a mixed landscape of farmland crisscrossed by hedges and trees, cider-apple orchards and small, scattered villages. Near Beauvais the chalky, silt-covered plateau suddenly reveals a verdant hollow: the **Pays de Bray**, a wooded area interspersed with meadows where stock-farming is the main activity.

Chalk cliffs of Ault

© G. Targat/MICHELIN

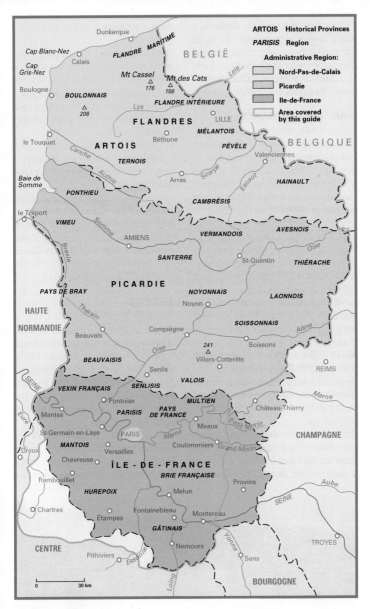

RIVERS AND VALLEYS

The verdant, wide-mouthed valleys are bisected by the Somme, Authie and Canche rivers.

These waters flow so slowly they have difficulty in making their way, losing themselves in ponds and marshes full of fish and waterfowl. The floors of the valleys are a mix of old peat bogs, rows of poplars, arable and stock-farming fields and in a few places, on the outskirts of towns like Amiens, floating vegetable gardens *(hortillonnages)* surrounded by canals.

Towns and cities have developed along the valleys: Montreuil on the Canche; Doullens on the Authie; Péronne, Amiens and Abbeville on the Somme.

The capital of Picardy is **Amiens**, a major industrial centre with factories producing tyres, electronics, video games, domestic appliances, car parts and chemical products. In Oise the main town is **Beauvais**, and in Aisne it is **Laon**.

MARITIME LANDSCAPE

To the south, near Ault, the Picardy plateau meets the sea, ending in a sharp cliff of white chalk banded with flint.

The bay, not surprisingly, is a huge and dangerous place to be, though it does seem to be suffering from coastal erosion. In 1878, it comprised 86sq m/ 33sq mi; in 1993 that was down to 73sq km/28sq mi, and today is about 70sq km/27sq mi – one estimate puts it at 40sq km/15.4sq mi. The tide goes out as much as 14km/8.7mi, the second largest ebb in France, leaving behind tricky sandbanks, muddy channels and large expanses of sea grass; when it comes back in it does so rather more quickly than it went out.

North of the Somme Bay a maritime plain called the **Marquenterre** area has been created by debris torn from the Normandy coast and carried northward by the currents, gradually forming an offshore bar.

Only the Somme, Authie and Canche rivers have carved a passage to the sea; there are therefore few large ports but several seaside resorts, the largest of them, Le Touquet, seated beside the dunes.

The coastal plain lies between the dunes and the old coastal bar, which is marked by a noticeable cliff. The drained and dried plain is now used for fields of wheat and oats, and for raising salt-pasture lambs on the grassy shores known as *mollières*.

In the past St-Valery-sur-Somme, Le Crotoy and Étaples were important ports; today they harbour only fishing boats and yachts.

NORD-PAS-DE-CALAIS

The northernmost region of France, Nord-Pas-de-Calais comprises two *départements*: **Nord** and **Pas-de-Calais**. The region roughly covers the former provinces of Artois and Flandre.

ARTOIS

The former province of Artois lies on an extension of the Picardy plateaux, a rise of land running northwest to southeast. It ends in an escarpment of about 100m/328ft (Vimy Ridge, Notre-Dame de Lorette Hill), which divides the Paris Basin from the Anglo-Belgian Basin. The great plain of Flandre begins at the foot of this escarpment.

The well-watered hills of Artois are however bare to the southeast, in the **Ternois** region where there are outcrops of chalk; to the northwest, the chalky

Parc du Marquenterre

© S. Sauvignier/MICHELIN

Landscape of the Boulonnais in spring

© Y. Tierny/MICHELIN

top layer of soil has decomposed into flinty clay resulting in lush, damp countryside, which includes Hesdin Forest and mixed agricultural and meadow land.

BOULONNAIS

The **Boulonnais** region forms an enclave in the chalk layer, revealing outcrops of harder, older rocks. The landscape here is very different from neighbouring areas. In the north, the Upper Boulonnais forms a chalky plateau which in places reaches over 200m/650ft in altitude. In the area where the land forms a hollow, the Lower Boulonnais, the wooded countryside is dotted with whitewashed farms. The clay has created meadows that are used for rearing the dappled-grey 'Boulonnais draughthorses' and for other stock-breeding. The soil also supports the Desvres and Boulogne forests, while the Hardelot Forest grows in sandier soil. Boulogne, France's foremost fishing port, stands at the mouth of the River Liane. To the north, the edge of the calcareous plateau forms the cliffs of the Opal Coast (&see La CÔTE D'OPALE).

HAINAUT AND CAMBRÉSIS

Hainaut (capital: Valenciennes) and **Cambrésis** (capital: Cambrai) are extensions of the chalky plateaus of Artois and Picardy. They are also covered with a thick layer of silt that is ideal for growing sugar beets and wheat, with excellent per-acre harvests. The plateaux are divided by wide river valleys such as those of the Scarpe, Sambre, Selle and Escaut (Scheldt). Meadows of fodder crops and pasture give them the look of farming country. The forests of St-Amand and Mormal appear where there is flinty clay, the result of decomposition of the chalk.

THIÉRACHE AND AVESNOIS

These two relatively hilly regions form the tail of the Ardennes uplands, covered at the western end by marl and chalk mixed with marl. The **Thiérache** is a damp region, part forest and part pasture. When carefully drained the cold, non-porous ground provides pasture for cows. The dairies produce butter, cheese and condensed milk.

The **Avesnois** is crossed by the River Helpe Majeure and River Helpe Mineure, tributaries of the River Sambre. This region resembles the Thiérache, but is marked by summits rising to over 250m/820ft in places. It is also an area of pastureland famous for its dairy cows and cheeses, especially Maroilles.

FLANDRE

The Flemish plain, which continues into Belgium, is bounded to the south by the hills of Artois and to the east by the plateaux of Hainault and Cambrésis.

COASTAL FLANDERS

The wet and windy *Blooteland* (bare land protected by dunes separating the area from the sea) has been gradually reclaimed from the sea since the Middle Ages. The engineers, including the famous **Coebergher**, who came mostly from the Low Countries, drained the land gradually using great dams, canals and pumps, thus creating the marshes *(Moëres)*. Today it is a low-lying region where the grey clay yields crops of sugar-beets, cereals, flax and chicory, and the nearby pastures are grazed by sheep, pigs, horses and cattle. The flat countryside, scattered with great isolated farms built around square courtyards, is dominated by belfries, bell towers, windmills and, on the coast, the factory chimneys and harbour cranes of Dunkerque and Calais.

INLAND FLANDRE

Known as *Houtland* (wooded land) in contrast to the bare coastal area, the 'Flemish lowlands' consist of lush countryside divided by rows of poplars, willows or elms. The censes, white-walled Flemish farms with red roofs, stand out against this green background.

A series of summits extends into Belgium, comprising the **Monts de Flandre** range. In addition to providing beautiful meadows where cows, horses and pigs thrive, the rich soil is also used for growing various crops such as cereals, fruit and vegetables in gardens among the St-Omer canals, and plants for industrial processing (hops near Bailleul, flax in the Lys Valley, chicory, sugar beets).

However, two small areas between Lille and Douai are different: the bare plateaux of the **Mélantois** and the **Pévèle** regions. The coal fields (*see Economy*) stretching from Béthune to Valenciennes have given rise to a 'black country' marked by slag-heaps, brick mining towns and mine-shaft frames. Between the Lys Valley and the River Escaut (Scheldt) lies the industrial conurbation of Lille-Roubaix-Tourcoing-Armentières. Once a major textile centre (*see LILLE*), it is currently undergoing extensive urban renewal.

ÎLE-DE-FRANCE
PAYS DE FRANCE

This arable plateau extending between St-Denis, Luzarches and the Dammartin-en-Goële ridge was in the heart of royal territory. The layer of marl covering the subsoil has made the area extremely fertile, and the huge fields are planted with wheat and beet.

PARISIS

Parisis lies between the River Oise and River Seine and the Pays de France. The area was once occupied by the Gauls, who gave it its name and christened the French capital. Parisis is an alluvial plain with few rivers that slopes toward the Seine. It is dominated by limestone hillocks covered in sand or grit.

Beyond the industrial suburbs of Paris, market gardens and orchards spread along the limestone slopes of the plain, while the sandy stretches are forested.

SENLISIS

Geographers and historians have often grouped this region with Valois, but in fact it was part of the Crown territory, the central core of Île-de-France. Senlisis, which is bordered by the Oise, the Dammartin-en-Goële ridge and the Valois itself, is one of the most picturesque regions near the capital. Arable land is found on the silty soils, while the sandy areas have favoured the development of forestry.

VALOIS

Valois is surrounded by Senlisis and the Oise, Automne and Ourcq rivers. It acquired strategic importance as early as Roman times and has remained one of the most important regions in French history. First a county, then a duchy, Valois was twice given to one of the king's brothers. On two occasions the descendants of this royal line, known as the Princes de Valois, acceded to the throne.

MULTIEN

Multien is an area of rolling landscapes and ploughed fields bounded by the River Marne, the Valois and the Goële ridge. It was the scene of fierce fighting in September 1914.

FRENCH VEXIN

Three rivers border this limestone platform: the **Oise**, the **Epte** and the **Seine**. West of the River Epte is the Normandy Vexin. The loess covering is an extremely fertile topsoil which favours cereal cultivation, especially wheat, and vegetable crops. Cattle rearing is concentrated in the valleys planted with poplar trees. The Buttes de Rosne, a series of outliers stretching from Monneville to Vallangoujard, are wooded. They include the strip of land running north of the Seine.

MANTOIS

Mantois is an enormous plateau situated between the River Eure and River Oise. It consists of forests to the east and arable land to the west. The small towns dotting its many valleys are well worth a visit.

HUREPOIX

Bounded by Mantois, Beauce, Fontainebleau Forest and the Seine, the **Hurepoix** region has suffered from recent urbanisation. However, by avoiding major roads and referring to *map no 106*, you will enjoy exploring its varied landscapes.

GÂTINAIS

The **Gâtinais** is defined by the River Seine and the Hurepoix, Beauce and Champagne regions. The French Gâtinais, a clay plateau, lies east of the River Loing while the Orléanais Gâtinais (to the west) is an area of sand and sandstone. This second area is covered by Fontainebleau Forest, popular because of its splendid groves and sandstone boulders. The lush valley of the Loing, which attracted a number of well-known artists to the area (Corot, Millet), is dotted with charming small towns.

FRENCH BRIE

French Brie is located between the River Seine and River Grand Morin and has Champagne Brie as its northern border. Historically, the former belonged to the King of France, while the latter was the property of the Comte de Champagne. The area is watered by four meandering rivers – Seine, Marne, Petit Morin and Grand Morin – and has many large farms specialising in large-scale wheat, sugar-beet and vegetable cultivation. French Brie contains sites as varied as the Chateau de Vaux-le-Vicomte and Disneyland Paris.

FORESTS

Île-de-France has some magnificent forests, including Rambouillet, Compiègne and Fontainebleau, which feature among the finest in the country. The forests form a 'green ring' around Paris that is a delight for weekend hikers, bikers and horse riders, among others.

Woods and forests have a timeless appeal: lush greenery in springtime, shaded groves in summer, the deep russet tones of autumn or the crisp frosts of winter. Forests also provide a multitude of fauna and flora to study, or flowers, fruit, nuts and mushrooms to harvest in season. Many also have charming picnic areas. Those who take time to understand the lifecycle of a forest also understand its infinite variety.

STATE AND PRIVATE FORESTS

Three types of forest exist in France: state, private and local. The most interesting for walkers are the state forests, as they have an extensive network of roads, paths and lanes, and their magnificent groves form a picturesque setting. The aim of the forest rangers is to preserve the natural habitat. The most beautiful French forests used to feature protected forest zones known as 'artistic reserves' in which unusually striking trees were left untouched by the axe, even when they died. This practice was given up in favour of 'biological reserves'. Forests on private estates are not open to the public, apart from the roads that run through them.

TREES

Like all living things, trees breathe, reproduce and need nourishment. Mineral nutrients are drawn from the earth by the roots and distributed to all parts of the tree via the sap running through the trunk and leaves.

Different trees require different kinds of soil. Chestnut trees, for instance, cannot survive on limestone sites, whereas oaks will flourish on a variety of soils.

Trees, like other plants, breathe through their leaves and reproduce through their flowers. Flowers will bear fruit if they are fertilised by pollen of their own species. Very few trees have hermaphrodite flowers – presenting both male and female characteristics – like roses, acacias, etc. Consequently the pollen is usually carried from the male flower to the female flower by insects, or sometimes by the wind. Trees may also reproduce by their shoots; thus, when a youngish tree trunk is razed to the ground, a number of stool shoots will emerge from the stump. Conifers do not produce offshoots.

The trees of Île-de-France fall into two categories: deciduous and coniferous.

Deciduous – These trees shed their leaves every autumn and grow them again in the spring. Beeches, oaks, hornbeams, birches and chestnut trees belong to this category.

Coniferous – In place of leaves, coniferous species have needles which they shed regularly throughout the year. The needles are renewed every four to five years. Their sap contains resin – they are also known as resinous trees – and the fruit is generally cone-shaped. Pines, cypresses, cedars and fir trees are all conifers, as is the larch, which loses its needles every year.

TREES OF THE ÎLE-DE-FRANCE FORESTS

Most species of deciduous trees can be found around Paris. The most common are listed below.

Oak – One of the most esteemed forest trees, the oak's hard but beautiful wood is used both for carpentry and ornamental woodwork. In former times oak bark was much sought after by local tanners. Some of the oaks tower 40m/132ft high with trunks over 1m/3ft in diameter. Trees can be felled up to the age of 250 years.

Beech – Although it resembles the oak in its habit, beech is slightly more elegant. The wood is mainly used for everyday furniture and railway sleepers but it is also popular as fuel. The trunk is cylindrical, the bark smooth and shiny; young shoots have a crooked, gnarled appearance. Beeches grow as tall as oaks but are not commercially viable beyond 120 years.

Hornbeam – A remarkably tough species, the hornbeam resembles the beech; it also lives to the same age, but is shorter and its bark features numerous grooves.

Chestnut – This tree can grow to great heights and can live for several hundred years, but is generally felled much younger as very old chestnut trees become hollow and prone to disease. Its wood was traditionally used by the cooperage industry for making staves, posts and stakes; nowadays it is used for the production of chipboard. Chestnut trees will grow only on siliceous soil.

Birch – Even when it reaches 25m/82ft in height the birch retains a graceful, slim trunk of white bark – which peels off in fine layers – and shimmering leaves. Damp, sandy soil is an excellent terrain for all varieties of birch. Although it is excellent firewood, it is mainly used in making wood pulp for the paper industry.

Scots Pine – This species, the most commonly found conifer in Île-de-France, is ideal for reafforestation, particularly in sandy terrain. Since the mid-19C it has been planted in plots of land where there is meagre or non-existent vegetation. Scots pines have short needles (4–6cm/1.5–2.5in) which grow in pairs, smallish cones (3–5cm/1–2in) and reddish-ochre bark.

Foresters often plant Scots pines alongside exotic or Mediterranean (maritime pine) resinous species. A great favourite is the Corsican pine, a tall, handsome tree with a perfectly straight trunk. It can grow to 50m/165ft, but old trees develop large grey patches on their bark.

THE SCIENCE OF FORESTRY

If a forest is not tended, it will invariably deteriorate. In order to develop fully and reach their proper size, trees must be given breathing space and be placed in an environment which meets their specific requirements. The first step in a reafforestation campaign is to plant fir trees, which have few needs and produce wood in a very short time. Their roots retain the earth, otherwise washed away by surface water, and the needles build up thick layers on the ground. Next, hornbeams, birches and beeches are planted to increase the fertility of the soil, and finally oaks. Many of the beech groves are left as this species is considered to be commercially profitable.

Rotations – The prime concern of foresters is always to have trees ready for felling. Consequently, when trees are felled foresters ensure they are immediately replaced with seedlings. For example, a forest may be divided into ten units, and every five years the unit with the oldest trees is cleared and then replanted. Thus, within 50 years the forest is entirely renewed while remaining commercially viable, a technique known as rotation.

Forest managers try to avoid exposing a large sector of the forest, as leafy plants such as hazel and mulberry trees can set in and choke the young shoots. Two, three or four groups within each sector are formed according to the trees' approximate age, and a programme of successive felling is planned. This ensures that only limited areas are deforested at any one time.

Whatever the rotation for a given forest, its appearance is bound to change depending on the thickness of the vegetation and the forestry techniques applied. There are three types of plantation in Île-de-France:

Groves – After the land has been sown, the weaker shoots are choked by the stronger ones in a process of natural selection. The trees, planted fairly close to one another, spread vertically.

After some time the land is cleared around the finer species to encourage them to develop, and eventually these are the only ones that remain. This grove, where the widely spaced trees are all the same age, is called a *futaie pleine*; the rotation is rather long, 50 or even 80 years for very tall trees. *Futaie jardinée* is another type of grove, in which the trees are planted and cut at different times, so that the sector features a variety of 'age groups'; older trees are always felled first.

A fully matured grove is a truly impressive sight, with its powerful trunks and its rich canopy of foliage producing subtle effects of light and shade.

Copses – The trees are younger. Rotation ranges from 5 to 30 years, depending on whether pit props, logs for heating or firewood is wanted. A copse is a sector of forest where a group of mature trees have been cut down. The shoots growing around the stump develop into a multitude of young, bushy, leafy trees.

Copses with Standards – If, when cutting a copse, the finest trees are left standing, these will dominate the new shoots. If they survive a series of fellings, they will grow to be extremely strong. The utilisation of copses with standards produces both fuel wood (from the copses) and timber for industrial purposes (from the older species).

FAUNA AND FLORA

Forests contain not only trees but also countless varieties of plants and animals. Hunts are still organised in certain forests.

Nature lovers will find forests fascinating as the rich, damp soil is remarkably fertile, sustaining moss, lichen, mushrooms, grasses, flowers, shrubs and ferns.

Flowers – April is the season of laburnum, hyacinths and daffodils. May brings hawthorn, lily-of-the-valley, columbine and the delightful catkins of the hazel tree. In June there is broom, heather, campanula, scabious and wild pinks. During the autumn, russet and gold leaves are as attractive as the forest flowers.

Fruit – Wild strawberries and succulent raspberries ripen during July and August, while blackberries can be harvested in August and September together with the new crop of hazelnuts. October is the time for sloes and sweet chestnuts.

Mushrooms – Some varieties of mushrooms – Russula virescens, chanterelle comestible and mousseron – are always edible. Other species are difficult to identify and may be dangerous. If in doubt, mushroom pickers should consult a professional mycologist or a local chemist (*pharmacien*), who is trained to identify mushrooms.

GARDENS IN ÎLE-DE-FRANCE

Three successive trends defined the official canons of ornamental gardening in Île-de-France, the home of many royal residences.

16C

During the 16C gardens were not considered as an essential part of an estate, but merely in the same category as outbuildings. They were generally of geometric shape and resembled a chessboard, where each of the squares contained carefully trimmed spindle and box forming arabesques and other elaborate patterns. These motifs were called *broderies*. Gardens were enclosed within a sort of cloister made of stone or greenery, from which visitors could enjoy a good view of the garden. Paths featuring fragments of marble, pottery and brick cut through the grounds. Though water did not play any significant part in the general appearance of the gardens, there were basins and fountains encircled by balustrades or tall plants. They were there to be ob-served in their own right and for people to admire the ornamental statues and water displays. Most of them have now disappeared, at least in Île-de-France. There is, however, an outstanding example in Villandry in the Loire Valley (see The Green Guide, *Châteaux of the Loire*).

17C–EARLY 18C: THE FORMAL GARDEN

Although **André le Nôtre** cannot be credited with 'inventing' the **formal French garden**, he was the one person who raised this art form to absolute perfection. Its purpose was twofold: to enhance the beauty of the château it surrounded and to provide a superb view from within. The garden's main features were fountains, trees, statues, terraces and a sweeping perspective.

The château was fronted by a 'Turkish carpet' of parterres, with flowers and evergreen shrubs forming arabesques and intricate patterns. These were flanked symmetrically by basins with fountains, usually adorned with statues. Fountains were also placed on the terrace bearing the château and the upper lawns, which was the starting-point of the central perspective along a canal or a 'green carpet of lawn' (*tapis vert*), lined with elegant groves of pretty, tall trees.

The groups of trees planted along the perspective were designed to be perfectly symmetrical. They were crossed by a network of paths, with clearings at the intersections offering splendid vistas extending into the far distance. Hedges lined the paths, concealing the massive tree trunks and providing a backdrop for marble statues. As hedges were fragile and expensive to maintain, most were later removed or greatly reduced in height from their original 6–8m/20–26ft. Each grove of trees featured a 'curiosity': perhaps a fountain with elaborate waterworks, a colonnade or a group of sculpted figures.

The enormous variety of designs and styles used for the parterres and surrounding trees, bushes and hedges ensured that these formal gardens were never monotonous. They were conceived as an intellectual pursuit, giving pleasure through their stately proportions and perspectives, the skilful design and the sheer beauty of each detail.

LATE 18C–19C:
THE LANDSCAPE GARDEN

In the 18C, manipulating the landscape into rigid geometric patterns was no longer fashionable. The tendency instead was to imitate nature. The landscape garden – also called the Anglo-Chinese garden – consisted of lush, rolling grounds dotted with great trees and rocks, pleasantly refreshed by streams and tiny cascades. A rustic bridge might cross a river flowing into a pond or lake covered with water-lilies and surrounded by willow trees, and a mill or dairy might add the final touch to this Arcadian scene.

The 18C fascination for philosophy, characteristic of the Age of Enlightenment, was also reflected in contemporary gardening, which saw the introduction of symbolic or exotic monuments or *fabriques* (a technical term originally referring to architectural works depicted in paintings).

Antique temples and medieval ruins were particular favourites, while tombs and mausoleums became popular just before the Revolution. Chinese and Turkish sculptures were also fashionable. An unfinished temple, for instance, would remind visitors of the limits of science, while an oriental pagoda standing beside a crumbling tower symbolised the fragility of human achievements.

Sentimentality, romance and melodrama were popular features of many art forms. Such trends also affected landscape gardens, giving rise to a number of new sights including the secret lovers' grotto, the bench of the tired mother, the grave of the rejected suitor, etc.

Most of these estates were ravaged during the Revolution, and few of their fragile monuments survived. Efforts are now being made to restore what was left. The most outstanding example of an 18C folly in the region is the Cassan Pagoda at L'Isle-Adam.

Particularly fine gardens may still be found at Versailles, Vaux-le-Vicomte, Chantilly, Courances, St-Cloud, Sceaux, Champs, Fontainebleau, Rambouillet and Ferrières.

Aerial view of Château de Fontainebleau and its gardens

© Arnaud Chicurel/hemis.fr

The Louvre and the pyramid
© Arnaud Chicurel/hemis.fr

PARIS

Paris is France's most populated city, its national capital, and the regional capital of Île-de-France. Lying on the banks of a loop formed by the Seine River, the ordinary Gallo-Roman village of Lutetia became an important urban centre during the 10C thanks to its location at a crossroads of trade routes, in the heart of a rich agricultural region. Two hundred years later, Paris' cultural influence was felt all over Europe. With the kings of France choosing it as their capital city (and the basilica of the neighbouring town of St-Denis as their necropolis), Paris' political weight continued to grow until it became a major focal point of the Christian world at the beginning of the 14C. As a centre of all powers in France, the only real challenge to Paris came from Versailles, where the monarchy settled from the late 17C until the French Revolution of 1789. A world capital of arts and leisure in the 19C and early 20C, Paris' unrivalled heritage and culture have given it the honour of becoming the world's most popular tourist destination.

Highlights

1 Visit one of the world's finest collections of Impressionist paintings at **Musée d'Orsay** (p130)

2 If you enjoyed the award-winning film *Amélie*, follow in the character's footsteps in **Montmartre** (p138)

3 Visit the Grand appartement de la Reine, Marie-Antoinette's private retreat from the pomp of **Versailles** (p176)

A Parisian Way of Life

Your mornings in Paris should begin with a *café-croissant* on a terrace, a Parisian institution since the 18C, when cafés attracted the likes of Voltaire and Rousseau. But the "City of Light" has far more in store for you, and not only for a shopping spree at the *Grands Magasins*. Looking for a good film? You'll have to choose from a hundred venues, one of the most emblematic being Le Grand Rex. Home of the Comédie-Française (17C), Paris always has a great classic on stage, but the city also harbours numerous smaller, avant-garde venues. The music scene ranges from classical concerts at Salle Pleyel or Salle Gaveau to jazz shows at the trendy New Morning Club. For opera and ballet, the 19C Opéra-Garnier and modern, more popular Opéra-Bastille offer a rich and varied repertoire. Night owls may want to check out the Champs-Élysées or the Bastille-République area as a starter, although you can happen upon hip nightclubs, cabarets, variety shows, reviews, cafés-theatres or charming old bars just about anywhere you roam.

Museums Galore

Magnificently restored in the 1990s, the Louvre is one of the largest art museums in the world. Don't miss the recent Egyptian and Assyrian collections, and make sure you have time for the French and Italian sculpture sections. Just across the Seine river, the Musée d'Orsay, a former railway station built in steel and glass, awaits with its outstanding collections of impressionist masterpieces. If modern art is more your speed, make a stop at the colourful Centre Georges Pompidou: both the permanent collection and temporary exhibits will sate your curiosity. The lesser-known Musée Guimet boasts an impressive collection of Asian art, while the recently created Musée du

Paris Museum Pass

This pass is valid for 2, 4 or 6 consecutive days (39€, 54€, 69€ respectively) and provides unlimited access to more than 60 museums and monuments in and around Paris. It is on sale at each of the featured sites and at city tourist offices. Passholders do not have to queue for admission.
www.parismuseumpass.com.

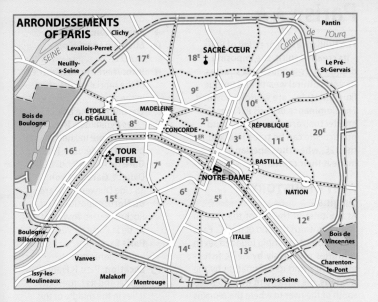

ARRONDISSEMENTS OF PARIS

Quai Branly is a vibrant tribute to indigenous arts from around the globe. Heading outside Paris, exploring the Palace of Versailles (Unesco World Heritage site) is a must. The National Museum of Archaeology in St-Germain hosts unique sculptures from prehistoric France. Why not pay a visit to the workshops of the National Manufacture of Porcelain in Sèvres? You might also explore Rodin's house in Meudon, where the sculptor produced some of his legendary works.

Urban Landscape

Can you imagine picnicking in the Gallo-Roman-era Arènes de Lutèce? Or relaxing on a lounge chair overlooking the Seine? Each summer, several kilometres of a usually busy road are converted into Paris-Plage, a sunny beach complete with palm trees and sand. Civil architecture in and around Paris ranges from the bizarre – witness the colourful pipes of Centre Georges Pompidou, built by Renzo Piano in the 1970s – to the pure classicism of Versailles and the Louvre. The fashionable Marais abounds in quaint 17C mansions, but the city's dominant style is 19C Haussmanian cut-stone buildings. But Paris isn't merely a city dwelling in its glorious past. The skyscrapers and imposing cubic Arche at La Défense and newborn Bibliothèque Nationale district remind us that Paris is a dynamic, continually evolving urban community.

Parks and Gardens

Paris' oldest public garden, the Jardin des Plantes, dates to the early 17C. But most green spaces in the Paris region were created in the 19C; outstanding examples include the Buttes-Chaumont, Bois de Vincennes and Bois de Boulogne. The royal park at Versailles is a remarkable composition of gardens, musical fountains and canals. Quiet Parc de Sceaux and Parc de St-Cloud also merit a visit. Finally, don't miss the castle at St-Germain-en-Laye: the splendid park terrace commands a sweeping view of the capital.

Paris★★★

The brilliance and prestige of Paris – its creative spirit, the imposing dignity of its avenues and squares, its vast cultural wealth and unique flair and style – are world-renowned. The dominance of Paris in France's intellectual, artistic, scientific and political life can be traced back to the 12C, when the Capetian kings made it their capital.

A BIT OF HISTORY
Origins

At the time of the fall of the Roman Empire towards the end of the 5C, Paris was a modest township founded seven centuries previously by Gallic fishermen. Following its occupation by the **Romans**, the settlement was extended south of the river to where the remains of the Cluny Baths and a 2C amphitheatre now stand: the **Quartier latin**. In the 3C, St Denis, Paris' first bishop, had met his martyrdom and the Barbarians had razed the place to the ground. This destruction, together with the threat posed by Attila's hordes (but supposedly averted by the intervention of St Geneviève, patron saint of the city), had prompted inhabitants to withdraw to the security of the Île de la Cité.

Clovis, King of the **Franks**, settled in Paris in 506. Two years later, he founded an abbey south of the Seine in honour of St Geneviève, just as 35 years previously a basilica had been erected over the tomb of St Denis. In 885, for the fifth time in 40 years, the Norsemen sailed up the river and attacked Paris; Odo, son of Robert the Strong, bravely led the local resistance, and was elected king of "France" in 888. From then on, Paris was the seat of royal power, albeit with some interruptions.

The Capetian Dynasty
(987–1328)

In 1136, Abbot Suger rebuilt the abbey church of St-Denis in the revolutionary Gothic style, an example soon followed by Maurice de Sully at Notre-Dame. Between 1180 and 1210, **Philippe**

▶ **Population:** 2 233 818

Michelin Local Map: 312 D 2.

Info: There are six branches of the official tourist office in the city. The **main office** is at 25 r. des Pyramides. The other branches are located at pl. du 11 novembre 1918, **Gare de l'Est**; 20 bd Diderot, **Gare de Lyon**; 18 r. de Dunkerque, **Gare du Nord**; opposite 72 bd. Rochechouart, **Anvers**; 1 pl. de la Porte de Versailles, **Paris Expo**. en.parisinfo.com.

Location: Paris is France's capital and its largest city. It lies in the middle of the Île-de-France region, which sits between the Centre, Bourgogne, Champagne-Ardennes, Picardy and Haute Normandie regions. Paris is 85.6km/53mi SW of Compiègne and 69km/42.8mi NW of Fontainebleau.

Don't Miss: Arc de Triomphe, Place de la Concorde, Eiffel Tower, Notre-Dame Cathedral, the Champs-Élysées, Quartier Latin, Montmartre, the Marais, the Opéra and Madeleine district, the Louvre and the Musée d'Orsay.

Kids: La Villette (encompassing the child-friendly Cité des Sciences et de l'Industrie, the spherical cinema La Géode and Cité des Enfants), Jardin de Luxembourg, Palais de la Découverte. Most major museums now organise special displays and activities for children.

Auguste surrounded the growing city with a continuous ring of fortifications anchored on the Louvre fortress. In 1215 France's first university was founded on the St-Geneviève hill.

House of Valois (1328–1589)

On 22 February 1358, Étienne Marcel, the merchants' provost, succeeded in rousing the townsfolk to break into the Law Courts (Palais de Justice); entering the Dauphin's apartments, he slew two of the future Charles V's counsellors before his eyes. On becoming king, **Charles V** quit this place of ill memory. In 1370, he built himself a stronghold in the eastern part of the city, the Bastille, which became the centrepiece of a new ring of fortifications.

Paris was taken by the English in 1418. **Joan of Arc** was wounded in front of Porte St-Honoré trying to retake the city in 1429. Paris was won back for France eight years later by Charles VII.

In 1492, the discovery of America marked the first beginnings of a new outlook and the modern age. The Neapolitan artists brought back by **Charles VIII** from his campaigns in Italy were introducing new trends in taste and thought; the influence of the Renaissance became apparent in many new buildings. In the 1560s, the brothers Androuet Du Cerceau drew up the plans for the Flore Pavilion abutting the Louvre to the west, then set about the construction of the Pont Neuf (New Bridge), which today is the city's oldest surviving bridge.

On 24 August 1572, bells rang out from the tower of St-Germain-l'Auxerrois to signal the start of the St Bartholomew's Day Massacre (of Protestants); Henry of Navarre, the future Henri IV, just married to Marguerite of Valois, barely escaped with his life. In 1589, Henri III was assassinated at St-Cloud in 1589 by the monk Jacques Clément. This violent act marked the end of the Valois line.

The Bourbons (1589–1789)

In 1594 Paris opened its gates to **Henri IV**, the new king who had renounced his Protestant faith and succeeded in pacifying the country. But on 14 May 1610 in the rue de la Ferronnerie, this monarch too fell victim to an assassin.

Under **Louis XIII** (1610–43), Métézeau designed an imposing Classical west facade for St-Gervais Church, the first of its kind in Paris; Salomon de Brosse built the Luxembourg Palace for Marie de' Medici; Jean Androuet Du Cerceau laid out the courtyards and gardens of the Hôtel de Béthune-Sully. As well as erecting a church for the Sorbonne with Classical columns on its courtyard side, Lemercier built the Palais-Royal for Richelieu. On the king's death in 1643, Anne of Austria became Regent, acting in concert with Mazarin and continuing the policies of Richelieu. Paris fell prey to the series of disturbances caused by unrest among the nobility and known as the Fronde; the young king concluded that it might be advantageous to separate Court from city.

The 23-year-old **Louis XIV** began his long and highly personal reign in 1661. Even more than the splendour of court life, it was the extraordinary advancement of the arts and literature at this time that gave Paris and France such prestige in Europe. Under the protection of a king keen to encourage artistic endeavour and promote creative confidence, writers, painters, sculptors and landscapers flourished as never before. In the space of 20 years, the great Le Nôtre redesigned the parterres of the Tuileries; Claude Perrault provided the Louvre with its fine colonnade and built the Observatory; Le Vau completed the greater part of both the Institut de France and the Louvre. France's "Century of Greatness" came to an end with Louis XIV's death in 1715.

The country now found itself, for the second time, under the rule of a five-year-old. The running of the country was therefore put into the hands of a regent, Philippe d'Orléans; the first action of the court was to pack its bags and quit the boredom of Versailles for the gaiety of the capital. A long period of peace accompanied the years of corruption; for 77 years France experienced no foreign incursions. Literary salons flourished, notably those of the Marquise de Lambert, Mme Du Deffand and Mme Geoffrin, all helping the spread of new ideas in what became known as the **Age of Enlightenment**. The Palais Bourbon (1722–28), which now houses the National Assembly, was erected at this time.

The personal rule exercised by **Louis XV** was discredited by his favourites, but Paris nevertheless provided a haven for a number of famous figures and important advances, such as Charles de la Condamine, a surveyor and naturalist responsible for the discovery of rubber (1751); Jussieu, incumbent of the Chair in Botany at the Botanical Gardens, responsible for a systematic classification of plants (1759) and for many advances in pharmacology; Diderot, author, together with d'Alambert, of the great *Encyclopaedia*, a splendid summary of the technology of the age; Chardin, who had lodgings in the Louvre, devoted himself to working in pastel; Robert Pothier, who wrote the *Treatise of Obligations*, or Ange-Jacques Gabriel, the last and most famous of a line of architects linked to Mansart and Robert de Cotte, who between them gave France a hundred years of architectural unity. it was Gabriel who designed the magnificent façades fronting the Place de la Concorde, the west front of St-Roch Church and the École Militaire (Military Academy). Finally there was Soufflot, creator of the dome which crowns the Panthéon. Distinguished furniture-makers were at work too: Lardin with his cabinets and commodes with rosewood inlay, and Boudin with his virtuose marquetry and secret compartments; they anticipated the masters who were to emerge in the following reign.

Revolution and Empire (1789–1814)

In 1788, King **Louis XVI (1774–92)** decided to convene the States-General. The delegates assembled at Versailles on 5 May 1789. As a result, on 17 June, the States-General transformed itself into a **National Assembly** which styled itself the Constituent Assembly on 9 July; the monarchy would eventually become a constitutional one.

On **14 July 1789**, in the space of less than an hour, the people of Paris took over the Bastille in the hope of finding arms there; the outline of the demolished fortress can still be traced in the paving on the west side of the Place de la Bastille (14 July became a day of national celebration in 1879). On 17 July, in the City Hall (Hôtel de Ville), Louis XVI kissed the recently adopted tricolour cockade. The feudal system was abolished on 4 August, and the Declaration of the Rights of Man adopted on 26 August; on 5 October, the Assembly moved into the riding-school of the Tuileries, and the royal family was brought from Versailles and installed in the Tuileries Palace.

On 12 July 1790 the Church became subject to the Civil Constitution for the Clergy. Two days later, a great crowd gathered on the Champ-de-Mars to celebrate the anniversary of the fall of the Bastille; Talleyrand, Bishop of Autun as well as statesman and diplomat, celebrated mass on the altar of the nation and the king reaffirmed his oath of loyalty to the country.

After his attempt to join Bouillé's army at Metz had been foiled, Louis was brought back to Paris on 25 June 1791; on 30 September, he was forced to accept the constitution adopted by the Assembly which then dissolved itself.

The Legislative Assembly – The new deputies met the following day in the Tuileries Riding School. On 20 June 1792, encouraged by the moderate revolutionary faction known as the Girondins, rioters invaded the Tuileries and made Louis put on the red bonnet of liberty. On 11 July, the Assembly declared France to be in danger, and during the night of 9 August the mob (sans-culottes) instituted a "revolutionary commune" with the status of an organ of government. The next day, the Tuileries were sacked and 600 of the Swiss Guards massacred. The Assembly responded by depriving the king of his few remaining responsibilities and confining him with his family in the tower of the Templar Prison (Tour du Temple).

Soon after, the "September Massacres" began; 1 200 prisoners, some "politicals", but most of them common offenders, were hauled from the city's jails and arbitrarily executed on the Buci crossroads in a frenzy of fear and panic precipitated by fear of invasion. This grisly event marked the beginning of a particularly violent period known as the Terror. On 21 September, the day after the French defeat at the Battle of Valmy, the Legislative Assembly gave way to the Convention.

The Convention – At its very first meeting, the new assembly, now in the hands of the Girondins, formally abolished the monarchy and proclaimed the **Republic**. This day, 21 September 1792, became Day 1 of Year One in the new revolutionary calendar (which remained in force until 31 December 1805). At the end of May, beset by difficulties at home and abroad and bereft of popular support, the Girondins fell, to be replaced by the "Mountain" (the extreme Jacobin faction, so-called because they occupied the upper tiers of seating in the Assembly).

In one of the faction's first acts, Louis XVI was guillotined on 21 January 1793 on the Place de la Concorde. On 17 September, the Law of Suspects was passed, legalising **the Terror**. The first to be executed by the revolutionary tribunals were the Girondins, in October 1793. On 8 June 1794, Robespierre the "Incorruptible" presided over the Festival of the Supreme Being. The event was orchestrated by the painter David, beginning in the Tuileries Gardens and proceeding to the Champ-de-Mars.

On 10 June (9 Prairial), the Great Terror began. Over a period of two months, the "national razor", as the guillotine was known, was to slice off 2 561 heads. Among those executed was Lavoisier, former Farmer-General and eminent chemist, responsible for the formulation of the theory of the conservation of mass on which much of modern chemistry rests, and André Chénier, the lyric poet who had condemned the excesses of the regime in his verse. The end of the Terror came with the fall and execution of Robespierre himself, on 27 July (9 Thermidor).

The Thermidorian Convention now attempted to put the sickening spectacle of the scaffold behind it with a policy calculated to promote stability. Among its most important achievements were measures designed to advance science and learning, including the founding of the École Polytechnique (School of Engineering); the creation of the Conservatoire des Arts et Métiers (National Technical Institution), and the setting up of the École Normale (the prestigious college). In 1795, the metric system was adopted and the Office of Longitudes founded. Just before the Assembly's dissolution on 25 October, public education was instituted and the Institut de France founded, embracing the nation's learned academies (including the Académie Française).

The Directory and the Consulate – The period of the Directory was marked, in 1798, by the very first Universal Exhibition, but was brought to an end with the *coup d'état* of 9 November (18 Brumaire) 1799, when the Council of Elders persuaded the legislature to move to St-Cloud as a precautionary measure against Jacobin plots. On the following day, **Napoleon Bonaparte** entered the chamber to address the delegates, but was booed; he was saved by the presence of mind of his brother Lucien, who used the guard to disperse the members. By the same evening, power was in the hands of three consuls; this marked the end of the Revolution. In less than five years, the Consulate allowed Napoleon to centralise power, opening the way to the realisation of his Imperial ambitions.

The Empire – Proclaimed Emperor of France by the Senate on 18 May 1804, Napoleon I was anointed on 2 December by Pope Pius VII at Notre-Dame, though it was he himself who actually put the crown on his head in a ceremony immortalised by David. His reign was marked by the promulgation in 1804 of the Civil Code, which he had helped draft himself when he was still First Consul, and which, as the *Code Napoleon*, has since formed the legal basis of many other countries. In order to make Paris into a truly imperial capital, Napoleon ordered the erection of a great column in the Place Vendôme; cast from the melted-down metal of guns taken at the Battle of Austerlitz (Slavkov), it commemorated the victories of his *Grande Armée*. Vignon was commissioned to design a temple which nearly became a railway station before ending up as the Madeleine Church; Chalgrin was put to work drawing up plans for a great triumphal arch (Arc de Triomphe); Brongniart built the Stock Exchange (Bourse); Percier and Fontaine, the promoters of the Empire style, constructed the north wing of the Louvre and the Carrousel Arch (Arc du Carrousel); Gros painted the battles and Géricault the cavalry of the *Grande Armée*.

On 31 March 1814, despite strong resistance offered by Daumesnil at Vincennes, the Allies occupied Paris. On 11 April, the Emperor, "the sole obstacle to peace in Europe", put his signature to the document of abdication at Fontainebleau.

The Restoration (May 1814–February 1848)
The reign of Louis XVIII – 1814–24
The period of rule by Louis XVI's brother was interrupted by the Hundred Days of Napoleon's attempt to re-establish himself between his sojourn on Elba and his final exile to St Helena. During the years of Louis XVIII's reign, Laënnec invented the stethoscope, wrote his *Treatise on Mediate Auscultation* and founded the anatomo-clinical school together with Bayle and Dupuytren; Pinel studied mental illness at the Salpêtrière Hospital; Cuvier put biology on a sounder footing, formulated the principles of subordination of organs to their function and established a zoological classification; Bertholet studied the composition of acids, Sadi Carnot thermodynamics and temperature equi-

librium, and Arago electromagnetism and the polarisation of light; Daguerre laid the foundations of his fame with his dioramas, and Lamartine conquered literary society with his *Méditations Poétiques* – its elegaic rhythms soothed Talleyrand's sleepless nights.

The reign of Charles X – 1824–30
Painting flourished with the brilliant sweep of Delacroix' great canvases and Corot's landscapes. At the same time, Laplace was establishing the fundamental laws of mathematical analysis and providing a firm basis for astronomical mechanics, and Berlioz was composing his *Fantastic Symphony*, the key work of the Romantic Movement in music.

On 21 February 1830, Victor Hugo's drama *Hernani* provoked a literary battle between "moderns" and "classicals" in which the latter were temporarily routed. In the summer, Charles' press ordinances provoked a crisis which led to his abdication; he was succeeded by Louis Philippe, a member of the cadet branch of the Bourbons.

Reign of Louis-Philippe – 1830–48
During the 1830s, the mathematician Evariste Galois put forward the theory of sets; Victor Hugo wrote *Notre-Dame de Paris* and Alfred de Musset *Caprices*. Chopin, the darling of Parisian society, composed scherzos, waltzes and his celebrated *Polonaises*. In 1838, while on holiday in Paris, Stendhal wrote *The Charterhouse of Parma*, a masterpiece of psychological observation which can be read on a number of levels. The first news agency was founded by Charles Havas. In 1839, a railway line was opened between Paris and St-Germain. The 1840s saw the publication of the *Mysteries of Paris* by Eugène Sue, the *Count of Monte Cristo* and the *Three Musketeers* by Dumas and many of the works of Balzac's prodigious *Human Comedy* as well as the *Treatise on Parasitology* by Raspail. The abuses of the July monarchy, meanwhile, were satirised in the drawings of Daumier. At the age of 79, Chateaubriand brought his finely chiselled *Memories from beyond the Tomb* to a triumphant

conclusion. On 23 February 1848, the barricades went up on the Boulevard des Capucines and the monarchy fell; the next day, at the City Hall, amid scenes of wild enthusiasm, Lamartine saluted the tricolour: "the flag which has spread the name of France, freedom and glory around the wide world".

Second Republic and Second Empire (1848–1870)
Second Republic
The abolition of the National Workshops in June 1848 led to rioting in the St-Antoine district, in which the archbishop of Paris was killed. In 1849, Léon Foucault proved the rotation and spherical nature of the earth by means of a pendulum (the experiment was repeated in 1855 from the dome of the Panthéon). On 2 December 1851 the short life of the Second Republic was ended by a *coup d'état*.

Second Empire – 1852–70
Two great exhibitions (in 1855 and 1867) proclaimed the prosperity France enjoyed under the rule of Bonaparte's nephew, Napoleon III. **Baron Haussmann**, Prefect of the *Département* of the Seine, was responsible for an ambitious programme of public works which transformed the capital, giving it many of the features which now seem quintessentially Parisian. Among

them were the laying out of the Bois de Boulogne and the Bois de Vincennes, and the building of railway stations and the North Wing of the Louvre. But the Baron is remembered above all for the ruthless surgery he performed on the capital's ancient urban tissue, opening up new focal points (Place de l'Opéra) and linking them with great axial roadways (Grands Boulevards), splendid exercises in traffic engineering and crowd control.

In 1852, Alexandre Dumas wrote *The Lady of the Camellias* at the same time Rudé was working on the memorial to Marshal Ney, which was to be placed on the spot where the great soldier had been executed in 1815; in Rodin's opinion, it was Paris' finest statue. In 1857 Baudelaire, the first poet of the teeming modern metropolis, published *Les Fleurs du Mal (The Flowers of Evil)*. In 1859, Gounod presented *Faust* at the Opéra Lyrique. In 1860, Étienne Lenoir registered his first patent for the internal combustion engine.

The year 1863 was marked by the scandals caused by Manet's *Déjeuner sur l'herbe* and *Olympia*; Baltard masked the masterly iron structure of the St-Augustin Church with the stone cladding still obligatory in a religious building. In 1896 Pierre de Coubertin created the International Olympic Committee.

Paris Commune – the Vendome Column was pulled down on 16 May 1871.

© UPPA/Photoshot

Famous artists

On 19 December 1915, Édith Giovanna Gassion was born to abject poverty at the Tenon Hospital (but popular legend had her come into the world under a lamppost on the steps of no. 72 r. de Belleville). She later sang in the streets, before becoming a radio, gramophone and music-hall success in 1935 under the name of **Édith Piaf**. Beloved for the instinctive but deeply moving tones of her voice, she came to embody the spirit of France (*La vie en rose, Les cloches*).

Another famous figure was **Maurice Chevalier** (1888–1972), film star, entertainer and cabaret singer; he paired with Jeanne Mistinguett at the Folies Bergère (1911) and sang at the Casino de Paris between the World Wars. Before attaining fame on Broadway in blacktie and boater, he was known at home for songs that are rooted in Belleville: *Ma Pomme, Prosper and un gars du Ménilmontant*.

Republican Continuity (1870 to the present day)

On 4 September 1870, the mob which had invaded the National Assembly was led by Gambetta to City Hall, declaring the Republic. The new government prepared to defend Paris against the advancing Prussians; the St-Cloud Château was set on fire and a fierce battle took place at Le Bourget.

The ensuing siege subjected Parisians to terrible hardships; food ran out and the winter was exceptionally severe. The city surrendered on 28 January 1871. The revolutionary **Commune** was ruthlessly suppressed by military force, but not before the Communards had burnt down the City Hall, the Tuileries and the Audit Office (Cours des Comptes – on the site of what is now the Orsay Museum), pulled down the column in the Place Vendôme and shot their prisoners at the Hostages' Wall in the Rue Haxo. They made their last stand in the Père-Lachaise Cemetery, where those Communards who had survived the bitter fighting were summarily executed at the Federalists' Wall (Mur des Fédérés).

Political institutions were re-established and the nation revived; the Republic was consolidated as France's political regime, notwithstanding Marshal Pétain's so-called French State (État Français), Nazi occupation and the provisional government following the end of World War II.

Third Republic – Carpeaux sculpted the Four Corners of the World for the Observatory Fountain, and Émile Littré completed the publication of his renowned *Dictionary of the French Language*. Bizet wrote *L'Arlésienne (the Woman of Arles)* for the Odéon theatre and followed it with *Carmen*, based on a short story by Mérimée.

In 1874, Degas painted *The Dancing Class* and Monet *Impression: Rising Sun*, which, when exhibited by his dealer Nadar, prompted the coining of the initially derisive term "Impressionism". Later, Renoir worked at the Moulin de la Galette, and Puvis de Chavannes decorated the walls of the Panthéon. Rodin sculpted the *Thinker,* followed by figures of Balzac and Victor Hugo.

In 1879, Seulecq presented the principle of sequential transmission on which television is based and Pasteur completed his vast body of work. Seurat's *Grande Jatte* heralded the establishment of the Pointillist school of painting. The engineer Gustave Eiffel completed his great tower, centrepiece of the Universal Exhibition of 1889. In the century's final decade, Toulouse-Lautrec painted cabaret scenes and Pissarro Parisian townscapes, and Forain gained fame as a marvellous caricaturist. At the Catholic Institute, Édouard Branly discovered radio conductors.

In 1891, René Panhard built the first petrol-engine motor car, which drove across Paris. In 1898, the young Louis Renault built his first car, then founded his Billancourt factory; in 1902 he patented a turbocharger. The factory turned out cars, lorries, planes and, in 1917, light tanks which contributed to the German defeat in 1918. In 1898 Pierre and Marie Curie isolated radium and established the atomic character of radioactivity; their laboratory has since disappeared, but its outline is shown in the courtyard of the school at 10 rue Vauquelin. Girault used steel, stone and glass to construct the Grand Palais and Petit Palais exhibition halls for the 1900 Exhibition. This occasion also saw the bridging of the Seine by the great flattened arch of the Pont Alexandre III. In 1906, Santos-Dumont took off in a heavier-than-air machine, staying aloft for 21 seconds and travelling 220m/721.7ft.

At Montparnasse, artists Soutine, Zadkine, Chagall, Modigliani and Léger took up studios; Brancusi's work was evolving towards abstraction *(The Sleeping Muse)*. In 1913, the Théâtre des Champs-Élysées theatre opened with a controversial performance of Stravinsky's *Rite of Spring*.

In 1914 construction of the Sacré-Cœur Basilica was completed. On 31 July, the eve of the outbreak of World War I, Jean Jaurès was assassinated.

The World Wars

World War I (1914–18) put civilians and soldiers to the severest of tests. After three years of conflict, Clemenceau assumed leadership of France, earning the title "Father of Victory". In 1920, the interment of an unknown soldier at the Arc de Triomphe marked France's recognition of the sacrifices made by ordinary soldiers.

In the 1920s, Le Corbusier built the La Roche Villa, Bourdelle sculpted *"France"* at the Palais de Tokyo; Georges Rouault completed *Miserere*, Maurice Ravel composed *Boléro* for the dancer Ida Rubinstein and Cocteau wrote *Les Enfants Terribles*. In 1934, André Citroën introduced the Traction Avant (Front-Wheel Drive) car.

In 1940, during **World War II**, Paris was bombed, then **occupied** by Nazi troops. In July 1942, police rounded up over 13 000 French Jews at the Vélodrome d'Hiver prior to deporting them to Nazi death camps; 4 500 members of the Resistance also perished in the clearing on Mount Valérien, where the National Memorial of Fighting France now stands. On 19 August 1944, Paris was **liberated**.

Fourth and Fifth Republics – Post-WWII thinkers like Jean-Paul Sartre, Simone de Beauvoir and Albert Camus brought new ideas in art and philosophy, including Existentialism, to the fore. In 1950, Alfred Kastler confirmed the principle of "optical pumping", subsequently used as a method for producing a laser beam. The *Symphony for a Single Man* by Maurice Béjart, presented at the Étoile Theatre in 1955, was danced to *musique concrète* composed by Pierre Henry and Pierre Schaeffer. In May 1968, a student-led revolt at the Sorbonne ushered in a major social and cultural revolution, propelled by others around the world.

GETTING AROUND PARIS

The Seine River flows east–west across the city. Places north of the river are on the *rive droite*, while those to the south are on the *rive gauche*. Paris is divided into 20 **arrondissements** (districts or neighbourhoods), each with its own local government and characteristics. Each arrondissement is further divided into a number of neighbourhoods determined by history and the people who live there.

The métro is the easiest and most economical mode of transport. **Line 1**, crossing Paris east–west, serves many famous attractions: the Louvre, Champs-Élysées and Arc de Triomphe. **Line 4** is useful for travelling north–south. The metro also serves the near suburbs, but for those a bit farther out, use the **RER** suburban trains.

Arrondissements 1–4

Harbouring the historic Île de la Cité, the awe-inspiring Notre-Dame Cathedral and Sainte-Chapelle, the Louvre, Tuileries, Palais Royal, and the Marais district with its heady mixture of Renaissance charm and hip urban culture, arrondissements 1-4 make up the heart of classical Right Bank Paris.

- **Michelin Map:** 312 D 2. See page 109.
- **Info:** en.parisinfo.com.
- **Location:** Stretching from the city centre, through the Sentier, Temple and Marais districts to the Île de la Cité and Île St-Louis.
- **Don't Miss:** Notre-Dame Cathedral, Louvre, Marais.
- **Kids:** Ice cream from Berthillon on the Île St Louis.

NOTRE-DAME CATHÉDRAL★★★

r. du cloître Notre-Dame. **Cathedral** *open Mon–Fri 8am–6.45pm, Sat–Sun 8am–7.15pm.* *No charge.* *Guided tours in English Wed & Thu 2pm, Sat 2.30pm.* **Towers** *open Apr–Sept 10am–6.30pm; Oct–Mar 10am–5.30pm.* *8.50€.* *01 53 10 07 00. www.notredamedeparis.fr.* *Notre-Dame is the point from which distances to Paris are measured.*

Maurice de Sully began work on the cathedral in 1163, but people have worshipped at the site for 2 000 years and the present building has witnessed the great events of French history.

Notre-Dame is the last great galleried church building and one of the first with flying buttresses. In 1245 the bulk of the work was complete and St Louis held a ceremony for the knighting of his son, also placing the Crown of Thorns in the cathedral until the nearby Sainte-Chapelle was ready to receive it. In 1250 the twin towers were finished.

In 1430, the cathedral hosted the coronation of the young Henry VI of England as King of France; in 1455, the late Joan of Arc was rehabilitated here in a ceremony; in 1558, Mary Stuart was crowned here on becoming Queen of France by her marriage to François II; in 1572, the Huguenot Henri IV married Marguerite of Valois; in 1594 the king converted to the Catholic faith.

Notre Dame has endured mutilations of various kinds throughout its history: in 1699 the choir screen was demolished, and later some of the original stained glass was removed to let in more light; the central portal was also demolished

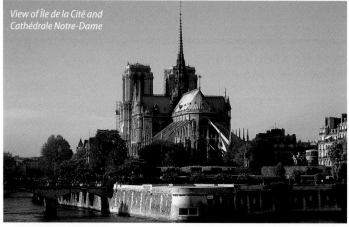

View of Île de la Cité and Cathédrale Notre-Dame

© G. Targat/MICHELIN

(18C) to facilitate processions. During the 1789 Revolution, statues were destroyed and the cathedral declared a Temple of Reason. It was in a much-dilapidated building that Napoleon Bonaparte crowned himself Emperor and the King of Rome was baptised. In 1831, Hugo's novel *Notre-Dame de Paris* sensitised public opinion to the poor state of the building, and in 1841 Louis-Philippe charged Viollet-le-Duc with its restoration. In the space of 24 years, he completed his work in accordance with his own, idealised vision of the Gothic style. Though often criticised, it should be seen in the context of the wholesale demolition of the medieval Île-de-la-Cité and its replacement with administrative buildings.

The magnificent Cloister Portal (Portail du Cloître–north transept) is 30 years older than the west front portals; with its richly carved gables and smiling figure of the Virgin – the only original large sculpture to have survived – it demonstrates how far the art of sculpture had advanced over the period. At the beginning of the 14C, the bold array of flying buttresses was sent soaring over the ambulatory and galleries to hold the high vaults of the east end in place.

Above the Kings' Gallery is the great rose window, which conserves its medieval glass. An enterprise of considerable daring – it was the largest such window of its time – it shows no sign of distortion after 700 years and has often been imitated. Inside, the rose window has particularly fine stained glass of a deep bluish-mauve.

SAINTE-CHAPELLE★★★

4 bd. du Palais. &⊙*Open Mar–Oct 9.30am–6pm; Nov–Feb 9am–5pm; Wed evenings 15 May–15 Sept last admission 9pm.* ⊙*Closed 1 Jan, 1 May, 1 and 25 Dec.* ☛*8.50€. sainte-chapelle. monuments-nationaux.fr/en.*

Only 80 years separate this definitive masterpiece of the High Gothic from the Transitional Gothic of Notre-Dame, but the difference is striking; in the lightness and clarity of its structure,

the Sainte-Chapelle pushes Gothic ideas to the limit. The chapel was built on the orders of St Louis to house the recently acquired relics of the Passion within the precincts of the royal palace; it was completed in a record time of 33 months.

The upper chapel resembles a shrine, with walls made almost entirely of remarkable stained glass covering a total area of 618sq m/6 672sq ft; 1 134 different scenes are depicted, of which 720 are made of original glass. The windows rise to a height of 15m/49ft. By 1240, the stained glass at Chartres had been completed, and the king was able to summon the master craftsmen who had worked on them to Paris. This explains the similarity between the glass of the cathedral and of the chapel, in terms of the scenes shown and the luminous colour which eclipses the simplicity of the design.

The theme is Christ's Passion, including its foretelling by the Prophets and John the Baptist, together with the episodes which lead up to it.

The original rose window is shown in a scene from the Très Riches Heures du Duc de Berry; the present rose window is a product of the Flamboyant Gothic, ordered by Charles VII, and depicts the Apocalypse of St John. It is characteristic of its age in the design of its tracery and in the subtle variations of colour which had replaced the earlier method of juxtaposing numerous small coloured panes.

PALAIS DE JUSTICE AND CONCIERGERIE★★

2 bd. du Palais. **Palais** ⊙*open Mon–Sat 8.30am–6pm.* ⊙*Closed public holidays. Visitors are normally allowed to attend a civil or criminal hearing.* ✆*01 44 32 50 50.* **Conciergerie** ⊙*open daily 9.30am–6pm.* ⊙*Closed late-Sept–late-Oct (check website for details), 1 Jan, 1 May, 25 Dec.* ☛*8.50€. conciergerie. monuments-nationaux.fr/en.*

Known as the Palace (Palais), this is the principal seat of civil and judicial authority. Before becoming the royal palace of the rulers of medieval France, it served as the residence of Roman governors, Merovingian kings and the children of Clovis.

The Capetian kings built a chapel and fortified the palace with a keep. Philippe le Bel (the Fair) entrusted Enguerrand de Marigny with construction of the Conciergerie as well as with the extension and embellishment of the palace; its Gothic halls of 1313 were widely admired. Later, Charles V built the Clock Tower (Tour de l'Horloge), the city's first public clock; he also installed Parliament here, the country's supreme court. Survivals from this period include the Great Hall (Salle des gens d'Armes) with its fine capitals, the Guard Room (Salle des Gardes) with its magnificent pillars, and kitchens with monumental corner fireplaces.

The great hall on the first floor was restored by Salomon de Brosse after the fire of 1618; it was refurbished again in 1840 and once more after the fire of 1871.

The First Civil Court is in the former Grand'chambre du parlement: this is where kings dispensed justice, where the 16-year-old Louis XIV dictated his orders to Parliament, where that body in its turn demanded the convocation of the States-General in 1788, and where the Revolutionary Tribunal was set up under public prosecutor Fouquier-Tinville.

The entrance to the royal palace was once guarded by the twin towers gracing the north front of the great complex; this is the oldest part of the building, albeit now hiding behind a 19C neo-Gothic façade.

The **Conciergerie** served as antechamber to the guillotine during the Terror, housing up to 1 200 detainees at a time. The Prisoners' Gallery (Galerie des Prisonniers), Marie-Antoinette's cachot (cell) and the Girondins' Chapel (Chapelle des Girondins) are particularly moving.

HÔTEL DE VILLE★

pl. de l'Hôtel de Ville.

Hôtel de Ville (City Hall) is home to the Parisian government. Municipal government was introduced in the 13C, under the direction of leading members of the powerful watermen's guild appointed by Louis IX.

The vast plaza outside City Hall has long been the epicentre of uprising and revolt (and was also the scene of gory executions during the Medieval period). Throughout the French Revolution it was in the hands of the Commune, and in 1848 it became the seat of the Provisional Government. The Republic was proclaimed from here in 1870, and, on 24 March 1871, the Communards burnt it down. It was rebuilt from 1874.

ARC DE TRIOMPHE DU CARROUSEL★

This delightful pastiche, inspired by the Roman triumphal arch of Septimus Severus, was built between 1806 and 1808. Six bas-relief sculptures commemorate the Napoléonic victories of 1805. On the platform, where Napoléon placed the four horses removed from the basilica of San Marco in Venice (until these were returned in 1815), **Bosio** sculpted an allegorical goddess, representing the Restoration of the Bourbons, accompanied by Victories and driving a quadriga.

The square takes its name from the lavish equestrian and theatrical tournament held there in honour of the birth of the Dauphin (Prince) in 1662.

Standing beneath the arch affords a magnificent **view★★★** along the axis that runs from the Louvre through the Tuileries, place de la Concorde, the Champs-Élysées and the Arc de Triomphe, as far as the Grande Arche at La Défense.

⊳ Descend one of the flights of stairs near the Carrousel, or go through the Pyramid and the main entrance.

La Galerie Carrousel du Louvre

The inverted crystalline pyramid provides a well of light in the central area of the arcade; concrete masonry, rows of windows and subdued lighting combine to give the main arcade the appearance of a large entrance hall.

▶ Go back towards the main entrance via the underground passage.

PALAIS DU LOUVRE★★★ (MUSÉE DU LOUVRE)

For eight centuries the Louvre was the seat of kings and emperors. Today it is famous for one of the richest collections of art and antiquities in the world.

Philippe Auguste (1180–1223) lived in the Palais de la Cité. In 1190 he had the Louvre fortress built on the north bank of the Seine, at the weakest point in his capital's defences against its English neighbours. This fortress was located on the southwest quarter of the present Cour Carrée. **Philip the Fair** (1285–1314) installed his arsenal and royal treasury in the Louvre, where they would remain for the next four centuries.

Charles V (1364–80) transformed the old fortress into a comfortable residence without changing its dimensions. Here he installed his famous **library** of 973 books, the largest in the kingdom. A miniature in the *Very Rich Hours* of the Duke of Berry depicts this attractive Louvre, surrounded by new ramparts, which put an end to its military career. After Charles V, the Louvre was not to be inhabited by royalty for the next 150 years.

François I (1515–47) lived mainly in the Loire Valley or the Marais. In 1528, in desperate need of money, he prepared to demand contributions from the Parisian population. To soften them up, he announced his intention to take up residence in the Louvre. Rebuilding began: the keep, a bulky form, which cast a shadow over the courtyard, was razed, and the advance defences were demolished; however, orders for a new palace for the King of France to be built on the foundations of the old fortress were not given to **Pierre Lescot** until 1546. Lescot's designs in keeping with the style of the Italian Renaissance, which had found such favour on the banks of the Loire, were new to Paris. By 1547, at the death of the king, construction was barely visible above ground level.

Henri II (1547–59) took up residence in the Louvre and retained Lescot as chief architect. The old great hall was transformed into the **Salle des Caryatides**; on the first floor, the Salle des Cent-Suisses, reserved for the Palace Guard, preceded the royal suite in the south wing (the queen's suite was on the ground floor).

Catherine de' Medici (1519–89) withdrew after the death of her husband Henri II. Once declared regent, she decided to take up residence in the Louvre, on the floor since known as the Logis des Reines (Queens' Lodging), but was not content to reside in the middle of Lescot's building site. In 1564, she ordered **Philibert Delorme** to build her a residence of her own on the site known as Les Tuileries, in which she would have greater freedom of move-

Arc de Triomphe du Carrousel

© A. Simpson/MICHELIN

Brief History of the Collections at the Louvre

François I was the first eminent patron of Italian artists of his day. Twelve paintings from his original collection, including the *Mona Lisa* by Leonardo da Vinci, *La Belle Jardinière* by Raphael and *A Portrait of François I* by Titian, are among the most important works presently in State hands. By the time Louis XIV died, over 2 500 paintings hung in the palaces of the Louvre and Versailles.

The idea of making the collection accessible to the public, as envisaged by Marigny under Louis XVI, was finally realised by the Convention on 10 August 1793, when the doors of the Grande Galerie were opened to visitors. Napoléon subsequently made the museum's collection the richest in the world by exacting a tribute in works of art from every country he conquered; many of these were reclaimed by the Allies in 1815.

In turn, Louis XVIII, Charles X and Louis-Philippe all further endowed the collections: scarcely had the *Venus de Milo* been rediscovered when she was brought to France by Dumont d'Urville. Departments for Egyptian and Assyrian art were opened. Gifts, legacies and acquisitions continue to enrich the collections of the Louvre, with over 350 000 works now catalogued.

ment. The Queen Mother planned to have a covered passage built between the two palaces to enable people to walk the 500m/547yd unnoticed and shelter from inclement weather. The connecting galleries were duly begun, but work was brought to a halt by the Wars of Religion. The old Louvre was to keep its two Gothic and two Renaissance wings until the reign of Louis XIV.

Henri IV (1589–1610) continued work on his arrival in Paris in 1594. **Louis Métezeau** added an upper floor to the Galerie du Bord de l'Eau; **Jacques II Androuet Du Cerceau** completed the Petite Galerie and built the **Pavillon de Flore**, with another gallery leading off to link it with the Tuileries Palace.

Louis XIII (1610–43) undertook to enlarge the Louvre fourfold. Lemercier built the **pavillon de l'Horloge** in 1640 and the northwest corner of the courtyard, a Classical statement in response to Lescot's design.

Louis XIV (1643–1715). After the death of Louis XIII, Anne of Austria moved to the Palais-Royal with the young Louis. Nine years later, they moved to the Louvre, intimidated by the *Fronde* uprisings. Louis XIV asked **Le Vau** to resume work on the extension; he had him build the **Galerie d'Apollon** and in 1662 ordered a grand new façade to close off the Cour Carrée (**Colonnade★★**). In 1682, the

king moved his court from the capital to Versailles. Construction was halted.

18C–19C – The Louvre was by now so dilapidated that there was talk of tearing it down. After the brief interval of the Regency (1715–22), Louis XV lived at Versailles, whence Louis XVI was brought to Paris on 6 October 1789, briefly occupying the Tuileries until his incarceration at the Temple prison. The Convention used the theatre and the Committee of Public Safety installed itself in the royal apartments of the Tuileries, until appropriated by Bonaparte, the Premier Consul.

Napoléon I (1799–1814), while living in the Tuileries, took great interest in the Louvre. The emperor commissioned architects **Percier** and **Fontaine** to complete the Cour Carrée, enlarge the place du Carrousel and build the Arc de Triomphe du Carrousel. Napoléon's fall in 1814 interrupted works.

Napoléon III (1852–70), also resident of the Tuileries, oversaw completion of the Louvre. He entrusted first **Visconti**, then **Lefuel** with closing off the Grande Cour to the north. The latter compensated for the difference in levels of the two arms of the Louvre by rebuilding the **Pavillon de Flore★** in a grandiose style (high relief by **Carpeaux, The Triumph of Flora★**) and modifying a section of the Galerie du Bord de l'Eau.

The Republic – The bloody uprising of the Paris Commune resulted in the Tuileries Palace being burned down in 1871, but collections were saved. In 1875, **Lefuel** began restoration of the Louvre, proposing to rebuild the Tuileries. In 1882 the Assembly removed the ruins, obliterating associations with the past regime.

François Mitterrand initiated the **Grand Louvre** project from 1981. Most work was finished by 1993, with the opening of the Richelieu wing and a new fashion museum.

☙ WALKING TOUR

The Louvre Palace Exterior
The exhibition on the History of the Louvre and the underground excavations provide insight into the palace. *For this you need an entrance ticket.*

▶ Start from the church of St-Germain l'Auxerrois, near Metro Louvre-Rivoli. From rue de Rivoli, head for the Seine. Opposite is the Louvre Palace.

Colonnade★★
See opposite.
The height and Classical harmony of the structure are fully apparent now that moats have been cleared to a depth of 7m/23ft around the rusticated base.

▶ Head towards the river and turn right. At Pont des Arts, cross the Jardin de l'Infante to the Cour Carrée.

☺ Guided Tours ☺

☙ English-language guided tours, activities and workshops are available. Tours for groups are conducted daily between 9.15am and 8pm and last 1hr30min. Visitors should buy their tickets at the window marked "Accueil des groupes" under the Pyramid, ☏01 40 20 51 77, ☜5€. In many rooms, there are explanatory texts for consultation in several languages, placed in racks near the door.

Cour Carrée★★★
The Renaissance façade is the work of **Pierre Lescot**. The expressive sculpture of the avant-corps (projecting bay) and upper storey are by **Jean Goujon**, depicting allegorical scenes, and animated figures. A nocturnal lighting system highlights the most impressive remnants of the old Louvre.

▶ Pass under the Clock Pavilion.

Pavillon de l'Horloge (*opposite*)

▶ Enter Cour Napoléon.

Pyramid★★
The Pyramid, 21m/69ft high and 33m/108.3ft wide at the base, was designed by architect **Ieoh Ming Pei**; it is built of sheet glass supported on a framework of stainless-steel tubes. An **equestrian statue of Louis XIV** stands on the axis leading to the Champs-Élysées.

Galerie d'Apollon

© Iipo Musto/Apa Publications

OPENING TIMES

♿ Open Wed–Mon 9am–6pm. Some sections open Wed and Fri until 9.45pm. Temporary exhibits in the Hall Napoléon: 9am–6pm (9.45pm Wed, Fri). Closed 1 Jan, 1 May, 25 Dec.

ADMISSION CHARGES

Permanent collection and temporary exhibits (single ticket, except for temporary exhibits in the Hall Napoléon): 12€, Hall Napoléon 13€ (under-18s no charge; under-26 no charge Fri 6pm–9.45pm; no charge the 1st Sun of the month or 14 Jul). Tickets valid all day long, even if you leave the museum.

Ticket sales until 5.15pm (9.15pm Wed, Fri). Advance ticket purchase from the **FNAC** store, www.fnactickets. com (1.50€ commission fee added to price), from Ticketnet ☏0892 390 100 (0.34€ per min), www.ticketnet.fr (1.10€ fee); tickets remain valid for an unlimited time.

PASSES AND DISCOUNTS

The **Paris Museum Pass** (valid 2, 4 or 6 days for over 60 museums and monuments) is for sale in the Carrousel du Louvre and allows you to enter the permanent collections immediately, without waiting. The **"carte Louvre jeunes"** pass: 15€ (valid one year for those under age 30, for sale under the Pyramid or by post) and **"Carte des Amis du Louvre"**: 70€ (valid one year, purchase from the Amis du Louvre booth between the Pyramid and the inverse Pyramid in the entrance area) allow entrance to permanent collections and temporary exhibits as well as activities reserved for museum members, discounts on auditorium events and for guided tours (www. amisdu louvre.fr).

Temporary exhibits – In the Hall Napoléon (under the Pyramid): 9am–6pm (9.45pm Wed, Fri), or in the Richelieu and Sully wings (during opening hours). 13€.

ACCESS

The main entrance is via the **Pyramid**. Direct access to the **Carrousel du Louvre** shopping centre is possible via the **Palais Royal Musée du Louvre** metro station, on either side of the **Arc du Carrousel** or at no. 99 rue de Rivoli.

PARKING

The **Carrousel-Louvre** car park (daily 7am–11pm) has space for 80 coaches and 620 cars. Access via the underground passage **avenue du Général-Lemonnier**, then enter the shopping centre through the old Charles V fortifications.

Hall Napoléon

Under the Pyramid, this hall is the nerve centre of the visitor network designed by the architect Pei. Visitors are immediately orientated towards one of three wings of the museum: **Denon**, **Richelieu** or **Sully**. This vast reception hall also houses a certain number of other services: bookshop, **Le Grand Louvre** restaurant, group facilities and an auditorium.

INFORMATION

General information can be obtained by calling or consulting the following: ☏01 40 20 51 51 (answering machine); ☏01 40 20 53 17 to speak to someone at the desk (six languages); internet: www.louvre.fr.

Some galleries are closed on certain days (or even for restoration); check the schedule of open rooms online or call in advance.

Fourteen video screens in the hall provide information about events on a daily basis in the museum. There is also a general **activity programme** (seven languages) available at the main information desk which comes out every three months.

Audio-guides can be hired (seven languages) on the mezzanine level in the various wings.

GETTING AROUND

The collections have been divided into three main sections: **Denon**, **Richelieu** and **Sully**, which make up the two wings and Cour Carrée. Within these three sections are four floors, from the medieval remnants of the Louvre in the lower level and the sculpture galleries and prehistoric arts on the ground floor to the French arts and European paintings on the first and second floors. The maze can be incredibly confusing, so be sure to pick up a floor plan at the information desk beneath the Pyramid.

Sully

- History of the Louvre: *Entresol.*
- Medieval Louvre: *Entresol.*
- Egyptian Antiquities: *Entresol, ground and 1st floors.*
- Greek Antiquities (Cariatides room, Hellenic period): *Ground and 1st floor.*
- Near East Antiquities (Iran and the Levant): *Ground floor.*
- Greek Antiquities (Bronze room, Campana gallery): *1st floor.*
- 17C–18C objets d'art: *1st floor.*
- 17C–19C French painting, including Graphic arts: *2nd floor.*
- Beistegui collection (room A): *2nd floor.*

Denon

- Italian sculpture: *Entresol and Ground floor.*
- Scandinavian sculpture: *Entresol.*
- Coptic Egypt: *Entresol.*
- The East Mediterranean in the Roman Empire: *Entresol.*
- Greek Antiquities: *Ground and 1st floors.*
- Etruscan and Roman Antiquities: *Ground floor.*
- Italian painting: *1st floor.*
- Spanish painting: *1st floor.*
- English painting: *1st floor.*
- 19C French painting (large sizes): *1st floor.*
- Decorative Arts (Apollon gallery): *1st floor. 18C section closed until 2014.*
- Islamic Art: *Entresol, Cour Visconti*

Richelieu

- Exhibitions documents: *Entresol.*
- French sculpture (Marly and Puget rooms): *Entresol and ground floor.*
- Near East Antiquities (Mesopotamia): *Ground floor.*
- Objets d'art (including Napoléon III's apartments): *1st floor.*
- 14C–17C French painting: *2nd floor.*
- Scandinavian schools: *2nd floor.*

▶ Cross the road that traverses place du Carrousel, in the direction of the Jardins des Tuileries.

CENTRE GEORGES-POMPIDOU★★★

pl. Georges-Pompidou. ◷*Wed–Sun 11am–10pm (ticket office closes 8pm). Atelier Brancusi 2pm–6pm.* ◷*1 May.* ♿ ℘*01 44 78 12 33.* *www.centrepompidou.fr.*

The "inside-out" building known to locals as "Beaubourg" is easily spotted on the Parisian skyline with its bright red, blue and white pipes and beams. Built in 1977 on the grounds that once served as parking for the marketplace at Les Halles, it's home to a modern art museum, public library, music research centre, café, several shops, an arthouse cinema and rooftop restaurant. A splendid panoramic **view★★** extends over Paris' rooftops (*◎3€ or free with museum ticket*).

The architects **Richard Rogers** (British) and **Renzo Piano** (Italian) achieved a totally futuristic building. The façade appears a tangle of pipes and tubes latticed along its glass skin, earning the establishment the nickname of "the inside-out museum".

The **Musée national d'Art moderne** (National Museum of Modern Art) occupies the 4th and 5th levels. The **Bibliothèque publique d'information**, the public library known as the BPI, is on the 1st, 2nd and 3rd levels. The **IRCAM** (Institute for Acoustic and Musical Research) lies beneath place Stravinski. The centre also houses several **temporary exhibition halls**.

In addition, the centre provides live entertainment (dance, music, theatre), cinema performances and spoken reviews. The library is especially popular with Parisians, thanks to its late hours, open access and up-to-date collection of printed and other resources. There's an arts bookshop on level 0, a design shop and mezzanine café (with view over the main entrance) on level one, and a good restaurant, Georges *(reservations required, ☎01 44 78 47 99, www. beaumarly.com)* on level 6.

Musée national d'Art moderne★★★
pl. Georges-Pompidou. Opening times the same as Centre Georges-Pompidou, see p125. Museum and exhibitions 11–13€; no charge for the museum 1st Sun of the month.

Ranking high among the most significant collections dedicated to modern art in the world (76 000 works and objects), this museum traces the evolution of art from Fauvism and Cubism to contemporary movements. The modern collection (1905–60) is housed on the fifth floor, whereas contemporary exhibitions from the 1960s onwards are on the fourth floor.

Outside the museum on the vast, sloping square, the Parisian sculpture workshop of **Constantin Brancusi** (1876–1957) has been entirely reconstituted in a small building, featuring the artist's tools, major works and personal art collection.

Modern collection – *Fifth floor.*
Forty galleries present around 900 works *(changes every 18 months)*. Throughout the exhibition, the juxtaposition of painting and sculpture with the design and architecture of the same decade enables the visitor to obtain an overview of 20C artistic creation. Galleries dedicated to a single artist (Matisse, Léger, Picasso, Rouault, Delau-

nay) alternate with thematic rooms. All the main movements of the first half of the 20C are represented here, including **Fauvism** (1905–10; Derain, Marquet, Dufy and Matisse); **Cubism** (**Braque** and **Picasso** in 1907), **Dada** (from 1913; **Marcel Duchamp**), the **Paris School** (1910–30; **Soutine**, **Chagall**, **Modigliani**, Larionov, Gontcharova), the Abstract School (from 1910; **Kandinsky**, **Kupka**, **Mondrian**, **Klee**), and the **Bauhaus School**.

Surrealism is represented by De Chirico, **Salvador Dalí**, Max Ernst, **Magritte**, Brauner, André Masson, Tanguy, Giacometti, Picasso and **Miró**.

The **Cobra** movement (1948–51) advocated spontaneous expression through the free use of bold colour and energetic brushstrokes (Alechinsky, Appel, Jorn). American art from the 1940s to the 1960s is represented by **Pollock**, **Rothko** and **Newman**.

Contemporary collection –
Fourth floor.

This collection is regularly changed and updated to reflect contemporary artistic trends and highlight the work of major personalities from around the world. The result is a dynamic, colourful world of form and movement linking art with everyday life.

Major works include *Requiem for a Dead Leaf* (Tinguely) and *Red Rhinoceros* (Veilhan). **Pop Art** is represented by **Warhol** and Rauschenberg, **New Realism** by **Klein**, **Arman**, **César**, **Niki de Saint-Phalle**, **Op** and **Kinetic Art** by **Agam** (Antechamber of the Élysée Palace private apartments) and Vasarely. There are also installations by **Dubuffet** *(The Winter Garden)*, **Beuys** *(Plight)* and **Raynaud** *(Container Zero)*.

Three rooms offer examples of design and architecture from the 1960s to the present (Starck, Nouvel, Perrault, Toto Ito). Space is also devoted to film, multimedia installations and Happening (**Gutaï** and **Fluxus**).

ÉGLISE ST-EUSTACHE★★
2 Impasse Saint-Eustache. Open Mon–Fri 9.30am–7pm, Sat, Sun 9am–

7pm. Audioguides available, suggested donation ☜3€. ✆ 01 42 36 31 05, saint-eustache.org.

This was once the richest church in Paris and the centre of a parish that included the areas around the Palais-Royal and the Halles market. It was modelled after Notre-Dame when construction began in 1532. But St-Eustache took over a hundred years to complete; tastes changed, and the building's Gothic skeleton is fleshed out with Renaissance finishes and detail.

The Flamboyant style is evident in the three-storeyed interior elevation, the vaulting of the choir, crossing and nave, lofty side aisles and flying buttresses. The Renaissance is exemplified in the Corinthian columns and in the return to the use of semicircular arches, and Classicism in P. de Champaigne's choir windows and in Colbert's tomb, designed by Le Brun in collaboration with Coysevox and Tuby. The Chapelle St-Joseph houses English sculptor Raymond Mason's commemoration of the fruit and vegetable market's move out of Paris in 1969.

MUSÉE DES ARTS ET MÉTIERS★★

60 r. Réaumur. ◷Open Tue–Sun 10am–6pm (9.30pm on Thu). ◷Closed public holidays. ☜6.50€. ✆01 53 01 82 00, www.arts-et-metiers.net.

This museum illustrates technical progress in industry and science. The visit begins with instruments used to explore the **"infinitesimal** and **infinitely remote"**. Next come **machines** and models showing **building techniques**. **Communication** is illustrated through printing, television, photography, etc. **Energy** is represented by a model of the Marly machine (1678–85), turbines, boilers and engines, while **locomotion** explores means of transport: cycles, cars, aircraft and 19C railways. The chapel displays the first steam buses and models of the Statue of Liberty, the engine of the European rocket Ariane and of Foucault's pendulum (the latter proved the Earth's rotation).

LE MARAIS★★★

Charles V's 14C move to the Hôtel St-Paul in the Marais district marked the incorporation of a suburban area into Paris. Charles VI, Henri IV and Louis XIII also resided here, making the former swamplands increasingly fashionable. The characteristic French town house, (hôtel) assumed its definitive form here; it became the setting for literary or philosophical salons.

The **Hôtel Lamoignon★** (24 r. Pavée) of 1584 is a typical example of a Henri III-style mansion. Jean-Baptiste Androuet Du Cerceau applied the Giant Order style with flattened pilasters, Corinthian capitals and sculpted string-course for the first time in Paris.

The Henri IV style emerges in the **Place des Vosges★★★** designed by Louis Métezeau, completed in 1612. The 36 houses retain their original symmetrical appearance with arcades, two storeys of alternating brick and stone facades and steeply pitched slate roofs pierced with dormer windows. The King's Pavilion (Pavillon du Roi) lies at the southern end, balanced by the Queen's Pavilion (Pavillon de la Reine) at the sunnier northern end.

Louis XIII's reign heralds the Classical style. In 1624, Jean Androuet Du Cerceau built the **Hôtel de Sully★** (62 r. Saint-Antoine) with a gateway framed between massive pavilions, and a main courtyard (**cour d'honneur★★★**) with triangular and curved pediments complemented by scrolled dormer windows.

The early Louis XIV style is seen in Mansart's 1648 **Hôtel Guénégaud★★** (60 r. des Archives), where a majestic staircase and small formal garden make it one of the finest Marais houses. Other examples include Le Pautre's **Hôtel de Beauvais★** (68 r. François Miron) with its curved balcony on brackets and its ingenious internal layout; the **Hôtel Carnavalet★** (23 r. de Sévigné), a Renaissance house rebuilt by Mansart in 1655, and Cottard's **Hôtel Amelot-de-Bisseuil★** (47 r. Vieille-du-Temple) of somewhat theatrical design with its cornice and curved pediment decorated with allegorical figures.

The later Louis XIV style features in two adjoining *hôtels* built by Delamair: the **Hôtel de Rohan**★★ *(87 r. Vieille-du-Temple)* with its wonderful sculpture of the *Horses of Apollo (Chevaux frémissants d'Apollon à l'abreuvoir)* by Robert Le Lorrain; and the **Hôtel de Soubise**★★ *(60 r. des Francs-Bourgeois)* with its horseshoe-shaped courtyard and double colonnade. They are characterised by raised ground floors, massive windows, roof balustrades and the sculpture of their projecting central sections.

Arrondissements 5–7

Moving across the Seine to the Left Bank, arrondissements 5-7 are home to many of the capital's legendary sights, from the quaint streets of the Quartier Latin and St-Germain-des-Prés with their dizzying intellectual heritage, to the Musée d'Orsay and Eiffel Tower, symbols of a city keen to embrace modernity.

- **Michelin Map:** 312 D 2. See page 109.
- **Info:** ℰ08 92 68 30 00 or http://en.parisinfo.com.
- **Location:** Beginning near St-Michel and heading west to St-Germain-des-Prés, then toward the Quai d'Orsay and the Eiffel Tower.
- **Don't Miss:** Quartier Latin, Musée d'Orsay, Eiffel Tower.
- **Kids:** The Jardin des Plantes and its quaint zoo.

QUARTIER LATIN★★★

Lying on the left bank of the Seine and the slopes of the mount **"Montagne" Ste-Geneviève**, the Quartier Latin concentrates many of the capital's most venerable institutions, notably the Sorbonne, one of Europe's oldest universities, founded 1253.

Though anchored in the past, the area is marked by the ebb and flow of students and other young people who make up the population of the "Latin" Quarter (so-called because Latin was the language of instruction up to the French Revolution).

The area also abounds in publishing houses, bookshops, and terrace cafés, including the legendary **Procope** *(13 r. de l'Ancienne Comédie)*, one of Paris' oldest cafés and former haunt of philosophers such as Voltaire.

Église St-Séverin★★

3 r. Prêtres St Séverin.
www.saint-severin.com.
This much-loved Latin Quarter church features a number of architectural styles. The lower part of the portal and the first three bays of the nave are High Gothic; while much of the rest of the building was remodelled in Flamboyant style. In the 18C, the pillars in the chancel were clad in wood and marble.

Luxembourg Palace★★

15 r. de Vaugirard.
The historic gardens of Luxembourg Palace (*see Parks and Gardens in Paris box, p139*), seat of the French Senate, are a magnificent oasis of greenery in the heart of the Latin Quarter, making it a popular place where one can sit and absorb the atmosphere of Paris.

In 1257 a community of Carthusians, with the help of St Louis, laid claim to the area and built a vast monastery with extensive grounds.

After the death of Henri IV, Queen Marie de' Medici, who wished to have a place of her own which would remind her of the Pitti Palace in Florence. Construction started in 1615, with a commission in 1621 for **Rubens** to paint 24 large allegorical pictures representing the queen's life (these are now in the Louvre).

In 1790 when the monastery was suppressed, the palace gardens were extended to the avenue de l'Observatoire.

Today the palace is the seat of the **Sénat** (the French Upper House), composed of 319 members.

The **Petit Luxembourg**, now the residence of the President of the Senate, comprises the original Hôtel de Luxembourg given to Richelieu by Marie de Medici, but also the cloister and chapel of a convent founded by the queen. The **Musée du Luxembourg** (enter at 19 r. de Vaugirard; ◷ open during exhibitions Tue–Thu, Sat–Sun 10am–7.30pm, Mon & Fri 10am–10pm.⊚11€. ℘01 40 13 62 00, www.museeduluxembourg.fr) houses temporary exhibitions in the former orangerie.

PANTHÉON★★

pl. du Panthéon. ◷ Open daily Apr–Sept, 10am–6.30pm; Oct–Mar, 10am–6pm. ☛ Guided tours in French. ◷ Closed public holidays. ⊚7.50€. ℘01 44 32 18 00. pantheon.monuments-nationaux.fr.

The Panthéon's distinctive silhouette on the hilltop and its role as the necropolis of France's greatest citizens make it a popular national monument.

Louis XV vowed, when desperately ill in 1744, that should he recover he would replace the semi-ruined church of the abbey of Ste-Geneviève. The project was given to the architect Jacques **Soufflot**. A lack of funds and cracks in the structure caused by ground movements delayed completion until 1789, after Soufflot's death (1780).

In April 1791 the structure's function as a church was suspended by the Constituent Assembly in order to "receive the bodies of great men who died in the period of French liberty" – it thus became a Pantheon. Voltaire and Rousseau are buried here, and Mirabeau and Marat were for a short while.

The Panthéon subsequently served as a church under the empire, a necropolis in the reign of Louis-Philippe, a church under Napoléon III, the headquarters of the Commune and finally as a lay temple to receive the ashes of Victor Hugo in 1885.

The **dome★★**, strengthened with an iron framework, can be best surveyed from a distance. Eleven steps rise to the peristyle, composed of fluted columns supporting a triangular pediment – the first of its kind in Paris.

The great edifice is built in the shape of a Greek Cross. The upper section has a fresco by Baron Antoine Jean Gros (1771–1835) depicting St Geneviève's Apotheosis. Stairs lead up to the dome from a place affording a fine **view★★** over Paris.

Although strangely eerie and empty, the crypt contains the tombs of great thinkers throughout France's history: La Tour d'Auvergne, Voltaire, Rousseau, Victor Hugo, Émile Zola, Marcelin Berthelot, Louis Braille, Jean Jaurès, the explorer Bougainville. More recent figures honoured here are Nobel Prize winners Pierre and Marie Curie, and French Resistance leader Jean Moulin.

Foucault's Pendulum – In 1851 Léon Foucault took advantage of the dome's height to repeat publicly his experiment that proved the rotation of the earth, which deviated from its axis during oscillation in a circular movement.

The pendulum can now be seen at the Musée des Arts et Métiers (⟳ see p127).

HÔTEL DE CLUNY (MUSÉE NATIONAL DU MOYEN ÂGE)★★

6 pl. Paul Painlevé. ◷ Open Wed–Mon 9.15am–5.45pm (last admission 30min before closing). ◷ Closed 1 Jan, 1 May, 25 Dec. ⊚8€, no charge 1st Sun of the month. ℘01 53 73 78 00. www.musee-moyenage.fr.

This museum encompasses the residence of the abbots of Cluny, the ruins of Roman thermal baths and a collection of medieval arts.

Together with the Hôtel de Sens, Hôtel de Cluny is one of only two remaining 15C private houses in Paris. Despite much restoration, original medieval details survive in features such as wall crenellations and turrets.

The left wing is articulated with arches; the central building has mullioned windows; a frieze and Flamboyant balustrade, from which gargoyles spurt, line the base of the roof. A pentagonal tower juts out from the central building.

QUARTIER DE ST-GERMAIN-DES-PRÉS★★

Antique dealers, literary cafés and chic niglife on side streets combine to maintain the reputation of this former centre of international Bohemian life. Notable landmarks include Café de Flore (172 bd. St Germain) and Les Deux Magots (6 pl. St Germain des Prés).

Église de St-Germain-des-Prés★★

pl. Saint-Germain des Prés.

With the exception of Clovis, this church was the final resting place of the Merovingian kings. The church was subsequently destroyed by the Normans, but was restored during the 10C and 11C. Not surprising, then, that the tower rising above the west front has a fortress-like character. Around 1160, the nave was enlarged and the chancel rebuilt in the new Gothic style. "Improvements" followed in the 17C and in 1822 a somewhat over-zealous restoration took place.

The church's years of glory were 1631–1789, when the austere Congregation of St Maur made it a centre of learning and spirituality: monks studied ancient inscriptions and writing, the Church Fathers, archaeology and cartography. Their library was confiscated during the French Revolution.

Église de Saint-Sulpice★★

33 r. Saint-Sulpice. ○Open daily from 7.30am–7.30pm.

The church, dedicated to the 6C Archbishop of Bourges, St Sulpicius, was founded by the abbey of St-Germain des-Prés as a parish church for peasants living in its domain. Rebuilding began in 1646 with the chancel. Six architects took charge over a period of 134 years.

The **interior** is impressive for its size. Of the 20 artists who worked on the interior paintings, Delacroix's genius dominates. His **murals**★, painted between 1849 and 1861, illustrate St Michael Killing the Demon (ceiling), Heliodorus Being Driven from the Temple, and Jacob Wrestling with the Angel (left).

Institut de France★★

quai Conti. www.institut-de-france.fr.

Founded by Mazarin for scholars for provinces incorporated into France during his ministry, the building (1662) was first called the College of Four Nations. Designed by Le Vau, it stands on the far side of the river from the Louvre. The Institute comprises five academies, including the highly exclusive Académie Française, founded 1635 and honouring France's great intellectual achievers.

FAUBOURG SAINT-GERMAIN★★

The Faubourg St-Germain was originally the aristocratic suburb (faubourg) of the abbey of St-Germain-des-Prés.

The Revolution closed its sumptuous town houses and today the district is known primarily for its government ministries. Curious travellers wandering outside the well-known St-Germain and St-Sulpice districts will find the elegant, residential Sèvres-Babylone district dotted with shops and lively cafes.

Palais Bourbon★

126 r. de l'Université.

This palace of 1722 has been the seat of the Lower House of France's parliament, the Assemblée Nationale, for more than 150 years.

MUSÉE D'ORSAY★★★

62 r. de Lille. ♿○Open Fri–Wed, 9.30am –6pm, Thu 9.30am–9.45pm. ○Closed 1 Jan, 1 May, 25 Dec. ♾9€ for the permanent collection, 12€ for access to the permanent and temporary collections; no charge 1st Sun in the month. ☏01 40 49 48 14. www.musee-orsay.fr.

The focus of this museum, which was fully refurbished in 2011, is the period

Musée d'Orsay

© Jean-Luc Bohin/age fotostock

1848 to 1914. The upper floor is dedicated to the Impressionists, with one of the world's finest collections. There is also a considerable collection of pre- and post-Impressionist works, as well as sections consecrated to decorative arts and photography.

Major artists include the sculptors Degas and Rosso and the painters Degas, Sisley, Cézanne, Manet, Berthe Morisot, Pissarro, Gustave Caillebotte, Pierre-Auguste Renoir, and Claude Monet. Among the best-known works from this group of artists are *Planing the floor* (1875) by Caillebotte (gallery 30), Renoir's *Le Moulin de la Galette* (1876), and the bronze *Little 14-Year-Old Dancer* (1881) by Degas.

LES INVALIDES★★★

129 r. de Grenelle. Open daily Apr–Oct, 10am–6pm; Nov–Mar, 10am–5pm. Closed 1st Mon of the month in Oct–Jun, 1 Jan, 1 May, 1 Nov, 25 Dec. 9.50€ price includes Église du Dôme, Musée de l'Armée, l'Historial de Gaulle, Musée des Plans-Reliefs and Musée de l'Ordre de la Libération. Guided tours available for groups: 0825 05 44 05. Multimedia guide 6€ www.invalides.org.

The plans for this vast edifice were drawn up by Libéral Bruant between 1671–76 and implemented under by Louvois. The main façade, nearly 200m/650ft long, is dominated by an attic storey decorated with masks and dormer windows in the form of trophies. Napoléon once paraded his troops in the main courtyard (Cour d'honneur); here the South Pavilion (Pavillon du Midi) forms the façade of the Église St-Louis, the resting-place of some of France's great soldiers, and the interior is hung with flags taken from the enemy. Berlioz' Requiem was performed for the first time in 1837 here.

Musée d l'Armée

Open Apr–Oct, 10am–6pm; Nov–Mar, 10am–5pm.

Containing over 500 000 military artefacts, this museum lies on either side of the main courtyard at the Invalides. Arms and armour (*west side*) illustrate the evolution of methods of defence and attack, with weapons and armour from prehistoric times to the 16C. The Ancien Régime and 19C (*east side*) section features weapons and uniforms from the 17C through to the Second Empire, including many of Napoléon's. Banners and artillery grace the courtyard, including 200 cannons in the **Salle Gribeauval** (*west side*).

The **World War I** and **II** (*west side*) sections feature displays showing the development of World War I, and three floors are devoted to World War II, following a chronological order.

Église du Dôme, Hôtel National des Invalides

© Y. Kanazawa/Michelin

Église du Dôme★★★

⊙Open Apr-May 10am–6pm; mid-Jun–Sept, 10am–6pm; Oct–Mar, 10am–5pm. ⊙Closed 1st Mon of the month.

The church of Les Invalides, designed by, **Jules-Hardouin Mansart**, was begun in 1677. With its beautiful gilded dome, it is one of the great works of the Louis XIV style, bringing to perfection the Classicism introduced in the churches of the Sorbonne and the Val-de-Grâce. In 1735, Robert de Cotte completed the building by replacing the planned south colonnade and portico with the splendid vista offered by the Avenue de Breteuil. On the far side he laid out the Esplanade, and set up the guns captured at Vienna in 1805 by Napoleon to defend the gardens and fire ceremonial salvoes on great national occasions.

The church became a military necropolis after Napoleon had Marshal Turenne (d. 1675) buried here.

Note the memorial to Vauban, the great military architect, and the tomb of Marshal Foch. In Visconti's crypt of green granite from the Vosges stands the "cloak of glory", the unmarked **Tombeau de Napoléon,** completed in 1861 to receive the Emperor's remains.

▲▲ EIFFEL TOWER★★★

7 r. de Belloy. ⊙Open daily. Lift: mid-Jun–Aug 9am–12.45am; Sept–mid-Jun 9.30am–11.45pm. Stairs: mid-Jun–Aug 9am–12.45am; Sept–mid-Jun 9.30am–6.30pm. ⊸8.20€; child 4€ (lift to 2nd floor), 14€, child 9.50€ (lift to top floor); Stairs 1st and 2nd floors only, 5€, child 3€. ℘01 44 11 23 23. www.tour-eiffel.fr.

The Eiffel Tower is Paris' most famous symbol. The first proposal for a tower was made in 1884; construction was completed in 26 months and the tower opened in March 1889 for the Universal Exhibition of that year.

The structure highlights Eiffel's imagination and daring; in spite of the tower's weight of 7 000 tonnes and a height of 320.75m/1 051ft and the use of 2.5 million rivets, it is a masterpiece of lightness. It is difficult to believe that the tower actually weighs less than the volume of air surrounding it and that the pressure it exerts on the ground is that of a man sitting on a chair.

⊙The best light for viewing is usually 1hr before sunset. At night the tower sparkles for the first 5 minutes of every hour. At level 3, Eiffel's newly-renovated sitting room can be seen through a window. The second floor houses a restaurant, brasseries and boutiques. On the first floor is a museum, a gift shop, a post office and another restaurant.

PALAIS DE CHAILLOT★★

pl. du Trocadéro.

This remarkable example of inter-war architecture was built for the 1937 Universal Exhibition. Its twin pavilions are linked by a portico and extended by wings which frame the wide terrace with its statues in gilded bronze.

From here there is a wonderful **view★★★** of Paris; in the foreground are the Trocadero Gardens with their spectacular fountains, and beyond the curving river the Eiffel Tower, the Champ-de-Mars, and the École Militaire. The Palais houses the **Théâtre de Chaillot** (℘01 53 65 30 00, www.theatre-chaillot.fr), the **Musée de l'Homme★★**, (closed for renovation until 2015), **Musée de la Marine★★** (⊸7€; ℘01 53 65 69 69, www.musee-marine.fr), and the **Musée des Monuments Français★★** (⊸8€; ℘01 58 51 52 00, www.citechaillot.fr).

ÉCOLE MILITAIRE★★

1 pl. Joffre.

Though the original design could not be fully implemented because of lack of funds, the Military Academy by Jacques-Ange Gabriel is one of the outstanding examples of French 18C architecture. It was begun in 1752, financed in part by Mme de Pompadour, and completed in 1773. Under the Second Empire, cavalry and artillery buildings of nondescript design were added, together with the low-lying wings which frame the main building. True to its original function, it now houses the French Army's Staff College. The superb main courtyard (**cour d'honneur★**), lined on either side by beautiful porticoes with paired columns, is approached via an exercise yard; the imposing central section and the projecting wings form a harmonious composition.

MUSÉE DU QUAI BRANLY★★

37 quai Branly. ⏱*Open Tue–Sun 11am–7pm (9pm on Thu, Fri, Sat).* ✆*8.50€; 13€ combined for the permanent and temporary exhibitions. Audioguides available in several languages.* ✆*5€.* ♿ ☎*01 56 61 70 00. www.quaibranly.fr.*

Designed by eminent architect Jean Nouvel, this museum dedicated to indigenous arts from around the world opened in summer 2006.

The setting is remarkable: undulating leather-clad low walls lead visitors through the glass and metal structure to sections dedicated to the arts and civilizations of Africa, Asia, Oceania and the Americas. The collection includes Aboriginal dreamtime maps, a shaman's costume from Siberia, and a club from Brazil used to kill captives before they were eaten as part of a ceremony of ritual sacrifice. Surrounding gardens add to a sense of luxurious distance from the bustle of the city.

Eiffel Tower

© Mark Soskolne/iStockphoto.com

Gustave Eiffel (1832–1923)

Engineer and entrepreneur in equal measure, Eiffel was to enjoy both success and failure during his long life. Mostly remembered today for his Tower, he was also responsible for several other massively impressive structures both in France and further afield. The Garabit Viaduct, the Pest Railway Station and the internal structure of the Statue of Liberty are just three examples of his fine work still in use. Unfortunately, Eiffel became embroiled in the scandal caused by the French Panama Canal Company. Although not involved in the finances of the enterprise, Eiffel was found guilty of fraud, a decision which was later reversed. He spent the rest of his life as a scientist, using his Tower for wind resistance experiments, as an aerial mast and a weather station.

Arrondissements 8–10 & 17

These prestigious arrondissements are synonymous with the pomp and grandeur of wealth and power. But notwithstanding the bustling, gilded settings of the Champs-Élysées, Madeleine and Grands Boulevards, this area is also home to quiet, off-the-beaten-track spots such as the Canal St-Martin and the little-known Batignolles district, from which artists like Edouard Manet drew their inspiration.

- **Michelin Map:** 312 D 2. See p109.
- **Info:** ℘08 92 68 30 00 or en.parisinfo.com.
- **Location:** Beginning near Madeleine and Champs Élysées; northeast to Opéra Garnier and Gare du Nord, Place de Clichy.
- **Don't Miss:** Voie Triomphale, Champs Élysées
- **Kids:** Science museum.

LA VOIE TRIOMPHALE★★★

The most famous thoroughfare in Paris is at once an avenue with a spectacular view, a place of entertainment and a street full of smart luxury shops. The vista extending down the Champs-Élysées, with the Arc de Triomphe silhouetted against the sky, is world-renowned, and Parisians call it the *Voie Triomphale* or Triumphal Way. The avenue continues to be the rallying point for protests.

Jardin du Carrousel

Burned down by the rioters of the Paris Commune in 1871, the ruins of the Tuileries were razed in 1883 and replaced by the Carrousel Garden, named after an equestrian parade, or carrousel, that took place here in the 18C. Two flowerbeds frame yew hedges radiating out from the Arc du Carrousel. 18 statues of female nudes by the sculptor Maillol are placed among the hedges, which are framed by the two wings of the Louvre Museum.

Jardin des Tuileries★

Catherine de Medici envisaged an Italian-style park, complete with fountains, maze, and grotto, populated with terracotta figures by Bernard Palissy, and a menagerie for her palace next to the Louvre. Henri IV later added an orangery and a silkworm farm. In 1664 Le Nôtre raised two lengthwise terraces of unequal height to level the sloping ground, creating the magnificent central axis; he also created the pools and formal flower beds, quincunxes and slopes. Colbert was so delighted that he intended the gardens to be kept for the royal family, but was persuaded by Charles Perrault to grant access to the public.

Musée de l'Orangerie★★

Open Wed–Mon 9am–6pm.
Closed 1 May, 25 Dec. 7.50€.
℘01 44 77 80 07.
www.musee-orangerie.fr.

Two pavilions, the Orangerie and the Jeu de Paume, were built during the Second Empire and have served as art galleries since the beginning of the 20C. Reopened in 2006 after extensive renovations, the two oval rooms on the ground floor are hung with panels from Claude Monet's water-lily series of his garden at Giverny, in Normandy, known as the Nymphéas. The lower-level galleries accommodate the Walter-Guillaume Collection (Impressionists to 1930). This famous collection presents the work of celebrated artists including Picasso, Cézanne, Renoir and Rousseau.

Place de la Concorde★★★

Everything about this square – site, size, general elegance – is impressive, particularly the obelisk, which dominates the scene. Place de la Concorde is one of the most beautiful squares in Paris, but also one of the busiest. The point of the obelisk indicates international time – it is the largest sundial in the world.

It was designed by Ange-Jacues Gabriel in 1755 and completed over a period of 20 years. On Sunday 21 January 1793, a guillotine was erected in the northwest corner (near where the Brest statue now stands) for the execution of **Louis XVI**. The colossal **mansions ★★** on either side of the opening to rue Royale are among the finest examples of the early Louis XVI style. The right pavilion, the **Hôtel de la Marine**, was until 1792 the royal store; it then became the Admiralty Office. Today it houses the Navy headquarters. The **Hôtel de Crillon**, across the street, was at first occupied by four noblemen. In the centre of the square stands an **obelisk★** from the ruins of the temple at Luxor, given to France in 1831 by Mohammed Ali, Viceroy of Egypt. The pink granite monument is 3 300 years old and covered in hieroglyphics.

The obelisk provides the best **views-★★★** of the Champs-Élysées, framed by the **Marly Horses** looking up the avenue. Coysevox's Winged Horses frame the view across the Tuileries. Replicas have replaced the two marble groups of horses, which are in the Louvre.

Grand Palais★

This great exhibition hall is formally fronted by an Ionic colonnade running the length of the building, before a mosaic frieze. Enormous quadrigae punctuate the corners; the Belle-Epoque building is elsewhere dotted with turn-of-the-19C decorative elements. Inside, a single glazed space is covered by a flattened dome. With an exhibition area of nearly 5 000sq m/5 980sq yd, the **Galeries du Grand Palais** (3 ave.du Général Eisenhower; ○Open Sun–Mon, 10am–8pm; Wed–Sat, 10am–8pm; ○Closed 1 May, 25 Dec; ⊜12€; www.rmn.fr) have become a cultural centre for major temporary exhibitions of artefacts and art from around the world.

★ Palais de la Découverte★★

Inside the Grand Palais; entrance on avenue Franklin D Roosevelt. ○Open Tue–Sat, 9.30am–6pm, Sun and public holidays 10am–7pm. ○Closed 1 Jan, 1 May, 14 Jul, 15 Aug, 25 Dec. ⊜7€; children 6€; Planetarium 3€. ✆01 56 43 20 20. www.palais-decouverte.fr.

This centre for scientific study and discovery is popular with children and adults. The **planetarium★** (level 2) provides an introduction to the skies.

Avenue des Champs-Élysées★★★

Today, the iconic Champs-Élysées is lined with restaurants and cafés, showrooms and banks, cinemas and nightclubs. Most of the shops are international chains, with the majority of the fashion boutiques found along the side streets like avenues George V and Montaigne.

The Second Empire private houses and amusement halls that once lined the Avenue have since vanished; the only exception is no. **25**, a mansion built by La Païva, a Polish adventuress, whose house was famous for dinners attended by philosophers, painters and writers. **Le Colisée**, an amphitheatre built in 1770 to hold an audience of 40 000, has left its name to a street, a café and a cinema.

Canal Saint-Martin

Napoléon ordered the construction of the canal in 1802 to provide much-needed fresh water from the Canal de l'Ourq. It was not completed until 1825. Subsequently allowed to deteriorate, the area received a boost in 1938 when it was refurbished for the Marcel Carné film *Hôtel du Nord*, starring the Parisian actress Arletty. However, during the 1960s the canal began to fall into disuse. New boutiques and trendy cafés opened in the past ten years have renewed its popularity with strolling tourists, locals with their picnics, and "bourgeois bohemian" professionals who snap up the canalside apartments.

Arc de Triomphe★★★

pl. Charles-de-Gaulle. ◐*Open daily Apr–Sept 10am–11pm; Oct–Mar 10am–10.30pm.* ◐*Closed public holidays.* ◑9.50€. ℘01 55 37 73 77.

The arch and **place Charles de Gaulle★★★**, which surrounds it, form one of Paris' most famous landmarks. Twelve avenues radiate from the arch, which explains why it is also called **place de l'Étoile** (*étoile* means star). The arch commemorates Napoléon's victories and the fate of the Unknown Soldier, laid to rest in the tomb in 1921.

Napoléon commissioned **Chalgrin** to construct a giant arch in 1806. It wasn't finished until 1836, under **Louis-Philippe**. In 1840 the carriage bearing the emperor's body passed beneath the arch. **Haussmann** redesigned the square in 1854, creating seven radiating avenues, while Hittorff planned the uniform façades which surround it. On 14 July 1919, Allied armies, led by the marshals, marched in victory here. The **arch platform** (◐*Open Apr–Sept 10am–11pm, last admission 30min before closing; Oct–Mar 10am–10.30pm;* ◐*Closed 1 Jan, 1, 8 May, 14 Jul, 11 Nov, 25 Dec;* ◑*9.50€, under 18s and EU citizens under-25 free;* ℘*01 55 37 73 77, arc-de-triomphe.monuments-nationaux.fr)* has an excellent **view★★★** of the capital: in the foreground, 12 avenues radiate from the square, you are halfway between the Louvre and La Défense.

Opéra Garnier

© S. Sauvignier/MICHELIN

PALAIS DE L'ÉLYSÉE

55 r. du Faubourg St-Honoré. ☞*Closed to the public.*

The mansion was constructed in 1718 for the Count of Évreux. During the Revolution it became a dance hall. It was home to Caroline Murat, Napoléon's sister, then Empress Josephine. Napoléon signed his second abdication here after his Waterloo defeat, on 22 June 1815, and the future **Napoléon III** planned his successful coup d'état of 1851 here. Since 1873 the Élysée Palace has housed the French president.

PALAIS-ROYAL★★

pl. du Palais-Royal.

In 1632, Richelieu ordered Lemercier to build what was first dubbed the Palais Cardinal (**Cardinal's Palace**), an edifice remarkable for its impressive central façade, surmounted by allegorical statues and a curved pediment. Richelieu bequeathed it to Louis XIII, whereupon its name was changed to the Palais-Royal. In 1783, Victor Louis laid out the charming formal gardens and arcades. In 1986, **Daniel Buren** designed the 260 striped columns of varying heights which occupy the outer courtyard.

PALAIS GARNIER – OPÉRA NATIONAL DE PARIS★★

pl. de l'Opéra, entrance on r. Scribe. ◐*Open mid-Jul–Sept daily 10am–5pm (except during matinée or special event); Sept–mid-Jul, 10am–6pm.* ☜*Guided tours Wed, Sat, Sun 11.30am, 3.30pm (daily Jul–Aug, 11.30am, 2pm, 3.30pm).* ◑*10€; 14€ with tour.* ℘*08 92 89 90 90. www.operadeparis.fr.*

This stunning building housed the Paris Opera from 1875 to 1989, and is now home to the city's ballet company. The architect **Charles Garnier** built it in 1861. The theatre accommodates up to 450 performers. The main façade overlooking the place de l'Opéra features a series of sculpted figures. Garnier used multicoloured marbles quarried in France for the **interior★★★**. The **Great Staircase** and **Grand Foyer** are often venues for sumptuous occasions.

Arrondissements 11-15

The heart of dynamic, contemporary Paris, arrondissements 11-15 are popular for their nightlife (Bastille, Oberkampf and Montparnasse), cutting-edge architecture and urban planning (Bercy, Bibliothèque Nationale), as well as quiet, village-like areas little-trodden by tourists.

BASTILLE

Scene of the historic revolutions of 1789, 1830 and 1848, the **place de la Bastille** remains a symbolic rallying point for demonstration and public celebrations, dominated by the commemorative **July Column** (52m/171ft high) and the **Opéra Bastille★**. It also has a lively bar and club scene.

BERCY

Bercy is home to the Palais Omnisports by architects Andrault, Parat and Gavan, the **Cinémathèque Française** (51 r. de Bercy; www.cinematheque.fr) – the world's largest film archive – and the imposing **Finance Ministry,** designed by Chemetow and Huidobro. The **Bibliothèque nationale de France-François-Mitterrand★** (Quai François-Mauriac; www.bnf.fr) by Dominique Perrault – four tower blocks resembling open books – was the last of President Mitterrand's "great projects".

ÉGLISE NOTRE-DAME-DU-VAL-DE-GRÂCE★★

1 pl. Laveran. Open Tue–Sat 2–6pm, Sun 9am–noon, 2–6pm. 01 43 29 12 31. www.valdegrace.org.
Anne of Austria commissioned this church to commemorate the birth of Louis XIV in 1638. Built in the Romanesque Renaissance style, the church features a dome with a double triangular pediment that is particularly ornate. The **cupola★★** was decorated by Mignard and features a fresco with 200 figures.

LES CATACOMBES★

Entrance: 1 pl. Denfert Rochereau. Open Tue–Sun 10am–5pm. Closed public holidays. 8€. 30mn audio guide in French, English and Spanish 3€. 01 43 22 47 63. www.catacombes.paris.fr.
Long stairways, no restrooms.
These Gallo-Roman quarries were filled with millions of skeletons from overcrowded Parisian cemeteries between 1785 and 1810. After descending 130 steps, visitors encounter countless femurs, skulls and tibias arranged along the walls by cemetery.

MONTPARNASSE★★

Although no longer the magnet for artists and philosophers it was in the early 20C, Montparnasse is still lively at night.

Tour Montparnasse★★

Open Apr–Sept, 9.30am–11.30pm; Oct–Mar, Sun–Thu 9.30am–10.30pm, Fri–Sat and day before holidays 9.30am–11pm (last admission 30min before closing). 13.50€. 01 45 38 52 56. www.tourmontparnasse56.com.
Completed in 1973, this 209m/685.7ft tower dominates Montparnasse. It takes 40 seconds to reach the 56th floor, offering a magnificent **panorama★★★** of Paris and its surroundings.
There is also a bar and panoramic restaurant. From the open-roof terrace (59th floor) the view can extend as far as 50km/31mi.

- **Michelin Map:** 312 D 2. See p109.
- **Info:** 08 92 68 30 00 or en.parisinfo.com
- **Location:** Beginning near Bastille, then crossing the Seine to Bercy, Gare de Lyon, and Montparnasse.
- **Don't Miss:** Bastille nightlife, the view from Montparnasse.
- **Kids:** View from Tour Montparnasse.

Arrondissements 18–20

The home of arty, romantic Montmartre with its winding cobblestone streets and precipitous views, but also of edgy, urban Belleville and quiet nooks like the Père-Lachaise Cemetery and Buttes-Chaumont park, arrondissements 18-20 set the scene for some of the capital's best preserved areas. It's also the traditional working-class bastion of Paris.

- **Michelin Map:** 312 D 2.
- **Info:** ℘08 92 68 30 00 or en.parisinfo.com.
- **Location:** Stretching from Montmartre hill to the Buttes-Chaumont park, and the bustling Belleville neighbourhood to Père-Lachaise.
- **Don't Miss:** Montmartre, Père-Lachaise Cemetery.
- **Kids:** The carrousel in Montmartre is great for kids.

MONTMARTRE★★★

The "Martyrs' Hill" was an independent village before becoming the haunt of artists in the late 19C. It retains the picturesque quality of a village in its steep, narrow lanes and precipitous stairways. The "Butte", or mound, rises from the city's sea of roofs; at its centre is the **Place du Tertre★★** with the former town hall at no. 3. The area still enjoys some semblance of local life, at least in the morning; by the afternoon, the "art market" is flooded with tourists.

Nearby rises the dramatic outline of the **Basilique du Sacré-Cœur★★** (r. du Chevalier-de-la-Barre; ℘01 53 41 89 00; www.sacre-coeur-montmartre.com), a place of perpetual pilgrimage. The dome gallery offers an incomparable **panorama★★★** over Paris.

LA VILLETTE★★

The city's largest park stretches between the Porte de la Villette and the Porte de Pantin, a vast green space boasting two modern museum complexes, concert venues, cinemas, and play areas.

▲▲ Cité des Sciences et de l'Industrie★★★

30 ave. Corentin-Cariou. ⟨Open Tue–Sat 10am–6pm, Sun 10am–7pm. ⟨Closed 1 May and 25 Dec. ⊜8€–17.50€. ℘01 40 05 70 00. www.cite-sciences.fr.* Built in an effort to educate young and old alike about scientific and industrial advances, this museum encourages visitors to investigate, learn and have fun through entertaining scenarios, and an updated programme of exhibits.

Cité des Enfants★ – *(*⟨*See above for opening times).* The ground floor of the Cité is designed to encourage young scientific discovery through experimentation, and is divided into two sections: ages 2–7 and ages 5–12.

▲▲ La Géode★★★

In the park just outside the museum. ⟨*Open Tue–Sun 10.30am–8.30pm (hourly sessions). ⊜10.50€, child 9€. www.lageode.fr.* This spherical cinema and circular screen (diameter: 36m/118ft), which rests on a sheet of water, is by engineer Chamayou.

MARCHÉ AUX PUCES DE SAINT-OUEN★

Espace Accueil et Information du Marché aux Puces, 7 Impasse Simon, St-Ouen. www.marcheauxpuces-saintouen.com. ⟨*The flea market is situated just outside Paris in the suburb of St-Ouen (five-min walk from metro Clignancourt – go north under bd. Périphérique to reach the markets).* ▰*Guided group or individual visits are available:* ℘01 40 11 77 36. www.st-ouentourisme.com.

The most famous flea market in Paris; there are between 2 500 and 3 000 stalls on display. If you are willing to search and bargain you may find something to treasure among the assorted bric-a-brac – a real collector's paradise.

Parks in Paris

The city boasts around 450 parks, public gardens and green spaces, many prestigious, historic or adorned with fine sculpture.

Jardin du Luxembourg

© S. Sauvignier/MICHELIN

Highlights include:

Bois de Vincennes, 4 458 acre/995ha including the Parc Floral.

Bois de Boulogne, 2 090 acre/846ha with the Bagatelle, iris and rose gardens.

Jardin des Plantes, historic Botanical Gardens of Paris (opened to the public in 1640).

Jardin des Tuileries, with its ancient and modern statuary.

Jardin du Luxembourg, a pleasant Latin Quarter park with a pond alongside the palace, popular with students and young children.

Parc Montsouris and Square des Batignolles, examples of "Jardins Anglais", albeit with a less formal layout.

Parc Paysager des Buttes-Chaumont, possibly the city's most picturesque, boasting dramatic bluffs and man-made grottos.

Jardin du Palais-Royal, a haven of elegance in the very heart of Paris.

Jardin japonais de l'UNESCO, a Japanese-style garden at the UNESCO headquarters, also known as "Garden of Peace".

Jardin du Musée Rodin, ideal spot to prolong your museum visit and discover magnificent city views.

Parc Monceau, offering memorable statues of Musset, Maupassant, Chopin and other noteworthy French figures.

Parc André-Citroën, sophisticated and contemporary, with several themed gardens.

Parc de La Villette, the largest in Paris.

Parc de Belleville, offering panoramic views of the whole city.

Parc de Bercy, recalling the wine-dealing past of this modernised district.

PÈRE-LACHAISE CEMETERY★

bd. de Ménilmontant; main entrances: Porte de Repos (Metro Philippe Auguste), Porte d'Amandiers (Metro Père-Lachaise) ◷*Open mid-Mar–Nov, 8am–6pm, Sat 8.30am–6pm, Sun and holidays 9am–6pm; Nov–mid-Mar, 8am–5.30pm, Sat 8.30am–5.30pm, Sun and public holidays 9am–5.30pm.* ◞*Guided tours (2hr) possible: ℘01 55 25 82 10. Maps at Repos and Gambetta entrances.*

Père-Lachaise Cemetery is the city's oldest and largest, sprawling across 44 hectares (109 acres) and housing the tombs of greats from Balzac to Molière,

Edith Piaf to Oscar Wilde. Addressing a problem of painfully overcrowded graveyards, Emperor Napoleon I ordered the creation of Père-Lachaise (along with several others) in the early 19C. The lush site – boasting thousands of trees, plants and flowers – was designed to resemble an English garden.

Père-Lachaise houses two important war memorials. The **Mur des Fédérés** is a wall commemorating the 147 insurgents of the Paris Commune who were executed at the site in 1871. In the cemetery's southeast corner, monuments dedicated to World War II deportees and victims of extermination camps bear witness to a still darker stretch of Paris history.

ADDRESSES

🛏 STAY

😑🛏 **Familia**– 11 r. des Ecoles, 75005. Ⓜ️Cardinal Lemoine. 𝄞01 43 54 55 27. www.familiahotel.com. 30 rooms. Notre-Dame and the Collège des Bernardins provide the backdrop for rustic rooms adorned with sepia frescoes of Paris monuments. Air conditioning, free wi-fi.

😑🛏 **Delambre**– 35 r. Delambre, 75014. Ⓜ️Edgar Quinet. 𝄞01 43 20 66 31. www.delambre-paris-hotel.com. 30 rooms. French poet André Breton frequented this hotel located close to the Montparnasse railway station. Simple, bright and spacious.

😑🛏 **Aberotel** – 24 r. Blomet, 75015. Ⓜ️Volontaires. 𝄞01 40 61 70 50. www.aberotel.com. 28 rooms. A popular hotel with stylish rooms and an inner courtyard for summer breakfasts. A lounge is adorned with paintings of playing cards.

😑🛏 **Nord et Est** – 49 r. Malte, 75011. Ⓜ️Oberkampf. 𝄞01 47 00 71 70. www.hotel-nord-est.com. 45 rooms. The warm family atmosphere and reasonable prices draw regulars to this hotel near Place de la République. Ask for one of the refurbished rooms.

😑🛏🛏 **Louvre Ste-Anne** – 32 r. Ste-Anne, 75001. Ⓜ️Pyramides. 𝄞01 40 20 02 35. www.louvre-ste-anne.fr. 20 rooms. In a street lined with Japanese restaurants, this hotel has well-equipped rooms decorated in pastel shades. Vaulted breakfast room.

😑🛏🛏 **Etats-Unis Opéra** – 16 r. d'Antin, 75002. Ⓜ️Opéra. 𝄞01 42 65 05 05. www.hotel-paris-opera.com. 45 rooms. Nestled by a quiet street, this 1930s hotel offers modern, comfortable rooms. Breakfast is served in the English-style bar.

😑🛏🛏 **Beaubourg**– 11 r. S. Le Franc, 75004. Ⓜ️Rambuteau. 𝄞01 42 74 34 24. www.hotelbeaubourg.com. 28 rooms. Nestled in a tiny street behind the Georges-Pompidou Centre, some of this hotel's rooms have exposed stone walls and wooden beams.

😑🛏🛏🛏 **7 Eiffel**– 17 bis r. Amélie, 75007. Ⓜ️La Tour Maubourg. 𝄞01 45 55 10 01. www.hotel-7eiffel-paris.com. 32 rooms and junior suites. Sleek contemporary design reigns in this elegant Left-Bank hotel. A rooftop summer terrace complete with bee hives affords great city views.

😑🛏🛏 **Le Hameau de Passy** – 48 r. Passy, 75016. Ⓜ️La Muette. 𝄞01 42 88 47 55. www.hameaudepassy.com. 32 rooms. A private lane leads to this hamlet with a charming inner courtyard overrun with greenery. Quiet nights guaranteed in small, well-maintained rooms. Free wi-fi.

🍴 EAT

😑🛏 **Pharamond** – 24 r. de la Grande-Truanderie, 75001. Ⓜ️Châtelet-Les-Halles. 𝄞01 40 28 45 18. www.pharamond.fr. Frequented by Hemingway, Fitzgerald and Mittérand, Pharamond serves traditional French dishes (tripe and offal a speciality). Authentic 1900s decor.

😑🛏 **Vaudeville** – 29 r. Vivienne, 75002. Ⓜ️Bourse. 𝄞01 40 20 04 62. www.vaudevilleparis.com. This large Brasserie with its sparkling Art Deco details in pure Parisian style is lively after theatre performances. Classic French fare.

😑🛏 **Le Carré des Vosges** – 15 r. St-Gilles, 75003. Ⓜ️Chemin Vert. 𝄞01 42 71 22 21. www.lecarredesvosges.fr. Friendly bistro a stone's throw from rue des Francs-Bourgeois and its trendy boutiques. Well-prepared market cuisine by chef Masahide Ikuta, with fish a speciality.

😑🛏 **Atelier Maître Albert** – 1 r. Maître Albert, 75005. Ⓜ️Maubert Mutualité. 𝄞01 56 81 30 01. www.ateliermaitrealbert.com. A huge medieval fireplace and spits for roast meat take pride of place in this traditional rotisserie. Guy Savoy is responsible for the mouth-watering fare.

😑🛏 **Bistro de la Muette** – 10 Chaussée de la Muette, 75016. Ⓜ️Mo La Muette. 𝄞01 45 03 14 84. www.bistrocie.fr. This elegant bistro's attractive, all-inclusive formula partly explains its appeal in the neighbourhood. Warm, modern decor in earthy tones. Veranda. Reservations recommended.

😑🛏 **Chardenoux** – 1, r. Jules Vallès, 75011. Ⓜ️Charonne. 𝄞01 43 71 49 52. Reopened under celebrity chef Cyril Lignac on its 100th anniversary, this bistro is bringing back traditional cuisine. Decor of yesteryear. Garden terrace.

😑🛏🛏 **La Coupole** – 102 bd. Montparnasse, 75014. Ⓜ️Vavin. 𝄞01 43 20 14 20. www.lacoupole-paris.com. The spirit of Montparnasse pervades this huge Art Déco brasserie opened in 1927. The 24 pillars were decorated by artists of the period. The cupola sports a new fresco.

ENTERTAINMENT

Consult publications such as *L'Officiel des Spectacles (www.offi.fr)* and *Pariscope (www.spectacles.premiere.fr)* for details of time and place of exhibitions. The Paris Tourist Office's website (*parisinfo.com*) lists exhibitions, shows and other events. Paris boasts a total of 100 **theatres**. Most of these venues are located near the traditional bastions of Opéra and the Madeleine, but from Montmartre to Montparnasse, Bastille to the **Latin Quarter★★★** and from Boulevard Haussmann to the Porte Maillot, state-funded theatres (**Opéra-Garnier★★**, Opéra-Bastille, Comédie Française, Odéon, Chaillot, La Colline) reside side by side with local theatres, singing cabarets and cafés-theatres. Over 400 **cinemas** are found in every part of the city, particularly in the same areas as the theatres and on the Champs-Élysées. There are also two open-air cinema festivals: one at **Parc de la Villette★**; the other, **Cinéma au Clair de Lune**, is held in parks and squares. **Music-hall**, **variety shows** and **reviews** can be enjoyed at such places as the Alcazar de Paris, Crazy Horse, Lido, Paradis Latin, Casino de Paris, the Folies Bergère and the Moulin Rouge. Aside from the **Opéra-Garnier★★**, the Opéra-Bastille and the Comic Opera (Opéra-Comique), there are a number of concert halls with resident orchestras.

SHOPPING

Champs-Élysées – On this celebrated avenue and in the surrounding streets (avenue Montaigne, avenue Marceau), visitors can admire dazzling window-displays and covered malls (Galerie Elysée Rond-Point, Galerie Point-Show, Galerie Elysée 26, Arcades du Lido).

Rue du Faubourg-St-Honoré – Here haute couture is displayed alongside perfume, fine leather goods and furs.

Place Vendôme – Some of the most prestigious jewellery shops (**Cartier**, **Van Cleef & Arpels**, **Boucheron**, **Chaumet**) stand facing the Ritz Hotel and the Ministry of Justice.

Place de la Madeleine and rue Tronchet – An impressive showcase for shoes, ready-to-wear clothing, luggage, leather goods and fine tableware.

The Marais – Designer boutiques, concept stores and high-fashion global chains. Main arteries are Rue des Francs-Bourgeois and Rue de Turenne.

Les Halles – In addition to a monstrous underground shopping mall, the area abounds with boutiques.

DEPARTMENT STORES

The city's great department stores – known as "les grands magasins" – are an ideal way to find a vast choice of high-quality fashions and other goods under one roof. Stores are usually open from Monday–Saturday 9.30am–7pm.
Bazar de l'Hôtel de Ville (52 r. de Rivoli)
Galeries Lafayette (40 bd. Haussmann)
Printemps (64 bd. Haussmann)
Le Bon Marché (r. de Sèvres)

ANTIQUE SHOPS AND DEALERS

Le Louvre des Antiquaires (1 pl. du Palais Royal), **Le Village Suisse** (r. du Général de Larminat), the **Richelieu-Drouot** auction room and the **rues Bonaparte** and **La Boétie** specialise in antiques. Good bargains can also be found at the flea market at the **Porte de Montreuil** and **Porte de St-Ouen** (Sat–Mon).

FAIRS AND EXHIBITIONS

Paris – Expo – *pl. de la Porte de Versailles. www.viparis.com*. Over 200 exhibitions, conventions and events per year including the Paris Nautical Trade Show, the Salon du Chocolat (Chocolate Trade Show) and the Salon de l'Agriculture.

Parc International d'Expositions – *Paris-Nord Villepinte. www.viparis.com*. Trade Show for Crafts (SMAC), the Maison & Objet home style expo, the International food industry exhibition (SIAL) and Japan Expo.

Parc des Expositions – *Le Bourget aerodrome. www.paris-air-show.com*. Paris Air Show (odd years, next 2013).

SPORT

Among the most popular sporting events held in and around Paris are the International **Roland Garros** Tennis Championship (French Open), the **Paris Marathon**, the legendary **Tour de France** and prestigious horse races. The **Parc des Princes stadium** (*24 r. Claude Farrère; www.leparcdesprinces.fr*) is host to the great football and rugby finals and the **Palais Omnisport de Paris-Bercy** (*8 bd. Bercy; www.bercy.fr*) organises the most unusual indoor competitions: indoor surfing, North American rodeos, ice figure-skating, tennis championships (Open de Paris), moto-cross races, martial arts, Six-day Paris Cycling Event, and pop concerts.

Visitors to Paris often save time for a day trip to the Château de Versailles *(see p76)* but miss out the many fascinating places within close reach of the city limits, in the near suburbs known in French as the "Petite Couronne" (little crown). Comprising three administrative *départements* circling the outskirts of Paris – Seine-St-Denis, Hauts-de-Seine and Val-de-Marne – the Petite Couronne is densely populated, connected by an efficient transport system and has lots to offer arts, culture and architecture enthusiasts. Its vast green spaces, from parks with natural or man-made lakes to quaint botanical gardens, are havens of peace amid the hustle and bustle of the city, and offer plenty of opportunities for hiking, watersports and other outdoor activities. Waterside areas such as L'Île de la Grande Jatte are so beautiful that they inspired paintings by Monet, Sisley and Seurat. Planning half-day trips from Paris to sites such as the St-Denis Basilica or the Bois de Boulogne is easy: most places are readily accessible by metro, commuter train (RER) or tramway. The area also affords the opportunity for some interesting and picturesque driving tours.

Highlights

Urban and Natural Environment

The 123 cities and towns that make up the "petite couronne" are remarkably diverse.

Some areas, such as the mostly working-class **Seine-St-Denis**, seem to epitomise urban grit, dominated by high-rise public housing complexes, industrial zones and bustling flea markets, and have seen waves of immigration since the 19C. The north and east Paris suburbs tend to be somewhat neglected by tourists and guidebooks, but nonetheless boast numerous cultural and architectural riches and a surprising dynamism.

The more affluent **west and south suburbs**, including Neuilly-sur-Seine, St-Cloud and Rueil-Malmaison, have largely conserved their historical and architectural patrimony, possessing chateaux (among them the magnificent Napoleonic residence of Malmaison), vast green spaces such as the Parc de Sceaux, pleasant riverside promenades and natural islands.

Rapid Development

Far more so than intramural Paris, the immediate suburbs are undergoing rapid development. The departure of major manufacturers from the "gates" of Paris have left ample space for ambitious urban planning initiatives. Filmmaker Luc Besson opened a new European film centre called the Cité du Cinéma on the site of a former nuclear power plant in St-Denis in 2012. The Seguin island in Boulogne-Billancourt, formerly a production site for automaker Renault, is being transformed into a contemporary arts centre and music conservatory in co-operation with celebrated architect Jean Nouvel.

In traditionally "gritty" suburbs such as Montreuil, the arrival of young urban professionals snapping up less expensive properties and artists' lofts is considerably changing the social and cultural landscape.

Monuments and Architecture

A wide range of architectural styles and periods can be found in this area, from early Gothic cathedrals and stately châteaux to whimsically innovative skyscrapers.

La Défense with La Grande Arche in the middle

St-Denis Basilica just north of Paris has a stunning early Gothic facade, and holds the recumbent effigies of over 70 Kings and Queens of France.

East of the city limits, the under-appreciated **Château de Vincennes** adjoins the famous wood, boasting a stunning medieval keep and moat. It is the only surviving royal residence from the period in France.

To the west, you can visit the royal estate most closely associated with Napoléon I and his first wife Josephine at **Rueil-Malmaison**.

If you're more interested in contemporary architecture and urban planning, head to the **La Défense** business district, where unusual buildings and skyscrapers from star architects are interspersed with modern sculptures and fountains by the likes of Alexander Calder and Busato.

Parks and Gardens

The densely populated ring around Paris thankfully counts numerous large parks and gardens. Known as "Paris' lungs" to locals, the **Bois de Vincennes** and **Bois de Boulogne** east and west of Paris, respectively offer large lawns, wooded areas, man-made lakes for boating, restaurants and open-air theatre.

South of the city, the lovely **Parc de Sceaux** and its once-royal chateau has beautiful formal gardens with sculpture, waterfalls, and a Grand Canal that rivals the one at Versailles.

Arts and Culture

The near suburbs have plenty to sate arts and culture enthusiasts. For contemporary art, the **MAC/VAL in Vitry-sur-Seine** is an underappreciated gem offering a fascinating look at some of the most exciting work being produced by artists worldwide.

Boulogne-Billancourt has a series of excellent museums dedicated to **20C art movements** such as Cubism and Modernism, while in Montreuil, small edgy theatres and innovative galleries abound, where novel art forms take pride of place, far removed from the dealings of the global art market.

Finally, if you're interested in the history of Impressionism, a stroll along the **Île de la Grande Jatte** and its marked Impressionist trail is a must.

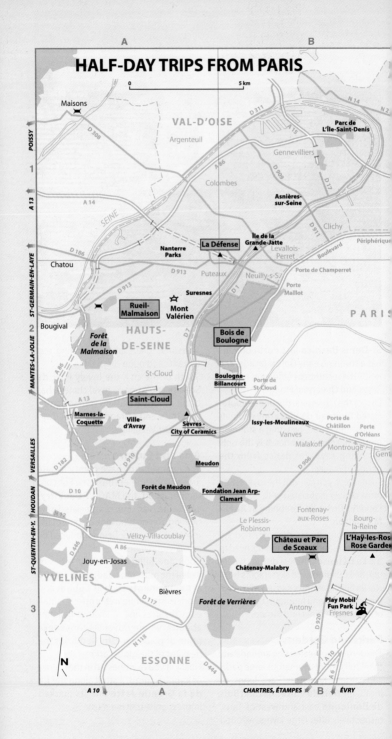

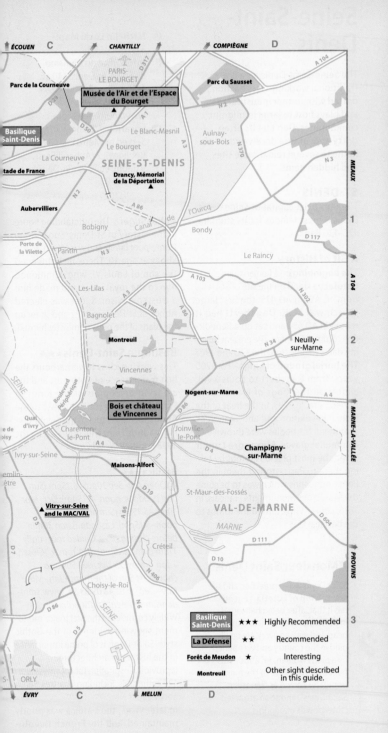

ÉCOUEN   C   CHANTILLY   COMPIÈGNE   D

A 104

PARIS-LE BOURGET

D 317

Parc de la Courneuve

Parc du Sausset

Musée de l'Air et de l'Espace du Bourget
▲

N 2

D 29

D 50

Le Blanc-Mesnil

Aulnay-sous-Bois

N 370

N 3

Basilique Saint-Denis

A 1

Le Bourget

A 3

MEAUX

Stade de France

La Courneuve

SEINE-ST-DENIS

Drancy, Mémorial de la Déportation
▲

N 2

A 86

de l'Ourcq

Aubervilliers

Bobigny

Canal

Bondy

D 117

1

Porte de la Vilette

Pantin

N 3

Le Raincy

A 104

A 103

Les-Lilas

A 3

N 302

Bagnolet

A 186

A 86

Neuilly-sur-Marne

N 34

Montreuil

2

SEINE

Vincennes

Boulevard Périphérique

Bois et château de Vincennes

Nogent-sur-Marne

A 4

MARNE-LA-VALLÉE

Quai d'Ivry

Charenton-le-Pont

D 86

Joinville-le-Pont

de Choisy

A 4

Champigny-sur-Marne

Ivry-sur-Seine

D 4

Gemlin-être

Maisons-Alfort

D 19

St-Maur-des-Fossés

VAL-DE-MARNE

D 604

▲ **Vitry-sur-Seine et le MAC/VAL**

A 86

MARNE

PROVINS

D 5

Créteil

D 111

D 7

D 10

N 406

D 6

Choisy-le-Roi

N 6

SEINE

3

D 86

D 5

ORLY

S-

ÉVRY   C   MELUN   D

Basilique Saint-Denis	★★★	Highly Recommended
La Défense	★★	Recommended
Forêt de Meudon	★	Interesting
Montreuil		Other sight described in this guide.

Seine-Saint-Denis

The Seine-Saint-Denis area is a traditional working-class bastion dotted with former industrial sites and plays host to large immigrant communities. Don't let its often gritty appearance deceive you – it's home to several remarkable sites and hidden gems.

ST-DENIS

The unofficial capital of Seine-Saint-Denis is most famous for its stunning 12C–13C Basilica.

A Bit of History

The beginnings – A Roman town called **Catolacus** stood on the site of St-Denis from 1C AD. In AD 475, the first large church was built. **DagobertI** had it rebuilt in AD 630 and set up a Benedictine community there. The present building dates mainly from the 12C and 13C.

The burial ground of kings – For 1200 years, from Dagobert to Louis XVIII, almost all the Kings of France were buried here. In 1793, in the heat of the French Revolution and anti-monarchy sentiment, the bodies were thrown into communal graves. **Alexandre Lenoir** saved the most precious tombs by taking them to Paris, storing them in the Petits-Augustins which was to become the Musée des Monuments Français. In 1816, Louis XVIII returned the tombs to the basilica.

"Monsieur Saint Denis"

Saint Denis was a preacher, and the first **Bishop of Lutetia**. Legend has it that, after being beheaded in **Montmartre**, he picked up his head and walked away. He finally died in the country and was buried by a pious woman. An abbey was built over the grave of the man popularly known as "Monsieur Saint Denis", and soon attracted large crowds of pilgrims.

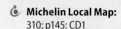

- **Michelin Local Map:** 310; p145: CD1
- **Info:** Office du tourisme de Seine-St-Denis: 140 av. Jean-Lolive, Pantin 93695. &01 49 15 98 98. www.tourisme93.com.
- **Location:** NE from Paris. Served by Metro lines 5 (to Bobligny), 7 (Aubervilliers), 9 (Montreuil), 13 (St-Denis); RER line B.

Abbot Suger – The outstanding figure in the history of St-Denis, Sugar came from a poor family and was "given" to the abbey at age 10. There, he befriended the son of Louis VI, who summoned him to the royal court and made him a trusted advisor. Suger was elected Abbot of St-Denis in 1122 and drew up the plans of the present minster himself.

Basilique Saint-Denis★★★

This working-class town harbours the first masterpiece of Gothic art and the amazing necropolis of the Kings of France. This is in stark contrast to the futuristic architecture of the neighbouring Stade de France, inaugurated for the 1998 Football World Cup.

Basilica★★★

Open Apr–Sep 10am–6.15pm (Sun and holidays, noon–6.15pm); Oct–Mar 10am–5.15pm (Sun and holidays, noon–5.15pm). Last admission 30min before closing. Guided tours daily 11am (Sun 12.15pm) and 3pm. Closed 1 Jan, 1 May, 25 Dec. 7.50€, no charge 1st Sun of the month Jan–May, Nov–Dec. &01 48 09 83 54. www.saint-denis.monuments-nationaux.fr.

Widely considered the first major monument showing evidence of the Gothic style, Saint-Denis is of prime importance in the history of architecture.

It provided inspiration for countless late-12C cathedrals, including Chartres, Senlis and Meaux.

In later years, the basilica was poorly maintained, and the **French Revolu-**

tion caused further damage. Napoléon ordered urgent repairs and returned the basilica to the Church in 1806.

Architect **François Debret** renovated the church in 1813, but knew little about medieval architecture, and his work raised public indignation. He began work on the magnificent spire, but used materials that were too heavy, disturbing the delicate balance. In 1846, the spire threatened collapse and was removed.

Replacing Debret in 1847, **Eugène Viollet-le-Duc** gathered documents enabling him to restore the building. From 1858 until his death in 1879, he made painstaking efforts, and the present incarnation is largely thanks to his work. The absence of the north tower mars the harmony of the **west front**. In the Middle Ages, the building was fortified and some crenellations are still visible at the base of the towers.

The tympanum on the **central doorway** represents the Last Judgment; the replicated carving on the right doorway depicts the Last Communion of Saint Denis, and on the left, the Death of Saint Denis and his companions Rusticus and Eleutherus (also recarved). The **door jambs** feature the Wise and Foolish Virgins (*centre*), labours of the months (*right*) and signs of the Zodiac (*left*). The cathedral is 108m/354ft long, 39m/

128ft wide in the transept and 29m/95ft high, making it slightly smaller than Notre-Dame in Paris.

The elegant nave features bays in the triforium opening to the exterior (one of the first such examples). The stained-glass windows in the nave are modern.

Tombs and recumbent effigies★★★– St-Denis houses the tombs of 46 kings, 32 queens, 63 royal children, and 10 French court members, including **Bertrand du Guesclin**. Until the Renaissance, the only sculpture adorning tombs were recumbent figures. Note the tombs of **Clovis** and **Frédégonde**, featuring a copper cloisonné mosaic made in the 12C for St-Germain-des-Prés Church.

In around 1260, St Louis commissioned effigies of his predecessors since the 7C. They include the tomb of **Dagobert**, the recumbent effigies of **Charles Martel**

Inside Basilique Saint-Denis

© Sylvain Sonnet/hemis.fr

and **Pépin the Bref**, and a female effigy carved in Tournai marble.

The tomb of **Isabelle of Aragon** and of **Philippe III le Hardi** shows an early concern for accurate portraiture.

From the 14C, it became customary to remove organs from the bodies of royals before embalming them. The inner organs, heart and body were buried in different places, but the bodies stayed in St-Denis. The life-like effigies of **Charles V**, and those of **Charles VI** and **Isabelle de Bavière** are representative of the mid-14C.

During the Renaissance, **mausoleums** took on monumental proportions. The upper level featured the king and queen, kneeling in full regalia. On the lower level, the deceased were pictured lying down as naked cadavers. Admire the monuments built for **Louis XII** and **Anne de Bretagne**, and that of **François I** and **Claude de France**.

Catherine de' Medici, surviving her husband Henri II by 30 years, gave orders to build the royal tomb. When she saw how she had been portrayed, she fainted in horror and ordered a new effigy substituting sleep for death. Both works are on display in the cathedral. Primaticcio and Germain Pilon oversaw their creation.

Chancel – The pre-Renaissance **stalls** and the carved wooden door were taken from the Norman Castle in Gaillon. On the right stands a 12C Romanesque **Virgin Mary★** in painted wood, brought from St-Martin-des-Champs.

The **bishop's throne** opposite is a replica of Dagobert's royal throne. At the end, the modern **reliquary** of saints Denis, Rusticus and Eleutherius flanks Suger's **ambulatory★**, featuring wide arches and slender columns.

Crypt★★ – The lower ambulatory was built by Suger (12C) and restored by Viollet-le-Duc. In the centre stands the vaulted **Hilduin's Chapel** (after the abbot who had it built in the 9C). Beneath the pavement lies the burial vault of the Bourbons, housing the remains of Louis XVI, Marie-Antoinette and Louis XVIII. In 1817, remains of the monarchs (Merovingians, Capetians

and members of the Orléans and Valois dynasties) pillaged during the French Revolution were reburied in a common **ossuary** in the north transept.

Musée d'Art et d'Histoire

22 bis r. Gabriel-Péri. ⏰*Open daily (except Tue) 10am–5.30pm, Thu 10am–8pm, Sat–Sun 2–6.30pm.* ⏰*Closed public holidays.* ✺*5€.* ✆*01 42 43 05 10.* *www.musee-saint-denis.fr.*

This museum is housed in the former **Carmelite convent** (1625). In the refectory and kitchen, artefacts unearthed in St-Denis are displayed. These come from the **Hôtel-Dieu** hospital in Beaune, including a reconstruction of an **apothecary**'s shop. The first floor features religious art, and a room devoted to painter **Albert André** (1869–1954).

The second floor features documents relating to the Paris Commune of 1871. The former Louis XV pavilion houses an exhibition commemorating poet **Paul Éluard,** who was born in St-Denis.

Stade de France★

🎧*Guided tours daily 11am, noon, 2pm, 3pm, 4pm (schedules may vary).* ✺*15€.* ✆*0892 700 900.* *www.stadefrance.com.*

The **1998 World Football Cup** inspired the construction of the stadium, now the biggest in France.

Designed by architects Zubléna, Macary, Regembal and Constantini, the elliptic structure is 270m/295yd long, 230m/240yd wide, 35m/115ft high and covers an area of 17ha/42 acres. Thanks to its variable capacity, it can host all kinds of sporting and entertainment events. The circle of stands (25 000 seats) nearest the track can be reconfigured to accommodate athletic competitions.

Parc de l'Île-Saint-Denis

Quai de la Marine, 93450 L'île St-Denis (A86 to Asnières - Villeneuve-la-Garenne exit). For more information on hours and events: ✆*01 48 13 14 49.*

During the 19C, the Saint-Denis Island and its traditional music-hall/restaurants (guinguettes) were favoured leisure spots. Impressionist painters Sisley, Berthe Morisot and Manet found inspiration here. The guinguettes have since disappeared, and the narrow park, created during the 1980s at the island's edge and measuring 23 ha/57 acres, is a haven of tranquility, especially during the week. An installation along the banks of the Seine traces the heritage of the Impressionists in the area through colourful, detailed panels, bringing the works to life and showing how the island landscape inspired painters. Sports equipment is available for free rental.

Parc de la Courneuve

2.5km/1.5mi E along r. de Strasbourg and N 301 (on the right).
This 350ha/865-acre stretch of greenery features a cycling track, bridlepath, a ski jump, a little train, sports facilities and playgrounds. Rowing boats and pedaloes may be hired to explore the 12ha/30-acre lake *(bathing prohibited)*. The park is home to some 100 varieties of trees and 250 shrub species and the floral gardens are also remarkable. The park regularly organises tours: visit the information desk at the park *(Maison du Parc: ℘01 43 11 13 00).*

Parc du Sausset

2 rue Raoul Dufy /Rte. Camille Pissarro (at Aulnay-Sous-Bois); alternative entrance av. du Sausset (Villepinte). Motorway A104 to exit Parc départemental de Sausset. For more information: ℘01 48 19 28 28.
This large park, measuring 200 ha/494 acres, encircles the Villepinte train station. Despite its proximity to heavily used roads and an airport, the park provides the pleasant sensation of a countryside stroll. The woody site has retained much of its original character, broken down into four areas.
The **Prés carrés**, vast fields easily accessible from the train station, offer wide lawns ideal for sprawling out or picnicking, or enjoying games of cricket or football. The park also features a large swamp, part of which is visible and harbouring many birds. In addition, there's a labyrinth, sports facilities including ping-pong tables and basket-

ball. A walk around the Savigny pond is also pleasant: a garden featuring plants indigenous to the Americas and a viewpoint offering a large overview of the park awaits. A grassy farmland area called the **Bocage** is accessible via the Observatoire bridge. Tall grasses, plants and tree-lined pathways abound.
The area known as the **Puits d'Enfer** (literally, "wells of hell") have few pathways, having been planted with numerous vineyards. A walking trail with signs along the way helps identify several varieties of trees.

MUSÉE DE L'AIR ET DE L'ESPACE DU BOURGET★★

&♿🕐*Open Tue–Sun 10am–6pm (Oct–Mar until 5pm).*🎟8€, 13€, 16€ *depending on selected activities; permanent collection free. ℘01 49 92 70 62. www.museeairespace.fr.*
Le Bourget airfield was created in 1914 and rapidly became an important airport and military airbase. Nungesser and Coli set off from here in their *White Bird* on 8 May 1927 in a doomed attempt to reach the American coast. On 22 May, Lindbergh successfully landed his *Spirit of St Louis* in Paris, completing the first non-stop solo flight across the Atlantic. Costes and Bellonte were the first to accomplish this feat in the opposite direction on 1 September 1930.
The museum is housed in the former terminal building at Le Bourget, with collections retelling the history of aviation. The adventure began with **hot air balloons★** after the 1783 experiment by Pilâtre de Rozier and Arlandes; a model of their balloon is displayed. Balloons proved useful during the Franco-Prussian War of 1870–71.
Grande Galerie★★ – This gallery traces the early years of aviation, boasting the world's largest collection. Some aircraft were inspired by bionics, notably Clément Ader's *Éole*, designed after observing a bat's flight. Among early aircraft, note Farman's *Voisin* (first round trip, 1km/0.6mi, in Issy-les-Moulineaux, 1907), the elegant *Levasseur Antoinette* (1908), and the *Blériot-XI*, which succeeded in flying across the Channel. With

the outbreak of World War I, aviation rapidly progressed as the skies became the setting for the first aerial battles.

▷ Proceed in chronological order via the Hall de l'Espace to the Hall de l'Aviation légère et sportive.

Hall 10 Inter-war aircraft – This hall contains the powerful *Caudron 714R* (900hp) and the *BreguetXIX* 'Nungesser-Coli', in which Costes and Le Brix made the first successful crossing of the South Atlantic in 1927.

Hall 7 Prototypes★ – This hall presents the history of the French Air Force since 1945 and features prototypes with thermopropulsion.

Hall 6 Concorde★★ – Some fearsome WWII fighters are represented here, such as the *Spitfire MK-16*, used by the Free French Airforce. The star is the prototype of supersonic aircraft *Concorde 001*.

Hall 11 Space exploration★ – The conquest of space is represented by launchers and space capsules (the famous **Sputnik** was the Earth's first artificial satellite). In 1965, France became the third nation to conquer space after the US and USSR with its *Diamant* launcher, replaced later by the *Ariane* launcher.

DRANCY DÉPORTATION MEMORIAL

Mémorial du camp de Drancy, Av. Jean Jaurès, Esp. Charles de Gaulle, Drancy. ⏴⏵*Guided tours of deportation cars and archives by reservation only:* *01 48 95 35 05 or 01 48 96 50 87.*
This memorial honours the 76 000 jews imprisoned at the Drancy internment camp outside Paris between 1941–1944 by Nazi and French forces, most of whom where later deported to the Auschwitz-Birkenau extermination camp.
A 1976 granite sculpture by Shélomo Selinger is the central feature. Railway tracks linking the work to a deportation car marked with a star of David allude to the victims' tragic fate – fewer than 2 000 would survive. The site also hosts a permanent exhibition. A Shoah memorial, museum and education space opened opposite the cité de la Muette in 2012 (www.memorialdelashoah.org).

AUBERVILLIERS
This working class town was once a hive of factories and warehouses.

Église Notre-Dame-des-Vertus
The present-day church was completed in the 17C; it was a prestigious place of pilgrimage visited by figures such as Francois I and Louis XIII. In 1900, a fire ravaged the church, which had already been damaged during wars.
The Jesuit-style facade dates to 1628.

MONTREUIL
Frequented by kings until the 16C, Montreuil was a farming village before becoming a working-class bastion in the 19C. Guided tours of its factories and workshops are organised by the local tourist office *(www.montreuilt-ourisme.fr)*.

Hôtel de Ville
Pl. Jean-Jaurès. www.montreuil.fr
The present-day City Hall was inaugurated in 1935. It is noteworthy for its 40m/131ft belfry and **Paul Signac**'s monumental painting, *Au Temps d'harmonie.*

Église St-Pierre-St-Paul
2 r. Romainville. ⏰*Open daily, except Tue.* *01 42 87 30 06.*
This church, which is based on the same layout as Notre Dame, features a remarkable chancel dating to the early 13C.

Murs à pêches (Peach walls)
The wall stretches from 23 r. St-Just to imp. Gobétue. ⬭*No charge.* *01 48 70 23 80. www.mursapeches.org.*
Montreuil was once famous for cultivating peaches, and the vestiges of this legacy are visible in the several preserved kilometres of its famed "peach wall".

Val-de-Marne

Just southeast of Paris, the Val-de-Marne region has a lot to offer, from the romantic greenery of the Bois de Vincennes to riverside walks at Nogent-sur-Marne and picturesque rose gardens.

BOIS ET CHÂTEAU DE VINCENNES★★

Unofficial capital of the Val-de-Marne region, the legendary Bois de Vincennes is at once a wooded area, floral park, and sporting centre. But Vincennes is equally well-known for its massive fortified château, a remarkably preserved former royal residence built in the 14C.

Bois de Vincennes: West Side

▶ *Begin at Metro Porte-Dorée (line 8).*
La Porte Dorée – Exiting the metro, note the Place Edouard-Renard, renovated for the Colonial Exposition of 1931. A fountain and golden statue commemorating France's colonial conquests remains.

Palais de la Porte Dorée – Built for the same Colonial Exposition, this is a fine example of Art Deco architecture. The sculpture decorating the façade was meant to illustrate the colonial power's role as a supposedly "civilising force". The reception hall was inspired by Moroccan palaces.
Cité nationale de l'histoire de l'immigration – *293 av. Daumesnil.* ◐*Open Tue–Fri 10am–5.30pm; Sat–Sun 10am–7pm.* ◐*Closed Mon, 1 Jan, 1 May, 14 July and 25 Dec.* ◉*6/4.50€ (Under 26s free). Aquarium combined ticket: 8/17€. www.histoire-immigration.fr.*
Former pavilion of the 1931 Colonial Exposition, the building now houses the National Museum of the History of Immigration, tracing waves of immigration to France since the 19C.
Porte Dorée Tropical Aquarium★ – *Same location as Immigration Museum.* ◐*Open Tue–Fri 10am–5.30pm, Sat–Sun 10am–7pm.* ◐*Closed Mon, public holidays (call ahead).* ◉*5€ (+ 2€ with temporary exhibit). www.aquarium-portedoree.fr.*

▶ **Population:** 1.3 million
⚲ **Michelin Map:** p145: C2.
🏣 **Info:** ☎01 55 09 16 20. www.tourisme-valde marne.com.
▶ **Location:** From Paris, line 1 or RER A services Bois de Vincennes; RER reaches many cities further out.
👥 **Kids:** Boat rides or puppet shows at the Bois de Vincennes.

This colonial-era Aquarium features some 5 000 species of marine life, including crocodiles.
Lac Daumesnil★ – This picturesque (man-made) lake boasts two islands, one with a café (accessible by bridges or rental boat).
Vincennes Buddhist Centre – *Rte de la Ceinture-du-lac-Daumesnil. org.* ◐*Open: call for opening dates and times.* ☎*01 43 41 54 48. www.kagyu-dzong.*
This massive pagoda opened for the Colonial Exposition of 1931. The 9m/29.5ft gold-leaf Buddha was donated in 2009 by the Patriarchs of Thailand.

Bois de Vincennes: East Side

▶ *If starting here, begin at Metro Chateau de Vincennes (line 1).*
Parc Floral★★ – ◐*Open Jan–Jun 9.30am–6.30pm; Jul–Dec 9.30am–8pm.* ◉*No charge (5.50€ Jun–Sep special events/exhibits).* ☎*01 49 57 15 15. www.parcfloraldeparis.com.*
This park harbours hundreds of floral species, including dahlias, irises, tulips and camelias. Contemporary sculptures like Calder's *Stabile* grace the grounds. The park frequently hosts jazz concerts and other events.
Lac des Minimes – The lake is named after the Minimes convent, which once formed an enclave in the royal wood. Take a bridge to the Ile de la Porte Jaune, where there's a restaurant.

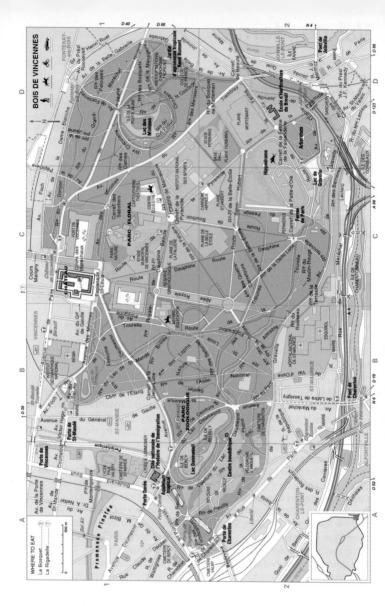

Jardin d'agronomie tropicale René-Dumont – *45 bis av. de la Belle-Gabrielle. Hours vary according to season.*

This garden, featuring an ornate Chinese-style gate, first opened in 1899 as a tropical plants nursery.

Arboretum de l'école du Breuil – 🕐*Open Mar–mid-Jun 9.30am–6.30pm; mid-Jun–Sept 9.30am–8pm; Oct–Feb 9.30am–7pm; rest of year: call for more*

information. 📞*01 53 66 14 05. www.ecoledubreuil.fr.* This 12 hectare park contains 500 species of trees and 300 varieties of lilacs.

Lac de Gravelle – Lying to the southeast of the Bois de Vincennes, this lake contains 28,000 cubic litres of water for the wood's hydraulic network.

Hippodrome – A must-see for horseriding enthusiasts.

Château★★

Av. de Paris. ⏲*Open Sep–May 10am–5pm; Jun–Sep 10am–6pm.* ⏲*Closed 1 Jan, 1 May, 1 and 11 Nov and 25 Dec.* ✎*8.50€; no charge 1st Sunday of the month (Nov–Mar).* ✎*Walking tour: contact for times. Audio guide available.* ✆*01 41 74 19 12. www.chateau-vincennes.fr.*

The château comprises two sections: a forbidding keep, the only medieval royal residence still standing in France, and a majestic complex dating to the 17C.

Keep★★

Guided tours daily.

This 14C masterpiece boasts a 50m/164ft tower flanked with four corner turrets. The ground floor houses royal kitchens and an exhibit exploring the life of prisoners in the keep. The first floor harbours the King's council chamber; the bedchamber is on the second floor. **Tour du village★** – The fortress guards resided here. The structure's military purpose remains evident: slots for drawbridge chains, portcullis grooves, etc. **Sainte chapelle royale★** – *Temporary exhibitions* ✎*7.50€.* Construction started under Charles V (14C), but was finished under Henri II (1552). The edifice is Gothic, aside from stained glass. Note Renaissance stained glass in the chancel representing the Last Judgement.

NOGENT-SUR-MARNE

This city on the Marne River maintains some of its Belle Époque Paris charm.

Nogent-sur-Marne Museum

36 bd Gallieni. ⏲*Open Tue–Thu and Sun 2–6pm, Sat 10am–12pm, 2–6pm.* ⏲*Closed public holidays.* ✎*No charge.* ✆*01 48 75 51 25. www.musee-nogentsurmarne.fr*

The permanent exhibit explores the landscapes and architecture of the Marne.

Pavillon Baltard

R. J.-L.-Labarbe. This pavilion formerly sat in the defunct market at Les Halles in Paris and now hosts shows and exhibits. It also boasts the restored Gaumont-Palace organ.

Carré des Coignard

150 Grande-Rue-Charles-de-Gaulle. Former private residence now a contemporary art gallery.

Marne Riverbank Walk★

✎A walk or bike ride on the banks of the Marne is always very pleasant.

CHAMPIGNY-SUR-MARNE

This town occupies the left bank of the Marne. Downstream from the Champigny bridge is a pleasant walking path. A monument honours the tragic events of 30 Nov–2 Dec 1870, when Parisians attempted to resist a Prussian attack.

Église St-Saturnin

This church boasts a 12C bell tower and 13C nave. On the altar of the chapel at left, a Gothic sculpture depicts Christ facing Pontius Pilate.

Musée de la Résistance Nationale

Parc Vercors, 88 av. Marx-Dormoy. ⏲*Open Tue–Fri 9am–12.30 pm 2–5.30pm; weekend 2–6pm.* ⏲*Closed Mon, holidays except 8 May, Sept and weekends in Aug.* ✎*5€.* ✆*01 48 81 00 80. www.musee-resistance.com.*

The museum traces the history of Resistance movements against fascism.

MAISONS-ALFORT

This town is known for the 1766 veterinary school situated in the grounds of a former manor.

Musée Fragonard de l'École nationale vétérinaire

7 av du Gén.-de-Gaulle. ⏲*Open Wed, Thu 2–6pm, Sat–Sun 2–6pm.* ⏲*Closed public holidays.* ✎*7€. Guided tour* ✎*5€.* ✆*01 43 96 71 72, www.musee-vet-alfort.fr.*

Explore a world of human skulls and animal skeletons before discovering the cabinet of curiosities built by Honoré Fragonard in 1766.

Botanical Garden – ⏰*Open Mar–Nov Wed–Thu, Sat–Sun, 1pm–6pm.* 👁*5€.* 📞*01 43 96 70 35.*
Created in 1766, the botanical garden contains medicinal and toxic plants.

Église Ste-Agnès

This cement church, built in 1932, boasts an irregular diamond shape and tall bell-tower. Stained glass by Max Ingrand.

VITRY-SUR-SEINE

Vitry is a centre of modern art: over 100 works grace the streets, from Jean Debuffet's sculpture *Chaufferie avec cheminée* to Alberto Magnelli mosaics.

MAC/VAL★

Pl. de la Libération. ⏰*Open Tue–Fri 10–6pm, weekends 12–7pm.* ⏰*Closed 1 Jan, 1 May and 25 Dec.* 👁*5€ (free for under 26s).* 📞*01 43 91 64 20. www.macval.fr.*
This contemporary art museum houses over 1 300 works, circulated bi-annually. The collection includes Christian Boltanski, Gina Pane and Gilles Barbier.

Galerie municipale Jean Collet

59 av. Guy Moquet. ⏰*Open Tue–Sun, 1.30pm–6pm, Wed 10am–12pm, 1.30pm–6pm during exhibitions.* 📞*01 43 91 15 33. galerie.vitry94.fr.*
This gallery hosts various exhibits and events focusing on contemporary arts.

Exploradôme

18 av. Henri-Barbusse. ⏰*Hours vary according to season; call ahead.* ⏰*Closed 1 Jan, 1st 2 weeks in Aug and 25 Dec.* 👁*6€.* 📞*01 43 91 16 20. exploradome.com.*
This museum introduces children to science with 60 fun experiments. Print your shadow on the wall, build a Roman bridge, or watch how sand dunes form.

Parc départemental des lilas

From Paris, Metro Bibliothèque-François-Mitterrand (line 14) or Mairie-d'Ivry (line 7), then bus 132 to "Cité Moulin-vert". ⏰*Open May–Aug 8am–9pm; Feb, Apr, Sept 8am–8pm; Mar, Oct 8am–7pm.*
This large park features gardens, plant specimens, wooded areas, a small canal, and mini-farm.

L'HAŸ-LES-ROSES ROSE GARDEN★★

R. Albert-Watel. ⏰*Open mid-May–mid-Sept 10am–8pm. Guided tours possible (1hr). Full bloom in Jun.* 👁*3€.* 📞*01 43 99 82 80. www.roseraieduvaldemarne.fr.*
This elegant rose garden c. 1892 was created by landscape artist Edouard Andé. It regularly introduces new breeds, and houses 3 300 varieties of roses.

PLAYMOBIL FUN PARK

22/24 allée des Jachères, ZA La Cerisaie. 94263 Fresnes. ⏰*Open Tue-Sun 10am–7pm, Mon school holidays.* 👁*2.50€ (free for under 3s).* 📞*01 49 84 94 44. www.playmobil-funpark.fr.*
At this park featuring Playmobil characters and backdrops, kids can visit the pyramids, embark on a safari and other fantasy-inspired scenarios.

Hauts-de-Seine

Home to some of the capital's most exclusive suburbs (Neuilly and St Cloud), green expanses like the former royal Parc de Sceaux, and the starkly metropolitan La Défense business district, this region is rich in more ways than one.

▶ **Population:** 1.5 million
🧭 **Michelin Map:** p144: B3.
🛈 **Info:** 📞01 46 93 92 92 www.tourisme92.com.
▶ **Location:** Comprises the western inner suburbs of Paris.
👪 **Kids:** The Piqueur farm teaches kids about animals.

CHÂTEAU ET PARC DE SCEAUX

The southen Paris suburb of Sceaux boasts many parks and gardens popular with families. The grounds of the picturesque château play host to a summer classical music festival, and the gardens are pleasant for a weekend stroll.

In 1670 Louis XIV's superintendent of buildings commissioned Claude Perrault, Le Brun, Girardon and Coysevox to build a residence in Sceaux. Two groups of sculptures flanking the entrance pavilion were created by Coysevox: the dog and the unicorn, representing loyalty and honesty. The château was inaugurated in 1677 at a reception attended by the Sun King.

In 1700, the estate became the property of the Duc du Maine, the legitimised son of Louis XIV. The Duchess of Maine, the Great Condé's granddaughter, surrounded herself with a large court of brilliant personalities and entertained on a grand scale. During the French Revolution, the domain was confiscated and sold and the château was razed.

In 1856, the Duc de Trévise built the château that stands today. In 1923 it was bought by the Seine département and restored. Physicists Pierre (1859–1906) and Marie Curie (1867–1934) lived in Sceaux.

Château and Park★★

⏱Park open from 7am–10pm depending on season. ♿ 𝄞06 64 40 56 66.

Main Entrance – Two entrance pavilions with sculpted pediments are flanked by two small lodges surmounted by **Coysevox**'s statues.

Orangerie – Designed by **Jules Hardouin-Mansart** in 1685 and decorated with carved pediments, it now hosts conferences and concerts.

Grandes Cascades★ – Waters spring out of carvings by **Rodin** and splash down to the **Octagonal Basin**.

Grand Canal★ – This canal is as long as Versailles' Petit Canal (1030m/3380ft), and flanked by Lombardy poplars.

Musée de l'Île-de-France★ – ⏱Open Nov–Mar Wed–Mon 10am–1pm, 2–5pm; Apr–Oct 10am–1pm, 2–6pm, Sat 10am–6pm (Sun 6.30pm). ⏱Closed Tue, 1 Jan, 1 May, 14 Jul, 15 Aug, 1 Nov, 25 Dec. 🎫3€ (no charge 1st Sunday of the month). ♿ 𝄞01 41 87 29 50. www.chateau-sceaux.fr.

Housed in the **château** that once belonged to the Duc de Trévise, the collections focus on four major themes: Sceaux and its owners; ceramics from the Paris Basin; royal and princely residences; and scenery in the Paris Basin from the 18C–20C. The museum boasts the largest existing collection of **Sceaux faience**. It also features 17C–18C porcelain, fine 19C faience, and works by Art Nouveau ceramist **Pierre-Adrien Dalpayrat**. Luxurious residences in the vicinity are illustrated with etchings by Rigaud, oils including the *Château de St-Cloud* by Troyon, and furniture by Riesenburg and the Jacob brothers.

CHÂTENAY-MALABRY

Architecture enthusiasts will appreciate this town for its 17C and 18C residences, while romantic souls will find inspiration in the Vallée-aux-Loups, former refuge of writers and artists such as Chateaubriand and Faudrier.

Église St-Germain-l'Auxerrois★ – Situated on the former village square, this church is remarkable for its simple lines and Roman-style belltower.

Maison de Chateaubriand – Vallée-aux-Loups★ – 87 r. de Chateaubriand. Guided tour (40min) no charge Sun and holidays. ⏱Open Mar–Oct Tue–Sat 10am–12pm, 2–6pm, Sun 11am–6pm; Nov–Feb Tue–Sun 2–5pm. ⏱Closed 1 May, 1 Nov and 25 Dec. 🎫3€ (guided tours during week until 5pm 5€). Park open 10am–5pm, 6pm or 7pm according to the season. 🎫No charge. 𝄞01 55 52 13 00, www.maison-de-chateaubriand.fr.

In 1807, French writer Chateaubriand (1768–1848) was forced to leave Paris after writing an article hostile to Napoléon's despotic regime. He bought the Domaine de la Vallée-aux-Loups near Paris and started his famed *Memoires* there.

The writer created a park evoking his world travels: the garden includes Lebanese cedars, Nile reeds and other far-flung species. The pavilion was the writer's workshop and library.

Plagued with financial problems, Chateaubriand sold the estate in 1818 to Mathieu de Montmorency. In 1826, Montmorency's daughter inherited the estate; the family expanded the park and added a left wing. The estate was sold to the region in 1967; the house and park opened to the public in 1987.

Parc boisé de la Vallée-aux-Loups – ⏱*Open all day.* ☎*06 64 40 57 52.*
The great "wood" of oaks and chestnuts surrounds Chateaubriand's English-style garden. Fauna abounds here, including game birds and their predators.

Arboretum – *102 r. de Chateaubriand.* ⏱*Open Apr–Sept 10am–7pm; Mar–Oct 10am–6pm; Nov–Feb 10am–5pm.* ☞*No charge.* &. ☎*01 49 17 20 63.* The 18C arboretum was conceived as an English-style garden, boasting grottoes and a waterfall. Remarkable rare trees, including bald cypresses whose strange roots emerge at the edge of the water, grace the grounds.

L'Île Vert – *34 r. Eugène-Sinet.* ☎*01 49 17 20 63.* This romantic garden is graced with green walls, ponds and lush vegetation. The main residence (1828) was acquired by playwright Jules Barbier in 1852. He created the garden and expanded the house. After Barbier's death, writer Marcel Arland rented the house in the 1930s. In 1945, painter Jean Fautrier (1898–1964) took up residence here.

Musée du Bonsaï – *25 r. de Châteaubriand.* ⏱*Open Mon–Sat, 10am–6pm.* ☞*No charge.* ☎*01 47 02 91 99. www.lebonsai.com.* Two greenhouses abound with miniature trees aged from 6 to 300 years. Some are arranged to create the impression of a forest, while others are placed among rocks, creating a sense of landscape in the tradition of China and Japan. While smaller bonsaïs remain affordable, trees such as a 150 year-old fig tree can run up to 7000€.

Forêt de Verrières

▶ *2km/1.25mi from Châtenay-Malabry. From the intersection at 11-Novembre-1918, follow the Plessis-Piquet road.*
🚶 Here you'll encounter chestnuts, oaks, ash trees, maples and cherry trees. The GR 11 allows you to cross the forest along 5km, and there's also a short, more rugged hiking trail. Enjoy beautiful **views** of Paris and the Bièvre *Valley.*

FONDATION JEAN ARP★

21 r. des Châtaigniers. ⏱*Open Fri–Sun 2–6pm.* ☞*8€.* ☎*01 45 34 22 63. www.fondationarp.org.*
The cubist-style house and workshop of sculptor **Jean Arp** (1886–1966) was designed by his partner **Sophie Taeuber** (1889–1943) in the 1960s. Arp collaborated with Kandinsky in the German Blaue Reiter movement; the two later joined the Dada movement in Germany and France.

Arp's sculptures, characterised by pure lines and curves, invite touch (special gloves provided at welcome desk).

ISSY-LES-MOULINEAUX

This town once harboured army barracks on its island, but it's now a major business centre close to the Seine River.

Musée français de la Carte à jouer – *16 r. Auguste-Gervais.* ⏱*Open Wed–Fri 11am–5pm, weekends 2–6pm (Jul Wed–Sun 1pm–6pm).* ⏱*Closed holidays and Aug.* ☞*4.50€, no charge 1st Sun of month.* ☎*01 41 23 83 60.* This museum presents a collection of rare **playing cards★**. Among the oldest is a 15C illuminated Tarot set attributed to the Ferrare school (Italy). The former Conti pavilion explores Issy's history. One section is devoted to artists who sojourned in Issy.

Église Saint-Étienne – *Pl. de l'Église. Call for opening times,* ☎*01 46 42 27 12.* The church and its 34m/111ft bell tower were completed in 1645. There is a 12C Roman-style tympanum in the left aisle.

Parc départemental de l'île St-Germain – *Tramway T2 Issy-les-Moulineauxl, Access via footbridge from quai de Stalingrad.* ⏱*Open daily 8am–8pm depending on the season.* ☎*01 55 95 98 92.*

The history of Meudon

Around 1540, the **Duchess of Étampes** built a Renaissance-style house at the edge of Meudon's Terrace. The **Cardinal de Lorraine** purchased it in 1522. In 1654, it was sold to **the Marquis de Sablé**, who commissioned **Le Vau** to renovate the château and build the great terrace. In 1659, the estate was sold to **Louvois**. He entrusted the gardens to **Le Nôtre**, then **Mansart**.

Louis XIV's son, the **Grand Dauphin,** renovated the **Château-Vieux** and added the **Château-Neuf.**

Under Louis XV and Louis XVI, and after the French Revolution, Meudon declined. The Château-Vieux was demolished after a 1795 fire.

During the **Franco-Prussian War** of 1870, Prussian forces used Meudon's terrace for defense. The Château-Neuf was arsoned in 1871. Only a few walls remain. It now houses the famed Observatory.

This park lies on Issy's St-Germain island. The northwest features lawns with playgrounds and a sculpture by Dubuffet. Southwest, thematic gardens are ideal for a stroll.

MEUDON★

Nestled on a plateau covered by the Meudon Forest, the Seine Valley unfolds below. From here you can spot Paris monuments such as the Eiffel Tower and Sacré-Coeur.

Avenue du Château – A plaque at left marks the house *(no. 27)* where **Richard Wagner** composed the score for the *Flying Dutchman* in 1841.

Terrace★ – The terrace (450m/1480ft long and 136m/ 447ft wide) boasts **panoramic views★** over the Seine Valley and Paris.

Observatory – Guided tour one *Sat per month 2.30pm. Call for details.* 6€. 01 45 07 75 30. www.obspm.fr. Founded by astronomer **Jules Janssen**, this observatory (1876) houses the astrophysics section of the Paris Observatory. A **revolving dome** crowns the centre of the Château-Neuf.

Musée d'Art et d'Histoire – *11 r. des Pierres. Museum refurbished in early 2012.* Tue–Sun 2pm–6pm. 01 46 23 87 13. The house that **Molière**'s widow **Armande Béjart** bought in 1676 is now a museum. Partly dedicated to Meudon's history, it also features a collection of 20C sculpture from greats like Rodin or César. French **gardens** are dotted with sculptures by Jean Arp and Stahly.

Musée Rodin – *19 av. Auguste-Rodin.* Open Fri–Sun 1pm–6pm (last admission 5.15pm). Closed 1 Jan, 1 May and 25 Dec. 4€. 01 41 14 35 00. www. musee-rodin.fr. A twin to the world-famous Rodin Museum in Paris, this Rodin museum stands next to the **Villa des Brillants**, Rodin's home and studio from 1895.

The 17C façade of the old Issy château that Rodin purchased after the castle was set on fire and reassembled in his garden, has been integrated to the museum's building.

Moulds, drawings, sketches and original plaster casts *(The Gates of Hell, Balzac, The Burghers of Calais)* fill the rooms. Rodin died in 1917 and his grave was laid in front of the museum, a cast of the famous *Thinker* on his tombstone.

FORÊT DE MEUDON★

This forest (1 150ha/2 841acre) covers a plateau stretching from Sèvres to Villacoublay and includes 16.5km/10 mi of hiking trails.

From the route des Bois-Blancs, reach the intersection known as the Etoile du Pavé de Meudon: from a nearby promontory, enjoy a view of the Viroflay woods. Next, take the route des Treize-Ponts to reach the "Chene des Missions", a megolithic site reconstituted in 1895. At the Etoile du Pavé, turn right on the route de la Mare-Adam; the intersection of the same name leads to the intersection of the Queue-de-l'Etang and passes under the expressway.

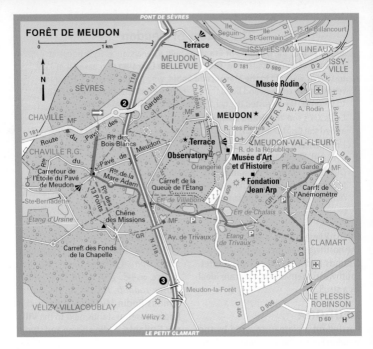

The forest road descends to the Ville-bon pond, before crossing the avenue de Trivaux and passing between two other ponds. It winds through the woods to the left just before reaching the D 2.

SÈVRES – CITY OF CERAMICS★★

2 pl. de la Manufacture. ⊙*Open Wed–Mon, 10am–5pm.* ⊙*Closed 1 Jan, 1 May and 25 Dec.* ⊛*6€; no charge 1st Sun of month.* ℘*01 46 29 22 00, www.sevrescitéceramique.fr.*

The porcelain factory located here since the 18C made Sèvres world-famous.The factory and museum, installed on the banks of the Seine were recently combined to create the "City of Ceramics".

Production workshops – ℘*01 46 29 22 05;* ☏*guided tours by reservation (1hr30).* Observe porcelain artists and learn about methods which have remained unchanged since the 18C.

Museum – Housing over 55 000 ceramic works, this museum offers a sweeping look at the craft, from humble Norman pitchers to Catherine of Russia's sumptuous tea service. Techniques using both porous clay (faience and pottery) and non-porous clay (hard and soft-paste porcelains) are explored.

Collections showcase ceramics from the Antiquity to the present, and boast rare pieces from around the world (Asia, Islamic world, Europe and France). Displays emphasise the development of techniques used through the ages, in both Europe and abroad.

VILLE-D'AVRAY

This refined holiday town has attracted grand thinkers from Balzac to Corot.

Maison des Jardies – *14 av. Gambetta.* ⊙*Open Thu–Sun 2.30–6.30pm.* ⊙*Closed public holidays.* ⊛*5.50€.* ℘*01 45 34 61 22. This gardener's lodge was part of the Jardies estate, where* **Honoré de Balzac** *(1799–1850) settled in 1838.* **Gambetta** *died here on 31 December 1882.*

The house is situated in a pleasant green area. The **forêt de Fausses-Reposes** is a lovely forest planted with oaks, chestnuts and birches. **Ponds★** are nestled in a valley bordering the forest. Corot often painted from a modest cabin here. Back in town, visit the Louis XVI-style **église St-Nicolas-St-Marc**. Corot's

Saint Jérôme in the desert hangs here, along with smaller works in the transept.

SAINT-CLOUD★

Situated on the west bank of the Seine across from the Bois de Boulogne, this affluent community is particularly renowned for its verdant park.

Clodoald, grandson of **Clovis** and Clotilda, escaped an assassination attempt by his uncle Clotaire I (but his two brothers were murdered). Clodoald became a disciple of the hermit **Severin**, then founded a monastery where he died in 560. His tomb became a place of pilgrimage and the town of Nogent was renamed St-Cloud. The saint bequeathed his seigniorial rights to the bishops of Paris.

The assassination of Henri III – In 1589 Henri III attacked Paris, which had fallen into the hands of the **Catholic League**. Following the king's alliance with his cousin, Protestant Henri of Navarre, Jacobin friar **Jacques Clément** stabbed the king, who died two days later.

Monsieur's Castle – In 1658, the episcopal building became the property of Louis XIV's brother. The Sun King's brother later married Charlotte-Elisabeth of Bavaria. He extended the grounds and asked **Jules Hardouin-Mansart** to plan a series of beautiful buildings. The park and cascade were designed by **Le Nôtre** during 1690–1695. **Marie-Antoinette** bought the estate in 1785; but it became State property during the Revolution.

The 18 Brumaire – When General **Bonaparte** returned from his Egyptian campaign, the French people thought he would restore peace. On 18 Brumaire of the year VIII in the new French calendar (9 November 1799), the **seat of the Consulate** was moved to St-Cloud. The next day, the Five Hundred held a meeting at the orangery, led by Napoleon's brother **Lucien Bonaparte**. The General met with hostility and was saved by his brother, who cleared the Assembly. The Directoire was abolished.

St-Cloud during the Empire – In 1802, Bonaparte was appointed consul for life, and St-Cloud became his favourite offi-

cial residence. He celebrated his civil wedding with Marie-Louise here, following it with a religious ceremony in the Square Salon of the Louvre (1810).

In 1814, Prussian **Marshal Gebhard Blücher** moved in to the château. He vengefully cut the silk hangings and wrecked the bedroom and library.

Charles X signed the **Ordinances of July 1830** at St-Cloud, abolishing the charter. On 1 December 1852, Prince-President **Louis-Napoléon** became Emperor. On 15 July 1870, a meeting was held here to declare **war on Prussia**. The building was damaged in a fire three months later, and razed in 1891.

Domaine National de Saint-Cloud★★

🕐*Open daily Mar–Apr and Sept–Oct 7.30am–9pm. May–Aug 7.30am–10pm; Nov–Feb 7.30am– 8pm. ☞5€ per car, no charge for pedestrians. ℘01 41 12 02 90. www.saint-cloud.monuments-nationaux.fr.*

The 450ha/1 112-acre national estate spreads from the Seine Valley to the Garches plateau. The château may be gone, but the gardens retain most of Le Nôtre 's classical layout.

Musée historique – 🕐*Open Wed–Sun, 10am–1pm and 2–6pm. ☞No charge. ℘01 41 12 02 90.* This museum tells the story of the estate its gardens and defunct château.

Jardin du Trocadéro★ – These gardens were laid out on the site of the former château. The end of the terrace commands a **view** of Paris. In the foreground, note the Pavillon d'Artois, partly built in the 17C.

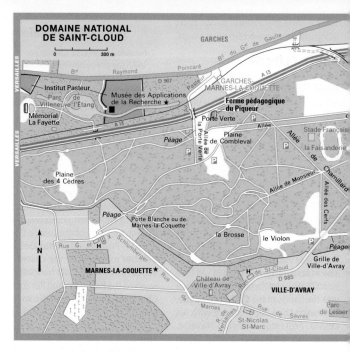

DOMAINE NATIONAL
DE SAINT-CLOUD

Grande Perspective – Yew trees and marble layout mark the château's former site, which was also the start of the "Grande Perspective", a succession of parterres, lawns and ponds stretching over 2km/1.2mi. The terrace offers a superb **panorama**★★ of Paris.

Terrasse de l'Orangerie – Some 50 orange trees and oleanders bloom here from May to October. In winter they take shelter in the Meudon orangery.

Tapis vert – Running from the Grande Gerbe to Rond-Point des 24 Jets, these lawns command a lovely view of the flower beds and of Paris.

Rond-Point de la Balustrade– Napoléon erected a monument here surmounted by a lantern, lit when the Emperor was staying at the château. It was blown up by the Prussians in 1870.

Lower Park

Grande Cascade★– Designed in the 17C by Lepautre, these impressive falls were enlarged by Jules Hardouin-Mansart. Dominated by statues, the waters flow into basins and troughs before reaching the lower falls.

The **Grandes Eaux**★★ is an impressive fountain display, staged every June.

Pont de St-Cloud

In the 8C, a bridge was built across the River Seine. According to tradition, no king was to set foot on it, or he would die a sudden death. Until the middle of the 16C, French rulers would cross the river in a boat. However, when François I died in Rambouillet, it was decided that the funeral procession would cross the famous bridge. No ill omens were feared as the king was already deceased.

François' son Henri II replaced the old wooden bridge with a magnificent stone construction featuring 14 arches. Local people were astonished by the display of stonework, claiming it the Devil's work, and thus the bridge was exorcised.

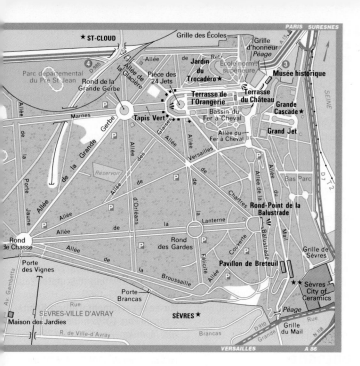

Grand Jet – Nestling near the Great Cascade, this is the park's most powerful fountain, rising 42m/138ft.

Pavillon de Breteuil – This 18C pavilion houses the **Bureau International des Poids et Mesures** (World Centre for Scientific Measurement). The Bureau still has the old standard metre.

Ferme pédagogique du Piqueur – ⓈOpen Sat–Sun and holidays 10am–12pm 1.30–5.30pm. ☜2€. Guided tours and workshops available. ℰ01 46 02 24 53. www.fermedupiqueur.fr.

Complete with orchard, vegetable garden and barnyard animals, this educational farm is tucked in the heart of the Domaine national de St-Cloud, housed in Napoléon III's former stud farm.

Town

Overlooked by the spire of the **Église St-Clodoald** (1865), the steep streets wind up the hillsides of the Valley.

Église St-Clodoald★ – Pl. de l'Église. ℰ01 41 12 80 80. In 550, a chapel stood here that was expanded by St-Clodoald. At the end of the 18C, Marie-Antoinette built a chapel and hospital in St-Cloud, where the first stones of a new church were laid. But the Revolution interrupted works. Napoléon III resumed construction in 1860, and the Romano-Gothic church was completed in 1865. The marble altar in the chancel was donated by Napoléon III.

Musée des Avelines - Musée d'Art et d'Histoire de St-Cloud – 60 r. Gounod. ⓈOpen Wed–Sat 12–6pm, Sun 2–6pm. Guided tours Sun 3pm. ☜No charge. ℰ01 46 02 67 18. www. musee-saint-cloud.fr. This museum celebrating the history of St-Cloud since the 17C is housed in the former Brunet villa (early 1930s). Highlights include porcelain from the 18C and paintings from 19C and early 20C artists including Duval Le Camus, Regnault, and Dantan.

Église Stella-Matutina★ – pl.Henri-Chrétien, av. du Maréchal-Foch. This church (1965) is shaped like a circular tent in wood, metal and glass.

MARNES-LA-COQUETTE★

Only 10km (6.2 mi) from Paris, this town is nonetheless a haven of peace. It's small but merits a detour.

👥 Institut Pasteur – Musée Pasteur★
– 25 rue du Docteur Roux. 🕐 Open
Mon–Fri, guided tours 2pm, 3pm, 4pm
(no reservation required). 🕐 Closed
public holidays, Aug. 👓7€. 📞01 55
18 46 42, www.pasteur.fr. Located in
Pasteur's former apartment on the site
of the Villeneuve-l'Étang estate, once
occupied by the troops of Napoléon III,
the museum at the **Institut Pasteur**
traces the fight against infectious
disease by Louis Pasteur.

Mémorial La Fayette – Entrance
on bd Raymond-Poincaré. 🕐 Open
7.30am–7.30pm. Crypt may be visited on
request. 👓No charge. 📞01 47 95 34 76.
www.lafayettepilotsmemorial.com. West
of the Parc de St-Cloud, this monument
honours the 209 American Air Force
volunteers who participated in the La
Fayette squadron during WW I. An arch
and colonnade reflect in a pool, and
a crypt holds the remains of 67 pilots
killed during the war.

BOULOGNE-
BILLANCOURT★

Former headquarters of automobile
maker Renault, Boulogne-Billancourt
has changed considerably since its heyday. The Seguin islands and the banks
of Billancourt are currently being turned
into a major centre of arts and culture.

Musée des Années 30★ – Espace
Landowski. 28 av. André-Morizet. 🕐Open
Tue–Sun, 11am–6pm. 🕐 Closed 1 Jan,
1 May, 25 Dec.👓 6€. 📞01 55 18 53 00.
www.annees30.com. This museum
celebrates the fertile overlap between
art and industry. The 4th floor features
hotel models by Dujarric de la Rivière
and Ternisien, including the famous
triangular building by Le Corbusier,
shaped like an ocean liner. The furniture
by designers Jules Leleu, Art Deco
master Ruhlmann (beautiful 1925 chair)
and Jean Prouvé (note the steel chaise
longue) are truly timeless.

The third floor explores sacred art
inspired by daily life. One section is
dedicated to the "Sundays in Boulogne",
recounting how Cubist art dealer Dan-
iel-Henry Kahnweiler brought together
important early 20C artists including

Antonin Artaud, Desnos, Gertrude Stein
and Picasso. The painting Panier
et siphon (1925) is by Juan Gris, who
designed fabric prints for Kahnweiler
to create a remarkable set of chairs.
Another section explores Orientalism
and the new enthusiasm for African and
Asian cultures.

The second floor abounds with neoclassical works, with an emphasis on female
nudes and traditional pastoral scenes.

Musée-jardin Paul-Landowski – 14 r.
Max-Blondat. 🕐Open Wed and weekends
10am–12pm, 2–5pm. 🕐 Closed some
public holidays (call ahead). 👓6€. No
charge 1st Sun of month. Combined pass
with Musee Paul Belmondo: 10€. 📞01
55 18 53 00. In a garden adorned with
monumental sculptures, a crypt houses
documents relating to sculptor Paul
Landowski (1875–1961).

Musée départemental Albert-Kahn★
– 14 r. du Port. 🕐Open Tue–Sun 11am–
7pm (6pm Jan–Apr). 🕐Closed 25 Dec–1
Jan, public holidays. 👓 4€; no charge
1st Sun of month. 📞01 55 19 28 00, www.
hauts-de-seine.net. Comprising some 72
000 photographs, 4 000 stereoscopic
images, and around 100 hours of film,
the **Archives of the Planet★** painstak-
ingly document social history, religion,
economics and politics of the 19C. Dig-
itising efforts are helping to preserve
the most fragile documents and present
them in different formats.

Gardens★ – Banker Albert Kahn commissioned this "map of the world" garden symbolising his efforts to foster
worldwide dialogue.

The grounds include a Japanese garden
with red bridge (repica of the sacred
Nikko bridge north of Tokyo) and tea
ceremony pavillion. There's an English
garden and French-style counterpart
designed by artists Henri and Achille
Duchêne, rose garden, "blue forest"
housing superb Atlas cedars, and other
thematic areas.

Expo-musée Renault - 27 r. des
Abondances. 🕐 Open Tue and Thu
2–6pm. 🕐Closed holidays and Aug. 👓No
charge. 📞01 46 05 21 58. The museum
retraces the human and technological
history of the company.

A royal Forest – Bois de Boulogne

In Merovingian times the forest was hunted for bear, deer, wolves and wild boar. Later, the royal forest became a refuge for bandits, and in 1556 Henri II enclosed it with a wall. In the 17C , Colbert adapted it for hunting with straight roads. Louis XIV opened the wood to the public as a place for country walks, but its reputation soon degraded. According to one chronicle, "marriages from the Bois de Boulogne do not get celebrated by the priest".

Decline – During the Revolution the forest again provided refuge to the destitute and poachers. In 1815, the English and Russian armies set up camp, devastating a great section. Oaks were replaced by horse chestnuts, acacias, sycamores and maples, though sadly many were destroyed in the storm of 26 December 1999 and 2003 heatwave.

Present day – When Napoléon III gave the forest to the city in 1852, Haussmann demolished the surrounding wall and created winding paths, ornamental lakes and ponds, the Longchamp racecourse, restaurants and pavilions. The Auteuil racecourse was built after 1870. The 20C saw the construction of the Jardin des Serres, **Roland-Garros** and **Parc des Princes** stadiums.

Musée Paul-Belmondo – *14 r. de l'Abreuvoir.* ○ *Open Tue–Fri 2–6pm, weekend 11am–6pm.* ○ *Closed 1 Jan, 1 May, 25 Dec.* ⊕*6€. No charge 1st Sun of month.* ℘*01 55 18 53 00.* This museum features original mouldings, bronze sculptures, ornate medals and other works from neoclassical artist Paul Belmondo (1898–1982). The artist's Paris workshop on rue Victor-Considérant has been recreated in the pavillion on the left.

The central building resembles a medal, with white sections on one side and surprising wood sections on the other.

The ground floor houses early works from the artist; ornate busts and sculptures are placed in niches.

The first floor features 15 busts of children and elongated bronzes characteristic of the 1950s. The last floor presents medals from the artist created for the Monnaie de Paris, as well as his famed red chalk drawings. The museum park is graced with contemporary sculptures.

Parc Edmond-de-Rothschild – *3 r. des Victoires.* ○*Opening times vary* ℘*01 46 94 81 50.* This pretty park is part of the old estate acquired by the Baron James de Rothschild around 1856. He adorned the park with sumptuous châteaux and gardens. Pillaged during the Occupation of WW II and halved in size by the construction of a nearby hospital

and motorway, the park conserves its romantic charm.

BOIS DE BOULOGNE★★

This 846ha/2 090 acre park laid out in the 19C is crossed by shaded roads and paths for pedestrians, horses and cyclists. Lakes and waterfalls, gardens, lawns and woodland, cafés and restaurants grace the grounds. Horseraces take place at the Longchamp and Auteuil tracks, and music concerts and theatre plays are regularly organised in the Bagatelle and Pré Catelan gardens.

Park Avenue Foch – This avenue completed by Haussmann is 120m/394ft wide. After its 1854 inauguration, it became a fashionable entry point to the Bois de Boulogne.

The Lakes★ – **Lac Supérieur** is a pleasant recreation area, as is **Lac Inférieur**. It has a landing-stage for motor boats heading to the islands and rowing boats for hire.

Pré Catelan★ – This park includes a café-restaurant, lawns, and a copper beech that's nearly 200 years old.

Longchamp – A man-made waterfall graces the crossroads (**carrefour de Longchamp**). Beyond the pond is a monument to 35 people shot by the Nazis in 1944. **Château de Longchamp** was given to Haussmann by Napoléon

III and houses the Centre International de l'Enfance.

The **Hippodrome de Longchamp** race-course opened by Napoléon III in 1857 hosts numerous racing events.

👫 **Jardin d'Acclimatation** – 🕐*Daily Apr–Sept 10am–7pm; Oct–Mar 10am–6pm.* ♿3€. ♿ 🕿*01 40 67 90 85. www. jardindacclimatation.fr.* This garden and children's amusement park includes a small zoo with a pets' corner, Norman farm and an aviary. The **Explor@dome** (🕐*Tue, Thu–Fri 10am–12pm, 1.30pm–6pm, Wed and Sat 10pm–6pm.* 🕐*Closed public holidays.* ♿6€. 🕿*01 43 91 16 20; www.exploradome.com)* is a science and multimedia area.

Parc de Bagatelle★★ – *Route de Sèvres à Neuilly.* 🕐*Jun–Sept 9.30am–8pm; Oct–Dec and Mar–May 9.30am–6pm; Jan–Feb 9.30am–5pm.* ♿5.50€. 🕿*01 53 64 53 80.* In 1775 the future Charles X waged a bet with sister-in-law, **Marie-Antoinette**, that he could have a house and gardens designed and built within three months. He won. Bagatelle survived the Revolution and was passed to Napoléon, then sold to the City of Paris in 1905. It is one of four botanical gardens run by the City of Paris.

RUEIL-MALMAISON★★

Rueil is famed for Malmaison, a superb Napoleonic estate.

Malmaison in Imperial times – Crowned Emperor in 1804, **Napoléon** divided his time between his official residences of St-Cloud, Fontainebleau and the Tuileries. Visits to Malmaison were too rare for the Empress Joséphine's liking; she began to miss her splendid botanical and rose gardens.

Malmaison after the divorce – After her divorce in 1809, Napoléon gave Joséphine Malmaison, the Élysée and a château near Évreux. She fled the estate in 1814, but the Allied powers persuaded her to return. She died on 29 May 1814, at 51, while visiting her daughter Hortense.

The farewell to Malmaison – Ten months after Joséphine's death, Napoléon escaped from Elba and revisited Malmaison. At the end of the Hundred Days he returned to the estate and stayed with Hortense, who had married Napoléon's brother, Louis, and would give birth to Napoléon III. In June 1815 the Emperor paid a last visit to his family before leaving for Rochefort and St Helena.

A succession of owners – After Joséphine's death, the Château de Malmaison and its lands passed to her son Prince Eugène, who died in 1824. The château changed hands until it was bought by Napoléon III, who restored it to its former glory.

By 1877 the château was dilapidated and the grounds reduced to 60ha/148 acres. Malmaison was sold as State property and saw another succession of owners, the last of these donated it to the State in 1904.

The site of the Mausoleum of the Imperial Prince was donated to Malmaison by Prince Victor-Napoleon. Mr and Mrs Edward Tuck, an American couple who owned Bois-Préau Château, donated their residence and its park, formerly part of Josephine's private gardens.

Museum – 🕐*Open Apr–Sept Mon, Wed–Fri 10am–12.30pm, 1.30–5.45pm (Sat–Sun 6.15pm); Oct–Mar Mon, Wed–Fri 10am–12.30pm, 1.30–5.15pm (Sat–Sun 5.45pm); last admission 45min before closing.* ♿6.50€; no charge 1st Sun of month and visitors under 26. 🕿*01 41 29 05 55. www. chateau-malmaison.fr.* When Joséphine bought it in 1799, the **château**, built around 1622, featured the central block and two jutting pavilions dating from the 18C. The museum, founded in 1906, houses items purchased for, donated to or taken from Malmaison, St-Cloud and the Tuileries, or from other palaces connected with the Imperial family.

Pavilions – The **Pavillon Osiris** contains antique pieces belonging to former owner Mr Osiris, a selection of snuff boxes, glass objects and caskets relating to the Napoleonic legend. The central area is dominated by Gérard's portrait of Tsar Alexander I. The **Pavillon des Voitures** displays Imperial carriages.

Musée d'Histoire Locale – *6 av. Paul-Vaillant-Couturier, inside former town hall.* 🕐*Open Mon–Sat 2.30-6pm.* 🕐*Closed Aug.* 🕿 *01 47 32 66 50. www.*

rueil-tourisme.com. Housed in a Second Empire-style building, this museum, which was once the town hall, traces Rueil's transformation from small village to imperial residence. One room on the first floor is devoted to the Consulate and Empire periods (impressive collection of tin soldiers representing Napoleon's Grande Armée). Another room illustrates the importance of Rueil in the early 20C (postcard-printing).

Musée Franco-Suisse – *5 pl. du Mar.-Leclerc.* ⏰*Open Sept–Jun by reservation only.* ✆*No charge.* ✆*01 47 32 66 50.* Documents, weapons, and uniforms illustrate the lives of Swiss guards stationed in the Rueil barracks over a period of 200 years.

🚗 DRIVING TOUR

PARK, FOREST AND RIVERBANKS PARC DE MALMAISON

Chateau grounds. ⏰*Open Wed–Mon 10am–6.30pm.* ✆*01 41 29 05 55.* ⏰*Closed 25 Dec, 1 Jan.* ✆*1.50€.* The park boasts a Marengo cedar planted following Napoléon's victory in 1800, a rose garden and rare plants. Skirted by century-old linden trees stands Napoléon's summer pavillion, used by the Emperor as an office.

▶ Exiting the estate, take a right and go round the park on av. Marmontel. At left is the Mausoleum of the Imperial Prince, holding the remains of Napoléon III's son, killed by Zulus in 1879.

Parc de Bois-Préau

This English-style garden near the château de Bois-Préau opens onto a monumental statue of Empress Joséphine. Église St-Pierre-St-Paul. Restored under Napoléon III, the interior dates to the Renaissance. Highlights include a 15C Florentine **organ sideboard★**, donated by Napoléon III. To the left of the chancel lies the marble tomb of Joséphine. At left is a funerary monument to Queen Hortense.

▶ Take the D 39 road (at left when exiting the church), then turn left on r. Massena to reach r. Charles-Floquet, turning into av. de Versailles. Enter the forest and drive to the St-Cucufa pond; leave the car there.

Forêt de la Malmaison

This forest is populated with oaks and chestnuts. According to legend, a chapel dedicated to St Cucufa, who died around 304, once stood here. The St-Cucufa **pond★** is carpeted with waterlilies in summer. Empress Joséphine built a dairyhouse here to supply milk to the château de Malmaison.

▶ Return to the forest edge and take the 1st road at right for 2km (1.2 mi). av. de la Châtaigneraie and r. du Colonel-de-Rochebrune (D 180) cross the Buzenval quarter, where defenders of Paris were beseiged in January 1871 during the Franco-Prussian war.

Seine and Impressionist Park

The banks of the Seine from Nanterre to Bougival are lined with pathways. The Parc des Impressionnistes is inspired by Monet's garden at Giverny. ⏰*Open Oct–Apr 9.30am–6pm; May–Sept 9.30am–8pm.* ✆*01 47 32 35 75.*

SURESNES

Wine from Suresnes once flowed at royal tables, and the town continues to produce one of the best regional vintages. But it remains associated with a tragic episode during WW II: over 4 500 hostages and Resistance members were executed at Mont Valérien in a clearing by the German army during World War II.

Mémorial de la France combattante – *Free guided tour by reservation.* ✆*01 47 28 46 35, www.mont-valerien.fr.* This monument commemorating heroes and victims of WW II was inaugurated by General de Gaulle on 18 June 1960. In the centre stands a Lorraine cross and a flame of memory lit every 18 June. A crypt houses the bodies of 16 soldiers and members of the Resistance and the ashes of anonymous deportees. In the chapel where prisoners were detained, wall graffiti is still visible; execution posts with bullet holes stand witness to the terror that took place here. In front of the chapel, a bronze bell names 1 008 known victims. There is also an exhibition tracing events in France during WW II.

At the foot of mont Valérien *(bd. Washington)*, the American cemetery honours the soldiers who fell here (over 1 500) during WW II.

Promenade Jacques Baumel – Access on av. du Professeur-Léon-Bernard. Circling Mont Valérien and its park affords a dramatic view of west Paris.

Musée d'Histoire urbaine et sociale Behind Hôpital Foch near station. *Museum refurbished in 2012.* ☜3.50€. 📞01 41 18 37 37, www.ville-suresnes.fr. The museum explores the history of Suresnes and its urban landscape. Highlights include 1905 Lalique crystal bottles for local perfume house Coty.

LA DÉFENSE★★

The La Défense business district juxtaposes traditional office space with experimental developments. The Grande Arche stands at the extreme west of an axis along the Champs-Élysées, which starts at the Louvre and passes through the Arc de Triomphe. After the Esso building opened in 1964, the number of towers has grown to 71 housing over 2,500 companies.

La Grande Arche★★

🕐*Apr–Aug 10am–8pm; Sept–Mar, 10am–7pm.* ☜10€. 📞01 49 07 27 55. www.grandearche.com.

The Grande Arche, designed by Otto von Spreckelsen, is one of the *Grands Projets* instigated by President François Mitterrand. This gigantic open cube (110m/361ft wide) weighs 300 000t, supported by 12 undergound piles. Notre-Dame Cathedral could fit into the arch. The top is occupied by galleries, a restaurant and belvedere offering exceptional views of the **capital's historic vista★★★**. (🕐*The rooftop is currently closed to the public for security reasons; no opening date has been announced).*

Comparitive dimensions of La Grande Arche and Notre-Dame Cathedral

🐾WALKING TOUR

Esplanade de la Défense

Take a **walk★★** on the Esplanade to admire modern architecture and 20C sculptures. Starting in place Carpeaux, note César's *Thumb* (**1**); right of the Arch is a metal sculpture by Japanese artist Miyawaki (**2**). Take the footbridge towards the Faubourg de l'Arche to see the *Colosse* (**3**) by Igor Mitoraj.

The **Palais de la Défense** (**CNIT**)★ features bold design. Its concrete vault (220m/722ft span) has only three points of support. At left on place de

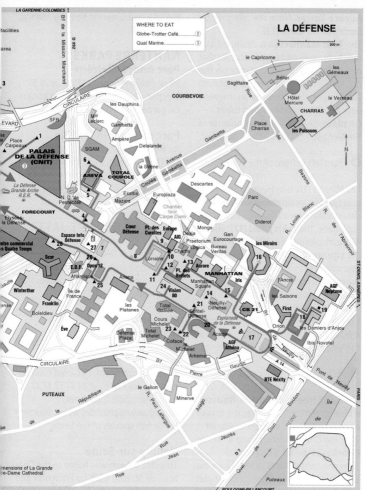

la Défense is **Calder**'s last work, a red stabile 15m/49.2ft high (**4**).

▶ Walk through the opening on the left to the Fiat Tower.

The **Tour Framatome** used to be the district's tallest building, rising 45 storeys to 178m/584ft (that honour now goes to Tour First, which is 231m/757ft high). At its foot, *The Great Toscano* (**5**), a bronze bust by Mitoraj, evokes an antique giant. Pass left round the tower to see *Les Lieux du Corps* (**6**), in polyester resin, by Delfino.

▶ Return to the esplanade.

In the centre of the esplanade is a monumental **fountain by Agam** (**7**) and an underground art **gallery**. The *Midday-Midnight* pond (**8**) by Clarus is a ventilation shaft decorated to represent the trajectory of the sun and moon.

The **place des Corelles** is named after the *Corolla* (**9**) copper fountain by Louis Leygue. A ceramic fresco, *The Cloud Sculptor* (**10**), by Attila adorns a low wall. Philolaos' *Mechanical Bird* (**11**) is on the terrace. Beyond the Vision 80 Tower is **place des Reflets** (**12**) reflected in the

Aurore Tower. Note the allegory by Derbré of *The Earth* (**13**).

The **Tour Manhattan** is designed as a series of curves and counter-curves that mirror the sky. In the distance on the right is the strange silhouette of *Moretti* (**14**), an aeration chimney augmented with 672 coloured fibreglass tubes.

On **place de l'Iris** lies the silhouette of the *Sleepwalker* (**15**) by Henri de Miller.

▷ Turn left in front of the **Tour GAN**.

Les Miroirs (**16**) is by Henri La Fonta: the courtyard fountain comprises ten cylinders decorated with mosaics. East of the esplanade, the **Takis pond** (**17**) reflects 49 multicoloured flexible light-tubes.

On **square Vivaldi** the *Conversation Fountain* (**18**) by Busato represents two bronze figures in conversation.

On place Napoléon-I at the foot of the Neptune Tower, a monument shaped like the Cross of the Légion d'Honneur medal (**19**) commemorates the return of the emperor's remains from St Helena.

▷ Return to the Takis pond.

The **Tour Hoechst-Marion-Roussel**, a blue-green high-rise, was the first to appear (1967) at La Défense. Ahead is *The Frog* (**20**) by Torricini and a bronze *Ophelia* (**21**) by Apel les Fenosa.

Skirt the Sofitel Hotel at left. From the terrace overlooking the cours Michelet is Venet's 14m/46ft-high painted steel sculpture (**22**) and to the right, Jakober's assemblage of welded iron (**23**).

In the square below the esplanade, 35 flower-planters (**24**) with faces and clasped hands are from Selinger. The white-marble *Lady Moon* (**25**) by Julio Silva sits between the Atlantique and Crédit Lyonnais Towers. Barrias' bronze group *La Défense* (**27**) is at the foot of the Agam fountain.

Facing the shopping centre is a colourful sculpture (**28**) by Miró.

On **place des Degrès**, sculptor Kowalski has created a *mineral landscape* (**29**). From the esplanade, take the passage de l'Arche to the KPMG building, framing

the the monumental head by Mitoraj, *Tindajo* (**30**).

NANTERRE PARKS
Parc André-Malraux
39 av. Pablo-Picasso. ℰ01 47 24 28 35.
This park near La Défense boasts botanical gardens and views of Mont Valérien.

Parc du Chemin-de-l'Île
Av. Hoche - RER A Nanterre-Ville.

⊠ This 14ha/34.5acre park was built over industrial wasteland. It's one of the starting points for the "Blue Promenade" trail, stretching from Issy to Rueil.

ÎLE DE LA GRANDE-JATTE
Impressionist painters often painted on this island. Take a **walk** along riverbanks lined with houseboats to familiarise yourself with the landscapes that inspired them.

Maison de la pêche et de la nature
22 allée Claude-Monet, downstream in Levallois-Perret. ◷*Open Wed and weekend afternoons.* ◷*Closed holidays and Aug.* ⊜*3.50€.* ℰ*01 47 57 17 32. www.maisondelapeche.net.*
This aquarium provides an introduction to the fish species of the Seine.

Neuilly-sur-Seine
This chic suburb was home to the Château de Madrid built by François I and destroyed during the Revolution in 1793.

ASNIÈRES-SUR-SEINE
This town was famous in the 19C when it attracted painters like Seurat, Monet and Van Gogh. In 1887, Van Gogh depicted its most famous guinguette in his eponymous painting "La Sirène".
Hôtel de Ville – *1 pl. de l'Hôtel-de-Ville. ℰ01 41 11 12 13.* The city hall was inaugurated in 1899 and boasts an impressive belfry and sumptuous interior decor.
Château d'Asnières – *89 r. du Château. Guided tours 1st Sun in the month by reservation. ℰ01 41 11 16 09.* In 1750, an art amateur commissioned Jacques Hardouin-Mansart de Sagonne (grandson of

the architect who created Versailles) to re-design his 18C leisure house. Nicolas Pineau created the interior design. Note the copies of *Apollo* and *Venus* gracing the entry.

Église Ste-Geneviève – *4 r. du Cardinal-Verdier.* This church was rebuilt in the 18C by Jacques Hardouin-Mansart II. Above the baroque portal with Tuscan colonnades, note the modern statue of Saint Geneviève (original at the Sacré-Coeur).

Pet Cemetery – *4 pont de Clichy.* ©*Open mid-Mar–Oct Tue–Sun 10am–6pm; Oct–mid-Mar10am–4.30pm.* ©*Closed Mon and public holidays.* ©*3.50€.* ₰*01 40 86 21 11.*

ADDRESSES

♈/ EAT

⊖ **La Vogue** – *1 r. du Vieux-Port, in the office buildings of the Cristallerie, right-side entrance near Seine, Sèvres.* ₰*01 46 26 90 07. Open Mon–Fri lunch. Closed Sat–Sun.* This small restaurant squeezed between buildings offers a haven of peace. Green terrace, trendy cuisine.

⊖⊟ **Le Bosquet** – *Parc floral, Metro Château-de-Vincennes.* ₰*01 43 28 87 15.* Pleasant terrace and buffet; good choice for a savory or sweet snack.

⊖⊟ **L'Heureux Père** – *47 bis bd. Semard.* ₰*01 46 02 09 43. www.lheureuxpere.com. Closed 8–30 Aug, Christmas holidays and public holidays.* The talented chef surprises the palate with unusual associations of flavours. Creole cuisine is a major influence.

⊖⊟⊟ **Le Bonheur de Chine** – *6 allée A.-Maillol, Rueil-Malmaison.* ₰*01 47 49 88 88. www.bonheurdechine.com. Closed Mon.* Chinese restaurant with lavish marble reception area and elegant dining rooms.

⊖⊟⊟ **La Rigadelle** – *23 r. de Montreuil. RER Vincennes.* ₰*01 43 28 04 23. Closed Sun–Mon, 28 July–17 Aug, 20–28 Dec.* Sunny restaurant serving up fresh dishes with an emphasis on seafood and shellfish.

⊖⊟⊟ **Le Garde-Manger** – *21 r. d'Orléans, Saint-Cloud.* ₰*01 46 02 03 66. www.legardemanger.com. Closed Mon on holidays and Sun.* This recently renovated restaurant offers generous bistro cuisine and a tempting wine list.

⊖⊟⊟ **Globe Trotter Café** – *16 pl. de la Défense, 92400 Courbevoie.* ₰*01 55 91 96 96. www.globetrottercafe.com. Open lunch Sun–Wed.* At the heart of La Défense, facing the Grande Arche this restaurant has a large dining room and huge terrace to soak up the atmosphere.

SHOPPING

Porcelaine de Sèvres – *Pl. de la Manufacture, Sèvres.* ₰*01 46 29 2210. www.sevrescitececeramique.fr. Open Wed–Mon 10am–5pm. Closed 25 Dec–1 Jan.* Factory shop selling porcelain and gifts.

Les Quatre Temps – *92400 Courbevoie, access by escalator. Underground parking and access by metro. www.les4temps. com. Open Mon–Sat 10am–8pm, Sun 11am–7pm.* One of the largest shopping centres in Europe with over 250 stores.

ACTIVITIES

Lac Daumesnil – Cyclorama bike rental: *5€/h.* ₰*06 81 34 47 19.* Boat rental: *Hours vary. 12€/h for 1–2 people. 13€/h for 3–4 people.* ₰*01 43 28 19 20.*

≗≗ Cercle hippique du bois de Vincennes– *8 r. de Fontenay. Nogent-sur-Marne.* ₰*01 48 73 01 28, www.chbv. fr. Open daily.* Horseriding centre offering lessons and excursions with poneys and horses.

Guignol (Puppets) – *Parc floral.* ₰*01 49 23 94 37. www.guignolparcfloral.com.* The programme changes weekly.

Hippodrome de Saint-Cloud – *1 r. du Camp-Canadien.* ₰*01 47 71 69 26.* 75 ha (185 acres) racetrack and golf course.

Île-de-France is the vast, fertile region around Paris. Despite a population of just over ten million, most of its residential areas are tightly concentrated, particularly close to the capital, giving much of the region the look and feel of rural countryside with its farms and forests. Hidden among these dense woodlands and ploughed fields are some of the most impressive royal châteaux and ancient abbeys in the country. Within an hour of leaving the French capital, discover medieval villages, charming towns straddling sleepy rivers, and some of the favourite haunts of writers and artists.

Highlights

1 Tour the manufacturing centre at **Peugeot** (p228)

2 Enjoy the horse stunts at **Buffalo Bill's Wild West Show** (p268)

3 Sample the best Brie cheeses in **Meaux** (p277)

4 Go on a romantic candlelit tour of **Vaux-le-Vicomte** (p283)

5 Attend a Gregorian music concert at **Chartres Cathedral** (p324)

The Landscape

Many of the towns in the Île-de-France grew up around the Seine river and its tributaries, such as the Marne, the Oise, the Loing, the Essonne and the Eure. Today, many new towns have been created on the outskirts of the Île-de-France, as regional councils work to maintain the balance of historic monuments and rural industries with much-needed modernisation and development.

Immediately outside Paris, the ring of administrative *départements* known as the Petit Couronne (Little Crown) is home to heavily populated suburbs, international airports and industrial zones. The larger *départements* beyond, called the Grand Couronne (Big Crown), are covered by farmland where a lot of the region's food is still produced, livestock reared and the famous Brie cheeses made. In addition to the more industrialised producers, small family farms can still be found along the country roads, often with signs advertising fresh eggs, free range chickens, or pick-your-own-fruit.

Parks and Forests – At the weekend Parisians often eagerly escape the hustle and bustle of the city to one of several important forests in the area (Fontainebleau, Rambouillet, Auvers-sur-Oise), where you can cycle or hike in the great outdoors. Many of these offer thematic trails allowing you to get better acquainted with the regional flora and fauna, and some, including the Sénart forest, offer a fascinating glimpse into royal hunting traditions.

For fishing, swimming and water sports aficionados, the region offers plenty of natural and man-made bodies of water, including the ponds of the Vallée de la Bièvre, Cergy-Neuville, or the Plage de l'Ile-Adam.

Horse lovers, meanwhile, will find ample opportunities for horseriding lessons, excursions and related activities in dedicated centres such as the Chevreuse regional park and the Fontainebleau forest.

Arts and Culture

Landed gentry and religious devotees weren't the only ones who wished to escape the crowded city: many artists and writers looking for inspiration, peace and quiet, or simply a bit of fresh air, made their home in towns like Barbizon, Moret-sur-Loing, Auvers-sur-Oise, Milly-la-Forêt, Jouy-en-Josas and L'Isle-Adam. Their contributions are remembered in the museums, galleries, and the very landscape of these towns.

The Impressionist Trail – Particularly for fans of the Impressionist movement in painting, Île-de-France is home to many of the scenes painted in works that radically broke with the conventions of the time. From Claude Monet, whose house and gardens in Giverny inspired some of his most iconic paintings, to Edouard Manet, Sisley and Pissarro, who depicted towns bordering the Seine, Oise and Marne rivers in their works, the Impressionist trail is rich and diverse.

Expressionism and Modern Art – Following the Impressionist experiment, Ile de France also served as a cradle for pioneers in Expressionism such as Vincent Van Gogh, who sojourned (and died) in Auvers-sur-Oise; later, the Nabis and Fauvist painters, headed by artists including Maurice Denis and Vlaminck, settled in towns outside Paris and marked the area with their bold, modern creations.

Concerts and festivals – Châteaux such as Versailles, Fontainebleau, Rambouillet and Vaux-le-Vicomte host seasonal festivals of music, dance and open-air theatre, while Chartres Cathedral and the Abbey of Pont-Royal-des-Champs are known for their religious music concerts. Far from the crowds of the capital, these cultural outings are a great way to mingle with the locals as well.

Faience and Fabrics – The region is also noted for its delicate faience ceramics, the speciality of towns such as Montereau and Creil, and for traditional fabric printing methods like the one used for the legendary *toile de Jouy*, made in the town of the same name.

Architecture

Île-de-France offers a remarkable diversity of architectural periods and styles, from dramatic fortified châteaux and moats to Baroque palaces, Belle-Epoque buildings, quiet riverside guinguettes and intriguing avant-garde structures hovering between art and architecture. Excellent examples of medieval architecture include the stunning Gothic cathedral at Chartres and the ruins of the 12C Abbaye de Chaalis. The Classical French style reached its pinnacle with the elegance and pomp of the Vaux-le-Vicompte and Versailles palaces. The Empire style, meanwhile, asserts itself in the still regal but slightly more sober Palais de Fontainebleau.

Entering the 20C, structures such as the Maison de Picassiette near Chartres, featuring mosaics made from 4 million shards of brightly coloured glass, are striking, while recent urban areas such as St-Quentin-en-Yvelines offer numerous examples of interesting buildings and urban planning concepts.

Visiting with Kids

The region is very child-friendly and family activities are fairly easy to come by with some advance planning. Aside from the world-famous Disneyland resort, amusement parks such as Parc Asterix, France Miniature and the Mer de Sable provide just as much stimulation and fun for adults as they do children. It's also easy to enjoy outdoor activities like pony rides, swimming, boating and bike rides in many of the region's parks, forests and waterside leisure centres.

Touring the Region by Car

While most of the major cities and towns in the region are accessible by regional and commuter trains from Paris, taking a driving tour gives you more freedom to explore some of the more remote sites.

Southwest: visit Chartres then Rambouillet with its château, forest and elegant town; side trips can be made to Dampierre, Maintenon and Breteuil châteaux, Montfort-l'Amaury and Port-Royal-des-Champs.

Northwest: Thoiry, Poissy, Malmaison and La Roche-Guyon can all be visited from Auvers-sur-Oise and the charming l'Isle-Adam.

Southeast: Provins and Fontainebleau deserve a full day, with excursions to Vaux-le-Vicomte, Moret-sur-Loing, Barbizon or Milly-la-Forêt worth an extra day trip.

East: Disneyland Paris; add an extra day if you want to visit Meaux and the Château de Ferrières.

West: Bask in the splendour of the Château de Versailles. Add an extra day by venturing to the striking Abbaye de Port-Royal-de-Champs or admire the delicate printed toile de Jouy fabrics in Jouy-en-Josas.

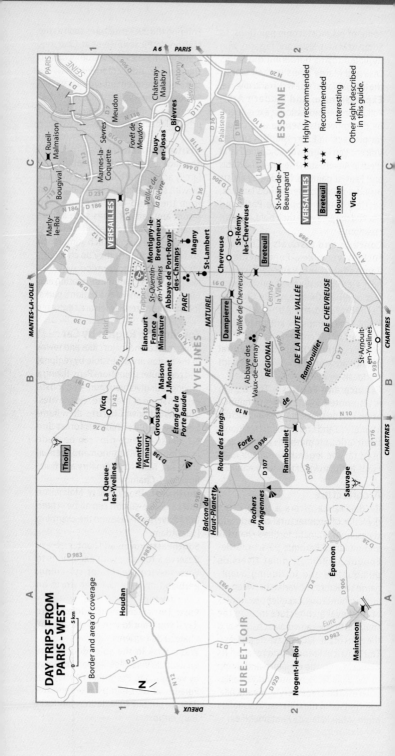

DAY TRIPS FROM PARIS - WEST

0   5 km

Border and area of coverage

N

★★★ Highly recommended
★★ Recommended
★ Interesting
    Other sight described
    in this guide.

VERSAILLES
Breteuil
Houdan
Vicq

Ville de
Versailles★★

The steady stream of visitors to the Château de Versailles too often overlook this charming town. Originally home to palace courtiers, the Royal City has retained a certain austere character, with three avenues converging on the Château, private mansions, imposing churches and narrow cobbled streets.

A BIT OF HISTORY

In 1671, Louis XIV decided that plots of land in Versailles would be granted to those citizens who put in a request, in exchange for a levy of five sous for each arpent (3 194sq m/3 833sq yd). The new buildings had to conform to the rules laid down by the **Service des Bâtiments du Roi**, a building commission answerable to the court. The purpose of these measures was to achieve architectural unity. Moreover, in order that the palace might continue to dominate the area, the roofs of the village houses were not to exceed the height of the Cour de Marbre.

Today very little remains of these 17C buildings. Most of the old town was completed in the 18C, enlarged and renovated in the 19C.

France's defeat in the 1870–71 Franco-Prussian War enabled Versailles to regain its political role as the seat of the French government. The population rose from 40 000 to 150 000 in a matter of days. Ministers, senators and members of the **National Assembly** occupied the palace which also housed the **Banque de France** and other official institutions. A **Salle du Congrès** was built in the middle of the castle's south wing to house the Parliament, but in 1879, the Parliament returned to the capital.

During the 3rd and 4th Republics, presidential elections were held here. And today, when the French Constitution needs to be amended, the Senate and the National Assembly are both required to meet here.

▶ **Population:** 89 490

Michelin Local Map:
p172 C1, 311:1-3, map 101 fold 23 or 106 folds 17, 18.

Info: Office du tourisme de Versailles, 2bis av. de Paris, 78000. ℘01 39 24 88 88. www.versailles-tourisme.com.

Location: From Paris: RER C (Versailles-Rive-Gauche), SNCF rail link from Gare Montparnasse (Versailles-Chantier) or from Gare St-Lazare (Versailles-Rive-Droite).

Versailles today – More than 200 years after the end of absolute monarchy in France, most of the old town dates from the 18C with 19C alterations. Having long suffered from being too close to Paris, Versailles has nevertheless managed to develop its own cultural programme. Many of its beautiful façades have been restored in Quartier St-Louis, for instance. The pedestrianised rue Satory, in the heart of the old town, is lined with antique dealers and cafés.

DISCOVERING VERSAILLES
AROUND THE CHÂTEAU
Place d'Armes★★

This huge square was the junction of three wide avenues leading to Paris, St-Cloud and Sceaux, separated by the **Écuries royales★**, the stables built in 1683. These imposing buildings housed some 600 horses.

Grande Écurie★

To the right of the square as you look towards the Château.
This is where the dressage of saddle horses for the king took place.
Musée des Carosses – *Call for opening times. ℘01 30 83 78 00. www.chateau versailles.fr. Re-opens 2014.*
Various sedan chairs and carriages can be seen (carriages used for Napoléon's wedding, Charles X's coronation, presidential elections, etc.).

Académie du Spectacle équestre★ –
🕐*Only open on certain dates.* 📞*08 92 681 891. www.acadequestre.fr.*
Visitors are treated to dressage or beautifully choreographed equestrian shows.

Petite Écurie
To the left of the square as you look towards the Château.
This was used for carriages and horses. It now houses a school of architecture.

Rue de l'Indépendance-Américaine
In the 18C this street housed buildings occupied by ministries and public services, in particular the **Grand Commun**, built by Mansart in 1684. At no. 5 stands the former **Ministry of the Navy and Foreign Affairs** (1761), fronted by a gate crowned by statues of Peace and War. It was here that an alliance was signed in 1762 between France and the American *insurrectionaries*, preceding the 1783 treaties granting the independence of the United States. Now a public library.

QUARTIER ST-LOUIS★
Rue du Vieux-Versailles, lined with craftsmen's workshops, leads to **rue Satory**: General Hoche's birthplace is at no. 18, near the Petite Écurie where his father took care of the horses; note the fine wrought-iron work (*no visits*). The St-Louis district boasts many **historic mansions** built during the reign of Louis XV, and the Jeu de Paume (*see below*) where the National Assembly took their oath on 20 June 1789.

Cathédrale St-Louis★
Built in 1754 to serve the "Old Versailles" and the Parc aux Cerfs.

Carrés St-Louis
Louis XV gave orders to create a shopping area along the streets named **rue Royale** and **rue d'Anjou** (1755). The **market** features shops with mansard roofs around four small squares.

Salle du Jeu de Paume
🚶*By guided tour only Sat 3pm. Call tourist office on* 📞*01 39 24 88 88 for details.*

This is one of the only remaining courts used to play *Jeu de Paume*, a predecessor of modern lawn tennis.
Built for the Court in 1686, it became famous on 20 June 1789 when the Members of the Tiers État (representing the people) and the lower clergy gathered here after having been excluded from the States General meeting. They vowed to not dissolve the Assembly until the French people a constitution.

Potager du Roi★
10 r. du Mar.-Joffre. 🕐*Open Jan–Mar, Tue and Thu 10am–1pm; Apr–Oct, Tue–Sun 10am–6pm; Nov–Dec, Tue and Thu 10am–6pm, Sat 10am–1pm (guided tours Sat, Sun and holidays at 11am, 2.30pm and 4pm).* 💶*4.50€ (6.50€ Sat–Sun and holidays).* ♿📞*01 39 24 62 62. www.potager-du-roi.fr.*
The King's Vegetable Garden was commissioned by Louis XIV to supply the king's table with fruits and vegetables, many of which have become quite rare. The kitchen garden, now housing the **École nationale supérieure du paysage**, sells produce in an on-site shop. Some 50 different species grow in the plots, surrounded by apple and pear orchards of 130 different varieties.

QUARTIER NOTRE-DAME★
This district features the oldest church in Versailles and houses built under Louis XIV, situated near the marketplace.

Église Notre-Dame★
The church built in rue Dauphine (renamed rue Hoche) by **Jules Hardouin-Mansart** in 1686 was the parish church to the king and his court. The king would attend Solemn Masses here. The Service des Bâtiments du Roi explains why the church has a flattened front flanked by truncated towers.

Hôtel du Baillage
On the corner of r. de la Pourvoirie.
Built by **Gabriel** in 1724, this mansion served as the bailiff's tribunal and municipal prison until it was turned into a residence in 1844.

Rue de la Paroisse leads to the **Marché Notre-Dame**; covered market halls surrounded by picturesque streets.

Musée de la Ville de Versailles - Hôtel Lambinet★

54 bd. de la Reine. ○*Open Sat–Thu 2–6pm.* ○*Closed public holidays.* ○*4€.* ⚹ *01 39 50 30 32.*

The **Hôtel Lambinet** was built in 1750. The atmosphere of an 18C town house has been recreated using period furniture, paintings and sculptures (Pajou, Houdon). The first floor houses a collection dedicated to the Revolution: **Marat**'s murder; **Charlotte de Corday**'s arrest; events in Versailles during 1789 including the Declaration of Human Rights. One room is devoted to the **Manufacture d'armes de Versailles**, created in 1793. A section devoted to **sacred art★** includes works by 19C landscape painter Eugène Isabey.

QUARTIER DE MONTREUIL
Orangerie de Mme Élisabeth

Impasse Champ-Lagarde.

The Orangerie formed part of the estate offered to Mme Élisabeth in 1783 by her brother, Louis XVI. In 1997, it was bought by the region and refurbished to house exhibitions of contemporary art.

QUARTIER DE CLAGNY
Osmothèque - Conservatoire international des parfums

From the château, av. de St-Cloud, turn left down r. de Provence (then r. du Parc-de-Clagny). ⚹ *01 39 55 46 99, www.osmotheque.fr*

This unique institution records existing perfumes, revives classic scents and creates new fragrances. Nearly 2 000 perfumes to discover.

EXCURSIONS
Arboretum de Chèvreloup

▶ *30 rte de Versailles, in Rocquencourt.* ○*Open Apr–mid-Nov Mon, Wed, Sat–Sun and holidays 10am–6pm.* ○*4€.* ⚹ *01 39 55 53 80. chevreloup.mnhn.fr.*

In 1924, land formerly belonging to the Grand Parc (⚹*see PARC DU CHÂTEAU DE VERSAILLES*) was donated to the Natural

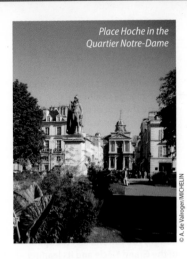

Place Hoche in the Quartier Notre-Dame

© A. de Valroger/MICHELIN

History Museum of Paris and is now home to 2 500 species and varieties. The **Maison de l'arbre** explores tree evolution.

Haras de Jardy

▶ *2km/1.2mi NE along N 182. Leave Versailles by av. de St-Cloud towards Paris.* ⚹ *01 47 01 35 30. www.harasde jardy.com.*

This stud farm forms part of a leisure complex (tennis, golf, horseriding).

ADDRESSES

🛏 STAY

🛏 **Mercure** – *19 r. Ph. de Dangeau.* ⚹*01 39 50 44 10. www.mercure.com. 60 rooms.* ⚺. Located in a quiet neighbourhood with smart rooms.

🛏 **Hôtel Le Versailles** – *7 r. Ste-Anne, Petite Place.* ⚹*01 39 50 64 65. www.hotel-le-versailles.fr. 46 rooms.* ⚺*14€.* Renovated hotel close to château. Spacious, bright and elegant Art Deco style rooms. Cosy lounge and terrace.

🍷 EAT

Place du Marché – This agreeable square is lined with bars, restaurants.

🍽 **Au Chapeau Gris** – *7 r. Hoche.* ⚹*01 39 50 10 81. www.auchapeaugris.com. Closed Tue eve, Wed. Reservations required.* Dating back to the 18C, this is a veritable institution. Quintessential Versailles ambience and appetising cuisine.

Château de
Versailles★★★

Who could predict that a humble hunting lodge would one day become the seat of royal power and the political centre of France, symbol of royal absolutism and one of the greatest achievements of 18C French architecture? The French Revolution and fall of the monarchy could have proved fatal to Versailles. The worst was avoided and today, as night falls over this UNESCO World Heritage site, subtly enhancing its elegant design, you can still feel the spirit of the Grand Siècle and its leading light: Louis XIV, the Sun King.

A BIT OF HISTORY

Louis XIII's hunting lodge – In the 17C, Versailles was the seat of a medieval castle perched on a hillock. At the foot lay the village, surrounded by marshes and woodland abounding in game. **Louis XIII** came hunting here often, and in 1624 bought the lordship of Versailles from the **Gondi family,** commissioning a small château. The castle was completed in 1634.

Taming nature – 1661 marked **Louis XIV**'s accession to power. The King hired the artists, builders, designers and landscape architects who had produced **Vaux-le-Vicomte** and entrusted them with an even more challenging task. Louis was wary of settling in Paris following the Fronde uprisings, and so searched for a site on the outskirts of the capital. He chose **Versailles** as he had spent happy days there as a boy and he was fond of hunting. It was by no means an ideal site – too narrow to allow Louis XIII's château to be enlarged.

An ambitious project – It took 50 years to complete the structural work on the palace. In the early stages (**1662–1668**), alterations were made to the old structure and the gardens to accommodate festivities. During the second building campaign (**1669–1672**), a stone "enve-

Michelin Local Map: p172 C1, 311:1-3, map 101 folds 22, 23 or 106 folds 17, 18.

Location: 18km/11mi west of the capital. From Paris, A 13 motorway toward Rouen (exit Versailles-Château), RER line C (Versailles-Rive-Gauche), SNCF rail link from Gare St-Lazare (Versailles-Rive-Droite) or SNCF rail link from Gare Montparnasse (Versailles-Chantiers). If you plan on enjoying Versailles gardens and Marie-Antoinette's Estate after you have visited the royal apartments, note that a little train departing from the château's North Terrace provides a convenient shuttle service between the palace, both Trianons and the Grand Canal.

Don't Miss: The King's Bedroom, where everyday, Louis XIV would submit himself to the rising and retiring ceremonies in front of the courtiers; the Baroque decor of his parade apartment, a seven-room prestigious enfilade full of allegorical compositions; the unforgettable Hall of Mirrors, which lent splendour to formal receptions and celebrations.

Timing: Versailles is definitely worth a full day's visit, not only for a peek at its refined interior, but also for an overview of the park, with the Trianon Palaces, Marie-Antoinette's Estate and the fabulous gardens.

lope" reminiscent of Italian architecture was built around the old château by **Louis Le Vau,** providing new lodgings for Louis XIV and his immediate circle. **Jules Hardouin-Mansart** was appointed head architect in 1678. This started the most important phase of construction **(1678–1684)**, which gave Versailles its current guise. **Charles Le Brun** supervised a team of painters, sculptors, carvers and interior decorators, while **Le Nôtre** embellished the grounds; when designing the waterworks, he joined forces with the **Francines**, a family of Italian engineers. A last building campaign **(1688–1697)** gave Versailles its final touch: the royal chapel.

It was necessary to build a **hill** to accommodate the length of the new palace (680m/2 230ft). Whole **forests** were transplanted, and the King's gardeners produced 150 000 flowering plants every year.

Water supply was a major concern. The waters of Clagny Pond proved insufficient, and builders were forced to divert the course of the Bièvre and drain the Saclay plateau. The famous **Machine of Marly** conveyed waters pumped from the River Seine.

Life at Court – When the king and entourage moved to Versailles, the palace and adjacent outbuildings were required to lodge at least **3 000 people**. The Fronde movement had been a humiliating experience for the king, who had witnessed many intrigues involving men in high places. Consequently, his main concern was to keep the aristocracy at court, in an attempt to stifle opposition. The lavish entertainments suited his extravagant tastes and served to keep the nobility under his thumb. For the first time in French history, the royal suites in the palace were given fixed, **permanent furnishings**. Thanks to Colbert's efforts to encourage the production of l**uxury goods** (tapestries, furniture, lace etc.) on a national scale, the palace – which remained open to the public – offered a standing exhibition of arts and crafts in France. Strict **etiquette** governed the visits that the French people would pay to Versailles.

Versailles in the 18C – When Louis XIV died in 1715, his successor was a young boy. The Regent **Philippe d'Orléans**

administered the king's affairs from the Palais-Royal in Paris. During this time, the court left Versailles and moved to the **Tuileries**.

In 1722, **Louis XV**, aged 12, settled at Versailles. He dreamed of having the front of the palace remodelled, a task he entrusted to **Jacques-Anges Gabriel**. No major alterations could be carried out owing to insufficient funds, but the **Petit Trianon** was built.

Louis XVI commissioned no major works. He gave Marie-Antoinette the Petit Trianon, completed by Gabriel in 1768, and had the **hamlet** designed for her in 1774. On 6 October 1789, the national insurrection forced the royal family to return to Paris and Versailles ceased to house the kings of France.

To the Glory of France – After the storming of the Tuileries and the fall of the monarchy on 10 August 1792, most of the furniture was removed and auctioned. The major works of art were kept for the art museum which opened at the Louvre in August 1793. After the renovation work undertaken by **Napoleon** and **Louis XVIII**, Versailles was threatened once more. It was spared demolition by **Louis-Philippe**, who turned it into a museum of French history in 1837.

More recently, Versailles was restored following World War I, thanks to generosity from the Academy of Fine Arts and contributions from wealthy patrons. The 1952–1980 period witnessed **restoration projects** such as the Royal Opera, the King's Bedroom and the Hall of Mirrors. Launched in 2003, a renovation project called **Grand Versailles** should be completed in 2020.

THE PALACE AND ITS SURROUNDS★★★

🕐*Open Tue–Sun Apr–Oct 9am–6.30pm; Nov–Mar 9am–5.30pm.* 🎟️*15€ ("Billet Château" including the most famous parts in the palace). Last admission 30min before closing time.* 🕐 *Closed 1 Jan, 1 May, 25 Dec.* 📞*01 30 83 78 00. www.chateauversailles.fr.* ♿*As soon as you arrive, proceed to the"Aile sud des Ministres" to purchase*

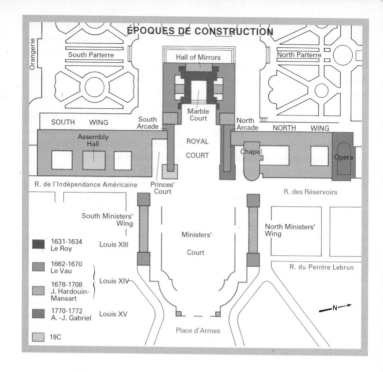

ÉPOQUES DE CONSTRUCTION

Orangerie

South Parterre

Hall of Mirrors

North Parterre

SOUTH WING
South Arcade

Marble Court

North Arcade NORTH WING

Assembly Hall

ROYAL COURT

Chapel

Opera

R. de l'Indépendance Américaine

Princes' Court

R. des Réservoirs

South Ministers' Wing

North Ministers' Wing

Ministers' Court

R. du Peintre Lebrun

1631-1634 Le Roy — Louis XIII

1662-1670 Le Vau

1678-1708 J. Hardouin-Mansart — Louis XIV

1770-1772 A.-J. Gabriel — Louis XV

19C

N →

Place d'Armes

your ticket, then to the visitors' entrance (Door A). If you have your ticket (online ticket sales at www.chateauversailles.fr), proceed directly to Door A.

Commissioned by Louis-Philippe in the 19C, Versailles's emblematic **equestrian statue** of Louis XIV was removed from its original location (near the newly-installed royal gate) in 2006 to undergo restoration. Since June 2009, it stands proudly on the **Place d'Armes**, facing the Avenue de Paris.

Courtyards★★

The wrought-iron railings date from the reign of Louis XVIII. Beyond them are three courtyards.

– The **Cour des Ministres** is flanked by two wings linking four pavilions which accommodated the king's ministers.

– Since 2008, the **Cour royale** is separated from the outer courtyard by a replica of the Baroque-style **royal gate** by Jules Hardouin-Mansart, which had disappeared during the French Revolution. Only persons of high rank could

pass through. The two wings lining this court were first used as outbuildings. They were joined to the main building and fronted by colonnades under Louis XV and Louis XVIII.

– Paved with slabs of black and white marble, the **Cour de Marbre★★** is surrounded by Louis XIII's old château, the façades of which were greatly improved by Louis Le Vau and Jules Hardouin-Mansart. On the first floor of the central pavilion, three windows belonging to the king's bedroom are fronted by a gilded balcony resting upon eight marble columns.

Garden Façade★★★

Walk under the North Arcade, skirt the main building and step back to get a good view of this façade.

The huge building measures 680m/2 230ft in length. The façade has rows of sculpted columns and pillars to break the rigidity of the horizontal lines. The flat, Italian-style roof is concealed by a balustrade.

Statues of Apollo and Diana surmount the central body which housed the Royal

Suite. Certain members of the royal family, including several of the king's children, stayed in the South Wing.

The terrace in front of the château commands an extensive view of the park. It bears two **giant vases★**, one at each end. The one to the north was executed by **Coysevox** and symbolises War, while the south vase, attributed to **Tuby**, represents of Peace.

At the foot of the main building lies a row of four sculptures, the first to be cast by the Keller brothers who drew inspiration from a classical model: Bacchus, Apollo, Antinoüs and Silenus.

The terrace offers a **view★** of the grounds: in the foreground, the Water Gardens (*Parterres d'Eau*), with a sweeping perspective as far as the Grand Canal: on the left, the South Parterre (*Parterre du Midi*); on the right, the North Parterre (*Parterre du Nord*) and groves (*Bosquets du Nord*), cut across by another canal leading to the Neptune Basin.

GRANDS APPARTEMENTS
Grand Appartement du Roi★★★

The king's formal apartment comprises six salons, built by **Le Vau** in 1668 and decorated by **Le Brun**. The apartment was formerly approached from the Royal Court by means of the Ambassadors' Staircase (destroyed in 1752). It provides a splendid example of early Louis XIV decoration.

The Grand Appartement symbolised the solar myth cultivated by Louis XIV. It was generally sparsely furnished. Three times a week, the King held court in the Grand Appartement. The ceremony included dancing and gaming.

Salon d'Hercule★★★ – This drawing room stands on the site formerly occupied by the fourth and penultimate chapel of the original château.

The room boasts two splendid compositions by Veronese. **Christ at the House of Simon the Pharisee★** was a present to Louis XIV from the Venetian Republic. On the ceiling, note the **Apotheosis of Hercules★** by François Lemoyne.

Salon de l'Abondance (a) – On days when Louis XIV held court, this reception

room contained buffets for hot and cold drinks. The walls are hung with winter furnishings in embossed velvet.

Salon de Vénus (b) – The ceiling of this salon and subsequent rooms were painted by Houasse. It features decorated panels framed by heavy gilt stucco.

Salon de Diane (c) – This was a billiard room under Louis XIV. Observe the Baroque **bust of Louis XIV** by Bernini (1665). Also note several paintings by De Lafosse and Blanchard.

Salon de Mars (d) – The lavish decoration shows that this room once belonged to the royal suite (guard-room). Louis XIV later used it for dances, games and concerts. The two galleries housing the musicians were placed on either side of the fireplace. They were dismantled in 1750. One of the Sun King's favourite paintings hangs here: Domenichino's *King David*, in which he is portrayed playing the harp.

Salon de Mercure (e) – It was here that Louis XIV lay in state for one week after his death in 1715.

Salon d'Apollon or Salle du trône (f) – The throne was placed on a central platform covered by a canopy. The king received ambassadors in this chamber. When he held court, it was used for dances and concerts. The ceiling sports a fresco by De Lafosse: *Apollo in a Sun Chariot*. This room marks the end of the king's formal suite.

Salon de la Guerre★

The War Salon is a corner room joining the Hall of Mirrors and the Grands Appartements. it features an oval low-relief sculpture by **Coysevox**, representing the king defeating his enemies.

Galerie des Glaces★★★

The Hall of Mirrors was completed by **Mansart** in 1686. It covered a short-lived terrace (1668–78) that Le Vau built overlooking the gardens. With the Salon de la Guerre and Salon de la Paix, it is **Le Brun's** most brilliant achievement.

17 large windows are echoed by 17 mirrors on the wall opposite. These are made up of 578 large pieces. This hall was designed to catch the golden rays of sunset. The ceiling fresco pays tribute

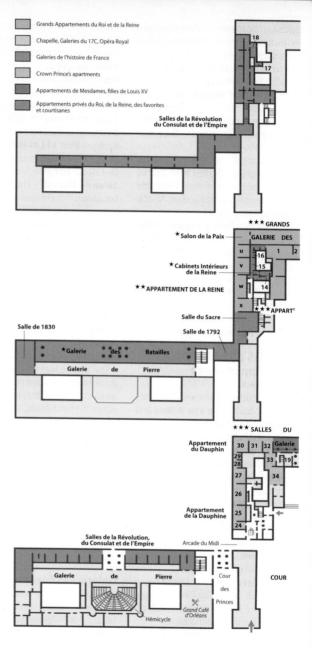

to the early reign of Louis XIV (from 1661 to 1678, up to the Treaty of Nijmegen). The Hall of Mirrors was used for court receptions, ceremonies and diplomatic encounters. On these occasions, the throne was placed under the arch leading into the Salon de la Paix.

It is easier to picture the hall during festivities, thronged with elegant visitors in formal attire, brightly lit by thousands of flickering candles. The tubs bearing the

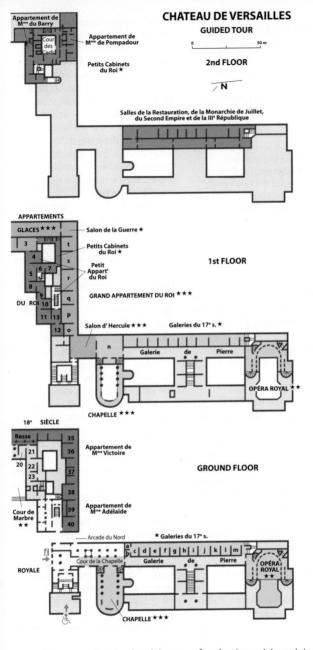

CHATEAU DE VERSAILLES
GUIDED TOUR

0 _____ 50 m

2nd FLOOR

N

Appartement de Mme du Barry

Appartement de Mme de Pompadour

Cour des Cerfs

Petits Cabinets du Roi ★

Salles de la Restauration, de la Monarchie de Juillet, du Second Empire et de la IIIe République

APPARTEMENTS

GLACES ★★★ — Salon de la Guerre ★

Petits Cabinets du Roi ★

1st FLOOR

Petit Appart^t du Roi

GRAND APPARTEMENT DU ROI ★★★

DU ROI

Salon d' Hercule ★★★   Galeries du 17e s. ★

Galerie   de   Pierre

OPÉRA ROYAL ★★

CHAPELLE ★★★

18e SIÈCLE

Basse

Appartement de Mme Victoire

GROUND FLOOR

Appartement de Mme Adélaïde

Cour de Marbre ★★

Arcade du Nord   ★ Galeries du 17e s.

ROYALE   Cour de la Chapelle   Galerie   de   Pierre   OPÉRA ROYAL ★★

CHAPELLE ★★★

orange trees, as well as the chandeliers and other furnishings, were made of solid silver in Louis XIV's time.

In 1980, the Hall of Mirrors was restored to its former glory. With its crystal chandeliers and new set of candelabra – cast after the six surviving originals – it presents the same dazzling appearance as in 1770, when Marie-Antoinette was married to the Dauphin, the future King Louis XVI.

The king's valets

The Sun King had 28 valets who served and assisted him according to a very precise timetable. They were close to him daily and could, if the need arose, request a favour from him. In addition, their office automatically made them members of the aristocracy, exempted them from paying the *taille*, a royal tax and provided them with a substantial income. The best known of the king's valets was **Marie Du Bois** (a man, despite his name), who left a diary, but the most renowned was **Alexandre Bontemps**, a valet for 60 years, whom Louis XIV trusted implicitly.

It was here that the German Empire was proclaimed on 18 January 1871, and that the **Treaty of Versailles** was signed on 28 June 1919.

The central windows offer a splendid **view★★★** of the Grand Perspective.

Salon de la Paix★

Placed at the southern end of the Hall of Mirrors, the Peace Salon counterbalances the War Salon.

Originally designed as an extension of the great gallery, it was made into an annex of the Queen's Suite toward the end of Louis XIV's reign; it communicated with the Hall of Mirrors by means of a movable partition.

Above the mantelpiece hangs *Louis XV Bringing Peace to Europe*, a painting by François Lemoyne.

Appartement du Roi★★★

Louis XIV's more private suite is arranged around the Cour de Marbre. It was designed by **Jules Hardouin-Mansart** and set up in Louis XIII's château between 1682 and 1701. The style shows a marked change in the Louis XIV period. The ceilings are no longer coffered but painted white, the marble tiling has been replaced by white and gold panelling, and large mirrors adorn the stately fireplaces.

The **salle des Gardes** or Guard-Room(1) and a **first antechamber** (2) lead to the a second, most famous antechamber.

Salon de l'Œil-de-Bœuf (3) – The Bulls'-Eye Chamber was originally two rooms: the king's bedchamber between 1684 and 170, and a small study. The two were united by Mansart and Robert de Cotte. Level with the famous bull's-eye is a frieze depicting children at play. Note Coysevox' bust of Louis XIV. It was here that courtiers assembled before witnessing the rising and retiring ceremonies of the king.

Chambre du Roi (4) – This became Louis XIV's formal bedroom in 1701. At the centre of the palace, this bedroom, which looks onto the Cour de Marbre, faces in the direction of the rising sun. Louis XIV, suffering from a gangrenous knee, died here on 1 September 1715. Ritual rising and retiring ceremonies (see sidebar p185) took place in this room from 1701 to 1789.

Daytime visitors were requested to make a small bow when passing in front of the bed, which symbolised the divine right of the monarchy.

The king's bedroom is hung with its summer furnishings of 1722 – Louis XV's second year at the palace. Beyond the beautifully restored gilded balustrade is a raised four-poster bed, complete with canopy and curtains.

Salle du Conseil (5) – This originally consisted of two rooms: the Cabinet des Termes and the Cabinet des Perruques. The decoration of the present room – created under Louis XV – was entrusted to **Gabriel**. The mirrors dating from Louis XIV's reign were replaced with wainscoting by **Rousseau**, who produced a splendid Rococo interior. Over 100 years, many grave decisions affecting the destiny of France were taken here, including that of France's involvement in the **American War of Independence** in 1775.

Grand appartement de la Reine★★

The Queen's suite was originally created for Louis XIV's wife **Marie-Thérèse**, who died here in 1683.

Chambre de la Reine (g) – The bedchamber was later occupied by the wife of the Grand Dauphin, the king's son; by the Duchesse de Bourgogne, wife of the Sun King's grandson; by Marie Leszcynska, wife of Louis XV (for 43 years); and by Louis XVI's wife **Marie-Antoinette**. Nineteen royal children – among them Louis XV and Philippe V of Spain – were born in this bedroom.

Salon des Nobles de la Reine (h) – The official presentations to the queen took place in this former antechamber. It was also here that the queens and dauphins of France used to lie in state prior to the burial ceremony. The original fresco on the ceiling, attributed to Michel Corneille, has been preserved.

The rest of the decoration was considered staid and old-fashioned by Marie-Antoinette, who had it entirely refurbished by the architect **Richard Mique** (1785). It was furnished with commodes and corner cupboards by **Riesener** and embellished with green silk hangings.

Antichambre du Grand Couvert (i) – This chamber was used as a guard-room under Marie-Thérèse. It was here that Louis XV and Marie Leszczynska – and later Louis XVI and Marie-Antoinette – would dine in full view of the public. A family portrait of Marie-Antoinette and her children (1787) by Mme Vigée-Lebrun hangs here.

Salle des gardes de la Reine (j) – The decoration was the work of Le Brun and N Coypel. It was moved from its original setting – the Salon de Jupiter – when the Hall of Mirrors was completed in 1687. The Salon de Jupiter was subsequently renamed the Salon de la Guerre. On 6 October 1789, several of the queen's guards were stabbed to death by a group of dedicated revolutionaries.

Escalier de la Reine – Towards the end of the Ancien Régime, the Queen's Staircase was the official entrance to the royal apartments. The decoration of the staircase is extremely ornate; from the top landing, admire the elegant display of multicoloured marble designed by Le Brun. The huge *trompe-l'œil* painting is jointly attributed to Meusnier, Poerson and Belin de Fontenay.

CHAPELLE, GALERIES DU 17C, OPÉRA ROYAL★★
Chapelle★★★

Only in 1710 was the chapel finished: Louis XIV was 72. Dedicated to **Saint-Louis** (Louis IX), it is an elegant display of stonework in white and gold.

This masterpiece is the work of **Mansart** and, completed by his brother-in-law **Robert de Cotte** in 1710. The pillars and arches bear exquisite bas-reliefs.

The organ stands instead at the east end in the gallery, a splendid piece by **Clicquot**. While the members of the royal family were seated in the gallery, courtiers stood in the nave. The ceiling, showing Hercules entering the Kingdom of the Gods, is by **François Lemoyne**.

Galeries du 17C★

These rooms – occupying the greater part of the north wing – feature a charming selection of paintings and portraits, busts and console tables.

Ground Floor – The vestibule by the chapel leads to this suite of 11 rooms. The first six were once occupied by the Duc de Maine, the son of Louis XIV, while the last four housed the apartments of the Princes of Bourbon-Conti. The series of portraits includes Henri IV, who enjoyed visiting the site of Versailles, and Louis XIII, the founder of the original château.

First Floor – Portraits of the royal family, Mme de Maintenon, Louis XIV's legitimised children and other celebrated figures, painted by Le Brun, Mignard Van der Meulen, Coypel, Rigaud Largillière etc, bring these rooms to life. Note the set of portraits of famous men (Colbert, Racine, Molière, La Fontaine, Le Nôtre and Couperin) and vast battle scenes by Van der Meulen.

Opéra Royal★★

Entirely made of wood, the Royal Opera can seat 700.

Gabriel started work on the Royal Opera House in 1768 and completed it in time for the wedding ceremony of **Marie-Antoinette** and the future **King Louis XVI** in 1770. It was the first oval-shaped opera house in France.

Pajou's decorative work, inspired by classical models, is strikingly modern. Although initially reserved for members of the court, the opera house at Versailles was later used for lavish receptions organised during official visits. Several foreign rulers were received at the palace, including the **King of Sweden** (1784), Marie-Antoinette's brother the **Emperor Joseph II** (1777 and 1781) and **Queen Victoria** (1855). Sessions of the **National Assembly** were held in the Royal Opera between 1871 and 1875. It was here that the **Wallon Amendment** was voted on 30 January 1875, laying the foundations of the Third Republic. The latest restoration was in 1957, marked by a reception honouring **Queen Elizabeth II** and **Prince Philip**.

CROWN PRINCE'S APARTMENTS

The entrance is through the **Salle des Gardes**, decorated with splendid Gobelins tapestries. A second antechamber exhibits portraits of Louis XV's daughters by Nattier.

Chambre du Dauphin (19) – Occupied from 1684, first by Louis XIV's son and then by subsequent heirs to the throne (the last occupant was Louis XVI's son), this has retained its original 1747 decor: wardrobe with lacquered panels (Bernard Van Rysenburgh – BVRB), commode by Boudin and an 18C canopied bed.

Grand Cabinet du Dauphin (20) – This room houses portraits of royal women by Nattier, as well as beautiful furniture by Jacob, taken from Louis XVI's gaming room at St-Cloud. The remarkable globe was commissioned by Louis XVI.

Bibliothèque (21) – The library boasts fine wood panelling in deep amber tones, enhanced by turquoise relief work.

Cabinet Intérieur de la Dauphine (22) – This room features Vernis Martin wainscoting. Note Gaudreaux' commode and a writing desk by Bernard Van Rysenburgh (BVRB). The back rooms were refurbished under Louis XVIII for the Duchesse d'Angoulême, the daughter of Louis XVI.

Chambre de la Dauphine (23) – The bedroom contains a Polish-style bed and a magnificent set of armchairs by Heurtaut. Note Nattier's two portraits of Mme Henriette and Mme Adélaïde, portrayed respectively as Flora and Diana.

Grand Cabinet de la Dauphine (24) – This room evokes the marriage of Marie Leszczynska to Louis XV. It also presents Lemaire's sculpted barometer, offered on the occasion of Marie-Antoinette's marriage to the Dauphin, and several corner cupboards by Bernard Van Rysenburgh (BVRB). If one compares the Savonnerie tapestry with that of the next room, one notices that the fleur-de-lis motifs have been replaced by stars (Revolution).

Deuxième antichambre (25) – The fireplace, adorned with a bust of the Regent, was taken from the Queen's Bedroom at the time of Marie Leszczynska. Savonnerie tapestry.

Première antichambre (26) – This houses a number of pictures representing the rulers who succeeded the Sun King: portrait of the five-year-old Louis XV by Alexis Belle (1723), *Cavalcade of the King (Louis XV) after His Coronation on 22 October 1722* by Pierre-Denis Martin.

APPARTEMENTS DE MESDAMES, FILLES DE LOUIS XV

These were the private suites of Louis XV's two unmarried daughters who lived here until the French Revolution.

Galerie basse – Divided into apartments under Louis XVI and partly restored under Louis-Philippe, the gallery now stands as it did under Louis XIV.

Appartement de Mme Victoire – The Sun King's former bathroom and its two marble piscinae underwent several alterations before being used as the antechamber to this suite, occupied by a daughter of Louis XV.

The **Grand Cabinet (27)** is an exquisite room with a cornice by Verberckt.

Mme Victoire's former **bedroom (28)** has some outstanding furnishings.

Appartement de Mme Adélaïde – These rooms housed the second suite of Mme de Pompadour, who died here in 1764. Mme Adélaïde later moved in. The **Salle des Hocquetons (29)** was an annex adjoining the former Ambassadors' Staircase, destroyed in 1752. The stately proportions of the room allude to how magnificent the flight of stairs once looked. Note the huge **clock★** by Passement and Roque with bronze ornamentation by Germain (1754); it illustrates the world's creation .

APPARTEMENTS PRIVÉS DU ROI, DE LA REINE, DES FAVORITES ET DES COURTISANS★

The private apartments of the king, queen, favourites and courtiers.

Appartement intérieur du Roi

This suite of rooms boasts superb wainscoting by Gabriel.

Chambre à coucher (6) – The absence of furniture makes it difficult to picture this room in its original state. Owing to the constraints of court etiquette, Louis XV and then Louis XVI daily had to leave this room and slip away to the formal bedroom. It was here that Louis XV died of smallpox on 10 May 1774.

Cabinet de la Pendule (7) – This was a games room until 1769. Passemant and Dauthiau's **astronomical clock★★★** was installed here in 1754. A copper line running across the floor indicates the Versailles meridian. In the centre of the room stands the equestrian statue of Louis XV by Vassé. It is a replica of Bouchardon's sculpture which initially adorned place Louis XV – now called place de la Concorde – in Paris and which was destroyed in 1792.

Antichambre des Chiens (8) – A charming passageway off the king's private staircase (known as *degré du Roi*). The decoration features Louis XIV panelling, in sharp contrast to the adjoining rooms.

Salle à manger dite des Retours de chasse (9) – Between 1750 and 1769 hunts were organised every other day in the forests surrounding Versailles. Louis XV and fellow hunters would come here to sup after their exertions.

Cabinet intérieur du Roi (10) – This masterpiece of 18C French ornamental art was commissioned by Louis XV and features stunning Rococo decor. The cel-ebrated **roll-top desk★★★** by Oeben and Riesener (1769) was spared in 1792. The **medal cabinet** is decorated with gilded bronze: it bears the 1783 candelabra commemorating France's role in the American War of Independence.

In 1785 the room was the scene of a formal encounter attended by Marie-Antoinette, at which the king informed **Cardinal de Rohan** that he would shortly be arrested for his involvement in the **Diamond Necklace Affair**.

The Corner Room leads to the study where Louis XV and Louis XVI kept confidential documents on State affairs, and where they granted private audiences.

Cabinet de Mme Adélaïde (11) – This was one of the first "new rooms" commissioned by Louis XV. It overlooks the Royal Court and was designed by Louis XV as a music room for his daughter Mme Adélaïde (1752). It features Rococo wainscoting and gilded panelling embellished with musical instruments, fishing and floral motifs. A young Mozart supposedly performed on the harpsichord before the royal family in this room during the winter of 1763–64.

Bibliothèque de Louis XVI (12) – Designed by the ageing Gabriel, this refined library is a perfect example of the Louis XVI style (1774). The austere bookcases, in which door panels are concealed by a set of false decorative backs, are countered by Chinese motifs on the upholstery and curtains. Next to Riesener's flat-top desk stands the

The rising ceremony

The Sun King was woken up at 7am by his first valet. The first visit he received was that of his **doctor**. Next came the **grandes entrées** (important guests including members of his family and those who held an office), then the **secondes entrées** (less important guests) and finally the **nobility**. **Breakfast** was followed by the **dressing ceremony**, then the king left his apartments to hear **Mass**.

mahogany table where the king spent hours correcting geographical maps.

Salon des Porcelaines (13) – This room was used as the Hunters' Dining Hall under Louis XV and Louis XVI. It houses numerous exhibits of Sèvres porcelain, painted after drawings by Oudry.

Salon des Jeux de Louis XVI (14) – Admire this perfect vignette of 18C furniture and ornamental art: corner cupboards by Riesener (1774), set of chairs by Boulard, curtains and upholstery in crimson and gold brocade.

Cabinets intérieurs de la Reine★

Also called "Appartements de Marie-Antoinette", these cramped interior apartments, looking onto two inner courtyards, were used as a daytime retreat by the queens of France who were not allowed to live anywhere but in their Grands Appartements.

Cabinet doré (15) – Panelling by the **Rousseau brothers** marks the revival of Antique motifs: frieze with rosettes, sphinx, trivets, small censers. A chandelier features among the magnificent bronze works. The commode was made by **Riesener**. Naderman's harp reminds visitors that the queen was an enthusiastic musician.

Bibliothèque (16) – Note the drawer handles shaped like a two-headed eagle, emblem of the House of Hapsburg.

Méridienne (17) – This octagonal boudoir was used for resting by Marie-Antoinette. It was designed in 1781 in honour of the birth of the first dauphin.

Petits cabinets du Roi★

These were originally Louis XV's interior apartments, where he could retire away from it all or receive intimate guests.

Appartement de Mme de Pompadour – This was the first suite occupied by Louis XV's mistress between 1745 and 1750. The Grand Cabinet features splendid carved woodwork by Verberckt.

Appartement de Mme du Barry – The wood panelling has been restored to its original colours. The suite consists of a bathroom, bedroom, library and a corner **drawing room** (18).

Appartements des ducs de Maurepas et Brissac– These apartments were occupied by two ministers of Louis XVI. Most of the furniture was donated by the Duke and Duchess of Windsor.

GALERIES DE L'HISTOIRE DE FRANCE

The collections of paintings and sculptures of the old **Musée de l'Histoire de France** at Versailles was set up by King Louis-Philippe in 1837. The galleries are open to the public. They also feature other galleries, such as the Salles de la **Révolution**, du **Consulat** et de l'**Empire** and the Salles de la **Restauration** and de la **Monarchie de Juillet**, which can only be visited by guided tour. *For more details, call ℘01 30 83 78 00.*

Galerie des batailles★

Created in 1837 in the south wing, this gallery houses the 33 paintings of **France's major victories** under the Ancien Régime, the Empire and the Republic, from Tolbiac *(first on the left when entering)* to Wagram *(first on the right)* by Horace Vernet.

Salle de 1792

This large, unfurnished room lies at the junction of the south wing and the main central pavilion.

Salle de 1830

Commissioned by Louis-Philippe, this room is devoted to the last king of France, known as the 'Citizen-king'.

Salle du sacre

The Coronation Room was used as a chapel between 1676 and 1682. The **Parlement of Paris** once held sessions here. Louis-Philippe altered it to accommodate huge paintings depicting the Emperor's coronation. David's second *Coronation of Napoleon* (1808–1822) lies left of the entrance. The original is exhibited at the Louvre.

Parc du Château de
Versailles★★★

For over a century, Versailles provided Europe with a model of the ideal royal residence. This included its gardens and park, born from the Sun King's determination to transform the marshland surrounding his château into a masterpiece.
The undertaking will forever be associated with André Le Nôtre, whose refined sense of balance between symmetry and fantasy, combined with the skilful play of shadow and light and abundant use of water, created what is perhaps the most beautiful example of 17C landscape architecture.

A BIT OF HISTORY

Versailles was built on top of a small hillock consolidated by vast loads of earth. Before the French Revolution, the park was surrounded by a 43km/27mi-long wall, punctuated by 22 royal gates. Beyond the actual **gardens** of the Château (93ha/230 acres), the Versailles estate once incorporated the **Petit Parc** (including the Grand Canal and the Trianon), and the **Grand Parc**, a vast hunting reserve dotted with villages. Under the Second Empire, the area of the park shrank to around 815ha/2 014 acres. Today, the distance between the palace and its perimeter is about 950m/1 040yd.

THE GARDENS★★★

Open Apr–Oct daily 7am–8.30pm; Nov–Mar 8am–6pm. 8€ entrance fee only required during the Grand Musical Fountain Display season (see Addresses). 01 30 83 78 00. www.chateauversailles.fr.
The terrace and parterres provide a perfect balance to the monumental front of the palace, which screens the town of Versailles. Lower down, the lawns and the Grand Canal cut across the middle of the grounds, creating a sweeping **perspective★★★** that extends into the

- **Michelin Local Map:** p172: C1, 311:1-3, map 101 folds 22, 23 or 106 folds 17, 18.
- **Info:** www.chateau versailles.fr and www.chateauversailles spectacles.fr.
- **Location:** The park lies northwest both of the town of Versailles and the château. If you plan on visiting the royal apartments prior to discovering the park and its major highlights, note that a little train departing from the château's North Terrace provides a convenient shuttle service between the palace, both Trianons and the Grand Canal (see Addresses).
- **Don't Miss:** Walking through Versailles' beautiful gardens to the sound of Baroque music, during the enchanting Grand Musical Fountain Displays (see Addresses); Marie-Antoinette's delicate, bucolic retreat at the Queen's Hamlet.
- **Timing:** If you only have a few hours to spare, treating yourself to a Segway tour of this large park (see Addresses) will enable you get a good overview of it in record time.

distance. Numerous groves and paths are laid out on either side of this central axis. The 300 sculptures which adorn the park make it one of the biggest open-air museums of classical sculpture. In order to return to Le Nôtre's original layout, Versaille's gardeners brought down the chestnut trees lining the Allée royale and replanted this stretch framed by six groves to recreate the decor: clipped box trees, high hornbeam hedges and trellis work.

Gardens outside Château de Versailles

© Timebacker/Dreamstime.com

AXE DU SOLEIL

Below are the major highlights found along the east–west axis of the gardens.

Parterre d'eau★★

The Water Parterres are two huge basins which front the stately palace and constitute a sort of aquatic esplanade where three main perspectives meet: the central view and the lines along the North and South Parterres.

Bassin et parterre de Latone★

The imposing Latona Staircase, flanked by two fountains and a double ramp flanked with yew trees and replicas of antique statues, lead from the Parterre d'Eau to the Bassin de Latone (see below).

The two fountains – Three statues decorate the two fountains (1687), originally called *Combats des animaux* (Animal Combats). Particulary noteworthy, **Le Point du Jour** (1) by Gaspard Marsy, features Dawn with his head crowned by a star, while Desjardins' statue of **L'Heure du Soir★** (2) portrays the hunting goddess Diana.

Bassin de Latone★ – This composition by Marsy was the first marble sculpture in the gardens (1670). It tells the story of Latona, mother of Apollo and Diana, who was showered with insults by the peasants of Lycea and prevented from quenching her thirst. She appealed to Jupiter, the father of her children, who avenged the offence by turning the culprits into aquatic animals. Originally, the statue of Latona looked toward the palace, a clear indication of how the kiing viewed the public or private insults concerning his love life. At the foot of the steps lies the **Nymphe à la coquille** (3), a replica of Coysevox' statue, featuring a nymph with a shell. The original work was moved to the Louvre.

Allée royale

The Royal Walk is run down the middle by the **Tapis Vert**, a stretch of lawn replanted according to Le Nôtre's plans. It is lined with a superb collection of ornamental **vases** and **statues**.

A stroll on the Allée du Midi leads to the **Vénus de Richelieu** (4), sculpted by Le Gros after a bust which featured among the Cardinal Richelieu's collections.

BOSQUETS DU MIDI

You will find below some of the south groves' main sights.

Bosquet de la Girandole

This is one of the oldest groves in Versailles. Its sculptures were commissioned by Nicolas Fouquet for his splendid castle in Vaux-le-Vicomte (see p283).

Bosquet de la Salle de Bal★ (5)

This Ballroom Grove was used as an outdoor theatre for performances or for dancing. It was part of Le Nôtre's original plans and his last creation (1682). Shaped as a circular stage, it is surrounded by gentle slopes, grassy banks and rockeries with small cascades.

Bassins des Saisons

Dedicated to the seasons, four fountains were laid out along paths parallel to the Tapis Vert. Their lead figures were re-gilded and decorated in natural tones. They are *Bacchus or Autumn* (6) by Marsy, *Saturn or Winter* (9) by Girardon, *Flora or Spring* (13) by Tuby, *Ceres or Summer* (14) by Regnaudin.

Bosquet de la Reine (7)

The Queen's Grove (1775) lies on the site of a former maze and was created at the time of the great replanting campaign. In features busts and bronze statues cast after Antique models: Aphrodite, a Fighting Gladiator, etc.

Bassin du Miroir (8)

Of the two fountains circling the Allée royale, the larger one began to silt up and Louis XVIII replaced it by a landscape garden, known as the Jardin du Roi. The only to survive is the Mirror Fountain, adorned handsomely with statues.

Jardin du Roi★

A dazzling sight in summer, when all the flowers are in full bloom, the King's Garden is a welcome change from the formal groves of Versailles.

The Colonnade★★

This grove boasts a peristyle with 32 marble columns, built by **Mansart** in 1685. Note the statue of *Proserpine Ravished by Pluto* attributed to Girardon.

Bassin d'Apollon★

This whole composition, created by Tuby after drawings by Le Brun, portrays Apollo the Sun God seated in his chariot, surrounded by marine monsters, rising from the ocean to bring Light to the Earth. From the Apollo Fountain, an esplanade bordered by statues leads to the Grand Canal.

BOSQUETS DU NORD

The north groves' major highlights are as follows.

Bosquet des Dômes (10)

The Grove of Domes was named after two pavilions crowned by domes which were designed by **Mansart**. They were demolished in 1820. A series of low-relief sculptures adorns the edge of the fountain, representing the weapons used in different countries. It has the elegant touch of Girardon. Among the statues feature two works by Tuby, *Acis* and *Galatea*.

Bosquet de l'Encelade★★ (11)

The realism of this Baroque composition by Marsy contrasts sharply with other groups in the gardens. A head and two arms is all that is visible of the Titan Enceladus, dragged down towards the bowels of the earth by the rocks of Mount Olympus – the same rocks the Titan had hoped to climb to reach the sky (a clear warning to Fouquet).

Bassin de l'Obélisque (12)

Designed by Mansart, this raised fountain is surrounded by a flight of stone steps and several lawns. When the fountains are in operation, the central sculpture lets out a gigantic spray of water which resembles a liquid obelisk.

Bosquet des Bains d'Apollon★★ (15)

Only open during the Grand Musical Fountain Display (see Addresses).
Designed by Hubert Robert in 1776, the Grove of Apollo's Baths heralded the Anglo-Chinese style, later adopted by Marie-Antoinette for the Trianon. On the edge of a lake, an artificial grotto houses the **Apollo Group★**.
Its lush setting is a far cry from the austere 17C Versailles. The Sun God, tired by the day's exertions, is portrayed resting, waited upon by a group of nymphs (Girardon and Regnaudin).

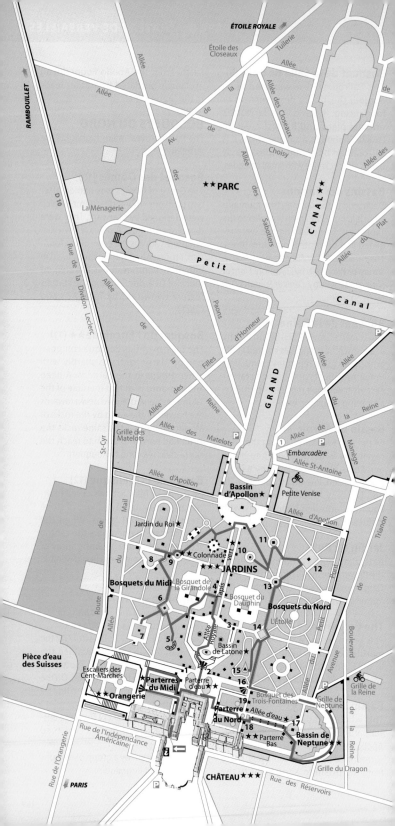

ÉTOILE ROYALE

DOMAINE DE
MARIE-ANTOINETTE ★★

★ Jardins

GRAND
TRIANON ★★

Jardin
du Roi

Glacières

★ Pavillon
Français

Salon Frais

Théâtre de
la Reine

Rocher

Jardin
Français

Chapelle

Belvédère

Orangerie

Grotte

PETIT TRIANON ★★

Ferme

★★ HAMEAU DE
LA REINE

Temple de
l'Amour

Jardin
anglais ★★

Grand
Lac

Tour de Marlborough
et Laiterie

Moulin

Maison de
la Reine

Colombier

Réchauffoir

Porte St-Antoine

Pépinières

Le Trèfle

Chateauneuf

Petite
Étoile

Grand
Carré

Grande
Étoile

Étoile de
la Reine

Étoile des
Ha!! Ha!!

Ha!! Ha!!

Arboretum

national

de Chèvreloup

Le Chesnay

ST-GERMAIN, A13

VERSAILLES

N

PARC DU CHÂTEAU
DE VERSAILLES

0   400 m

SE RESTAURER

Carrefour des Philosophes (16)

Flanked by impressive statues, the Philosophers' Crossroad offers an interesting sideways **view★★** of the palace (*northwest corner*).

BASSINS DE NEPTUNE ET DU DRAGON – ALLÉE D'EAU
Bassin de Neptune★★

The Neptune Fountain was designed by **Le Nôtre**, but acquired its present appearance in 1741, during the reign of Louis XV. It is by far Versailles' largest fountain. Its proportions are extravagant by classical standards, and it extends northwards beyond the rectangle formed by the gardens.

Bassin du Dragon (17)

This allegorical sculpture evoking the victory over deep-sea monsters is an allusion to the crushing of the Fronde Revolt, symbolised by a wounded dragon.

Allée d'Eau★

The Water Walk is a double row of 22 small white-marble fountains bearing bronze groups of three children, each holding pink marble vessels.

PARTERRES – ORANGERIE
Parterre du Nord

The very first royal suite looked out onto the North Parterre, a 'terrace of greenery' created in 1668.

Bassin des Nymphes de Diane (18)

The cascade known as the Bath of Diana's Nymphs is surrounded by fine **low-relief carvings★** by Girardon, which inspired 18C and 19C painters such as Renoir.

Parterre Bas★★

Close to the groves, this terrace is flanked along its northern and western boundaries by bronze statues representing the four Continents, four Poems, four Seasons and four Temperaments. The lead **Pyramid Fountain★** (19), made by Girardon from a study by Le Brun, combines grace with originality: dolphins, crayfish and tritons. At the top

of the steps leading to the Parterres d'Eau, note **Le Rémouleur** (the Knife-grinder), a bronze replica of a Classical statue. Coysevox' **Vénus à la tortue** (Venus on a tortoise), is a bronze cast, also inspired by Antique sculpture.

Parterres du Midi★

The flower beds of the South Parterre, with their vivid blossoms and pretty boxwood patterns, were laid out in front of the queen's apartments.

The terrace running along the Orangery offers a good **view★** of the octagonal **Pièce d'Eau des Suisses**. Designed to embellish the north–south axis of the gardens, the 700m/2 275ft-long Swiss Ornamental Lake was named after the Swiss guards who built it in 1678.

Orangerie★★

One of **Mansart**'s creations (1684), the south-facing Orangerie has retained its original double glazing. It extends south by means of two corner pavilions set at right angles which support the colossal **Escalier des Cent-Marches**, a flight of 100 steps.

At the time of Louis XIV, the Orangerie housed 3 000 rare trees in tubs; 2 000 of these were orange trees. The Orangerie looks splendid during the summer season, when its 1 055 orange trees, palm trees, oleanders and others are brought outside and arranged around the restored flower beds.

THE PARK★★

🕐*Open Apr–Oct daily 7am–8.30pm; Nov–Mar 8am–6pm.* 🚗*No charge for pedestrians; 4.50€/5.50€ car (restricted parking areas; access from bd. de la Reine or Grille St-Antoine). 📞01 30 83 78 00. www.chateauversailles.fr.*

Grand Canal★★

Built from 1668 to 1679, the Grand Canal was designed by **Le Nôtre** in the shape of a large cross: the long canal is 1 670m/5 480ft long by 62m/204ft wide; the shorter one measures 1 070m/ 3 500ft long by 80m/263ft wide. Years ago, the 1 872 trees lining the Grand Canal were clipped back to a height of

15m/49ft in order to return to the initial perspective.

DOMAINE DE MARIE-ANTOINETTE★★

🕐 *Open Apr–Oct Tue–Sun noon–6.30pm; Nov–Mar Tue–Sun noon–5.30pm.* 💳 *10€. Ticket includes access to both Trianon Palaces, the Queen's Hamlet, the French and English Gardens, the French Pavilion, the Temple of Love and the Belvedere.* ✆ *01 30 83 78 00. www.chateauversailles.fr.*

Formed by the **Petit Trianon** and its **gardens** and **hamlet**, the area called Marie-Antoinette's Estate underwent intensive renovations and reopened in 1996, restored to its original arrangements. This is where Louis XVI's wife would retire, away from the Court's rigorous etiquette, injecting her own distinctive taste and theatrical whimsy into the place.

PETIT TRIANON★★

Louis XV's love of gardening and farming prompted construction of the Petit Trianon. **Gabriel** completed the project in 1768, shortly before Louis XV's reign ended. Mme de Pompadour, the woman behind the project, never saw the château. Louis XVI gave the Petit Trianon to his wife **Marie-Antoinette** in 1774. The queen often came here with her children and sister-in-law, relieved to escape the pomp and intrigue of Versailles.

Exterior – Overlooking the formal gardens, the somewhat austere façade facing the courtyard shows a transition from the Rococo style to the more sober Neoclassic style in the latter half of the 18C. Four regularly spaced columns are crowned by a balustrade; two fine flights of steps lead to the gardens.

Interior – This masterpiece of the Louis XVI style offers many highlights. Among these, Guibert's craftsmanship is particularly evident in the superb **panelling★★** of the dining room and drawing room. In the dining room, decor includes fruit, flower and foliage motifs against a pale green background. The drawing room, partly refurnished by

Empress Eugénie in the 19C, houses one of **Riesener**'s greatest achievements, the famous astronomical writing desk (1771).

The **queen's apartment** at the Trianon shows Marie Antoinette's intense need for privacy: the boudoir was fitted with mirrored panels that could be easily turned to automatically obscure the interior from view.

GARDENS AND HAMLET★★
Pavillon français★

Built in 1750 by Gabriel for Louis XV and Mme de Pompadour, this pavilion houses a circular room, boudoir and kitchen. Note the cornice and frieze representing farm animals raised on the estate. The pavilion is surrounded by **French gardens**.

Orangerie de Jussieu

Louis XV commissioned **Claude Richard** to design this experimental greenhouse (1759) which was entrusted to the famous botanist **Bernard de Jussieu**.

Petit théâtre de Marie-Antoinette

As the queen loved acting, a small theatre, accommodating a hundred spectators, was designed for her by **Mique** in

---

"Ten thousand trees for Versailles"

The park was severely damaged by storms, which hit the Île-de-France region in December 1999. Thousands of trees, particularly old, tall ones, were brought down. However, the devastating action of the storm had one very positive effect: the renovation programme launched in 1990 was brought forward with the invaluable help of numerous patrons, among them Americans, Koreans, Canadians and a whole village in Switzerland. And today, quite a few sections of the park have been restored to their original condition.

1780. The machinery used for the scenery changes has survived.

Hameau de la Reine★★

Reminiscent of a Norman village, this bucolic composition, which forms the Queen's Hamlet, was built in 1783.
The grounds around the lake (Grand Lac) are dotted with pretty cottages featuring cob walls and thatched or tiled roofs: the **Queen's House**, the Boudoir, the Malborough Tower, the Mill, the Warming Room, the Refreshments Dairy, the Dovecote, the Guards' Room, and last but not least, the Farm, the products of which actually supplied Versailles' kitchens.

Jardin anglais★★

In 1774, Louis XV's former **botanical garden** was torn up to make room for this English Garden.
Created between 1777 and 1787 by **Richard Mique** and painter **Hubert Robert**, this succession of artificial landscape scenes includes the Belvedere (a bandstand with statues by Deschamps), the Rock and the Grotto (affording pleasant garden views) and the **Temple of Love**, a Neoclassical marble building housing a replica of Bouchardon's *Cupid cutting his bow from the Club of Hercules*.

GRAND TRIANON★★

Known as the **Trianon de Porcelaine**, the first pavilion (1670) built on this site, faced with blue-and-white Delft tiling, was a secluded meeting place for Louis XIV and his favourite, Mme de Montespan. When she fell from favour, the pavilion was dismantled in 1687. In six months, **Jules Hardouin-Mansart** completed the **Trianon de Marbre**, built by Louis XIV for the royal family.

Château★★

This "pink marble and porphyry palace with delightful gardens", as Mansart described it, is widely regarded as the most refined set of buildings within the compound.
Walk past the low railings and enter the semicircular courtyard to discover two buildings with a flat terrace roof, joined by a **peristyle**.

Interior – The austere interior decoration has changed little since the days of Louis XIV. The apartments were occupied by **Napoleon**, **Louis-Philippe** and their families. The furniture is either Empire, Restoration or Louis-Philippe, and the paintings are by 17C French artists. Here are just a few highlights. In the left pavilion, the **Salon des Glaces** was used as a council chamber. Admire the splendid Empire furniture and lavish silk hangings, rewoven according to the pattern ordered by Marie-Antoinette. The **bedroom** contains the bed Napoléon commissioned for his apartments at the Tuileries.
The right-wing **reception rooms** were remodelled by Louis-Philippe. The salons are enhanced by a collection of 17C mythological paintings. The **Salon des Malachites** owes its name to various objects encrusted with malachite given to Napoléon by Tsar Alexander I.
The north-facing **drawing room** houses paintings representing the early days of Versailles. The two filing cabinets (1810) and console table (1806) were made by Jacob Desmalter from a drawing by Charles Percier. The **Salon des Sources**, used by Napoléon as a topographical study, leads to the Imperial suite.
The **Galerie des Cotelle★** houses a precious collection of 21 paintings by Cotelle. They offer a vivid picture of the palace and its grounds at the time of Louis XIV. The Empire chandeliers were manufactured in the town of Le Creusot. At the end of the gallery, the **Salon des Jardins** features a fine set of chairs from the Château de Meudon.

Gardens★

These derive their charm from the simple displays of flower beds. Some of the flowers in fashion during the 17C-18C have been reintroduced. The terrace of the **Jardin Bas** or Lower Gardens (**20**) commands a good view of the **Bassin Bas** or Lower Basin (**21**), which is reached via a horseshoe staircase, and of the Grand Canal beyond, seen from the side. Beyond the *parterres* lies a wood featuring fine avenues, rows of trees and several small ponds. The only sculpture with a mythological theme is Mansart's **Buffet d'Eau (22)**, a fountain completed in 1703.

Skirt **Trianon-sous-Bois** and walk through what was once the King's private garden, flanked by two pavilions that housed the apartments of Mme de Maintenon and Louis XIV toward the end of the Sun King's reign.

ADDRESSES

⏉/EAT

🍴🍴 **La Flotille** – *Parc du Château de Versailles.* 🖉*01 39 51 41 58. www.la flotille.fr. Closed evenings except during evening events. Reservations required Sun.* On the edge of the Grand Canal, in the château's park, this small, late 19C house is brightened by a glass roof. This establishment offers three options: restaurant, brasserie and tearoom. The food is unremarkable, but the summer terrace is utterly delightful!

FOUNTAIN DISPLAYS

🍂 You may purchase your ticket for either of the following events on the day you come *(at the entrance of the Gardens)* or in advance, by using the online reservation service. *www.chateauversaillesspectacles.fr.* 🖉*01 30 83 78 89.*

Les Grandes Eaux musicales – *Apr– end Oct, Sat–Sun and holidays (except 1 May), 11am– noon, 3.30pm–5.30pm; end May–end Jun, Tue 11am– noon, 2.30pm– 4pm; check website for other dates. 8.50€.* The Grand Musical Fountain Display takes the spectator back to the magical fountains and groves of 17C Versailles, accompanied by Baroque music. As soon as the Bassin de Latone fountain begins gushing, follow the map without dawdling, and make sure not to miss the *bosquets* (groves) that are only open for these events, especially La Salle de Bal and the Bosquet d'Apollon (invisible from the alleys). The end – and climax – of the show *(at 5.20pm, lasting 10min)* takes place in the Bassin de Neptune and the Bassin du Dragon: 99 jets, one reaching 28m/92ft high.

Les Grandes Eaux nocturnes – *End Jun–mid-Aug, Sat 9pm–11.30pm. 23€.* On summer evenings, visitors can enjoy the enchanting sight of musical fountains and illuminated groves and terraces. Beautiful fireworks over the Grand Canal add a stunning final touch to the Grand Evening Fountain Display.

A DIFFERENT VIEW OF VERSAILLES

Petits trains de Versailles – *Daily year round. Schedules and frequency of trains vary depending on the season: from 10am at the earliest to 6.15pm at the latest, every 10 to 25min. Optional audio commentary. 6.70€ round trip (children 11–18 5.20€). Free for children under 11. These tickets are not valid for Versailles visits.* 🖉*01 39 54 22 00, www.train-versailles.com.* From the château's North Terrace, this little train takes you to the **Petit Trianon** *(from, there, you can walk to the Queen's Hamlet)*, to the **Grand Trianon** and the **Grand Canal.** This 5km/3.1mi tour lasts 50min. You may get off at any stop and take the next train with the same ticket.

Bicycle rentals – *Parc du Château de Versailles.* 🖉*01 39 66 97 66, www. versailles-tourisme.com/activites-ludiques. Open daily (weather permitting) Feb–Nov 10am–5.30pm to 7pm (depending on the season). 6.50€ (1hr), 15€ (4hr), 17€ (8hr).* There are three rental points within the park: Petite Venise, Grille St-Antoine (on boulevard St-Antoine) and Grille de la Reine (on Boulevard de la Reine).

Grand Canal Boat rentals – *Parc du Château de Versailles.* 🖉*01 39 66 97 66. Open daily Mar–Nov 10am (at the earliest) –7.30pm (at the latest); opening hours vary depending on the season. 15€ (1hr) or 11€ (30min) for 4-person boats.* Rental point near La Flotille restaurant.

Segway Tours – 🖉*01 78 52 54 00, www.versaillesevents.fr. Open daily, 10am–6pm. Call for prices. Reservations required 24hrs in advance.* What about using this self-balancing electric vehicle for an original guided tour of the royal park? It will allow you to see its major highlights, including the gardens and Marie-Antoinette's Estate, in record time!

Jouy-en-Josas

With its tidy houses and elegant estates, this town was once favoured by writer Victor Hugo. His stay here inspired the writing of *Olympio*. Former French President Léon Blum and bacteriologist Albert Calmette, who discovered the tuberculosis vaccine, are buried here. But the town is most famous for its *toile de Jouy* fabrics.

- ▶ **Population:** 8 055
- **Michelin Local Map:** p172: C1 or map 106 fold 30.
- **Info:** 29 bis av. Jean-Jaurès, 78350 Jouy-en-Josas. ℘01 39 56 62 69. www.jouy-en-josas.fr.
- **Location:** 6km/3.7mi SE of Versailles.
- **Parking:** Limited parking in town centre *(fee)*.
- **Don't Miss:** The Musée Français de la Photographie.
- **Timing:** Allow an hour or so for each museum.

A BIT OF HISTORY
A textile centre

In the 17C, printed cotton was largely imported from India. In 1760, **Christophe-Philippe Oberkampf** founded his first textile workshop, specialising in printed calico known as *toile de Jouy*. In 1783 the factory became the Royal Works, and business prospered. The manufacturer employed up to 1 300 workers. However, the Napoleonic wars, invasions and competition dealt a deathblow. In 1843 the company declared bankruptcy; the factory was demolished 20 years later.

SIGHTS
Musée de la Toile de Jouy★

54 r. Charles-de-Gaulle. ⏱*Open Tue–Sun 11am–6pm.* ⊛*7€.* ♿ ℘*01 39 56 48 64.* www.museedelatoiledejouy.fr. The museum is housed in the 19C Château de l'Églantine. Ground-floor displays explain the techniques used to make the famous fabrics. Copper plates and cylinders or blocks of wood were used to print the patterns. The Salon d'Oberkampf has been reconstructed with waxwork figures, Jouy hangings and family portraits. The first floor showcases 18C and 19C dresses, shawls and panels.

Église Saint-Martin

11 r. Bonnard. ⏱*Open daily 9am–6pm, except during services.* ℘*01 39 56 42 64.* http://jouysm-catholique-yvelines.cef.fr. The oldest vestiges date to the 13C, but by the 15C the church fell into ruin after the Hundred Years' War and Plague. It

was rebuilt in 1549. In 1960 some elements were restored. Don't miss the gorgeous 17C marble statue of St. Sébastien.

Maison de Jeanne et Léon Blum

4 r. Léon-Blum. ⏱*Open May–Jun and Sep–Oct Sun 2–5pm.* ⊛*3.80€.* ℘*01 39 20 11 11.* The former French president lived here from 1945 until his death in 1950 with his wife Jeanne (whom he married in 1943 in Buchenwald concentration camp). Documents recall Blum's early days, literary works and his role in French Socialist politics and current affairs. The main room houses his writing desk and collection of books.

EXCURSIONS
Maison littéraire de Victor Hugo

45 r. de Vauboyen. ⟿*Guided tours Mar–Nov, Sat–Sun 2.30–6.30pm.* ⊛*4€.* ♿ ℘*01 69 41 82 84.* www.maison litterairedevictorhugo.net. The museum founded in 1991 has been restored to its original romantic style and houses mementoes of the writer: letters written by Hugo and his contemporaries, drafts, annotated proofs of *Les Misérables* and *Les Contemplations* and photos.

Musée Français de la Photographie★

78 r. de Paris, in the direction of Le Petit Clamart. ⏰Open Wed–Sun 1.30–5.30pm. ⏰Closed public holidays. ⊜3€. ✆01 69 35 16 50. www.museedelaphoto.fr.

This museum dedicated to photography houses some 15 000 items, including 300 Kodak cameras, and about a million photographs. Exhibits range from Da Vinci's studies to the latest technology. The discoveries of Nicéphore Niepce, who took the first photograph in 1816, are explained in detail.

The museum explores the quest for technical advancement, including large-format cameras, which are masterpieces of cabinetmaking and leatherwork. The first aerial photograph was taken in 1858 by Félix Tournachon from a hot-air balloon over Bièvres. A stele at the intersection of RN 118 and A 86 recalls his achievement. Every June, Bièvres hosts a renowned photography fair.

BIÈVRE RIVER VALLEY

The river, once populated with beavers, takes its name from the Gallic word brebos.

🚶 The GR 11 winds for 50km (31mi) from Neauphle-le-Château to Sceaux. It passes through the Bièvre valley and crosses forestland. Heading up the river on the Jouy road, you'll pass by the porte de Jouy, a guardhouse of the 17C royal hunting estate. Further on, note the **aqueduc de Buc**: an aqueduct built in 1684 to supply water to the Château de Versailles. After crossing the town of Buc, you'll reach the Geneste pond (reserved for fishing). Three other ponds are reserved for fishing and sailing.

SAINT-QUENTIN-EN-YVELINES

The new agglomeration St-Quentin-en-Yvelines is an example of urban art and planning in the latter half of the 20C.

La Ville Nouveau

The "new city" comprises of seven towns linked by simultaneous urban planning efforts.

Élancourt

This town boasts a lively pedestrian shopping zone and library with brick belfry.

Montigny-le-Bretonneux

On the place Georges-Pompidou stands a modern theatre by Stanislas Fiszer.

Réserve naturelle de l'étang de St-Quentin

Maison de la réserve. Rd-pt Éric-Tabarly. RD 912. ⏰Closed public holidays. ✆01 30 16 44 40, www.basedeloisirs78.fr.

This 90ha/222acre natural reserve east of the St-Quentin pond harbours several species of nesting and migratory birds, including snipes and grebes.

Musée de la Ville

Quai François-Truffaut. ⏰Open Wed–Sat 2–6pm. ⏰Closed mid-July–end of Aug. ⊜Free. ✆01 34 52 28 80. www.museedelaville.sqy.fr.

This museum boasts an eclectic collection with themes as diverse as urban design, feminist art and skateboarding. It also offers guided tours of the city, allowing visitors to appreciate the area's history, architecture, etc.

FRANCE MINIATURE★

Bd. André-Malraux. 78990 Élancourt. ⏰Open daily Mar–Aug, 10am–6pm (7pm Jul-Sep); Sep–Nov Wed, Thu, weekends and holidays. ⊜19.50–20.50€ (4–14 years 13.50–14.50€). ✆08 26 302 040 (0.15€/min). www.franceminiature.com.

Much like Gulliver stumbling on Lilliput in the famed tale by Jonathan Swift, visitors at this amusement park dedicated to the world of miniatures find themselves in a strange land. Climb to the top of the Alps (9m/30ft high), where a panoramic view of France awaits, reduced to 5ha/12.3acre and representing 158 important sites at a scale of 1/30, including the Eiffel Tower, Mont St-Michel and the Château de Versailles.

Abbaye de
Port-Royal-
des-Champs★

Little remains of this famous abbey, which was the scene of a major religious dispute for more than 100 years.

A BIT OF HISTORY
An Abbess aged eleven

In 1204 a Cistercian convent was founded in Porrois, a town later known as Port-Royal. Although this order was supposed to be strict, the rules grew extremely lax over a period of five centuries and by the turn of the 17C, the ten nuns and six novices who resided at the abbey were leading a most unsaintly life; the cloisters had become a promenade, fasting was a bygone practice and the vows of poverty were hardly compatible with the entertaining carried out at the abbey, including Carnival celebrations. In 1602 **Angélique Arnauld**, the 11-year-old daughter of an influential family of lawyers was passed off as 17-years-old and appointed Abbess of Port-Royal.

Racine at Port-Royal

Poet and classical playwright Jean Racine (1639–99) lived at Port-Royal from age 16 to 19. He was taught Greek, Latin, French versification, diction and rhetoric. The French poet soon became an outstanding reader. Louis XIV was spellbound by his beautiful voice.

🔲 A 7km/4.3mi footpath dedicated to Racine starts from the Granges de Port-Royal, with his poems about the natural beauty of the area inscribed on panels along the way. The path crosses the D 91, runs through the hamlet of La Lorioterie, past the Fauveau mill, then across the Roi de Rome and Madeleine crossroads and ends at the church in Chevreuse.

🔵 **Michelin Local Map:** 311:1-3, p172: BC 2, map 101 fold 22 or 106 fold 29.
🔲 **Info:** ☎01 30 43 74 93. www.port-royal-des-champs.eu.

A reformer without mercy

Recovering from a bout of ill health, Mother Angélique began a series of reforms at the convent, reinstating the enclosure and imposing Cistercian rule, meditation and manual labour. From 1648 the growing community split its time between Port-Royal-des-Champs and Paris.

Theological battles

Over the course of the 17C, Port-Royal-des-Champs became a hotbed of theological controversy as the 'Petites Ecoles' at the abbey produced some of the greatest minds of the day, promoting **Jansenism** to the great indignation of the Jesuits. The monastery buildings were razed to the ground in 1710 by order of Louis XIV. Ongoing renovations have restored several buildings, the orchards and meadows.

RUINS AND MUSEUMS
Musée national de Port-Royal des Champs

🕐*Open Nov–Mar, Wed–Fri, Mon 10am–noon, 2–5.30pm, Sat–Sun 10.30am–6pm; Apr–Oct, Wed–Fri, Mon 10.30am–12.30pm, 2–6pm, Sat–Sun 10.30am–6.30pm* 🕐*Closed 21 Dec–4 Jan.* ✆*4.50€. No charge for visitors under 25 on 1st Sun of month.* ☎*01 39 30 72 72. www.port-royal-des-champs.eu.*

A tour of the Port-Royal estate comprises a visit to the abbey ruins and the park, followed by the former Petites Ecoles building situated higher up, on a plateau, which now houses the Musée de Port-Royal des Champs.

Starting at the **site of the ruined abbey,** avenues of lime tree, victims of the great storm of 1999, once marked the site of the former cloisters. The graveyard where the Cistercian nuns were buried after 1204 has been planted with grass. The church adjoined the cloisters. When the building was demolished, the original floor level and pillar bases were revealed, which now provide an outline of the building. An oratory was built on the site of the choir in 1891. Next, visit the dovecote, a 17C barn housing a collection of paintings, engravings and memorabilia.

La ferme des Granges lies above the valley on the north side screened by trees, and connected to the abbey by the **Hundred Stairs**. The **Petites écoles**, built by the Solitaires to provide religious education in 1651–1652, presents a suitably austere front. A Louis XIII-style wing was added in the 19C. It now houses France's smallest national museum, **Musée de l'Abbaye**. Most of the rooms have been restored and contain books, engravings and drawings on the history of the abbey and

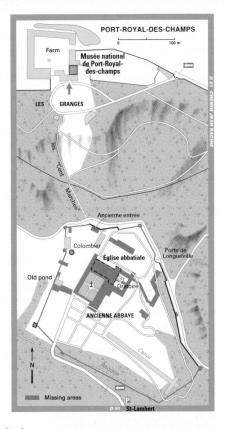

PORT-ROYAL-DES-CHAMPS

the Jansenist movement. The display also features the death mask of a former abbess, Angélique Arnauld.

The exhibition dedicated to Philippe de Champaigne (two paintings, *Ecce Homo* and *Mater Dolorosa*) reminds visitors of the strong ties that linked this painter to the abbey.

Since the beginning of the 21C, the museum has begun restoring the gardens, including an orchard planted by the Solitaires in front of the logis, where they lived. The orchard features rare and traditional tree species, such as pear trees.

Blaise Pascal came to the abbey on a retreat to write his *Mystery of Jesus* in 1655. His knowledge of mathematics proved useful at the abbey when he produced calculations for a new winch for the well: this enabled the nuns to draw a huge bucket as big as nine ordinary buckets, from a depth of 60m/197ft.

Musée National des Granges de Port-Royal

© S. Sauvignier/MICHELIN

Chevreuse

Capital of the Haute-Vallée de Chevreuse regional nature park, this pretty town is situated on the edge of the Essonne department. Dominated by an impressive fortified château, Chevreuse has retained a village-like charm, centred around the delightful place des Halles.

SIGHTS
Église St-Martin

Direct access to car park by narrow covered passageway of the priory, beginning at the central crossing. Enter to the right.

The interior of this church boasts a remarkable ambulatory chancel. Fragments of stained glass dating to the 16C grace the apse. The organs were built in 1732, and feature a tribune decorated with 18C panelling. The lovely stairway leading to the tribune dates to the 15C. Nearby, admire the ruins of the prieuré St-Saturnin, edifice dating to the 11C.

Promenade des Petits-Ponts

Taking a walk alongside the banks of the Yvette river, you'll see small bridges which once led to tanneries and artisanal mills.

These attest to the goat-skin tannery industry which once thrived here and gave its name to Chevreuse ("chèvre" means goat in French).

A haunt for Jean Racine

Playwright and poet Jean Racine (1639-1699) sojourned in Chevreuse in 1661 and found it intensely boring. To remedy this, he often holed up at the **Cabaret de Lys** – the house still stands at no. 3 r. Lalande (plaque).

From Chevreuse, the poet enjoyed walking through the woods to Port-Royal. *For details of the walk, see Abbaye de PORT-ROYAL-DES-CHAMPS.*

▶ **Population:** 5 809.

Michelin Local Map: 172: C2.

Info: Tourist Office- Pl. de Luynes. ✆01 30 52 02 27 or www.chevreuse.fr/office-de-tourisme.aspx.

Location: 28 km (17 miles) SW of Paris on N 118 to Christ de Saclay, then D306 and D 906. RER B St-Rémy-lès-Chevreuse, then bus 39.

Timing: Allow at least a half-day.

Château de la Madeleine

Accessible by car by departing from no. 30, r. de la Porte-de-Paris, then by following the steep street marked with an arrow. Open Mar–Oct, Wed–Sat, 2–5.30pm, Sun and public holidays 10am–6pm; Nov–Mar, Wed–Sun, 2–5.30pm.

Erected between the 11C and 15C, this château, which belonged notably to the feudal lords of Chevreuse, Louis XIV and the Duke of Luynes, has been restored following a period of deterioration. Today, four of six original towers remain. The rectangular 11C keep was remodelled in the 18C, adding a two-sided roof that gives it the appearance of a chapel from afar. The west tower remains crowned with machiolations. In the basement, a chronological frieze traces the history of the château.

EXCURSIONS
St-Rémy-lès-Chevreuse

▷ *2km/1.2mi E of Chevreuse on the D 906 and D 938.*

Château de Coubertin

Open mid-Sept–mid-Nov: call ahead for more info. ✆01 30 85 69 89. www.fondation-coubertin.asso.fr.

This 17C château houses the **Coubertin Foundation**, open to the public only for temporary exhibitions and during 'Heritage Days'. An ideal opportunity to explore the park and its lovely sculptures.

Château de
Dampierre★★

The château is closely associated with two distinguished families, the Luynes and the Chevreuse, who still own it today. From 1675 to 1683 Jules Hardouin-Mansart rebuilt the Château de Dampierre for Colbert's son-in-law the Duke of Chevreuse, a former student at Port-Royal and the mentor of the Duke of Burgundy. The castle and its park, laid out by Le Nôtre, form one of the rare well-preserved estates close to Paris.

- **Michelin Local Map:** p172: B2, map 101 fold 31 or 106 fold 29.
- **Info:** ℰ01 30 52 53 24. www.chateau-de-dampierre.fr.
- **Location:** Situated in the narrow upper part of the Chevreuse Valley, 43.4km/27mi southwest of Paris; accessible by the A 12.
- **Timing:** You should allow half a day to get the best out of your visit.

VISIT
Château★★

Open Apr–Sep Mon–Sat 11am–6.30pm; Sun, public holidays 11am–noon, 2–6.30pm. 12.50€; grounds only, 9€. ℰ01 30 52 53 24. www.chateau-de-dampierre.fr.

The main body of the château, surrounded by a moat, opens onto a courtyard flanked by stables and outbuildings. In front of it are two buildings with arcades. The pinkish tones of the brick harmonise with the sober stone string courses and columns, contrasting sharply with the darker hues of the park.

On the ground floor, visitors can admire Cavelier's statue of Penelope (1848) in the hall leading to the drawing rooms embellished with Louis XV wainscoting, the suite occupied by Marie Leszczynska, and an imposing dining room decorated with Louis XIV panelling.

The first floor houses the **Royal Suite**, which accommodated Louis XIV, Louis XV and Louis XVI. The splendid 17C and 18C furnishings are beautifully preserved and reminiscent of the king's suite at Versailles. Note the furniture, portraits, wainscoting, medallions and overdoor panels by old masters.

The most amazing achievement lies at the top of the great staircase.

The Salle de la Minerve is a formal reception room dating from the 19C when the castle was restored by Duban. Ingres was commissioned to paint a fresco representing the Golden Age; it was never completed. The Duc Honoré de Luynes, who conceived the whole project, ordered a colourful 3m/9.8ft statue of Minerva, a miniature replica of the legendary gold and ivory goddess of the Parthenon executed by Phidias in the 5C BC.

Park★

A walk round the castle starting from the right will lead you to a large ornamental pond, a favourite spot of many anglers. Water is omnipresent in this vast romantic park: canals, fountains and waterfalls embellish the green open space in the heart of the forest, in the middle of the picturesque Chevreuse Valley. The park and the castle form one of the rare protected estates near the capital.

EXCURSION
Vaux de Cernay

4km/2.5mi S by D 91 to Cernay-la-Ville, then right onto D 24

The road weaves up the wooded narrow valley, past a restaurant and across a brook by a mill, Moulin des Roches.

Park near the Chalet des Cascades.

Étang de Cernay

30min–2hr.

The pond was created by the monks of the local abbey to stock fish. A memorial to the 19C landscape painter Léon-Germain Pelouse stands at the top of the embankment, near a stately oak tree. The walk may be continued for another 30min or 1hr by following the wide path, which veers right and leads straight up to the wooded plateau. From the edge of the plateau turn back, bear right and return along the cliff path that skirts the promontory.

Abbaye des Vaux-de-Cernay★

Now a hotel, the abbey was founded in the early 12C. It came under Cistercian rule and reached its heyday in the 13C, but in the 14C it suffered from epidemics of plague and successive wars and slipped into decline. In 1791 it was abandoned by its last 12 monks and sold. The Rothschild family who bought the abbey in 1873 restored and preserved it until World War II. The ruins of the abbey church include a late-12C **façade** with rose window, as well as the monk's building, now a concert hall.

Château de
Breteuil★★

Owned by the Le Tonnelier de Breteuil family since 1712, Breteuil is one of the most charming châteaux in the Île-de-France region. The estate boasts fine architecture and furniture, souvenirs of a family of famous diplomats, a pleasant park and – a special treat for children – an exhibit dedicated to well-known fairytale characters.

VISIT

Open daily 2.30–6.30pm. *Guided tours (last visit 5.30pm). Grounds open at 10am. 15.50€ (chateau, gardens and storytelling). Gardens and storytelling session only: 9.90€ (children over 4, 8.90€). 01 30 52 05 02. www.breteuil.fr.*

ADDRESSES

STAY

Abbaye des Vaux de Cernay – *78720 Cernay-la-Ville, 2.5km/1.5mi W. 01 34 85 23 00. www.abbayedecernay.com. 57 rooms. 18€. Restaurant.* To fall asleep in the superb Cistercian abbey and awake to the monastic quietude of its magnificent park is heavenly! The spacious rooms are a successful blend of modern comfort and antique furniture. The restaurant serves traditional cuisine and offers a buffet lunch on Sundays and public holidays.

EAT

Salon de Musique - *West of Cernay via the D 24, Cernay-la-Ville 01 34 85 23 00.* Make the most of the abbey and park by stopping off for tea, a herbal infusion or coffee in the vaulted splendour of a former cellar fronted by an airy terrace.

Michelin Map: p172: BC2.

Info: 01 30 52 05 02. www.breteuil.fr.

Location: 43 km from Paris on N 118 or pont de Sèvres ; exit Saclay, follow D 306 and D 906 toward Chevreuse.

Timing: Allow 2–3 hours to visit.

The château is built in the Louis XIII style in brick and stone. It consists of a main building flanked by two low wings.

On the first floor, waxwork figures bring to life a few historical events. Louis XVI is shown with Louis-Auguste de Breteuil and Marie-Antoinette, signing the arrest warrant for the Cardinal de Rohan who was implicated in the affair of the Queen's necklace.

In the smoking room, the figures represent Henri de Breteuil, Gambetta and the future Edward VII laying down the basis of the Entente Cordiale in 1881.

A Renaissance in French-Style Gardens

Henri Duchêne (1841-1902) was one of the pioneering figures in the renaissance of French classical gardening techniques. After earning an engineering degree from the Arts et Métiers in Paris, he began working for the city. He next turned to the study of parks and gardens for private clients. While the fashion at the time was to partially or entirely overhaul the landscape, Henri Duchêne looked back to traditional techniques, ordering the gardens according to the layout of the house. His son Achille would join him in his efforts and the two men went on to become a household name. They produced a total of over 6 000 parks and gardens around the world, including those of 480 grand estates, such as Vaux-le-Vicomte, Champs, Courances, Le Marais and Breteuil, to name but a few.

The château's most outstanding exhibit remains the **Teschen table★★★**, inlaid with stones, gems and petrified wood, given to Louis-Auguste de Breteuil (1730–1807) by Empress Maria Teresa of Austria after successfully mediating the Treaty of Teschen (1779), which put an end to a serious regional conflict between the Empire and Prussia.

👥 Service Quarters

The kids will love it! Special rooms dedicated to the beloved fairytales of Charles Perrault, from Little Red Riding Hood to Puss in Boots, have been set up in outbuildings known as 'Les Communs'. To reach these, follow the boot icon on the path to the stables, laundry quarters, hunting lodges and labyrinth. Here, fantasy-inspired scenes await – *Sleeping Beauty, Bluebeard* and *Cinderella*. A

storyteller brings the tales to life each Sun at 4.30pm *(in French only; dates vary: call ahead for more info)*. The medieval dovecote at the château houses numerous temporary exhibits year-round.

👥 The Park★★

The 75ha/185-acre park, where deer roam freely, provides beautiful views and diverse landscapes. Near the château are the **formal French gardens**, created by the Duchênes (father and son) in accordance with Le Nôtre's principles. They include a lake, 16C dovecote, statues and topiary. The **Princes' Garden** harbours flowering cherries, roses and peonies. A box **maze** occupies one of the terraces of the orangery. Two ponds lower down offer an ideal setting for a romantic stroll.

Château de Breteuil

© Arnaud Chicurel/hemis.fr

Rambouillet★

With its stunning château, park and forest, Rambouillet is one of the most coveted sights in Île-de-France. Since 1883 it has been the official summer residence of the President of the French Republic. Distinguished guests include Nelson Mandela (South Africa, July 1996), Boris Yeltsin (Russia, October 1995), George H. W. Bush (United States, July 1991) and Mikhail Gorbachev (USSR, October 1990).

CHÂTEAU

Guided tours (30min). Open Wed–Mon 10am–11am, 2–4pm (Apr–Sept 5pm). Closed during presidential visits. 8.50€; no charge first Sun in the month from Oct–May. 01 34 83 00 25. www.chateau-rambouillet. monuments-nationaux.fr.

Leave from place de la Libération, the site of the town hall *(if the car park is full, leave the car in the Château's park)*.

The château is triangular in shape: this is due to Napoleon dismantling the left wing. The large round tower, where François I is believed to have died, belonged to the 14C fortress. It is difficult to distinguish because of the numerous additions made by the Comte de Toulouse. The façades are essentially 19C.

Mezzanine

The reception rooms commissioned by the Comte de Toulouse are embellished with superb Rococo **wainscoting★**. Note the charming boudoir designed for the Comte's wife.

> **Population:** 25 661
> **Michelin Local Map:** p172: B2 or map 106 fold 28.
> **Info:** Hôtel de Ville, pl. de la Libération, 78120 Rambouillet. 01 34 83 21 21. www.rambouillet-tourisme.fr.
> **Location:** 53km/33mi SW of Paris, via the A 13 and A 12. Access from Paris: SNCF rail link from Gare Montparnasse.
> **Parking:** Near the château or on the place Jeanne d'Arc (charge).
> **Don't Miss:** Visit the deer observation points in the Forêt des Cerfs.
> **Kids:** Espace Rambouillet, shows. The toy train collection (Musée Rambolitrain).
> **Timing:** The château itself will not take more than an hour.

The corridor adjoining the François I tower leads through to the Imperial bathroom suite, adorned with Pompeian frescoes. This opens onto the Emperor's Bedchamber, where he spent the night of 29 June 1815, and the study. It was in the dining room – the former ball-room – that Charles X signed the abdication document. The view of the park is stunning.

International meetings in Rambouillet

Let to various persons after the abdication of Charles X, Rambouillet Château came back into State ownership on the fall of the Second Empire. In 1897, it became one of the official country residences of the presidents of the Republic. De Gaulle organised hunting parties on the estate. On the initiative of Valéry Giscard d'Estaing, the château was the venue of the first summit meeting of industrialised countries, which began as an informal get-together of six western heads of state. More recently, the Rambouillet conference of March 1999 attempted to find a solution to the Kosovo problem, unfortunately without success.

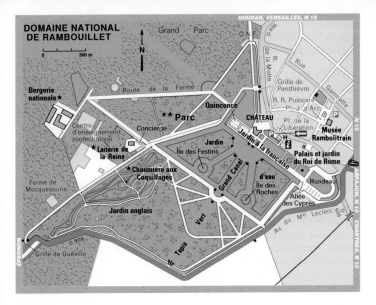

DOMAINE NATIONAL
DE RAMBOUILLET

PARK★

🕐*Open daily Apr–Sep 8am–7.30pm (Oct–Mar 5pm).* ♿ 🕿*01 34 83 00 25.*
The château is set in a pleasant park, renowned for the variety of its gardens remodelled throughout the 17C and 18C. These remodellings reflect the evolution of taste during that period, from the formal parterres to the winding alleyways lined with exotic trees.

Jardin à la française

Walking back towards the château, pass through the 'petit bosquet' (small copse), the 'miroir' (mirror) and the 'grand bosquet' (large copse) forming a French-style garden.

Quinconce

This quincunx, situated to the east of the château and created in 1710, comprises a group of lime trees from Holland planted according to a chequered pattern known as a 'quinconce'. In its centre stands *La Barque* solaire, a bronze sculpture by Karel, inaugurated in 1993.

Jardin à l'anglaise

In 1779, Hubert Robert designed an English-style garden beyond the green carpet of lawn. It is essentially planted with exotic species. The **Grotte des Amants** (Lovers' grotto) was named after a couple of lovers who took refuge inside during a thunderstorm. Canals crisscross the park, forming small islands: Île des Festins, Îles des Roches, etc. 18C follies are scattered among the greenery.

Chaumière des Coquillages★

🕐*Open same hours as château.* 🕿*01 34 83 00 25. www.chateau-rambouillet. monuments-nationaux.fr.*
The **landscape garden** in the park features a charming cottage built for the Princesse de Lamballe. The walls of the rooms are encrusted with a variety of sea shells, chips of marble and mother-of-pearl. A small boudoir with painted panelling adjoins the main room.

Laiterie de la Reine★

🕐*Open same hours as château.* 🕿*01 34 83 00 25, www.chateau-rambouillet. monuments-nationaux.fr.*
Louis XVI had the dairy built in 1785 to amuse his wife Marie-Antoinette. The small sandstone pavilion resembling a neo-Classical temple consists of two rooms. The first – which houses the actual dairy – features marble paving and a marble table from the First Empire.
The room at the back was designed as an artificial grotto adorned with luxuriant

vegetation. It includes a marble composition by Pierre Julien depicting a nymph and the she-goat Amalthea (1787).

ADDITIONAL SIGHTS
Palais du Roi de Rome
🕐 *Open during exhibitions only: Wed–Sun 2–6pm. Park open Mon–Sat 2–6pm, Sun 10am–2pm, 2–6pm.* ✆ *01 34 83 10 31. www.rambouillet-tourisme.fr.*

This mansion was first built in 1784 on the orders of Louis XVI and rebuilt in 1813 at the request of Napoleon, who intended to give it to his son, the King of Rome. It was only very briefly used before he left for Austria with his mother, Maria-Louise. The right wing stages themed exhibitions. The garden was restored to its original layout in 1991.

Musée du Jeu de l'Oie
⚲ *Currently closed for restoration: call for opening date.* ✆ *2.50€.* ✆ *01 30 88 73 73. www.ot-rambouillet.fr.*

The left wing houses Pierre Dietsch's collection including 80 games of snakes and ladders dating 17C–20C.

Jardin
🕐 *Open daily 2–7pm.*

Laid out according to its original plan, this romantic garden covering 5 000sq m/ 5 980sq yd contains a stele erected in memory of the "young king of Rome".

🚹🚼 Musée Rambolitrain
4 pl. Jeanne-d'Arc. 🕐 *Open Wed–Sun 10am–noon, 2–5.30pm.* 🕐 *Closed 1 Jan, 25 Dec.* ✆ *3.50€.* ✆ *01 34 83 15 93. www.rambolitrain.com.*

An astounding collection of more than 4 000 toy trains and models explains the history of the railway from its early beginnings to the present day.

Bergerie Nationale★
🕐 *Open Wed and Sat–Sun 2–5.30pm.* 🕐 *Closed 24 Dec–mid-Jan.* ✆ *5.50€.* ♿ ✆ *01 61 08 68 00. www.bergerie nationale.educagri.fr.*

In 1785, Louis XVI added Spanish merino sheep, Angora goats and Swiss cows to his experimental farm to produce wool. The sheep buildings were completed during the Second Empire.

Forêt de
Rambouillet★

This vast forest has some delightful footpaths for those who enjoy walking, as well as 60km/37mi of cycle tracks, 20 or more lakes with picturesque banks, and villages with historic houses. The forest is home to a thriving game population.

A BIT OF HISTORY
Rambouillet is part of the ancient Yveline Forest, which in Gallo-Roman times stretched as far as the outskirts of Nogent-le-Roi, Houdan, Cernay-la-Ville and Etampes. A large part of it is now included in the Parc Naturel Régional de la Haute Vallée de Chevreuse.

Of the total 20 000ha/49 421 acres, 14 000ha/34 595 acres are state owned.

- 🚲 **Michelin Local Map:** p172: A1 to B2 or map 106 fold 28.
- 🛈 **Info:** Hôtel de Ville, pl. de la Libération, 78120 Rambouillet. ✆ 01 34 83 21 21.
- ▶ **Location:** 53km/33mi SW of the centre of Paris, Rambouillet is reached via the A 13 and A 12. Access from Paris: SNCF rail link from Gare Montparnasse.
- 🚹 **Kids:** Espace Rambouillet.
- 🕐 **Timing:** 1 day.

They cover a clay plateau with an altitude of between 110m/358ft and 180m/585ft, crisscrossed by sandy valleys. In the Middle Ages, wide-scale deforestation took place and the vast clearances now divide

Forêt de Rambouillet

© Jean-Luc Bohin/age fotostock

it into three main areas of woodland: St-Léger and Rambouillet itself, the most popular areas with tourists situated north of Rambouillet, and Yvelines to the south, which is more divided up into private estates.

Flora and fauna

The forest around Rambouillet is damper and has more rivers, lakes and ponds than the one at Fontainebleau. It has long been well stocked with game such as deer, roe-deer and wild boar – and it remains so today.

VISIT
Espace Rambouillet

Open Apr, Jul–Oct daily 10am–6pm (Sat–Sun 6.30pm); May–Jun 9.30am–6pm (Sat–Sun 6.30pm); Feb–Mar, Nov, Tue–Sun 10am–5pm. 17€ (children 14€). 01 34 83 05 00. www.onf.fr/espaceramb. Visitor centre 500m/540yd SW of the Rambouillet-Clairefontaine road (D 27).

This 250ha/625-acre wildlife park has been divided into various areas (binoculars are recommended):

Forêt des Cerfs, where observation hides provide a view of deer, stags and wild oxen.

Forêt Sauvage, a 180ha/450-acre site in which the animals roam free.

Forêt des Aigles, with more than 100 birds of prey in aviaries. Free flight shows.

Coin des Fourmis, where young children can get acquainted with these industrious insects (ants).

HIKES AND TOURS

The **GR 1** trail runs through the forest from north to south between Montfort-l'Amaury and Rambouillet. The **GR 22** trail runs northwest/southwest from Gambaiseuil to St-Léger-en-Yvelines.

Rochers d'Angennes

8.5km/5.3mi from Rambouillet via D 936 then D 107. Leave from the parking area of the 'Zone de Silence des Rabières'. Walk 100m/110yd through the village up the steeper slope of the valley to find the path leading to the summit.

Go past an arena-shaped shelf to reach the crest: **view** of the Guesle Valley and Angennes Lake, bordered by reeds and other aquatic plants.

Balcon du Haut-Planet★

12km/7.4mi from Rambouillet along D 936 to Carrefour du Haut-Planet, then turn right onto the unsurfaced road which crosses rough, hilly ground and leave your vehicle in the car park at La Croix Pater.

After passing the Blue Fountain spring on the right, the lane reaches a terrace on the plateau's edge, revealing a panorama: the **view** extends north across the Vesgre Valley and the Château du Planet.

Route des Étangs

8km/5mi from Rambouillet along N 10 then D 191 to St-Hubert; leave car near the Étang de St-Hubert. For information on regulations for pond fishing, contact the Fédération des Yvelines pour la Pêche et la Protection du Milieu Aquatique. 01 34 77 58 90.

4hr there and back.

The ponds were part of Vauban's projects to create reservoirs for Versailles. Six ponds separated by paths was laid out near the **Étangs de Hollande**. Only the two end basins are filled with water. In summer, the ponds offer **swimming** and **fishing** facilities.

Head west from St-Hubert, follow the Corbet forest track, cross the Villarceau alleyway; walk to the Petites-Yvelines crossroads then the Malmaison crossroads. Turn left towards the Bourg-

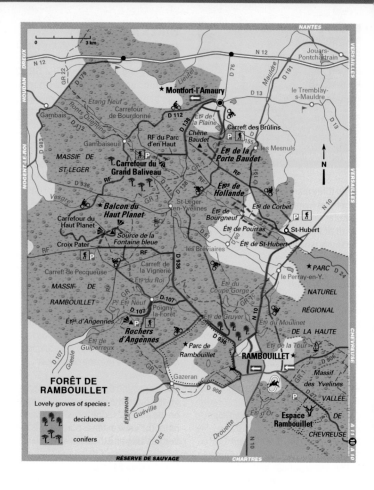

neuf crossroads and, to the southeast, the Route des Étangs, skirting the **Bourgneuf** pond. Follow D 60 to the **Corbet** pond. Walk past the sluice-gate which separates it from the **Pourras** pond and skirt the Pourras woods to Croix Vaudin. A path on the left runs through the woods to the Pont Napoléon; on the right lies the **St-Hubert** pond. This leads back to the Corbet forest track.

Carrefour du Grand Baliveau

8km/5mi from Montfort-l'Amaury via D 138. At the crossroads, follow the path to the right of the panel marked 'Route forestière du Parc-d'en-Haut'. 30min there and back.

The path offers a walk through a lovely green glade. One of the clearings affords a good **view**★ of a secluded valley.

Étang de la Porte Baudet ou des Maurus

4km/2.5mi from Montfort by D 112 and D 13: go past the turning to Gambais (right) and turn left on r. du Vert-Galant. Follow the plateau along the road. Starting point: parking des Brûlins; 45min there and back.

This is one of the forêt's finest sites; farther on, Route Belsédène then Route Goron lead (1km/0.6mi) to Chêne Baudet, a splendid 550-year-old oak tree with an impressive girth.

Maintenon★

This charming town on the banks of the River Eure is renowned for its château, irrevocably linked to the incredible destiny of **Françoise d'Aubigné**. Born in 1635 to a family with Calvinist views, she was orphaned at the age of 12, became the widow of the burlesque poet Paul Scarron at the age of 25, the clandestine governess of Mme de Montespan's children by the age of 34 and, in a secret ceremony, the wife of Louis XIV at the age of 48.

▶ **Population:** 4 427
Michelin Local Map: p172: A2 or map 106 fold 26.
Info: Mairie, pl. Aristide-Briand, 28130 Maintenon. ☎02 37 23 05 04. www.mairie-maintenon.fr.
Location: 80km/50mi from Paris, along the A 10. Access from Paris: SNCF rail link from Gare Montparnasse.
Timing: Allow 1–2hr to visit the château.

A BIT OF HISTORY

When her clandestine charge, the Duc de Maine, was legitimised, Françoise Scarron made a public appearance at court. Thereafter Louis XIV, who was extremely fond of his son, would visit with her every day. Initially, he found her a trifle pedantic, but soon revised his opinion of 'the Scarron widow' and succumbed to her charm, intelligence and strong temperament.

After the queen's death, Louis XIV secretly married Mme de Maintenon in the winter of 1683–1684. The morganatic queen acceded to the rank of peer and marquise in 1688 and from then on she became an extremely powerful figure in the country's political life.

VISIT
Château★

Open Apr–Jun Wed–Mon 10.30am–6pm; Jul–Aug daily 10.30am–6pm; Sep Wed–Fri, Mon 2pm–5pm, Sat–Sun 10.30am–6pm; Oct–Nov Wed–Mon 2pm–5pm. 7.50€ (children 3€). ☎02 37 23 00 09. www.chateaudemaintenon.fr.

The present château occupies the site of a former stronghold, circled by the waters of the Eure. The construction work was undertaken by Jean Cottereau, Minister of Finance to Louis XII, François I and Henri II, and completed around 1509 in the Renaissance style.

The estate passed to the d'Angennes family until Louis XIV bought it In 1674 and gave it to the future Marquise de Maintenon. The Marquise left it to her niece, who was married to the Duke of Ayen, son of the first Maréchal de Noailles. The château has remained in the family ever since.

The archway flanked by two protruding turrets and bearing Jean Cottereau's coat of arms (three lizards) leads to the inner court which is the starting-point for tours. The square 12C keep is all that remains of the original stronghold.

The adjoining wing was built by Mme de Maintenon and the narrow door in the tower still sports the Marquise's emblem, a griffin's head. A door depicting St Michael and bearing the lizard emblem gives onto a staircase leads to Mme de Maintenon's suite, consisting of a bedroom – where Charles X spent the night on 3 August 1830 when he fled Rambouillet – and antechamber.

After leaving the central building, visitors are shown round the first floor of the Renaissance wing, redesigned to accommodate the apartments of Mme de Montespan and her royal charges.

In the Portrait Gallery, a collection of paintings represents the illustrious members of the family.

EXCURSIONS
👤👤 Réserve zoologique de Sauvage

▶ 1km/0.6mi from Émancé via r. de la Fontaine-aux-Graviers. Open Nov–Mar Sat–Sun 10am–5pm; Mar–Oct daily 10am–5pm ☎01 34 94 00 94.

The Drouette valley harbours the châ-teau, built under Louis XIII and reno-vated in the 19C. Its 40ha/90acre Eng-lish-style park dominated by oak trees features antelope, kangaroos and deer.

Épernon

▶ *6 km/3.7mi NW of Émancé on D 176.*
Take a long walk in the old town, whose serpentine streets zigzag on the hillside: here you'll see numerous 15C half-tim-bered houses.

Remarkable both for its location and its architectural coherence, the **church** of Epernon mostly dates to the 16C, although some elements can be traced to the 13C, including the arc of the chan-cel. The 16C nave rests on octognal pil-lars which lack capitals.

The modern plaster vaulting was destroyed by a bomb in WW II; resto-ration artists were able to reconstitute the 16C painted wood panelling of the principal vaulting and the aisles.

Nogent-le-Roi

▶ *8km/5 mi NE of Maintenon along the D 983.*
This town owes its name to a defunct royal chateau where Philippe Auguste and Saint Louis often paid visits.

From the south car park, enjoy an inter-esting view of the **Église St-Sulpice** and its chevet, propped up with flying but-tresses and transept dating to the late 15C. The church edifice is dominated to the east by a heavy 17C clock tower. St-Sulpice was once part of a fortress built along a natural moat.

Enter via the transept door, surmounted by crenellations. Inside, the windows are designed in Flamboyant style. The simple nave comprises two bays and is decorated with wood vaulting reproduc-ing the Renaissance rib vault keystone. Looking out from the facade, Epernon boasts a series of **wood houses** dating to the same period as the church. The house located on the corner of rue du Marché-à-la-Volaille is particularly interesting.

ADDRESSES

⑲ EAT

◉◉ **Le Petit Marché**– *2 bis pl. Omer et Noé-Sadorge. Closed mid-Feb–mid-Mar, Sun eve. (Nov-Mar).* ℘*02 37 23 17 38.* Friendly eatery serving bistro-style cuisine, including meat specialities. Generous portions served in a dining room with a view on the open kitchen.

Montfort-l'Amaury★

This historic town, now an elegant holiday resort, is built on a hill dominated by castle ruins. Before the French Revolution, Montfort was an important town enjoying far more power than nearby Rambouillet. Composer Maurice Ravel and Jean Monnet, co-founder of the European Union, were among the town's distinguished residents.

A BIT OF HISTORY

The district was fortified in the 11C by Amaury de Montfort. The most famous descendant of this illustrious family was

▶ **Population:** 3 076
⑥ **Michelin Local Map:** p172: B1 or map 106 north of folds 27, 28.
🅩 **Info:** 6 r. Amaury, 78490 Montfort-l'Amaury. ℘01 34 86 87 96. www.ville-montfort-l-amaury.fr.
▶ **Location:** 48km/30mi almost due west of Paris, via the A 12/N 12.

Simon IV, leader of the Albigensian Cru-sade against the Cathars of Languedoc. In 1312 the marriage of the Breton Duke Arthur to one of the Montfort daugh-ters made this citadel a part of Brittany.

When Anne of Brittany, Comtesse de Montfort married Charles VIII and then Louis XII, Montfort-l'Amaury became a French fief. The duchy became Crown property after the accession of Henri II.

SIGHTS
Église St-Pierre★

www.st-pierre-montfort-l-amaury.fr.
The rebuilding of the church was commissioned by Anne of Brittany in the late 15C; work continued through the 17C. Observe the gargoyles that adorn the walls of the apse and the high flying buttresses supporting the chancel. The pretty doorway on the south front bears medallions portraying benefactors André de Foix and his wife. The interior features a superb set of Renaissance **stained-glass windows★**.

Ancien charnier

This old cemetery is enclosed within an arcaded gallery surmounted by splendid timbered roofing in the shape of an upturned ship. These galleries were intended to receive the bones of the dead when there was a lack of space in the graveyard.

Castle ruins

Take the narrow road to the hilltop. Ivy-covered walls are all that remain of the 11C keep. The stone and brick turret belonged to the building commissioned by Anne of Brittany. The summit offers a good **view★** of the town.

Musée Maurice-Ravel★

5 r. Maurice-Ravel. Guided tours by reservation only, Sat–Sun, 10am, 11am, 2.30pm, 3.30pm, 4.30pm. 7.30€. 01 34 86 00 89. www.ville-montfort-l-amaury.fr.
In 1920 French composer **Ravel** bought a tiny villa in Montfort. It was in this house that he wrote most of his music: *L'Enfant et les Sortilèges*, *Boléro*, etc. The interior decoration has remained intact. Exhibits include the composer's piano, gramophone and mementoes.
Jardin zen – The tiny garden was relaid in the Japanese style, boasting bamboos and azaleas, irises and small trees.

Ancien charnier

© S. Sauvignier/MICHELIN

EXCURSIONS
Maison Jean-Monnet (Centre d'information sur l'Europe)

▶*In Houjarray, 4.5km/3mi E of Montfort via D 13.* ⊙*Open Mon–Fri 10am–5pm, Sat 1–6pm, Sun and public holidays 10am–6pm.* 01 34 86 12 43. www.ajmonnet.eu.
Economist and diplomat Jean Monnet (1888–1979) bought this country retreat in 1945; it has a thatched roof and garden.

Maison Louis Carré

▶*Continue on D 13 to Bazoches-sur-Guyonne. 2, ch. du St-Sacrement.* ⊙*Open Mar–Nov, weekends 2–6pm by reservation.* Guided tours every hour (until 5pm) by reservation only. 15€. 01 34 86 79 63. www.maisonlouiscarre.fr.
Collector and gallery owner Louis Carré commissioned Finnish architect Alvaar Alto to build this beautiful villa in 1959.

Houdan★

▶*18km/11mi W of Monfort on the N12.*
Office du tourisme – *4 pl. de la Tour, Houdan.* 01 30 59 53 86.
Houdan boasts a charming village centre dominated by a 12C keep, as well as many rustic old houses and a church with a rare organ dating from 1582.

Château et Parc de
Thoiry★★

Thoiry is a vast estate comprising a large Renaissance château and 250ha/ 625 acres of gardens and parkland. Owned by the same family for the past 400 years, it's a magical spot where history and nature merge.

SIGHTS
Château

🕐Open Feb–mid-Nov daily, hours vary. See website or call for details. ✆Combined tickets for château, gardens, labyrinthe, wildlife park, etc., 27.50€. ♿ ✆01 34 87 49 26. www.thoiry.net.

The 16C Renaissance château de Thoiry, which has remained in the La Panouse family for 16 generations, was built on a small hill by Raoul Moreau, renowned for his passionate interest in alchemy and esoterics. It was he who had this 'solar house' built on a magnetic fault, to designs using the Golden Section. This hilltop position enables the château to act as a solar instrument, with spectacular sights such as the sunrise or sunset in line with the façade at the solstices. The house is also a 'time machine', which gives an insight into an eventful history. The ancestors conversing from their picture frames in the portrait gallery, and the tales uncovered in the 50 trunks full of family archives, are all means of examining history.

- **Population:** 1 120
- **Michelin Local Map:** p172: B1 or map 106 folds 15, 16.
- **Info:** www.thoiry.net.
- **Location:** 53km/33mi W of Paris. By car, take A 13 then A 12 to St-Quentin-en-Yvelines. Leave the motorway at the Bois d'Arcy exit towards Dreux and follow N 12 to Pontchartrain, then turn onto D 11 to Thoiry.
- **Timing:** Make a day of it.

👥 Zoological Gardens
♿🕐See Château for details.

The area of park adjacent to the château has been laid out as a zoo, with numerous special events. The most impressive section is the tiger enclosure.

Various trails pass the elegant but fearsome black panthers, the emus and cassowaries, the mandrill island, and a tribe of free-frolicking lemurs.

👥 Safari
♿🕐See Château for details.

The château's 1 200 acres are home to an African wildlife zoo, vast botanical gardens and forested trails.

The château is richly decorated with antique furnishings, including a magnificent Gobelins tapestry. The wildlife park is accessible by car only (you must keep your windows closed and refrain

Elephants at Château et Parc de Thoiry, Safari

© Bertrand Gardel/hemis.fr

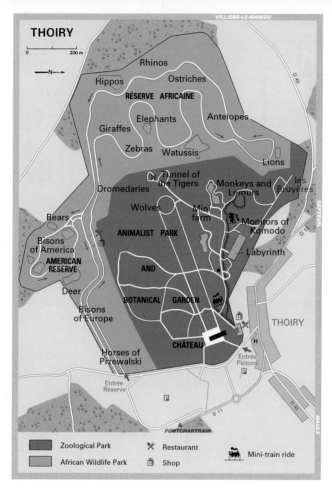

THOIRY

0   200 m

→ N →

VILLIERS-LE-MAHIEU

Rhinos

Hippos   Ostriches

RÉSERVE AFRICAINE

Elephants   Antelopes

Giraffes

Zebras   Watussis

Lions

Tunnel of
the Tigers   Monkeys and   les
Lemurs   Bruyères

Dromedaries

Wolves   Mini
farm   Monitors of
Komodo

Bears

ANIMALIST PARK   Labyrinth

Bisons
of America

**AMERICAN
RESERVE**   **AND**

Deer   **BOTANICAL GARDEN**

Bisons
of Europe   THOIRY

CHÂTEAU

Horses of
Przewalski   Entrée
Piétons

Entrée
Réserve

P

PONTCHARTRAIN

▨	Zoological Park	✗	Restaurant
▨	African Wildlife Park	▥	Shop
		🚂	Mini-train ride

from feeding the animals) as the animals are permitted to roam freely. Allow an entire day to visit Thoiry.

The park is so huge that many species of African, North American and European wildlife are able to live together quite happily.

There are over 1000 animals throughout the park, including antelopes, bison, giraffes, zebras, elephants, rhinos, hippos and much more. A drive through two high-security enclosures provides a close-up view of lions and bears.

There are regular events at the château and gardens, including summer and winter solstice festivals.

ADDRESSES

ⵌ/ EAT

☻ **Good to know** – Located at the park entrance, snack bar **Le Jardin d'hiver** offers a selection of snacks and drinks for takeaway. There is a sandwich bar in the African wildlife zoo. There are also picnic tables dotted around the park.

⬭ *La Licorne* – *Pl. du 8-Mai-1945. 78650 Beynes. 6km/3.7mi east of Thoiry along the D 119. ☎01 34 89 96 17. Closed Sun eve, Wed eve and Monday, mid-Jul–mid-Aug. Reservations required on weekends.* This restaurant situated just a few kilometres from the African wildlife zoo is a good address to know. Simple, fresh cuisine prepared with market ingredients. The service is friendly.

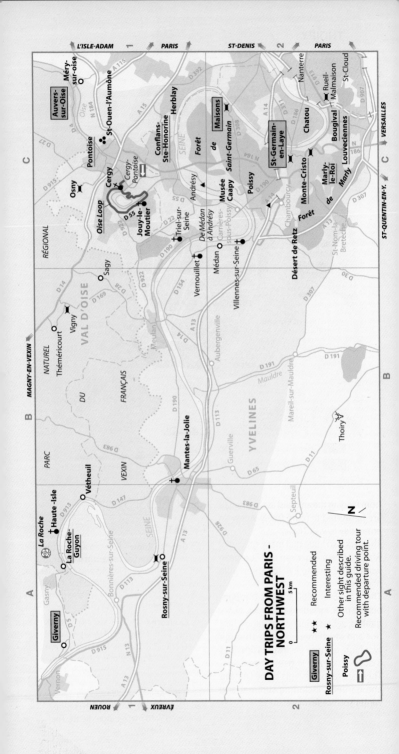

DAY TRIPS FROM PARIS – NORTHWEST

★★ Recommended

★ Interesting

✝ Other sight described in this guide.

⊞ Recommended driving tour with departure point.

Giverny

Rosny-sur-Seine

Poissy

Saint-Germain-en-Laye★★

Nestled on a loop of the Seine River, amid a forest of oaks, this residential suburb west of Paris was once an important royal town. Several monarchs made Saint-Germain-en-Laye their residence, including Louis XIV, who was born in its castle, grew up and lived there for many years until he and the court left for Versailles in the last quarter of the 17C. Very popular with the locals, St-Germain's famous stone terrace, designed by Le Nôtre, unfolds sweeping views of the capital, some 20km/12.4mi away.

▸ **Population:** 43 207
⚭ **Michelin Local Map:** p214: C2, map 101 fold 12 or 106 folds 17, 18.
▤ **Info:** Office du tourisme de St-Germain-en-Laye, Maison Claude Debussy, 38 r. au Pain, 78100. ℘01 30 87 20 63. www.ot-saint germainenlaye.fr.
◖ **Location:** From Paris, access via the A 14 and N 13, or RER line A 1 (terminus).

A BIT OF HISTORY
The old castle (château Vieux)

In the 12C, **Louis VI le Gros**, eager to exploit the strategic position of the St-Germain hillside, built a fortified stronghold on the site of the present château. The fortress was destroyed during the **Hundred Years War** and restored by **Charles V** around 1368. In 1514, **Louis XII** married his daughter Claude de France to the Duc d'Angoulême, who became **François I** the following year. The young ruler was acquainted with Italian culture, and the ancient citadel was hardly suited to his taste for palatial comfort and luxury. In 1539, he had the whole building razed, with the exception of Charles V's keep and the chapel built by **St-Louis**.

The new castle (château Neuf)

The new building was fortified, equipped with machicolations and defended by a garrison of 3 000 men. **Henri II**, who wanted a real country house, commissioned **Philibert Delorme** to draw up plans for a new château on the edge of the plateau. The château became famous on account of its fantastic location and the terraces built along the slopes overlooking the River Seine.

The area beneath the foundation arches was arranged into artificial grottoes where hydraulically propelled automatons re-enacted mythological scenes:

Château de St-Germain-en-Laye

© H. Le Gac/ MICHELIN

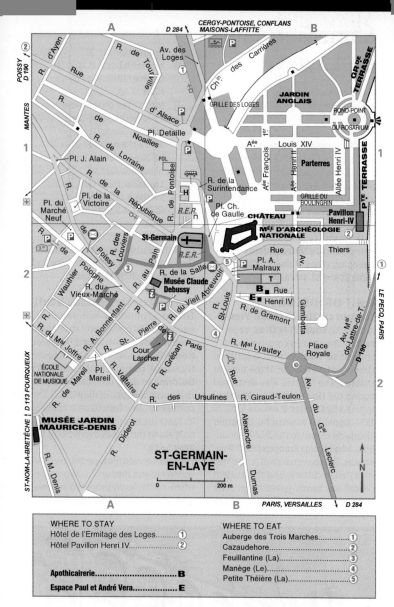

Orpheus playing the viola and attracting animals who came to listen, Neptune's chariot in full motion, etc.

Chronology of court events – The court occupied both the new château and the old castle, which were used as a palatial residence, or a safe retreat when riots broke out in Paris. Henri II, **Charles IX** and **Louis XIV** were all born at St-Germain. **Louis XIII** died here. **Mary Queen of Scots** lived here between the ages of 6 and 16. In 1558, she married the Dauphin François, aged only 15, and was crowned Queen of France the following year.

Mansart's improvements – Louis XIV, who was christened and brought up at St-Germain, grew fond of the château. As king, he paid frequent visits to the estate. The apartments of the old castle had become too cramped for Louis' liking, and he commissioned **Jules Hardouin-Mansart** to build five large pavilions to replace the five corner turrets adjoining the outer walls. **Le Nôtre** drew up the plans for the park, the terrace and the forest. In 1665, the grounds were replanted with five and a half million trees. In 1682, the court moved from St-Germain to Versailles. In 1689, the deposed King of England **James II** came to stay at the old castle, where he died in great financial straits in 1701, a well-loved figure (funeral monument in St-Germain Church, facing the château).

Final developments – In 1776, the badly dilapidated new château was ceded to the Comte d'Artois by his brother **Louis XVI**. The future king **Charles X** had the building demolished, except for the Henri IV pavilion on the terrace and the Sully Pavilion, in Le Pecq. The remains, together with the park, were sold during the Revolution. The old castle was stripped of its furniture. Under **Napoleon I**, it was the seat of a cavalry college. Under **Louis-Philippe**, it housed a military penitentiary, but **Napoleon III** ordered its closure in 1855. It was then entirely restored under the guidance of the architect **Millet**, succeeded by **Daumet**.
In 1862, Napoleon III inaugurated the National Museum of French Antiquities which he had set up on the premises. The signing of the 1919 **peace treaty** with Austria took place in the château at St-Germain.

SIGHTS
The most striking approach to the château is from the north, along the road from Les Loges. The tour starts from the square beside the château, on the **place Charles-de-Gaulle**.

Château★
The château forms the shape of an imperfect pentagon. The feudal foundations are distinguishable together with the covered watch-path and a series of machicolations restored by Daumet. The roof is laid out as a terrace edged with vases and a balustrade and dominated by tall chimneys – an innovative idea in its time. The royal suites were on the first floor; the king and the dauphin lived in the wing facing the parterres, the queen's suite looked toward Paris, and the children's rooms were in the wing which now faces rue Thiers. Under Henri IV, 12 of the 14 royal infants, born to five different mothers, romped noisily here.

Ste-Chapelle★
Built by Saint-Louis from 1230 to 1238, this chapel precedes the Ste-Chapelle in Paris by a decade. It was probably designed by the same architect, **Pierre de Montreuil,** but its tall windows do not have the stained glass that gives such dazzling splendour to its counterpart in Paris. Within the thickness of the keystones are carvings of figures thought to represent St-Louis, his mother Blanche of Castille, his wife, and other kin. If this is true, it would make these precious images the oldest pictures of royal families in existence.

Musée d'Archéologie nationale★★
pl. Charles-de-Gaulle. ⏱*Open Wed–Mon 10am–5pm.* ⏱*Closed 1 Jan and 25 Dec.* ♿☎*7€.* ☎*01 39 10 13 00. www.musee-archeologienationale.fr.* Particularly famous for its collection of carved or engraved prehistoric artefacts, the French National Archaeology Museum displays a fine array of antiquities ranging from the early settlements of France to the reign of Charlemagne.
– Toolmaking techniques of the **Palaeolithic Age** (from the origins till around 8000 BC) were characterised by the use of materials such as stone (flint), quartz, bone and antlers. Major works of art dating from that period are surprisingly small, as illustrated by the world-famous **Lady of Brassempouy** (3.6cm/1.44in high), the oldest representation of a human face found to date (c. 21 000 BC).

The Last Judicial Duel

Now the site of a pillbox, St-Germain castle's east esplanade was the scene of the last judicial duel during which the will of God was invoked. The duel between **Jarnacc** and **La Châtaigneraie** was attended by **Henri II**, accompanied by his retinue of courtiers. La Châtaigneraie, one of the finest swordsmen in Europe, was confident about the outcome of the battle. Jarnac, however, had learnt a new tactic: he severed the left hamstring of his adversary, who collapsed and slowly died.

– The **Neolithic Age** (6000 BC–3000 BC) saw the growth of farming and cattle rearing, community life in huts and the use of ceramics. Man produced arms and tools by polishing very hard stones. Found in Bernon (Brittany), a set of 16 large polished axe blades (15–18cm/5.9–7.1in) dating from around 5000 BC offers a fine illustration of this practice.

– The discovery of an alloy combining copper and tin led to the early stages of metallurgy, called the **Bronze Age** (2000 BC–c. 800 BC). Gold was also widely used, and the museum displays several objects and pieces of jewellery made of solid gold or gold leaf. Also note numerous weapons (daggers, axes with curved blades), metal necklaces and other decorative objects.

– Roughly ending with the Roman conquest, the **Iron Age** (750 BC–1C AD) is marked by profound mutations in traditional rural society, and by the rise of fortified *oppida*. One of the highlights of this section is the remains of a chariot burial from c. 400 BC excavated at La Gorge-Meillet in the Marne region.

– In **Roman Gaule** (1C–5C AD), the lengthy period of Roman peace, the indulgence of the victors and the deeply rooted religious feeling for indigenous gods gave rise to a flourishing industry of mythological and funerary sculpture. Ceramic pieces played an important role in domestic life. The museum offers a fairly comprehensive presentation of "sigillate" ceramics, decorated with stamped motifs, made in workshops at Lezoux, La Graufesenque, etc.

– Gaul progressively became France with the **Merovingians** (5C–8C AD) whose heritage mainly consists of burial places rich in arms – swords with damascene blades – and items of finery: heavy flat buckles for belts, S-shaped clasps, etc.

Grounds

Parterres – Enter the gardens through the gate on place Charles-de-Gaulle and skirt the château. Built into the façade is a loggia opening onto the inner main staircase. The moat contains restored megalithic monuments and replicas of Roman statues.

Pavillon Henri-IV – This brick pavilion was built on the very edge of the escarpment. It is crowned by a dome, and, together with the **Sully Pavilion** set lower on the hillside at Le Pecq, is all that remains of the new château. It contains the Louis XIII **oratory** where Louis XIV was baptised the same day of his birth, on 5 September 1638.

The **hotel,** (*see Addresses on opposite page*) which opened in this historic building in 1836, became an important meeting place for 19C writers, artists and politicians. Alexandre Dumas wrote *The Three Musketeers* and *The Count of Monte Cristo* while he was staying here, Offenbach composed *The Drum Major's Daughter* and Léo Delibes produced the ballet *Sylvia*. The statesman and president Thiers died here in 1877.

Terraces★★ – The **Small Terrace** starts beside the hotel and extends to the Rosarium roundabout. There, a worn Touring Club of France viewing table is a reminder of past views toward the western suburbs of Paris.

The **Grand Terrace** extends beyond the roundabout. Completed in 1673 after four years of large-scale construction work, this is one of **Le Nôtre**'s finest accomplishments. Lined with stately lime trees, it is also one of the most famous promenades around Paris (400m/8 000ft long). The **vista★** from the terrace being the same all the way along, visitors pressed for time may return to their car through the lovely **English-style garden★**.

ADDITIONAL SIGHTS
Musée Claude Debussy
38 r. au Pain. ⏰*Open Tue–Sat 2–5.30pm.* ⏰*Closed holidays.* 👜*No charge.* ☎*01 30 87 20 63.*
ThIs restored building was the birthplace of **Claude Debussy** (1862–1918). The museum features mementoes of the composer and houses the tourist office.

Musée départemental Maurice-Denis★
2 bis, r. Maurice-Denis. ⏰*Open Tue–Fri 10am–5.30pm (1st Thu in the month 9pm), Sat–Sun and holidays 10am–6.30pm.* ⏰*Closed Jan 1, May 1, Dec 25.* 👜*4.50€ (no charge 1st Sun of the month).* ☎*01 39 73 77 87. www.musee-mauricedenis.fr.*
Founded in 1678 as a royal hospital, this old **priory** became the property of the painter **Maurice Denis** (1870–1943), who moved here with his family and freely entertained his friends from the **Nabis movement**.
The museum explains the origin of this group of post-Impressionist artists, founded by **Paul Sérusier** in 1888, which became influential in the field of graphic art, rejecting Realism and Naturalism and putting feeling at the centre of every work of art.
A key work here is *Eternal Spring*, a set of ten panels by Maurice Denis, depicting women bathing near fountains or in a garden, gathered together for music or conversation.

ADDRESSES

🏨 STAY

🍴🛏🍴🛏 **Ermitage des Loges** – *11 av. Loges.* ☎*01 39 21 50 90. www.ermitagedesloges.fr. 56 rooms. Wifi.* ☐*13€. Restaurant*🍴🛏🍴. Hotel made up of two buildings on the edge of the St Germain forest. The main building dates from the 19C. Rooms in the more modern annexe

have views over the garden. Restaurant closed on weekends, special Fri eve fixed-price menus with drinks, 34€.

🍴🛏🍴🛏 **Pavillon Henri IV** – *21 r. Thiers.* ☎*01 39 10 15 15. www.pavillonhenri4.fr. 42 rooms.* ☐*17€. Restaurant*🍴🛏🍴🛏. This building (1604) was the birthplace of Louis XIV. High-class atmosphere in the nicely refurbished lounges and rooms. The comfortable dining room affords superb views over the River Seine valley and Paris.

🍴 EAT

🍴🛏 **La Petite Théière** – *1 pl. André-Malraux* ☎*01 39 21 79 10. Open 9.30am–7pm. Closed Mon and throughout Aug.* Just a few steps from the château, this restaurant provides a warm family ambiance in a Provencal-style setting. Traditional cuisine and a delicious American or Norwegian-style Sunday brunch.

🍴🛏 **La Feuillantine** – *10 r. des Louviers.* ☎*01 34 51 04 24. www.lafeuillantine.com. Closed Mon, Tue lunch, 3rd week in Aug.* This modern restaurant boasts a menu with a large variety of dishes, from country fare to seafood.

🍴🛏 **Le Manège** – *5 r. St-Louis.* ☎*01 39 73 22 12. www.restaurant-le-manege.com. Closed 1st week of Jan and week of 15 Aug.* Traditional cuisine served in a distinguished building decorated in bistro style, 200m/656ft from the château. Vaulted ceilings in dining room, terrace seating for warmer weather. Well-rounded wine list.

🍴🛏🍴 **Auberge des Trois Marches** – *15 r. J.-Laurent. Le Vesinet.* ☎*01 39 76 10 30. www.auberge-des-3-marches.com. 15 rooms*🍴🛏🍴. The restaurant serves traditional cuisine in a dining room with a fresco evoking the 1930s. You can expect warm service and village ambience in this discreet inn, and the functional rooms are well-kept.

🍴🛏 **Cazaudehore** – *Hôtel La Forestière. 1 av. du Prés.-Kennedy.* ☎*01 30 61 64 64. www.cazaudehore.fr. Closed Mon and Sun evening from Nov–Mar.* A family restaurant opened in 1928, offering pleasant terrace seating under acacia trees. Chic, cosy ambiance, refined cuisine and comprehensive wine list.

Marly-le-Roi★

Although a number of major property developments have spread across the Grandes Terres plateau since 1950, stretching towards Le Pecq, the name of Louis XIV remains firmly attached to this town. Marly was the Sun King's favourite residence. Unfortunately, its golden age lasted barely twenty years. After the First Empire, only the park remained, an impressive display of greenery bordering the old village, which has welcomed many writers and artists: Alexandre Dumas senior and junior, Alfred Sisley, Camille Pissarro and the sculptor Maillol.

A BIT OF HISTORY

The early stages – Marly's construction was a result of **Louis XIV**'s desire to retreat from the formal etiquette of Versailles. In 1678, at the peak of his glory, tired of the pomp and circumstance of Versailles, the king dreamed of a peaceful country residence, far from the madding crowd. His barony at Marly offered a deep, lush valley which suited the purpose, and he entrusted **Jules Hardouin-Mansart** with the plans. Mansart came up with an ingenious idea: instead of designing one enormous pavilion, which he knew the king would refuse, he conceived a series of 13 separate units. The royal pavilion would stand on the upper terrace, while the remaining 12, smaller in size and all identical, would be arranged along a stretch of water.

To promote his idea, Mansart proposed that the decoration of the king's pavilion symbolise the sun – Louis XIV's emblem – and that the surrounding buildings represent the 12 signs of the zodiac. It was agreed to replace the carved bas-reliefs with cheap *trompe-l'œil* frescoes. The king was delighted and gave orders to start building in 1679. It took nine years for the project to be completed. After working relentlessly all his life, Mansart died at the château in 1708.

Further embellishments – Right until the end of his reign, Louis XIV applied himself to the improvement of his Marly

- ▶ **Population:** 16 759
- ⚙ **Michelin Local Map:** p214: C2, map 101 fold 12 or 106 fold 17.
- ⓘ **Info:** Office du tourisme de Marly-le-Roi, 2 av. des Combattants, 78160. ℘01 30 61 61 35. www.pays-des-impressionistes.fr.
- ◗ **Location:** From Paris, SNCF rail link from Gare St-Lazare.

residence and kept a close watch on the various projects under way.

Behind the royal pavilion rose the steep, wooded slopes of the hillside. The Sun King gave orders to build the River, also called the **Grande Cascade**, the Wonder of Marly, which was served by the famous "Machine": starting from the top of the hill, a series of falls cascaded down a flight of 52 steps of pink marble set into the terraced slope. The ensemble – adorned with statues and rockeries – was completed in 1699.

Life at Marly – Apart from his close relatives, Louis XIV brought very few guests to Marly; the facilities for accommodation were limited to **24 apartments**. The king himself drew up a list of guests and personally determined where they should stay; the nearer they were to the royal pavilion, the greater the honour. The 'happy few' were not necessarily members of the aristocracy or dignitaries, but intelligent personalities whose charm would enliven the king's stays. The formal etiquette of Versailles was dropped at Marly. The king shared his meals with his guests, with whom he conversed in a free, casual manner. Hunts, outdoor games, card games and concerts were a regular feature. The standard of comfort at the place, however, was poor; in summer the guests caught fever, in winter they shivered with cold and damp. Louis XIV, who personally tackled the problem, introduced new systems every year, in vain.

The end of Marly – On 9 August 1715, the king suffered a bout of exhaustion after following the hunt in his carriage. He was taken to Versailles, where he died on 1 September, aged 77.

Louis XV and **Louis XVI** stayed at Marly from time to time. The costly Grande Cascade was abandoned in favour of the present "green carpet." The furniture was sold during the Revolution.

In 1800, an industrialist bought the estate and set up a mill. Having failed in business, he offered **Napoléon I** the opportunity to buy Marly, but he was turned down. He then proceeded to demolish the château and sell the building materials. A year later, Napoleon retrieved the estate which has since been the property of the French State.

Famed "Marly horses"

© Ph. Gajic/MICHELIN

SIGHTS
Marly Park★★

🕐 *Open daily Nov–Mar 8am–6pm; Apr–Oct 7.30am–7.30pm.*

A large esplanade flanked by lime trees in the centre of the park marks the former site of the **royal pavilion**. A series of slabs defines the layout of the building; the large octagonal drawing room in the centre is surrounded by four corner rooms, separated by vestibules.

This is where the two perspectives of the park meet: across to the drive leading to the **Royal Gates**, and along the route running from St-Germain and the Seine Valley up to the **Grand Mirror** fountains and the green 'carpet' of lawns.

Further information can be obtained from the museum (👤 *see below*).

Grille Royale

Louis XIV would use this entrance. Admire the perspective of the steep road climbing up the hillside and its continuation on the opposite slope, slicing its way through the trees.

Musée-Promenade de Marly-le-Roi-Louveciennes

🕐 *Open Wed–Sun 2–5.30pm.* ⊚*4€.* ♿ 📞*01 39 69 06 26. www.musee-promenade.fr.*

This museum contains precious material on the 13 pavilions and garden statues which no longer exist. The plans drawn up in 1753 and a miniature model of the whole project give a fairly clear idea of what the king's country residence looked like. The interior decoration of the royal pavilion is represented by Van der Meulen's *Capture of Gray* and by Mme Vigée-Lebrun's *Summer* and *Autumn*, which both hung at Marly. Before leaving the museum, visit the small room presenting the 'Machine of Marly' (drawings and plans, together with a model).

Abreuvoir

After a steep descent – known as Côte du Cœur-Volant – the D 386 leads to the **horse-pond,** once used as a spillway for the waters of Marly park. From here, the water was conveyed back to the Seine by a system of pipes and drains. The terrace flanked by yew trees was used to display Coysevox' *Winged Horses* and at a later date, Guillaume Coustou's *Rearing Horses*. Two replicas stand in their place. The original statues once adorned Place de la Concorde in Paris.

EXCURSIONS
Château de Monte-Cristo★

▶ *Located in Port-Marly.* 🕐*Open Apr–Oct Tue–Fri 10am–12.30pm, 2–6pm, Sat–Sun and holidays 10am–6pm; Nov–Mar Sun only 2–5pm.* 🕐*Closed 1 Jan and 25 Dec.* ⊚*6€. (Sun pm 7.50€ by guided tour only).* 📞*01 39 16 49 49. www.chateau-monte-cristo.com.*

Built in 1846 on a hill overlooking the Seine Valley, this extravagant folly expressed the eccentricity of **Alexandre Dumas** through a wonderfully eclectic combination of Gothic, Renaissance and Moorish styles. After holding sumptuous receptions for the fashionable Paris set when his works *The Count of Monte-Cristo* and *The Three Musketeers* were enjoying great success, Dumas ran up enormous debts and was finally forced to sell up. The delightful building, which houses a library and information centre, is decorated with medallions representing the famous writer and the great minds whom he particularly admired, Homer, Aeschylus, Sophocles.

Some of the rooms contain portraits and documents. Visitors can also see the great man's study and the splendid **Moorish drawing room★** in which the exuberance of the carvings and brilliant stained glass are equalled only by the furniture.

Louveciennes★

◗ *2km/1.2mi E of Marly on the D 7.*
This small town on the edge of Marly Forest still features several large estates. Many famous people were attracted by this charming place including Impressionist painters such as Renoir.
◖◣ Two itineraries guide you in the footsteps of the Impressionists and help you discover the town's history: the *"Chemin des Impressionnistes" (4km/2.5mi starting from the town hall)* and the *"Liaison Verte" (6km/3.7mi starting from the Musée-promenade at Marly-le-Roi).*
The **church** (12C–13C) on the village square retains a Romanesque look, but the polygonal bell-tower is 19C.
Walk through the public gardens, along rue de l'Étang and down rue du Pont for a pleasant view of the 16C **Château du Pont** (⊶ *private*), groves of trees and rippling moat waters. Follow rue du Général-Leclerc to the town hall, opposite which stand arches of the disused aqueduct which conveyed the waters of the Seine to Versailles. Return to the church and walk along rue du Professeur-Tuffier, then follow the signposts to reach **Field Marshal Joffre's Tomb**. Known as the "Victor of the Marne", this World War I hero insisted on being buried here rather than at the Invalides in Paris.

Forêt de Marly

This State forest covers a picturesque plateau planted with oaks, beeches and chestnut trees. The area measures approx 2 000ha/5 000 acres. The thicker groves lie west from St-Germain to St-Nom-la-Bretèche, between Étoile des Dames and Étoile de Joyenval.

Désert de Retz

◗ *Not accessible by car: park near Chambourcy Cemetery. Shuttle twice daily (2pm and 4pm). May–Oct, 2nd and 4th Sat in the month: guided tours (1h30) at 2pm, 2.30pm and 4.30pm. Reservations required. ℘01 39 22 31 37. www.chambourcy.fr.*
This park was visited by notable personalities in the 18C. On the outskirts of the Marly forest, it was divided into 17 fantasy-inspired themes, following the fashion of the time. It's one of the few surviving "deserts": places created to enjoy freedom from the constraints of social etiquette.

André Derain House

◗ *Chambourcy, 10km/6.2mi NW of Marly-le-Roi on the N 13, 64, Grande Rue. Visit (1hr) by reservation only, 4th Sun in the month at 3pm. ℘01 30 74 70 04, www.maisonderain.free.fr.*
Not far from the Seine riverbanks adored by the Impressionists, Fauvist painter André Derain made Chambourcy his home and studio in 1935. Co-founder of the bold movement in painting, Derain invited many notable artists here.

ADDRESSES

ⴼ/ EAT

⊜⊜ **Le Cottage** – *7 bis Grande Rue. ℘01 39 16 34 89. Closed Mon, 3 weeks in Aug, 1 week at Easter and 1 week in Dec. Call ahead.* This cosy tearoom serves up lunch between 12–3pm, and in the afternoon, enjoy hot chocolate, tea or a pastry.

ACTIVITIES

Boat Cruise: Impressionist Country
℘*01 30 61 61 35. www.marlyleroi-tourisme.fr.* ⊜*15€ (children 10€).* Explore the sites that inspired Sisley.

Bougival★

In the 19C, Bougival was a centre of art, fêtes and bohemian life. Bizet, Corot, Meissonier and Renoir lived here. Boaters and young Parisian men and women who flocked to the dances at La Grenouillère were portrayed by Maupassant in his novels and short stories, and captured on canvas by Impressionists (Renoir, Berthe Morisot, Monet).

▶ **Population:** 8 532
⚄ **Michelin Map:**
   p214: C2; 311.
▤ **Info:** Bougival Tourist
   Office: ☎01 39 69 21 23.
   www.tourisme-bougival.com.
◉ **Location:** 7km/4.3mi W of
   Paris from St Lazare by train
   or by the A 86 and D 113.
👪 **Kids:** A boat cruise with
   the whole family can
   be entertaining and
   educational.

SIGHTS
Musée Tourgueniev

16 r. Ivan-Tourgueniev. Access on foot via alleyway off N 13, near Holiday Inn. ◷*Open Apr–Oct, Sat 2–6pm, Sun 10am–6pm.* ⊚*6€.* ☎*01 45 77 87 12. www.tourgueniev.fr.*

Built on the heights, the house where Russian novelist **Ivan Turgueniev** (1818–1883) lived during his exile was part of the property owned by friends Louis Viardot and his wife Pauline, a singer. The ground floor displays the writer's personal documents, engravings, and his piano. His works are evoked through extracts from novels and essays, among them *A Sportsman's Notebook* (1852), in which he predicted the abolition of serfdom in Russia.

On the first floor, the writer's study and the room where he died on 3 September 1883 have been recreated.

The Machine of Marly

The **Île de la Loge** road bridge affords a good view of the buildings *(quai Rennequin-Sualem at Bougival)* which contained the Machine of Marly. From there, observe a white lodge: this was **Madame du Barry's Music Pavilion**. The pavilion was inaugurated in September 1771 during a sumptuous banquet attended by Louis XV.

EXCURSION
Chatou

◉ *5km/3mi from Bougival on the A 86.*

Cherished by the 19C Impressionists, the town of Chatou subsequently saw the birth of Fauvism in the 20C with artists Derain and Vlaminck. Artists often assembled here at the recently renovated Fournaise house, situated on the still-bucolic Île des impressionistes, Renoir called it "the prettiest place in Paris' surrounds" and painted one of his masterpieces, *Le Déjeuner des Canotiers*, here.

Musée Fournaise

On l'île des Impressionnistes. ◷*Open Wed–Fri 10am–12pm and 2–6pm, weekends and public holidays 11am–6pm.* ◷*Closed public holidays.* ⊚*6€; children under-12 free.* ☎*01 34 80 63 22. www.musee-fournaise.com.*

The Fournaise family lodged artists such as Renoir, Caillebotte, Maupassant and Offenbach. A small museum on the 2nd floor and in the former "boat garage" hosts exhibits retracing the history of the house and artworks inspired there.

Musée de la Grenouillère

Espace Chanorier, 12 Grande Rue. Croissy-sur-Seine. ◷*Open Wed and Sun 2.30–6pm, and daily for groups by reservation only.* ◷*Closed 15 Dec–15 Jan, early Aug.* ⊚*4€/2.50€ (under 12s free).* ☎*01 30 53 61 02. www.grenouillere-museum.com.*

A small museum bringing back to life the spirit of the famed "guinguette". Paintings, engavings and other objects trace its spirited history.

Château de Maisons-Lafitte ★★

Set on the western outskirts of Paris in a loop on the River Seine, Maisons-Lafitte is a residential town at the edge of St-Germain Forest. Particularly famous for its castle, a fine example of French neo-Classical architecture built by Mansart in the 17C, the town is also known as the birthplace of horse racing in France.

▶ **Population:** 21 856

🎯 **Michelin Local Map:** p214: C2; 311; map 101 fold 13 or 106 fold 18.

▣ **Info:** Office du tourisme de Maisons-Laffitte, 41 av. de Longueil, 78600. ℘01 39 62 63 64. www.tourisme-maisonslaffitte.fr.

◐ **Location:** From Paris, SNCF rail link from Gare St-Lazare or RER line A 3/A 5.

A BIT OF HISTORY

Maisons-Laffitte castle was built between 1642–1651 for **René de Longueil**, Governor of the royal châteaux at Versailles and St-Germain. Louis XIV, who took up residence at St-Germain, frequently visited, as did successors. The Comte d'Artois, brother of Louis XVI, acquired the estate in 1777 and built the famous racecourse. In 1818, banker **Jacques Laffitte** (1767–1844) bought the estate. He aided in securing Louis-Philippe d'Orléans' accession to the throne during the Revolution of July 1830, which overthrew Charles X. Made Prime Minister in 1830, Laffitte proved unable to calm the disturbances that had broken out in Paris. Mistrusted by both the Orleanists and the moderates, he was forced to resign in March 1831. Ruined, he dismantled the imposing stables and used the stone to build houses in the Grand Parc.

VISIT
Château de Maisons★

ⓞOpen mid-May–mid-Sep Wed–Sun 10am–12.30pm, 2–6pm (mid-Sep–mid-May 6pm). ⓞClosed 1 Jan, 1 May, 1 and 11 Nov, 25 Dec. ⌧7.50€ (no charge 1st Sun in month Jan–May, Nov–Dec. ℘01 39 62 01 49. http://maisons.monuments-nationaux.fr.

Dating to Louis XIV's reign, the château has long been considered a model of French architecture. From the main driveway, there is a splendid **view** of the high-pitched roofs.
The **façade** features a dry moat, a terrace and the main staircase. The stone exterior presents Classical ornamentation: Doric on the ground floor, Ionic on the first floor, and Corinthian on the attic storey level. Alternating fluted columns and engaged pilasters form a well-balanced composition. The **interior** boasts highlights such as the Grand Staircase and Mirror Room.

Racecourse and Park

The Maisons-Lafitte racecourse is located on the banks of the Seine; stables and riding trails are at the borders of the forest, north of the park. An early morning stroll (around 7am) often permits you to watch grooms exercising groups of horses along the paths.

ADDRESSES

🛏STAY

⊜⊜**Hôtel Ibis**– 2r. de Paris. ℘01 39 12 20 20. www.ibishotel.com. 68 rooms. This well-placed hotel is located close to the chateau and racecourse.

🍴EAT

⊜⊜**Le Cosy** – 37av. de Longueil. ℘01 39 12 44 59. www.lecosy.fr. Closed 1 Jan and 24–25 Dec. This traditional French brasserie near the river boasts Baroque-style decor.

⊜⊜⊜**Tastevin** – 9av. Églé. ℘01 39 62 11 67. www.letastevin-restaurant.fr. Closed 22 Feb–8 March, 3–26 Aug, Mon and Tue. Headed by Michel Blanchet for over 30 years, this restaurant offers classic cuisine with a creative twist, using produce of the finest quality.

Conflans-Sainte-Honorine★

Situated at the meeting point of the Seine and Oise rivers, the town is perched on a bank overlooking the former, downstream from Paris. While boating activity has diminished significantly, Conflans nonetheless remains the capital of inland water shipping in France. Its quays are still lined with barges.

- ▶ **Population:** 34 305
- ⚲ **Michelin Local Map:** p214 C1.
- 🚹 **Info:** Tourist Office. René-Albert. ☎01 34 90 99 09. www.conflans-tourisme.com.
- ▶ **Location:** 38 km from Paris on the A 15, exit 7. Train connection from Paris-St-Lazare or RER A Conflans-Fin-d'Oise.
- 👪 **Kids:** Le musée de la Batellerie; a boat ride on the Seine or Oise river.

SIGHTS
Where Rivers Meet: Le Pointil
1.5km/1mi W of Conflans: follow the quai de la République and the quai E.-Le-Corre.

Pass the railroad viaduct and continue to the left until you reach the "Pointil": a mound of land where the Seine and Oise cross paths. Here, a monument stands in memory to military boatmen who perished during WWI. From here, interesting views of the river traffic and various structures abound: note the metallic Eiffel bridge, originally built in 1890, destroyed during WWII in 1944 and entirely rebuilt in 1947. Upstream, admire the imposing structures of the **Andrésy** lock and dam (1957). Just acros the way, the Nancy island harbours numerous birds.

Tour Montjoie
Jutting out from a plateau in Conflans, this 11C Roman tower most likely belonged to the "old chateau" owned by the counts of Beaumont. It's a rare regional example of a residential keep. Its walls are thinner than counterparts used for defensive purposes.

Église St-Maclou
Due to renovations, the church is currently closed to visitors.

Upstream from the tower, this 11C church (remodelled through the 19C) houses the tombstones of Mathieu IV of Montmorency and of Jean Ier (14C) as well as stained glass dating to 1860 and illustrating the arrival of the relics of **Sainte Honorine** (3C) in Conflans.

Harbour, Conflans-Sainte-Honorine

© Yann Guichaoua/age fotostock

Château du Prieuré
This château sits on the site of the priory which formerly housed the Saint's relics. Renovated in 1869 in Neo-Renaissance style, it now houses the Musée de la Batellerie (👁 *see below*). From the Place Jules-Gévelot, enjoy a lovely **view★** of the river and church.

👪 Musée de la Batellerie
3 pl. Jules-Gévelot, Château du Prieuré.
🚫 Closed for renovation until 2014.
Contact for details. ☎01 34 90 39 50.

This museum houses an impressive collection of old model boats, paintings, photos, etc. tracing the history of river navigation in France.

Ground floor – Several models demonstrate the mechanisms of locks, dams and canal reaches. An adjoining courtyard displaying barge parts (anchors, jacks, etc).

First Floor – The right-side room illustrates barge propulsion mechanisms across the centuries, from sails to water vapour and contemporary motors. The rooms to the left retrace the history of river tourism, starting with 18C Parisian cruiseliners. A last room is consecrated to industrial river transport.

Le Jaques and le Triton 25

⊙Open May–Sept weekends and holidays 3–6pm. ⊛2.50€. ☎01 34 90 39 73. http://perso.orange.fr/vexin.fr/AMB.

A non-profit organisation associated with the Musée de la Batellerie restored these two tugboats: the first, built in 1904, is doubtless the oldest steam tugboat to remain in operation; the second, built in 1955, is the last river tugboat to have been designed for traction.

"Je Sers" Chapel-Boat

⊙Hours vary; call for information. ☎01 39 72 62 83. www.bateaujesers.org.

Anchored on the Quai de la République, this barge made of reinforced cement and measuring 70m/230ft was built following WW I. Capable of accommodating loads of 1 100 tonnes, it's one of only six 'chapel-boats' in France, and one of the oldest. The boat houses a church complete with stained glass.

EXCURSIONS
Herblay

▶ 7km/4.3mi W of Conflans along D 48. Situated above a loop of the Seine, this town once cultivated wine, fruit trees, lilacs and figs. Herblay and neighborhing town **La Frette-sur-Seine** were both appreciated by painters such as Cézanne, Pissaro, and Vlaminck, who lived here.

The **St-Martin** church (11 r. Jean XXIII) looms above the river banks. The chancel and left side of the church, dating to the 16C, house Renaissance-era stained-glass.

From the church cemetery, enjoy a **view★** of the river and nearby St-Germain forest.

⬤From rue Jean XXIII, continue until you reach the river banks; follow the old towpath for a pleasant waterside stroll (around 1hr30mins). The water has long been much-appreciated by bathers and boaters. On the avenue, enjoy the view of some remarkable villas.

ADDRESSES

⚑EAT

⊖ **Le Paris**– 36 r. Maurice-Bertaux. ☎01 39 72 60 24. Closed Sun and 25 Jul–15 Aug. On Conflans' main street, this restaurant offers French-Oriental specialities. You'll find a large choice of tagines, spit roasts, couscous (including one vegetarian) and grills, as well as a selection of traditional recipes. Takeways available.

⊖⊖⊖ **Au Bord de l'Eau** – 15 quai des Martyrs-de-la-Résistance. ☎01 39 72 86 51. This old farm on the banks of the Oise houses a family-run restaurant. The interior pays homage to Conflans' canal boats. Traditional cuisine.

SHOPPING

Osmont– 41 r. Maurice-Berteaux. ☎01 39 72 61 39. www.patisserie-osmont.fr. Open Tue–Sat 9am–1pm, 3–7.30pm, Sun 9am–1pm. This pastry and chocolate maker has long been renowned as one of the best in France. Specialties include Les Rochers de la Tour (caramelised almonds covered in chocolate) and 12 flavours of macaroons.

ACTIVITIES
CRUISES

Reservations and info at the Tourist Office: ☎01 34 90 99 09. www.conflans-tourisme.com.

Cultural Cruise – Sundays, Jun–Sept. 13€ (children 9€). 1hr tour with commentary.

Lunch Cruises – Jun–Oct. Cruise on the Seine to Poissy or on the Oise to Auvers-sur-Oise: lunch followed by music and dancing.

Poissy

Situated on the banks of the Seine, Poissy was a royal residence as early as the 5C. St Louis was christened here in 1214; the king's private correspondence was even signed "Louis de Poissy". The castle once stood on place Meissonnier but it was demolished by Charles V. Up to the middle of the last century, Poissy was the main cattle market serving Paris. Today, it is the site of a Peugeot automobile plant.

▶ **Population:** 35 860
◔ **Michelin Local Map:**
p214 C2; 311; map 101 fold 12 or 106 fold 17.
🛈 **Info:** 132 r. du Gén.-de-Gaulle, 78300 Poissy.
📞 01 30 74 60 65.
www.ville-poissy.fr.
◖ **Location:** 32km/20mi from the centre of Paris, on the Seine. Access from Paris: RER line A 5 or SNCF rail link from Gare St-Lazare.
👥 **Kids:** Musée du Jouet.
🕐 **Timing:** Half a day.

SIGHTS
Collégiale Notre-Dame★

🕐Open 8am–7pm. 🔍Guided tours Sun 3–6pm. www.poissy-tourisme.fr.
The greater part of the collegiate church is Romanesque, dating from the 11C and 12C. The front tower, built in the Romanesque style, once served as a belfry-porch. The square base of the tower develops to an octagonal section on the highest level, ending in a stone spire. The central tower is eight-sided and ends in a timberwork spire.

Interior – The nave is a rare example of transitional style. The capitals of the south columns in the first two bays were recarved in the 17C. The other capitals feature interlacing monsters and foliage motifs. Some are thought to be older than the building itself and were probably taken from another church. The nave is very well-lit , owing to the installation of a triforium by Viollet-le-Duc in the three bays nearest to the chancel, which is circled by an ambulatory with crossed vaulting. The side chapels – added in the 15C – pay homage to various trade guilds: butchers, fishermen, etc.

The first chapel to the right of the doorway contains fragments of the font used for St Louis' christening. For many centuries, the faithful would scrape the stone sides of the font, dissolve the dust in a glass of water and drink the potion as a remedy for high fever. This explains why the font is in such bad condition.

The most impressive furnishings are in the first chapel on the right: majestic 15C statues of John the Baptist and St Barbara, and a superb 16C Entombment (see below) portraying Mary, John, Mary Magdalene, the Holy Women, Nicodemus and Joseph of Arimathea.

Royal Priory

Only a few vestiges remain of this vast assembly of churches and convent buildings built in 1304. The most interesting is the porter's lodge, which now houses the Musée du Jouet (◔see below).

👥 Musée du Jouet

1 enclos de l'Abbaye. 🕐Open Tue–Sun 9.30am–noon, 2–5.30pm. ◉4€ (children 3€). 📞01 39 65 06 06.
The toy museum is housed in the building flanked by two towers that used to be the entrance to the abbey. The toys and games exhibited here cover the period from 1850 to 1960. A large number of dolls show changes in fashion over a century. The first floor features a display case full of clockwork toys, another filled with teddy bears and yet another with lead and paper soldiers dating from the 19C. On the top floor are collections of cars and trains, some clockwork, others powered by steam. An electric train track from the 1930s operates automatically as visitors approach.

Parc Meissonier

Av. du Bon-Roi-St-Louis.
This 10ha/25acre English-style park boasts a large reservoir of water (with

The Poissy Symposium

An Augustinian convent founded in the 11C was given to the Dominican order by Philip the Fair. From 9 September to 13 October 1561 the abbey refectory hosted the Poissy Symposium; Catholics and Protestants were invited to discuss their differences at the instigation of Chancellor Michel de l'Hôpital. The debate was attended by the papal legate, 16 cardinals, 40 bishops and the general of the Jesuit order on the one side, and by an important group of theologians led by Theodore Beza on the other. The symposium lasted 17 days, but these talks proved to be in vain; the divide between the two parties was even greater after the conference.

a stream descending to the Seine) and a rose garden. It's also well-known for its beautiful trees, including a Lebanese cedar planted around 1740. Formerly owned by the St-Louis royal monastery, the park was already beloved during the Middle Ages: it's notably mentioned in medieval poetess Christine de Pisan's Dict de Poissy (1400).

Villa Savoye★

82 r. de Villiers. ⏰*Open Tue–Sun May–Aug 10am–6pm; Mar–Apr and Sept–Oct 10am–5pm; Nov–Feb 10am–1pm, 2–5pm.* ⏰*Closed 1 Jan, 1 May, 1 and 11 Nov, 25 Dec* ⏰*7.50€. Free 1st Sun of month Jan-May, Nov-Dec.* ☎*01 39 65 01 06. http://villa-savoye.monuments-nationaux.fr.*

This masterpiece of modern architecture was designed in 1929 by **Le Corbusier** and **Pierre Jeanneret** for the industrialist Savoye. The use of cylindrical piles made it possible to eliminate load-bearing walls and introduce huge glass surfaces. The main rooms are located on the first floor, at a height of 3.5m/12ft, arranged around a large terrace which opens onto the countryside. A solarium occupies the top level of the house.

Musée Caapy, Carrières-sous-Poissy

On the PSA Peugeot site. From Poissy, take the D 190 then D 55, 212 bd Pelletier. ⏰*Open Mon 2pm–5pm, Sat 9am–noon, 2pm–5pm.* ⏰*Closed Aug and public holidays.* ⏰*5€.* ☎*01 30 19 41 15. www.caapy.net.*

A display of 70 cars that have marked the history of this production site, including a large number of Talbot models.

Centre de Production Peugeot

45 r. J.-P.-Timbaud. ☎*Guided tours by appointment a week in advance, Mon–Fri, 9am, 2pm.* ⏰*11€.* ☎*01 30 19 30 00.*

PSA Peugeot-Citroën is the second-largest car maker in Europe. The Peugeot brand's roots go back to the 19C, when it was making coffee and bicycles. In 1974, Peugeot took over Citroën, although both brands have maintained their identities. The group then bought Chrysler's European subsidiaries, including Talbot. Like the Renault factory in Flins, the PSA Peugeot Citroën factory in Poissy has contributed to shaping the Seine Valley. Today, this ultra-modern car plant has a large number of industrial robots producing over 1 200 cars every day.

ADDRESSES

⏷ EAT

☕☕ **Saint-Martin**– *22 r. Galande, Triel-sur-Seine.* ☎*01 39 70 32 00, www.restaurantsaintmartin.com. Closed 1–20 Aug, around Christmas, Wed and Sun.* This tiny yet cosy restaurant near a 13C gothic church has gained a loyal local following for its home-made bread and creative mix of old and new French specialities.

SHOPPING

Noyau de Poissy – *105 r. du Gén.-de-Gaulle.* ☎*01 39 65 20 59. www.noyaude-poissy.com. Daily except Sun afternoon and Mon, 10am–1pm, 3–7pm; Sun 9.30am–12.30pm.* Come and visit this hundred year-old distillery to learn how the famous Noyau de Poissy liqueurs are made. Enjoy the guided tour before browsing in the adjoining shop.

Mantes-la-Jolie

Mantes-la-Jolie, traditionally a royal city, has preserved many of its riches. The collegiate church rivals certain cathedrals, with a bright and elegant nave that reveals the transition from the Romanesque to the Gothic style, and is almost as high as the nave of Notre Dame in Paris.

SIGHTS
Collégiale Notre-Dame★★

Guided tours by appointment. Contact tourist office. ℰ01 34 78 86 70.
This church inspired one of Corot's finest paintings, now exposed at the Musée des Beaux-Arts in Reims. Construction began in 1170, with the naves and chancel dating to as late as the 13C. The chapels were added in the 14C.

Exterior – The **facade** is the oldest section of the church. The left tower and slender corridor which connects it to the right tower were reconstructed in the 19C. Three badly damaged portals open at the front. The central portal, dedicated to the Virgin, was created between 1170 and 1195. Note the delicate perfection of the foliage motifs sculpted on the abutments and column bases of the central and left portals. On the right side, forming a projection, stands the 14C Chapelle de Navarre. Admire the magnificent **chevet** and its complex, detailed design: powerful apses, buttresses and flying buttresses overlap to support the upper part of the chancel.

Interior – At 33m/108ft high, the nave is almost as high as its counterpart at Notre-Dame Cathedral in Paris (35 m/115ft). It features a succession of large corridors, high windows and brightly lit galleries. The lovely rose window on the facade represents the Last Judgement and dates to the early 13C. Advancing further into the nave, note the six-part vaulting structure. The beams supporting the heaviest weights are situated at the edges and meet with the largest pillars; those supporting lighter weights meet with the round columns. Above

- **Population:** 42 365
- **Michelin Map:** p214 AB1; 331.
- **Info: Maison du tourisme du Mantois**: 1 r. Thiers, Mantes-la-Jolie. ℰ01 34 77 10 30. www.manteslajolie.fr.
- **Location:** 53km/33mi from Paris along the A 13. Train from Paris-St-Lazare or Paris-Montparnasse stations.
- **Don't miss:** La Collégiale Notre-Dame; the Old Bridge of Limay.
- **Kids:** Playtime in the gardens of the Collégiale Notre-Dame.

the aisles, well-lit, deep galleries in the Romanesque style open onto the nave via triple bays. Note the archaic structure of the galleries in the apse and north side of the chancel, covered in barrel vaults.

Four delicate 14C statues of crowned female figures grace the entry of the Chapelle de Navarre. These likely depict Jeanne de France, the Countess of Évreux (1312-1349), and Jeanne d'Évreux, who became Queen of France when she married Charles IV le Bel in 1324. The two other young women may be the daughters of Jeanne de France: Blanche, Queen of France through her alliance with Philippe VI of Valois, and Agnès, wife of Gaston Phébus, Count of Foix.

Most of the stained glass in the chapel was destroyed during the French Revolution; the radiant windows that today illuminate the chapel are primarily reconstructions. The chapel was named in honour of the kings of Navarre, of the Évreux lineage (the counts of Évreux served as the lords of Mantes from 1328 to 1364).

Square du Château

The Collégiale Notre-Dame once stood within the fortified walls of the royal château, which rose from the site of the current public gardens. It was destroyed in the 18C. From the rue de l'Abbé-Hua which stretches across the garden, enjoy a lovely view of the Seine and the chevet of the Collégiale Notre-Dame.

Renaissance Fountain

Rue Heuse, perpendicular to r. Thiers.
The current fountain is a reproduction of the original, built in 1520. The original, still conserved in Mantes, is the only known remaining fountain from the period boasting two basins. From this vantage point, admire the ornate rooftops of the Collégiale.

Tour St-Maclou

This 16C tower, last vestiges of a church that once stood here and was originally built in the 11C, has been exceptionally well-preserved.

Old Bridge of Limay

This slightly crooked bridge, dating to the 11C at the latest, is one of the oldest in France. It was badly damaged during WWII and was never reconstructed; the bridge has since been cut off. It was used to transport agricultural and fishery goods until 1870. It's all that remains of a much larger bridge that once connected Mantes to the town of Limay, and inspired several paintings by Corot, including Le Pont de Mantes, now at the Louvre. A porter's house c. 1750 still stands here.

Musée de l'Hôtel-Dieu

1 r. Thiers. ○*Open Mon–Fri 1–6pm, Sat 10am–12.30pm, 1.30–7pm, Sun and public holidays 1–7pm.* ○*Closed Mar, 1 Jan, 11 Nov and 25 Dec.* ⊜*5€.* ⧗. ℘*01 34 78 86 60. www.manteslajolie.fr.*
The former Hôtel-Dieu, whose facade dates to the 17C, houses a museum consecrated to neo-Impressionist painter **Maximilien Luce** (1858–1941). With ties to fellow painters Seurat and Pissarro, he was also a friend to many French Anarchist writers. The collection boasts over 150 works, from paintings to drawings

and lithographies. Luce was above all concerned with social issues of his time; in paintings such as *Fonderie à Charleroi, La Coulée* (1896), *L'Exécution de Varlin*, and the series *Gare de l'Est*, he portrays the daily lives of common workers, as well as bloody civil conflicts like the Paris Commune.

Another section of the museum is dedicated to Mantes during the medieval period, housing pottery, tombstones from the old Jewish cemetery (13C), and other artefacts.

Église Sainte-Anne

This 12C Roman-style church once belonged to a Benedictine priory attached to the Abbey of Cluny. Bossuet, bishop of Meaux and private tutor to Louis XIV's eldest son, was an Abbot here from 1664 to 1703. The church has been remarkably restored following damage during bombing raids in 1944. Inside, 13C stained glass is among the most beautiful in France.

EXCURSION

Château de Rosny-sur-Seine★

▶ *6km/3.2mi W of Mantes-la-Jolie along the D 113. Private property/ no visits permitted.*
Maximilien de Béthune, marquis of Rosny (1559–1651), was no doubt born in the feudal château that once stood here. In the early 17C, he commissioned the Louis XIII-style château that replaced it, surrounding it with dry moats, and created the first gardens, filled with lush groves and caves.

In 1820, Marie-Caroline de Bourbon-Sicile, widow of the Duke of Berry, was pregant with a "miracle child": the Duke of Bordeaux, future Count of Chambord. She retired to Rosny, where she restored the château, built a hospice and remodeled the park in the fashionable English style. She fled Rosny at the outbreak of the 1830 Revolution.

La Roche-Guyon★

This village was developed at the foot of an old stronghold; its crumbling keep still dominates the precipitous, rocky ledge. Life at La Roche-Guyon has resumed its peaceful character since the bombings of July 1944 and the Battle of Normandy, when Marshal Rommel established his headquarters in the castle.
The village has retained some of its cave dwellings and fine old houses.

A BIT OF HISTORY
The La Rochefoucauld estate

In the 13C, a residential château was erected at the foot of the cliff not far from the fortress; it was linked to the keep by a flight of steps carved in the rock. François I and his numerous retinue took up residence here in 1546. La Roche-Guyon was made a duchy peerage in 1621. In 1659, the title came into the hands of **François de La Rochefoucauld**, who wrote many of his famous *Maximes* at the château.

SIGHTS
The banks of the Seine★

The quayside promenade commands a good **view★** of the sleepy countryside and the meandering river. Behind, the two castles stand side by side. The abutment pier of the former suspension bridge (dismantled in the 19C) provides a good observation point.

▸ **Population:** 550
Michelin Local Map: p214: A1; map 106 fold 2.
Info: 8 r. du Général Leclerc, 95780 La Roche-Guyon. ☏01 34 79 70 55. www.larocheguyon.fr.
Location: Between the Seine and the Vexin plateau, 80km/50mi W of Paris, via the A 13.
Parking: Large free car park at west side of the village.
Don't Miss: A visit to the troglodyte caves along the Route des Crêtes.
Timing: Allow at least 1–2 hrs to see the village and château.

Château★

Open daily Feb–Mar 10am–5pm; Apr–Oct Mon–Fri 10am–6pm, Sat–Sun and public holidays 10am–7pm; Nov daily 10am–5pm. ☞7.80€. ☏01 34 79 74 42, www.chateaudelarocheguyon.fr.
The superb wrought-iron gates bearing the La Rochefoucauld crest open onto the courtyard and 18C stables, which now house the reception desk and temporary exhibitions. The house still has some 13C features, such as the towers flanking the main apartments. Built in the 16C, they stand on a terrace supported by arcaded foundations. The parapet walkway and 'southeast' tower

The Duke and the young Romantic writers

In 1816 Louis-François Auguste, **Duc de Rohan-Chabot**, acquired the estate. He lost his wife in 1819 and took holy orders at the age of 31. He continued to entertain at the château, combining acts of charity with the fashionable manners of pre-Revolutionary France. Among the guests were fellow students at St-Sulpice Seminary and the young Romantic authors Victor Hugo, Alphonse de Lamartine, Hugues Lamennais, Henri Lacordaire and Father Dupanloup. They delighted in the grand services celebrated in the underground chapel to the strains of a superb Italian organ. In 1829 the duke was appointed Archbishop of Besançon, and then Cardinal; he sold the château and its grounds to François de la Rochefoucauld-Liancourt. La Roche-Guyon has remained in this family ever since.

provide some wonderful panoramic views of the Seine Valley. A newly restored corridor leads to the three chapels. The main one is dedicated to "Our Lady of the Snows". During the German Occupation, numerous pillboxes were built into the cliffs. They now house a retrospective look at Rommel's stay at the château. The remainder of the buildings in the cliffs are now used as the backdrop for a sound and light show on regional art, entitled **Parcours de lumière en Vallée de Seine**.

EXCURSIONS
Route des Crêtes★
⟡ *Round trip of 4km/2.5mi.*

Take the road to Gasny which passes the entrance to the famous troglodyte caves or stables , called **boves**, carved in the chalk. On reaching the pass, turn right onto D 100, also known as *Route des Crêtes*. When the estates no longer conceal the view of the river, park on the belvedere near a spinney of pine trees.

From here, enjoy a **view★★** of the Seine carpeted with the trees of the Forêt de Moisson and, further along the promontory, of the spurs of the Haute-Isle cliffs. in the foreground, you'll see the truncated **keep** of the Château de La Roche-Guyon.

Continue along D 100. At the first junction, turn right onto Charrière des Bois, which leads back to the starting point. The road follows a steep downward slope and passes under the 18C aqueduct that supplies water to the village and the château.

Arboretum de La Roche
⟡ *On D 37 towards Amenucourt.*

The arboretum, which spreads over 12ha/29 acres, has been planted to reproduce the geography of the Île-de-France area. Each *département* is distinguished by a different species: oak for Seine-et-Marne, maple for Essonne, hornbeam for Val-de-Marne, ash for Val-d'Oise, cherry for Seine-Saint-Denis, lime for Les Hauts-de-Seine, and beech for Yvelines. The plane trees in the middle represent Paris. There is one 20-year-old Lebanese cedar at the central roundabout.

Haute-Isle
⟡ *2km/1.2mi E of La Roche-Guyon along D 913.*

This troglodytic village harbours seven levels of man-made caves, or **boves,** carved into the cliffside. The houses lining the lone street here only appeared in the 18C. Behind a small cemetery, a church dating to 1670 is one of only a handful of churches in France to be entirely dug into a cliffside. Its tiny bell tower emerges from the rocky cliff.

Vétheuil
⟡ *6km/3.7mi E along D 913.*

This former wine-growing village has a lovely riverside setting on the steep banks of one of the Seine's meanders. The village houses are characteristic of the French Vexin region. The town was made famous by the Impressionists; Monet lived here for three years.

Domaine de Villarceaux
⟡ *10km/6.2mi NE. from Chaussy, follow D 71 towards Magny-en-Vexin. Follow signposted road 'La Comté'. A little further on the right, a new access road leads to a vast parking area.* ⟡*Open Apr–Jun, Sep–Oct Wed, Sat, Sun 2–5pm; Jun–Aug Tue–Sun 2–5pm. ☏01 53 85 51 85 (Mon–Fri). villarceaux.iledefrance.fr.*

Villarceaux estate is graced by a magnificent setting and two châteaux: a 15C-16C manor house which belonged to the celebrated beauty Ninon de Lenclos, and a Louis XV château. Approaching the estate from the south, the road from Villers-en-Arthies offers a glimpse of a third edifice, the Château du Couvent. The Manoir de Ninon replaced a former fortified house now reduced to the Tour St-Nicolas. Ninon's pavilion ends with a tower which houses an Italian closet. The **gardens★** illustrate the evolution of gardens through the centuries. The terraces on the left of the entrance are overlooked by the St-Nicolas Tower, known as the 'tower of the condemned' because witches were hanged there. The path circling the large pond leads past Ninon's pool, and reveals a **view★** of the south front of the Louis XV castle.

Giverny★★

Giverny preserves the memory of legendary painter Claude Monet, who lived here from 1883 to his death in 1926. His rose-hued house with green shutters and adjoining lush garden transport you to some of his most beautiful works. It was here that Monet created his legendary series of poplars and haystacks, as well as one of his great masterpieces, *Nymphéas*.

▶ **Population:** 550
◔ **Michelin Local Map:** p214 A1 or map 106 fold 2.
▯ **Info:** Office de tourisme des Portes de l'Eure: In the car park facing the Musée des Impressionnismes. www.cape-tourisme.fr. ☏02 32 51 39 60. Apr–Oct: 9.30am–1pm, 2–5.30pm; Sep–Oct: 10am–1pm, 2.30–5.30pm.
◖ **Location:** A small village located on the right banks of the Seine and Epte rivers, which meet here; 72 km from Paris along the A 13. By train from Paris-St-Lazare to the Vernon station; 7 km from Vernon to Giverny by shuttle, taxi or bus number 240.

SIGHTS
Maison de Claude Monet★

84 r. Claude-Monet. ◔*Open Apr–mid-Nov 9.30am–6pm.* ◔*Closed mid-Nov–Mar.* ◒*9.50€ (under 7s free).* ☏*02 32 51 28 21. www.fondation-monet.com.*

The long house overlooking Monet's famed gardens features several reproductions of the artist's works, as well as a large series of Japanese woodblock prints (18C–19C) collected by Monet. Also of note is the sitting room, the studio-workshop, the dining room in warm yellow hues and painted wood furniture, and, above all, the splendid kitchen, with walls covered in blue tiles from Rouen.

The true highlight, however, are the gardens, which change beautifully in accordance with the seasons, and include the water garden and the area known as the Clos normand. Monet frequently drew and painted the latter in full bloom. Rectangular pathways bursting with colour lead to the man-made, Japanese-style water garden, supplied with waters from the Epte river. Japanese-inspired bridges stretch across the Nymphéas pond, carpeted with waterlilies. The iconic weeping willow and banks lined with bamboo and rhododendrons are to further poetic effect.

Musée des Impressionismes★

90 r. Claude-Monet. ◔*Open Apr–Oct 10am–6pm.* ◔*Closed Nov–Mar.* ◒*7€ (7–12 years 3€, 13–18 years 4.50€). No charge 1st Sun of month. www.mdig.fr.*

This new museum dedicated to the Impressionist movement has been seamlessly incorporated into Giverny's lush green landscapes, yet boasts remarkably futuristic architecture. The building was designed against the natural slope of the hillside and features a lush green roof. Large glass doors open onto a splendid contemporary garden created by landscape painter Mark Rudkin, dominated by thujas and beechtrees. Rosebushes, aromatic and wild plants, poppies and other varieties grace the garden beds.

The museum comprises three galleries and a large auditorium. The collection traces the history of Impressionism and related movements. Temporary exhibits dedicated to the great Impressionist painters permit visitors to better appreciate this diversity.

🏃 *After visiting the museum, two marked trails allow visitors to discover the flora and fauna in Giverny and surrounds:*

Sentier du Lézard Vert *(5km/3.1mi).*
Sentier de l'Astragale *(5.5km/3.4mi). Reach the trail heads by taking a left at r. Blanche-Hoschedé from the Auberge Baudy. For more info: call or visit the Tourist Office.*

Musée A.-G.-Poulain

12 r. du Pont, Vernon. ⏰*Open Apr–Sep Tue–Fri 10.30am–12.30pm, 2–6pm, weekends 2–6pm; Oct–Mar Tue–Sun 2–5.30pm.* 🎫*2.50€.* 📞*02 32 21 28 09. www.giverney.org/museums/poulain.* This museum dedicated to painting and drawing is situated in renovated buildings dating from the 15C to the 18C. The courtyard boasts an impressive forged iron portal; this once graced the château de Bizy. Works from painters of the Nabi school, including Pierre Bonnard, Rosa Bonheur and Maurice Denis, are of particular interest Also don't miss two key works by Claude Monet: *Falaises à Pourville* and *Nénuphars.*

Pontoise and the Oise Loop★

The historic city of Pontoise is part of the modern agglomeration of Cergy-Pontoise. Built on a plateau, its fortified walls once dominated the Oise and the city has preserved its medieval layout, boasting noteworthy monuments, elegant squares and narrow, winding streets. The old city forms an interesting contrast to the "Axe Majeur" in Cergy: an immense public garden laid out in 1980 and an excellent example of contemporary landscape design.

SIGHTS
Cathédrale St-Maclou

This cathedral, of mixed style due to successive remodellings, has dominant architectural elements dating to the 15C –16C. A flamboyant tower, central portal and rose window are crowned with a Renaissance dome.

Skirting the right side of the facade, note the lovely Renaissance windows. The pilasters, decorated with and separated by sculptures, boast a frieze graced with gargoyles.

Go around the 12C chevet via rue de la Pierre-aux-Poissons: note the Renais-

ADDRESSES

🏠 STAY

🛏🛏**La Musardière –** *32 r. Claude-Monet.* 📞*02 32 21 03 18. www.lamusardiere.fr.* *10 rooms.* Lodging in a house c. 1880 at the village edge, in the middle of a small park. Warm, old-style service and rustic ambience. The restaurant has a large, pleasant terrace.

▸ **Population:** 30 376
⊙ **Michelin Map:** p214 C1; 305.
🛈 **Info:** Tourist Office – 6 pl. du Petit-Martroy. 📞01 34 41 70 60. www.ot-cergypontoise.fr.
▸ **Location:** 35 km from Paris along the A 15. Train from Paris-St-Lazare or Paris-Nord station; RER Cergy Pontoise. For Cergy, RER A: Cergy-Préfecture or Cergy-St-Christophe.
👁 **Don't miss:** The musée Tavet-Delacour and the musée Pissarro; l'Axe majeur.
👥 **Kids:** The ponds at Cergy-Neuville.

sance portal onto the ambulatory. The nave is marked by 15C–16C elements, notably the north capitals decorated with human figures.

The chancel and ambulatory form the only discernable 12C elements. On the other side of the facade, a chapel presents sculptures deciated to the theme of the Passion of the Christ.

Musée Tavet-Delacour

4 r. Lemercier. ○*Open Wed–Sun 10am–12.30pm; 1.30–6pm.* ○*Closed public holidays.* ⊛*5€.* ☎*01 30 38 02 40. www.ot-cergypontoise.fr.*

Housed in a 15C manor, this municipal museum is dedicated to the works of **Otto Freundlich** (1878–1943), a German artist who lived in Paris from 1908, as well as other contemporary artists (Arp, Gleizes, Matisse etc).

Musée Pissarro

17 r. du Château. ○*Open Wed–Sun 2–6pm.* ○*Closed public holidays.* ⊛*Free.* ☎*01 30 32 38 33. www.ot-cergypontoise.fr.*

Dedicated to painter **Camille Pissarro** (1830–1903), who worked and lived in Pontoise from 1866, the museum also hosts several temporary exhibits a year focusing on other 19C Impressionists and post-Impressionists. The museum occupies a residence on the site of a royal chateau, destroyed in 1740.

 WALKING TOUR

The Oise Loop

▷*This itinerary takes approx 30 minutes. Begin at RER A station Cergy-Préfecture. Take the bd. du Port southwest on Bus 38 (Menucourt stop).*
Highlights in **Cergy-Village** include the St-Christophe church and square, graced with a 16C nave that was never completed. The church (○—Closed for renovations) is accessed by a Renaissance-era portico.

▷ Continue toward the Port-Cergy: bus 48, Base de Loisirs stop.

The Cergy marina in **Port Cergy** houses some 100 boats and is perfect for a leisurely stroll. Cross the footbridge to reach the ponds at **Cergy-Neuville**. The 250ha/618acre ponds offer supervised swimming and waterskiing.
Created in 1985 by Ricardo Bofill and Dani Karavan, **L'Axe Majeur** is a jewel of contemporary architecure. It boasts a 3km/1.8mi promenade and urban gar-den, "sculpted" into the landscape. The Axe was envisioned as a prolongation of the "Voie Triomphale" in Paris – the line stretching from the Louvre to Place de la Concorde and La Défense. The start-point is the Tour-Belvédere, a 36m/118ft column at the centre of amphitheatre-style buildings. The top affords a pano-rama. L'Axe is divided into 12 "stations", including the Impressionists park, the "astronomical island" and a pyramid. A footbridge connects the amphitheatre to the island. The Cergy-St-Christophe station, meanwhile, has gained acco-lades for its monumental clock.

EXCURSIONS
St-Ouen-l'Aumône

▷*3km/1.8mi SW of Pontoise along av. du Gén.-Leclerc.*

Abbaye de Maubuisson – *r. Richard-de-Tour. Take the A 15, exit 7 or 8; RER A, Cergy-Préfecture, then bus 56 and 57, to Mairie.* ○*Open Mon–Fri 1–6pm; week-ends and holidays 2–6pm.* ○*Closed Sep, 1 Jan, 1 May and 25 Dec.* ⊛*No charge.* �& ☎*01 34 64 36 10. wwwvaldoise.fr.*

It's difficult to imagine the lost beauty of this Cictercian abbey founded in 1236 by Blanche de Castille. Originally named Notre-Dame-la-Royale, it was led by a succession of powerful abbesses in the Middle Ages.

Closed by Louis XVI in 1787, the abbey was progressively dismantled. Only a few buildings survived, including the elegant **chapter house★** and an impressive 13C **barn★**. The building now exhibits contemporary art shows.

Château de Grouchy

▷*Osny. 4km/2.5mi W of Pontoise along D 92. From Cergy: bus 44 to Osny-Gare.* ○*Open 1st Sun of the month, 2–6pm.* ○*Closed Jul–Aug.* ☎*01 34 25 42 00.*

Now housing the town hall, this build-ing dates to the medieval period: the only vestige is a tower now serving as a dovecote. The top floor houses a small museum dedicated to William Thornley.

Auvers-Sur-Oise★★

In the early 19C, this pleasant riverside village just outside Paris became the favoured stomping ground for a new generation of painters known as the 'Impressionists' (&see Introduction), including Monet, Van Gogh and Corot. You're bound to recognise many of the sights as you walk through the narrow streets. Here and there, panels indicate the scenes portrayed by Impressionist painters, while the district around the church is a favourite 'place of pilgrimage' for art lovers.

IN VAN GOGH'S FOOTSTEPS

During his stay in Auvers, Vincent Van Gogh was extremely active. The restful countryside, where he hoped to find peace after his internment in Provence, encouraged his quest for freedom and his frantic need to work. He completed over 70 paintings in a very short time.

Auberge Ravoux★

pl. de la Mairie. ○Open Mar–Oct Wed–Sun 10am–6pm. ◎6€. ℘01 30 36 60 60. www.maisondevangogh.fr.
Known as the **Maison de Van Gogh**, this is the inn where Van Gogh stayed for two months before his tragic death. Feeling guilt towards his brother Theo, upon whom he was entirely dependent, Van Gogh shot himself in the chest while he was out in a field; he died two days later in his room. He was 37 years old. The inn has been carefully restored and

▶ **Population:** 7 082
⌖ **Michelin Local Map:** p214:C1 or map 106 fold 6.
▯ **Info:** Manoir des Colombières, r. de la Sansonne, 95430 Auvers-sur-Oise, ℘01 30 36 10 06. www.auvers-sur-oise.com.
▶ **Location:** Auvers-sur-Oise lies just 32km/20mi NW of Paris, along the A 115. SNCF depart from Gare du Nord or Gare St-Lazare, changing at Pontoise.
⊛ **Don't Miss:** Use the map available at the tourist office to locate the various sites with ease.
👥 **Kids:** The 17C Château d'Auvers.
🕑 **Timing:** Spend a full day here to explore the home of Dr Gachet and the Maison du Pendu.

has retained its interior decoration and restaurant. Outside are panels describing the artist's dramatic life.
The small garret he occupied has remained unchanged and, despite the absence of furniture, gives an insight into the ascetic conditions in which he lived. The tour ends with an audio-visual presentation of Van Gogh's stay in Auvers.

▶ Follow r. des Colombières past the museum and studio of Charles-François Daubigny (& see Additional Sights).

A path to the right leads to a cemetery set among the corn fields that Van Gogh loved to paint.

Vincent and Theo Van Gogh's Graves

r. Émile-Bernard.
The famous Dutch painter's tomb stands against the left-hand wall. His brother Theo, who supported him and who died soon after him, rests by his side.

© Renaud Visage/age fotostock

EXCURSIONS
Méry-sur-Oise
▶*1km/0.6km S of Auvers along the D 928 (av. Marcel-Perrin). No visits.*

The château de Méry, built on the site of a 14C priory, was redesigned in the 17C and 18C, then renovated in 1999. While visits to the chateau are not possible, the **château park** affords pleasant views of the river winding through the landscapes. *℘01 30 36 23 00. www.merysuroise.fr.*

Additional Sights
Musée de l'Absinthe
44 r. Alphonse Callé. ◐*Open mid-Jun–mid-Sept Wed–Fri 1.30–6pm, Sat–Sun 11am–6pm; mid-Sept–mid-Jun Sat–Sun 11am–6pm.* ⬤*5€. Guided tour and absinthe tasting: 12€.* *℘01 30 36 83 26. www.musee-absinthe.com.*

The famous green liqueur, dubbed the **green fairy,** reached the peak of its popularity in 19C cafés. Documents, posters and objects recount the history of a drink which had a profound social and artistic influence until it was banned (at least in its true form) in 1915.

Musée Daubigny
r. de la Sansonne. ◐*Open Apr–Oct Wed–Fri 2–6pm, Sat–Sun 10.30am–12.30pm, 2–6pm; Nov–Mar Wed–Fri 2–5pm, Sat–Sun 2–5.30pm.* ⬤*4€. ℘01 30 36 80 20. www.musee-daubigny.com.*

This collection of 19C paintings, drawings and engravings illustrates the birth of Impressionism, concentrating on works by landscape painter Daubigny. There are also contemporary works.

Maison-Atelier de Daubigny★
61 r. Daubigny ◐*Open Apr–mid-Jul, mid-Aug–Oct Thu–Sun 2–6.30pm.* ⬤*6€. ℘01 30 36 60 60. www.atelier-daubigny.com.*
Charles-François Daubigny (1817–78), settled in Auvers in 1861 on the advice of his friend Camille Corot. Paintings from Charles, Corot, Daumier and others grace the walls of the house. In 1890, Van Gogh painted Daubigny's garden.

👥 Château d'Auvers
50 r. de Léry Audio tours (1hr30min); last admission 1hr30min before closing. ◐*Open Apr–Sept Tue–Sun 10.30am–6pm; Oct–Mar Tue–Sun 10.30am–4.30pm.* ⬤*13.50€ (children 9.40€).* ℘*01 34 48 48 40. www.chateau-auvers.fr.*

This 17C château takes visitors on a **Journey Back to the Days of the Impressionists★**. Using reconstructions of interiors, audiovisual materials and the projection of some 600 works of art, it brings to life Paris during its transformation by Baron Haussmann.

ADDRESSES

🛏 STAY

😴😴😴😴 **Hostellerie du Nord –** *6 r. du Gén.-de-Gaulle.* ℘ *01 30 36 70 74. www.hostelleriedunord.fr. Closed Sat, Sun eves, Mon. 8 rooms.* This former post house once lodged renowned painters. Artworks adorn the dining area and rooms. Traditional French cuisine.

🍴 EAT

😋😋😋 **Auberge Ravoux** – *Opposite the town hall.* ℘*01 30 36 60 60. www.maisondevangogh.fr. Closed Mon–Tue, Fri–Sat lunches, mid-Nov–mid-Mar. Reservations required.* This old artists' café was Van Gogh's last home. Serving solid traditional cuisine and wine from small vintners.

😋😋 **Le Chemin des peintres** – *3 bis r. de Paris.* ℘*01 30 36 14 15. www.lechemindespeintres.fr. Wed–Fri 11.30am–4pm, Sat 11.30am–11pm, Sun and holidays 11.30am–7pm. Closed Mon, Tue and 20 Dec–5 Jan.* Refined country bistro cuisine made from local farm and organic products. Bright, modern decor.

ACTIVITIES
Val d'Oise Impressionist Trail – ℘*01 30 29 51 00. www.valdoise-tourisme.com.* Auvers-sur-Oise, L'Isle-Adam, La Roche-Guyon and Argenteuil are situated along the regional "Impressionist Trail", which allows visitors to follow in the footsteps of painters who worked or lived in the region, including Monet, Daubigny, Pissarro, Renoir and Van Gogh. Visit the website for suggested itineraries.

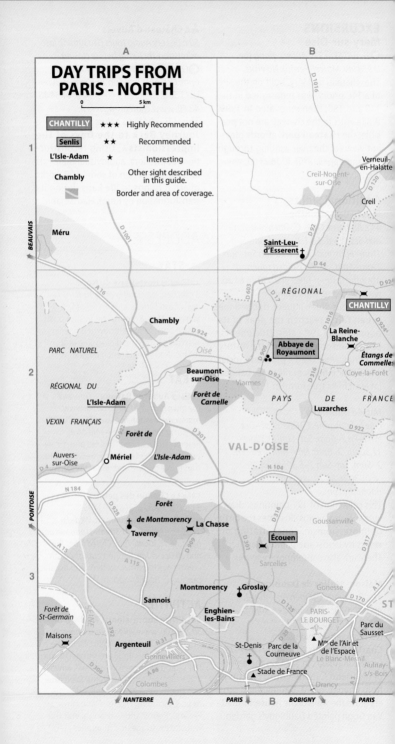

**DAY TRIPS FROM
PARIS - NORTH**

0   5 km

CHANTILLY	★★★	Highly Recommended
<u>Senlis</u>	★★	Recommended
<u>L'Isle-Adam</u>	★	Interesting
Chambly		Other sight described in this guide.
		Border and area of coverage.

BEAUVAIS

Méru

D 1001

Verneuil-
en-Halatte

Creil-Nogent-
sur-Oise

Creil

D 120

D 1016

A 16

**Saint-Leu-
d'Esserent** ✝

D 92

D 44

RÉGIONAL

D 603

D 17

D 924

CHANTILLY

D 1016

D 924

Chambly

D 924

Oise

D 609

**Abbaye de
Royaumont**

**La Reine-
Blanche**

*Étangs de
Commelles*

Coye-la-Forêt

**Beaumont-
sur-Oise**

Viarmes

D 922

D 316

PARC NATUREL

RÉGIONAL DU

*Forêt de
Carnelle*

PAYS

DE

FRANCE

<u>L'Isle-Adam</u>

Luzarches

D 922

VEXIN FRANÇAIS

D 301

D 922

Forêt de

VAL-D'OISE

Auvers-
sur-Oise

○ **Mériel**

L'Isle-Adam

N 104

D 4

PONTOISE

N 184

D 928

Forêt

de Montmorency

La Chasse ✕

D 316

Goussainville

✝
Taverny

D 909

Écouen ✕

D 301

D 317

A 15

A 115

Sarcelles

A 1

**Forêt de
St-Germain**

Montmorency ✝**Groslay**

Sannois

Gonesse

D 170

ST

Maisons ✕

D 392

Argenteuil

**Enghien-
les-Bains**

D 125

PARIS-
LE BOURGET

**Parc du
Sausset**

Gennevilliers

N 31

SEINE

St-Denis ✝

Parc de la
Courneuve

▲ Mᵉᵉ de l'Air et
de l'Espace

Le Blanc-Mesnil

Aulnay-
s/s-Bois

Colombes

D 308

A 86

▲ Stade de France

Drancy

A 3

NANTERRE   A   PARIS   B   BOBIGNY   PARIS

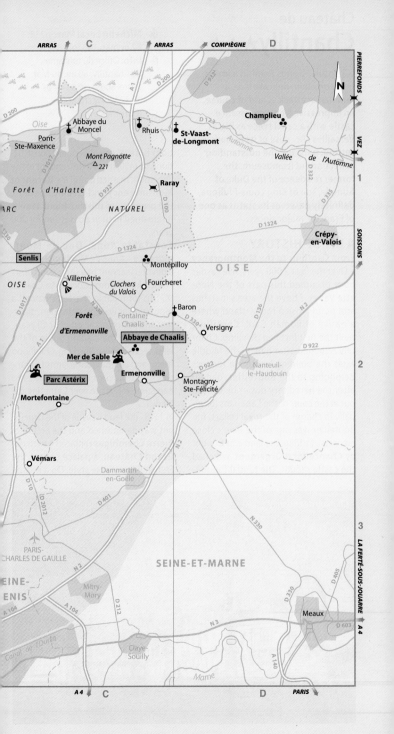

Château de
Chantilly★★★

"Chantilly" brings to mind a forest, fine porcelain, delicate lace, a famous racetrack… and of course, an impressive Neo-Renaissance castle with a canal twice as big as Versailles'. Because of its remarkable setting, park and the outstanding collections of its museum, the former residence of the Duke of Aumale, son of King Louis-Philippe, definitely deserves its status as one of France's major sights.

A BIT OF HISTORY

From Cantilius to the Montmorency – Over the past 2 000 years, five castles have occupied this part of the Non-ette Valley. Above the area's marshes and ponds rose a rocky island where a native of Roman Gaul, **Cantilius,** built the first fortified dwelling. Chantilly is named after him. In the Middle Ages the building became a fortress belonging to the **Bouteiller**, named after the hereditary duties he carried out at the court of the Capetians (originally in charge of the royal cellars, the Bouteiller was one of the king's close advisers). In 1386, the land was bought by **Chancellor d'Orgemont**, who had the castle rebuilt. The feudal founda-

> ♿ **Michelin Local Map:** p238: B2 or map 106 fold 8
>
> 🅸 **Info:** Office du tourisme de Chantilly, 60 av. du Mar. Joffre, 60631. ✆03 44 67 37 37. www.chantilly-tourisme.com.

tions bore three subsequent constructions. In 1450, the last descendant of the Orgemont married one of the **Barons of Montmorency** and Chantilly became the property of this illustrious family. It remained in their possession for 200 years.

Constable Anne, Duc de Montmorency – Anne de Montmorency was a devoted servant to a succession of six French kings from Louis XII to Charles IX. This formidable character gained a reputation as warrior, statesman, diplomat and patron of the arts. For 40 years, he remained the leading noble of the land, second only to the king. Childhood friend and companion-in-arms to François I, close adviser to Henri II, he even had some influence over Catherine de' Medici.

In 1528, the feudal castle of the Orgemont was demolished and the architect **Pierre Chambiges** replaced it with the **Grand Château**, a palace built in the French Renaissance style. On a nearby

Château de Chantilly

© Steve Vidler/age fotostock

island, **Jean Bullant** erected a charming château which still stands today: the **Petit Château**. It was separated from the Grand Château by a moat (now filled in) which was spanned by two superimposed bridges. New gardens were designed, the best artists were called to decorate both castles, and Chantilly became one of the most prestigious estates in the kingdom of France. Constable Anne died in 1567, during the second of the Wars of Religion.

The last love of Henri IV – Henri IV often stayed at Chantilly, with his companion-in-arms **Henri I de Montmorency**, the son of Constable Anne. At the age of 54, the king fell in love with his host's daughter Charlotte, aged only 15. He arranged for her to marry Henri II de Bourbon-Condé, a shy and gauche young man, whom the king hoped would prove an accommodating husband. The day after the wedding, however, Condé left the capital with his wife. Henri IV ordered them to return to Paris. The young couple fled to Brussels, where they stayed under the protection of the King of Spain. Henri IV raged, implored, threatened and went as far as to ask the Pope to intervene. Only when Henri IV was murdered by Ravaillac did the two fugitives return to France.

Encouraged by Louis XIII's brother, the scheming Gaston d'Orléans, **Henri II de Montmorency** plotted against Richelieu. He was defeated at Castelnaudary near Toulouse and made a prisoner after receiving 18 wounds. By way of an apology, he bequeathed to Cardinal Richelieu the two *Slave* statues by Michelangelo, now in the Louvre; those at Chantilly and Écouen are replicas.

The Great Condé – Charlotte de Montmorency and her husband the Prince of Condé – the couple persecuted by Henri IV – inherited Chantilly in 1643; the château remained family property until 1830. Descendants of Charles de Bourbon like Henri IV, the Princes of Condé were of royal blood and the heir apparent to the title was called the Duke of Enghien.

The Great Condé was the son of Charlotte and Henri II. He applied himself

Statue of Henri IV

© S. Sauvignier/MICHELIN

to renovating the Château de Chantilly with the same energy and efficiency he had shown in military operations. In 1662 he commissioned **Le Nôtre** to redesign the park and the forest. The fountains at Chantilly were considered the most elegant in France and Louis XIV made a point of outclassing them at Versailles. The work lasted 20 years and the result was a splendid achievement, part of which still stands today.

The Last of the Condés –The Prince of Condé died at Fontainebleau in 1686, to the king's great dismay. During the religious ceremony preceding the burial, Bossuet delivered a funeral oration which became famous.

The great-grandson of the Great Condé, **Louis-Henri de Bourbon**, alias "Monsieur le Duc", was an artist with a taste for splendour, who gave Chantilly a new lease on life. He asked **Jean Aubert** to build the Grandes Écuries, a masterpiece of the 18C, and set up a porcelain factory which closed down in 1870.

The **Château d'Enghien** was built on the estate by **Louis-Joseph de Condé** in 1769. His newborn grandson, the Duke of Enghien, was its first occupant. The infant duke's father was only 16, his grandfather 36. The young prince died tragically in 1804; he was seized by the French police in the margravate of Baden and shot outside the fortress of Vincennes on the orders of Bonaparte. During the **French Revolution**, the main building was razed to the ground, though the Petit Château was spared. Louis-Joseph was 78 when he returned from exile. His son accompanied him back to Chantilly and they were dismayed to find their château was in ruins. Vowing to renovate the estate, they bought back the plots of their former land, restored the Petit Château, redesigned and refurbished the grounds.

The prince died in 1818, but the duke continued the renovation work. He was an enthusiastic hunter and at the age of 70 he still hunted daily. Thanks to his efforts, Chantilly became the lively, fashionable place it had been in the years preceding the Revolution. As in former times, the receptions and hunting parties attracted elegant visitors.

The Revolution of 1830 raised his cousin Louis-Philippe to the throne, and the Duke considered returning to England. Days later, he was found hanging from a window at his castle in St-Leu. He was the last descendant of the Condé.

The Duke of Bourbon had left Chantilly to his great-nephew and godson the **Duke of Aumale**, the fourth son of Louis-Philippe. This prince gained recognition in Africa when he captured Abd el-Kader and his numerous relations. The Revolution of 1848 forced him into exile and he returned only in 1870.

From 1875 to 1881, the duke commissioned **Daumet** to build the Grand Château in the Renaissance style. This castle, the fifth in a succession, still stands today. The duke died in 1897 and the Institute of France inherited Chantilly, together with the superb collections that constitute the Condé Museum.

CHÂTEAU★★★

○*Open daily Apr–Oct Wed–Mon 10am–6pm; Nov–Mar Wed–Mon 10.30am–5pm.* ✆14€ *(château, park and museum),* 18€ *whole estate.* ✆03 44 27 31 80. www.domainedechantilly.com. The two main buildings were once divided by an arm of water: the 16C Petit Château (or barbican) and the Grand Château, for which Daumet used the foundations of the former stronghold.

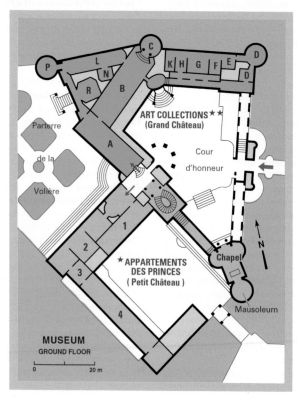

MUSEUM
GROUND FLOOR
0 — 20 m

Cross the constable's terrace, which bears the equestrian statue of Anne de Montmorency, and enter the main courtyard through the gateway flanked by the two copies of Michelangelo's *Slaves*.

The Duke of Aumale never intended to create a museum for educational purposes; he merely wanted to build up a fine art collection. He therefore hung the works in chronological order of purchase, though favourites were sometimes placed in a separate room. The curators have respected his layout. According to the terms of the duke's legacy, the Institute must agree "to make no changes to the interior and exterior architecture of the château." Moreover, it is not allowed to lend any of the exhibits.

The reception hall is the starting point for guided tours of the chapel and various apartments as well as for unaccompanied tours of the collections. if a group has already formed, it is best to join it . It is advisable to interrupt a visit to the collections if the custodians announce a guided tour of the apartments.

Appartements des Princes★ (Petit Château)

The **Grands Appartements,** occupied by the Great Condé and his descendants, were embellished with Regency and Rococo **wainscoting★★**, especially in the 18C thanks to the Duke of Bourbon.

The Duke of Aumale took up residence in the **Petits Appartements** on the ground floor, and had them designed and decorated by painter Eugène Lami specially for his marriage in 1844.

Below are a few highlights; a visit to the Petit Chateau promises far more. **Cabinet des Livres★** (Library) **(1)** – Open Mon–Fri 9.15am–5pm. Reservations only. 03 44 62 62 69. This gallery has a splendid collection of manuscripts, including **The Very Rich Hours of the Duke of Berry** (*Les Très Riches Heures du duc de Berry*) with 15C illuminations by the Limbourg brothers. This extremely fragile

Library

D. Pazery/ MICHELIN

document is not permanently exhibited, but visitors may see a facsimile by Faksimile Verlag of Luzern. Another interesting reproduction is the psalter of Queen Ingeburge of Denmark.

Notable ornamental motifs include the monogram of the Duke of Aumale (H O for Henri d'Orléans) and the Condé coat of arms (France's "broken" coat of arms with a diagonal line symbolising the younger branch of the family).

Chambre de Monsieur le Prince (2) –This title referred to the reigning Condé Prince, in this instance the Duke of Bourbon (1692–1740), who installed a wainscot at the far end of the room, into which were embedded panels painted by C Huet in 1735. The famous Louis XVI commode was designed by Riesener and made by Hervieu.

Salon des Singes (3) –This collection of monkey scenes *(singeries)* dating from the early 18C, is a masterpiece by an anonymous draughtsman.

Galerie de Monsieur le Prince (4) –The Great Condé had ordered his own battle gallery, which he never saw completed (1692). The sequence was interrupted from 1652 to 1659 during his years of rebellion.

Chapel

An **altar★** attributed to Jean Goujon and some 16C wainscoting and stained-glass windows from the chapel at Écouen were brought here by the Duke of Aumale.

The apse contains the **mausoleum** of Henri II de Condé and the stone urn which received the hearts of the Condé princes.

The Collections★★ (Grand Château)

As you cross the **Galerie des Cerfs (A)**, dedicated to hunting themes, note the 17C Gobelins tapestries.

Galerie de Peinture (B) – The variety of paintings reflect the tastes of the Duke of Aumale. Military events are illustrated on huge canvases (*Battle on the Railway Line* by Neuville, Meissonnier's *The Cuirassiers of 1805*). Orientalism is well represented with Gros' work, *The Plague Victims of Jaffa*, H Vernet's *Arab Sheikhs holding Council*, and *The Falcon Hunt* by Fromentin. Note, too, the famous portrait of *Gabrielle d'Estrées in her Bath* (16C French school), the portraits of Cardinals Richelieu and Mazarin by Philippe de Champaigne, and *The Massacre of the Holy Innocents* by Poussin.

Rotonde (C) – The *Loreto Madonna* by **Raphael, Piero di Cosimo's** portrait of the ravishing Simonetta Vespucci, who is believed to have been Botticelli's model for his *Birth of Venus*, and Chapu's kneeling statue of Joan of Arc listening to voices are exhibited here.

Salle de la Smalah and Salle de la Minerve (D) – Family portraits of the Orléans (17C, 18C and 19C) and of Louis-Philippe's kin in particular: Bonnat's picture of the Duke of Aumale at the age of 68.

Cabinet de Giotto (E) – A room devoted to Italian Primitives: *Angels Dancing in the Sun* (Italian School, 15C).

Salle Isabelle (F) – 19C paintings including *Moroccan Guards* by Delacroix, *Horse Leaving the Stables* by Géricault, and *Françoise de Rimini* by Ingres.

Salon d'Orléans (G) – The cabinets contain **soft-paste Chantilly porcelain** manufactured in the workshops founded in 1725 by the Duke of Bourbon.

Salle Caroline (H) – 18C painting has pride of place here, with portraits by Largillière and Greuze, *Young Woman Playing with Children* by Van Loo, *The Worried Lover* and *The Serenade Player* by Watteau, or *Snowstorm* by Everdingen.

Salle Clouet (K) – A precious collection of extremely rare **paintings★★** executed by the **Clouets**, Corneille de Lyon, etc. portraying François I, Marguerite of Navarre and Henri II as a child.

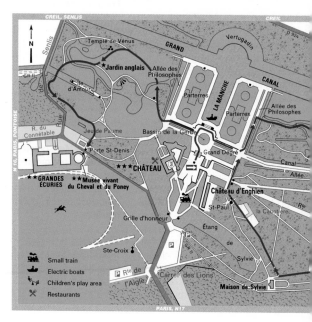

Galerie de Psyché (L) – The 44 **stained-glass windows** (16C) that tell the story of the loves of Psyche and Cupid came from Constable Anne's other family home, Château d'Écouen.

Santuario★★★ (N) – This houses the museum's most precious exhibits: **Raphael**'s *Orléans Madonna*, and *The Three Ages of Womanhood*, also known as *The Three Graces*, by the same artist; *Esther and Ahasuerus*, the panel of a wedding chest painted by **Filippino Lippi**; and 40 miniature works by **Jean Fouquet**, cut out of Estienne Chevalier's book of hours, a splendid example of French 15C art.

Cabinet des Gemmes (P) – This area contains stunning jewels. The Pink Diamond, alias the Great Condé (*a copy of which is permanently on show*), was stolen in 1926 and subsequently found in an apple where the thieves had hidden it.

Tribune (R) – Above the cornice of this polygonal room are painted panels representing episodes from the life of the Duke of Aumale and the house of Orléans. The paintings include *Autumn* by **Botticelli**, *Love Disarmed* and *Pastoral Pleasures* by **Watteau**, a portrait of Molière by **Mignard**, and on the "Ecouen

Wall", three superb works by **Ingres**: a self-portrait, *Madame Devaucay* and *Venus*.

PARK★★

🕐 *Open Apr–Oct Wed–Mon 10am–8pm; Nov–Mar Wed–Mon 10.30am–6pm.* 🎫*7€.* 📞*03 44 27 31 80. www.domainedechantilly.com.*

Take a stroll in this huge park (115ha/ 284acre) designed at the end of the 17C by Le Nôtre, and discover some of its highlights.

Maison de Sylvie – This charming 18C house was named after the duchess of Montmorency's nickname from the French poet Théophile de Viau.

👥 **Kangaroo Enclave** – Finding kangaroos in the park may seem a bit surprising, but it is a reminder of the Princes de Condé's *ménagerie*, which was destroyed during the French Revolution.

Chapelle St-Jean – This chapel was erected by Constable Anne in 1538 along with six others; they commemorate the seven churches of Rome he had visited to gain the indulgences granted to pilgrims. Two other chapels still stand here: **Ste-Croix**, on the racecourse, and **St-Paul**, located behind the **Château d'Enghien**, built in 1769 by Jean-François Leroy to house the Princes of Condé's numerous guests.

Cascade – These tiered waterfalls mark the start of the **Grand Canal** that Le Nôtre created in 1671–1673 by canalizing the waters of the Nonette River.

Hameau – This charming miniature village (1775) was renovated in 2008.

Parterres à la française – The 2009 renovation of these French gardens, including the restoration of Le Nôtre's **hydraulic system**, has given them a new lease of life. Both parterres are framed by the **Allée des Philosophes**, named after the great writers who visited Chantilly. The circular Vertugadin lawns lie along the line of **La Manche**, flanked by stretches of water.

Between La Manche and the round **Bassin de la Gerbe** stands Coysevox's statue of the Great Condé, framed by effigies of La Bruyère and Bossuet (statues of Molière and Le Nôtre in the near distance). The **Grand Degré** is a large

THE PARK

0 ——— 150 m

VINEUIL

le Hameau

Labyrinthes
Morfondus

Blanche

Cascade

St-Jean

Enclos des
kangourous

du

Pont

du

Roi

WHERE TO EAT
Aux Goûters Champêtres .... ①
La Capitainerie "Les Cuisines de Vatel" .... ③

stairway leading from the parterres to the terrace.

Jardin anglais★ – Designed by **Victor Dubois** in 1819 for Prince Louis-Joseph de Condé, this English-style garden was laid out on the surviving relics of Le Nôtre's park. Its charm derives from the pleasant groves rather than from its symbolic monuments: remains of the **Temple de Vénus** and **Île d'Amour**.

ADDITIONAL SIGHTS
Grandes écuries★★

◷*Open to the public; equestrian shows. www.museevivantducheval.fr.*
Designed by **Jean Aubert** for Louis-Henri de Bourbon, the Great Stables constitute the most stunning piece of 18C architecture in Chantilly.

Nouveau musée du Cheval★★ – This new 15-room museum features interactive exhibits and audiovisual displays exploring the evolution of horses and horseracing around the world, technological advances and the role of horses in power, warfare and hunting.

Le Potager des Princes

17 r. de la Faisanderie. ◷*Open daily (except Tue) Feb–Nov, 2–7pm.* ◉*8.50€.* ℘*03 44 57 39 66. www.potagerdesprinces.com.*
Designed in 1682 for the Grand Condé's **pheasantry**, this garden includes an orchard, rose and vegetable gardens.

SURROUNDS
Forêt de Chantilly

Managed by the Office National des Forêts, this vast wooded area (6 300 ha) shelters deer, wild boars and other animals, and offers paths ideal for country walks and horseriding. Hikers will appreciate nature walks around **Coye-la-Forêt**, **Orry-la-Ville** and **Pontarmé**.

Étangs de Commelles – Located near the village of Coye-la-Forêt, this 19C recreational site (40 ha/98.8 acre) features four ponds: these were built in the 13C by monks from the Chaalis Abbey (*see Abbaye de CHAALIS*) who used them as fishponds.

Château de la Reine Blanche – The ponds of Commelles are home to this former watermill restored in the Troubadour Style in 1825 by the last of the Condés, the Duke of Bourbon, who used it as a hunting lodge. It stands on the site of a legendary château believed to have been built by Queen Blanche of Navarre in around 1350.

An avenue of age-old beeches completes this delightful **site★**.

ADDRESSES

🛏 STAY

🍷🍷🍷🍷 **Château de la Tour** – *Chemin de la Chaussée, Gouvieux.* ℘*03 44 62 38 38. www.lechateaudelatour.fr. Wi-fi. 41 rooms.* This early 20C domain overlooks a park. Elegant dining rooms with a Louis XIII flair.

🍴 EAT

🍷🍷 **Le restaurant du Hameau** – *Au Hameau.* ℘*03 44 57 46 21. www. domainedechantilly.com. Daily except Tue 12–6pm. Closed mid-Nov–Mar.* In a decor of thatched roofs, half-timbering and greenery, enjoy local teatime snacks: foie gras, deer pâté, cider, jams or local honey, delicious fruit tarts, etc.

🍷🍷 **Le Boudoir** – *100r. du Connétable.* ℘*03 44 55 44 49. www.leboudoir-chantilly.fr. Mon 11am–6pm, Tue–Sat 10am–7pm, Sun 11am–7pm. Closed 1 Jan and 25 Dec.* This cosy dining room in beige and raspberry tones offers quiches, salads and hot dishes, as well as teas, cakes and sweets.

🍷🍷 **La Capitainerie "Les Cuisines de Vatel"** – ℘*03 44 57 15 89. www.domaine dechantilly.com. Closed Tue and eves.* Dine under the ancestral arches of kitchens once overseen by illustrious chef Vatel.

SHOPPING

Chantilly is a major porcelain manufacturing centre known for soft-paste porcelain, made without kaolin.
Maison de la porcelaine – *1r. de Creil.* ℘*03 44 57 54 19. www.maisonporcelaine.com. Open Tue–Sat 9.45am–12.15pm, 2.30–7pm.* Silkscreen porcelains.

Porcelaine de Chantilly – *Pl. Omer-Vallon.* ℘*03 44 67 16 16. Open daily except Sun 9.45am–12.15pm, 2.30–7pm. Closed Aug and public holidays.* This boutique specialises in hand-painted porcelains.

Senlis★★

A tributary of the Oise, the River Nonette runs through this picturesque medieval town surrounded by the rich cornfields of Valois and the wooded expanses of Ermenonville, Chantilly and Halatte forests. Strolling along the winding streets of the Old Quarter, paved with flagstones and lined with relics of its past, you may still feel the powerful presence of the Frankish rulers and cathedral builders who left behind an invaluable legacy for us to enjoy.

A BIT OF HISTORY

The election of Hugues Capet – The conquerors of Senlis built a massive stronghold over the first Gallo-Roman ramparts of the town. The kings of the first two **Frankish dynasties** would often take up residence here, lured by game in the nearby forests. The Carolingian line died out when Louis V suffered a fatal hunting accident. In 987, the Archbishop of Reims called a meeting at Senlis Castle in which he and the local lords decided that **Hugues Capet**, then Duke of France, would be the next king. The last king of France to have stayed in Senlis was Henri IV. The city went out of fashion as a royal place of residence and was gradually replaced by Compiègne and Fontainebleau.

VISIT
Cathédrale Notre-Dame★★

○Open daily (except during religious office) 8.30am–7pm. ℘03 44 53 15 38. The construction of Senlis cathedral started in 1153 – 16 years after St-Denis and 10 years before Notre-Dame in Paris – but progress was slow. The cathedral was not consecrated until 1191. It was only toward the mid-13C that the right tower was crowned with the magnificent **spire★★** which was to have such a strong influence over religious architecture in the Valois area. The **main doorway★★** is strongly reminiscent of the doorways at Chartres, Notre-Dame in Paris, Amiens and Reims.

- ▶ **Population:** 16 327
- ⌚ **Michelin Local Map:** p239: C1; map 106 folds 8, 9.
- **Info:** Office du tourisme de Senlis, pl. du Parvis-Notre-Dame, 60300. ℘03 44 53 06 40. www.senlis-tourisme.fr.
- ▷ **Location:** Access from Paris: by car, via the A 1 (51.5km/32mi); by train, from Gare du Nord to Chantilly, then bus link to Senlis.
- 🅿 **Parking:** The car park near the cathedral fills early in the day. Try those off the r. de la République.
- **Don't Miss:** Notre-Dame's magnificient spire; the Gallo-Roman and Merovingian collections of the Musée d'Art et d'Archéologie; St-Frambourg Royal Chapel and its stained-glass windows by Joan Miro.

South front – Constructed by **Pierre Chambiges** (1509–1544) in the 16C, the **transept façade★★** contrasts sharply with the main façade. One may follow the evolution of Gothic architecture from the austere 12C to the 16C, when Late Flamboyant already showed signs of Renaissance influence, introduced after the Italian wars. The clerestory and its huge Flamboyant windows were also completed in the 16C.

The lower part (12C) of the east end and the radiating chapels are intact. The galleries – dating from Romanesque times – support the nave and chancel with the help of Gothic flying buttresses.

Interior – The church interior is 70m/230ft long, 19.2m/63ft wide and measures 24m/79ft to the keystone. Above the organ, the 12C vaulting which escaped the ravages of a fire in 1504 marks the original height of the church. The nave and the chancel are graced with an airy lightness.

Detail of Cathédrale Notre-Dame

© Wysocki-Frances/hemis.fr

The first chapel to the right of the south doorway features superb vaulting with pendant keystones, a 14C stone Virgin Mary and a lovely set of stained-glass windows. These are the only original panes to have remained intact. A statue of St Louis from the 14C is placed in the south aisle of the ambulatory.

North side – The cathedral's setting on this side is much less solemn. It features several patches of greenery and is extremely picturesque.

Skirt the little garden that follows the east façade of what was once the bishop's palace. The building rests on the ruins of the old Gallo-Roman ramparts; the base of one tower remains. Lovely **view** of the cathedral's east end.

👣 WALKING TOUR

OLD QUARTER
Jardin du Roy
These gardens occupy the former moat of the Gallo-Roman ramparts which, at their widest point, measured 312m/1 024ft across and at their narrowest 242m/794ft. Twenty-eight towers (7m/23ft high and 4m/14ft thick) defended the city walls; 16 remain today, some still intact, others badly damaged.

Place du Parvis★
This is a charming little square at the foot of the cathedral.

Eglise St-Pierre
Built in the 12C, heavily rehandled in the 17C, and deconsecrated during the French Revolution, this church now houses a centre for Romanesque, Gothic and Renaissance culture.

Ancien Château Royal
Before entering the courtyard of the old Royal Castle, take time to walk up rue du Châtel to see the original **fortified entrance** to the stronghold, now walled up. Adjoining the old doorway, the 16C **Hôtel des Trois Pots** proudly sports its old-fashioned sign.

The castle where Hugues Capet was proclaimed King of France in 987 was built on a site which had already been fortified under the Romans at the time of Emperor Claudius (AD 41–54).

The castle was unfortunately taken apart bit by bit to the benefit of more comfortable residences. Included within the compound, an old priory now houses the Musée de la Vénerie (🕭 *opposite*).

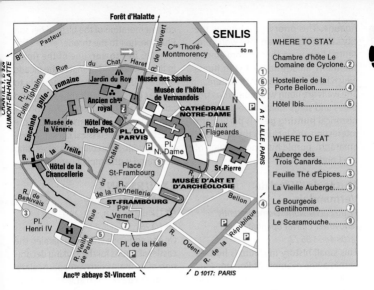

Old Streets★

Rue du Châtel used to be the main street through Senlis for those travelling from Paris to Flanders, until the opening of rue Neuve-de-Paris (now rue de la République) in 1753. Rue Vieille-de-Paris thus refers to the ancient thoroughfare. Take the charming **rue de la Treille** and walk to the "Fausse Porte", which was the postern of the former Gallo-Roman ramparts. On the left stands the Hôtel de la Chancellerie, flanked by two towers. The **town hall** (Hôtel de Ville), on place Henri-IV, was rebuilt in 1495.

SIGHTS
Musée d'Art et d'Archéologie★

2 pl. Notre-Dame. ⏰*Open Mon, Thu–Fri 10am–noon, 2–6pm, Wed 2–6pm, Sat –Sun 11am–1pm, 2–6pm.* ⏰*Closed 1 Jan, 1 May, 25 Dec.* ⮑*2€.* ℘*03 44 24 86 72. www.musees-senlis.fr.*

This museum is housed in the old bishop's palace (13C–18C buildings). It features a **bronze base★** dating from AD 48 and engraved with a dedication to Emperor Claudius, along with other Gallo-Roman artefacts. Its medieval collection includes striking sculptures such as the **Head of a Bearded Man★** (early 13C), a majestic marble **Virgin and Child** (late 14C), and mid-12C stained-glass windows. Paintings dating from

the 17C to the 20C include the works of artists such as Philippe de Champaigne, Luca Giordano, Francesco Solimena, Corot, Boudin, Sérusier, and **Thomas Couture** (1815–79), a native of Senlis.

Musée des Spahis

By the entrance to the former royal château. ⏰*Open Tue 2–6pm, Wed–Fri 10am–noon, 2–6pm. Sat –Sun 11am–1pm, 2–6pm.* ⏰*Closed 1 Jan, 1 May, 25 Dec.* ⮑*2€.* ℘*03 44 26 15 50. www.musees-senlis.fr.*

This museum traces 150 years of the North African cavalry, which held a special place in the French Army from 1780 to 1814 and from 1830 to 1964. It concentrates on the old **Spahis** (native Algerian horsemen), **Goumiers** (indigenous horsemen and foot soldiers), **Meharists** (dromedary riders) and **Saharans** (cameleers).

Musée de la Vénerie

Former royal château, pl. du Parvis-Notre-Dame. ⏰*Open Tue 2–6pm, Wed–Fri 10am–noon, 2–6pm; Sat –Sun 11am–1pm, 2–6pm.* ⏰*Closed 1 Jan, 1 May, 25 Dec..* ⮑*2€.* ℘*03 44 29 49 93. www.musees-senlis.fr.*

In the 13C, King Saint-Louis had a **priory** built next to the Royal Castle to keep the precious relics of Saint Maurice of

Agaune. This priory now houses the city's **Hunting Museum**. The works presented here were chosen from among the many illustrations of stag hunts which have enriched French culture. The walls are hung with numerous trophies and stags' heads. The display of historical **hunting gear** is particularly interesting and includes the fawn and amaranth-purple hunting costume of the Condé.

Musée de l'Hôtel de Vermandois

Pl. du Parvis-Notre-Dame. Recently renovated. Call for opening dates.
℘ *03 44 24 86 72.*

This small history museum is housed within a fine example of Romanesque civil architecture (12C). Visitors are introduced to the history of Senlis and its cathedral through audio-visual accounts. Don't miss the rich **statuary collection** including the 12C head of an angel from a doorway of Notre-Dame.

Chapelle Royale St-Frambourg★

1pl Saint-Frambourg. ⏰*Open Mar–Jun, Sep–Nov last Sat of month 2–6pm.* ⬤*6€.* ℘ *03 44 53 39 99.*

This chapel was founded before 990 by the wife of Hugues Capet.
Through the efforts of the pianist Georges Cziffra, the chapel was restored and turned into the **Franz Liszt auditorium** in which concerts and exhibitions are organised. Note the Gothic church with beautiful **stained-glass windows★** by Joan Miro, and the archaeological crypt, with remnants of a sanctuary dating back to year 1000.

Ancienne abbaye St-Vincent

30r. de Meaux. ⏰*Open weekends, public holidays and school holidays. Call ahead for weekend visits.* ⏰*Closed 1 Jan, 1 May, 25 Dec.* ⬤*6€.* ℘ *03 44 53 06 40. www.senlis-tourisme.fr.*

A private secondary school now occupies this remarkable abbey, founded in 1060 by Anne of Kiev, wife of King Henry I of France. She may have had it built in commemoration of the birth of her son Philippe, heir to the throne.

The 12C **belltower**, one of the finest in Île-de-France, dominates the facade of the church, made subsequently to appear grander by modifications and additions to the structure. The former abbey buildings, reconstructed in the 17C, comprise a classical cloister ennobled by doric-style columns and vaulting decorated with simple beams.

EXCURSIONS

Château de Raray

▷ *13km/8mi NE by D 932A, D 26E and D 26.*

On the edge of a charming hamlet, the castle is famous for the striking decoration of its main courtyard, particularly the **porticoes★**, used in Jean Cocteau's film *Beauty and the Beast*.

St-Vaast-de-Longmont

▷ *16km/10mi NE by D 932A.*

Seen from the village cemetery, the Romanesque bell tower and stone spire appear extremely ornate: cornices with billet moulding and arcades resting on finely decorated columns.

In nearby **Rhuis** (*W on D 123*), the 11C Romanesque **church** has a bell tower with a double row of twinned windows, one of the oldest in Île-de-France.

⬤ Forêt d'Halatte★

This large forest (4 300ha/10 626acre) north of Senlis includes beech groves, oaks, hornbeams and other species.

Pont-Ste-Maxence

▷ *11km/7mi N by D 1017.*

The **Abbaye du Moncel★** was built by Philippe le Bel next to a royal castle, two towers of which still remain. The main façade still looks medieval. The **courtyard★** is surrounded by three wings crowned with tall roofs of brown tiles. Other noteworthy elements include the 14C **timberwork★** above the nuns' dorter, made with oak from Halatte Forest. *Guided tours (1hr) Apr–Oct Wed–Sun. Call for times and prices.* ℘ *03 44 72 33 98. www.abbayedumoncel.fr.*

Abbaye de Royaumont★★

Royaumont Abbey is an impressive symbol of the wealth that often accrued to the great French abbeys in the Middle Ages. Founded in 1228 and completed in 1235, the abbey was occupied by members of the Cistercian order. Six of St Louis' relatives – three children, a brother and two grandsons – were buried in the abbey. Their remains have since been moved to St-Denis.

In 1793 Royaumont was sold as State property and the church dismantled. In 1964 the last owners Isabel and Henri Gouïn (1900–77) created the Royaumont Foundation for the Advancement of Human Science, to which they donated the estate.

- **Michelin Local Map:** p238: B2; map 106 fold 7.
- **Info:** ℘01 30 35 59 90. www.royaumont.com.
- **Location:** Located 35.4km/ 22mi N of Paris, 27km/17mi from Paris CDG Airport and the Roissy TGV train station. The Abbey is easy to reach by the A1 and A16 autoroutes.
- **Timing:** Allow yourself 1hr to tour the abbey.

VISIT

Open Mar–Oct Mon-Fri 10am–12.45pm, 1.45pm–5.30pm, (weekends 6pm); Nov–Feb daily 10am–12.45pm, 1.45pm–5.30pm. 6.50€ (children 5€). Guided tours.

Church ruins

See plan p252. Royaumont Church, consecrated in 1235, is, unlike traditional Cistercian churches, an unusually large edifice (101m/330ft long) in keeping with its royal origins. The chancel and its radiating chapels break with Cistercian tradition in that they have no flat east end. A corner turret (1) belonging to the former north transept gives an idea of the church's elevation (the keystone was 28m/91ft above ground).

Cloisters

These surround a garden. The west gallery *(opposite the entrance)* is paralleled, at the back, by a narrow, uncovered passageway. It was built for the lay brothers to have access to their wing and church without passing through the cloisters, habitually reserved for the monks.

Refectory

This spacious dining hall is a masterpiece of Gothic architecture. It could accommodate 60 monks without difficulty. St Louis would take his turn serving the monks at table while they sat in silence listening to the reader, who stood in a pulpit carved out of the thick stone wall.

Abbaye de Royaumont

© SuperStock/age fotostock

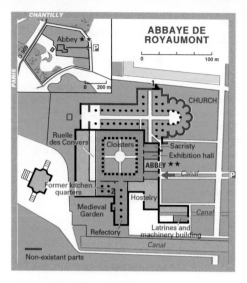

ABBAYE DE ROYAUMONT

A cultural mission

In 1978 the Centre Culturel de Rencontre set up on the abbey's premises to ensure its preservation. It also organises concerts, lectures, training seminars and exhibitions in its regional vocal arts centre, literary centre and ethnology centre.

Former kitchen quarters

The kitchens house a statue of the Virgin of Royaumont (2), carved in the 14C. The strange building resting on 31 semicircular arches astride the canal is the **latrines and machinery building**. In former times, the water reached a higher level and activated the machinery.

Abbot's Residence (Palais Abbatial)

Not open to visitors. Built for the last commendatory abbot of Royaumont, this cubic construction is reminiscent of an Italian villa. The façade facing the road to Chantilly is reflected in the waters of a charming pond.

EXCURSION
Luzarches

6km/3.7mi S of Asnières-sur-Oise by taking the D 909 and D 922.

Tourist Office – *6 r. St-Damien. ℘01 34 09 98 48, www.tourisme-luzarches.org. Open 10am–12pm, Sat 10am–12pm, 3–5pm. Closed Aug, public holidays and Sun in Jan–Feb.*

Robert de Luzarches (13C), who designed the cathedral at Amiens, was born in this village. From the bridge at the juncture with the D316, there's a great **view** of the **church**, comprising a 12C belltower and chevet, with three apses of varying heights and design. The church is dedicated to the patron saints of surgeons, Saint Côme and Saint Damien. Their relics were brought back from Rome by a Crusader and lord of Luzarches. The nearby tourist office is housed in the **Château de la Motte**.

Botanical Garden – Allée Lamartine. Open 8am-6pm. This garden houses over 400 varieties of plants. Don't miss the remarkable and rare purple beech, planted in the 18C.

ADDRESSES

☕ EAT

Auberge La Renaissance. *16 av. J.-F. Kennedy. ℘01 30 35 40 24. www.aubergelarenaissance.com. Closed Sat and Sun evening, 25 Dec to 1 Jan.* Enjoy semi-gastronomic cuisine in a modern, warm atmosphere. Garden seating.

SNACKS

Bar-Salon de thé – *At the Abbaye de Royaumont. Open weekends and holidays from 12pm.* Enjoy la bite in this 13C space, serving tea, pastries and sandwiches. View of the water.

ENTERTAINMENT

The Fondation Royaumont organises concerts, shows and other events year-round. ℘01 30 35 59 00, www.royaumont.com.

Abbaye de
Chaalis★★

This estate lies on the edge of Ermenonville Forest, near the Mer de Sable theme park (🗘 see p262). During the 19C, it evoked the gentle, romantic charm of religious contemplation. Up to 1912, Chaalis inspired its last owners to put together a remarkable art collection.

A BIT OF HISTORY
A Royal Abbey

Chaalis was a Cistercian abbey built on the site of a former priory in 1136 by Louis the Fat. The monks led a modest country life, husbanding the land, cultivating vines, keeping bees and fishing in the lakes.

During the 16C the abbey was held *in commendam* and the abbots were appointed by the king. The first was Cardinal Ippolito d'Este, son of Alfonso d'Este and Lucrezia Borgia. Known as **Cardinal of Ferrara**, this enthusiastic art lover commissioned fine gardens and had his private chapel decorated with murals. In the 18C the ninth abbot, one of the Great Condé's grandsons, attempted to restore the abbey to plans by **Jean Aubert**, the architect who designed the Great Stables at Chantilly. It was a disaster; after only one side of the building had been completed (1739,

> 🗘 **Michelin Local Map:** p238: C2; map 106 fold 9.

currently the Château-Museum), work stopped owing to lack of funds. This financial crisis prompted Louis XVI to close down the abbey in 1785. During the French Revolution, Chaalis was badly pillaged and the greater part of the building destroyed.

The estate frequently changed hands. In 1850, **Mme de Vatry** bought the ruins, converted the 18C building into a château, had the park refurbished and entertained lavishly. Later, a couple of art lovers (🗘 see sidebar below) would transform Chaalis.

VISIT

1hr. 🕐 *Park, rose garden and church: open daily year-round 10am–6pm. Museum: Mar–mid-Nov daily 11am–6pm; rest of year, Sun and holidays 10.30am–12.30pm, 1.30pm–5.30pm.* 🕐 *Closed 25 Dec.* 🎫 *7€ (museum, park and rose garden).* 📞 *03 44 54 04 02. www.chaalis.fr.*

Church ruins★

Consecrated in 1219, Chaalis was the first Cistercian church built in the Gothic style. Of the original buildings there remain a staircase turret, the northern transept arm surrounded by radiating

Patrons of the arts

Of humble origin, **Nélie Jacquemart** (1841–1912) lived for long periods, during her childhood, in the home of Mme de Vatry, who treated her like a daughter. She became acquainted with members of the aristocracy and the upper middle-class who were very useful in her career as a fashionable portrait painter, having studied with Léon Cogniet. In 1872, **Édouard André**, the heir to one of the largest fortunes in banking, commissioned a portrait from her, which still hangs in the private apartments of his Parisian mansion, and they met for the first time on this occasion. In 1881 they got married and their union was a happy one. Having no children, the couple devoted their efforts to collecting beautiful objects, mainly from Italy, for their sumptuous mansion on boulevard Haussmann. Nélie André completed this collection after the death of her husband. In 1902, she realised one of her dreams: going to India; however she gave up the idea of a world tour when she learned that the Chaalis estate was for sale. She acquired it and devoted the last years of her life to it.

Abbaye de Chaalis, Oise

© Arnaud Chicurel/hemis.fr

chapels, part of the chancel and the altar.

Chapelle Ste-Marie de l'abbé★

Built between 1255–1260, the chapel is a fine example of Gothic splendour from the time of the Sainte-Chapelle in Paris. Note the extraordinary cycle of murals by 16C Italian master **Francesco Primaticcio** (1504–1570) and the bronze bust of Nélie André by Denis Puech (1972).

Rose garden and park

Beyond the chapel, a strange 16C crenellated wall with asymmetrical merlons sets the boundaries of the rose garden. Above the heavy archway, the coat of arms of Cardinal Louis d'Este is displayed. From north of the château, there is a fine view of the park with its flowerbeds and dazzling lake.

Château-Musée★★

The **Salle des Moines** houses many marvels, including Italian 15C Gothic furniture, two panels from an altarpiece painted by Jean de Bellegambe, religious statues (14C–16C French) and above all, the famous Giotto's **painted panels ★★**, depicting St John the Evangelist and St Lawrence. Do not miss Nélie André's **private appartments,** and the **Jean-Jacques Rousseau Gallery**, with some exceptional documents.

ADDRESSES

TAKING A BREAK

Abbaye de Chaalis Cafeteria – ☏034454 0402. Apr–11 Nov: 12–5pm. Enjoy lunch here in the romantic setting of the Abbey.

Château d'
Écouen★★

Nestled in a 17ha/42 acre park overlooking the Île-de-France plain, the Château d'Écouen was originally built in the 16C for Constable Anne de Montmorency, supreme commander of the French Army. Confiscated during the Revolution and salvaged by Napoleon I, who founded here the first school for the daughters of members of the Légion d'Honneur, the castle now houses some of the most prestigious Renaissance art collections in the country.

- **Michelin Local Map:** p238: B3, map 101 fold 6 or 106 fold 19.
- **Parking:** Cars must be parked at the entrance to the forest. Access is through the forest, on foot.

THE CASTLE

The Château d'Écouen reflects the transition of French art from the **Early Renaissance** period (Château of the Loire) to the **High Renaissance** (during Henri II's reign). The buildings feature pavilions at each corner, and are surmounted by elaborate dormer windows with carved pediments. The beautiful east range was destroyed in the 18C and replaced by a low entrance wing.

Porticoes with Classical-style columns decorate the buildings. The most outstanding one is to the left, on the south wing (Anne de Montmorency's residence), built by **Jean Bullant** to house Michelangelo's famous *Slaves* in the niches on the ground floor. The statues (*the originals are in the Louvre*) were a gift to Anne de Montmorency from King Henri II. The North Terrace affords a sweeping **view** of the surrounding grain-growing countryside.

Musée National de la Renaissance★★

⊙*Open Wed–Mon 9.30am–12.45pm, 2–5.15pm (5.45pm in summer).* ⊙*Closed Tue, 1 Jan, 1 May and 25 Dec.* ⊛5€ *(no charge 1st Sun of the month).* ⅙ ℘*01 34 38 38 50. www.musee-renaissance.fr.*

This outstanding museum presents a wide range of works dating from the 16C and early 17C, which introduce visitors to the various branches of the decorative arts: furniture, tapestries and embroidery, silver and gold work, ceramics, enamels , glasswork, stained glass, paintings, weapons, etc. Most of the pieces, made in France, Italy or the Netherlands, were carefully selected to recreate the ambience in keeping with the life of wealthy nobility during the Renaissance.

The original interior decoration mainly consists of **grotesque paintings** on friezes below the ceiling and the embrasures of the windows. But Ecouen is most renowned for its **painted fireplaces★**. Representative of the first Fontainebleau School, these chimneypieces feature a central biblical scene painted on a medallion, surrounded by grotesques, garlands of fruit, motifs in leather, and hazy landscapes depicting antique ruins, fortresses and humble cottages.

Ground Floor – The monograms A and M (Anne de Montmorency and Madeleine of Savoy, the former's wife) were included in the decoration of the **chapel** (1544), covered with painted vaulting resting on diagonal arches. This heraldic motif reappears in different rooms. The Passion Altarpiece is adorned with enamelling and a copy of Leonardo da Vinci's *Last Supper*.

Several rooms are devoted to a particular trade or technique. Note a clock of German origin in the shape of a ship known as Charles V's clock, now incorporated into a 16C collector's cabinet. In the reconstruction of a 16C goldsmith's workshop, a work bench is set in an inlaid chest.

First Floor –The south wing features the constable's bedroom and Madeleine of Savoy's suite, with period furniture. The west wing is almost entirely toccupied by the **Tapestry of David and Bathsheba★★★** (1510–20) which runs from the Abigail pavilion to the king's bedchamber, along the Psyche Gallery. The 75m/246ft hanging divided into 10 sections recounts the romance between King David and Bathsheba. The outstanding quality of the tapestry is equalled only by that of *The Hunts of Maximilian* in the Louvre: these two are doubtless the two outstanding examples of 16C Brussels tapestry work in France.

The hanging ends in the **King's Apartment**, in the northwest pavilion. The king's suite occupied tahe northern wing. Note the floor tiles made specially for the château in 1542 by potter Masséot Abaquesne, and two tapestries which were part of the famous *Fructus Belli* made in Brussels to cartoons by Jules Romains.

Second Floor – In the northeast pavilion, Iznik pottery (mid-16C to early 17C) illustrates the exotic tastes of 16C collectors. The first room in the north wing presents religious stained glass painted in *grisaille*; admire the Virgin and Child, dated 1544.

The second hall deals entirely with French ceramics. It features St-Porchaire ceramics, pieces by Bernard Palissy and Masséot Abaquesne, and a reconstruction of the second-floor tiled floor, showing the arms of the Constable, those of his wife, of Henri II and Catherine de' Medici.

15 **marriage chests** in the northwest pavilion form a remarkable ensemble. The west pavillion features beautiful enamel pieces by Léonard Limosin, while the southwest pavilion showcases silverware mainly of German origin (note the extraordinary Daphné by Nuremberg goldsmith Wenzel Jammitzer).

Also see – Rarely opened to the public (ask for opening days), some rooms give unusual insight into life in the Renaissance. Note the former **library** of Constable Anne (above the chapel), with original gilded wainscoting, and a suite of **private bathrooms** (in the basement) to which rain water from the central courtyard was ingeniously channelled.

ADDITIONAL SIGHTS
Église St-Acceul

This is Ecouen's second architectural-masterpiece. The **chancel** by Jean Bullant is the most interesting feature. The complex rib patterns of the vaulting date the church to the 16C. St-Acceul features several Renaissance **stained-glass windows★**.

Colonie des peintres

Mairie d'Écouen. ○ *Closed Thu and Sat afternoon, Sun. Call tourist office for more information.*

Some forty 19C artists made Écouen their home and formed the movement known as the Ecole d'Écouen. Rejecting academic painting techniques, they privileged everyday rural scenes. The space houses around thirty works from artists such as A. Schenck, G.Seignac, G.Haag, Ch.-E. Frère and L. Chialiva.

Parc Astérix★★

Astérix the Gaul, hero of the world- famous cartoon strip by Goscinny and Uderzo, translated into several languages, provides the theme for this 50ha/123 acre fun park, opened in 1989. It's a fantasy world for all ages. The Gauls, and in particular Astérix's friends – the mighty Obelix who follows him everywhere, Panoramix (Getafix) who prepares magic potions, Assurancetourix (Cacofonix) the bard and Abraracourcix (Vitalstatistix) the chief of the tribe – are all here. But beware: the Romans are never far away!

👫 VISIT

○ *Open late Mar–early Nov, 10am–6pm (7pm depending on visitor numbers).* 🎫*44€ (under-12s 33€).* ℘*08 26 30 10 40 (0.15€/min). www.parcasterix.fr.* Divided into five "historical" sections, complete with various attractions and shows, the park also offers a choice of snacks and meals.

- 🎡 **Michelin Local Map:** p238: C2 or map 106 fold 9.
- ▷ **Location:** 30km/18.6mi N of Paris. By **car**: 30min from central Paris on autoroute A1; by **Métro**/RER train: line B3 from Châtelet or Gare du Nord stations (alight at Roissy-Charles de Gaulle 1 station); by **coach**: from Roissy coach station with Courriers Île-de-France (CIF; www.cif-bus.com).
- 👫 **Kids:** Camp de Petitbonum, La Ronde des Rondins, Les Petits Drakkars, La Forêt des Druides, Au Pied du Grand Huit, La Petite Tempête, Les Petits Chars Tamponneurs.

Start at **Via Antiqua**, a "street" lined with stalls symbolising Asterix's journeys across Europe, leading to a giant rock where the hero welcomes his visitors.

Gaul

At the very heart of the park, Astérix's **Village Gaulois★** consists of huts where visitors can meet the little hero and his fellow characters. The **Forêt des Druides** includes toboggan rides, while the **Grand Splatch★** offers more water fun. Next, tour the Stone Age village (**ZAG**), built on piles, on the **Menhir Express★★**, which takes you on a trip through a network of canals bristling with surprises! The **Trace du Hourra-★★★** train races along a bobsleigh track at 60kph/37mph.

Roman Empire

In the arena, witness a charming young Gallic spy become the heroine of acrobatic fights in **La Légion recrute★★**. Next, join the **Espions de César★** who have devised a very efficient surveillance system above ground level, then meet the four spying challenges of the **Défi de César**. Finally, brave a tumultuous river on board buoys at **Romus et Rapidus**.

Ancient Greece

The entrance to this part of the park is marked by the colonnade from the Temple of Zeus. The **Vol d'Icare** (Icarus' flight) takes you out of Daedalus' labyrinth, but you still have to defeat the terrible **Hydre de Lerne**. Next, embark on a daring journey aboard a giant roller coaster called **Tonnerre de Zeus★★**, with the angry god watching you from atop Mount Olympus! Then relax and enjoy a **dolphin show★★** at the Theatre of Poséidon or a trip down the **Elis River**.

The Vikings

Highlights in this section of the park include **Goudurix★★**, a gigantic roller coaster taking visitors through a succession of vertiginous drops and loops. **La Galère** is a swing shaped like a boat. **Les Petits Drakkars** (boats on water) and **Les Petites Chaises Volantes** (flying chairs) are perfect for young children.

Egypt

Opened in spring 2012, this section devoted to the adventures of Astérix and Cleopatra offers two attractions:

Sos Numérobis for young children and **Oziris★★** for anyone "over 1.30m" (4ft 3in). After crossing through an Egyptian temple, visitors sit with their feet in the void before being lifted 40m (130ft) into the air and sent hurtling down an impressive series of loops at 90km(55mi) per hour. A dizzying experience!

Across Time

Take a journey through time along **Avenue de Paris★★**. Ten centuries of history are illustrated here, each represented by characters in period costume and typical shops. The Middle Ages come to life with street entertainers and **artisans★** working in dark, mysterious streets.

Going on holiday has not always been plain sailing, as you can see from the **Nationale 7** main road to the south of France. If you'd rather not leave the city, the **Oxygénarium★★** has been specially designed to offer city dwellers the combined benefits of water and fresh mountain air!

This trip through time ends in 1930, in **Main basse sur la Joconde★★**, a splendid enactment of a historical detective story during which a gang of thieves attempts to steal the *Mona Lisa*.

ADDRESSES

🛏 STAY

🍴🍴🍴**Hôtel des Trois Hiboux** – *Parc Astérix, 60128 Plailly. ☏03 44 62 68 00. 100 rooms. Room and park packages available. Restaurant* 🍴🍴🍴. According to legend, each of the three forests surrounding the amusement park used to be the territory of an owl (hibou). Perhaps you'll fall asleep to the lullaby of their songs in one of the cosy bedrooms of this hotel where they are said to convene. Sweet dreams!

🍴 EAT

All this fun is guaranteed to stimulate your appetite, and there are plenty of places to enjoy a snack or light lunch at the park. Three on-site restaurants and numerous taverns await you. You can even choose your desired ambience: Ancient Rome or Gallic village?

L'Isle-Adam★

Founded by Adam de Villiers in 1014, when a castle built on one of the islands in the River Oise was ceded to him by Robert II the Pious, L'Isle-Adam is famous as the inspiration for several novels by Honoré de Balzac, and the 19C author of Cruel Tales, Villiers de L'Isle-Adam. It is also the site of one of France's largest inland beaches. The old bridges – in particular Cabouillet Bridge, a 16C stone construction with three arches – command a pleasant view of the Oise.

SIGHTS
Musée d'art et d'histoire Louis-Senlecq
31 Grande-Rue. ⏰*Open Wed–Mon 2–6pm.* ✆*3.70€.* ✆*01 34 69 45 44. www.musee.ville-isle-adam.fr.*
Housed in a former 17C school, this museum features paintings by Émile Boggio, Jules-Romain Joyant and Vlaminck.

Centre d'Art Jacques-Henri-Lartigue
31 Grande-Rue. &⏰*Open Wed–Mon 2–6pm.* ✆*3.20€ (no charge Sun).* ✆*01 34 08 02 72. www.ville-isle-adam.fr.*
Jacques-Henri Lartigue (1894–1986) was a photographer and painter: 300 of his paintings are exhibited here in rotation. His work is recognisable for its vigorous brushstrokes and bright colours.

Pavillon Chinois de Cassan
Follow r. de Beaumont. Enter through the main gateway of the former park.
This pavilion overlooking a lake was built to adorn the landscaped park of Cassan; the rest of the estate is now residential. A pagoda stands on arches that house the spillway for the park's waters.

Forêt de L'Isle-Adam
Covering an area of 1 500ha/3 800 acres, this forest is dominated by oak trees. Other varieties include beech, chestnut and lime.

▸ **Population:** 11 231
✆ **Michelin Local Map:** p238: A2; map 106 fold 6.
ℹ **Info:** 18 av. des Ecuries de Conti, L'Isle-Adam. ✆01 34 69 41 99. www.ville-isle-adam.fr.
▸ **Location:** Situated N of Paris along the Oise Valley.
🄿 **Parking:** There are plenty of free parking areas.

EXCURSION
Beaumont-sur-Oise
▸*6km/3.7mi NE of L'Isle-Adam on the D 922. Visitor Info: 2 r. Basse-de-la-Vallée.* ✆*01 34 70 08 08.*
One of the towns set up by Julius Caesar during his conquest of Gaul, Beaumont has an amphitheatre (1–3C) and other impressive archaeological sites. The ruins of the medieval castle include a Roman keep. St-Laurent Church (12C–16C), with its Renaissance dome and bell tower, dominates the Oise valley.

ADDRESSES

🛏 STAY
🛏🛏 **Chambre d'hôte Maison Delaleu** – *131 av. Foch-in Parmain, 2km/1.25mi W of L'Ile-Adam.* ✆*01 34 73 02 92. 4 rooms.* Traditional farmhouse with large, minimalist rooms; enjoy breakfast at a large communal table.

🍴 EAT
🍴🍴🍴 **Le Cabouillet** – *5 quai de l'Oise.* ✆*01 34 69 00 90. www.lecabouillet.com. Closed Feb school holidays, Sun eve, Mon. Reservations Sat–Sun.* Popular 200-year-old establishment. Tables upstairs overlook the River Oise.

ACTIVITIES
L'Isle-Adam Beach – *1 av. du Gén.-de-Gaulle.* ✆*01 34 6901 68. www.ville-isle-adam.fr. Activities and games: Apr–mid Jun, weekends 2–7pm; mid-Jun–Aug 2–7pm; Swimming: mid-Jun–Aug 10am–7pm. Day pass 11.30/15.50€ (children 7.20/9€).* The region's largest riverside beach has the allure of chic Deauville, with its cabins and striped chaises longs.

Saint-Leu-d'Esserent★

The Archbishop of Sens, Saint Leu (d. 623), gave his name to several French localities, including this one. Located on the banks of the River Oise, St-Leu-d'Esserent boasts a magnificent church that the philosopher and historian Ernest Renan compared to a Greek temple on account of its harmonious lines.

ABBEY CHURCH★

The bridge over the Oise affords the best **view** of the church from a distance. Nearby quarries produced the lovely stone, which was used for the construction of many other churches and cathedrals, as well as the palace at Versailles. During World War II, German troops converted the quarries into workshops for their V1 missiles. As a result, the town was repeatedly bombed and the church destroyed in 1944.

Exterior – Significantly restored since the 19C, the façade is separate from the nave. It forms a Romanesque block (12C) presenting a porch and, on the upper level, a gallery, each consisting of three bays. Two square towers frame the chancel.

Interior★ – The nave houses modern stained glass (1960). The chancel and first two bays of the nave are Romanesque (12C) while the rest of the nave is 13C.

ADDRESSES

🛏STAY

😊😊 **Hôtel de l'Oise** – *25 quai d'Amont. ℘03 44 56 60 24. www.hoteldeloise.com Closed first week of Feb and 3 first weeks of Aug; restaurant closed Fri eve, Sat at noon and Sun eve. 17 rooms.* This elegant hotel is housed in a brick building dating to the 1930s and situated on the banks of the Oise. A beautiful original staircase leads to impeccably kept, discreetly decorated rooms; pleasant restaurant serving traditional cuisine based on fresh market products.

> **Population:** 4 867
> **Michelin Local Map:** p238: B1 or map 106 folds 7, 8.
> **Info:** Office du tourisme St-Leu-d'Esserent, 7 av. de la Gare, 60430. ℘03 44 56 38 10. www.pierresudoise tourisme.fr.

🍴 EAT

😊😊😊 **Ô Relais de la Côte** – *9 r. de Chantilly. Gouvieux. ℘03 44 57 01 19. Closed last week of Jul and ten days in Aug, 1st week of Feb, Sun eve, Mon eve, Tue.* Just outside the city, this modern-style restaurant boasts a tree-lined terrace. Cuisine will please contemporary palettes.

SHOPPING

Ercuis – *142r. des Tilleuls. Ercuis, 12km/7.5mi NW on the D 92, D 44 or D 929. ℘03 44 26 54 92. www.ercuis.fr. Mon and Wed 1–3.45pm. Closed Aug; other additional closures- call ahead.* Created in 1867 by the parish priest of Ercuis, this gold and silversmith has become an institution. Artisans carry out tradition with passion and inventiveness, creating tea and coffee sets, champagne buckets and fine silverware. The store offers wholesale prices: expect to pay 20–50 percent less than in traditional boutiques.

ACTIVITIES

Leisure Centre – *R.de la Garenne. ℘03 44 56 77 88. www.basestleu.com. May–Aug: 10am–6.30pm; Sep: Wed and Sat, 10am–6.30pm; Oct–Nov and Feb–Apr: Wed and Sat 1.30–5.30pm. Closed Dec–Jan. 2.40–6.90€ (children 1.90–3.80€).* This leisure centre offers 50ha/123 acres of green space to play in for all ages. On the relaxing side: supervised swimming, picnics and animal park. Water sports and activities (paddleboats, canoes, kayaks and mini-golf). Peckish? Head for the large picnic area or snackbar.

Montmorency

Ancient fief of the Montmorency family, one of the most distinguished branches of the French nobility, this wealthy suburb of Paris and its beautiful forest once attracted artists, politicians, socialites and writers fleeing Paris, the "town of noises, of mud and smoke". Among these was celebrated 18C author and social theorist Jean-Jacques Rousseau, who came here, closer to nature, to write some of his greatest works.

> ▸ **Population:** 20 599
> ⚅ **Michelin Local Map:** p238: AB3, F-7, map 101 fold 5 or 106 fold 19.
> ▯ **Info:** Office du tourisme de Montmorency, 1 av. Foch, 95160. ℘01 39 64 42 94. www.montmorency-tourisme.fr.
> ◐ **Location:** N of Paris, between St-Denis and Sarcelles, on D 301. From Paris, SNCF rail link from Gare du Nord (Enghien-les-Bains), then bus 13 (Mairie-de-Montmorency).

A BIT OF HISTORY

The First Christian Barons – The Bouchard family, who held the lordship of Montmorency, had the reputation of being difficult vassals, and it was only after the 12C that they served the French crown loyally. Over a period of 500 years, the **Montmorency family** produced six constables, 12 marshals and four admirals. They had connections with every ruler in Europe and chose to call themselves the "first Christian barons".

The oldest branch of the family died out in 1632 when the constable's grandson **Henri II de Montmorency**, governor of Languedoc, was beheaded at the age of 37 for having plotted against **Cardinal Richelieu**. Although the duchy passed into the hands of Henri de Bourbon-Condé, King Louis XIV decided that the prestigious title of Duke of Montmorency should remain in the **Montmorency-Boutteville** family.

Jean-Jacques Rousseau's Literary Retreat – Rousseau (1712–18) lived in Montmorency from 1756 to 1762. Invited by **Mme d'Épinay**, a society woman who moved in literary circles, the 44-year-old author took up residence in the **Ermitage,** a small garden pavilion which has since been taken down. He was living with **Thérèse Levasseur**, a linen maid whom he later married, but fell passionately in love with his hostess' sister-in-law **Mme d'Houdetot**, who was nearly 20 years his junior. His romantic involvements caused him to fall out with Mme d'Épinay in 1757, at which point he moved to the **maison du Mont-Louis**, a house in the village, where he completed *The New Eloisa* and published *Emilius and Sophia* and *A Treatise on the Social Contract*. These were his three major works.

In 1762, *Emilius and Sophia* was qualified as subversive literature by the Parlement de Paris and a warrant was issued for Rousseau's arrest. Fortunately, the author was forewarned. He fled Mont-Louis with the help of **Marshal de Montmorency-Luxembourg**, an influential figure who had taken the writer under his wing, and sought refuge in Switzerland.

SIGHTS

Collégiale St-Martin★

Started in the 16C by **Guillaume de Montmorency** and completed by his son **Constable Anne**, this collegiate church is characteristic of the Flamboyant Gothic style. It was originally designed to be the mausoleum of the Montmorency family.

The chapel was intended to receive the remains of the Montmorency family and, in the 18C, the tombs of several members of the Condé family. The tombs were destroyed during the Revolution. Some were salvaged and moved to the Louvre, including those of Constable Anne and his wife Madeleine. The others have disappeared, save for the funeral slab of Guillaume de Montmorency and his wife Anne Pot, of the famous Burgundian family; it has been placed at the top of the south aisle.

Stained-glass windows★ – The 14 windows that adorn the apse and the five nearest right-hand bays of the chancel provide fine examples of Renaissance decoration, tastefully restored in the 19C. The family connections of the Montmorency are illustrated by the effigies of their ancestors, the brightly coloured coats of arms and the saints they worshipped. The other windows in the nave – executed in the 19C – harmonise well with the earlier Renaissance windows.

Polish connection – In the chancel, you may be surprised to see a copy of the statue of **Our Lady of Czestochowa**, patron saint of Poland. This is a reminder that the Polish elite, exiled after the failed insurrection of 1830–1831 against the Russian rule, had settled in Montmorency in the 19C.

Musée Jean-Jacques-Rousseau

5 r. Jean-Jacques-Rousseau.

Guided tours (1hr) Tue–Sun 2–6pm.
Closed1 May, 20 Dec–3 Jan.
4€. 01 39 64 80 13.
www.museejjrousseau.montmorency.fr.

This is the Mont-Louis House where French writer **Jean-Jacques Rousseau** lived from 1757 to 1762, and where he wrote his major works. Partly recreated with period furniture, the interior evokes the daily life of Rousseau and his wife. The old part of the house affords a good **view** of the valley.

A little arbour, planted with lime trees, leads through to the small garden pavilion Rousseau used as a **study**, which he sardonically called his "keep".

In the modern part of the house, the exhibition hall and audio-visual room present particular aspects of Rousseau's life and work. On the edge of the grounds, a 18C house called the "maison des Commères" (House of Gossips) contains a library with numerous studies on Rousseau, and houses the town's historic research centre.

EXCURSIONS
Enghien-les-Bains

▶ 9km/5.6mi from Montmorency on the D 938 then D 911.

Not far from Paris, the only true waterside city of Île-de-France offers splendid Belle Époque villas and reputed thermal baths – but also a casino, theatre, arts centre and horseracing tracks. The banks of its large lake, filled with canoes and sailboats, promises romantic strolls.

Lake★ – The lake is 43ha/106 acres wide and 1 to 5m/3.316 ft deep. From the walking path on rue du Gén.-de-Gaulle, the view of the water and its lush green setting is very pleasant. You can take a walk around the lake (3.5km/2.2mi) via the central belt and the Boulevard du Lac, but the villas and gardens generally prevent views of the water, except from the north bridge and the "Muse" bridge. There's also a large sporting and nautical activities centre (visit www.ot-enghien-lesbains.fr for more information).

Forêt de Montmorency

Extending over 2 000ha/4 942 acres north of the Seine, the Montmorency Forest covers the highest hill (195m/640ft) in the Paris region. The area west of Domont and N 309 is the most interesting section, with deep wooded vales and patches of moist undergrowth. Oaks, planted in vast quantities in the 18C, and chestnut trees are the dominant species. The forest has several footpaths (GR1, various hiking trails) for long and shorts rambles; a road known as the **Route du Faîte**, opened to both cyclists and walkers, which cuts through the forest; and the Caesar's Camp recreational area.

Château de la Chasse – 30min on foot from N 309 (green gate on the left, 2km/1.2mi beyond Montlignon Church). This oddly shaped castle (12C), flanked with truncated towers, stands in a picturesque setting on the edge of a pond.

Église St-Martin Groslay

▶ Groslay, 2km/1.2mi E of Montmorency. This church dating to the 12C–13C features stained glass, including an **Arbre de Jessé** inspired by the one at the St-Étienne de Beauvais church.

Taverny

▶ *12km/7.4mi NW of Montmorency on the D 109, D 144 and D 928.*

Southwest of the Montmorency forest, Taverny boasts a remarkable hillside **church★** (✆*01 30 40 71 79; ⟿guided tours possible*). In the early 13C, the Montmorency family built the current church beside a chateau that has since disappeared. Remodelled in the 15C, the gothic-style church was restored by Viollet-le-Duc in the 19C. The chancel boasts a Renaissance stone **altar★**. The lower frieze features the Passion, the monogram of Henri II and the crescent seals of Diane de Poitiers. The upper part depicts the Evangelists.

Sannois

▶ *4km/2.5mi W of Enghien.*

An 18C **windmill** (*currently under restoration*) stands on a 162m/531ft-high knoll. The village church houses the tombstone of **Cyrano de Bergerac**, who died here in 1655.

Argenteuil

▶ *5.5km/3.4mi SW of Enghien.*

Situated on a loop of the Seine, Argenteuil inspired numerous painters including Boudin *(Bassin d'Argenteuil)*, Caillebotte *(Le Pont d'Argenteuil et la Seine)*, Manet *(Argenteuil)* and Monet *(Vue d'Argenteuil)*.

ADDRESSES

⏦/EAT

⊜⊜⊜⊜ **Au Cœur de la Forêt** – *Av. du Repos de Diane. Access via a forest lane.* ✆*01 39 64 99 19. www.aucoeurdelaforet. com. Closed 15–25 Aug, Thu dinner, Sun dinner and Mon.* Traditional seasonal menus served in two rustic rooms and on a shaded summer terrace.

Ermenonville and Mer de Sable

Ermenonville, situated on the outskirts of the eponymous forest, owes its fame to French philosopher Jean-Jacques Rousseau, who frequently enthused about its "shady trees" and natural beauty. The town is also home to the Mer de Sable amusement park.

▶ **Population:** 938

◔ **Michelin Map:** p238 C2.

▤ **Info:** Ermenonville Tourist Office: ✆03 44 54 01 58. www.otsi-ermenonville.com.

▶ **Location:** 52km/32.3mi N of Paris on the A 1, D 126 and D 922.

♟♟ **Kids:** Mer de Sable amusement park.

ERMENONVILLE

In May 1778, **Jean-Jacques Rousseau** was invited to stay at the Château d'Ermenonville (*private*) by the Marquis de Girardin, who had acquired the estate in 1763, and it is here that Rousseau rekindled his passion for nature; he walked, daydreamed in the park and taught music to his host's children. The **Parc Jean-Jacques Rousseau** (◔ *open Apr–Sept Mon–Fri 10am–6.30pm (weekends 7.30pm), Oct–Mar Mon–Sat 1pm–5.30pm, Sun 10am–5.30pm); ✆03 44 10 45 15; ⊜2€*) was transformed by the marquess from sandy, swampy land into a landscaped garden in the French style with shaded paths, graceful vistas, elegant rockeries and follies.

♟♟ MER DE SABLE★

0.5km/0.25mi S on N 330. ◔*Open daily Apr–Sept 10am–6pm.* ⊜*23.50€ (no charge children under 3).* ♿ ✆*08 25 25 20 60 (0.15€/min). www.merdesable.fr.*

This family theme park was created in the middle of the Ermenonville forest, in a sandy clearing dating from the Tertiary Era – at the end of the Ice Age when this region was probably a vast sandy moor covered with wild heather. The park has three worlds to explore: the **Wild West**, the **Sahara** and the great **Jungle**. Ride through the desert aboard the little **Train des Sables** and expect lots of shows (re-enactments of Western movies) and attractions (thrill-seeker rides, pony rides, toboggan, Merry Go Round, Ferris wheel, canoe rides, etc).

Mer de Sable

© Gérard Labriet/Photononstop

EXCURSIONS
Forêt d'Ermenonville
◐ *Follow the signs at the central car park in the village of Ermenonville to reach the forest.*

The state-owned Ermenonville Forest (3 300ha/8 154 acres) is one of the most beautiful in the region, alongside Chantilly and Halatte. The terrain consists mostly of sandy, poor soil, and the forest of today is the result of some 150 years of planting former moorlands with woody and maritime pines (17 00ha/42 00 acres). The trunks have a distinctive reddish hue near the base.

The national forest authority has designated several hiking trails, particularly concentrated at the crossroads of the "Baraque de Chaalis". Outside of the "Longue Route" which provides access to this intersection of trails, the forest roads are forbidden to vehicles. Cars are however permitted to circulate on the path leading from the Baraque de Chaalis to the memorial commemorating the 346 people who died in a plane crash at the site in 1974.

Mortefontaine
◐ *7.5km/4.6mi W of Ermenonville on the D 922 and D 126.*

To the southwest, the forest merges with the wood and ponds of the Domaine de Mortefontaine. These sites, which enhanted romantic thinkers Corot and Gérard de Nerval, are unfortunately not accessible, but it is possible to follow the **route de Mortefontaine in Thiers-sur-Thève**: from here, sublime views of the Vallière pond, rocky, rugged hills, moorlands and mysterious thickets.

François Mauriac House
◐ *Vemars, 15km/9.3mi SW of Ermenonville by D 922, D 126, D 10 and D 16. Mairie de Vémars, r. Léon-Bouchard. Call town hall for info on opening hours. ℘01 34 68 33 40.*

Situated across from the cemetery where French writer **François Mauriac** (1885-1970) was laid to rest, the Vémars town hall is housed in the house where the writer frequently sojourned from 1913 to 1970. It was in this house, owned by his wife's family, that he learned of his nomination for the 1952 Nobel Prize for Literature, and also where he wrote his last novel, *Un adolescent d'autrefois*. The author's memorabilia and artefacts are displayed in one of the rooms.

ADDRESSES

ℙ/ STAY

◖◖◖ **Hôtel des Trois Hiboux** – *Parc Astérix, 60128 Plailly. ℘03 44 62 68 00. 100 rooms. Room and park packages available. Restaurant◖◖◖.* According to legend, each of the three forests surrounding the amusement park used to be the territory of an owl (hibou). Perhaps you'll fall asleep to the lullaby of their songs in one of the cosy bedrooms of this hotel where they are said to convene. Sweet dreams!

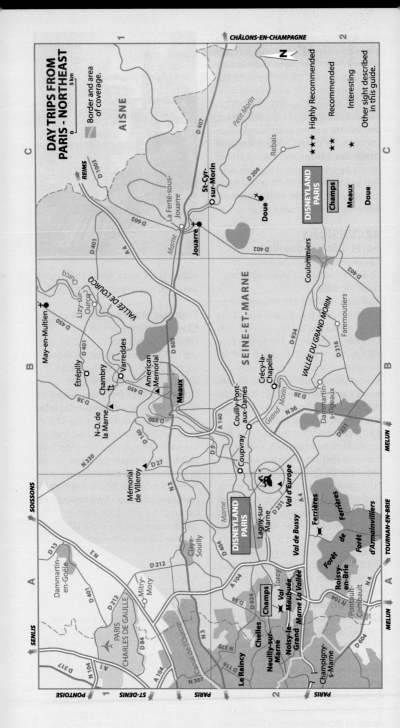

DAY TRIPS FROM PARIS - NORTHEAST

0   5 km

Border and area of coverage.

★★★ Highly Recommended
★★   Recommended
★   Interesting
     Other sight described in this guide.

DISNEYLAND PARIS

| **Champs** |
| Meaux |
| Doue |

C

AISNE

CHÂLONS-EN-CHAMPAGNE

REIMS

D 1003

D 603

La Ferté-sous-Jouarre

Petit Morin

Rebais

St-Cyr-sur-Morin

D 204

Doue

Marne

Jouarre

D 402

Coulommiers

D 402

B

May-en-Multien

D 450

Lizy-sur-Ourcq

Ourcq

VALLÉE DE L'OURCQ

Étrépilly

D 38

Chambry

N.-D. de la Marne

D 405

Varreddes

American Memorial

Meaux

D 603

SEINE-ET-MARNE

Couilly-Pont-aux-Dames

Crécy-la-Chapelle

VALLÉE DU GRAND MORIN

D 934

D 216

Faremoutiers

Grand Morin

N 36

Dammartin-s-Tigeaux

D 231

A

SOISSONS

SENLIS

Dammartin-en-Goële

D 13

N 2

D 212

D 401

D 212

Mitry-Mory

Claye-Souilly

Mémorial de Villeroy

D 27

N 330

N 3

D 140

A 140

D 5

Coupvray

Marne

DISNEYLAND PARIS

Lagny-sur-Marne

Val d'Europe

Val de Bussy

Ferrières

Forêt de Ferrières

Forêt d'Armainvilliers

Roissy-en-Brie

Pontault-Combault

D 604

N 4

TOURNAN-EN-BRIE

MELUN

MELUN

2

PONTOISE

ST-DENIS

PARIS

PARIS

PARIS CHARLES DE GAULLE

Canal de l'Ourcq

A 104

N 3

D 84

D 317

N 104

A 1

N 2

Val Torcy

Champs

Val Maubuée

Marne La Vallée

Chelles

Noisy-le-Grand

Neuilly-sur-Marne

Le Raincy

Champigny-s-Marne

N 370

N 302

N 307

D 934

D 34

A 104

Disneyland Paris★★★

This 53ha/acre park will transport you to another world, where life is a series of fairytales, adventures and futuristic inventions. Ideal for children of all ages, as well as "big kids".

A BIT OF HISTORY
A Magician called Walt Disney

Walt Disney's name is linked to innumerable animated cartoons that have entertained children throughout the world. No one can forget the heroes of his creations (Mickey Mouse, Minnie, Donald, Pluto, Pinocchio and others).

Born **Walter Elias Disney** in Chicago in 1901, Walt soon showed great ability at drawing. After World War I, in which he served as an ambulance driver in France, he returned to the US where, in Kansas City, he met a young Dutchman called Ub Iwerks. In Hollywood in 1923, the pair produced a series of short films called *Alice Comedies*. In 1928, Mickey Mouse, the future international star, was created. Next followed the era of Oscar-winning, full-length animated films: *The Three Little Pigs* (1933), *Snow White and the Seven Dwarfs* (1937), and *Dumbo* (1941).

Disney also produced films starring real people, such as *Treasure Island* (1950). In 1966 Disney died, but Walt Disney Studios continued to make films, remaining faithful to his ideas. The parks dotted around the world keep the fantasy alive for young and old alike.

♟♜ DISNEYLAND PARK★★★

Opening times vary according to the season. Check the website for details. Disneyland: Mon–Fri 10am–6pm, weekend 10am–8pm. 1 day/1 park 61€ (child 55€); 1 day/2 parks 74€ (child 66€). www.disneylandparis.com. Disney Studios: See Disneyland for opening times. Guided tours: contact the City Hall (Disneyland Park) on Town Square in Main Street, or the Studio Services in Walt Disney Studios.

Michelin Local Map: p264: A2 or map 106 fold 22.

Info: +33 01 60 30 60 53 (from outside France), 0825 300 500 (in France). www.disneylandparis.com.

Location: The resort is 32km/20mi E of Paris, with excellent transport links. On arrival, find the information desk in City Hall (Disneyland Park) where a programme of the attractions is provided.

Parking: Car parks are available in the northeast portion of the park, although thanks to its train and bus terminals, Disneyland Paris is easily accessible by public transport.

Timing: To avoid long queues, visit popular attractions during the parade, at the end of the day or with a Fast Pass *(free)* issued by machines at the entrance to attractions; this ticket bears a time slot of one hour during which time you have priority access to the attraction.

1 day/1 park 57€ (child 51€).
Disneyland Passport *(Passeport Annuel) 300 days 119€, 365 days 199€. Passports allow total freedom of movement between both parks.*

The large Disneyland Paris site (over 55ha/135 acres) comprises five territories or 'lands', each with a different theme. As well as the spectacular shows featuring amazing automatons in detailed settings, each region has shops, ice cream vendors and restaurants.

Every day, the **Disney Parade★★**, a procession of floats carrying all the favourite Disney cartoon characters, takes place. On some evenings, during holiday periods and throughout the

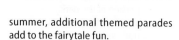

How old is Mickey?

The famous young mouse hasn't a single wrinkle, yet he was born in 1928. Mickey first appeared in a small film entitled *Plane Crazy*, based on Charles Lindbergh's achievement in aviation. However, it was on 18 November of the same year that the world's favourite mouse made his star debut, together with Minnie, in the first silent cartoon film entitled *Steamboat Willie*. Age has caused Mickey to lose not his hair, but his tail!

summer, additional themed parades add to the fairytale fun.

Main Street USA

The main street of an American town at the turn of the 20C, lined with shops and restaurants with Victorian-style fronts, is brought to life as though by magic. Horse-drawn cars, limousines, police cars and fire engines shuttle visitors from Town Square to Central Plaza while a talented troupe of musicians play favourite ragtime, jazz and Dixieland tunes. On either side of the road are **Discovery Arcade** and **Liberty Arcade** (exhibition and diorama on the famous Statue of Liberty).

From Main Street station a small steam train, the **Disneyland Railroad**★, travels across the park and through the **Grand Canyon Diorama**, stopping at the station in each land.

Frontierland

The dangerous exploration of the American Far West, the gold rush and the Wild West with its legends and folklore come back to life in Thunder Mesa, made to resemble a typical western town. The waters here are plied by two handsome old paddle **steamboats**★, the *Mark Twain* and the *Molly Brown*.

Big Thunder Mountain★★★ – In the mountains of the far west, there's an old gold mine. On the banks of the lake, in the buildings belonging to a mining company, crowds of travellers patiently wait to board the **Mine Train**. The daredevil trip in hurtling carriages racing down the track at top speed includes explosions and risks of falling rocks – not to mention chilling brushes with rattlesnakes and coyotes.

Phantom Manor★★★ – A dilapidated, foreboding manor house stands high above the Rivers of the Far West. Inside, strange things begin to happen: the walls stretch and shrink. The tour through the rooms and basement continues in small black 'haunted' chairs, bringing you into a ghostly world you won't soon forget. When you leave, take a stroll to the **Boot Hill** cemetery and have a look at the strange tombstones.

Adventureland

Adventureland conjures up images of exotic adventures, travel to distant lands, treasure island, and pirates. Children and adults alike will be thrilled by the spirit of this far-flung and wild land.

Pirates of the Caribbean★★★ – Long before the box-office topping movie franchise starring Johnny Depp hit the screens, this ride was a classic. The fortress is easy to spot – a skull and crossbones fly atop its walls. Cross the underground passages which reserve a few surprises , then board a small boat and watch the attack and ransacking of a Spanish harbour town by pirates. At your own risk, of course, matey!

Pirate's Beach – A pirate-themed playground for the youngest visitors.

Indiana Jones and the Temple of Peril★★★ – In the jungle lies a ruined temple; courageous archaeologists in wagons enter it in reverse, defying laws of gravity. This ride is not for the faint-hearted (or for those under age 8).

La Cabane des Robinson★★ – The Swiss Family Robinson survived a shipwreck and were able to salvage a few objects and building materials that enabled them to build a tree house in a giant banyan tree (an Indian fig).

Le Passage Enchanté d'Aladdin – In the colourful city of Agrabah, revisit the magic world of Aladdin and the enchanted carpet.

Fantasyland

The land of fairytales, Sleeping Beauty's Castle and your favourite Disney characters 'in the flesh': Mickey, Minnie, Donald, Goofy and Pluto are ready to pose for photos.

Sleeping Beauty's Castle★★ – On the upper floor, stained-glass windows and Aubusson tapestries recount episodes from this beloved tale. Below, in the depths of the castle, a giant dragon appears to be sleeping. A magnificent view from the ramparts.

It's a Small World★★ – A 'cruise' takes visitors past dolls dressed in national costume, singing and dancing in sets that represent their home countries.

Alice's Curious Labyrinth★ –An episode from *Alice in Wonderland* in which the path to the Queen of Heart's castle is full of surprises. Also don't miss the nearby Mad Hatter's teacup ride!

Peter Pan's Flight★★ – Like the flight of Peter Pan, the boy who never grew up, the trip takes visitors over the rooftops of London and Never-Never Land.

Snow White and the Seven Dwarfs★ – In a mysterious forest crossed by small wagons, a wicked witch lurks, plotting to cast a spell on Snow White.

Discoveryland

A fascinating land of tomorrow paying homage to inventions and Science Fiction.

Space Mountain Mission 2 ★★★ – This superb attraction was inspired by Jules Verne's novel *From the Earth to the Moon*. A huge copper and bronze mountain encompassing a gigantic cannon pointing skywards awaits the most audacious visitors. After being catapulted toward the cosmos, experience a mind-bending, acrobatic, intergalactic trip.

Star Tours★★★ – A breathtaking trip on a spaceship. Based on George Lucas' *Star Wars*. Use the **Photomorph** to change your looks (laughter guaranteed) and have your photo taken.

Captain EO starring Michael Jackson – Back by popular demand and updated with new special effects : an exceptional 3D and musical experience starring the King of Pop himself.

Buzz Lightyear Laser Blast – Save the universe of toys using your lasergun to target in on the pesky Emporer Zurg.

WALT DISNEY STUDIOS PARK★★★

Inaugurated on 16 March 2002, this park is entirely dedicated to the wonders of cinema. Discover the secrets of filming, animation techniques and television.

Front Lot – The park entrance is overlooked by a 33m/108ft-high water tower, a traditional landmark in film studios. In the centre of the Spanish-style courtyard stands a fountain dedicated to Mickey.
Disney Studio 1 reconstructs a famous Hollywood film set, Hollywood Boulevard.

Toon Studio

Disney contributed much to the development of 20C animation: here, its secrets are unlocked!

Animagique★★★ – Transport yourself to the centre of a 3D cartoon, next to Mickey, Donald Duck and others!

Art of Disney Animation★★ – Discover the secrets of animation.

Toy Story Playland – A colourful paradise of toys awaits the youngest visitors inspired by the film franchise.

Crush's Coaster – A dashing deep-sea adventure inspired by the animated film *Finding Nemo*.

Flying Carpets over Agrabah★★ – Guests are taken onto a film set where Aladdin's Genie guides them onto flying carpets!

Production Courtyard

Here spectators are plunged behind the scenes at film and TV studios, learning how film sets and special effects are created.

Sleeping Beauty's Castle

© Disney

Cinémagique★★★ – Spectators literally go through the screen and become film heroes.

Playhouse Disney – Younger visitors delight as their favourite Disney Channel cartoon characters come to life on a live toon set!

Studio Tram Tour★★ – Sit back and enjoy this guided tour through amazing film sets, until you reach **Catastrophe Canyon**★★★!

The Twilight Zone Tower of Terror – A terrifying visit to the fourth dimension as you ride the elevator of an old Hollywood hotel… then free-fall 13 floors!

BackLot

This is where the action is!

Armageddon★★ – The Russian space station is threatened by meteorites: hang on tight!

Rock 'n' Roller Coaster★★★ – A unique 'musical' experience awaits you inside a recording studio; be prepared to be propelled at full speed.

Moteurs… Action!★★★ – A hero chases villains through a village in the south of France: superb stunts.

DISNEY VILLAGE★

The main street of this American town offers continuous entertainment, particularly once the theme parks close. Night-owls can hit the discotheque **Hurricanes**. The quality of the shows, cinemas, and the reputation of establishments such as **Planet Hollywood** have ensured the success of this 'village'.

Buffalo Bill's Wild West Show★★ – The adventures of William Frederick Cody (1846–1917), alias Buffalo Bill, inspired this dinner-show, which evokes the epic days of the Wild West. Mickey, Sitting Bull and Annie Oakley are all there too.

MAKING THE MOST OF THE THEME PARKS

To avoid long queues at popular attractions, visit them during the parade, at the end of the day, or better still, get a **Fast Pass**, issued by distributors outside popular attractions in both parks. This ticket bears a time slot of one hour during which time you have priority access to the attraction.

Disneyland Park: Indiana Jones (Adventureland); Peter Pan's Flight (Fantasyland); Big Thunder Mountain (Frontierland); Space Mountain and Star Tours (Discoveryland).

Walt Disney Studios Park: Rock 'n' Roller Coaster (Backlot); Flying Carpets (Production); Studio Tram Tour (Production).

GENERAL INFORMATION

Booking a show – Entertainment programmes and booking facilities can be found at City Hall, in Town Square, just inside Disneyland Park.

Currency exchange – Facilities are available at the main entrance to the park.

Visitors with Disabilities – A guide detailing special services available can be obtained from City Hall (Disneyland Park) or from the information desk inside Walt Disney Studios Park.

Storage areas – Near the main entrance, beneath Main Street Station.

Animals – Pets are not allowed in the theme parks, in Disney Village or in the hotels. The Animal Care Centre is located near the visitors' car park.

Baby Care Centre, Meeting Place for Lost Children, First Aid – Near the Plaza Gardens Restaurant (Disneyland Park) or in Front Lot (Walt Disney Studios Park).

ADDRESSES

🏨 STAY

🐭 For the total Disney experience, choose one of the park's own hotels, with decor inspired by different regions of the USA.

➤ **L'International** – *77450 Jablines, 6km/3.7mi N. ℘01 60 26 09 37. www.camping-jablines.com. Closed Oct–Mar. Reservations advisable. 150 pitches.* Offers water sports, camping and bungalow rentals; the site also has the region's biggest beach, right around the corner from Disneyland.

➤ **Bellevue Bed and Breakfast** – *77610 Neufmoutiers-en-Brie, 10km/6mi S. Take A 4, D 231 then D 96. ℘01 64 07 11 05. www.domaine-de-bellevue.net. 7 rooms.* Nestled in an attractive garden on the edge of a small village, this 19C residence is simple and elegant, close to Paris and Disneyland, and makes a charming stopover in the heart of the Brie region.

➤ **Les Hauts de Montguillon** – *22 r. de St-Quentin, in Montguillon, St-Germain-sur-Morin, 3km/1.8mi NE. ℘01 60 04 45 53. www.les-hauts-de-montguillon.com. ✉. 3 rooms. Meals ➤➤.* This restored farmhouse located a few minutes from Disneyland is a comfortable stop. Bedrooms blend old and new; bathrooms are stylish and ultra-modern.

➤➤➤ **Hôtel Santa Fé** – *In Disneyland. ℘01 60 45 78 00. 1 000 rooms.* Welcome to New Mexico! A larger than life poster of Clint Eastwood, straight out of *The Good, The Bad and The Ugly*, welcomes you to rooms cooled by ceiling fans. The Tex-Mex restaurant features *mariachi* bands.

➤➤➤➤ **Hôtel Cheyenne** – *In Disneyland. ℘01 60 45 62 00. 1 000 rooms.* Come and learn how cowboys live with your kids at this reconstructed Far West town! Simple rooms designed for family visits.

➤➤➤➤➤ **Hôtel Sequoia Lodge** – *In Disneyland. ℘01 60 45 51 00. 997 rooms.* Inspired by the wild landscape of the Rocky Mountains, this hotel enjoys comfortable rooms, two restaurants with buffet service, a swimming pool and fitness centre.

Neuilly-sur-Marne

Situated on the verdant banks of the Marne and boasting one of the region's most pleasant riverside beach areas, this unassuming town holds unsuspecting riches, including a large waterside park and fine 12C church.

SIGHTS
Église St-Baudile
Pl. du Chanoine-Héroux.
This small church dating to the late 12C is surprising for its harmonious blend of the Romanesque and Gothic styles. In the Romanesque section, three columns grace the chancel, stretching upwards towards the vault. The three arches connecting the pillars that support the bell tower mark a transition from the Roman to the Gothic style. The latter style is visible in the nave's monocylindrical pillars, carved in the same proportions and style as those found at Notre-Dame de Paris.

♣♣ Parc de la Haute-Île
To reach the park, exit at Quelles on the N 34; follow the tree-lined road until you reach a small road at right, just before the traffic light at the Chelles business district: this leads to the park car park (inaccessible from the other side of the motorway). ◥◥ *Allow at least 1hr to visit the park.* ⊙*Open daily Jun–Sept; Oct–May: weekends, school and public holidays.* ℘*01 43 93 98 20.*
Nestled between the Marne river and the canal de Vaires, this tranquil park and natural reserve provides opportunities for pleasant strolls. Observatories invite visitors to get a close look at numerous species of birds living here, among wild plants.
The park has a human history stretching back 8 000 years. A **mesolithic exhibit** at the centre allows visitors to understand the relationship between human beings and their environment during this period, and reconstitues the habitat and daily life of mesolithic humans. Walking paths are accessible to disabled visitors and strollers.

EXCURSION
Le Raincy
◗ *6.5km/4mi N of Neuilly-sur-Marne.*
In the 17C, Le Vau built a beautiful château, which has since disappeared, but which in part inspired the sublime Vaux-le-Vicomte chateau.
Église Notre-Dame★ – *Av. de la Résistance.* Built by **Auguste Perret** in 1923, this church consists of breeze-block and trellised screens covered in small, stained-glass windows replicating scenes from paintings by Maurice Denis.

Musée Alfred-Bonno, Chelles
◗ *7km/4.5mi NE of Neuilly-sur-Marne. Pl. de la République.* ⊙*Open Wed 10am–12pm, 2–6pm, Sun 2-5pm* ⊙*Closed Aug.* ℘*01 64 72 65 80.*
This museum houses a collection of local archaeological artefacts.

▶ **Population:** 33 680
⚙ **Michelin Map:** p264: A2.
🚩 **Info:** Seine-Saint-Denis Tourist Office, 140 av. J.-Lolive, 93695 Pantin. ℘01 49 15 98 98. www.tourisme93.com.
◗ **Location:** 10km/6.2mi from Paris on the N 34. Neighbouring Neuilly-Plaisance and across from Noisy-le-Grand, Neuilly-sur-Marne is on the banks of the Marne and the canal de Vaires RER A Neuilly-Plaisance.
👁 **Don't miss:** The architecture of the Eglise Notre-Dame in Raincy.
♣♣ **Kids**: The parc de la Haute-Île and its playground.

Château de Champs★★

Built at the end of Louis XIV's reign, the château de Champs is widely regarded as a model of 18C architecture. Its magnificent park is one of the masterpieces of French landscape gardening, with its elegant flowerbeds, groves and ornamental lakes.

VISIT
Château★

Open Wed–Mon 10am–12.15pm, 1.30–5pm (summer 6pm). Times may vary. Check website for details. 7.50€. 01 60 05 24 43, www.champs-sur-marne.monuments-nationaux.fr.

Following a six-year restoration project, the château reopened in summer 2013 and offers a high-tech visitor experience. When the château de Champs was completed by **J.-B. Bullet** in 1708, it gained attention for its unusual design, which placed a high importance on comfort. Each room boasts a bathroom and cloakroom; a more intimate style of dining room also appeared with this chateau. At the end of the wings, on the courtyard side, mezzanine levels connected to the ground floor by hidden staircases, served as quarters for servants. The ground floor includes the Grand drawing room, dining room, and a smoking room with a portrait of Louis XV from the Van Loo school. The **Chinese drawing room★★** is furnished with chairs upholstered with Beauvais tapestries illustrating La Fontaine's fables. The boudoir, meanwhile, is decorated with blue cameo paintings representing Chinese pastoral scenes. On the first floor, the music room affords a lovely view of the gardens.

Next in the visit follow the ceremonial room of Madame de Pompadour and the corner drawing room, decorated with magnificent **woodwork★**. The drawing room houses a portrait of the Marquise in "garden" attire, painted by Drouais.

Michelin Map: p264: A2.

Info: 01 60 05 24 43 or www.champs-sur-marne.monuments-nationaux.fr.

Location: 24km/15mi from Paris along the A 4. By commuter train: RER A Noisiel-le-Luzard.

The Marquise's Château

The most famous inhabitant of the Château de Champs was, without contest, Madame de Pompadour, who rented the residence in 1757 for the tidy sum of 12 000 livres. The marquise stayed only two or three years, but in that time spent lavishly. In 1760, she purchased the château de Mesnars in France's Loir-et-Cher region: she died there four years later.

The château served as a set for the 1989 film, Dangerous Liaisons, adapted by Stephen Frears from the book by Choderlos de Laclos.

Park ★★

Open Feb–Oct Wed–Mon 9.45am–5.30pm; Nov–Feb 9.45am–5.30pm weekends only.
Closed 1 Jan, 1 May, 1 and 11 Nov and 25 Dec. Free. 01 60 05 24 43.

Designed by **Claude Desgots**, nephew of Le Nôtre, this magnificent park was recreated in the beginning of the 20C by Duchêne, who strove to replicate the park's original 'embroidered' flowerbeds, waterbasins and groves. A marked walking path points visitors to principal sites of interest at the park and affords pleasant views of the chateau and surrounds. Allow around 2 hours for the 5.5 km/3.4mi walk.

A descriptive pamphlet is available at the main entrance of the park.

Marne-la-Vallée

The location of Disneyland Paris Resort, Marne-la-Vallée, a vast area comprising 26 towns, draws crowds from all over the globe. The area is worth exploring for its other riches, however, including bucolic strolls along the Marne river and an aquarium with some 300 marine species.

▶ **Population:** 282 150
⚅ **Michelin Local Map:** p264: A2.
🖹 **Info:** Seine et Marne Tourist Office: ☏ 01 60 39 60 39. www.tourisme77.net
▶ **Location:** Marne-la-Vallée comprises 26 cities broken into four zones along the Marne river, the Autoroute de l'Est et and the RER Line A. 27 km/16.7mi from Paris along the A 4. RER A Marne-la-Vallée.
👥 **Kids:** The Sea Life Aquarium.

NOISY-LE-GRAND

The modern architecture dominating the new centre of this city confirms its place as a commercial and administrative hub in the region. Some noteworthy architectural achievements include the **Palacio d'Abraxas** by Ricardo Bofill (pl. des Fédérés, just west of RER station Noisy-Mont-d'Est), the **Arènes de Picasso** by Manolo Núñez (in the Pavé-Neuf district, south of the same RER station), and the École supérieure d'ingénieurs en électronique et électrotechnique, an engineering school whose building was conceived by architect Dominique Perrault (located south of RER station Noisy-Champs).

Arènes de Picasso by Manolo Núñez, Noisy-le-Grand

© ARCO/J.Hildebrandt/age fotostock

VAL MAUBUÉE

Six towns make up this central area of the Marne-la-Vallée agglomeration; the Val Maubée is well-appreciated thanks to its proximity to the Marne river, combining relatively spacious residential zones with leisure and sports facilities. The waterside leisure centre in **Torcy** is especially popular.

Noisiel

This town is the location of the **Menier chocolate factory**★ *(headquarters of the Nestle corporation; no visits; from RER Noisiel, bus n 211 toward Torcy; stop at Chocolaterie),* a noteworthy example of 19C industrial architecure. A bustling centre during the Industrial Revolution, Noisiel housed a vast **workers' village**

The Meniers: A Large Family

Jean Antoine Menier (1795-1853) is at the centre of what has been called the Menier Empire. This Paris pharmacist developed a revolutionary process for pulverising medicines from plant and animal-based materials. He later had an idea to apply it to the processing of cocoa. This is how a mill acquired in 1825 was transformed into a chocolate factory, and eventually evolved into an industrial empire that would invigorate the economy of the whole region.

with over 300 small red-brick houses, an English-style park and **agricultural zone**.

Promenade historique des berges de la Marne

The historical Marne riverside walk gives visitors a good overview of the main industrial buildings of the former chocolate factory: the Saulnier mill, with its ceramic and glazed brick facade; the "cathedral" on the Menier island, which accommodated visitors wishing to observe the industrial mixing of sugar and cocoa; the Hardi bridge in reinforced concrete, which was a technical feat in its time. Also of note: the former city hall and old stables.

La Ferme du Buisson

Follow signs from the RER Noisiel station. Ticket office open Sat–Sun 2–6pm. Closed end Jul–end Aug. *01 64 62 77 77. www.lafermedubuisson.com.*
Once a vast farm, this assemblage of striking buildings in brick and timber-wood (18C) has been converted into a large contemporary arts centre comprising exhibition rooms, a cinema, theatre, studios and a restaurant.

VAL DE BUSSY

This area is made up of several old villages, including Bussy-St-Georges, Montenain and St-Thibault: their old-world charm remains palpable.

Église N.- D. du Val

33 bd. Thibaud-de-Champagne, in Bussy-St-Georges. Open Sat 10.30am–12.30pm. *01 64 66 39 92. www.notredameduval.fr.*
Completed in 2001, this church overlooks the Val pond in a lush green setting in the modern city centre. Architects H. Gonot and P. Marcenac conceived this ultramodern edifice which nonetheless evokes traditional religious iconography. Columns emerge from the water, encircling a rounded nave and climb up to the bell tower, evoking the spiritual quest.

Moulin Russon

r. du Lavoir, Bussy. Open Oct–May Wed and weekends 2–5pm; summer call for details. *01 64 77 27 14. www.marneetgondoire.fr.*
Situated in a bucolic setting, this 15C watermill was recently renovated. Admire the mechanisms of the wheel and external runnel, whose speed is regulated by a sluice gate and millstone system.

Take a leisurely stroll along the rue de la Brosse to enjoy the countryside ambience in the area.

Parc culturel de Rentilly

1 r. de l'Étang, Bussy-St-Martin. Open Apr–Sep 9am–7pm; Oct–Mar 9am–5.30pm. *01 60 35 44 12. www.parcculturelrentilly.fr.*
This recently opened park and contemporary arts centre is set in an unusually lush natural area. The verdant grounds offer lovely views of the Brosse valley, and comprise a French-style park, English-style counterpart and wooded pathways. There's also a château in the grounds (built in the 1950s after a fire decimated the original) and attached buildings: stables, Turkish baths, trophy room, etc. These have been refurbished to accommodate a contemporary arts centre, documentation room and artists' studios. Temporary exhibits and permanent works inside and out.

VAL D'EUROPE

This area is home to attraction parks Disneyland Paris and Walt Disney Studios (*see DISNEYLAND PARIS*), as well as an enormous shopping centre in Serris.
The **Sea Life aquarium**★ (open 10am–5.30pm; closed on the mornings of 1 Jan, 25 Dec; 16€ (13€ for children under 12); *01 60 42 33 66; www. sealife.fr*) provides a showcase for over 300 species of fish housed in 50 tanks, including a 360 degree glass "tunnel". Some of the tanks are "interactive", meaning visitors can touch and interact with the animals. The aquarium also hosts regular shows and special events.

Château de
Ferrières★

The Ferrières estate's shooting parties, the château's luxurious furnishings and the precious collections gathered by the members of the Rothschild dynasty were the talk of the town for over a century. The landscaped park, created at the same time as the Bois de Boulogne, is stunning, particularly around the lake. The nearby town of Ferrières draws its name from the iron ore *(fer)* extracted in great quantities during the 16C and 17C.

VISIT
Exterior
The castle's architecture reflects the various styles of the Renaissance period, including the odd eccentricity that was acceptable in the 19C. Although balus-

- **Michelin Local Map:** p264: A2; map 101 fold 30 or 106 folds 21, 22.
- **Info:** ✆01 64 66 31 14. www.ferrieres-en-brie.fr
- **Location:** Rue Rucherie, 25 km/15.5mi from Paris along the A4, exit 12: Ferrières-Val de Bussy.

ters, galleries and colonnades reigned supreme, the façades were each different.

The most striking and the most typically English is the main front overlooking the lake, with its centrepiece flanked by turrets and its display of superimposed galleries.

Step back to take in the tall decorative stone chimneys, reminiscent of the Château de Chambord.

A Challenge to Tradition

In 1829 James de Rothschild, founder of the French line of the family, acquired 7 500 acres/3 035ha of hunting grounds formerly belonging to Fouché, with a view to building a villa which would accommodate his invaluable collections.

The baron did not choose a professional architect; he broke with tradition and hired **Joseph Paxton**, the English glasshouse and garden designer with a penchant for modern materials such as iron and glass. Already famed for the Crystal Palace in London *(destroyed by fire in 1936)*, Paxton erected a rectangular building flanked by square towers, with a central hall equipped with zenithal lighting. Construction work was completed in 1859. The decoration, left in the hands of the baroness, was entrusted to the French specialist Eugène Lami.

On 16 December 1862, Napoleon III paid an official visit to the Rothschilds in their new residence. Delighted by the splendid apartments and the 800 head of game for his day's shoot, the Emperor planted a sequoia tree as a commemorative gesture. Less than ten years later, Jules Favre – in charge of Foreign Affairs in the new National Defence government – turned up at the gates of the château on 19 September 1870. In his capacity as Minister, Favre came to see Kaiser Bismarck, who was staying at Ferrières with Kaiser Wilhelm I of Prussia, to ask him to agree to an armistice.

The chancellor however made this conditional on the surrender of Strasbourg, Toul and Bitche, and further implied that the cession of Alsace and part of Lorraine was inevitable. Jules Favre left the premises the following morning. On 28 January 1871, Paris fell to the hands of the enemy.

In 1977 Baron Guy de Rothschild and his wife Marie-Hélène donated their château and part of the estate to the Confederation of Paris Universities.

Interior

⚿ *Closed to the public.*

📞 *01 64 66 31 25.*

A pavilion sporting a large clock is fronted by the main entrance porch, which bears the baron's monogram (JR) and the family coat of arms (the five Rothschild arrows).

The main staircase leads to the central hall under the glass ceiling. Above the main door, a row of telamones and caryatids support a musicians' gallery. The Salon Bleu houses busts of the Empress Eugénie and Bettina de Rothschild, the château's first proprietress. The Louis XVI salon features, a painted ceiling inspired by Boucher and Louis XVI-style furniture. Opposite is the Salon Rouge, in which the 1870 negotiations took place.

Park★

🕐 *Call for times.* 📞 *01 64 66 31 25.*

The park designed by Paxton boasts superb compositions, mainly consisting of ornamental coniferous trees: cedars of Lebanon, numerous Atlas cedars, and sequoias, introduced into France around 1850.

Note a Lebanese cedar with long, spread-eagled branches, swamp cypresses with twigs which turn deep russet and drop off in winter and, on the far side of the lake, feathery weeping species.

EXCURSIONS
Forêt de Ferrières

In 1973, the Île-de-France region acquired this forest covering 2 800ha/ 6 919 acres. It now includes parking and picnic areas, as well as numerous footpaths and cycle paths accessible year-round. 15km/9.3mi of paths stretch between the woods of Beaubourg, Pontcarré, Villeneuve-St-Denis and the GR 14. Other trails are usable only during dry periods. The paths can be accessed along the D 471, D 21 and D 10. The Allée des Séquoias to the north of Pontcarré and the Orme plains are the principal sites of interest, while the Étang de la Planchette is an angler's paradise (*fishing permits delivered on-site*).

Forêt d'Armainvilliers

South of Pontcarré, this forest of conifers and oaks is in the process of being regenerated. Picnic sites are found along the D 471, near the Trois-Mares pond.

ADDRESSES

🏠 STAY

🛏️🍽️💰 **Hôtel Tulip Inn Marne-la-Vallée** – *44 bd A.-Giroust, 77600, Bussy-St-Georges-* 📞*01 64 66 11 11. www.tulipinnmarnela vallee.com. 87 rooms.* Opposite the RER railway station, this hotel offers well-equipped, sound-proofed rooms. Restaurant serves Italian-style cuisine in a dining room decorated in pastel colours.

Château de Ferrières

© Arnaud Chicurel/hemis.fr

Meaux★

Nestled inside a bend of the River Marne, Meaux is best-known for its world-famous Brie de Meaux cheese. In the summer, a **sound and light performance** featuring a cast of more than 2 000 re-enacts Meaux's moments of glory.

EPISCOPAL PRECINCT
Cathédrale St-Étienne★

Exterior – Construction of the church stretched from the 12C to the 16C, covering the gamut of Gothic architecture. The façade (14C–16C) is Flamboyant. The limestone used for the stonework has partially crumbled and the exterior decoration is badly damaged. The south transept façade is an elegant example of the Radiant Gothic style. The damaged south doorway is dedicated to St Stephen. Only the left tower (68m/ 223ft) was completed. On the right, the Black Tower: its dark shingles gave it its name.

Interior – Last restored in the 18C, the interior contrasts sharply with the weathered exterior. The lofty, well-lit nave is impressive. The two bays of the nave next to the transept date from the early 13C. Below the enormous stained-glass window runs an openwork triforium allowing a full view of the lancets. A walk round the ambulatory leads to Bossuet's tomb, marked by a slab of black marble.

Old Episcopal Palace

5 pl. Charles-de-Gaulle. ○*Open Apr–Sept Wed–Mon 10am–noon, 2–6pm. Oct–Mar Wed–Sun 10am–noon, 2–5pm, Sun 2–5pm.* ⊚*3€, no charge Wed.* ℘*01 64 34 84 45.*

The palace houses a **museum** largely dedicated to Bishop Bossuet. The building was completed in the 12C and altered in the 17C. The two magnificent **Gothic rooms** facing the park on the ground floor, the lower and the upper chapel are the oldest parts. The remarkable brick ramp leading to the first floor was designed in the 16C to enable mules loaded with grain to reach the attics.

▶ **Population:** 50 673
◉ **Michelin Local Map:** p264: B1; map 106 folds 22, 23.
▯ **Info:** 1 pl. Doumer, 77100 Meaux. ℘01 64 33 02 26. www.tourisme-paysdemeaux.fr.
◐ **Location:** In Île-de-France, 55km/34mi E of Paris, along the A 4. Access from Paris: SNCF rail link from Gare de l'Est.
▣ **Parking:** Limited town centre parking.
◕ **Timing:** Allow 1–2hr to visit the cathedral and episcopal palace.

Musée des Beaux-Arts

The Salle du Synode and the Grands Appartements have been turned into a Fine Arts Museum (15C–19C). Artists include Boullogne, De Troy, Bouchardon, Courbet and Van Loo. The Petits Appartements in the west wing house 19C works by Orientalist painters Gérôme and Decamps and landscape artists Daubigny and Millet.

Bossuet's Apartment

Bossuet's east-wing apartment has retained its original layout, but the decor was renewed in the Louis XV style. Admire Mignard's portrait of the bishop and a splendid Cressent commode (early 18C).

Old ramparts

Only accessible on guided tours.
At the top of the steps stands the 17C pavilion which Bossuet used as a study. The bishop would retire here to collect his thoughts or write during the night. The centre of the terrace affords a good **view★** of the gardens, Bishop's Palace and cathedral.

EXCURSION
Château de Montceaux

◐*8.5km/5mi E. Leave Meaux by N 3 (east). Beyond Trilport, in Montceaux Forest, turn right onto D 19 (signposted Montceaux-les-Meaux).*

Brie Cheese

One of France's most-celebrated cheeses, Brie had already secured its reputation by the 13C. As much appreciated by common Parisians as by royal tables, the cowsmilk cheese won a fierce competition pitting European varieties against each other at the 1815 Congress of Vienna. Little by little, several varieties appeared, notwithstanding common characteristics (namely the use of partially skimmed raw milk, a white rind lined with red marks, a soft, light-yellow interior, and aging not exceeding seven weeks). Brie de Meaux is the most famous, and boasts the largest wheels: measuring around 70cm/27in. in diameter, and weighing up to 3kg/6lb. Brie de Melun, another certified variety, is smaller but denser, with a pronounced aroma and saltier taste. It's also produced in much smaller quantities. Bries from Montereau and Nangis are both much smaller, and produced on a non-industrial, artisanal scale. Coulommiers, produced in the eponymous town, is a variety of brie that has been widely commercialised. It's also the smallest, with a diameter of around 14cm/5in. **Don't Miss:** The best seasons for tasting Brie de Meaux are the autumn, winter and the beginning of the spring. Try pairing Brie with a fresh baguette and Pinot Noir or Beaujolais wine.

Catherine de Medici had this chateau built (1547-1559). Upon her death, King Henry IV gave the château to his bride Marie de Medici. The château then fell into disrepair and became uninhabitable. Handsome ruins now stand here.

ADDRESSES

⬛ STAY

⬭⬕ **Chambre d'hôte M. et Mme.Cantin**– *2r. de l'Église, 77450 Trilbardou. ℘01 60 61 08 75. 3 rooms.* This 19C residence has a view of the canal de l'Ourcq from the garden. Elegant, refined rooms.

⬭⬕⬗ **Hôtel Le Richemont**– *43 quai de la Grande-Île. ℘01 60 25 12 10. www.hotel-lerichemont.com. 42 rooms.* This hotel sits on the banks of the Marne in the city centre. Well-equipped spacious rooms, buffet breakfast.

⬩/ EAT

⬭⬕ **La Péniche**– *Facing 6 quai Sadi-Carnot, near the pont du Marché. ℘01 60 01 16 16. http://la.peniche.free.fr. Capitaine: closed Sun eve, Mon. Sundeck: closed Sun eve and and from Oct to Feb.* This restaurant situated on a traditional river barge offers pleasant dining, especially in warmer months. Enjoy traditional fare in the "Capitaine" dining room, or light brasserie dishes on the sundeck.

⬭⬕⬗ **Le Canotier**– *2r. du Chemin-du-Bac, Précy-sur-Marne. ℘01 60 01 62 12. www.lecanotier.fr. Open Sun; groups accommodated by reserv. Lunch and dancing 24/29€. Tea dances: 12€.* This authentic restaurant-guinguette on the banks of the Marne offers pleasant waterside dining and "tea dances" bringing back a bygone era.

⬭⬕⬗ **La Grignotière**– *36r de la Sablonnière. ℘01 64 34 21 48. Closed Aug, Sat lunch, Tues and Wed.* A pleasant, rustic restaurant serving solid traditional dishes and shellfish platters.

SHOPPING

Market – *Pl. du Marché.* Open Sat all day, Wed morning. Traditional market is housed in two halls, including one c.1879.

Fromagerie de Meaux – *4r. du Gén.-Leclerc. ℘01 64 34 22 82. Open Tue–Thu 9am–12.30pm, 3.30–7pm; Fri–Sat 9am–7.15pm; Sun 9.30am–12.30pm. Closed Mon, July, Aug.* This shop is known for its Brie de Meaux, but also for other delicious cheeses.

ACTIVITIES

🚶 **Walking paths** – The regional walking trail known as the sentier de l'Île-de-France (GR1) runs through Meaux, stretching for some 207km/129mi. Greenery and pleasant waterside views abound. Contact Tourist Office for more information.

Jouarre★

Jouarre stands on a hilltop above the Petit Morin River, which flows into the Marne. The town already had two abbeys in the 7C. The monastery was short-lived, but the convent adopted the Benedictine rule and survived, soon gaining prestige. The great ladies of France, among them Madeleine d'Orléans, François I's half-sister, received the title of abbess. Badly damaged during the Hundred Years' War, the abbey was rebuilt several times. Seized during the Revolution, it was the residence of a fervent religious community, close observers of monastic rules. It resumed its activity in 1837.

VISIT
Tour romane

ⓘ *Open Wed–Mon 2–6pm, weekends and public holidays 11.15am–12.15pm, 2.30–6pm.* ✆4.50€. ✆01 60 22 06 11.
The only remaining tower from the old medieval sanctuary, it served as the bell-tower of the 12C Romanesque church. The restored interior comprises three vaulted rooms, furnished by Madeleine d'Orléans in the 16C; these house abbey relics and temporary exhibitions.
From the top, enjoy a superb panorama of the surrounding area. The tower served as an observation post during the Battle of the Marne in 1914.

Crypt★

🔈 *Guided tours (30min). Apr–Oct Wed–Mon 10am–1pm, 2–6pm; Nov–Mar Wed–Sun 10am–1pm, 2–5pm.* ⓘ*Closed public holidays.* ✆4.50€. ✆01 60 22 64 54. www.tourisme-jouarre.com.
The crypt lies behind the parish church, at the end of place St-Paul. The square presents an imposing 13C cross resting on a stone base with the Virgin and Child in the centre of a four-lobed medallion. The crypt consists of two formerly underground chapels, linked in the 17C. **Crypte St-Paul**, mausoleum of the founding family, is believed to be one of the oldest religious monuments in

📷 **Michelin Local Map:** p264: C1; map 106 fold 24.
ℹ **Info:** ✆01 60 22 64 54. www.tourisme-jouarre.com.
▷ **Location:** Just under 1hr from Paris via the autoroute A4 (leave at the exit for St Jean les deux Jumeaux) then take the RN3 (direction La Ferté sous Jouarre), and then D 402.
🕐 **Timing:** Allow 2hr.

France. The crypt is divided into three aisles by two rows of Gallo-Roman columns, made of marble, porphyry or limestone.
The famous Merovingian wall near the entrance presents a primitive stone mosaic with geometric motifs.
The most striking sarcophagus is the Tomb of St Agilbert, Bishop of Dorchester and later of Paris: Christ sits enthroned, surrounded by the Chosen Few with upraised arms. One of the galleries affords a good view of the bas-relief at the head: Christ circled by the four Evangelists' symbols (man, lion, bull, eagle). The tomb of St Osanne – an Irish princess who allegedly died in Jouarre – presents a 13C recumbent figure. The most elaborate decoration is the sarcophagus of Theodechilde, the first abbess of Jouarre.
The **crypte St-Ébrégésile** is a small Romanesque church beyond the first crypt. An archaeological dig in 1989 revealed that it had been built between Merovingian walls. The capitals in the crypt are also Merovingian, as is Bishop Ebrégésile's sarcophagus.
Recent excavations have revealed the nave of the St-Ébrégesile Church and several Merovingian sarcophagi.

Musée de la Civilisation Paysanne-Briard

R. de la Tour. ⓘ *Apr–Oct Wed–Mon 10am–1pm, 2–6pm; Nov–Mar Wed–Sun 10am–1pm, 2–5pm.* ✆3€. ✆01 60 22 64 54. www.tourisme-jouarre.com.

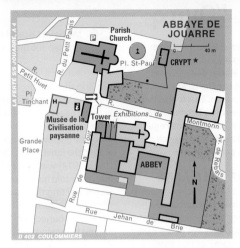

This museum explores regional folklore, customs and history: costumes, tools, paintings, etc.

Église Paroissiale

Enter by the south transept (⛅see plan above) at the end of the cul-de-sac.
This was rebuilt after the Hundred Years' War and completed in the early 16C. The north arm of the transept features a 16C Entombment, 15C *Pietà* and two reliquaries (12C and 13C) covered in silver-gilt with enamels, cabochons and filigree work.

EXCURSION
Doue

⏵*12km/7mi SE of Jouarre.*
Doue hill (181m/594ft) offers a view of the Plateau de la Brie des Morins. The squat nave of the **Église St-Martin** contrasts with its Gothic chancel and transept. Inside, the luminosity of the chancel and openwork design is characteristic of the Early Gothic style (13C).

St-Cyr-sur-Morin

⏵*7km/4.3mi SW of Jouarre along the D 114 and D 31.*
French writer **Pierre Mac Orlan** (1882–1970) spent his final days in this town: you can see his house at the edge of the village.
👥**Musée des Pays de Seine-et-Marne★** – *17 av. de la Ferté-sous-Jouarre.* ⏰*Open Sun–Fri 10am–12.30pm;*

2–5.30pm (Jul–Aug 6pm). ⏰*Closed 1 Jan, 1 May and 24 Dec.* 🎫*3€.* ♿ ☎*01 60 24 46 00. www.seineetmarne.fr.* The life, times and friendships of Mac Orlan are explored in the permanent exhibition on the first floor. The ground floor focuses on daily life and customs in the Seine-et-Marne region: folklore, traditional costumes and crafts and agricultural history.

ADDRESSES

🏠 STAY

🛏🛏🍽**Hôtel Château des Bondons** – *47 r. des Bondons, 77260 La Ferté-sous-Jouarre. 2km/1.2mi E by D 70. rte de Montménard.* ☎*01 60 22 00 98. www.chateaudesbondons.com. Wi-fi. 11 rooms.* This 18C chateau houses rooms of varying sizes, each with distinctive decor.

🍴 EAT

🛏**Auberge St(Eloi** – *1 pl. de Verdun, 77510 Doué.* ☎*01 64 20 99 77. www.auberge-saint-eloi.com. Closed Mon, Tue all day, Wed, Thu, Sun lunch.* Traditional cuisine served in a rustic setting: exposed beams, fireplace and tiled floor.

ACTIVITIES

🥾**Hiking** – The Tourist Office can recommend 6 hiking circuits around the city. Visit website to download maps. *www.tourisme-jouarre.com.*

Vallée de l'Ourcq

Beyond La Ferté-Milon, the River Ourcq follows a winding course through the Marne Valley. **Canal cruises** along the Ourcq are available in season. This is also the site of the devasting Battle of the Marne in 1914. Poet Charles Péguy was one of some 80 000 French soldiers who perished here.

BATTLE OF THE MARNE

The first Battle of the Marne originated with the Battle of the Ourcq, which in fact took place on the heights of the Multien plateau and not in the valley itself. The outcome of this battle did much to secure the success of the general Allied offensive launched between Nanteuil-le-Haudouin, north of Meaux, and Révigny, northwest of Bar-le-Duc. A little-known fact is that this battle began – on both sides – with the engagement of large reserve units (55th and 56th French Divisions, 4th German Corps). Owing to the hazards of drafting and the movement of retreat, many of the French soldiers were in fact defending their native territory.

≈ DRIVING TOUR

THE BATTLEFIELD AND THE OURCQ VALLEY

Round trip starting from Meaux. 96km/58mi. Allow 4hr. Local map, see overleaf.

Meaux★
& See MEAUX.

▶ From Meaux take N 3 (W) towards Paris. Turn right onto D 27, towards Iverny, then right again towards Chauconin-Neufmontiers.

Mémorial de Villeroy stands on the site of the early operations of 5 September 1914. The vault houses the remains of 133 soldiers who died nearby.
The 19th Company of the 276th Regiment was called in to relieve the Moroc-

& **Michelin Local Map:** p264: B1; map 106 folds 12, 23, 24.

can Brigade who accompanied them and who were dangerously engaged in battle near Penchard. It launched an attack towards Monthyon, under the fire of the enemy, sheltered in the valley around the Rutel brook. **Charles Péguy** (1873–1914) was the only surviving officer. He told his men to lie down and was inspecting the German positions when he was struck by a bullet.
Péguy was buried with his comrades-in-arms belonging to the 276th Infantry Regiment. Their collective grave lies to the right of the vault. The cross celebrating the memory of the writer, philosopher and social reformer now lies at the intersection of D 27 and D 129.

▶ At the next crossroads, turn left towards Chauconin-Neufmontiers. Drive through Penchard and follow signs to Chambry.

Cimetière National de Chambry is where the soldiers who died defending the village of Chambry, between 6–8 September, were buried. The village was taken and lost several times. The road offers a view of the Chambry-Barcy Plateau covered in war graves that seem to mark the progression of the Allied troops beneath the fire from the lines of German defence.
Located 500-m/550-yd east of the crossroads, the German military cemetery marks the place where the main German line – roughly following the dirt track – crossed the road to Varreddes.

▶ Turn back, towards Barcy.

Monument Notre-Dame-de-la-Marne, erected in 1914, dominates the battlefield.
Go toward Puisieux. At the crossroads after the factory, turn right to Étrépilly. In the village centre, 200m/220yd before reaching the church, turn left towards Vincy and Acy-en-Multien.

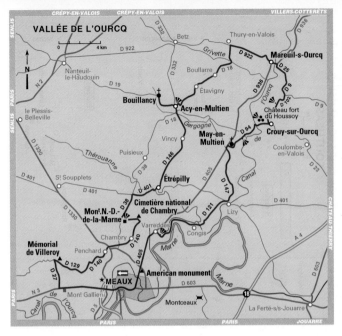

The small cemetery and memorial at **Étrépilly** evoke the battle over the night of 7–8 September, reaching a climax near the graveyard.

Acy-en-Multien was the scene of intensive warfare on 7 September 1914. The winding alleys, hillsides planted with small spinneys and château walls resulted in fatal close combat.

▶ Take the left-hand fork out of Acy towards Nanteuil-le-Haudouin.

The early Gothic church (12C–13C) **Église de Bouillancy** is situated In the valley.

▶ Turn back to Acy and take D 18 up to the plateau.

Enjoy the view of **Acy** and the elegant village spire. Beyond Étavigny, the road moves away from the battlefield.

▶ Just before Thury-en-Valois take D 922 to the right.

The road leads to **Mareuil-sur-Ourcq**, marking the start of the canal.

▶ Cross Varinfroy to Crouy-sur-Ourcq.

Just after the level crossing, the road skirts the ruins of the **Château Fort de Houssoy** in **Crouy-sur-Ourcq**. To see the separate **keep**, park and walk to the courtyard gates. Enjoy a fine view of the surrounds from the top of the tower. **Crouy Church** (visits by reserv: ℘01 64 35 63 02) features a Gothic interior with two 16C aisles.

▶ Turn back and turn left towards May after the bridge.

The winding road affords extensive **views** of the surrounding landscape. **May-en-Multien** is well situated 100m/330ft above the River Ourcq. Its church tower is visible from afar.

▶ Drive down to Lizy. Don't cross the bridge: go up the hill on |the N bank along the road to Congis (D 121). Cross Congis and Varreddes and join D 405, S.

On the left stands the huge **American memorial** commemorating the Marne combatants.

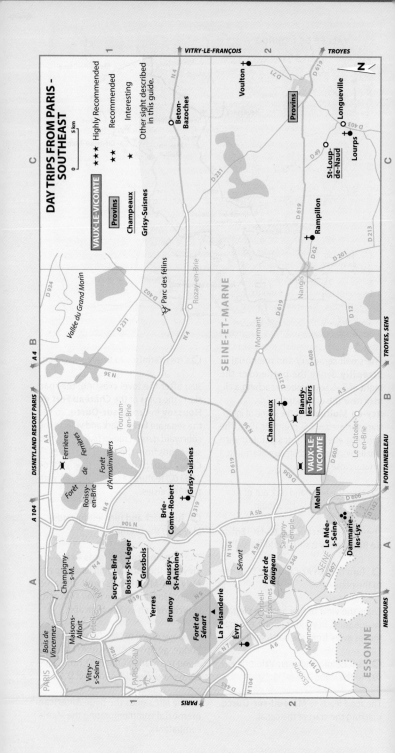

Château de
Vaux-le-Vicomte★★★

This château, built by Fouquet, foreshadowed the splendour of Versailles and remains one of the greatest masterpieces of the 17C. A walk through the gardens laid out by Le Nôtre offers an unforgettable experience, as does a tour of the château by candlelight.

A BIT OF HISTORY
The rise of Nicolas Fouquet

Fouquet became a member of the Paris Parliament by the age of 20. He was later appointed Superintendent of Finances under Mazarin. Intoxicated with success, Fouquet moved in 1656 to grace his own seignory of Vaux with a château he deemed worthy of his new social standing. He chose architect **Louis Le Vau**, decorator **Charles Le Brun** and landscape gardener **André Le Nôtre** to complete the endeavour. Construction, took five years to complete.

Royal offence

On 17 August 1661 Fouquet organised a fête for the king and his court. After a banquet, the guests feasted their eyes on the garden, boasting 1 200 fountains. The king was vexed by such an extravagant display of pomp and luxury, unparalleled at his own court. His first impulse was to have Fouquet arrested immediately, but Anne of Austria managed to dissuade him.

The fall of Nicolas Fouquet

Nineteen days later, the Superintendent of Finances was jailed and all his belongings were sequestrated. The artists who designed and built Vaux would later produce the Palace of Versailles. At the end of a trial, Fouquet was banished from court, but this sentence was altered by the king to perpetual imprisonment. Vaux survived the Revolution without suffering too much damage.

- 🚹 **Michelin Local Map:** p282: B2; map 106 folds 45, 46.
- 🚻 **Info:** ☎01 64 14 41 90. www.vaux-le-vicomte.com
- 🔵 **Location:** 6km/3.7mi NE of Melun, and 57km/36mi S of Paris via the D 51 and then A 5.
- 🅿 **Parking:** On site.
- 🕐 **Timing:** Allow half a day.

VISIT
Château ★★

🕐Open mid-Mar–mid-Nov 10am–6pm; Dec–Jan 10.30am–6pm (times may vary). 🕐Closed 25 Dec. ⊜14–16€; (gardens only 8€; candlelight visit 17–19€). ☎01 64 14 41 90. www.vaux-le-vicomte.com.

Surrounded by a moat, the château is approached via a main drive that leads towards the imposing northern front, with tall windows indicating the *piano nobile*.

The first floor is occupied by the **suites of Mr and Mme Fouquet**. The superintendent's anteroom is decorated with golden copper. Fouquet's office and bedroom boasts a beautiful ceiling likely designed by Jean Cotelle. Next are Mme Fouquet's office, Louis XV-style bedroom, and a Louis XVI-style counterpart. Returning to the ground floor,

Château de Vaux-le-Vicomte

© Béatrice Lécuyer-Bibal/Château de Vaux-le-Vicomte

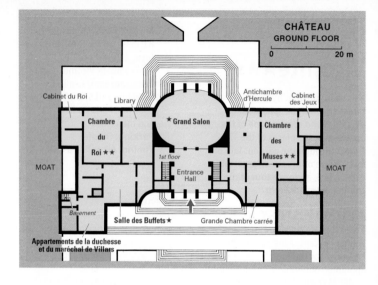

CHÂTEAU
GROUND FLOOR

0   20 m

Cabinet du Roi

Library

★ Grand Salon

Antichambre
d'Hercule

Cabinet
des Jeux

Chambre
du
Roi ★★

Chambre
des
Muses ★★

MOAT

MOAT

1st floor

Entrance
Hall

Basement

Salle des Buffets ★   Grande Chambre carrée

**Appartements de la duchesse
et du maréchal de Villars**

pass through the square-shaped Grande Chambre, the château's only example of the Louis XIII style.

Next, walk through the six grandiose rooms surrounding the Grand Salon. Their decorative coherence is visible in the ceiling paintings by Le Brun: *The Nine Muses* (in the **Muses★★** room), *Sleep* (game room), *The Entry of Hercules at Olympus* (in the antichambre d'Hercule). In the Salon d'Hercule, admire the equestrian statue of Louis XIV by Girardon, a bronze model of the monument that was destroyed during the Revolution at Place de la Vendôme. Other rooms on the ground floor and in the basement house costumed mannequins illustrating the history of Fouquet.

Grand Salon★ – The great drawing room, located in the central rotunda, was left incomplete following Fouquet's arrest. The walls were left without paint (but Le Brun's studies remain). Supporting columns symbolise the seasons.

King's Chamber★★ – The splendid chamber once occupied by Louis XIV adjoins the former antechamber, now an elegant library with Regence furniture. In the chamber, note Le Brun's magnificent ceiling painting.

Salle des Buffets★ – This was once Fouquet's dining room; it adjoins a corridor graced with fine wood panelling and paintings. The basement below houses large kitchens.

Outbuildings – A museum displaying vehicles and equipment (carriages, saddelry, etc.) is located in the west wing near the main entrance.

Gardens ★★★

🕐*Open mid-Mar–mid-Nov 10am–6pm; rest of the year: call for information.*
🕐*Closed 25 Dec, 1 Jan.* ✺*8€.* ✆*01 64 14 41 90. www.vaux-le-vicomte.com.*

Le Nôtre's superb gardens boast several "trompe l'oeil" effects, including the Water Mirror, designed to perfectly reflect the château. Take some distance from the upper terrace to appreciate the south facade, with its central rotunda and cupola, pavillions and sculptures.

First, pass through two knot gardens, Le **Boulingrin**. Three main bodies of water, including the **Grand Canal,** become visible at the last moment. Next come **Grottes** which seem to hover on the edge.

When you arrive at the Grand Canal, known as "the pan" due to its unusually rounded edges, skirt the canal and walk to the foot of the statue of the Farnese Hercules. Enjoy a magnificent **view★** of the château and gardens.

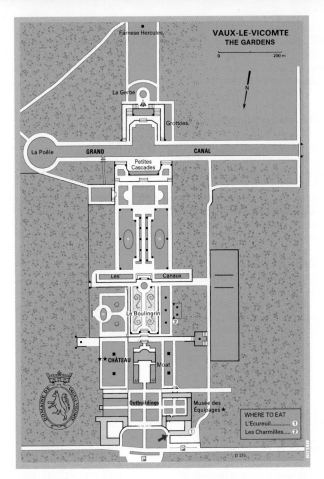

EXCURSIONS
Melun

▶ *6km/3.7mi from Vaux-le-Vicompte. Shuttlebuses (every 15min) between the château and Melun.*

Former home of the Capetian kings, Melun is home to the famed Brie de Melun cheese.

Musée municipal – *4 quai de la Courtille.* ⏰ *Open Wed–Sun 2–6pm.* ⏰ *Closed public holidays.* ☞ *Guided tours possible (1hr30).* ⊙ *2€. No charge 1st Sun of the month.* ✆ *01 64 79 77 70.* This museum is housed in the 16C Hôtel de la Vicomté, which belonged to Fouquet. Highlights include Gallo-Romancut stone vestiges and paintings of old Melun.

Collégiale Notre-Dame – *East side of the l'île St-Étienne. Guided tours by reservation with Tourist Office.*

Built in the 10C, this collegiate church is one of Melun's oldest buildings. The Renaissance-style facade boasts remarkable stained glass; the nave is supported by Gothic vaulting with archways originating at the chancel. Make sure to see the copy of the famed Melun Diptyque to the right of the chancel. Completed around 1450, this work by Jean Fouquet was commissioned by Étienne Chevalier, head treasurer of Charles VII. Agnès Sorel, the king's mistress, reportedly inspired the features of the Virgin portrayed in the diptyque.

Église St-Aspais – *Dating to the early 16C and built by Jehan de Felin, archi-*

tect of the tour St-Jacques in Paris, this church presents a beautifully coherent flamboyant Gothic design. Its original layout derives from the architect working around irregular foundations. Five progressively larger naves lead to an imposing chancel.

Musée de la Gendarmerie – 8 r. Émile-Leclerc. ☛ Closed for inventory until 2014. ℘01 64 14 33 17. From the 18C, military orders including the Hussars and Mamelukes settled in Melun. In 1945, the French police force set up a school here. Renovations at the museum will unveil an exhibit tracing the site's history from the 11C and highlight its compelling collection.

Le Mée-sur-Seine

▶3km/1.8mi W of Melun on D39, then take av. de la Courtilleraie.
The town's **museum** (937 r. Chapu; ☏open weekends 2–5pm; ☏closed Aug and public holidays; ☜no charge; ℘01 64 39 52 73) is dedicated to sculptor Henri Chapu (1833–1891), a prominent artist during the 3rd Republic.

Dammarie-les-Lys

▶3km/1.8mi S of Melun on D372.
The Abbey of Lys was founded in 1244 by Blanche de Castille. Only the ruins remain.

ADDRESSES

🛏 STAY

☻☻ **La Ferme du Couvent** –484 r. de la Chapelle-Gauthier, 77720 Bréau. (14.5km/9mi E of the château on D408 and D227 to the left. ℘01 64 39 22 28. www.la fermeducouvent.com. ☒☍. 15 rooms. ☚. Relaxing sojourn guaranteed in this 18C farm set in a 7ha/12-acre park. Rooms with sloping roofs and modern decor.

🍴 EAT

☻☻☻ **L'Écureuil**– At the château. ℘01 64 14 41 90. Open Apr–Oct, 10am–6pm, open until 12am during candlelight visits. Casual eatery named after Fouquet's personal emblem (the squirrel). Salads, grilled meats, hot dishes and pastries.

Blandy-les-Tours★

This 13C feudal château in the Brie countryside fell into complete ruin over the years, but recent renovations have restored much of its beauty. Be aware, though, that the château is reportedly haunted by former feudal lords!

VISIT
Château★

Place des Tours. ☏Open Apr–Oct Wed–Mon 10am–12.30pm, 1.30–6pm (Nov–Mar until 5pm). ☏Closed 1 Jan, 1 May and 25 Dec. Guided tours (1hr15min) possible. ☜6€ plus 4€ guided tour (free for visitors under 7). Free shows every Sun: call ahead to reserve. ℘01 60 59 17 80. www.chateau-blandy.fr.
The castle was enlarged and fortified at the end of the 14C on the orders of

▶ **Population:** 766
♿ **Michelin Local Map:** p282: B2.
🚩 **Info:** ℘01 60 59 17 80. www.tourisme77.fr.
▶ **Location:** 70 km from Paris by the A 4 and N 104. The Châteaubus shuttle links the Melun station Blandy-les-Tours via Vaux-le-Vicomte chateau, from April-Nov on weekends and holidays. 7€ return ticket.
🕐 **Timing:** Allow at least a half-day to explore the château and other sights.

Charles V, subsequently becoming a model for fortified medieval châteaux. Dominated by five towers, including a dramatic keep, it lost its military function in the 15C and 16C, falling gradually into ruin. Major restoration efforts were undertaken starting in 1992, and visitors now witness the chateau and its fortified walls as they likely appeared in the 17C. A permanent exhibit on the site traces the history of the elegant feudal monument. From the top of the keep (140 stairs), enjoy a magnificent panorama of the Brie plains.

The church, dedicate to Saint Maurice, shows the progression of religious art from the 12C to 18C: the nave and bell tower date to the end of the 14C, while the chancel is designed in 16C flamboyant Gothic style.

EXCURSION
Collégiale de Champeaux★

▶ 4 km/2.5mi NE of Blandy. ○Open 9am –7pm (6pm in winter), except Sunday mass from 10am–12pm; other important religious holidays. ℘01 60 66 96 07. www.collegialedechampeaux.com.

Built between 1160 and 1315, this collegiate church was founded by theologian Guillaume de Champeaux, who was first the instructor, then the enemy of the notorious Abélard.

The nave is both elegant and luminous, and boasts a six-part vaulting system that is unusually light and gracious for Gothic architecture.

The collegiate church's **stalls★** dating to 1522, depict angels in various guises, sculpted with a humorous qnd irreverant spirit. These depictions, which were considered very bold and perhaps insufficiently holy for their time, nearly led to their censorship during the 18C.

The chancel boasts a flat chevet and houses several engraved tombstones dating to the 13C–14C. In the apse, the tombs of Rose des Marets, her husband, son (decked in knightly garb), and daughter are moving spectacles in their own right.

Provins★★

Whether approaching Provins from the Brie plateau to the west or from Champagne and the Voulzie Valley, this medieval town presents the eye-catching and distinctive outlines of the Tour César and of the dome of St-Quiriace Church. Splendid remparts contribute to the town's medieval atmosphere, and the rose gardens add to its visual appeal.

The lower town, a lively shopping centre, sits at the foot of the promontory and extends along the River Voulzie and the River Durteint. The town, which boasts 58 historic monuments, is now a UNESCO World Heritage Site.

A BIT OF HISTORY
The Provins fairs

In the 10C Provins became one of the economic capitals of the Champagne region, thanks to its two annual fairs which, with those of Troyes, were among the largest in the region. Traders from the north and from the Mediterranean

▶ **Population:** 12 219
◐ **Michelin Local Map:** p282: C2.
▤ **Info:** Chemin de Villecran, 77160 Provins. ℘01 64 60 26 26. www.provins.net.
◑ **Location:** In the Île-de-France, 87km/54mi SE of Paris via the A 4 and then D 231. Access from Paris: SNCF rail link from Gare de l'Est.
🅿 **Parking:** Place Honore de Balzac, the rue Vieille Notre-Dame or the rue de Temple. Or park near Porte St-Jean, near the tourist office.
◉ **Don't Miss:** A tour of the ramparts and the upper town. If you're staying for a few days, consider buying a Provins Pass (Office du Tourisme); it can save you money.
◐ **Timing:** Allow at least a day to get the most from your visit.

came here with their linens, silks, spices from the Orient and wine, attracting people from all walks of life, including money agents and merchants from among the hard-working bourgeoisie of the region. These fairs prospered until the 14C, when the economic weight shifted to Paris, eclipsing the Champagne region.

Roses

According to tradition it was **Thibaud IV** the Troubadour who brought roses back from Syria and grew them here in Provins. Edmund Lancaster (1245–96), brother of the King of England, married Blanche of Artois and was suzerain of Provins for a time. He introduced the red rose into his coat of arms.

WALKING TOUR

UPPER TOWN★★

It is advisable to park in the car park near Porte St-Jean, location of the tourist office and departure point for the tourist train.

Porte St-Jean – St John's Gateway was built in the 13C. This stocky construction is flanked by two projecting towers which are partially hidden by the buttresses that were added in the 14C to support the drawbridge.

▶ Follow allée des Remparts which overlooks the old moat.

Remparts★★ – The town walls were built in the 12C and 13C along an existing line of defence, then altered on several occasions. They constitute a fine example of medieval military architec-

ture. A house straddling the curtain wall was the home of the Provins executioners. The last one to live here was Charles-Henri Sanson who executed Louis XVI. The most interesting part of the ramparts runs between Porte St-Jean and Porte de Jouy. The Tour aux Engins, on the corner, links the two curtain walls; it derives its name from a barn nearby in which engines of war were housed. In summer, on a space behind this tower the falconers of the 'Aigles de Provins' company put on a show of birds of prey; other birds are displayed in shelters. Beyond the 12C Porte de Jouy, take r. de Jouy, which is lined by picturesque low houses with long tiled roofs or an overhanging upper storey.

Place du Châtel – This vast, peaceful square, rectangular in shape, is bordered by attractive old houses: the 15C Maison des Quatre Pignons (southwest corner), the 13C Maison des Petits-Plaids (northwest corner), and the Hôtel de la Coquille to the north. The Église St-Thibault (12C) ruins stand on the northeast corner. Walk past the **Musée de Provins et du Provinois** (*see Additional Sights*), housed in one of the town's oldest buildings, the 'Maison Romane'.

Tour César (Caesar's Tower)★★

Open mid-May–mid-Sep Tue–Sun 11am–6.30pm; Oct–Apr call for information. 3.80€. 01 64 60 26 26.

Tour César

© M. Gaspar/MICHELIN

☺ Guided tour of the city ☺

Provins, an official City of Art and History, offers two-hour tours led by guides certified by the Ministry of Culture and Communication. Contact the Office du Tourisme *01 64 60 26 26 or visit www.provins.net.*

This superb 12C keep, 44m/144ft high and flanked by four turrets, is the emblem of the town.

The guard-room on the first floor is octagonal and 11m/36ft high; it is topped by vaulting comprising four arcades of pointed arches ending in a dome and pierced by an orifice through which the soldiers on the floor above were passed supplies. The **view★** extends over the town and the surrounding countryside.

▶ Return to Porte St-Jean via place du Châtel, then rue St-Jean on the left.

Knights Templar Residence – *R. de la Madeleine. Closed to the public.* ✆*01 64 20 26 26 or 01 60 58 80 32.* The legendary Knights Templar order may have been founded in the Middle East in 1119, but it has its origins in the Champagne region. During the First Crusade (1095), 12 knights came together to defend the Mont Moriah; included among them was the Count of Champagne. The order possessed two residences in Provins: Val de Provins in the Lower city, and **La Madeleine** in the High City, near the porte de Jouy. The fortified house included a hospital during the 15C.

Turn back to the Porte de Jouy and continue along rue de Jouy, lined with low houses with elegantly tiled roofs. The **caveau St-Esprit** *(no visits allowed)* belonged to a former hospital ravaged by a fire during the 17C.

Jardin des Brébans – This garden situated on a rocky spur affords a splendid **view** of the lower city and buildings, as well as structures surrounding it, notably the former palace of the Counts of Champagne (today a high school).

▶ Walk down the rue du Collège, alongside the fortified wall. Take rue d'Enfer (follow signs) to reach the former religious hopsital (Hôtel-Dieu).

Collégiale St-Quiriace – This collegiate church was constructed in the 12C on the initiative of Henri "the liberal". The transept and the nave date to the 13C; the rose window on the north wall was destroyed by a fire. The dome dates to the 17C. The church walls were originally decorated with polychrome materials; in the 18C these were refurbished with distemper. The stucco decor and finely-worked grilles also date to the 18C. On the square outside, a cross marks the spot of the former royal portal.

LOWER CITY
Descend the steep rue St-Thibault. To the left, enjoy a beautiful view of the Couvent des Cordelières (convent).

Couvent des Cordelières – *Only open to the public on special occasions. Call Tourist Office for more info.*
This convent was built between the 13C–15C by count Thibault IV of Champagne to accommodate the poor, and became a hospital under Louis XI; it maintained that role until 1977. The building now houses National Monuments archives. At 30, rue St-Thibault, on the corner of the the rue de la Pierre-Ronde, note the **census stone** which was used to pay feudal and church taxes and rents.

▶ Turn left on rue des Jacobins and continue along rue des Petits-Près to reach the rose garden.

Roseraie de Provins – *11 r. des Prés.* ◷*Open May–Oct 10am–7pm; Apr and Nov–24 Dec weekends 2–6pm.* ◷*Closed from 25 Dec–Mar.* ⊚*5€ (guided tour by reservation) 4.80€ with the Pass Provins. Half-price from Apr–mid-May.* &✆*01 60 58 05 78. www.roseraie-provins.com.*
The **Provins** rose is of course the star here *(blooming in June)*, but multiple other varieties of roses crowd the garden, making for a very pleasant stroll across 3ha/7.4acre.

▶ Continue along rue St-Thibault, which turns into rue du Val along a canal). Turn left on rue Ste-Croix.

ADDITIONAL SIGHTS
Grange aux Dîmes★
r. St-Jean. ◷*Open Apr–Aug 10am–6pm; Sep–Oct Mon–Fri 2–6pm, Sat–Sun*

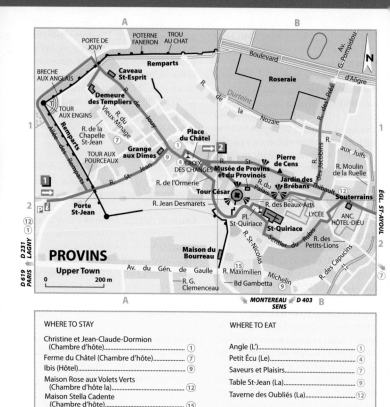

10am–6pm; rest of year Sat–Sun 2–5pm.
☞4.30€. ℘01 64 60 26 26.
www.provins.net.
This massive 13C building belonged to
the canons of St-Quiriace, who hired the
space to merchants during major fairs.
When the fairs fell into decline, the barn
became a store for the tithes (dîmes)
levied on the harvests of the peasants.
The vast hall on the ground floor houses
a permanent exhibition recreating the
atmosphere of the town's famous fairs.

Musée de Provins et du Provinois

⊙Open Apr–mid-Jun noon–5.30pm;
mid-Jun–mid-Sep 11am–6.30pm; mid-
Sept–Oct noon–5.30pm; rest of year
Sat–Sun noon–5.30pm. ☞3€.
℘01 64 01 40 19. www.provins.net.
The ground floor houses **sculpture
and ceramic collections★**. Exploiting
the underground clay quarries enabled potters to produce pieces now

noted for their remarkable variety and
timelessness.

Graffiti Passageways

Entrance in r. St-Thibault, left of the
doorway to the Ancien Hôtel-Dieu.
Guided tours (45min): hours vary
throughout the year, call for times.
☞4.50€. ℘01 64 60 26 26.
www.provins.net.
A network of underground passages
lies beneath Provins, some marked with
ancient graffiti. The section open to the
public runs through a layer of tufa that
lies parallel to the base of the spur on
which the Upper Town stands.

EXCURSIONS
Voulton Church

▷ 7km/4.3mi N of Provins along D 71.
⊙Open daily 9am–6pm. ℘01 64 00 17 72.
After travelling on a road dotted with
monastic names – from les Filles-Dieu

to St-Martin-des-Champs – you come to this gothic church and its bell tower. In the nave, archways are supported by round columns. The eight-part structure of some of the vaulting is noteworthy.

Beton-Bazoches

◗ *18km/11.2mi N of Provins on D 55.*
This village houses a large cider press built in 1850. It comprises a millstone measuring 2m/6.5ft in diameter which was powered by a horse, and two oak and elm presses featuring a wheel mechanism. ◷*Weekends 2.30–6pm. Visits by reservation.* ☏*01 64 01 06 96/01 92.*

St-Loup-de-Naud★

◗ *9km/5.6mi SW of Provins along D 106.*
This village, once fully fortified, is perched on a spur. Make sure to admire its dramatic outline as you approach from the southwest on the D 106.
Church – ◷*Open daily 9am–7pm.* Constructed at the outset of the 11C, this church was part of a Benedictine priory. The porch and two bays of the nave were built in the 12C. The well-preserved portal under the porch is analagous in design to the Royal Portal at Chartres: it features the Christ in a majestic pose, surrounded by symbols of the Evangelists (tympanum), apostles nestled under the arcades supported by lintels, column-statues in the splays and additional religious figures in the arches. Architectural advances between the 11C and 12C were significant, and this church provides an example of transition to increased technical prowess.

Rampillon

◗*18km/11.2mi W of Provins along the D 619, then the D 76 to the left.*
This village, situated on a knoll, once belonged to the counts of Champagne and the Diocese of Sens before falling into the hands of the Knights of St-Jean-de-Jérusalem in the 13C. During that century, the church was part of a commandery run by the Knights Templar; it was burned by the English in 1432. A tower attributed to the Templar order is attached to the church. The dramatic bell tower rises from the right. The portal is remarkable for its sculptures: on the tympanum, an illustration of Christ as judge; on the lintels, the Resurrection of the dead, and on the trumeau, Saint Éliphe, patron of the church.

ADDRESSES

🛏 STAY

🛏 **Ferme du Chatel (B&B)** – *5r. de la Chapelle-St-Jean.* ☏*01 64 00 10 73.* 🅿🚭. *5 rooms* 🍽. This farm, built between the 12C–18C, is in the heart of the medieval town. The rooms, with exposed timberwork, are quiet and impeccably maintained. Vast, tranquil garden planted with fruit trees.

🛏 **Hôtel Ibis** – *77av. du Gén.-de-Gaulle.* ☏*01 60 67 66 67.* 🅿⛐. *51 rooms* 🍽. In a calm district, with a medieval architectural style and contemporary rooms. Neo-rustic restaurant.

🛏 **La Maison Rose aux Volets Verts (B&B)** – *3 & 5 r. Maximilien-Michelin.* ☏*01 64 08 92 95. 5 rooms.* At the foot of the medieval city, two 19C houses provide modern comforts and historic charm. Tastefully decorated rooms, some overlooking the pretty gardens.

🛏 **Maison Stella Cadente**– *28r. Maximilien-Michelin.* ☏*01 60 67 40 23. www.bedandstyle.com. Reservations required. 5 rooms* 🍽. In this large 19C house situated in the centre of a park, dive into the luxurious world of the Stella Cadente fashion house. Rooms are inspired by fairly tales: *Snow White, Alice in Wonderland,* and other magical tales. Impeccably decorated rooms.

🛏 **Christine and Jean-Claude Dormion (B&B)** – *2 r. des Glycines, 77650 Lizines, 15km/9mi SW of Provins.* ☏*01 60 67 32 56.* 🚭. *5 rooms.* Agriculture is still the mainstay of this 300 year-old farm offering perfectly maintained, rustic bedrooms, each with a kitchenette. Garden and orchard.

⊰⊱ EAT

🛏 **Le Petit Écu** – *9pl. du Châtel.* ☏*0164089500. www.lepetitecu.com. Closed 3 Jan.* Located on the charming Place du Châtel in the heart of old Provins, this fine half-timbered house offers a weekend special in season that includes a country buffet.

○◎◎ **L'Angle**– *1 r. Saint-Jean.*
☏01 64 01 43 58. Restaurant offering a modern, cosy ambience: leather seats, lit fireplace during winter. Upstairs, a small space resembles a cigar room. The fare is simple and of good quality; salads and bruschetta are solid choices.

○◎◎ **Saveurs et Plaisirs** – *6pl. St-Ayoul.*
☏01 60 58 41 70. Closed 2 weeks in Aug, 1 week in Autumn, 1 week in winter, Mon eve and Sun. A contemporary restaurant with a dedicated, self-taught chef, with a choice between traditional or 'creative' menus. Among the fish specialties, the red tuna steak is very popular.

○◎◎ **La Table Saint-Jean** – *1r. St-Jean.*
☏01 64 08 9677. www.table-saint-jean. com. Closed in early Nov (call ahead), Sun eve, Tue eve and Wed. Located in the upper town, opposite the grange aux dîmes (tithes barn), this half-timbered house purportedly dates to the 11C. Depending on the season, you may dine in the decidedly rustic decor of the dining room or on the terrace, set up in a pretty, flower-filled courtyard.

○◎◎ **La Taverne des Oubliées**–
14 r. Saint-Thibault. Info at the Tourist Office ☏06 70 50 08 58 . www.provins-banquet-medieval.com. Open Apr–Oct (Sat eve only). Enjoy a medieval-style banquet in a beautiful 12C dining room. Sample an array of specialties from the Middle Ages – and get out your costumes! Troubadours, knights and jugglers provide the entertainment.

ENTERTAINMENT

▲▲ **Les Lueurs du Temps** –
☏01 64 60 26 26. www.provins.net. Open 1st Sat of Jul and of Aug. Guided tours 6.50€ (children 3€). Tour César only 3€. During the evening, the city and the Tour César are lit by candlelight. Guided tours, street entertainment and performances.

▲▲ **La Légende des chevaliers** –
☏01 64 60 26 26. www.provins.net. Closed late Aug–Jul. Tickets and schedule at the Tourist Office. 11€ (children 7.50€). Jousting match set within the rampart ditches.

Évry★

This urban agglomeration offers a striking insight into recent developments in contemporary architecture. Major urban planning commenced here in the 19C and accelerated thereafter. Don't miss Mario Batto's ultramodern cathedral, the large mosque and Buddhist pagoda.

SIGHTS
Cathédrale d'Evry★
12 clos de la Cathédrale. ◷Open Fri 2–5.30pm; weekends and public holidays 2–6pm. ◎3€. ☏01 60 75 02 71. www.museepauldelouvrier.com. Consecrated in 1996, the youngest of French cathedrals is striking for its cylindrical form; the roof is a slanted plane with a ring of 24 silver linden trees. The cathedral was designed by Swiss architect **Mario Botta**. Inside, note the altar and bapistry in Carrare marble. In the chapelle du St-Sacrament, a cross, tabernacle and statue of the Virgin Mary are the work of Gérard Garouste.

▸ **Population:** 51 900
⚭ **Michelin Local Map:** p282: A2.
🛈 **Info**: Hôtel de Ville Pl. des Droits de l'Homme. ☏01 60 91 63 98. www.tourisme-essonne.com.
◐ **Location**: Four cities make up the Evry urban area on the left bank of the Seine: Bondoufle, Courcouronnes, Évry and Lisses. 35 km from Paris par along A 6. RER D: évry-Courcouronnes.
▲▲ **Kids**: The area offers several parks.

Place des Droits-de-l'Homme
This square celebrating human rights features a series of monuments: the **chambre de commerce et d'industrie** resembles a ship with transparent tubing. **Hôtel de ville** is shaped like a capital "A" with a large glass roof.

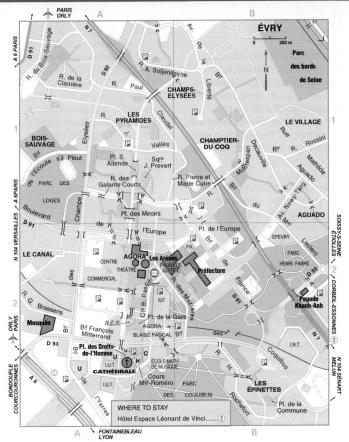

ÉVRY

Parc
des bords
de Seine

WHERE TO STAY
Hôtel Espace Léonard de Vinci.......②

Centre Culturel Desnos/Agora

This large leisure centre comprises a swimming pool, theatre, cinemas, bowling alley, restaurants and cafés. The sports arena, **Les Arènes**, is shaped like a horse saddle. Built around a rectangular body of water, the **Préfecture** is the work of architect Lagneau.

Mosquée d'Évry-Courcouronnes

20 r. Georges-Brassens, Courcouronnes. Visit upon reservation. ⓧ*Open 12–5pm daily except Fri, weekend and during prayer hours.* ℘*01 60 77 14 19.*
This is one of Europe's largest mosques. Mosaic in green, a glass cupola, and marble floors grace the patio. The prayer room has a lace-like stucco decor.

Nouvelle Pagode Khanh-Anh

R. François-Mauriac. ℘*06 84 97 80 08. www.gdptquangduc.info.*

This pagoda has been under construction since 1995 and is slated to become Europe's largest. Since 2002, a 4m/13ft gold-leaf Buddha has graced the site.

Parc des bords de Seine

♨♨This family-friendly park boasts playgrounds and many paths for strolls.

ADDRESSES

STAY

⬠⬠⬠⬠**Hôtel Espace Léonard de Vinci** – *Av. des Parcs, 91090 Lisses. 4km/2.5mi SW of Evry on N 7, D 26 and D 153.* ℘*01 64 97 66 77. http://espace-leonard-de-vinci.com.* 🅿. *73 rooms* ⌂. Just outside Évry, hotel complex offering complete spa facilities: indoor pool, hammam, jacuzzi. Modern rooms.

Brunoy

The charming Yerres Valley frames this lush, tranquil town, which attracted late 19C Parisians such as the actor Talma, friend of Napoléon I. Bordering the beautiful Sénart forest, Brunoy also boasts some of the region's most interesting museums and gardens.

VISIT

Musée Robert Dubois-Corneau – *16 r. du Réveillon.* ◷*Open Wed–Sun 2–6pm (5pm from Nov–Apr).* ◷*Closed public holidays and Aug.* ◓*No charge.* ✆*01 60 46 33 60. www.ville-brunoy.fr*
This museum, situated in the former residence of collector Robert Dubois-Corneau (1876–1951), traces the history of Brunoy and the Yerres Valley. The permanent collection includes paintings, drawings, sculpture, engravings and objets d'art, including a lovely series of 19C landscape paintings depicting the Yerres valey.

Église St-Médard – First built in the 12C and reconstructed several times, this church today shows its 18C decor, featuring Louis XIV and Louis XV-style panelling in white and gold. Inside, admire the Baroque pulpit and two paintings from Restout: Virgin and Child and Saint Jospeh with Jesus.

EXCURSIONS
Boussy-St-Antoine

◖ *4 km/2.5mi E of Brunoy.*
A partially intact historic estate is the highlight of this town. The **Town Hall** is housed in a property once owned by the Dunoyer de Segonzac family. Painter **André Dunoyer de Segonzac** (1884–1974) spent his childhood there. The **old bridge** is one of numerous old structures still crossing the Yerres river – part of it dates to at least the 15C.

Musée Dunoyer-de-Segonzac

5 pl. des Droits-de-l'Homme. ◷*Open Tue–Wed, Fri–Sat 3–6pm; Jul–Aug Tue and Sat 3–6pm.* ◷*Closed public*

holidays. ◓*No charge.* ♿ ✆*01 69 00 13 17. www.biblio-dunoyer.net.*
Just around the corner from where artist André Dunoyer de Segonzac was born, this museum explores the great illustrator's work across a permanent exhibition that includes drawings and engravings.

Caillebotte Estate

◖*In Yerres, N of Brunoy along the D 32.* ◷*Park: open from 9am daily, closes between 5.30–9pm depending on season. Vegetable garden: open Jun–Sep, Sun 3–6.30pm.* ✆*01 69 48 93 93.*
Gustave Caillebotte (1848–1894) produced some 80 paintings here – boating scenes on the Yerres, views of the park and surrounds, and other local landscapes. The Caillebotte family bought the property in 1860; it was later sold in 1879. It features a large English-style garden, close to the banks of the Yerres river which meanders through the eponymous town.

Near the park entrance, a house boasting neoclassical-style columns and known as **Le Casin** was recently renovated. It houses reproductions of some of Caillebotte's paintings. Across from the house, note the swiss **chalet** which once served as a dairy. In the park, stroll among an **orangery** hosting temporary exhibits and a kiosk-gazebo.

▸ **Population:** 26 324
✜ **Michelin Local Map:** p282: A1.
▮ **Info: Tourist Office** – 2 r. Philisbourg. ✆01 69 43 71 21. www.brunoy.fr.
◖ **Location**: 30 km from Paris along N 6. RER D: Brunoy.
✿ **Don't miss**: A stroll in the Senart forest; Fondation Dubuffet with its monumental sculptures and models.
◷ **Timing:** Allow a half-day to a day.

Fondation Dubuffet

▶ *In Perigny, 5 km/3.1mi E of Brunoy.
R. du Moulin-Neuf, sente des Vaux,
ruelle aux Chevaux, 94520 Périgny-
sur-Yerres. Visits by appointment only.*
*Guided tours (1hr30mins). 8€
(free for children under 10). 01 47 34
12 63. www.dubuffetfondation.com.*
The Dubuffet Foundation, created by the
eponymous artist in 1973, houses over
1 000 works. The former studios of
Dubuffet and his team in Périgny display architectural models; an adjoining museum features paintings and
decor created for animated painting
Coucou Bazar, perhaps Debuffet's
most-recognised work. But the major
highlight at the Foundation is the monumental, open-air **Closerie Falbala**, built
between 1971 and 1973 as part of the
artist's famed series, l'Hourloupe; it harbours between its tormented, strange
walls the Villa Falbala and Cabinet log-
ologique (1967–1969).

🚗 DRIVING TOUR

FROM FOREST TO TOWN

Allow 1 day.

The **Forêt de Sénart** previously served
as royal hunting grounds. It was during
a hunting expedition here that Louis
XV met Mme Lenormand d'Étiolles,
the future marquise de Pompadour.
The current forest, covering 3 100ha/7
660acres, spreads across a vast zone
between the Seine river and the N6. To
the north lie the towns of Draveil and
Brunoy; Corbeil-Essonnes and the "new
city" of Sénart are to the south.
Predominating trees include oak, birch,
pine and chestnut. Hares, foxes, wild
boars, squirrels and other animals are
commonly sighted.
Points of interest are mostly situated in
the area accessible from the Pyramide
de Brunoy *(this is the only access point
along the N6)*: here you'll find hundreds
of kilometres of walking paths, bike
paths, and educational nature trails.

La Faisanderie

🕐 *Open Mon–Fri 2–5pm; during school
holidays hours vary.* 🕐 *Closed 1 Jan,
1 May and 25 Dec. Sculpture park entry:
1€.* ♿ ☎ *01 60 75 54 17.*
The park's central pavillion, dating to
1778, houses the main **information**
centre on the forest. The surrounding
park houses monumental open-air
sculptures dating to the 1970s.

Forêt de Rougeau

*From the D 446 (D 346 in Seine-
et-Marne region) and the D 50, access
roads to rest areas. Marked woodland
sporting trail and pond trail.*
Domaine du Pavillon Royal – In the
south of the forest. 🕐 *Open Apr–Oct
9am-6.30pm; Nov–Mar Wed, weekends
and public holidays, 9am–5pm.*
Michel Bouret, secretary to Louis XV,
built this sumptuous hunting lodge for
the king. To realise the works, he laid out
the l'Allée Royale, connecting the forests
of Sénart and Rougeau (accessible to
pedestrians, bikes and horses). Today,
the lodge and adjoining buildings are
private property, but the large park is
open to the public.

Sénart

The youngest town in Île-de-France,
Sénart is situated on a plateau overlooking numerous wooded areas (forêt
de Sénart, forêt de Rougeau and the
bois de Bréviande), and includes several rural towns. The ten communities
which make up the new city boast a total
population of 98 000.
In contrast to other newly created cities,
the construction of Sénart has occurred
in several stages. There's no real city centre; instead, two new agglomerations
were created: **Sénart-Ville nouvelle**
and **Rougeau-Sénart**. These are mainly
new houses clustered around existing
villages. The landscape architecture is
distinctly bucolic, featuring ponds and
canals, and in some respects resembles
Western France.

Château de Grosbois★

This 16C château, rebuilt in the 17C, is situated in the centre of a verdant wood. It once belonged to the count of Provence and future Louis XVIII. Since 1962, the château and its grounds have housed an enormous equestrian training centre.

- ⛪ **Michelin Local Map:** p282: A1.
- **Info:** ℘01 49 77 15 24. www.museedutrot.com.
- **Location:** 20km/ from Paris along N 19. RER A: Boissy-St-Léger, then bus 4012, 4021, 4022 or 4023.
- **Kids:** The Musée du Trot equestrian museum at the château.

VISIT
Château
Domaine de Grosbois, Boissy St-Leger. Open Sun and holidays, 2–5pm. Under renovation until late 2013. Call for details. ⚲*5€ (includes guided tour); 8€ combined ticket with Musée du Trot.* ℘*01 49 77 15 24. www.letrot.com.*

Built in 1597 by the Baron de Sancy, a superintendent to Henri IV, the château de Grosbois was acquired in 1625 by Charles de Valois, who enlarged it. It looms at the end of a long avenue lined with chestnut trees (the park is not open to the public). The central part was completed in the early 17C by architect Florent Fournier. Two protruding Louis XIII-style wings surround it, framing the courtyard of honour and dry moats.

Interior– Some of the original decor dating from various periods remains, including opulent furniture.

The Huissiers room features portraits of one-time owner Maréchal Berthier and his family.

The Emperor's room displays portraits of Napoléon. The galerie des Batailles, meanwhile, owes its name to eight paintings ordered by Berthier to commemorate battles he had participated in. Berthier's library, at the end of the gallery, has largely retained its original design and houses some 3 000 books, maps and battle plans.

At the centre of the château, the ballroom offers a lovely view of the park and is flanked by the hunting room. These two rooms both boast a ceiling decorated with visible balks. The Salon Régence is adorned with white and gold wood panelling; a display

case holds fans from the 18–19C. Only the dining room has conserved the Louis XIII style. Large frescoes attributed to Abraham Bosse and completed in 1644, portray the second marriage of Charles de Valois at the château.

Musée du trot – ⊙*Open Sun and holidays 2–5pm.* ⚲*5€.* ℘*01 49 77 15 24. www. museedutrot.com.* The right wing of the château houses this museum dedicated to equestrian history.

EXCURSIONS
Boissy-St-Léger
▶ *3km/1.8mi N of the château on N 19.* Boissy-St-Léger has been the orchid capital of France since 1886, when royal gardener Henri Vacherot founded a horticultural centre in Boissy. His son Maurice developed the techniques that led to the hybridisation of the plant.

Établissements Vacherot-Lecoufle – *29r. de Valenton.* ⊙*Open Mon 2–6pm; Tue–Sat 10am–12pm and 2–7pm.* ⊙*Closed public holidays.* ⚲*No charge.* ℘ *01 45 69 10 42. www.lorchidee.fr.* New varieties of orchids have been developed here since 1886. Visit the dedicated greenhouses and get precious cultivation advice.

Château de Sucy-en-Brie
▶ *1.5km/1mi from Boissy on D 33. Av. Georges-Pompidou. Visits organised 2nd Sun of month from 4.30pm.* ℘*01 45 90 29 39.*

This 17C château was created par François Le Vau for Nicolas Lambert de Thorigny, counsellor to LouisXIV. It comprises a central lodge flanked by two rectangular pavillions. The hall opens onto the two façades and is decorated with doric columns, in the style of a Palladian villa. The ceiling paintings are likely the work of Charles Le Brun. It is now the home of the Conservatoire de musique and regular concerts are held in the Orangerie.

Musée de Sucy – av. Winston-Churchill. ○*Open Sat 2.30–5.30pm.* ℘*01 45 90 14 42.* ⊗*Free.* This former farmstead features an exhibition on the history of Sucy and rural occupations.

Fort de Sucy – *allée du Gén.-Séré-de-Rivière.* ○*Open 1st Sun of month 3pm. 2.30–5.30pm.* ℘*01 49 82 24 50.* Built between 1879 and 1881, this fort was part of the second ring of defences around Paris. The building includes stone barracks, a lower ground pillbox and firing platforms.

Brie-Comte-Robert

⊙ *9km/5.6mi S of the château de Grosbois on the N 19.* ⓘ *Tourism office open Tue–Sat 10am–12pm, 2.30–5.30pm, Sun 10am–12pm. Pl. Jeanne-d'Évreux.* ℘*01 64 05 30 09. Pick up a brochure of walking tours around the town.*

Former capital of the Brie region, this town remains an important agricultural centre. Along with its walls and the towers of its feudal castle, the cobbled streets around the market square reveal its medieval past.

Église St-Étienne – *www.eglisedebrie. org.* This Gothic church is noteworthy for its imposing presence, with a hollowed-out bell tower which lets light through and dramatic flying buttresses. Construction began in the 13C; the flat chevet is adorned with a grand rose window. The western facade boasts a 13C portal left undecorated, topped by a gallery and a Renaissance-era rose window. Inside, the rectangular nave owes its Gothic refinement to the triforium. The 13C rose window is made of 12 sections. Around the Christ figure on the central medallion, the 12 apostles are gathered; at the edges the 12 months of the year are illustrated. Saint Étienne's martyrdom is alluded to in the wooden

and gold sculpture in front of the altar (17C) and in a nearby painting dating to 1723.

Château – ○*Open Sat–Sun, 10am–12pm, 2.30–6.30pm. Guided tours possible by reservation.* ○*Closed Aug and public holidays.* ⊗*Free.* &℘*01 64 05 63 31. www.amisduvieuxchateau.org.* Construction of this château began at the close of the 12C under the orders of Robert I, brother of LouisVII, who also gave the city its name. His son Robert II completed the château in the beginning of the 13C, at the same time that he was working to develop the town.

Boasting a square design, the château is surrounded by a fortified wall converted into gardens and water-filled moats. Only a few vestiges of the original fortified wall that once stood here remain: the foundations of eight towers, including four corner towers, are still visible. The tower-portal of Saint-Jean, whose foundations remain visible, once housed the chapel. Inside the fortified walls, archeolohical digs have revealed several large rooms, two columned fireplaces and a bread oven. The south tower houses a tank powered by subterranean canals. The chateau prison, meanwhile, is situated on the first floor of the northwest tower.

A permanent exposition at the château traces the history of the château, displaying numerous artefacts unearthed during archeological digs, or retrieved from archives. Among these, note the decorative tiles that adorned the room of Jeanne d'Évreux in the 14C.

Ancien hôtel-Dieu – ○ *Open Wed–Sat 3–6pm, Sun 10am–1pm, 3–6pm.* ℘*01 60 34 15 81.* This former religious hospital, lining the rue des Halles, has conserved its impressive 13C Gothic facade featuring five decorative arcades.

Grisy-Suisnes

⊙ *5.5km/3.4mi E of Brie-Comte-Robert on D 319, then left toward Grisy. Bus route 21.*

This village houses a modern church built in 1966 that boasts an unusual knarled roof with a 42m/138ft spire.

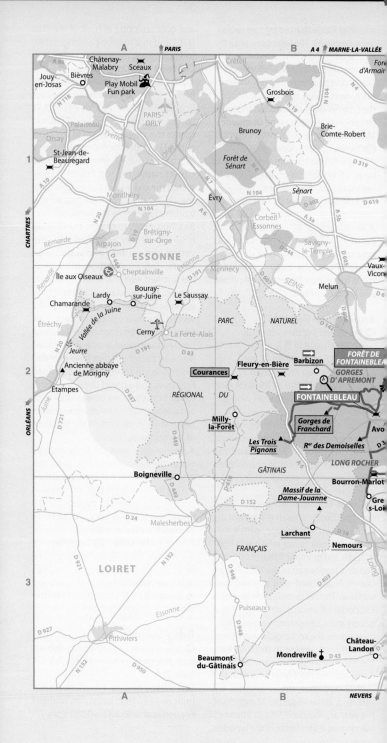

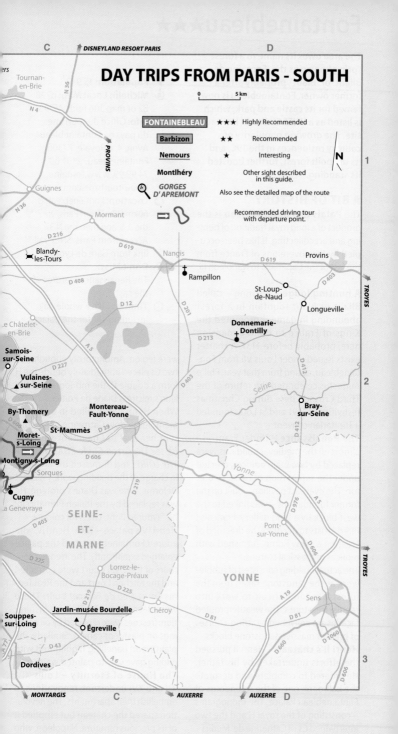

DAY TRIPS FROM PARIS - SOUTH

0   5 km

FONTAINEBLEAU	★★★	Highly Recommended
Barbizon	★★	Recommended
Nemours	★	Interesting
Montlhéry		Other sight described in this guide.
GORGES D'APREMONT		Also see the detailed map of the route
		Recommended driving tour with departure point.

N

DISNEYLAND RESORT PARIS

Tournan-en-Brie

PROVINS

Guignes

Mormant

Blandy-les-Tours

Nangis

Rampillon

St-Loup-de-Naud

Provins

Longueville

le Châtelet-en-Brie

Donnemarie-Dontilly

Samois-sur-Seine

Vulaines-sur-Seine

By-Thomery

Montereau-Fault-Yonne

Bray-sur-Seine

Morets-Loing

St-Mammès

Montigny-s-Loing

Sorques

Cugny

La Genevraye

SEINE-ET-MARNE

Seine

Yonne

Pont-sur-Yonne

Lorrez-le-Bocage-Préaux

YONNE

Jardin-musée Bourdelle

Chéroy

Sens

Souppes-sur-Loing

Égreville

Dordives

Fontainebleau★★★

The area owes its name to a forest spring known as the 'Fontaine de Bliaut' or 'Blaut', probably after a former owner. Fontainebleau is now famed for its castle and park, which is listed as a UNESCO World Heritage site. The growing popularity of country residences in the 19C, and its unspoilt forest, further boosted its standing.

A BIT OF HISTORY

The **Palais de Fontainebleau** is the product of a long royal tradition of hunting and art collecting. It has been occupied by the sovereigns of France from the last of the Capetians to Napoléon III.

A hunting lodge – A spring – called Bliaut or Blaut fountain in a forest abounding in game – prompted the Kings of France to build a mansion here, probably before 1137. A charter exists issued under Louis VII from Fontainebleau, dating from that year. Philip Augustus celebrated the return of the Third Crusade here during Christmas festivities of 1191 and St Louis founded a Trinitarian convent.

The Renaissance – Under François I almost all the medieval buildings were replaced by two main edifices, erected under the supervision of Gilles Le Breton. The oval east pavilion – built on the former foundations – was linked to the west block by a long gallery. François I hired artists to decorate; he dreamed of creating a 'New Rome' furnished with replicas of Classical statues.

The actual building consisted of rubblework as the sandstone taken from the forest was too difficult to work into regular freestones. The weatherproofed façades are enlivened by string-courses of brick or massive sandstone blocks.

Henri II's château – Henri II pursued the efforts undertaken by his father. He ordered to complete and decorate the ballroom, one of the splendours of Fontainebleau Palace. The monograms – consisting of the royal H and the two intertwined Cs of Catherine de' Medici –

- ▶ **Population:** 15 942
- **Michelin Local Map:** p298: B2 or map 106 folds 45, 46.
- **Info:** Office du tourisme du pays de Fontainebleau-Avon, 4, r. Royale, 77300 Fontainebleau. ℘01 60 74 99 99. www.fontaine bleau-tourisme.com.
- **Location:** Fontainebleau is 60km/37mi from Paris, via the A 6, and then the N 37. Access from Paris: SNCF rail link from Gare de Lyon.
- **Don't Miss:** The Renaissance features of the castle.
- **Timing:** Take a whole day, including 1hr for the palace.

were legion. Ambiguously enough, the two Cs placed immediately beside the H form a double D, the monogram of the king's mistress Diane de Poitiers.

When Henri II was killed in a tournament, his widow Catherine de' Medici sent her rival to Chaumont-sur-Loire (*see The Green Guide CHÂTEAUX OF THE LOIRE*) and dismissed the architect in charge of the building work, Philibert Delorme, who was Diane's protégé. He was replaced by the Italian Primaticcio; he favoured light, cheerful colours.

Henri IV's palace – 17C – Henri IV, who adored Fontainebleau, had the palace enlarged significantly. The irregular contours of the Oval Court were corrected and the Kitchen Court and the Real Tennis Court (*Jeu de Paume*) built. These were decorated with Flemish inspiration: frescoes were replaced by oil paintings on plaster or canvas. Similarly, the plain wood panelling highlighted with gilding gave way to painted wainscot.

The House of Eternity – Louis XIV, XV and XVI undertook renovations to embellish their apartments. The Revolution spared the château but emptied it of its precious furniture. Napoléon, who became consul, then emperor, enjoyed staying at the palace and preferred it to Versailles, where he felt haunted by a rival. He called Fontainebleau 'The House of Eternity' and commissioned further refurbishments. The last rulers of France also took up residence here.

THE PALACE★★★
Exterior
Cour du Cheval Blanc or des Adieux★★ – This former bailey was first used only by servants, but it was soon earmarked for official parades and tournaments. It was sometimes called the White Horse Court after Charles IX installed a plaster cast of the equestrian statue of Marcus Aurelius in Rome; a slab in the central alley marks its former location.

Golden eagles hover above the pillars of the main gate: the Emperor had this made into his main courtyard. He razed the Renaissance buildings that lay to the west of the court, but kept the end pavilions. The right wing – which boasted the Ulysses Gallery decorated under the supervision of Primaticcio – was dismantled by Louis XV and rebuilt by Jacques-Ange Gabriel.

The façades show a certain unity of style. The large horizontal planes of the blue slating are broken by white façades, trapezoidal roofs and the tall chimneys of the five pavilions.

The horseshoe staircase executed by Jean du Cerceau under Louis XIII is a curved, extravagant composition.

Cour de la Fontaine★ – The fountain at the edge of the pond (*Étang des Carpes*) used to yield remarkably clear water. This was kept exclusively for the king's use and to that end the spring was guarded by two sentinels. The present fountain dates to 1812 and is crowned by a statue of Ulysses. The **Aile de la Belle cheminée** on the right was built by Primaticcio around 1565. The name originated from the fireplace that adorned the first-floor hall until the 18C. At that point, Louis XV – who had turned the room into a theatre and rechristened it Aile de l'Ancienne Comédie – dismantled the fireplace, and the low-relief carvings were scattered. The external steps consist of a dog-legged staircase with two straight flights in the Italian style.

On the left, the **Aile des Reines-Mères et du Pape** (Queen Mothers' and Pope's wing) ends in the Grand Pavilion.

Étang des Carpes★ (Carp Pond) – In the centre of the carp-filled pond stands a small pavilion built by Henri IV, renovated by Louis XIV and then by Napoléon. Today, it is possible to rent boats on the pond.

Porte Dorée★ – Dated 1528, this gatehouse is part of an imposing pavilion. It was the official entrance to the palace until Henri IV built the Porte du Baptistère. The paintings by Primaticcio have all been restored and the tympanum sports a stylised salamander, François I's emblem. On the two upper levels are Italian-style loggias. The first floor once housed Mme de Maintenon's suite. The ballroom is flanked by lime trees. The east end of the chapel dedicated to St Saturnin can just be seen.

Military and Equestrian Tradition

Throughout French history, whether under monarchic or republican rule, independent units have been posted to Fontainebleau. Tradition, it seems, favoured the cavalry, present in the 17C with the king's bodyguard. A number of racecourses and riding schools were created under Napoléon III; the Centre National des Sports Équestres perpetuates this tradition (*see Calendar of Events*), while the forest caters to riding enthusiasts.

The history of the town has been marked by several military organisations, notably the École Spéciale Militaire (1803–1808, before St-Cyr), the polygon-shaped École d'Application d'Artillerie et du Génie (1871–1914) and the SHAPE (Supreme Headquarters, Allied Powers, Europe) headquarters of NATO, which gave the town a cosmopolitan touch from 1947 to 1967.

The Farewell

On 20 April 1814, Emperor Napoléon Bonaparte appeared at the top of the horseshoe staircase; it was 1pm. The foreign army commissioners in charge of escorting him away were waiting in their carriages at the foot of the steps. Napoléon started to walk down the staircase with great dignity, his hand resting on the stone balustrade, his face white with contained emotion. He stopped for a moment while contemplating his guards standing to attention, then moved forward to the group of officers surrounding the Eagle, led by General Petit. His farewell speech, deeply moving, was both an appeal to the spirit of patriotism and a parting tribute to those who had followed him throughout his career. After embracing the general, Bonaparte kissed the flag, threw himself into one of the carriages and was whisked away amid the tearful shouts of his soldiers.

Porte du Baptistère★ – The gateway opens onto the Oval Court. The base of the gateway is the entrance with decorative sandstone that once held the drawbridge across the old moat. Designed by Primaticcio, It opened onto the Cour du Cheval-Blanc. It is crowned by a wide arch surmounted by a dome. The gateway is named after the christening of Louis XIII and his two sisters, celebrated with great pomp on a dais in 1606.

Cour Ovale★ – This is by far the oldest courtyard of Fontainebleau. The site was the bailey of the original stronghold; of the latter only the keep remains, named after St Louis, although it was probably built prior to his reign. François I incorporated it into the structure he had erected on the foundations of the old castle, shaped like an oval or rather a polygon with rounded corners.

Under Henri IV, the courtyard lost its shape, though not its name; the east side was enlarged, and the wings were aligned and squared by two pavilions framing the new Porte du Baptistère. The layout of the palace was preserved.

Cour des Offices – The entrance faces the Porte du Baptistère and is guarded by two sandstone heads depicting Hermes, sculpted by Gilles Guérin in 1640. The Cour des Offices was built by Henri IV in 1609; it is a huge oblong, sealed off on three sides by austere buildings alternating with low pavilions. With its imposing porch executed in the style of city gates, it strongly resembles a square. Admire the gate's architecture from place d'Armes; the sandstone front presents rusticated work and has a large niche as its centrepiece.

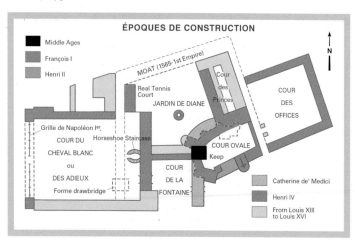

ÉPOQUES DE CONSTRUCTION

Middle Ages
François I
Henri II

MOAT (1565–1st Empire)

Real Tennis Court
JARDIN DE DIANE

Cour des Princes

COUR DES OFFICES

Grille de Napoléon Ier
COUR DU CHEVAL BLANC ou DES ADIEUX
Horseshoe Staircase
Forme drawbridge

COUR OVALE
Keep

COUR DE LA FONTAINE

Catherine de' Medici
Henri IV
From Louis XIII to Louis XVI

N

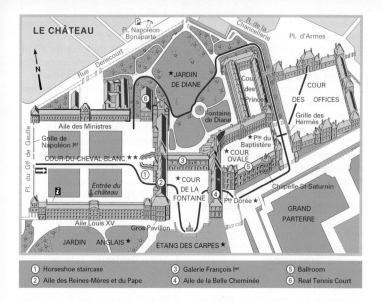

① Horseshoe staircase	③ Galerie François Ier
② Aile des Reines-Mères et du Pape	④ Aile de la Belle Cheminée

① Horseshoe staircase
② Aile des Reines-Mères et du Pape
③ Galerie François Ier
④ Aile de la Belle Cheminée
⑤ Ballroom
⑥ Real Tennis Court

Jardin de Diane★ – The queen's formal garden created by Catherine de' Medici was designed by Henri IV and is bordered by an orangery on the north side. In the 19C the orangery was torn down and the park turned into a landscape garden. Diana's fountain, an elegant display of stonework dated 1603, has survived in the middle.

It has now resumed its original appearance; the four bronze dogs formerly exhibited in the Louvre Museum sit at the feet of their mistress, the hunting goddess.

Grands Appartements★★★

⊙*Open Wed–Mon Apr–Sep 9.30am–6pm; Oct–Mar 9.30am–5pm; last admission 45min before closing. ⌕11€ (children and Paris Museum Pass holders no charge); no charge 1st Sun of the month. ⌕⌕01 60 71 50 70. www.chateaudefontainebleau.fr.*
The main apartments are reached by the stucco staircase (**a**), the Galerie des Fastes (**b**) and the Galerie des Assiettes (**c**), which features 128 beautifully decorated pieces of Sèvres porcelain.

Chapelle de la Trinité★ – The chapel takes its name from the Trinitarian church set up on the premises by St Louis. Henri IV had the sanctuary reinforced by vault-

ing and decorated. Martin Fréminet (1567–1619), a follower of Michelangelo, painted the arches with vigorous scenes representing the mystery of the Redemption and figures from the Old Testament. It was in this chapel that Louis XV wed Marie Leszczynska in 1725 and that Louis Napoléon, later known as Napoleon III, was christened in 1810.

Galerie de François I★★★ – This gallery was built from 1528 to 1530 and was originally open on both sides, resembling a covered passageway. When Louis XVI enlarged it in 1786, he filled in the windows looking onto Diana's garden. The greater part of the decoration – closely combining fresco and stucco work – was supervised by Rosso, while the wood panelling was entrusted to an Italian master carpenter. François I's monogram and his emblem the salamander were widely represented.

The scenes are difficult to interpret (there are no explanatory documents), though they seem to split into two groups, one on either side of the central bay, which is adorned with an oval painting depicting two figures: Danaë by Primaticcio and *The Nymph of Fontainebleau* (1860) after Rosso.

The east side features mostly violent scenes, perhaps referring to the recent misfortunes of the French king (the defeat of Pavia, the king's captivity in Madrid), the inescapable nature of war and death (the battle between the Centaurs and the Lapiths, Youth and Old Age, the Destruction of the Greek fleet). Beneath the vignette depicting Venus and Love at the edge of a pond, note the miniature picture set in a tablet, representing the château around 1540. On the west side, near the entrance, the decor exemplifies the sacred qualities of the royal function – Sacrifice, the Unity of the State – and the concept of filial piety, in the old-fashioned sense of the word (the twins Cleobis and Biton): the king, his mother Louise of Savoy and his sister Marguerite d'Angoulême were devoted to one another.

Escalier du Roi★★ – The staircase was built in 1749 under Louis XV, in what was once the bedchamber of the Duchess of Étampes, François I's favourite. The murals – the history of Alexander the Great – are by Primaticcio (note Alexander taming Bucephalus above the door) and dell'Abbate (Alexander placing Homer's books in a chest, on the far wall). Primaticcio's stucco work is highly original; the upper frieze features caryatids with elongated bodies.

Salle de Bal★★★ (Ballroom) – This room (30m/98.4ft long and 10m/33ft wide) was traditionally reserved for banquets and receptions. It was begun under François I and completed by Philibert Delorme under Henri II. A thorough restoration programme has revived the dazzling frescoes and paintings by Primaticcio and pupil dell'Abbate. The marquetry of the parquet floor, completed under Louis-Philippe, echoes the coffered ceiling, highlighted with silver and gold. The fireplace features two telamones, cast after Antique statues in the Capitol Museum in Rome.

Chapelles St-Saturnin – *Access via Cour Ovale* – Completed in 1546 under François I and situated behind the ballroom, this chapel is divided into two levels, the upper chapel and lower chapel. The organ tribune was designed by Philib-ert Delorme, and the stained glass from cartoons by Marie d'Orléans.

Appartements de Mme de Maintenon – Note the delicate wainscoting in the Grand Salon, dating to the 17C.

Appartements royaux★★ – At the time of François I, Fontainebleau featured a single suite of apartments laid out around the Oval Court. Towards 1565, the regent Catherine de' Medici gave orders to double the curved building between the Oval Court and Diana's Garden. Subsequently, the royal bedrooms, closets and private salons overlooked Diana's Garden. The original suite now houses antechambers, guard rooms and reception rooms where the king once entertained his guests.

Salle des Gardes (1) – Late 16C ceiling and frieze.

A wide arch leads from the **Salle du Buffet** (2) to a chamber in the oldest tower of the castle.

Salle du Donjon (3) – Until the reign of Henri IV this sombre room was occupied by French kings, who used it as a bedroom, hence its other name, the St Louis Bedroom. The equestrian low-relief sculpture (c. 1600) portraying Henri IV on the fireplace came from the 'Belle Cheminée'.

Salon Louis XIII (4) – Louis XIII was born here on 27 September 1601. His birth is evoked by the coffered ceiling which depicts Cupid riding a dolphin (the word *dauphin* means both dolphin and heir to the throne). The panel with painted wainscoting is crowned by a set of 11 pictures by Ambroise Dubois; the romance between Theagenes and Chariclea, works dating from c. 1610.

Salon François I (5) – Of Primaticcio's work there remains only the fireplace.

Salon des Tapisseries (6) – This room, once the queen's chamber, the guard room and the queen's first antechamber, became the empress's principal drawing room in 1804, the guard room once more in 1814 and Tapestry Salon in 1837. The Renaissance ceiling in pine wood is the work of Poncet (1835). The furniture was made during the mid-19C. The tapestries telling the story of Psyche were made in Paris in the first half of the 17C.

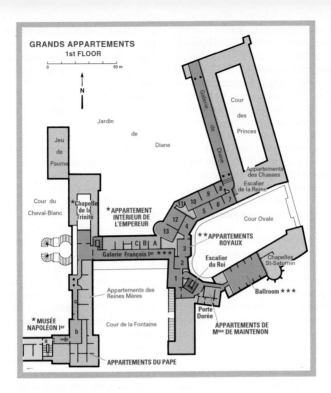

GRANDS APPARTEMENTS
1st FLOOR

0   50 m

N

Jardin

de

Diane

Cour
des
Princes

Galerie de Diane

Jeu
de
Paume

Cour du
Cheval-Blanc

Appartements
des Chasses

Escalier
de la Reine

★Chapelle
de la
Trinité

★ APPARTEMENT
INTÉRIEUR DE
L'EMPEREUR

Cour Ovale

10   9   8   7

11   6

12   5

13   4

★ ★ APPARTEMENTS
ROYAUX

Chapelles
St-Saturnin

C | B | A

★ Galerie François Ier ★ ★ ★

3

Escalier
du Roi

2

Appartements des
Reines Mères

1

★ MUSÉE
NAPOLÉON Ier

c

Cour de la Fontaine

b

a

Porte
Dorée

Ballroom ★ ★ ★

APPARTEMENTS DE
Mme DE MAINTENON

APPARTEMENTS DU PAPE

Antichambre de l'Impératrice (7) – Formerly the queen's guard room, this chamber was built on the site of the old royal staircase; the ceiling and panelling are both dated 1835. The Gobelins tapestries, executed after cartoons by Le Brun, illustrate the four seasons. The Second Empire furniture features a console, carved-oak writing desk, and a set of armchairs of English inspiration. Note the two Indian-style enamel vases produced by the Sèvres factory.

Galerie de Diane – This long, gilt passageway (80m/263ft) was decorated during the Restoration and turned into a library under the Second Empire.

Salon blanc- Petit salon de la Reine (8) – In 1835 the room was decorated with furnishings from an earlier period: Louis XV wainscoting, Louis XVI fireplace inlaid with bronze, etc. The furniture is Empire: chairs in gilt wood by Jacob Frères, settee, armchairs and chairs from St-Cloud, mahogany console and animal heads in bronzed, gilt wood (Jacob Desmalter).

Grand Salon de l'Impératrice (9) – This drawing room, formerly the queen's gaming room, features a ceiling painted by Berthélemy; the scene is Minerva crowning the Muses.

The furniture dates from the reign of Louis XVI (chests by Stöckel and Beneman, seats upholstered with painted satin, a carpet made by the Savonnerie works) or from the First Empire (seats and chests by Jacob Desmalter, the so-called 'Seasons Table' made of Sèvres porcelain and painted by Georget in 1806–7, and a carpet rewoven to an old design). The two sets of furniture are displayed in turn.

Chambre de l'Impératrice (10) – This used to be the queen's bedroom. Most of the ceiling was designed for Anne of Austria in 1644; the wood panelling, fireplace and top of the alcove were created for Marie Leszczynska in 1747 and the doors with arabesque motifs were installed for Marie-Antoinette in 1787. Among the furniture note Marie-Antoinette's bed, designed in 1787 by Hauré, Sené and Laurent, a set of armchairs attributed to Jacob Frères and several commodes by Stöckel and Beneman (1786). The vases are Sèvres porcelain.

Boudoir de la Reine (11) – This room was designed by Marie-Antoinette. The wainscoting was painted by Bourgois and Touzé after sketches by the architect Rousseau. The ceiling – representing sunrise – is the work of Berthélemy. The roll-top writing desk and the work table were made by Riesener in 1786.

Salle du Trône (12) – This was the king's bedroom from Henri IV to Louis XVI; Napoléon converted it into the throne room. Above the fireplace is a full-length portrait of Louis XIII.

Salle du Conseil (13) – This room was given a semicircular extension in 1773. The ceiling and panelling are Louis XV-style decoration. Five pictures by Boucher adorn the ceiling, representing the seasons and Apollo, conqueror of Night. The wainscoting presents an alternation of allegorical figures painted in blue or pink monochrome by Van Loo and Jean-Baptiste Pierre.

Appartement Intérieur de l'Empereur★ – *Visit included in the tour of the Grands Appartements.* **Napoleon** had his suite installed in the wing built by Louis XVI, on the garden side running parallel with the François I Gallery.

Chambre de Napoléon (A) – Most of the decoration – dating from the Louis XVI period – has survived. The furniture is typically Empire.

Petite chambre à coucher (B) – A little private study which Bonaparte furnished with a day bed in gilded iron.

Salon de l'Abdication (C) – This is the room in which the famous abdication document was signed on 6 April 1814. The Empire furniture in this drawing room is from that momentous time.

The François I Gallery leads to the Vestibule du Fer-à-cheval, at the top of the curved steps. This was the official entrance from the late 17C onwards.

Appartements du Pape – *First floor of the Gros Pavillon* – This part of the château is named for Poe Pie VII, who stayed here twice during the First Empire. It consists of a string of rooms created under the Renaissance in a pavillion

constructed by Gabriel. The Henri II bedroom retained its sculpted wood ceiling, that of Anne of Austria its painted ceiling, and stamped leather wall coverings from the Second Empire.

Musée Chinois★ – *Admission included in visit to the Grands Appartements.* ♿ 🖉 01 60 71 50 70.

This small museum on the ground floor of the Gros Pavillon includes heavy furniture and elegant objets d'art and artefacts. The collection originally comprised booty captured during the Franco-British conflict with China in 1860. The next year, Siamese ambassadors completed it with opulent presents, an event recorded in a painting by Gérôme.

The **antechamber** is decorated with Siamese palanquins. The **nouveaux salons** house crimson wall hangings, armchairs, ebony furniture and objects from China and Siam. The **cabinet de laque** is decorated with 15 panels from an 18C Chinese fan. Note the four large tapestries on the ceiling and the huge glass-fronted cabinet filled with objects, including a copy of the Siamese royal crown.

Musée Napoléon I★

The **museum** (♿ 🖥️ *price included in ticket for Grands Appartements*) is dedicated to the Emperor and his family, occupying the ground level and first floor of the Louis XV wing. Exhibits include portraits, silverware, arms, medals, ceramics (Imperial service), clothing (coronation robes, uniforms) and memorabilia. First-floor rooms evoke the Coronation, military campaigns, the Emperor's daily life, the Empress Marie-Louise in formal attire or painting the Emperor's portrait, and the birth of Napoléon's son.

The ground floor rooms are devoted to a member of the Imperial family: Napoleon's mother, his brothers Joseph, Louis and Jérôme and sisters Elisa, Pauline and Caroline.

Petits Appartements et Galerie des Cerfs

🖥️ *Guided tours (1hr15min) daily. Call for details.* 👓 6.50€. 🖉 01 60 71 50 70.

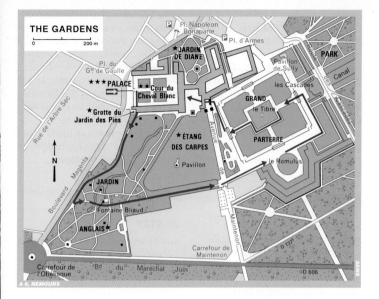

These rooms, on the ground floor are only accessible by guided tour.

Petits Appartements de Napoléon I – This suite comprises François I's former bathroom suite and ground floor of the Louis XVI wing. Rooms have Louis XV wainscoting and Empire furniture.

Appartements de l'Impératrice Joséphine★ – These rooms situated below the grand royal suite, designed for Joséphine in 1808, boast Louis XV panelling. The study with its large rotunda is located beneath the Council Chamber. The Empire furniture includes Marie-Louise's tambour frame, easel, etc. The Salon Jaune is an outstanding example of Empire decoration.

Galerie des Cerfs★ – The gallery is decorated with partly artificial deer heads. The mural paintings were renovated under Napoléon III and show palatial residences under Henri IV. Queen Christina of Sweden had her favourite, Monaldeschi, assassinated here in 1657.

GARDENS★

🕐Open daily Nov–Feb 9am–5pm; Mar, Apr and Oct 9am–6pm; May–Sept 9am–7pm. The Jardin anglais closes 1hr before the rest. 🕐Closed 25 Dec, 1 Jan. ℘01 60 71 50 70.

Grotte du Jardin des Pins★ – This ornamental sandstone composition reveals the popular taste for ponds, man-made features and bucolic landscapes toward the end of François I's reign. Rusticated arches are supported by giant telamones. The frescoes have disappeared.

Jardin anglais★ – The English-style garden was created in 1812 on the site of gardens abandoned during the Revolution. The Bliaut or Blaut fountain, which gave its name to the palace, plays in an octagonal central basin.

Park – The park was created by Henri IV, who filled the canal (in 1609) and planted trees. Preceding the Grand Canal at Versailles by 60 years, this was a novelty, as were the aquatic displays.

EXCURSIONS
Croix du Calvaire

▶5km/3mi from the château. Depart from bd. du Mar.-Leclerc. Turn on 2nd road to left (rte de la Reine-Amélie. 1 500m/1 640yd before the climb, turn left to reach l'esplanade du calvaire Lovely view of the city through the forest.

Avon

▷ *Depart Fontainebleau by bd. du Mar-Juin; at crossroads of Maintenon, turn left on D137E.*

Musicians including Claude Debussy and Maurice Ravel sejourned here at the manoir de Bel-Ébat. The manor's park is open daily from 10am to 7pm.

Church - The 11X Église St-Pierre boasts a nave with ribbed vaulting. Admire the bell tower (13C) and the Renaissance portal (15C). The chancel was completed in 1555, the porch in the 18C.

Atelier Rosa-Bonheur

▷ *In By-Thomery, 8km/5mi E of Fontainebleau on the D 137 which passes through Avon. Turn right at the entrance to By-Thomery.* ◷*Open Jan–Oct: Wed, Sat and holidays 2–5pm: call ahead to confirm hours. Closed 1 Jan, 25 Dec.* ⊜*3€.* ℘*01 64 70 80 14. www.systhome.free.fr/musee.php.*

Rosa Bonheur (1822–1899), renowned animal painter, purchased the château de By in 1859 to accommodate the large number of animals she raised. Empress Eugénie came in person to award Bonheur the Légion d'honneur, and Buffalo Bill gave her one of his constumes. The visit comprises the artist's office, workshop (taxidermied animals and her last, incomplete painting), and the study, housing her bed and personal objects. Note the official permit allowing the artist to "cross-dress" as a man.

Musée départemental Stéphane-Mallarmé

▷ *Vulaines-sur-Seine, 6km/3.7mi NE of Fontainebleau, toward Avon. Take first road at left after the pont de Valvins (bridge). 4 prom. Stéphane-Mallarmé.* ◷*Open Wed–Mon 10am–12.30pm, 2–6pm. Closed Mar, end of Dec to early Jan and 1 May.* ⊜*3€.* ℘*01 64 23 73 27.* This museum, installed in the former house of poet Mallarmé on the banks of the Seine, traces his life and work.

Samois-sur-Seine

▷ *10km/6.2mi NE of Fontainebleau on D 210 to Valvins, then D 137 at left.*

In the 15C, Samois boasted 5 000 inhabitants. It once had a fortified bridge arching over the Seine; this disappeared in the 19C. Samois is today a residential town featuring flower-lined houses along the rue du Bas-Samois, an old paved street descending directly toward the river. The jazz musician Django Reinhardt (1910–1953) lived at no.3.

L'île du Berceau★ is an island linked to the mainland by two footbridges. An annual jazz festival is held here.

ADDRESSES

⌂ STAY

⊖⊖ **Chambre d'hôte de la vallée Javot** – *27 r. de Montceau. 77133 Féricy.* ℘*01 64 23 65 91.* 🅿 ⌷. *4 rooms* ⌷. A tastefully restored former farmhouse serving meals made from market fresh produce.

⊖⊖⊜ **Hôtel Victoria** – *112 r. de France.* ℘*01 60 74 90 00. www.hotelvictoria.com.* 🅿. *20 rooms.* Hotel in 19C building offering comfortable rooms; seven have marble fireplaces. Breakfast served on veranda or garden terrace.

�/EAT

⊖ **Frédéric Cassel** – *21 r. des Sablons.* ℘*01 60 71 00 64. Closed Sun eve and Mon.* Charming teahouse serving savory dishes, hot drinks, chocolates and pastries.

⊖⊖⊜ **Le Dénécourt** – *7 r. Dénécourt.* ℘*01 64 22 27 85. Closed Tue and Mon eve.* A small restaurant close to the château serving generous, straightforward cuisine.

SHOPPING

Market – *Pl. de la République. Open Tue, Fri and Sun morning.* This is one of the region's most pleasant and beautiful outdoor markets.

ACTIVITIES

A la Petite Reine– *14 r. de la Paroisse.* ℘*01 60 74 57 57. www.alapetitereine.com. Open Tue–Sun 9am–7.30pm (Sun 6pm).* Bicycle hire store (mountain bikes, road bikes, children's models). Ideal for trips around Fontainebleau forest.

Forêt de **Fontainbleau**★★★

This 25 000ha/62 000 acre forest surrounding Fontainebleau is largely State-owned and has magnificent hunting grounds. It is popular with ramblers and climbing enthusiasts. The forest was ravaged by the violent storm of December 1999, but conscientious replanting has restored the damaged areas.

GEOLOGY OF THE FOREST

The forested area comprises parallel sandstone ridges thought to be the result of a tropical spell during the Tertiary Era, when winds gradually accumulated sand deposits. The sand dunes solidified into a hard sandstone matrix, creating the area's rolling landscape. Where the limestone has eroded revealing the sandstone, the resultant rocky areas are known locally as **platières**. These **moorlands** covered with heather and other shrubs are often cracked and dotted with ponds. When the sandstone has many crevices and holes, water seeps through and washes away the underlying sands. The upper sandstone stratum is no longer supported and crumbles, producing rocky clusters, the famous Fontainebleau **rochers**. **Vales** or **plains** averaging 40–80m/130–260ft in height lay where the sandstone layer has eroded, exposing the sand or the Brie marl and limestone beneath. The planting of conifers fertilises the soil, making it possible to grow beeches. These produce humus and are eventually replaced by oaks.

Forest Layout – The forest is divided into 747 plots of copses and thickets, moorland and rock. Sessile oak covers 8 000ha/19 768 acres, Norway pines 7 500ha/18 532 acres, and beeches 1 500ha/3 706 acres. Other species include birch, maritime and Corsican pine, chestnut and acacia. Some 416ha/1 433 acres constitute a natural reserve.

Denecourt-Colinet Footpaths

These footpaths take you to the most famous spots. Sylvain Denecourt served with Napoléon's Grande Armée.

- 📍 **Michelin Local Map:** p298: BC2 or map 106 folds 44, 45 and 46.
- 🛈 **Info:** Office du tourisme du pays de Fontainebleau-Avon, 4 r. Royale, 77300 Fontainebleau. ℘01 60 74 99 99. www.fontainebleau-tourisme.com.
- ▶ **Location:** Fontainebleau is 60km/37mi from Paris, via the A 6, and then the N 37.
- 🅿 **Parking:** There are few designated parking areas in the forest, but ample opportunity to pull off the road (leave no valuables in the car).
- 🙄 **Don't Miss:** The chance to take a walk in the woodlands.
- 🕐 **Timing:** Allow as much time as you want; the area is excellent for walking. Take a picnic and make a day of it.

He removed rocks and boulders from caves and created 150km/93mi of footpaths. On carefully selected trees or rocks, discreet blue lines topped by numbers (1 to 16) indicate main paths. Blue letters and stars also mark sights. Sylvain Colinet continued, adding white signposts at all the main junctions.

'Bleau' and 'Bleausards'

By 1910, a few climbing enthusiasts from the Club Alpin Français began to train at Fontainebleau. In the inter-war years, a rock climbing school was suggested among climbers. Fontainebleau was the ideal spot for climbers living in Paris. There are more than 100 climbs marked with arrows on the rocks. Each of them is a succession of climbs, descents and, in some cases, jumps; there are never any walks along these paths.

🚶 HIKING TOURS

1 GORGES DE FRANCHARD★★

🚶 *30min–2hr round trip.*

From the Croix de Franchard crossroads, drive to the esplanade at the Ermitage de Franchard. Note the cedar trees from the Atlas mountain range (North Africa), pine trees from Vancouver (Canada) and horse-chestnuts.

Ancien Ermitage de Franchard

A hermitage developed here in the 12C; in the 13C a community moved in. By the 19C, the pilgrimage had become a country fête held on the Tuesday after Whitsun. Only the chapel walls remain.

Grand Point de vue★

🚶 *30min round trip.*

Beyond the warden's garden, skirt the sandy track on the left and climb towards the rocks without changing direction. This leads to a sandy road (*route de Tavannes*); after 300m/330yd a mushroom-shaped rock will appear. At the plateau turn right; bear left at the rock. A breathtaking view.

▷ To return to the hermitage, walk down three steps and bear left. This path returns to the rte de Tavannes.

Circuit des Druides★★

🚶 *2hr.*

Beyond the Grand Point de Vue on the map, go down three steps and turn right. Follow the blue markings indicating Denecourt-Colinet path 7, winding through half-splintered boulders, some forming overhangs. At the bottom of the 'gorge', cross a sandy road beside an oak tree and climb back up to the rocks to the 'second belvedere'.

From the plateau edge, there is a wonderful view of the gorge and across the **Belvédère des Druides** (marked 'P'). Go down to the easterly footpath and, at the bottom of the gorge, join the *route Amédée*. Turn right. At the first crossroads, turn left onto the route de la Roche-qui-Pleure which climbs up the hill and through a gap in the side of the plateau to the hermitage. *Do not follow the path with the blue signs; it zigzags its way up through the rocks on the left.*

2 GORGES D'APREMONT★

🚶 *10km/6mi round trip – about 4hr.*

Leave Barbizon by allée aux Vaches, the continuation of Grande Rue, a tree-lined avenue well known to artists. This leads to the carrefour du Bas-Bréau, an intersection near a cluster of trees.

Chaos d'Apremont★

🚶 *45min round trip from the crossroads.*

Follow the path marked in blue left of the refreshment chalet *(buvette)* and continue up amid the rocks; at the top

Rocher du Bilboquet in the massif des Trois Pignons

© Jacass/MICHELIN

bear right and follow the plateau's edge. Enjoy views over the wooded slopes of the gorge and the Bière plain. The path veers left: a clump of acacia and pine trees marks the entrance to the **Caverne des Brigands** (☺*take a torch*).

▷ Return to the car. Take the Sully road through the woods to the bare plateau high above the distant ravines.

Grand Belvédère d'Apremont★
🚶 *15min.*
About 1.7km/1mi from the crossroads called Le Bas-Bréau, park at the junction with the 'road' to Le Cul-de-Chaudron. Progress along the plateau and turn left onto the path with blue markings. At a crossroads with a Denecourt-Colinet sign, turn right.
The path runs downhill. Bear left, remaining above the rocks. Below is the gorge.

▷ Return to the car and to carrefour du Bas-Bréau.

Circuit du Désert★
🚶 *3hr30min.*
This area is famous for its barren, desert-like terrain, appreciated by artists.
Take the old road from Barbizon to Fontainebleau; after 1.6km/1mi turn south onto the road to Le Clair Bois. Take the first lane on the right, route de la Chouette, over a pass and to the Désert d'Apremont, dotted with oddly shaped boulders. Bear left onto path no. 6 marked in blue. On reaching the rock resembling an animal with two snouts (trail marker N), bear right. At the carrefour du Désert take the blue-marked path that lies between route du Clair-Bois and route de Milan; it leads to a ravine framed by boulders.
Immediately after the Grotte des Dry-ades, marked with a star, bear left and walk down path '6-6' and up the far side of the valley to the raised platform; the pond called Mare aux Sangliers lies to the left. The prominent part of the plateau offers a good **view** of the Désert d'Apremont and the Bière plain.

▷ Return to the car via carrefour du Désert and rte de Clair-Bois.

⑤ LE LONG ROCHER
🚶 *1.5km/0.9mi – then 2hr30min round trip. From rte Ronde, branch off towards Bourron-Marlotte (D 58).*
Start from carrefour de Marlotte. After 1km/0.6mi, before reaching a steep slope, turn left onto route du Long Rocher, a sandy forest lane (ONF board: 'Zone de Silence de la Malmontagne').

▷ Park at the next crossroads (barrier). Take route des Étroitures (first turning on the right). After 100m/110yd, turn right onto path no. 11, marked in blue.

Belvédère des Étroitures
🚶 *Trail marker U.* Admire the view of Marlotte and the Loing Valley.

▷ Turn round and follow the blue-marked path, which soon begins to wind its way between the boulders in the shade of the trees. It then winds here and there along a seemingly aimless route until it reaches the top of the plateau, the 'Restant du Long-Rocher'.

Restant du Long Rocher★★
The edge of the plateau, strewn with boulders, offers several good views of the southern and northern areas of the forest. Return to the blue path and continue in an easterly direction. Leave the plateau via the steep slope which includes Grotte Béatrix. Walk past a series of boulders used for exercise by mountaineering schools *(red arrows)*. Further along, the path rises slightly; branch off left and take the steep, clearly marked track down. This leads back to route du Long Rocher; bear left to return to the starting point.

Suggestions for Additional Tours:
♦ North of Fontainebleau ③ **Hauteurs de la Solle★** along **route Louis-Philippe★** and **route du Gros-Fouteau★** through ancient groves and then to the

Rochers du Mont Ussy★ where a path leads through pine trees;

◆ A round trip northeast of the town **4** taking in **Tour Dénecourt**, a 19C tower offering **panoramic views★**, and **Samois-sur-Seine**, an attractive town on the banks of the river;

◆ To the southwest **6**, pleasant rambles through the Cirque des Demoiselles and to the **Rocher des Demoiselles★**.

◆ From the southern end of Arbonne **7**, admire the geological peculiarities of **Les Trois Pignons★**. This stony, barren sandstone landscape with dry valleys and eroded peaks leads to the starting point of the Denecourt-Colinet path (no. 16). The path follows the impressive Gorge aux Chats and leads to the edge of the plateau. The **Point de vue de la Vallée Close★★**, which has a good **view★★** of the uplands. In the foreground, a monument honours the local Resistance network. The blue path then turns north and descends eastward, this time leading through oak coppices and heather back to the starting point.

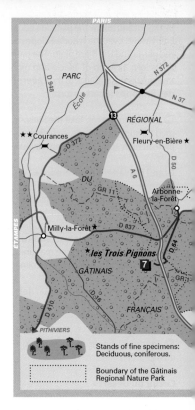

Stands of fine specimens: Deciduous, coniferous.

Boundary of the Gâtinais Regional Nature Park

ADDRESSES

🛏 STAY

🍽🛏 **Hôtel du Pavillon Royal** – 40 av. Gallieni, 77590 Bois-le-Roi, 10km/6mi N of Fontainebleau via N 6, D 116 and D 137. ☎01 64 10 41 00. 26 rooms �. Modern hotel with well-soundproofed, spacious rooms. Pleasant pool and garden.

🍽🛏🛏 **Chambre d'hôte Château de Rouillon**– 41av. Charles-de-Gaulle, 77590 Chartrettes. ☎01 60 69 64 40. www.chateauderouillon.net.⊿. 5 rooms ⊇. 17C château and majestic French park on the banks of the Seine. Stylish furniture and antiques create a refined decor in rooms.

🍴 EAT

🍽 **Le Baroque**– 79av. Gallieni, 77590 Bois-le-Roi. ☎01 64 87 12 65. http://restaurant.lebaroque.free.fr. Closed Sun eve, Sat and Mon. Restaurant offering reasonably priced lunch special. Dining room with avant-garde paintings creates original ambience.

🍽🛏 **La Marine**– 52 quai O.-Metra, 77590 Bois-le-Roi. ☎01 60 69 61 38. Closed 25

Oct–5 Nov, 25 Feb–5 Mar, Sun eve (Oct–Apr), Mon and Tue. On the banks of the Seine, just opposite the lock gate, an engaging restaurant whose terrace resembles the prow of a barge. Dining room with exposed beams; traditional cuisine.

ACTIVITIES

😊 **Caution!** The fragile ecosystem must be respected. Making fires, leaving litter behind, gathering plants, cutting branches off trees and wandering off trails are all prohibited!

RAMBLES

Over time, an increasing number of paths have been cleared. Their markings sometimes overlap, making orientation difficult.

Grande Randonnée (GR): Red and white.
Petite Randonnée (PR): Yellow. **Tour du Massif de Fontainebleau (TMF):** Green and white (vertical lines). Denecourt and Colinet's original trail markers (blue), much older than the current ones, have been maintained on certain trails.

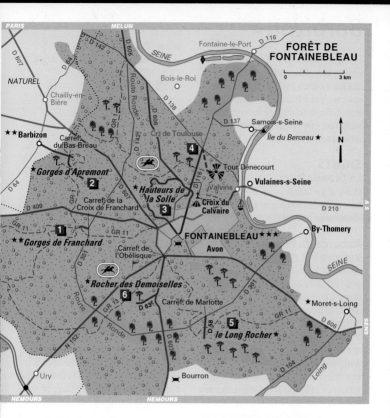

Les Amis de la forêt de Fontainebleau–
*26r. de la Cloche. BP 14, 77301
Fontainebleau Cedex.* ℰ*01 64 23 46 45
(answering machine). www.aaff.org. Staff
hours Tue 10am–12pm, Fri 2.30–4.30pm
(except summer holidays).* This organisation
publishes a *Guide des sentiers de promenade*
(A Guide to the Fontainebleau Forest's
Hiking Trails). It may be purchased in the
Office de Tourisme.

**Maison de l'environnement de Seine-
et-Marne** – *Prugnat Site. 18 allée Gustave-
Prugnat, 77250 Moret-sur-Loing.* ℰ*01 64 31
11 18. www.me77.fr. Registration required.
No charge.* This association organises
walks around the region. Visit Moret-sur-
Loing Office de Tourism.

CYCLING

The asphalt roads criss-crossing the forest,
many open to bicycles and closed to
cars, are much appreciated by cyclists.
A map is available at the Office National
des Fôrets. Trailbikes are also permitted
on certain trails. For more information
contact the Centre d'initiation à la forêt -
La Faisandrie - ℰ*01 64 22 72 59.*

HORSERIDING AND RACES

Centre équestre de Recloses – *Ch. Clos-
de-la Bonne, 77760 Recloses.* ℰ*06 85 01
59 08. www.cheval-en-foret.com.* Horseriding lessons and guided trail rides.

Le Grand Parquet - Stade équestre
– *Rte d'Orléans. D 152, turn right after
golf course. 77300 Fontainebleau.*
ℰ*01 64 23 42 87.* Sporting equipment
for high-level equestrian competitions.
Programme available at Fontainebleau
tourist office.

**Hippodrome de Fontainebleau-
La Solle** – *on D606.* ℰ*01 64 22 29 37.
www.hippodrome-fontainebleau.com.
Free for visitors under 16.* Racetrack.

ROCK-CLIMBING

Cosiroc – *www.cosiroc.org.* This rock-
climbing organisation is very active in
the "Bleau" area.

Club alpin français, Île-de-France – *24
av. Laumière. 75019 Paris.* ℰ*01 53 72 87 00.
www.clubalpin-idf.com.* Mountaineering
club organising outings.

Barbizon★

Lying on the edge of Fontainebleau forest, the village of Barbizon, part of Chailly until 1903, was a popular spot with landscape painters (*see Introduction: Landscape Painting*) and harbours memories of the artists who made it famous.

> ▸ **Population:** 1 571
> ⚲ **Michelin Local Map:** p298: B2 or map 106 fold 45.
> ▶ **Location:** 10km/6mi NW of Fontainebleau – Local map, *see Forêt de FONTAINEBLEAU.*
> ℹ **Info:** 55 Grande-Rue, 77630 Barbizon. ℘01 60 66 41 87. www.barbizon-tourisme.com.

SIGHTS
La Grande Rue
Many of the buildings on the high street bear plaques showing where the town's artists once lodged.

Auberge du Père Ganne★
92 Grande Rue. ◷Open Wed–Mon 10am–12.30pm, 2–6pm. ⊛3€. ℘01 60 66 22 27.

Once a popular meeting place for artists, this former inn is now the **Musée Municipal de l'École de Barbizon**. On the ground floor, three rooms show how the artists decorated cupboards, doors and other flat surfaces as payment. The first floor features paintings showing the influence of Barbizon on Impressionists through the 'Back to Nature' theme: works by Camille Corot, Charles Jacque, Jules Dupré, Ferdinand Chaigneau and Georges Gassies.

Maison-atelier de Théodore Rousseau - *55 Grande-Rue - ℘01 60 66 22 27 ⊛3€.* This small house, once occupied by Rousseau, hosts temporary exhibitions.

Maison-atelier de Jean-François Millet
27 Grande-Rue. ◷Open Wed–Mon 9.30am–12.30pm, 2–5.30pm. ⊛4€. ℘01 60 66 21 55.

Millet's home and studio contains etchings of famous paintings, including *The Angelus* and *The Gleaners*, along with drawings and engravings.

Monument de Rousseau et Millet
A medal embedded in the rock is the work of Henri Chapu. Another plaque commemorates the centenary of Rousseau's first artistic reserve in 1853.

EXCURSION
Château de Fleury-en-Bière
▷ *5km/3.1mi W of Barbizon. Take D 64 south to Macherin, then left on D 11.*

This chateau was built in the 16C by Cosme Clausse, finance secretary under Henri II. It's not possible to visit, but from

---

The Barbizon School

Breaking the rules of studio work, the Barbizon artists were landscape painters who perfected the technique of working directly from nature, a style typified by its two great masters, Théodor Rousseau (1812–67) and Jean-François Millet (1814–75).

The local people were happy to welcome these nature-loving artists, who rose at dawn and whose genius and mischievous nature enlivened local weddings and banquets. Next came the writers, seduced by the beauty of the forest and the congenial atmosphere of this small, international community: George Sand, Henri Murger, the Goncourt brothers and Taine, for example. Thereafter, Barbizon remained a fashionable spot.

Millet died after a life of hard work, his eyes forever riveted on the landscapes of the Bière plain. Like Rousseau, he was buried at Chailly Cemetery (2km/1mi north along D 64; plan of graveyard at entrance).

the entrance gate you can admire the majestic layout of the courtyard, closed on the street side by a large wall.

ADDRESSES

🏠 STAY

⊜⊜ **Chambre d'hôte La Bastide** – *52 r. du 23-Août (N via D 64).* ℘*06 84 95 14 54.* 🅿️. *5 rooms.* 🔁. *Restaurant.* Set in a lovely 1930s house, this comfortable inn combines old-fashioned and exotic appeal.

🍷 EAT

⊜⊜ **La Bohème** – *35 Grande-Rue.* ℘*01 60 66 48 65. Closed Sun eve and Mon.* In a typical Barbizon house, this restaurant offers copious traditional dishes.

⊜⊜⊜ **L'Angelus** – *31 Grande-Rue.* ℘*01 60 66 40 30. www.langelus-restauration.com. Closed Mon and Tue.* 🅿️. This inn takes its name from a Millet work painted at Barbizon. Traditional cuisine to enjoy in the smart dining room or on the shady terrace.

Château de Courances★★

The still-inhabited château de Courances is a dramatic example of the Louis XIII style. Famous for its park and numerous ponds and lakes, which make up its boldly geometric "water garden", Courances is at once contemporary and a rare vestige of a little-known 16C landscaping style.

VISIT
Château
R. du Château, 5km/3mi N of Milly-la-Forêt via D 372. 🔹🔹*Guided tours (40min) Apr–Oct Sat–Sun and holidays 2–6pm.* 🕐*Gardens Apr–Oct Sat–Sun and holidays 2pm–6.30pm.* ⊛*9€ (7€ for gardens only; children under 13 no*

- ♿ **Michelin Map:** p298: B2.
- 🚹 **Info:** ℘01 64 98 07 36, www.courances.net.
- ◗ **Location:** 60km/37mi from Paris on A 6. By train: RER D to Boutigny then taxi or train connection from Paris-Gare de-Lyon to Fontainebleau-Avon, then bike.
- 🕐 **Timing:** Allow a half-day.

charge). ℘*01 64 98 07 36. www.courances.net.*
This 16C castle on the edge of the Fontainebleau forest was the residence of the royal secretary to the king and his heirs. Its Louis XIII architecture was restored in the 19C. The exterior features brick panels in sandstone and narrow

Château de Courances

rooves. The entrance was adorned in the 19C with a stairway imitating the horse-shoe counterpart at Fontainebleau.

The castle served as a field hospital in World War I, and in World War II it was occupied by the Germans then Field Marshal Montgomery from 1947–1954.

Gardens★★

The chateau is best known for its **French formal gardens** and Grand Canal, considered among the best in Europe.

Laid out in the 16C by **Cosme Clausse**, the gardens have been renovated several times by various owners, and owe their beauty to waters which are carefully controlled and pooled from the École river, and to its 14 springs hidden in the gardens. The effect is distinctively unique: vast green spaces are bordered with towering rows of trees which have been left untrimmed; the branches hang and reflect in the pools of water.

Grotesque figures with monstrous faces spit out spring water thanks to a carefully designed system of levels in the garden; statues can be admired around the many bodies of water.

In front of the château, a walkway lined with plantains is overtaken by two canals. On the park side, the château leads to the boxwood garden beds designed by landscape artist **Achille Duchêne** in 1908. A path leads to the Grand Canal, measuring 600m/1 968 ft, where the École river flows. Another path perpendicular to the first heads through small cascades and leads to the garden beds. From here, enjoy a lovely view of the château reflecting in the "Mirror", a splendid rectangular body of water created in the 18C.

Before returning to the entrance gate, turn right near the château and the ruins of an old mill. To the left, at the top of an embankment, is a lovely English-Japanese garden created in the early 20C. Rare trees and lovely colours abound here. Not far, another small garden lies in the undergrowth (accessible to persons with limited mobility).

Milly-La-Forêt★

This village developed around the old covered market, Les Halles. Milly has long been a centre for medicinal plants, including peppermint. As part of the *Parc Naturel Régional du Gâtinais Français*, it's now an important starting-point for many of the forest paths crisscrossing the wooded uplands of Les Trois Pignons and Coquibus. It's also the long-time home and workplace of artist Jean Cocteau.

SIGHTS
Halles

The oak and chestnut market building dates to 1479. The roof structure resting on 48 pillars almost slopes down to the ground. Rue Jean-Cocteau leads to rue du Lau, ending in front of a Romanesque doorway flanked by turrets, linked to the residence where Jean Cocteau lived from 1947 to his death in 1963.

▶ **Population:** 4 728
🕭 **Michelin Local Map:** p298: B2 or map 106 fold 44.
🛈 **Info:** 60 r. Jean-Cocteau, 91490 Milly-la-Forêt.
𝄞01 64 98 83 17.
www.milly-la-foret.fr.
▶ **Location:** Milly-la-Forêt lies 64km/40mi S of Paris, via the A6.

Maison de Jean Cocteau

15 r. du Lau. 🕒*Open Wed–Sun Mar–Oct 10am–7pm; Nov–15 Jan 2–6pm.* 🕒*Closed 16 Jan–28 Feb.* ⌾*7€.* 𝄞*01 64 98 11 50. www.jeancocteau.net.*
Jean Cocteau bought this house in 1947 with partner Jean Marais; upon Cocteau's death in 1963, adoptive son and companion Édouard Dermit inherited it. He conserved the house and 500 of Cocteau's works until his own death in 1995. In 2010, the new museum opened

to the public. Drawings, oil paintings, sculptures and photos, notebooks and sketches are among the works and artefacts.

The portrait of Colette (1944) was drawn in coal and flour on a wood table.

Espace culturel Paul-Bédu

8 bis rue Farnault. **○***Open Wed–Sun Apr–Oct 2–6pm; rest of year 2–5pm.* ✆*No charge* ᗷ*. ℰ01 64 98 75 52.* Late-19C to early 20C works collected by Paul Bédu. Lithographs, drawings and ceramics by Cocteau are also on display.

Chapelle St-Blaise-des-Simples★

At the city exit by the rte de La Chapelle-la-Reine. **○***Mar–Oct Wed–Sun 10am–12.30pm, 2–6pm; Nov–15 Jan Wed–Sun 2–5pm.* **○***Closed rest of the year.* ✆*2.50€. ℰ01 64 98 84 94. www.chapelle-saint-blaise.org.*
In the 12C this chapel was part of the leper colony of St. Blaise. In 1959, **Jean Cocteau** (1889–1963) decorated the walls with herb patterns (mint, valerian, buttercup and monkshood). The artist's tomb is shared with companion Édouard Dermit (1925–1995).

Le Cyclop

🐾 *Guided tours only (45min) May–Oct Sat–Sun 1.30–6pm, Aug Fri–Sun 1.30–6pm.* ✆*7€* ⓕ*Note: children under-8 not allowed. ℰ01 64 98 95 72. www.lecyclop.com. Leave Milly on the Étampes road (D 837); follow the signs.*
This giant sculpture was donated in 1987 by artists Jean Tinguely and Niki de Sainte-Phalle. Its enormous, sparkling head (22.5m/73ft high) is made with 300t of steel The sculpture is topped with a water-filled basin dedicated to post-war artist Yves Klein (1928–62).

Conservatoire National des Plantes Médicinales Aromatiques et Industrielles

rte. de Nemours. **○***Open Apr–Oct Tue–Sun 10am–6pm; Mar and Nov Sat–Sun 10am–5pm.* **○***Closed Jan, Feb, Dec.* ✆*7.50€.* ᗷ*. ℰ01 64 98 83 77. www.cnpmai.net.*

A 2ha/5 acre park dedicated to preserving over 1 200 species of plants, including culinary and medicinal herbs.

EXCURSIONS
Boigneville

▶ *11km/6.8mi S of Milly on D1 and D449.* This village boasts the early 13C **N.-D.-de-l'Assomption** (*ℰ01 64 99 40 07;* 🐾*combined ticket with Ecomuseum*), remarkable for its paintings (1677) and **crypt★**. The latter was re-discovered in the 17C by a parish priest who covered it with frescoes depicting the Virgin. The 14C tombstone of la Dame de St-Val was also unveiled.

Écomusée – *ℰ01 64 99 40 07.* **○***1st Sun of the month 2–6pm.* ✆*3.80€.* Housed in a former bar, this museum explore the lives of people living in this district from the early 20C. Don't miss the collection of World War II propaganda posters.

ADDRESSES

🛏 STAY

🍽 **M. Lenoir (B&B)** – *9 r. du Souvenir, 91490 Moigny-sur-École. 3.5km/2mi N of Milly-la-Forêt. ℰ0164 98 47 84. www.compagnie-des-clos.com. 4 rooms* ☲*.* High walls ensure privacy at this stone house and garden. Tastefully decorated, peaceful rooms. Summer pool.

🍽🍽 **Chambre d'hôte La Ferme de Clercy**– *40r. de Clercy, 91590 Guigneville-sur-Essonne. 13km/8.7mi NW on D 105, rte de La Ferté-Alais. ℰ01 64 57 61 84. www.lafermedeclercy.fr.* 🅿 ☷*. 3 rooms and 2 suites* ☲*.* 18C farm in the regional natural park. Rustic decor, access to park and river.

🍴 EAT

🍽🍽🍽 **Auberge d'Auvers Galant**– *7r. d'Auvers, 77123 Noisy-sur-École. 4km/2.5mi S on D 948. ℰ01 64 24 51 02. http://perso.orange.fr/auvers-galant. Closed 21 Jan–12 Feb, 20 Aug–4 Sept, Sun eve, Mon and Tue.* Rustic inn bordering the forêt de Fontainebleau serving classic dishes.

SHOPPING

Market – The Milly herb market is held in early June, but each Thursday afternoon you can find herbs and medicinal plants at the Milly outdoor market.

Larchant★

Situated in a wooded basin, Larchant is recognisable by the dramatic, broken tower of the gothic St-Mathurin church, once favoured by pilgrims. Popular with climbers, it is home to a 15m/49ft-high boulder known as Dame-Jouanne, on the border of Fontainebleau forest.

VISIT
Église St-Mathurin★

Open summer 9am–7pm, winter 10am–4pm. ☎01 64 24 30 21.

Saint Mathurin is said to have been born around 250. Having miraculously saved Emperor Maximilian's daughter, his relics were brought to Larchant, believed to heal the possessed and mentally ill. The basilica was a place of pilgramage until the 17C. The church was arsoned in 1568 during the Religious Wars, and the tower crumbled in 1675.

Portail du Jugement dernier

This 13C portal opens to the nave. Its composition shows the influence of Notre-Dame de Paris : the Christ dominates over other figures. Two angels surround him. The Virgin and St John kneel around the angels. The tympanum shows the Resurrection of the dead; the arches depict St John the Baptist with a lamb and Moses holding the Ten Commandments.

Gated windows dominate the south side. Legend has it that these were used to imprison dangerous mentally ill individuals, but in reality they likely served as an archive.

Interior – Only the chancel, apse and chapel of the Virgin have retained vaulting. Two floors of windows complement fine columns jutting from the walls.

Chapelle de la Vierge – Built around 1300, the chapel opens onto the transept via two ornate arcades.

▶ **Population:** 728
⊚ **Michelin Map:** p298 B3.
▤ **Info:** Seine et Marne Tourist Office, ☎01 60 39 60 39 or www.tourisme77.fr
◑ **Location:** 72km/44.7mi from Paris on A 6. Train from Paris-Gare-de-Lyon to Nemours; Larchant is 13km/8mi away (take taxi).
◷ **Kids:** Allow 2 to 3 hours to visit the church and town; half-day to a full day for climbing excursion.

Marais de Larchant

◑ *NE of Larchant. Swamplands are accessible on rare occasions (only with guide). Call l'Association de la réserve naturelle du marais de Larchant for information. ☎09 60 45 00 38. www.maraisdelarchant.fr.*

Larchant houses one of the last swamplands of Fontainebleau. It's now a natural reserve harbouring birds, poplars and willows.

Massif de la Dame-Jouanne★

◑ *From Larchant, 3km/1.8mi N on car-accessible path (Recloses), marked Dame-Jouanne, then 1 hour return on foot.*

The trail departs on the right from the chalet Jobert, a restaurant popular with climbers, then ascends through woodstoward the plateau. After a sharp right turn, leave your car at the entrance to a large prairie to the right.

🚶 Follow the trail through the prairie and enter the wood: continue straight. At the bottom the path you will come to a bare *platière*: cross it and continue in the same direction. You'll reach marked trail GR 13 (red and white markings); take it to the right. The path leads to a rocky escarpment. The area is suitable for all levels of climbers, from children to experts. When returning to the car, don't miss the forking path on the trail back.

Moret-Sur-Loing★

Immortalised by the 19C painter Alfred Sisley, Moret is a fortified medieval town perched at the meeting point of the Loing and Seine rivers.

> ▸ **Population:** 4 478
> 🕭 **Michelin Local Map:**
> p298: C2 or map 106 fold 46.
> 🛈 **Info:** Pl. de Samois, 77250 Moret-sur-Loing. ✆01 60 70 41 66.
> ◖ **Location:** Near Fontainebleau, 80km/50mi S of Paris via the A 6/N 6. Access from Paris: SNCF rail link from Gare de Lyon.

A BIT OF HISTORY

Moret and its fortified castle defended the king's territory from the reign of Louis VII up to Philip the Fair's marriage to Jeanne of Navarre, daughter of the Comte de Champagne, which ended the family feud. Its keep and curtain wall lost their strategic value, and Fontainebleau became the official place of residence for French rulers. Fortifications remained until the mid-19C.

Moret's history is marked by famous women, including Jacqueline de Bueil (1588–1651), one of the loves of Henri IV, who founded the Notre-Dame-des-Anges hospital and convent. Marie Leszczynska met Louis XV here on 4 September 1725; an obelisk marks the place where the betrothed met (at the top of the rise along N 5). The next day they married in Fontainebleau.

SIGHTS

The river banks★

Branch off the road to St-Mammès and proceed towards the Pré de Pin, along the east bank of the Loing. Admire the **view** of the lake, islets, fishermen, church and keep. Alfred Sisley chose Moret as the theme for some 400 paintings.

Bridge over the Loing

One of the oldest bridges in Île-de-France, this was probably built around the same time as the town fortifications. On the approach to the Porte de Bourgogne, ramparts and several houses with overhangs come into view.

Église Notre-Dame

The **chancel** was likely consecrated in 1166. The original elevation is visible in the apse and south side; the main arches are crowned by a gallery opening onto triple arching, surmounted by clerestory windows. The arches and bays on the north side were walled to better support the unsound bell tower erected in the 15C.

Ancien Hospice (Hospital)

The corner post at rue de Grez bears an effigy of St James. A few steps further, a modern cartouche shows the hospital's founding date (1638).

Maison de Sisley

Alfred Sisley (1839–99), Impressionist painter of English parentage, spent his later life in Moret, in a studio at 19 rue Montmartre (⌒►private).

Rue Grande

At no. 24 a plaque marks the house where Napoléon spent the night on his way back from Elba (19 to 20 March 1815).

Maison François I

Walk through the town hall porch and into the small courtyard.
Note the Renaissance decoration, and the door crowned by a salamander.

Porte de Samois

A statue of the Virgin Mary adorns the inner façade.

🚗 DRIVING TOUR

FOREST AND LOING RIVER

◖ 40 km/25 miles loop from Moret. Cross Loing bridge; turn right on D 40.

The route takes you along the **canal du Loing** which descends to Montargis and ends at the canal de Briare.

After **Épisy**, the road crosses woods before arriving at **La Genevraye**. Stop at the crossroads before turning right toward Montigny and admiring the small, Roman-style **église de Cugny**, stranded in the middle of picturesque fields (*you can take the car or walk*).

The bridge at **Montigny-sur-Long** is particularly striking: view of the church, riverbanks and Loing islands, many converted into private gardens.

▻ Head W toward Bourron-Marlotte.

Château de Bourron

In Bourron-Marlotte. ◐*Park open: Jul-Sept 9am–12pm, 2–5pm. Château: guided tour by reservation (30 people min, 45min).* ◐*Closed weekends and holidays.* ✏*Château: 5€ (children 4€) + 80€ for tour guide. Park 2€ (1€ for children under 10).* ✆*01 64 78 39 39. www.bourron.fr.*
Built in the late 16C on the ruins of a medieval fortress, the brick and stone design and horseshoe-shaped staircase of the south facade evoke the Cheval-Blanc courtyard at the château de Fontainebleau. Facing the north façade, a drawbridge between the moats leads to another horseshoe stairway. The south grounds show off the château's harmonious, sober design; at the north end of the park lies the Ste-Sévère spring, which flows into the Great Canal.

▻ Head S to Grez-sur-Loing.

The small town of **Grez-sur-Loing** was part of the estate of several queens of France. It was re-incorporated into the royal estate in 1478 before being ceded to the Dukes of Nemours in 1672.
Église N.-D.-et-St-Laurent – This 12C church was part of the St-Jean de Sens abbey, and has a bell tower-porch.
Tour de Ganne – ◐*Open 8am–6pm.* ✏*No charge.* ♿✆*01 64 45 95 15.* Part of the former fortified château, this tower lodged Blanche de Castille and Louise de Savoie, mother of François I, who

died here in 1531. Its riverside gardens were painted by Corot and Karl Larsson. In the 19C, numerous artists sojourned here. From the bridge, enjoy a **view** of the river, village and tower.

▻ Return to Bourron-Marlotte and head toward Fontainebleau. At first crossroads, turn right toward Champagne-sur-Seine. Turn right toward Épisym then left at Sorques.

Before returning to Moret, you'll pass by the **plaine de Sorques**, a conserved natural area with two marked trails.

EXCURSIONS
St-Mammès
▻*2.5km/1.5mi NW of Moret.*
Take bus "Comète" line 3.
Situated at the meeting point of the Seine and Loing, St-Mammès is a boating centre. Enjoy the pleasant riverside walking path here.

Montereau-Fault-Yonne
▻*12km/7.4mi W of Moret along D 606.*
🛈*10 r. Jean-Jaurès. 77130 Montereau-Fault-Yonne.* ✆*01 64 32 07 76. www.ot-montereau77-cc2f.fr.*
This town had a château from the 11C. A pleasant stop near the Yonne river, it harbours the memory of gruesome events, including the assassination of John the Fearless in 1419.
Collégiale N.-D.-et-St-Loup– This collegial church (13–16C) combines Gothic and Renaissance styles. From the new centre of Montereau, follow the main avenue to the school complex. Walk around the lycée walls. From the hill, enjoy magnificent **panoramic views★** of the ruins of the château, bridges and church.

Donnemarie-Dontilly
▻*17km/10.5mi NW on D 403.*
Nestled in a hilly, wooded area, this town's 13C **N.-D.-de-la-Nativité** church has an imposing bell tower (60m/197ft), and a lovely rose window. Some of the stained glass dates to the 12C–13C.

Bray-sur-Seine

▶ *26km/16mi E of Montereau on D 411.*
This harbour on the Seine boasts paths bordered with linden trees. The market on rue Taveau has its original chestnut roof (1842). The collegial **church★** dates as far back as the 10C and was consecrated in 1171. The portal and bell tower date to the 17C. The nave is surrounded by 12 Roman-style columns.

ADDRESSES

Nemours★

Surrounded by deep forests, the historic town of Nemours is an ideal starting point for a tour of the Loing river valley. Situated on the edge of the Fontainebleau forest, the land consists of sandy knolls and rocky terrain.

VISIT
Château
Enter through 18C portal on rue Gauthier-1er. ◷*Open Wed–Sat 10am–12.30pm, 2–6pm, Sun 2–6pm; Tue groups only.* ◷*Closed Mon, 1 Jan, 1 May and 25 Dec.* ⊛*3€ (5€ for tour). ℘01 64 28 27 42. www.ville-nemours.fr.* This château boasts a main body flanked with round towers dating to the 12C–13C. The more decorative aspects, including the windows, are characteristic of 15C architecture. The château is linked to the keep by a wall topped with a covered gallery. Passing through vast

- ▶ **Population:** 12 813
- ⵛ **Michelin Local Map:** p298: B3.
- 🛈 **Info: Tourist Office** – 16 r. Gaston-Darley. ℘01 64 28 03 95. www.nemours-saint-pierre.com.
- ▶ **Location:** 82km/51mi from Paris on A 6.
- ⫯ **Kids:** Prehistoric Museum of Île-de-France.
- ◷ **Timing:** Allow a half-day.

rooms, you reach the **gothic oratory** (around 1150) situated within a tower. The château now houses an exhibit tracing the edifice's transformations over the centuries.

Église Saint-Jean-Baptiste
Dominated by a dramatic spire, the Nemours church dates to the 16C, excepting the tower foundations (12C).

The chancel boasts prominent chapels. The decorative vaulting in the nave, elevated in the 17C, bears wood ribs. On the largest pillar of the chancel, an inscription commemorates the visit of Pope Pie VII on 25 novembre 1804. Behind the altar is a bronze pieta (1870) from Justin Chrysostome **Sanson**.

♟♟ Musée départemental de Préhistoire d'Île-de-France★

E on the route de Sens. You can take the bus from the station: stop at "cité scolaire". 48 av. Étienne-Dailly. ◉*Open daily 10am–12.30pm, 2–5.30pm.* ◉*Closed Wed morning, Sat morning, 1 Jan, 1 May and 25 Dec.* ⊙*3€.* ℘*01 64 78 54 80.*

A modern concrete building houses this museum on the border of the Nanteau forest, at the centre of one of the region's richest prehistoric sites. The area abounds with megalithic monuments, notably "polissoirs": boulders with grooves created by sharpening stone tools on the surface.

After climbing a ramp tracing human evolution, enjoy a reconstitution of archeological digs in Étiolles.

Paleolithic rooms (800 000 to 9 000 BC) – These offer a picture of regional pre-history. A simulation shows how to date plant fossils by studying strata. A short presentation explores the daily life of local prehistoric communities.

Mesolithic (9 000 to 5 000 BC) – This section explores the lives of mesolithic hunters and fishermen across wooden objects found in the muddy deposits of Noyen-sur-Seine, as well as miniscule flint objects from sites.

Neolithic (5 000 to 2 300 BC) and **Metal Age** (2 300 to 25 BC) – This section provides information on village life, agriculture, arms or burial rites.

Domestic ceramics and funerary objects discovered in Châtenay-sur-Seine are notable.

⚑ HIKES

Gréau Boulders ★

⚑ *1h30 by foot (return trip) from stadium parking lot on av. d'Ormesson,* or from City Hall *(from station, pass by railroad tracks, turn left, then cross the Rochefontaine park.)*

From the parking lot, take the route de Nemours for 100m/328ft; enter the parc des Rochers via a passageway between two properties. From the entrance, take a slight left to reach the point between the two boulders *(you'll see an old hydrant and bench).* This path will lead you to the famed "tortoise". Climb to the right from there. If your starting point is city hall, turn right and continue until you reach a small stone house to the left. Go up a paved path to the Grande École.

▶ Descend to the hydrant and continue to the right.

Once you're back on flat ground, between the hydrant and the shelter, take the path marked by red and white double lines (GR 13) to the left and toward the woods. The path leads up to the Plat boulder, whose upper part is shaded with large pines. You can descend by following the path, but be careful: the slope is slippery.

Rochers de Nemours★

This rocky formation is the last prolongation in the south of the Fontainebleau sandstones. ⚑ The GR 13 marked trail crosses most of the masses; various trails along the way offer different possibilities, including the **Soulès Boulder Tour★**. *Forest map with 5 ideas for hikes available at the tourist office for 1€.*

ADDRESSES

SHOPPING

Market – *Champ-de-Mars. Wed and Sat morning.* An ideal place to procure fresh local products.

ACTIVITIES

♟♟ **Fami-Parc**– *D 403, at château de Nonville, 77140 Nonville.* ℘*01 64 29 02 02. www.fami-parc.com. Open Apr–Oct: dates vary according to season: call ahead.* This park is ideal for a family outing. Roller-coasters, shows and on-site dining.

Château-Landon

The elegant silhouette of the town's bell tower is reminiscent of Tuscany. This historic town is best explored at a leisurely pace.

WALKING TOUR

Place du Larry
This square leads to the place du Marché (marketplace), offering views of the town, the St-Turgal tower (vestige of a Roman church once part of the defensive wall), and the St-Séverin Abbey.

Église Notre-Dame
The church's **tower★** (15C) has open archways. Stand on place du Marché to admire the bell tower and chancel.

▷ Return to place du Marché and take the route de Souppes at left.

Pass in front of the tourist office and turn right onto a square. Take the staircase at right to rue Moïse on the left. At the street's end, take the stairway which descends to rue du Bas-Larry, then another stairway to the Fusain river. Head east to the bridge.
The **defensive site★** of Château-Landon was raised by the **St-Séverin abbey**.

EXCURSIONS
Souppes-sur-Loing
▷5.5km/3.4mi N on D 207.
🖪67 av. du Mar.-Leclerc.
Bordering the Loing Canal, this town's 12C–13C church has a 16C wood altarpiece, copy of a 14C work from the old Cistercian abbey of Cercanceaux (12C).
⊶Private property: guided tour one Sat per month, info at Tourist Office. ☜6€.

Dordives
▷7km/4.3mi E on D 43.
Musée du Verre et de ses métiers – 12 av. de Lyon. ◷Open May–Aug Wed–Thu, Sat–Mon 2–7pm; Sept–Apr Wed, Sat–Sun 2–6pm. ◷Closed Tue, Jan–Feb, 1 May,

▶ **Population:** 3 072
🚴 **Michelin Map:** p298: B
🖪 **Info:** Office de tourisme. 6 r. Hetzel. ℘01 64 29 38 08.
◐ **Location:** 103km/64mi from Paris on A 6. Train from Paris-Gare-de-Lyon to Souppes-sur-Loing, then take line 34 tourist bus from tourist office.
◔ **Timing:** Around a half-day.

25 Dec. ☜3.30€. ℘02 38 92 79 06. www.musee-dordives.fr. This industrial glassmaking museum features pieces made in glass workshops in nearby Bagneaux-sur-Loing.

Égreville
▷ 16 km/10mi E on D 43 then D 219.
The marketplace in this agricultural town dates to 16C. On the same square, the church (13C–15C) is graced by a massive bell tower-porch.

Jardin-musée départemental Antoine-Bourdelle★
▷ From Egreville, take NW exit off of D 58 toward Remauville, to Le Coudray.
◷Open May–Oct 10.30am–1pm, 2–6pm. ⊷Guided tours possible.
◷Closed Mon, Tue, 1 May, Pentecostal Monday and 15 Aug. ☜3€.
℘01 64 78 50 90.
This magnificent garden was completed in 1973. Sublime sculptures grace the park, from the **Heracles archer★★** to Saphho or the Dying Centaur.

Mondreville
▷7km/4.3mi W on D 43.
Mondreville's charming church, with its bell tower dominating a semi-circular chevet, has a beautiful Roman porch.

Beaumont-du-Gâtinais
▷18 km/11mi W on D 43.
This town has a lovely 17C wooden marketplace building. The church faces it: vestiges of a former fortified chateau (private property), with monumental portal and water-filled moats.

Chartres★★★

Capital of Beauce, France's corn belt, Chartres is famed mainly for the Cathedral of Our Lady, a magnificent edifice and UNESCO World Heritage Site which rises majestically over picturesque monuments.

A BIT OF HISTORY
A Town with a Destiny

Since ancient times Chartres has had a strong influence over religious matters. It is believed that a Gallo-Roman well on the Chartres plateau was the object of a pagan cult, and that in the 4C this was transformed into a Christian cult by the first evangelists. Adventius, the first known bishop of Chartres, lived during the mid 4C. A document from the 7C mentions a bishop Béthaire kneeling in front of Notre-Dame, which points to the existence of a Marian cult.

In 876 the chemise said to belong to the Virgin Mary was given to the cathedral by Charles the Bald, confirming that Chartres was already a place of pilgrimage. Up to the 14C the town of Chartres continued to flourish.

Chartres Cathedral was consecrated to the Assumption of the Virgin Mary in 1260; in the Middle Ages it attracted many pilgrims.

During 1912–1913 the writer and poet **Charles Péguy** (1873–1914) visited the cathedral. The strong influence it had on his work inspired a small group of enthusiasts to follow suit and led, in 1935, to the establishment of the 'Students' Pilgrimage' (during Whitsun).

An exceptional man

In the **Église St-Jean-Baptiste** in the Rechèvres district to the north of the town lies the body of the abbot **Franz Stock**. This German priest, chaplain to the prisons of Paris from 1940 to 1944, refused to retreat with the Wehrmacht and was taken prisoner. At the Morancez prison camp near Chartres, he founded a seminary for prisoners of war and was the Superior there for two years. He died in February 1948 at the age of 43.

▸ **Population:** 40 022
◔ **Michelin Local Map:** 311: D1. 106 folds 37 and 38.
▯ **Info:** pl. de la Cathédrale, 28000 Chartres. ℘02 37 18 26 26. www.chartres-tourisme.com.
◖ **Location:** Chartres lies off the A11, SE of Paris. The town is situated on a knoll on the left bank of the River Eure, in the heart of the Beauce. The cathedral dominates the Old Town, known as the Quartier St-André.
ℙ **Parking:** There is a large underground car park at Le Bouef Couronne, and street parking *(fee)* along the boulevard de la Résistance and the boulevard Maurice Violette.
◉ **Don't Miss:** For a bird's-eye view of the cathedral, stand behind the Monument aux Aviateurs Militaires, a memorial to the French Air Force high above the east bank of the river. The view is impressive.
◔ **Timing:** Allow 1.5–2hr to visit the cathedral and at least 4hr to visit the Old Town.

CATHÉDRALE★★★

Allow 1hr30min. ◔*Open daily 8.30am–7.30pm; Jul–Aug Tue, Fri and Sun 10pm.* ℘*02 37 21 59 08. www.cathedrale-chartres.org* ◎*No charge.* The 4 000 carved figures and 5 000 characters portrayed by the cathedral's magnificent stained-glass windows demanded a lifelong commitment from the specialists who studied them.

A Swift Construction

The building rests upon the Romanesque cathedral erected by Bishop Fulbert in the 11C and 12C. There remain the crypt, the towers and the foundations

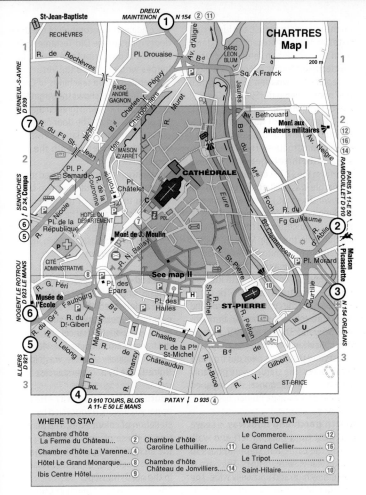

WHERE TO STAY		WHERE TO EAT	
Chambre d'hôte La Ferme du Château... ②	Chambre d'hôte Caroline Lethuillier.........⑪	Le Commerce................. ⑫	
Chambre d'hôte La Varenne..④		Le Grand Cellier.............. ⑯	
Hôtel Le Grand Monarque.....⑧	Chambre d'hôte Château de Jonvilliers....⑭	Le Tripot........................ ⑦	
Ibis Centre Hôtel.................⑨		Saint-Hilaire....................⑩	

of the west front, including the Royal Doorway, and fragments of the Notre-Dame-de-la-Belle-Verrière stained-glass window. The remaining sections of the cathedral were built in the wake of the Great Fire of 1194; princes and dignitaries contributed generously to the work, while the poor offered their labour.

These efforts made it possible to complete the cathedral in 25 years, and to add the north and south porches 20 years later. The resulting architecture and decoration of Notre-Dame forms a harmonious composition almost unparalleled in the history of Gothic art. By a seeming miracle, the Wars of Religion, the French Revolution and the two World Wars spared the famous cathedral, which Rodin referred to as 'the Acropolis of France' on account of its aesthetic and spiritual value.

Only the cathedral's 'forest' – the superb roof timbers – were destroyed by flames in 1836, and subsequently replaced by a metal framework.

Beneath the cathedral close, archaeological excavations covering around 1.2sq km/0.46sq mi are currently in progress. The remains of two 13C houses have so far been uncovered.

Exterior

West front –The two tall spires and the Royals Doorway form one of the most perfect compositions encountered in French religious art. The New Bell Tower on the left was built first; the lower part dates to 1134. Its present name dates from the 16C, when Jehan de Beauce erected a stone spire (115m /377ft high) to replace the wooden steeple, which had burned down in 1506. The Old Bell Tower (c. 1145–64), rising 106m/384ft, is a masterpiece of Romanesque art, forming a stark contrast to the ornate Gothic construction. The Royal Doorway and the three large windows above date from the 12C. Everything above this ensemble was built at a later date: the rose window (13C), the 14C gable and the king's gallery featuring the kings of Judah, the ancestors of the Virgin Mary. On the gable, the Virgin Mary is depicted presenting her son to the Beauce area.

The **Royal Doorway★★★** (Portail Royal), is a splendid example of Late Romanesque architecture (1145–70). The Christ in Majesty on the central tympanum and the statue-columns are famous throughout the world. The elongated features of the biblical kings and queens, prophets, priests and patriarchs peer out from the embrasures. The statues were primarily decorative and allegorical, not designed to realistically depict human beings.

North porch and doorway – Leave the west front on your left and walk round the cathedral, stepping back to get a clear view of its lines. The nave is extremely high and unusually wide. The problem of how to support it was brilliantly resolved with the construction of three-tiered flying buttresses; the lower two arcs were joined together by colonnettes.

The elegant Pavillon de l'Horloge near the New Bell Tower is the work of Jehan de Beauce (1520).

The ornamentation of the north porch is similar to that of the doorway, executed at an earlier date. Treated more freely than those on the Royal Doorway, the characters are elegant and extremely lively, illustrating a new, more realistic approach to religious art. The statue of St Modesta, a local martyr, who is pictured gazing up at the New Bell Tower, is extremely graceful.

Once again, the decoration of the three doors refers to the Old Testament. The right door pays tribute to the biblical heroes who exercised the virtues recommended in the teachings of Christ. The central panel shows the Virgin Mary and the Prophets, who foretold the coming of the Messiah. The door on the left presents the Annunciation, Visitation and Nativity, together with the Vices and Virtues.

In the bishop's garden, the raised terrace commands a view of the town below lying on the banks of the lower River Eure. Before reaching the garden gate, look left and note the archway straddling a narrow street: it used to open into the Notre-Dame cloisters.

East end – The complexity of the double-course flying buttresses – reinforced here with an intermediate pier as they cross over the chapels – and the succession of radiating chapels, chancel and arms of the transept are stunning. The 14C St-Piat Chapel, originally separate, was joined to Notre-Dame by a stately staircase.

South porch and doorway – Here, the upper stonework is concealed by a constellation of colonnettes. The perspective of these planes, stretching from the arches of the porch to the gables, confers a sense of unity that is lacking in the north transept.

The theme is the Church of Christ and the Last Judgment. In the Middle Ages, these scenes would usually be reserved for the west portal, but in this case the Royal Doorway already featured ornamentation. Consequently, the scenes portraying the Coming of a New World, prepared by the martyrs, were destined for the left-door embrasures, while those of the Confessors (witnesses of Christ who have not yet been made martyrs) adorn the right door.

Christ reigns supreme on the central tympanum. He is also present on the pier, framed by the double row of the 12 Apostles with their lean, ascetic faces, draped in long, gently folded robes. Among the martyrs, note the statues standing in the foreground: St George and St Theodore, both admirable 13C representations of knights in armour. These figures are quite separate from the columns – the feet are flat and no longer slanted – and were designed for purely decorative purposes.

The most delightful feature of the sculpted porch is the display of medallions, grouped in sets of six and placed on the recessed arches of the three doorways: these depict the lives of the martyrs, the Vices and Virtues, etc.

Returning to the west front, note the Old Bell Tower and its ironical statue of a donkey playing the fiddle, symbolising man's desire to share in celestial music. At the corner of the building, stop to admire the figure of the sundial Ang

Access to the Bell Tower★

◷*Open daily 9am–12pm, 2–6pm (Sept–Apr 2–5pm); last ascent 30min before closure.* ◷*Closed holidays.* ☞*3€. No charge for children under 18 with adult.* ℘*02 37 36 08 80.*

The tour *(195 steps)* leads round the north side and up to the lower platform of the New Bell Tower. Seen from a height of 70m/230ft, the buttresses, flying buttresses, statues, gargoyles and Old Bell Tower are impressive. It is still possible to recognise the former Notre-Dame cloisters thanks to the old pointed roof. Enclosed by a wall up to the 19C, this area was frequented by clerics, especially canons.

Interior

The nave (16m/52ft) is wider than any other in France (Notre-Dame in Paris 40ft; Notre-Dame in Amiens 46ft), though it has single aisles. The vaulting reaches a height of 37m/121ft and the interior is 130-m/427-ft long. This 13C nave is built in early or lancet Gothic style. There is no gallery; instead, there is a blind trifovrium (ℭ*see illustration in the INTRODUCTION: Religious Architecture).*

In a place of pilgrimage of this importance, the chancel and the transept had to accommodate large-scale ceremonies; they were therefore wider than the nave. In Chartres, the chancel, its double ambulatory and the transept form an ensemble 64m/210ft wide between the north and south doorways.

Note the gentle slope of the floor, rising slightly towards the chancel; this made it easier to wash down the church when the pilgrims had stayed overnight.

The striking state of semi-darkness in the nave creates an element of mystery which was not intentional: it is due to the gradual dimming of the stained glass over the centuries.

The floor of the nave houses an intriguing **labyrinth**, dating to around 12C and made of flagstones and black marble.

Stained-glass windows★★★ – The 12C and 13C stained-glass windows of Notre-Dame constitute, together with those of Bourges, the largest collection in France. The Virgin and Child and the Annunciation and Visitation scenes in the clerestory at the far end of the chancel produce a striking impression.

West front – The three 12C windows here once threw light on Fulbert's Romanesque cathedral and the dark, low nave that stood behind, which explains their considerable length.

The scenes *(bottom to top)* illustrate the fulfilment of the prophecies: *(right)* the Tree of Jesse; *(centre)* the childhood and life of Jesus (Incarnation cycle); and *(left)* Passion and Resurrection (Redemption cycle).

Feast your eyes on the famous 12C 'Chartres blue', with its clear, deep tones enhanced by reddish tinges, especially radiant in the rays of the setting sun. For many years, people believed that this particular shade of blue was a long-lost trade secret. Modern laboratories have now established that the sodium compounds and silica in the glass made it more resistant to dirt and corrosion than the panes made with other materials and in other times.

Transept – This ensemble consists of two 13C rose windows, to which were added a number of lancet windows featuring tall figures. The themes are the same as those on the corresponding carved doorway: Old Testament (north), the End of the World (south).

The north rose (rose de France) was a present from Blanche of Castille, mother of St Louis and Regent of France, and portrays a Virgin and Child. It is characterised by the fleur-de-lis motif on the shield under the central lancet and by the alternating Castile towers and fleurs-de-lis pictured on the small corner lancets. The larger lancets depict St Anne holding the infant Virgin Mary, framed by four kings or high priests: Melchizedek and David stand on the left, Solomon and Aaron on the right.

The centre roundel of the south rose shows the risen Christ, surrounded by the Old Men of the Apocalypse, forming two rings of 12 medallions. The yellow and blue chequered quatrefoils represent the coat of arms of the benefactors, the Comte de Dreux Pierre Mauclerc and his wife, who are also featured at the bottom of the lancets.

The lancets on either side of the Virgin and Child depict four striking figures – the Great Prophets Isaiah, Jeremiah, Ezekiel and Daniel – with the four Evangelists seated on their shoulders.

The morality of the scene is simple: although they are weak and lacking dignity, the Evangelists can see farther than the giants of the Old Testament thanks to the Holy Spirit.

Notre-Dame-de-la-Belle-Verrière★

(1) – This is a much-lauded stained-glass window. The Virgin and Child, a fragment of the window spared by the fire of 1194, was mounted in 13C stained glass. The range of blues is quite superb.

Other stained-glass windows

– The aisles of the nave and the chapels around the ambulatory are lit by a number of celebrated stained-glass windows from the 13C verging on the sombre side. On the east side, the arms of the transept have received two recent works, in perfect harmony with the early fenestration: St Fulbert's window (south transept) (2), donated by the American Association of Architects (from the François Lorin workshop, 1954), and the window of Peace (north transept) (3), a present from a group of German admirers (1971).

The Vendôme Chapel (4) features a particularly radiant 15C stained-glass window. It illustrates the development of this art, which eventually led to the lighter panes of the 17C and 18C.

Parclose ★★

– The screen was started by Jehan de Beauce in 1514 and finished in the 18C. This fine work consists of 41 sculpted compositions depicting the lives of Christ and the Virgin Mary. These Renaissance medallions, evoking biblical history, local history and mythology, contrast sharply with the Gothic statues of the doorways.

Chancel

– The marble facing, the Assumption group above the high altar and the low-relief carvings separating the columns were added in the 18C.

Organ

(5) – The case dates from the 16C.

Vierge du Pilier

(6) – This wooden statue (c. 1510) stood against the rood screen, but has sadly disappeared. The richly clothed Virgin is the object of an annual procession.

Treasury

– Closed to the public. Chapelle St-Piat was built to house the cathedral treasury. It is linked to the east end of the cathedral by a Renaissance staircase.

Chapelle des Martyrs

– This chapel has been refurbished and now contains the **Virgin Mary's Veil**, laid out in a glass-fronted reliquary. Pilgrims used to pray to this veil, calling it a 'Holy Chemise'

Crypt★

Guided tours (30min) Apr–Oct Mon–Sat 11am, 2.15pm, 3.30pm, 4.30pm, (Jun–Sep 5.15pm). 2.70€. 02 37 21 75 02. The entrance is outside the cathedral, on the south side (see plan).

This is France's longest crypt (220m/722ft long). It dates largely from the 11C and features Romanesque groined vaulting. It forms a curious shape; the two long galleries joined by the ambulatory pass under the chancel and the aisles

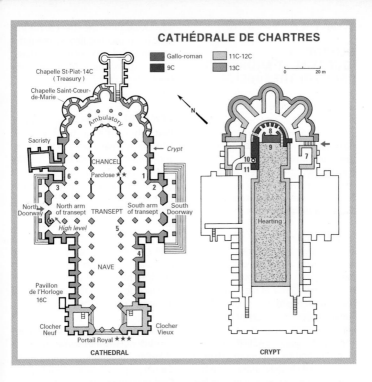

CATHÉDRALE DE CHARTRES

Gallo-roman   11C-12C
9C   13C

0   20 m

Chapelle St-Piat- 14C
(Treasury)

Chapelle Saint-Cœur-
de-Marie

Ambulatory

Sacristy

Crypt

CHANCEL

Parclose ★★

6   1

3   2

North
Doorway

North arm
of transept   TRANSEPT   South arm
of transept   South
Doorway

High level

5

NAVE

4

Pavillon
de l'Horloge
16C

Clocher
Neuf   Clocher
Vieux

Portail Royal ★★★

CATHEDRAL

8

9

10

11

7

Hearting

CRYPT

and give onto seven chapels. The central area, which has been filled in, remains unexplored. Of the seven radiating chapels, only three are Romanesque. The other four were added by the master architect of the Gothic cathedral to serve as foundations for the chancel and the apse of the future building.

St Martin's Chapel (**7**) – Located by the south gallery, this chapel houses the originals of the statues on the Royal Doorway.

▶ A staircase, starting from the ambulatory, leads to a lower crypt.

Crypt St-Lubin (**8**) – This crypt served as the foundations of the 9C church. A thick, circular column with a visible base backs onto a Gallo-Roman wall (**9**), its bond easily recognisable by the alternating bricks and mortar. The crypt was a safe place that protected the cathedral treasures in times of social unrest or natural disaster.

Puits des Saints-Forts (**10**) – The lower part of this 33m/108ft deep shaft has a square section characteristic of Gallo-Roman wells. The coping is contemporary. The name dates back to 858; it is believed that several Christian martyrs from Chartres were murdered during a Norman attack, and their bodies thrown down the well.

Chapelle Notre-Dame-de-Sous-Terre (**11**) – A sacred retreat where pilgrims indulge in fervent praying. Since the 17C the chapel, together with the north gallery of the crypt, has played the part of a miniature church. It originally consisted of a small alcove where the faithful came to venerate the Virgin Mary.

The interior of the chapel and its decoration were refurbished in 1976. On this occasion, the 19C statue of the Virgin Mary was replaced by a more hieratic figure, based on the Romanesque model, enhanced by a Gobelins tapestry.

WALKING TOURS

OLD TOWN★ (QUARTIER ST-ANDRÉ AND BANKS OF THE EURE)

▶ Follow the route on the map.

This pleasant walk leads past the picturesque hilly site, the banks of the River Eure, an ancient district recently restored and the cathedral which is visible from every street corner. In the summer season, a small **tourist train** circles the old town.

Église St-André

This Romanesque church *(deconsecrated)* was the place of worship of one of the most active and densely populated districts in town. Most of the trades were closely related to the river: millers, dyers, curriers, cobblers, tanners, drapers, fullers, tawers, serge makers, etc.

The church was enlarged in the 13C, and in the 16C and 17C it received a chancel and an axial chapel resting on arches that straddled the River Eure and Rue du Massacre.

Unfortunately, both these structures disappeared in 1827, leaving a much less picturesque church.

▶ Cross the Eure by a metal footbridge.

There is a good **view★** of the old humpback bridges. At the foot of the shortened nave of St Andrew's lie the remains of the arch that supported the chancel.

▶ Wander upstream.

The washhouses and races of former mills have been prettily restored. **Rue aux Juifs** leads through an ancient district that has recently been renovated, featuring cobbled streets bordered by gable-ended houses and old-fashioned street lamps.

Rue des Écuyers – This is one of the most successful restoration schemes of the old town. At nos. 17 and 19 the houses have 17C doorways with rusticated surrounds, surmounted by a bull's-eye window. Stroll along the street to rue aux Cois. The corner building is a delightful half-timbered villa, with an overhang in the shape of a prow. Opposite stands Queen Bertha's stair turret, a 16C structure, also half-timbered.

CENTRAL DISTRICT

Place du Cygne has been widened into a little square planted with trees and shrubs *(flower market on Tue, Thu and Sat)* and is at present an oasis of calm in this lively shopping district in the town centre.

At the end of rue du Cygne, on place Marceau, a monument celebrates the memory of the young local general who died at Altenkirchen (1796) at the age of 27. His ashes have been shared among Chartres (funeral urn under the statue on place des Épars), the Panthéon and the Dome Church of the Invalides in Paris.

The 12C and 13C Gothic **Église St-Pierre★** once belonged to the Benedictine abbey of St-Père-en-Vallée. The belfry porch dates from pre-Romanesque times. The **Gothic stained-glass windows★** can be traced back to the late 13C and early 14C, before the widespread introduction of yellow staining.

The oldest stained glass is in the south bays of the chancel, portraying tall, hieratic figures from the Old Testament. **The Monument de Jean Moulin** celebrates the *préfet* (chief administrator) of Chartres during the German invasion of WWII. On 8 June 1940, despite having been tortured, Moulin refused to sign a document claiming that the French troops had committed a series of atrocities. As he was afraid of being unable to withstand further torture, he attempted to commit suicide.

Moulin was dismissed by the Vichy government in November 1940 and, from then on, he planned and coordinated underground resistance efforts, working in collaboration with General de Gaulle who was exiled in England. Arrested in Lyon on 21 June 1943, he was murdered by the Gestapo. From the 12C onwards, the half-timbered barn **Grenier de Loëns**, with treble

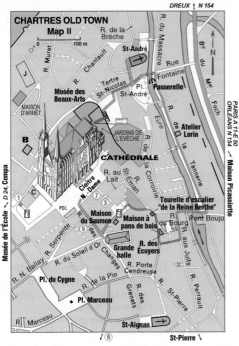

DREUX † N 154

CHARTRES OLD TOWN
Map II

WHERE TO EAT

La Brasserie Bruneau.....⑨
La Vieille Maison...........③
Le Café des Arts............⑤
Le Pichet 3..................①
Le Serpente.................⑦

Centre international
du Vitrail.......................B

gables in the courtyard of the old chapter house was used to store the wine and cereals offered to the clergy as a tithe. Renovated to house the **Centre international du Vitrail** (○Open Mon–Fri 9.30am–12.30pm, 1.30–6pm, Sat 10am–12.30pm, 2.30–6pm, Sun and public holidays 2.30–6pm; ☜6.50€; ♿ ℘02 37 21 65 72; www.centre-vitrail. org), which organises stained-glass exhibitions, the building now features a large hall with beautifully restored roof timbering and a magnificent 12C cellar.

ADDITIONAL SIGHTS
Musée des Beaux-Arts

○Open Mon–Sat 10am–noon, 2–5pm. ○Closed holidays. ☜7€ (ticket combined with the Maison Picassiette 9€). ℘02 37 90 45 80. www.ville-chartres.fr.

The museum is housed in the old bishop's palace and occupies the first terrace of the bishopric's gardens. The large, handsome edifice, which was built over four centuries consists of a 15C section arranged around an interior courtyard,

a 17C and 18C façade, and an early 18C wing overlooking the garden.
The old sacristy, close to the chapel, houses 12 unusually large **enamels**★ representing the Apostles, by Léonard Limousin.
The museum's new rooms house permanent modern art collections as well as temporary exhibitions.

Conservatoire de l'Agriculture

W by D 24. ☛Guided tours (1hr30min). ○Open Tue–Fri 9am–12.30pm, 1.30–6pm, Sat–Sun 10am–12.30pm, 1.30–7pm). ☜3.80€. ♿ ℘02 37 84 15 00. www.lecompa.com.

This museum is located in a converted former railway shed, and houses gleaming old machines and tools.
Tools and machines – Machines are grouped according to function: seeders, binder-harvesters, combine-harvesters.
Land, men and methods – A comparison of two farming concerns in different regions of France, in 1860 and today, provides insight into rural life.
Galerie des inventeurs et des inventions – The gallery introduces the fig-

ures responsible for major agricultural developments over the centuries. The ideas and innovations of Pliny the Elder, Olivier de Serres, Henri de Vilmorin, and Ferguson and the national agricultural research centre (INRA) are explained through information panels.

The tour ends with an exhibition of tractors dating from 1816 to 1954.

Musée de l'École

🕐Open Mon–Fri 10am–noon, 2–5pm; one weekend a month, call for details. 🎫3€. ♿ 🎷02 37 32 62 13.

A classroom of the old teacher training college houses teaching aids and furniture evoking the schools: abacuses, magic lanterns using paraffin, books advocating humanist ethics, etc.

Maison Picassiette

22 r. du Repos. 🕐Open Apr 10am–noon, 2–5pm; May–Jun, Sept 10am–noon, 2–6pm; Jul–Aug 10am–6pm; Oct Sat 10am–noon, 2–6pm, Sun 2–6pm. 🕐Closed holidays. 🎫5.40€ (ticket combined with the musée des Beaux-Arts 7.30€). 🎷02 37 34 10 78. www.ville-chartres.fr.

Built and decorated by Raymond Isidore (1900–64), this house offers an amazing medley of naive art. Isidore transformed the modest lodge by using 4 million pieces of broken dishes and coloured glass, binding them with cement. After visiting the interior, you'll find yourself in the black courtyard, featuring a raised tomb modelled after the Chartres cathedral. The garden, meanwhile, boasts a Jerusalem wall and a breathtaking blue tomb, le Tombeau de l'Esprit.

EXCURSIONS
Église de Meslay-le-Grenet

▶14 km/8.7mi S of Chartres on N 10.

Discovered in 1864 and renovated in 1979, this church boasts a captivating wall painting of the **Danse macabre.** The painting likely dates to the 15C. A confrontation between living and dead begins, on the south wall, with depictions of the Pope and Emperor, and ends on the other side with a child, hermit

and usurer. The upper section recounts the adventure of three sinners shocked into repentance by an encounter with three dead souls. In the chancel, the Passion of the Christ is evoked.

Gallardon

▶20km/12.4mi NE on D 32.
🏛Impasse de la Tour. 🎷02 37 31 11 11.

This pretty medieval town affords a pleasant stroll. A church with a high spire lies near an old twisted tower seeming to defy the laws of gravity.

▶ Turn right before the first bridge to follow the Voise river. You'll soon be privy to a lovely *view*★ of the Gallardon church and the tower.

Take the rue Notre-Dame; to the left lies the residence known as the "Little Louvre" where Louis XIV passed a night. A wooden house boasts 16C decor.

L'épaule de Gallardon – This elegant round tower, 38m/125ft high, dates to the middle of the 12C. Dubbed "the shoulder" (l'épaule) for reasons that are less than clear, It was once part of a fortified chateau and its remparts. The tower was partially destroyed in 1421 on the orders of the future Charles VII, then mined in 1443 by Dunois.

Church – The spire measures 76m/249ft and is best seen from afar. Approach the chevet. The tower with its spire and chancel with flying buttresses combine to produce an effect of lightness. The **chancel**★ attracts the eye for its 12C ambulatory, but above all for its extreme elevation, characteristic of the gothic style under Saint Louis. The wood-panelled vaulting of the nave was painted in 1709 with several striking motifs.

As in many countryside churches with visible woodwork elements, horizontal beams of wood (entraits) and vertical beams (poinçons) are fitted with animal heads of fantastic inspiration. This decor dates to the 15C.

ADDRESSES

🏨 STAY

🛏️🍴🛁🛋️🔔 **Hôtel Le Grand Monarque** – 22 pl. des Épars. ℘02 37 18 15 15. www. bw-grand-monarque.com. ♿🅿️. Wi-fi. 50 rooms. Built in the 16C, this former coaching inn was recommended in the Michelin Guide in 1900! Individually decorated rooms and a lively atmosphere, much like the Madrigal bar.

🛏️🔔 **Ibis Centre Hôtel** – 14 pl. Drouaise. ℘02 37 36 06 36. www.ibishotel.com. ♿🅿️. 82 rooms. Located in the city's historic district, close to the cathedral, this well-maintained hotel enjoys a pleasant restaurant terrace next to the Eure.

🛏️🍴 **La Varenne (Bed and Breakfast)** – 20r. de Tachainville. 28630 Ver-lès-Chartres. 6km/3.7mi S of Chartres on D935 and D114. ℘02 37 26 45 32. www.lavarenne28.free.fr. 🍴. Sited in the middle of the wheat fields, this single-storey renovated home has four simple yet elegant rooms. Heated indoor pool.

🛏️🍴 **Chambre d'hôte Caroline Lethuillier**– 2r. des Prunus in Cherville, 2km/1.25mi W. ℘02 37 31 72 80. www. cherville.com. 🅿️🍴. 4 rooms. Wooden beams and vintage furniture lend cachet to converted farm attic rooms dating to 1800.

🛏️🍴🛁 **La Ferme du Château (Bed and Breakfast)** – À Levesville. 8km/5mi W on D954 then D134. ℘02 37 22 97 02. www. ferme-levesville.com.🍴. Closed 1 Jan and 25 Dec. 3 rooms. This elegant farm offers tastefully decorated, comfortable and extremely quiet rooms. Neighbouring a small château.

🛏️🍴🛁🔔 **Chambre d'hôte Château de Jonvilliers**– 17r. L.-Petit Jonvilliers. 28320 Écrosnes. 4km/2.5mi NE of Gallardon on D32. ℘02 37 31 41 26. www.chateaudejonvilliers. com. Closed 24 Dec–2 Jan. 🅿️. 5 rooms🛏️. 18C mansion house a few kilometres from Gallardon with pretty, well-decorated rooms. Very calm. Copious breakfast.

🍴 EAT

🍴 **Le Grand Cellier**– r. de la Porte-de-Chartres. 28320 Gallardon. ℘02 37 31 40 89. Closed Tue, 3 weeks in Aug and 1 week in winter. Pleasant bar-brasserie serving authentic French dishes.

🍴 **Le Tripot** – 11pl. Jean-Moulin. Entry on r. Collin-d'Harleville. ℘02 37 36 60 11. www. Letripot.monsite-orange.fr. Closed last week Jul, 2 weeks in Aug, 19–26 Dec, Mon, Wed eve and Sun eve. This house built in 1553 once housed a tennis court called 'Le Tripot'. Rustic interior and contemporary cuisine.

🍴🍴 **La Brasserie Bruneau** – 4r. du Mar.-de-Lattre-de-Tassigny. ℘02 37 21 80 99. Closed 1st 2 weeks in Aug, 24 Dec–4 Jan, Sat lunch, Sun and holidays. A 1930s brasserie outside Hôtel de Ville. Traditional dishes; laid-back atmosphere.

🍴🍴 **Le Café des Ats** – 45r. des Changes. ℘02 37 21 07 05. Closed Mon and Sun in winter. This fashionable bar next to the the cathedral enjoys a streamlined decor inspired by the owner's travels to the Saharan desert. Savoury tartine specialities.

🍴🍴 **Le Pichet** – 19r. du Cheval-Blanc. ℘02 37 21 08 35. www.info28.com. Open 10am–7pm. Closed Tue eve and Wed; 25 Dec–1 Jan. Friendly bistro near cathedral. Pleasant decor; French cuisine. Tearoom.

🍴🍴 **Saint-Hilaire** – 11r. du Pont-St-Hilaire. ℘02 37 30 97 57. www.saint.hilaire.ifrance. com. Closed 26 Jul–17 Aug, Sun, Mon, early Nov and Easter holidays♿. 16C house has exposed wooden beams, clay tile floors and traditional French cuisine.

🍴🍴 **Le Serpente** – 2r. du Cloître-Notre-Dame. ℘02 37 21 68 81. www.le-cafe-serpente.com. An impressive collection of 365 teapots to admire to a soundtrack of classical music. Salads, traditional French dishes and a new take-away section.

🍴🍴🛁 **La Vieille Maison** – 5r. au Lait. ℘02 37 34 10 67. www.lavieillemaison.fr. Closed Sun eve and Mon. Exposed stone walls, fireplace and wooden beams afford rustic feel. Traditional French cuisine.

🍴🍴🛁 **Le Commerce** – 18pl. de l'Église. 28320 Gallardon. ℘02 37 31 00 07. Closed 2 weeks in Aug and Mon–Wed eve. This convivial inn houses both a bistrot-style dining room and a formal counterpart.

SHOPPING

Market – Pl. Billard. Near the cathedral. Each Saturday morning, this open-air market abounds with fresh local products.

ACTIVITIES

Atelier Loire– 16r. d'Ouarville. 5km/3.1mi N of Chartres. 28300 Lèves. ℘02 37 21 20 71. www.loire-vitrail.fr. Open Fri 2–5pm, closed in Aug. No charge. An estate in the middle of a pleasant park houses this workshop created in 1946. The art of stained glass is demonstrated.

Domaine de Saint-Jean-de-Beauregard

Hidden away on a vast estate, a third of which is covered by forest, Saint-Jean-de-Beauregard's château, vegetable garden and botanical festival attract thousands of visitors every year. The estate owes its charm to its landscaped garden, stunning panorama, architecture and pigeon house. Visitors enjoy an intriguing insight into the daily lives of the estate's former owners during the 17C and 18C.

VISIT
Château

In 1610, royal attorney François Dupoux purchased the former seigneury of Montfaucon, situated in wooded heights above the vallée de la Salmouille. He began construction of the current château with the two most elevated sections: the central part of the building and two pavilions at the edges date to the reign of Louis XIV. The château derives its name from the high bay windows which open onto a vast panorama. Inside, the reception halls boast elegant 18C furniture, including a lovely old library holding literary and historical tomes.

Vegetable Garden★

The east side of the château has been adorned with a lovely French-style garden offering views from the west side. The domaine de St-Jean-de-Beauregard is perhaps best-known, though, for its 17C vegetable garden, where a variety of quite rare vegetables continue to be cultivated on a plot measuring 2ha/4.9 acres.

Pigeonnier

This 17C pigeon house has some 4 500 pigeon holes and is the region's largest. Admire the imposing wooden structure of the building.

- **Michelin Local Map:** 312: D1
- **Info:** ✆01 60 12 00 01. www.domsaintjean beauregard.com.
- **Location:** 32km/20mi from Paris along A 10. RER B, Orsay station, then taxi or bus to "centre commercial Ulis 2". 1km/0.6mi walk to reach the estate.
- **Timing:** Allow a half-day.
- **Kids:** The 17C vegetable garden is fun.

EXCURSION
Briis-sous-Forges

10km/6.2mi S of Saint-Jean-de-Beauregard on D 35 to Gometz-la-Ville, then take D 131.

This formerly fortified village lies in the Prédecelles valley, south of the Chevreuse valley. The town's name probably comes from celtic terms meaning "clay of the earth" or "rich earth": this is indeed a fertile region whose agricultural heritage has not disappeared.

Church – The square-shaped bell tower dates to the 12C. Featuring 12 gables pointing to the cardinal directions, the tower measures 39m/128ft.

Beneath the bell tower is a beautiful Romanesque chapel; the chancel features quarter-sphere vaulting and the right-side beams have overlapping vaulting.

Keep – *Private property.* This is the only remaining vestige of the fortified château that once stood here.

Its walls are 3m/9.8ft thick at the base. The keep is topped by four sentinels adorned with conical roofs.

Vieille Bourse, Place du Général-de-Gaulle, with the bell tower in background, Lille
© Clément Philippe/agefotostock

France's fourth largest metropolitan area, covering 85 towns and villages, and home to 1.1 million people, Lille Métropole combines big city status with small town convenience. Linked by a ruthlessly efficient metro, tram and bus network, this agglomeration of hip neighbourhoods, river harbours and rural hamlets is a day-tripper's dream: you can breakfast in a barge, explore the biggest fine art collection outside Paris, have lunch overlooking the plain of Flanders, explore an eco-farm and be back in Lille in time for a plate of mussels and a concert by a professional orchestra. Although there's every reason to stay much longer, of course: its restored neo-Baroque belfries, brick-and-stone Flemish houses, Renaissance churches, citadels and forts regularly form the backdrop to traditional festivals and parades, while its museums explore everything from the forests that carpeted the region 300 million years ago to Charles de Gaulle's christening robe. Add a dynamic arts scene and retail credentials and you've got a metropolis that's as fascinating and varied as Paris with all the practicality of a young and compact city.

Highlights

1 Visit Lille in a **vintage 2CV** (p348)

2 Buy **designer clothes** in Roubaix (p349)

3 Climb a **bell tower** in Tourcoing (p350)

4 **Picnic** next to a Picasso in Villeneuve d'Ascq (p351)

5 Explore a **19C fort** in Seclin (p355)

Quick Links

Stepping off the train and into the glass-and-steel bubble of Lille-Europe station, it's hard not to feel that Lille Métropole has the future firmly in its sights. Plugged into the transcontinental high-speed rail network, Lille Métropole is a European live wire: as close to London and Brussels as it is to Paris, you're almost as likely to bump into a Brit, Belgian or a Dutchman in its cobbled streets as you are a Frenchman. Open, accessible and on the move, it's little wonder that Lille Métropole is now France's youngest urban area, with 42 percent of the population below the age of 25. Attracted by affordable rents and reasonable transport costs (including the world's first fully automatic metro system), 100 000 students, three universities and several high-tech industries have now made Lille Métropole their home.

Capital of Culture 2004

The city even out-partied Paris during its year as European Capital of Culture in 2004. Attracting 9 million visitors and organising a staggering 2,000 different exhibitions and performances in venues spanning everything from a renovated early-20C opera house to an abandoned postal sorting centre, Lille 2004 set the trend for the region's artistic revival. Its gifted offspring, Lille 3000, holds countless exhibitions, happenings and digital arts festivals, while the region's permanent art centres have nothing to envy their counterparts in Paris or London: just stand in the vast white atrium of Lille's fine arts museum or next to the poolside statues in La Piscine, a former swimming baths for textile workers in Roubaix, now an acclaimed arts and industry museum, to get a feel for how Lille Métropole is using culture to reinvent its future.

Even Lille Métropole's architectural heritage is looking bright-eyed and bushy-tailed. From the 15C Hospice Comtesse and the 17C Flemish townhouses of Old Lille to the renovated belfry of Roubaix and the magnificent bells of Tourcoing, all of the region's major historic buildings have now been restored, including many in private hands, as a visit to the family-run Fort de Seclin or a stay in a converted barn or mill go to prove. Some things, on the other hand, never change. No town or neighbourhood is without its own centuries-old festival or *ducasse*, ranging from ladle tossing

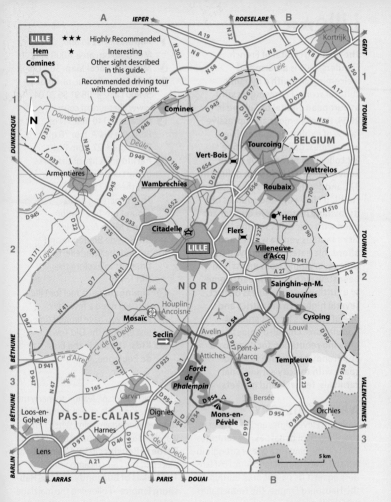

in Roubaix to the parading of the giants Phinaert and Lydéric, Lille's legendary founders, through the city's streets. Even the Grande Braderie, Europe's biggest flea market, would not be complete without the traditional mussels festival when restaurant owners compete to build the highest pile of empty mussel shells, with a little help from their hungry customers.

Rural Heritage

Lille Métropole has also remained close to its rural roots: the Flemish landscape is dotted with experimental farms, distilleries, organic producers, windmills and rural museums where you can explore the ingenuity of farming folk. Even if you're planning on staying in town, you're never far from a garden, park or square, such as the Bois de Boulogne that circles the citadel in Lille and the sculpture park at the LaM, where you can picnic next to a Picasso.

But Lille Métropole's rising star has to be its shopping scene. Whether you prefer the luxury brands lining the alleyways of Lille's Old Town, the design workshops run by stylists in the Faubourg des Modes, the chain stores of rue de Béthune – France's third busiest shopping street – or the outlet stores of Roubaix, Lille Métropole has something to satisfy the most ardent of retail enthusiasts.

Lille★★★

The bustling capital of French Flanders, Lille is a warm and welcoming city with a dynamic cultural scene. Following its stint as European Capital of Culture in 2004, the city enjoys an impressive range of exhibition spaces, live arts venues, galleries and a fine art collection second only to the Louvre in Paris. Lined with delightful 17C and 18C Flemish houses, the cobbled alleyways and squares of its lovingly restored old quarter are filled with chic cafés serving the city's famous vanilla waffles and affordable eateries where you can order everything from mussels to beer stew with gingerbread. Home to a cutting-edge business district, several high-tech industries and one of France's largest student populations, Lille also enjoys a growing reputation for its relaxed and trendy bars which jostle for space with the city's traditional carnivals, festivals and markets.

▶ **Population:** 226 800; Metropolitan area 1 000 900

Michelin Local Map: 302: G4.

Info: Palais Rihour, pl. Rihour, 59000 Lille. ✆08 91 56 20 04. www.lilletourism.com.

Location: 140 miles N of Paris, via the A 1, or 70 miles W via the A 27 from Brussels.

Parking: Plenty of car parks in the centre of the city, but these fill up early. Try the parking areas around the TGV station.

Don't Miss: A walk in the Bois de Boulogne and around the Citadelle; take time out to explore the Old Town.

Timing: To get a feel for Lille you will need a few days here. If you have limited time, just explore the Old Town.

Kids: The zoo in the Bois de Boulogne.

A BIT OF HISTORY

Besieged eleven times and ruled over by countless rival dynasties, for centuries Lille was the pawn in a power struggle in which France fought for control of Flanders against its neighbours Burgundy, the Habsburg Empire, the Netherlands and England.

The Counts of Flanders – The name "l'Isle" (pronounced "lille"), meaning "island" in French, is first mentioned in a charter of 1066, in which Baudoin V, Count of Flanders, who owned a château on an island on the River Deûle, founded the collegiate church of St Peter (*Collégiale St-Pierre*). A town soon sprang up around the château and its busy river port, now the av. du Peuple-Belge. As the town grew and the marshland on which it stood dried up, the port was gradually transferred to its current location. On the death of the Count of Flanders, Baudoin IX, in 1205, King Philippe Auguste of France tightened his grip over Flanders by forcing Baudoin's 5-year old successor, Jeanne, to marry the son of the King of Portugal, Ferrand, who soon rebelled against him. When Ferrand was defeated by Philippe Auguste at the **Battle of Bouvines** in 1214, Flanders was placed in the French camp.

The Dukes of Burgundy and the Habsburg Empire – Following the marriage of Marguerite of Flanders to Philip the Bold in 1369, Flanders became part of the Duchy of Burgundy. **Philip the Good** (1419–67) had Rihour Palace built, where he was surrounded by a court that included the painter **Van Eyck**. The marriage of Mary of Burgundy, daughter of Charles the Bold, to Maximilian of Austria in 1477 brought the Duchy of Burgundy, including Flanders, under Habsburg control; it later became Spanish territory when Charles V of Spain became the Habsburg Emperor. Following the Wars of Religion (1562–1598), gangs of peasants devastated the countryside and sacked the churches. Lille escaped the assault of the "Howlers" (*Hurlus*) thanks only to the inhabitants' energetic defence, led by the innkeeper **Jeanne Maillotte**.

Lille becomes French – Following his marriage to Maria-Theresa of Spain in 1663, Louis XIV laid claim to his wife's inheritance in the Low Countries. In 1667 he personally directed the siege of Lille and triumphantly entered the city after just nine days of resistance, after which Lille became the capital of the Northern Provinces. The Sun King hastened to have a citadel built by Vauban to consolidate his hold on the town. Lille was taken by the Dutch during the War of the Spanish Succession (1701–1714) and only became French permanently in 1713 after the signing of the Treaty of Utrecht.

Lille under Siege – In **September 1792**, 35 000 Austrians laid siege to Lille which was defended by a small garrison. Cannonballs rained down on the town and many buildings were destroyed; nevertheless, the courageous inhabitants held on and the Austrians eventually raised the siege.

In early **October 1914**, when six Bavarian regiments tried to breach the city's fortifications, Lille was obliged to submit after three days of bloody resistance in which 900 buildings were destroyed. Prince Ruprecht of Bavaria, receiving the surrender, refused the sword of Captain de Pardieu "in recognition of the heroism of the French troops."

In **May 1940**, seven Nazi divisions and Rommel's armoured tanks attacked Lille. 40 000 French soldiers held the city for three days before surrendering with military honours on June 1.

Traditional economy – During the Middle Ages Lille was famous for its cloth-making; high-warp weavers forced out of Arras by Louis XIV later established their tapestry workshops in the city.

Lille devoted itself to cotton and linen milling in the 18C, whereas nearby Roubaix and Tourcoing specialised in wool. Large-scale industry came to Lille at the end of the 18C, creating an impoverished urban proletariat: by 1846 the rate of infant mortality in the slums of St-Sauveur had reached 75 percent and the cellars where workers laboured achieved a notoriety which Victor Hugo evoked in tragic verse.

Another of Lille's specialities was the milling of linseed, rapeseed and poppyseed to produce oil. Last but not least, the town was famous for the production of lace and ceramics.

VISIT
Palais des Beaux-Arts★★★

🕐*Open Mon 2–6pm & Wed–Sun 10am–6pm.* 🕐*Closed 1 Jan, 1 May, 14 July, first weekend in Sept, 1 Nov, 25 Dec.* ✆*6.50€.* ♿ ☎*03 20 06 78 00. www.pba-lille.fr.*

This Neoclassical art museum was designed by architects Bérard and Delmas in 1892.

A narrow building 70m/228ft long and 6.5m/19.5ft wide was added to the rear in 1997. It contains the café and restaurant on the ground floor. Between the two buildings is the garden.

The middle section has been given a glass surface that lets light into the temporary exhibition halls below. The vast entrance hall extending the whole length of the façade is lit by two large coloured-glass chandeliers by Gaetano Pesce. There is free access to the atrium where the bookshop, tearoom and café-restaurant are located (*garden entrance in rue de Valmy*).

Basement
Archaeology – Works from the Mediterranean basin: Egypt, Cyprus, Rome and Greece. Don't miss the child's sarcophagus and skyphos drinking vase.

Middle Ages and Renaissance – Start with the chased-bronze Lille incense-burner (12C Mosan art) in the centre of the first room and the selection of ivory artefacts from abbeys in northern France such as the *Old Man of the Apocalypse*. Gothic art is particularly well-represented, including the most beautiful Donatello bas-relief in France, the *Feast of Herod*. Two wings of a 15C triptych by Dirk Bouts offer an explicit vision of heaven and hell.

Relief maps★ – Commissioned by Louis XIV for his military strategists, these scale models of 15 towns on France's northern borders are so detailed they even show carrots growing in a garden.

Ground floor
Ceramics – A superb collection of 18C faience from Lille, Nevers, Strasbourg, Delft and Rouen, as well as German and Walloon sandstone exhibits and 18C porcelain from China and Japan.

Sculpture – The collection provides an overview of 19C French sculpture, with works by Frémiet (*The Knight Errant*), Houdon (bust of *Le Fèvre de Caumartin*), David d'Angers (models for the Gutenberg memorial in Strasbourg), Camille Claudel (*Giganti, Mme de Massary*) and Bourdelle (*Penelope*, c. 1909).

First floor
The collections are displayed around the atrium by period, style and theme.

16C–17C Flemish School – The canvases by Jordaens explore religious (*The Temptation of Mary Magdalene*) mythological (*The Abduction of Europa*) and rustic (*The Huntsman*) themes; his study of cows was later taken up by Van Gogh. Don't miss Rubens' masterpiece *The Descent from the Cross.*

17C Dutch School – The finest collection outside Paris. Don't miss the genre scene by De Witte (*Nieuwe Kerk in Delft*), a landscape by Ruysdael (*The Wheat Field*) and still-life paintings by Van der Ast and Van Beyeren.

17C French School – Works by Charles de la Fosse (*The Keys to Paradise Are Given to St Peter*), Le Sueur, Philippe de Champaigne (*Nativity*), La Hyre (*Pastoral Landscape*) and Largillière (*Jean-Baptiste Forest*).

18C to 19C French School An extensive area is given over to Boilly (1761–1845), born at La Bassée near Lille. After his racy style was condemned as obscene by the revolutionary authorities, he produced a number of patriotic paintings including *Marat's Triumph*. Don't miss the charming paintings by Louis Watteau (*View of Lille*), who adopted Lille as his home. Other painters include David, Delacroix, and the symbolist Puvis de Chavannes (*Le Sommeil*).

Italian and Spanish Schools – Italy is represented by Liss' *Moses Saved from the Waters*, Tintoretto's *Portrait of a Senator* and a Veronese sketch, *Heaven*. Although small in number, the Spanish collection is of a rare quality: two **works★** by **Goya**, *Time or The Old Women* and *The Letter or The Young People*, reveal the cruel and kind satirist at his best, while El Greco's *St Francis Praying* is filled with spiritual intensity.

Impressionists – The end of the 19C is represented by works from the **Masson Bequest**. Covering pre-Impressionism and Impressionism, the collection starts with Boudin (*The Port of Camaret*) and Jongkind (*The Skaters*) before exploring, Renoir (*Young Woman in a Black Hat*) and Monet (*The Disaster, The Houses of Parliament*). Vuillard and several Rodin sculptures complete the collection.

Modern Artists – Figurative and abstract works by Léger (*Women With a Blue Vase*), Sonia Delaunay (*Colour Rhythm 1076*) and Picasso (*Portrait of Olga, 1923*).

Drawings – One of the largest collections in France (about 4 000 works), shown on a rotating basis as temporary exhibitions.

Cathédrale Notre-Dame★
Place Gilleson ◷*Open 10am–6.30pm.*
The **bronze door★★** of this neo-Gothic cathedral is the last work of Georges Jeanclos (died 1997).

🐾 WALKING TOURS

OLD LILLE★★ *3hr.*
The regeneration of Old Lille began in the 1970s when a handful of architecture enthusiasts decided to restore the 17C and 18C façades, revealing the wealth of Lille's architectural past.

Place Rihour
The main building on this square is the **Palais Rihour** (◷*open Mon–Sat 9am–6pm, Sun & holidays 10am–noon, 2–5pm; ⊶no charge; ☎08 91 56 20 04. www.lilletourism.com*), now home to the tourist office. This Gothic palace was built between 1454 and 1473 by Philip the Good, Duke of Burgundy.

The façade features mullioned windows and a graceful octagonal brick turret. The groundfloor guard-room has tall, pointed arches. Upstairs, the Conclave Room and the Duke's private chapel are reached by an elegant stone staircase.

Place du Général-de-Gaulle★

As you head towards the Place du Général-de-Gaulle, admire the 17C houses combining Flemish and French styles on the left. The Grand'Place served as marketplace in the Middle Ages. The **Grand' Garde** (1717) once housed the king's guard. Don't miss the triangular pediment decorated with the Sun King's symbol, a stamp of royal authority on the recently captured town. The **Colonne de la Déesse** (1845) recalls the city's resistance during the 1792 siege.

Vieille Bourse★★

Built in 1653 by Julien Destrée to provide the tradesmen of Lille with an exchange to rival those of the Low Countries, this masterpiece consists of 24 mansard-roofed houses around a courtyard. A wood sculptor, Destrée added a profusion of decoration. The caryatids and telamones, garlands and masks above the outer windows, and fruit and flowers on the inner court are reminiscent of a Flemish chest. The arcades house bronze busts, medallions and tablets honouring scientific achievement.

Place du Théâtre

The square is dominated by the Nouvelle Bourse with its neo-Flemish bell tower and the Louis XVI Opera (1923). Opposite the Nouvelle Bourse stands the "**Rang de Beauregard**" (1687). A terrace of houses adorned with pilasters and cartouches.

Rue de la Bourse

Note the cherubs and masks decorating the 17C houses lining this street.

Rue de la Grande-Chaussée

Many of these renovated arcaded sandstone houses have intricately worked window lintels. Don't miss nos. 9, 23 (ship on the window keystone) and 29.

Lille Style

The **Lille style** is a particular mix of bricks and carved stone. Façades decorated with quarry stones shaped into lozenges (place Louise-de-Bettignies) first appeared in the early 17C, followed by the Flemish Renaissance (Vieille Bourse, the Maison de Gilles de la Boé) when ornamentation reached its peak. By the late 17C the French influence began to be felt in the decoration of houses and their alignment in rows. Ground floors consist of arcades in close-grained sandstone that prevents humidity reaching the upper floors.

Rue des Chats-Bossus

The street acquired its curious name ("Street of the Humpback Cats") from an old tanner's sign. **L'Huîtrière** has a typical Art-Deco front dating from 1928.

Place du Lion-d'Or

Head for no. 15, the "House of the Fishmongers", which dates from the 18C.

Place Louise-de-Bettignies

The square bears the name of a World War I heroine. Decorated with cornices and prominent pediments, the **Demeure de Gilles de la Boé★** (1636) at no. 29 is an example of Flemish Baroque. This building once stood on the busy Basse-Deûle river port.

Rue de la Monnaie★

Named after the Mint that once stood here, this street is lined with 18C houses. Note the apothecary's shop sign at no. 3 and the statue of Notre-Dame-de-la-Treille on the façade of no. 10. The neighbouring early 17C houses include the Hospice Comtesse.

▶ Take the passageway opposite the Hospice Comtesse. Take the Cours à l'Eau to the right of the cathedral to the Place aux Oignons.

Weavers used to work in the poorly lit basements of these 17C and 18C houses, protected by simple wooden shutters.

WHERE TO STAY

WHERE TO EAT

STREET INDEX

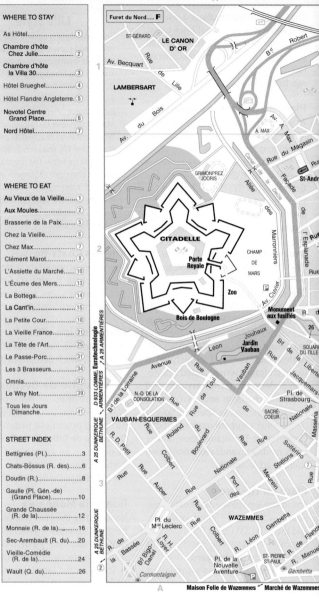

Maison Folie de Wazemmes — Marché de Wazemmes

◗ Take rue au Péterinck, turn left into rue de la Monnaie. Continue along rue de la Collégiale, then left onto rue Négrier.

Rue Royale

Built between the citadel and the old town in the 18C, this street is lined with French-style mansions. No. 68 is the for- mer Hôtel de l'Intendance, built in 1787 by Lequeux.

Rue Esquermoise

This street is lined with 17C and 18C houses. At nos. 6 and 4 cherubs are shown embracing or turning their backs on each other. Opposite is a restored house that belonged to a furrier (Gailliaerde).

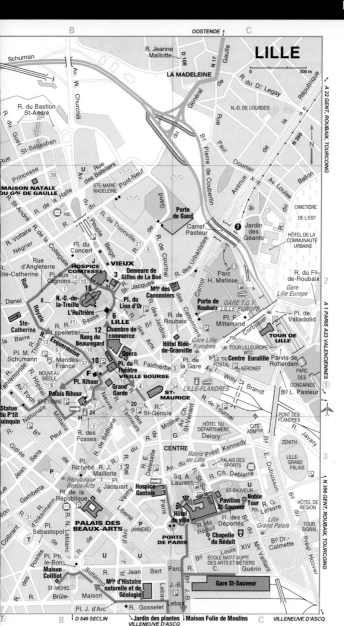

Statue du P'tit-Quinquin

Sq. Foch, r. Nationale. A tribute to *P'tit Quinquin*, a lullaby composed by Alexandre Desrousseaux in 1853, about a lacemaker singing her child to sleep.

QUARTIER ST-SAUVEUR

Allow 1hr 30min.

Now a smart business district, this former working-class slum inspired the author of the lullaby *Le P'tit Quinquin*, Emile Desrousseaux.

Hospice Gantois★

Line2 Mairie-de-Lille. 224 r. de Paris. ♿
☏ *03 20 85 30 30.* 🚶‍♂️ *Guided tour Tue 2pm.* ⊘ *No charge.*

Founded in 1462 by Jean Gantois, this hospice is now a prestigious hotel. Beneath an imposing 15C gable flanked by 17C buildings *(r. de Paris)*, the elaborately carved Flemish doorway (1664) opens onto the hospital ward with its 15C fresco. The spacious 17C chapel leads to a series of inner courtyards.

Porte de Paris★

Built by Simon Vollant in honour of Louis XIV, this is the only example of a town gate (1685–1692) which also served as a triumphal arch. Decorated with the arms of Lille (a lily) and France (three lilies) surmounted by Victory preparing to crown the Sun King on the outside, the inside forms a simple lodge.

Hôtel de Ville

Line 2 Mairie-de-Lille.
The belfry of the town hall (1924–1927) is 104m/341ft high (Open 10am–1pm, 2–6pm, 5pm in winter, closed Mon; 6€; audioguide in English). The giants of Lille, Lydéric and Phinaert, are sculpted at its base.

Pavillon St-Sauveur

The remaining wing of an 18C cloister, these brick and stone arches are topped by clerestory windows.

Noble Tour

This keep with its truncated appearance is the only relic of the 15C fortifications.

Chapelle du Réduit

This chapel with a Louis XIV façade bearing the arms of France and Navarre is all that remains of the Fort du Réduit, built to intimidate the rebellious locals.

Gare Saint-Sauveur

Line 2 Lille-Grand-Palais. Bd. Jean-Baptiste-Lebas. Open Mar–Oct Wed–Sun 2–7pm. No charge. 03 20 31 30 00. www.mairie-lille.fr.
Run by "Lille 3000", this former station has been turned into an events venue with a screening room, concert hall and temporary exhibition spaces.

Parc Jean-Baptiste Lebas

Bd. Jean-Baptiste Lebas. Open Apr–Sept 7.30am–10pm; Oct–Mar: 7.30am–9pm.
Renovated by Rotterdam landscapers West 8, this 3ha/7acre children's park has a mini-climbing wall and belfry.

Maison Folie de Moulins

47–49 r. d'Arras. Open Wed–Fri 2–7pm. 03 20 95 08 82. www.mfmoulins-lille.fr.
A "Lille 2004" venue, this former 19C brewery hosts shows, temporary exhibitions, workshops and concerts.

Natural History and Geology Museum

19 r. de Bruxelles. 03 28 55 30 80. Open Mon, Wed–Fri 9am–noon, 2–5pm, Sun 10am–5pm. No charge 1st Sun in the month.
After sizing up the whale skeletons in the entrance, move on to the **zoology** collection on the left, where stuffed mammals, reptiles and fish await you. The **geology** section features 100 000 fossils, minerals and rocks. Don't miss the plant fossils from forests that carpeted the region 300 million years ago.

Maison Coilliot

14 r. de Fleurus (not open to the public).
Built in 1898 by Hector Guimard, architect of the Paris metro, for Mr. Coilliot, a Lille ceramist, this Art nouveau masterpiece is decorated with porceliron.

Jardin des plantes

From bd. J.-B.-Lebas, take r. de Douai, r. A.-Carrel after bd. des Défenseurs-de-Lille. R. du Jardin-des-Plantes. Open Apr–Sept 8am–9pm; Oct–Mar 8am–6.30pm. No charge. 03 20 52 06 83.
This glass-and-concrete hothouse set in 12ha/30 acres of lawns, trees and flowers is home to tropical flora.

ADDITIONAL SIGHTS
East of the Town Centre
Euralille

Just outside Lille city centre is a new 70ha/173-acre urban district designed by Dutch architect Rem Koolhaas.

Since May 1993, Lille's railway station, renamed **Lille-Flandres**, has served the bulk of high-speed trains from Paris, while the new **Lille-Europe** station, recognisable by its huge glass frontage, was built for the Paris/Brussels-London routes and the high-speed train services between Lille and Lyon, Bordeaux, Nice, etc. Two towers span the new stations, the **Tour Lille-Europe WTC** by Claude Vasconi and the L-shaped **Tour du Crédit Lyonnais★** by Christian de Portzampac. The **Centre Euralille** was designed by Jean Nouvel. Its spacious walkways serve more than 130 shops, a cultural centre, a theatre and apartments.

Don't miss Japanese artist Yayoi Kusama's Tulips of Shangri-La on the esplanade.

Le Tri postal

Av. Willy-Brandt. Line 1 or 2 Gare-Lille-Flandres. ℘*0320 14 4760.*
A live performance and contemporary art venue, this former postal sorting office was turned into an exhibition and festival space during "Lille 2004".

Euralille II

La maison de l'architecture has put together an audio guide to the area. Available Mon–Fri 10am–4pm, Sat 11am–4.30pm. Identity card or deposit required. Contact www.mav-npdc.com.
If you're keen on contemporary architecture, don't miss Gilles Neveu's new regional government offices, the Hôtel de Région, and Signal Tower, the city's "third belfry" on the new 22ha/54 acre extension to the Euralille site.

Porte de Roubaix

Part of the 1621 Spanish fortifications, this gate has a sandstone base topped by a dripstone and a brick layer. It was enlarged to accommodate the tramway in 1875. A similar gate, the **Porte de Gand**, lies 600m/656yd to the north, via rue des Canonniers and rue de Courtrai.

The Wazemmes district

A great place to head on a Sunday morning, the Wazemmes outdoor market *(pl. de la Nouvelle Aventure, Line 1 Gambetta;* Open Tue, Thu, Sun 7am–2pm*)* and covered market *(Tue–Sun)*sell everything from satsumas to second-hand curios. The **Maison Folie★** *(70 r. des Sarrazins, Line 1 Wazemmes;* open Wed–Sat 2–7pm, Sun 10am–7pm)* hosts workshops, exhibitions and shows.
Don't miss the Oriental steam room in the brick-vaulted basement.

Hospice Comtesse★

Open Mon 2–6pm, Wed – Sun 10am–12.30pm & 2–6pm. 3.50€ *(no charge first Sun in month).* ℘*03 28 36 84 00.*
Founded by Jeanne, Countess of Flanders in 1237 and rebuilt extensively from 1470 to 1724, the hospice reveals 300 years of building techniques Lille. The **hospital ward** and its high-panelled timber **vault★★** reflect the medieval belief that open spaces reduced the spread of disease. The **chapel** gives onto the ward so that bedridden patients could celebrate mass. The **museum** offers an insight into daily life in a 17C Flemish religious establishment.

Maison Natale du Général de Gaulle

9 r. Princesse. Open Sept–Jun Wed–Sat, 10am–noon, 2–5pm, Sun 1.30–5pm (Jul–Aug Wed–Sun). Audio guide in English 6€. ℘*03 28 38 12 05. www.charles-de-gaulle.org.*
Charles de Gaulle was born on 22 November 1890 in this whitewashed brick house where his grandfather had a lace works. Memorabilia includes De Gaulle's christening robe.

Citadelle★ (Citadel)

The citadel is occupied by the military. Open 1st and 3rd Fri of the month 3pm and 5pm. 7€. ℘*08 91 56 20 04.*
Designed by Vauban (1667–70), this is the largest citadel in France. It took three years to build its five bastions and five demi-lune fortifications. The **Bois de Boulogne** has a small **zoo** and playground (open daily Apr–Oct 9am–

6pm, Nov–Mar 10am–5pm; ✆no charge; &03 28 52 07 00). Patriots executed during WWI are commemorated on the **Monument aux Fusillés** (1915).

Musée des Canonniers

🕐*Open Mon–Sat 2–5pm.* 🕐*Closed public holidays, mid-Dec to mid-Feb.* ✆5€. &03 20 55 58 90.
Museum exploring the sieges of Lille.

EXCURSIONS
Mosaïc - Jardin des cultures in Houplin-Ancoisne

▶️*7km/4mi to the S via D 147 then D 63 on the right.* 🕐*Open Apr–May, Sept–Oct 10am–6pm Wed–Sat, Sun 10am–7pm; Jun–Aug Mon–Sat 10am–7pm, Sun 10am–8pm.* ✆5€ Mon–Sat, 6€ Sun. ♿&03 20 63 11 24.
33ha/81-acre park with gardens from around the world. Play areas galore. 🚤*Garden tours by boat in summer.*

Wambrechies★

▶️*7km/4mi N of Lille via the NW bypass, exit 9 or 10. Bus routes 3/9.* 🄸*2 pl. Gén-de-Gaulle. 59118 Wambrechies.* &03 28 38 84 21. *www.valdedeule-tourisme.fr.*
Perched on the banks of the Deûle canal, this town has an elegant Grand'Place and neo-Renaissance Flemish brick town hall (1868).

Muséé de la poupée et du Jouet ancien★ – ♿🕐*Open Wed, Sun and public holidays 2–6pm; school holidays (ex. Jul-Aug) 2–6pm.* ✆4€ *(child 2€).* &03 20 39 69 28. Discover a vast collection of toys from 19C lead soldiers to Barbie dolls in the late-18C Château de Robertsart.

Distillerie Claeyssens – *1r. de la Distillerie. 59118 Wambrechies. Via town centre and pl. de L'Église close to the canal.* 🕐*10am–noon, 2–4pm.* ✆6€ *with tasting sessions.* &0320149191. *www.wambrechies.com.* Visit one of the last juniper berry distilleries in France.

ADDRESSES

🏠STAY

🛏 **As Hôtel** – *98 r. Louis-Braille. 59790 Ronchin. 3km/2mi SE Lille via m/way*

heading towards Paris, exit 1 Ronchin. &03 20 53 05 05. *www.ashotel.com.* ♿🄿 *62 rooms.* ⊒*8€.* This contemporary hotel offers functional, comfortable rooms and a pleasant dining room. A convenient stopover just off the A1 motorway.

🛏 **Chez Julie** – *8 r. de Radinghem, 59134 Beaucamps-Ligny. 12km/7mi to the W of Lille via A 25, exit 7 and D 62 rte du Radinghem.* &03 20 50 33 82. *www.chezjulie.fr.* 🄿🍴. *3 rooms.* ⊒. This homely red-brick smallholding on the edge of a village near Lille boasts well-maintained bedrooms.

🛏🛏 **Nord Hôtel** – *48 r. du Fg-d'Arras.* &0320535340. *www.nord-hotel.com.* 🄿 *80 rooms.* ⊒*8€.* Conveniently located near the Porte d'Arras metro station and easily accessible from the road. Modern, spacious rooms.

🛏🛏 **Hôtel Flandre Angleterre** – *13 pl. de la Gare.* &0320060412. *www.hotel-flandreangleterre-lille.com. 44 rooms.* ⊒*8€.* Situated opposite the train station and near the pedestrian streets, this family-run hotel presents modern rooms that are comfortable and cosy.

🛏🛏 **Hôtel Novotel Centre Grand Place** – *116 r. de L'Hôpital-Militaire.* &03 28 38 53 53. *www.novotel.com.* Wi-fi. *104 rooms.* ⊒*15€.* This renovated hotel boasts spacious, contemporary rooms with modern bathrooms.

🛏🛏 **Chambre d'hôte la Villa 30** – *24 r. du Plat.* &03 66 73 61 30. *www.lavilla30.fr.* Wi-fi. *4 rooms.* ⊒*15€.* Stylish Art Deco house close to the old town and fine arts museum. Excellent value for money.

🛏🛏 **Hôtel Brueghel** – *Parvis St-Maurice.* &03 20 06 0669. *www.hotel-brueghel.com.* Wi-fi. *65 rooms.* ⊒*8.50€.* This Flemish-style house near the train station marries bygone charm with modern facilities.

🍽 EAT

🍴 **Aux Moules** – *34 r. de Béthune.* &03 20 57 12 46. *Closed 1 Jan, 24–25, 31 Dec.* ♿. Steamed mussels and other Flemish specialities await customers in this 1930s style brasserie set in a lively pedestrian street.

🍴 **La Cant'in** – *36 r. St-Nicolas.* &06 34 63 79 39. *Closed eve., Sun, Aug.* Seasonal, simple dishes. All produce locally sourced.

🍴 **Omnia** – *9 r. Esquermoise.* &03 20 57 55 66. *http://omnia-restaurant.com. Closed 24, 25 Dec.* ♿. Successively a cabaret, brothel, movie theatre and microbrewery, this Baroque-Rococo bar and restaurant serves traditional fare.

🍽 **Brasserie de la Paix** – *25 pl. Rihour. 03 20 54 70 41. Closed Sun.* This friendly brasserie kitted out with banquettes and Desvres earthenware serves bistro cuisine.

🍽 **Les 3 Brasseurs** – *22 pl. de la Gare- 03 20 06 46 25. www.les3brasseurs.com. closed 24 Dec (eve) and 25 Dec.* &. The pungent scent of hops greets visitors to this brasserie. Sample one or four kinds of beer from the tuns.

🍽 **La Petite Cour** – *7r. du Curé-Saint-Étienne. 03 20 51 52 81.* A covered courtyard and chic terrace with a vintage vibe. Generous, hearty portions.

🍽 **Tous les Jours Dimanche** – *13r. Bartholomé-Masurel. 03 28 36 05 92. Noon–6.30pm. Closed Sun and Mon (Oct–Apr) eve.* Bohemian chic. Lunch menus prepared using fresh produce, a wide selection of teas and the best brunch in town!

🍽 **La Bottega** – *8 r. Péterinck. 03 20 21 16 85. www.la-bottega.com. Until 10pm. Closed Sun eve and Mon.* Italian restaurant serving up perfect pizzas and white pasta (piles of mozzarella, no tomato sauce). Italian deli opposite.

🍽 **Chez Max** – *164 r. de Solferino. 03 20 77 59 86. Closed Sun and Mon.* Spare a thought for Max as he shuttles up and down the stairs in this new eatery serving traditional cuisine.

🍽 **La Vieille France** – *51 r. de Gand. 03 20 31 00 57. Closed Tues & Wed lunch.* Old school regional dishes chalked up on a blackboard and served on chequered tablecloths.

🍽 **Chez la Vieille** – *60 r. de Gand. 03 28 36 40 06. Closed Aug, 24 Dec– 2 Jan, Sun and Mon.* Step back in time in this friendly Flemish estaminet favoured by locals for its authentic local cuisine.

🍽🍽 **L'Assiette du Marché** – *61 r. de la Monnaie, 59000 Lille. 03 20 06 83 61. www.assiettedumarche.com. Closed 2–24 Aug, Sun (contact for details).* &. Contemporary decor and a large skylight over the inner courtyard complements the 18C architecture of this former treasury mint. Seasonal dishes.

🍽🍽 **La Tête de l'Art** – *10 r. de l'Arc. 03 20 54 68 89. www.latetedelart-lille. com. Closed Mon, Tue & Sun eves.* Behind the pink façade of this 1890 house hides a cosy dining room serving traditional cuisine.

🍽🍽 **Le Passe-Porc** – *155 r. de Solferino. 03 20 42 83 93. Closed 3 wks in Aug, Sun and eve (ex. Fri).* &.The enamelled wall plaques act as the backdrop for a vast collection of pigs. Plentiful fare.

🍽🍽 **Le Why Not** – *9 r.Maracci. 03 20 74 14 14. www.lewhynot-restaurant.fr. Closed 1–6 Jan, 28 Jul–Aug, Sat lunch, Sun and Mon.* The trendy vibe of this relaxed eatery in Old Lille matches the cutting-edge cuisine prepared by its globe-trotting chef.

🍽🍽 **L'Ecume des Mers** – *10 r. du Pas. 03 20 54 95 40. www.ecume-des-mers. com.* Not far from the Grand' Place, this elegant restaurant specialises in seafood and seasonal game.

🍽🍽 **Clément Marot** – *16 r. de Pas. 03 20 57 01 10. www.clement-marot. com. Closed Sun eve.* A traditional menu served in a friendly restaurant run by the descendants of poet Clément Marot.

🍽🍽 **Au Vieux de la Vieille** – *2–4 r. des Vieux-Murs. 03 20 13 81 64. Closed Mon and Tue.* A candle-lit estaminet serving hearty northern fare. Very popular.

TAKING A BREAK

Chocolat Passion – *67 r. Nationale. 03 20 54 74 42. www.chocolatpassion. com. Open 9.15am–7pm, Wed 10am–7pm, Mon 1.30–7pm. Closed Sun and public holidays.* Chocolate in all its states of delicious decadence from juniper berries and Jenlain beer to flowers, teas and spices.

Chez Méo – *5 pl. du Gén.-de-Gaulle (Grand'Place). 03 20 57 34 54. www. meo.fr. Open 9.30am–7pm, Mon noon–7pm. Closed Sun.* Purveyors of coffee, tea, confectionary and regional specialities since 1928.

A les Echopes – *355 r. Léon Gambetta. 03 20 74 14 65. Call for opening times.* A huge range of French, Belgian and regional beers. Recipe sheets supplied on request.

SHOPPING

Euralille – *100, centre commercial. 03 20 14 52 20. www.euralille.com. Mon–Fri 10am-8pm; Sat 9am–8pm.* 120 stores, cafés, baby changing areas and nursery.

Marché de Sébastopol – *Pl. Sébastopol. Line 1 République-Beaux-Arts. Wed & Sat 7am–2pm.* Pleasant little market.

Marché du Vieux-Lille– *Pl. du Concert. Wed, Fri, Sun 7am–2pm.* Food market selling regional produce.

Marché aux livres anciens– *Line 1 Rihour. Tue–Sun afternoons.* The Vieille Bourse is a haven for second-hand book lovers.

ON THE TOWN

L'Échiquier (*Bar of the Alliance Hotel*), *17 quai de Wault. ☎03 20 30 62 62. www. alliance-lille.com. Mon–Sat 10am–1am, Sun 10.30am–11pm. Contact hotel for musical events.* Set in the divine 17C surroundings of a former convent, this bar offers a selection of champagnes and cocktails

Maisons de Mode– *R. du Faubourg-des-Postes. Lille Sud. ☎0320999120. www. maisonsdemode.com. Le Jardin des Modes: Tues-Sat noon–7pm; shops: Wed–Sat 2–7pm.* Twice yearly sales nights and fashion markets. (*See EVENTS*).

SHOWTIME

Good to know: The weekly journal, *Sortir*, lists all of the city's current events.

Orchestre National de Lille – *30 pl. Mendès-France. ☎03 20 12 82 40. www. onlille.com. Closed Aug. ≈26€ per show.* The Orchestre National de Lille gives an average of 120 concerts per season.

Théâtre Le Grand Bleu – *36av. Marx-Dormoy. ☎03 20 09 88 44. www. legrandbleu.com.* Dance, circus, theatre, storytelling and hip-hop performances for everyone from toddlers to teens.

Théâtre de Marionnettes du Jardin Vauban – *1 av. Léon-Jouhaux. Jardin Vauban. ☎03 20 42 09 95.* An outdoor puppet show.

Casino Barrière– *777 pont de Flandres. ☎03 28 14 47 77. www.hotel-casino-barriere-lille.com.* Recently-opened 1 200-seat theatre and casino.

L'Aéronef– *168 av. Willy-Brandt. Line 1 Gare-Lille-Flandres. ☎08 92 56 01 50 (0.34€/min). Ticket office ☎0328 38 5050. www.aeronef-spectacles.com.* Two concert halls showcasing a medley of music.

Le Biplan– *19 r. Colbert. Line 1 Gambetta. ☎03 20 42 02 27. Reservations ☎03 20 12 91 11. www.lebiplan.org.* Theatre, comedy and contemporary music.

La Malterie– *42r. Kuhlmann. Line 1 or 2 Porte-des-Postes ou Wazemmes. ☎03 20 15 13 21. www.lamalterie.com.* A former industrial site converted into performance and exhibition areas and artists' studios

ACTIVITIES

Hippodrome Serge-Charles– *59700 Marcq-en-Barœul.☎03 20 45 45 45.* One of the 15 busiest racecourses in France with over 200 races and 30 meetings a year.

Planet Bowling– *R. du Grand-But. 59160 Lomme. ☎08 92 70 70 04. www. planetbowling.com. 10am–2pm, Fri–Sat 10am–4am. ≈5.40€ (Sat & Sun 9€).* Europe's biggest bowling complex: 40alleys, 25 pool tables, karaoke Sat eve.

Tradi'Balade – *☎06 18 00 77 76. www.tradibalade.com.* Visit Lille in a 2CV.

EVENTS

Grande Braderie de Lille – *www. lilletourisme.com. 1st weekend of Sept.* Europe's biggest flea market attracting 2.5 million visitors every year.

Lille 3000 – *☎03 28 52 30 00. www.lille 3000.com.* Every 2 to 3 years, Lille 3000 organises several months of exhibitions, festivals and concerts. Next event: 2012.

La Nuit des soldes– *www.lillelanuit.com. 1st day of summer sales. 7pm–midnight.* Organised by the Maisons de Mode an evening with cocktails and a DJ.

Marché de Noël– *www.noel-a-lille.com. Mid-Nov–late Dec.* Chalets line pl. Rihour and the Grand'Place in the festive period.

TRANSPORT

Aéroport de Lille-Lesquin – *☎08 91 67 32 10. www.lille.aeroport.fr. Bus stop Euralille. 7€ single, 9€ return, every hr on the hr. Journey 20min. Daily.*

Transpole– *www.transpole.fr. ≈Single ticket, day pass (3.60€), evening pass (1.60€), "Braderie" pass (4.70€), Lille3000 day pass (7€), family card (2€ see conditions on website).* Lille Métropole public transport network. Tickets from machines in metro and tram stations or from the tourist office.

Lille Métropole City Pass – Access to tourist attractions in Lille, Roubaix, Tourcoing, Villeneuve-d'Ascq and Wattrelos. Passes valid 1 day (20€), 2 days (30€) or 3 days (45€). *☎08 91 56 20 04 (0.225€ /min). www.lilletourisme.com.*

Roubaix★

Revisiting the past to reinvent its future, Roubaix is not afraid of change. Once a world capital of the textile industry, the "town of a thousand chimneys" has converted its cotton mills into fashion design studios and its Art Deco swimming pool into a world-class art and design museum.

SIGHTS

La Piscine-musée d'Art et d'Industrie André-Diligent ★

23 r. de l'Espérance. ⏰*Open Mon–Thu 11am–6pm, Fri 11am–8pm, Sun & Sat 1–6pm. Guided tours in French (60–90 min) Sun 4–5pm.* ⏰*Closed 1 Jan, 1 May, Thu after Easter, 14 Jul, 15 Aug, 1 Nov, 25 Dec.* ✒*4.50€. No charge 1st Sun of the month.* ♿✆*03 20 69 23 60. www.roubaix-lapiscine.com.*

Built as a "temple of hygiene" for textile workers, this Art Deco swimming pool (1927–1932) has been transformed into an art gallery. 19C sculptures stand where swimmers once dived into the pool. Nip into a changing cabin to admire a Picasso pot or Pignon vase.

Quartier des Créateurs

✆*03 20 65 31 90.*
www.quartierdescreateurs.com.
The neighbourhood around La Piscine is home to some 20 contemporary design studios, along with galleries, artists' studios and fashion boutiques. Shoppers are advised to visit on Wed–Sat afternoons for a full selection of stores.

Église Saint-Martin

⏰*Open Tue–Sat from 11am.*
This neo-Gothic church features works from the 16C to the 18C, including a rare cenotaph by François de Luxembourg (1472).

Hôtel de ville

Designed in 1911 by Victor Lalaoux, the architect of the Gare d'Orsay in Paris, this town hall breasted by 12 slender iconic columns was built to match the town's soaring early-20C ambitions. Don't miss the **frieze**★ on the second floor illus-

▶ **Population:** 96 959
ⓘ **Michelin Map:** 302 H3.
🅸 **Info**: 12 pl. de la Liberté. 59100 Roubaix. ✆03 20 65 31 90. www.roubaix tourisme.com.
Guided tour – Year-round, Sat & Sun (details from office de tourisme) - 5€. Allovisite mobile phone tour; mp3 tour.
▶ **Location:** Between Lille and Tourcoing. From Lille, access via D 656; from Tournai via N 509. Alternative routes: E 42 then D 710; A 1/E 17. Expressways D 700, D 9 and D 656 circle the town.
⊘ **Don't Miss:** A shopping trip to the Créateurs district and a factory outlet; the frieze on the façade of the town hall; the stained-glass walls of Hem chapel.
🕐 **Timing:** Allow at least 2hr for the Musée d'Art et d'Industrie, 1hr for the manufacture des Flandres.
👫 **Kids**: The Piscine-musée d'Art et d'Industrie has areas specially designed for children.

trating scenes from Roubaix's glorious textile past.

Motte-Bossut wool mill

A cross between a cruise liner and a fortress, this 19C castle of industry was converted into an international centre for labour archives *(78 bd. du Gén Leclerc;* ⏰*Open Mon–Fri 1–6pm.* ✒*6€;* ✆*03 20 65 38 00)* in 1993 by the architect Alain Sarfati.

Parc Barbieux

This English-style park hidden in the hollow of a valley is dotted with ponds, play areas and tributes people of Roubaix.

Villa Cavrois

60 av. J.-F.-Kennedy. 59170 Croix (4km/2mi to the S). Scheduled to open 2013 (contact the Centre des Monuments Nationaux for details).

Now a showcase for modern furniture and contemporary design, this modernist home (1929–1932) in the suburbs of Lille, designed by **Robert Mallet-Stevens**, was inspired by an 18C castle.

Église Saint-Joseph

🕐*Open Sat 9am–11am.*
📞*03 20 24 92 84.*

Behind the sober exterior of this brick neo-Gothic church (1878), the walls, columns and vaults are alive with colour.

Manufacture des Flandres – Flemish Tapestries

25 r. de la Prudence. 1hr guided tours.
🕐*Open Tue–Sun 2–6pm.* 💶*6€ free 1st Sun of the month.* 📞*03 20 65 31 90.*
www.manufacturedesflandres.fr.

Explore the history of weaving from 17C looms to 21C digital machines in this tapestry museum running weekend workshops for budding weavers.

EXCURSIONS

Chapelle de Hem★

▷ *7km/4mi via av. Jean-Jaurès and D 64.* 🕐*Open 9am–6pm.* 🗣*Guided tour (1hr) available by request (1 month in advance).* 💶*No charge.* 📞*03 20 75 56 00 (M. Duquesne).*

Built to a design by Hermann Baur, this chapel (1958) flanked by a row of limewashed Flemish houses, resembles a Beguine convent. The **stained-glass walls★★** were designed by the painter Manessier. Note the warm, vibrant tones on the right and the lighter, more delicate hues on the left.

Wattrelos

▷ *10km/6mi to the NE.* 📋*189 r. Carnot. 59150 Wattrelos.* 📞*03 20 75 85 86.*
www.wattrelos-tourisme.com.

Step back in time at the **Musée des Arts et Traditions populaires**, a late-19C farmstead housing a watchmaker's workshop, a weaver's studio and a noisy estaminet. *96 r. François-Mériaux.*

🕐*Open Tue–Sat 9am–noon, 2–6pm, Sun 10.30am–12.30pm, 3–6pm.* 🕐*Closed Sun morning Oct–Mar.* 💶*No charge.* ♿📞*03 20 81 59 50. www.wattrelos.com.*

Tourcoing

▷ *4.6km/2.8mi N via D 775.*

Once a giant on the global textile stage, Tourcoing is an ambitious showcase for 19C industry architecture. Now one of Europe's leading mail order centres, this town enjoys a lively arts scene.

Hôtel de ville

2 pl. Victor-Hassbroucq. 🕐*Open Mon–Fri 8am–5.30pm.* 🕐*Closed public holidays.* 💶*No charge.* ♿📞*03 20 23 37 00. www.tourcoing.fr.*

An example of the French Eclectic style popular under the Second Empire, this neo-Renaissance town hall is home to several paintings.

Musée des Beaux-Arts Eugène-Leroy

2 r. Paul-Doumer. 🕐*Open Wed–Mon 1.30–6pm.* 💶*5€.* ♿📞*03 2028 9160.*
www. muba-tourcoing.fr.

The museum's collection of 16C and 17C masterpieces from the Northern school and 19C paintings (including *35 têtes d'expression* by Boilly) is displayed alongside contemporary artists. The vast display of works by **Eugène Leroy** explores the artist's distinctive technique.

Église Saint-Christophe

Pl. de le République. 📞*03 59 63 43 43.*

The 16C bell tower of this neo-Gothic church is host to a **bell museum** and a peal of 62 bells (4th largest in France). A mere 200 steps for a **panoramic** view.

Maison du Broutteux

19r. Jules-Watteeuw.
🔒*Not open to the public.*

The citizens of Tourcoing presented this Alsatian-style house to their prolific bard, **Jules Watteeuw**, "Le Broutteux" (1849-1947), in 1909. Watteeuw wrote in the local dialect.

👁*Look out for the bronze plaque marking his birthplace on the Grand'Place.*

Hospice d'Havré

100 r. de Tournai. Ope Wed–Mon
1.30–6pm. Closed public holidays,
Aug. No charge. *03 59 63 43 53.*
Founded in 1260, this former hospice is
set around a delicious cloister fringed
with sculpted culs-de-lampe. Transformed into a "Maison Folie", it now
hosts contemporary exhibitions, workshops and concerts.

ADDRESSES

TRANSPORT

Metro – Roubaix is linked to Lille Métropole by metro: allow 20min to the centre
of Lille and 10min to Tourcoing. 5 metro
stations serve the centre of Roubaix,
5.30am–midnight (Gare Lille-Flandres),
every 2min at rush hour, every 4-6min at
other times. *www.transpole.fr*

Tramway and bus – *08 20 42 40 40.
www.transpole.fr.* Roubaix is also linked
to Lille by tram (6 stations in the Roubaix
area) and numerous bus routes.

Villeneuve-d'Ascq★

Formed in 1970 from three villages,
Annappes, **Flers** and **Ascq**,
Villeneuve-d'Ascq is renowned for
its post-modern architecture and
cutting-edge contemporary arts
centre. Linked to Lille by the Val metro
system, its traditional farmsteads,
windmills, rolling parkland and
five lakes make it a popular country
getaway for stressed city dwellers.

SIGHTS
Musée des Moulins

R. Albert-Samain. Guided tour
(90min). Open Mon–Fri 10am–noon,
2–5pm. Closed public holidays, Aug.
6€. *03 20 05 49 34.
www.aram-nord.asso.fr.*
Out of the 200 mills that once dotted
the region in the 19C, Villeneuve-
d'Ascq is home to three fine examples:

- **Population:** 65 042
- **Michelin Local Map:**
  302: G4.
- **Info:** Office du tourisme
  de Villebeuve-d'Ascq,
  Château de Flers, Chemin
  du Chat-Botté, 59652
  03 20 43 55 75.
  www.villeneuvedascq-
  tourisme.eu.
- **Location:** The town lies
  8km/5mi to the E of Lille,
  close to the border
  with Belgium.
- **Parking:** See map for
  location of parking in the
  centre of the new town.
- **Don't Miss:** The windmill
  museum.
- **Timing:** Visit in the morning,
  and stay for lunch.
- **Kids:** Forum des Sciences.

Flour mill, Musée des Moulins

the **Moulin des Olieux** (an oil mill dating from 1743), a traditional **flour mill** (1776) and a water mill. The museum exhibits the various mechanisms and tools used by carpenters, millers, and woodcutters in the 18C and 19C.

Musée du Terroir

12 carrière Delporte. Access via r. du 8-Mai. Open Mar–Nov Mon–Fri 2.30–6pm, 2nd and 4th Sun 3–6pm; Dec–Feb Sun 9.30am–noon. 3€. 03 20 91 87 57. www.shvam.asso.fr.
Built from Lezennes stone and brick, **Delporte Farm**, once part of Annappes, now houses a folk museum. Get hands-on with agricultural tools and explore a range of workshops from a foundry to a locksmith's and a joinery.

Farms of Yesterday

Chemin du Chat-Botté. Château de Flers. 03 20 43 55 70.
Villeneuve-d'Ascq has more than 70 farms. Start with **Ferme Lebrun** (1610), now home to race horses (*rue de la Liberté*), before moving on to the **Ferme du Grand-Ruage** (19C), a modern working farm (*rue Colbert*). Other farms have been converted into a theatre (**Ferme Dupire**, *80 rue Yves-Decugis*), artists' studios (**Ferme d'En-Haut**, *rue Champollion*), and a **nature centre** (**Ferme du Héron**, 1816, *east of the lake*) - an ideal starting point for guided nature walks.

Lille Métropole musée d'Art Moderne, d'Art contemporain et d'Art brut (LaM)★★

1 allée du Musée. Open Tue–Sun 10am–6pm. Guided tours (2hr) by request. Closed 1 Jan, 1 May, 25 Dec. 10€, free 1st Sun of the month. 03 20 1968 68. www.musee-lam.fr.
Modernised and reopened in 2011, LaM boasts a new white extension by Manuelle Gautrand that cups the existing gallery like a giant hand. Its walls open onto a sculpture park featuring a stabile by **Alexander Calder** and a colossal concrete idol by **Picasso**.

The **modern art collection** contains over 210 works mainly from the first half of the 20C. Start your visit with a portrait of Roger Dutilleul by Modigliani before moving on to the **Cubist** room, with works by Braque, Picasso and Fernand Léger.

Continue to the **Modigliani** room where, among his many paintings and drawings, you'll find his poignantly unfinished white marble *Head of a Woman* (1913).

The modern section ends with surrealists and abstract painters, including **Miro, Kandinsky, Klee, De Staël** and **Jean Dubuffet**'s *Hourloupe* cycle.

The **contemporary art** collection begins with the heirs to the Cubist movement, **Jacques Villeglé, Mimmo Rotella and François Dufrêne**, known for their groundbreaking use of collage and other materials, and moves on to works by **Annette Messenger**, who has created a map of France using 200 mutilated stuffed toys, **Jacques Villeglé**'s torn street posters and the multicoloured "exploded cabin" by **Daniel Buren**.

The extensive **outsider art** collection, containing over 4 000 works by 170 artists, is unique in France. A concept invented by Dubuffet, "outsider" art refers to works by people not belonging to the art world. Examples on display include mental patient **Henry Darger**'s cartoonesque images of girls running across a landscape of exotic flowers and exploding bombs.

👥 Musée de Plein Air

143r. Colbert. 🕐*Open Jun–Aug Mon–Sat 10am–6pm (Sun 7pm); Apr–May, Sept–Nov Wed–Sat 10am–6pm (Sun 7pm).* 🚶*Guided tour by request.* 🎫*4€.* 📞*032063 11 25.*

If you're keen on the countryside, don't miss this truly original open-air museum devoted to the rural heritage of Flanders, Artois, Picardy and Hainaut. The museum saved twenty-two buildings from ruin and trucked them to Villeneuve where you can discover how talented rural folk built bakeries, barns, estaminet and forges without the help of architects.

Parc Archéologique Asnapio

r. Carpeaux. 🕐*Open Apr–Sept Wed 2–5pm, Sun 3–7pm; Sept–Oct Wed 2–5pm, Sun 2–6pm.* 🎫*3.60€.* 📞*03 20 47 21 99.*

This 6ha/15 acre park contains reconstructions of regional dwellings from the Neolithic Era to the end of the Middle Ages: houses, barns, workshops.

Château de Flers

Ch. du Chat-Botté. 🕐*Open Tue–Fri 2.30–5.30pm, Sun 3–6.30pm.* 🚶*Guided tour (1hr) by request 7 days in advance.* 🕐*Closed public holidays.* 🎫*No charge.* 📞*03 20 43 55 75.*

This Flemish château built in 1661 is surrounded by a moat once spanned by a drawbridge. The brick buildings with stone clamping surmounted by stepped gables house the tourist office and an **archaeological museum**.

Mémorial Ascq 1944

77 r. Mangin in Ascq. 🕐*Open Jul–Aug Tue–Thu (Sun – contact for details) 2–5.30pm; Sept–Jun Sun 2–5.30pm.* 🎫*3€.* ♿📞*03 20 91 87 57.*

This museum is dedicated to the memory of 86 inhabitants of Ascq killed in 1944 and the trial of those accused of their murder. Eighty-six stones line the railway to commemorate the tragedy.

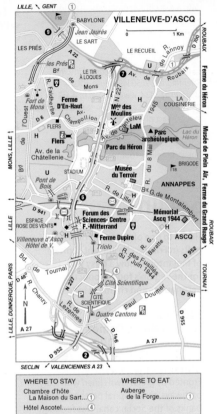

WHERE TO STAY	WHERE TO EAT
Chambre d'hôte	Auberge
La Maison du Sart....①	de la Forge..............①
Hôtel Ascotel..............④	

👥 Forum des Sciences

1 pl. de l'Hôtel-de-Ville. 🕐*Open Tue–Fri 10am–5.30pm, Sat, Sun and public holidays 2.30–6.30pm.* 🎫*3€ to 5€ depending on the activities.* ♿📞*03 20 19 36 36. www.forum departementaldessciences.fr.*

This educational centre devoted to new technology includes a children's workshop, an early learning space and an information centre.

ADDRESSES

🏨 STAY

🛏 **La Maison du Sart** – *64 av. de Flandre.* 📞*0320723504. www.maisondusart.com.* 🅿 🍴 *3 rooms* 🍽. A quaint 1930s residence with heaps of charm. Paved with beautiful marble tiles and graced with a real church organ, the hall opens into a rustic dining room. The bedrooms are comfortable, despite the separate bathroom on the landing. Practical and reasonably priced.

⊜⊜🛏 **Ascotel** – *Av. P.-Langevin-Cité-Scientifique. 59650 Villeneuve-d'Ascq.* 📞*03 20 67 3434. www.ascotel.fr.* ♿🅿 *Wi-fi. 83 rooms* ⊊*12.50€. Restaurant*⊜⊜. In the heart of town and close to local transport links, Ascotel is an unpretentious hotel built in red brick. The pale yellow rooms are spacious and well-appointed.

🍴 EAT

⊜ **L'Auberge de la Forge** – *160r. de Lannoy.* 📞*03 20 19 19 69. www.auberge-de-la-forge.com. Closed Sun–Thu eve.* ♿. Ample portions and a traditional menu with Flemish specialities await you at this tucked-away address. Friendly service.

ACTIVITIES

👥 **Découverte nature au parc du Héron**– *Lac du Héron. U 1 (Pont-de-Bois), then bus 41 (Contrescarpe).* Try your hand at boating, windsurfing and other nautical delights at the Héron.

Seclin

Home to one of the finest peals of bells in France, the ancient capital of Mélantois is now a busy hub for the region's food production, aeronautics and chemical industries.

SIGHTS
Hôpital Notre-Dame
Av. des Marronniers. 🕐*Open Sat–Sun 9am–6pm.* 👥*Guided tour.* ⊚*3€.* 📞*03 20 90 12 12.*
Fronted by green lawns lined with leafy pathways, this hospital perched on the banks of the Seclin canal was founded in the 13C by Marguerite de Flandre, sister of Jeanne, founder of the Hospice Comtesse in Lille. The current brickstone Flemish Baroque building (17C) has an elaborate sculpted design.
Enter by the **courtyard★** lined with arcades and look up to the right where a corbie-stepped gable marks out the hospital ward. This "Salle des Malades" (15C) is located immediately next to the chapel to allow the bedridden sick to celebrate mass. The chapel, also 15C, is topped by a wooden barrel vault.

Collégiale Saint-Piat
Bd Joseph-Hentgé. Bell concert by M. Mulier every Mon (market day) 11am–noon and civil & religious holidays. ⊚*No charge.* 📞*03 20 90 00 02.*
Begin your tour in the nave lined with long, slender capitals, then walk to the right of the choir, renovated in the 18C, where you'll find the entrance to

> ▶ **Population:** 12 083
> 🧭 **Michelin Map:** 302 G4.
> 🗊 **Info:** Office de tourisme –9 bd Hentgès. 59113 Seclin. 📞03 20 90 00 02. www.seclin-tourisme.com.
> ◖ **Location:** 10km/6mi S of Lille, on a chalk plateau to the west of Mélantois. From Lille, access via D 549 and A 1.
> ◉ **Don't Miss:** The crypt of the Saint-Piat collegial church; the courtyard of the Hôpital Notre-Dame.
> 🕐 **Timing:** Visit the town on Monday to hear the bell recital, 11am–noon.

the pre-Romanesque **crypt** housing the tomb of St Piat. A 12C tombstone covers the original sarcophagus. The chapter house (14C–15C) to the right of the ambulatory is worth lingering over. Made from a single bronze casting, the church's **peal of bells** (42 bells) was made in England – the only one of its kind in France. These bells are so highly esteemed they are used as a diapason to fine-tune bells across France.

🚗 DRIVING TOUR

LA PÉVÈLE AND LE MÉLANTOIS
52km/32mi circuit – 1hr30min.

La Pévèle, a humid region with a sandy clay soil, forms a slight bump in the Flemish landscape. As well as experimental crops, farmers here produce chicory and seeds. Le Mélantois sits on a band of chalky soil covered by a blanket of alluvium.

▷ Leave Seclin heading E to the D 8 towards Attiches.

Begin your tour with the young **Forêt de Phalempin** of oak and silver birch dotted with visitor areas.

▷ Following D 8 until your reach D 954 on the left.

Hunkered on a low hillock (alt. 107m/350ft), the town of **Mons-en-Pévèle** is the highest point in La Pévèle. Philippe le Bel defeated a group of Flemish "communiers" (craftmen) here in 1304. Take in the view over La Pévèle and the plain of Flanders beyond.

▷ Continue along D 954 then bear left down D 917. At Pont-à-Marcq, return to D 549 on the right then take the D 19 on the left until you reach Templeuve.

Book ahead to get an insider's view of the staggering proportions of the Vertain mill (17C) at **Templeuve**, with its 10m-/32ft-high tower, 1.25m-/4ft-thick walls and 24m-/78ft-diameter sails. ◷ *Open May–Sept: Sun 3.30–6.30pm.* ☞*Guided tour (30min).* ☜*2€ (under 12yrs no charge).* ✆*03 20 79 23 23.*

▷ Leave Templeuve to the NE and return to D 94. After Louvil, branch off right down D 94A.

An Augustinian abbey stood to the south of the modest village of **Cysoming** where Louis XV stayed in May 1744, a year before his victory at the battle of **Fontenoy**, which secured France's grip on the region.
Head down the "*pyramide de Fontenoy*" pathway to admire the 17m/22ft high **obelisk** raised by the local canons to celebrate his achievement. Placed on a rocky pedestal, it is topped by a fleur de lys.

▷ Leave Cysoing to the west via D 955.

If you're curious about how France first got a foothold in Flanders, head to the Saint-Pierre church on arrival in **Bouvines** where 21 **stained glass windows** reveal the story of Philippe Auguste's victory in 1214.

End your tour in the unassuming village of **Sainghin-en-Mélantois**: lime-washed Flemish houses with tiled roofs and a vast Gothic church (15C–16C) rebuilt after a devastating fire in 1971.

▷ Go back the way you came and turn right down D 19. Continue along D 54. In Avelin, join D 549 back to Seclin.

EXCURSION
Fort de Seclin
▷*A1 from Lille towards Paris. Exit 19 heading towards Seclin. Continue straight over the 1st roundabout, then right at the 2nd roundabout. F-59113 Seclin.* ◷*Sun & Sat 2–6pm. Mon–Fri by reservation (minimum 5 pers).* ☜*5€ (child 4€). Tours in English available.* ✆*03 20 97 14 18. www.fortseclin.com.* This family-owned fort (1870) houses one of the finest private collections of uniforms and weapons (1870–1918) in France. Occupied by a Bavarian regiment during World War I, the fort was used to supply the frontline. Climb the ramparts for a view of the Canadian memorial at Vimy on the horizon.

ADDRESSES

SHOPPING
Le Domaine Mandarine Napoléon – *204 r. Burgault.* ✆*03 20 32 54 93. www. domainenapoleon.com. Mon–Sat 10am– 5pm. Closed public holidays.* Explore a museum dedicated to Napoléon before discovering the secrets of mandarin liqueur at the tasting bar. The emperor loved it so much they named it after him. Direct sales to the public.

LA FLANDRE

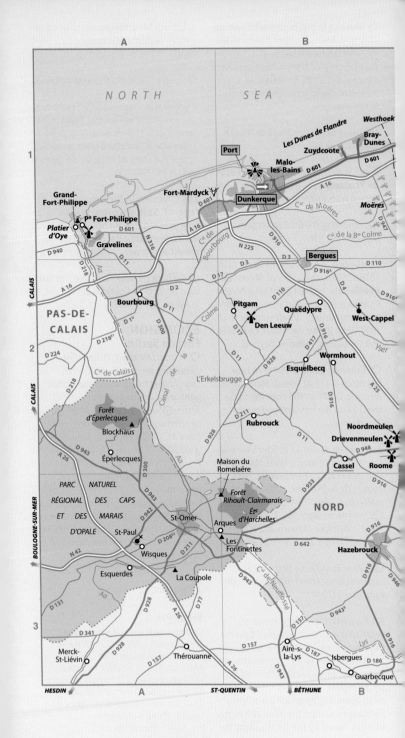

NORTH SEA

Westhoek
Bray-Dunes
Les Dunes de Flandre
Zuydcoote
Port
Malo-les-Bains
Fort-Mardyck
Dunkerque
D 601
A 16
Moëres
Cal de Moëres
Cal de la Bse Colme
Grand-Fort-Philippe
Platier d'Oye
Plt Fort-Philippe
D 601
A 16
Cal de Bourbourg
Bergues
D 916A
Gravelines
D 940
N 316
N 225
D 916
D 3
D 110
D 4
D 916A
CALAIS
A 16
D 218
Aa
D 11
D 17
D 2
D 3
PAS-DE-CALAIS
Bourbourg
D 11
Colme
Pitgam
Den Leeuw
Quaëdypre
West-Cappel
D 1D
D 300
D 218EL
D 110
D 417
D 916
D 928
Wormhout
Esquelbecq
A 25
D 224
CALAIS
D 218
Cal de Calais
Forêt d'Éperlecques
Blockhaus
Canal de la Hte Colme
L'Erkelsbrugge
Rubrouck
Noordmeulen
Drievenmeulen
Roome
Cassel
D 211
D 928
D 11
D 948
D 916
A 26
D 943
Éperlecques
D 300
Aa
Maison du Romelaëre
Forêt Rihoult-Clairmarais
Étg d'Harchelles
D 933
NORD
D 916
PARC NATUREL RÉGIONAL DES CAPS ET DES MARAIS D'OPALE
St-Omer
Arques
Hazebrouck
BOULOGNE-SUR-MER
St-Paul
Wisques
Esquerdes
La Coupole
Les Fontinettes
D 642
D 916
D 916
D 946
D 942
D 943
D 208cr
D 211
Cal de Neuffossé
N 42
D 131
D 928
A 26
D 77
Aa
D 341
D 157
Lys
D 157
D 943s
Merck-St-Liévin
Thérouanne
Aire-s-la-Lys
Isbergues
Guarbecque
D 157
A 26
D 943
D 187
D 186
HESDIN
ST-QUENTIN
BÉTHUNE

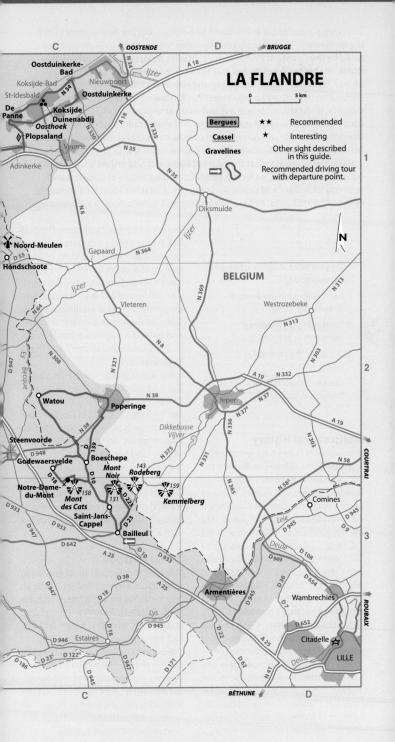

LA FLANDRE

OOSTENDE

BRUGGE

0   5 km

Bergues	★★	Recommended
Cassel	★	Interesting
Gravelines		Other sight described in this guide.
⇨		Recommended driving tour with departure point.

N

Oostduinkerke-Bad
Koksijde-Bad
St-Idesbald
De Panne
Oosthoek
Plopsaland
Koksijde
Duinenabdij
Oostduinkerke
Nieuwpoort
Veurne
Adinkerke

BELGIUM

Diksmuide
Noord-Meulen
Hondschoote
Gapaard
Vleteren
Westrozebeke

Watou
Poperinge
Ieper
Steenvoorde
Godewaersvelde
Boeschepe
Mont Noir
Rodeberg
Comines
Notre-Dame-du-Mont
Mont des Cats
Saint-Jans-Cappel
Bailleul

143
159
131
158
Kemmelberg

Dikkebusse Vijver

COURTRAI

Armentières
Wambrechies

Lys
Deule
Estaires

ROUBAIX

Citadelle
LILLE

BÉTHUNE

LA FLANDRE

Stretching from France in the south to Belgium and the Netherlands in the north, Flanders is a uniquely cosmopolitan region. Once a single territory ruled by the Counts of Flanders, for centuries its strategic position on the North Sea trade routes placed it at the centre of a gigantic territorial tug-of-war between France, Burgundy, the Habsburg Empire and England. The succession of so many foreign rulers has bestowed the region with a unique culinary, linguistic, architectural and cultural heritage, along with an endless round of carnivals, fascinating legends and more traditional dishes and beers than a single restaurant could ever fit on its menu. The region's talent for absorbing new influences has continued into the 21C. The region is now a major commercial hub at the heart of Europe. It also enjoys a stimulating natural environment, including several classified nature reserves, dunes teeming with flora and fauna, and vast sandy beaches ideal for a complete range of boardsports, from sand yachting and windsurfing to sailboarding.

Highlights

1 Try your hand at sand yachting in **Dunkerque** (p363)

2 Ramble through the dunes in **Gravelines** (p365)

3 Stroll along the **medieval ramparts** in Bergues (p367)

4 Celebrate the **carnival** in Cassel (p369)

5 Discover Flanders from a **hot air balloon** in Bailleul (p375)

Multicultural History

Few regions of France have welcomed so many different cultures or decided the fate of so many nations. Settled by the Romans, Saxons and Franks, Flanders passed under the control of the French crown in the 12C. After losing ground to the Burgundians and Habsburgs in the 15C to 17C, France tightened its grip in 1678, when Louis XIV divided the region into French Flanders in the south and what is now Belgian Flanders in the north. The distinctive star-shaped forts designed by France's greatest 17C military architect, Vauban, which you will come across throughout your visit, bear witness to France's determination never to lose control of the region again. The rise of another rival nation, Germany, and the outbreak of World War I and II, have left Flanders with a fascinating network of fortresses, bunkers, memorials and museums of military history.

Despite its tumultuous history, Flanders has always been a prosperous trading centre, a fact reflected in its remarkable civic architecture. The elaborate town halls and towering belfries which you will find all along your route were deliberate displays of wealth and power, while its flamboyant gothic churches and gabled houses owe much to the mobility between the French and Dutch Flemish peoples.

A few words of old French Flemish dialect have snuck into the French vocabulary, such as "estaminet" (café-bar). And, like their counterparts in Belgian Flanders, carnivals in French Flanders often feature "giants" or papier-maché effigies of their local heroes.

No carnival would be complete, of course, without a *potjevleesch* – a traditional Flemish dish of potted meat – washed down with one of the region's speciality beers or a *bistouille* – a coffee with a dash of alcohol.

Travel Hotspot

Still very much open to its European neighbours, French Flanders is now an international transportation hub for Paris, Brussels, Antwerp, Amsterdam and London, as well as a steel and petrochemical powerhouse centred around the port of Dunkerque, its gateway to the North Sea. The region's flat sandy beaches, invigorating winds and boisterous seas attract boardsports enthusiasts from across Europe, while its dunes have built an international reputation as a unique coastal nature reserve.

Dunkerque★★

Almost totally destroyed during World War II, Dunkerque has bounced back to become France's third largest port and a thriving industrial and commercial centre. A key player in European maritime history, the town is now home to three unique museums. Boasting the biggest carnival in northern France, Dunkerque also enjoys excellent cultural and sports facilities and a growing reputation as a mecca for sand yachting and sailing enthusiasts.

> ▶ **Population:** 70 834
> ⊙ **Michelin Local Map:** 302: C, p356 B1.
> 🏠 **Info:** Beffroi, r. de l'Amiral-Ronarc'h, 59140 Dunkerque. ℘03 28 66 79 21. www.dunkerque-tourisme.fr.

A BIT OF HISTORY
Church of the Dunes

Dunkerque, which means "church of the dunes" in Old Flemish, was founded in the 7C. Starting life as a sleepy fishing port, its strategic location on the North Sea soon placed it at the centre of a power struggle between France and its immediate neighbours. On a single day in June 1658, it passed under Spanish, English and finally French control during the famous Battle of the Dunes. Subsequently fortified by the French military architect Vauban, in the late 17C it entered a brief period of stability.

Jean Bart, "the king's privateer" – Unlike pirates, who attacked ships from any and every nation, often murdering the crews in the process, privateers were granted "letters patent" by the sovereign entitling them to hound enemy warships and merchant vessels. During the Franco-Dutch wars (1672–1678), the privateers of Dunkerque destroyed and captured 3 000 ships, took 30 000 prisoners and wiped out Dutch trade. The most intrepid of all the privateers was **Jean Bart** (1650–1702). During the Battle of Texel in 1694, Bart saved the kingdom from famine by capturing 130 ships loaded with wheat. As a result, he was raised to the nobility and given the rank of Commodore.

The stage for pioneering feats of maritime engineering during the 18C, the port was further expanded to accommodate the town's burgeoning shipbuilding industries in the 19C. Shelled by the Germans during World War I, Dunkerque's fortunes swung from heroism to despair during World War II.

Evacuation of Dunkerque (May–June 1940) – From 25 May to 4 June, the Allied forces were forced to beat a humiliating retreat from Dunkerque by advancing German forces. Despite limpet mines, torpedoes, bombs and the pounding of heavy shells, almost 350 000 men, about two-thirds of them British, were rescued by merchant ships, fishing vessels and pleasure boats sailing back and forth between French and English coasts.

THE PORT★★

France's third largest port, Dunkerque serves the local steel, petroleum and petrochemical industries. The shipyards closed down in 1987 after turning out more than 300 ships. Since then, the eastern and western ports have been linked by a **deep-water canal** to the Nord-Pas-de-Calais region of France, Belgium and the Paris Basin. The port installations extend along 15km/9mi of coastline.

Port-Est

The eastern port is served by an outer harbour (80ha/198 acres) and three locks, with the largest, the Charles-de-Gaulle Lock (365×50m/400×55yds), able to accommodate ships up to 115 000 tonnes. The **harbour basin** (6km/4mi long) is divided into six open basins and specialised industrial basins, in addition to storage installations. Equipped for ship repairs, the port has four dry docks and one floating dock.

Dunkerque Carnival

The carnival dates back to well before the 19C, when shipowners treated the 'visscherbende' (groups of fishermen in Flemish) to a hearty feast before they set out for several months to catch cod in the frozen Icelandic waters. Today the Dunkerque Carnival is one of the most popular in the north of France. Held over five weeks in winter, it's renowned for its rowdy street processions and crowds of dancers carried along by the sound of pipes and drums.

WALKING TOURS

MARINA TOUR

Approx. 1hr.

Start from place du Minck (fish market) between the Bassin du Commerce and the Cale aux Pêcheurs and cross the old citadel district, where the customs offices are based today. The channel and marina are on the right. Cross Trystam Lock and turn right toward the lighthouse. Housed in a former tobacco warehouse, the **Musée Portuaire** (*Harbour Museum;* open Wed–Mon 10am–12.45pm, 1.30–6pm (daily during school holidays); 10€, 7–12 years, 8€; 03 28 63 33 39; www.museeportuaire.com) explores the port's tumultuous past and industrious present. Clamber aboard the "Duchesse Anne" for the full sea-faring experience.

Boat trips

Guided boat tours. Approx. 1hr. Open Jul–Aug Mon–Sat 10.30am, 2:30pm & 4pm, Sun and public holidays; rest of the year: contact the tourist office. 8.50€ (child 6.50€, family 25€). 03 28 66 79 21. le-texel.fr.
The Texel leaves from the Place du Minck at the Bassin du Commerce, the largest of the three old basins, and cruises the entire length of the port.

Belfry

Guided panoramic visits (30min) Mon–Sat 9.30–11.15am, 2– 5.30pm, Sun 10–11.15am, 2–3.15pm. 3€ (7–12yrs, 2€). 03 28 66 79 21. www.dunkerque-tourisme.fr.
Built in the 13C and heightened in 1440, this belfry was once the bell-tower of the **Église St-Éloi** which burnt down in 1558. Listed as a UNESCO World Heritage Site, this soaring tower (58m/190ft) houses a peal of 50 bells which play popular tunes on the quarter hour. Don't miss the original concerts and recitals. Visit the tourist office on the ground floor for dates and times.

Église Saint-Éloi

Open Mon–Sat 10–11.30am, 2–5pm. No charge. Guided tour in French (contact tourist office). 03 28 66 79 21. Rebuilt after a fire in 1558 and renovated during the 18C and 19C, the church has a neogothic facade and three pyramid-shaped roofs. Due to the removal of the transept, the church is curiously proportioned (68m by 53m/62yds by 48 yds). Admire the volume of the naves and rib vaults supported by elegant pillars, and the radiating chapels of the apse. The restored lancet windows feature stained glass by the master glazier Gaudin. On the north side of the choir, under a white marble slab, lies the **tomb of Jean Bart**. Don't miss the strange 17C money box in the shape of a chained captive to the left of the entrance.

▶ Turn left on leaving the church.

Place Jean-Bart – A statue of the famous privateer by David d'Angers (1845) in the centre of this square lined with shops and businesses.

▶ Return to rue Georges-Clemenceau and head towards the town hall.

Town Hall – The town hall and its impressive 75m tower were build in neo-Flemish style in 1901 by regional architect Louis Cordonnier. A stained glass window by Félix Gaudin depicts the return of Jean Bart following his victory at the Battle of Texel in 1694.

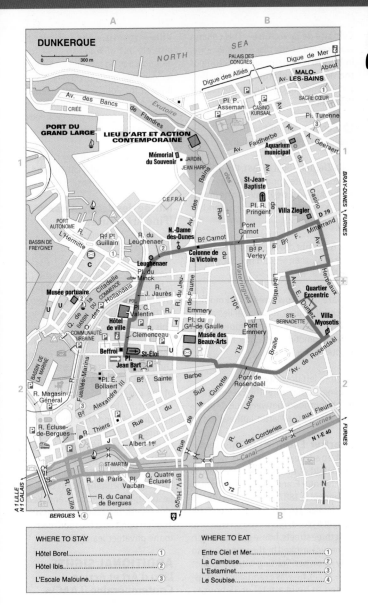

◗ Continue down rue Jean-Jaurès.

Leughenaer – Dunkerque's oldest monument, the Leughenaer is the last of 28 towers that once crowned the town's 14C Burgundian ramparts. Its Flemish name, "Liar's Tower", probably refers to the old privateering practice of sending false signals to passing shipping to lure them onto the sandbanks.

◗ Continue right down rue du Leughenaer.

Chapelle N.-D.-des-Dunes (◔ *open Mon–Fri 10am–noon, 2.30–4.30pm;* ☎ *03 28 63 76 41*). Rebuilt in the 19C, this chapel contains a wooden statue of N.-D. des Dunes, venerated by sailors since 1403. Don't miss the votive offerings left by generations of seafarers.

Colonne de la Victoire – This column was erected on the place de la Victoire, in 1893 to commemorate the lifting of the siege of Dunkerque after the Battle of Hondschoote during the French Revolution.

▶ Continue straight on to the boulevard François-Mitterrand.

Villa Ziegler – Built in 1881, this opulent wooden painted house now plays host to the **Maison de l'environnement**. It marks the entrance to the Rosendaël neighbourhood.

▶ Turn right down avenue Louis-Herbeaux, then second right down rue Marcel-Hénaux.

A maze of narrow streets and modest blocks of houses, Rosendaël lies at the residential heart of Dunkerque. Its varied and sometimes eccentric houses are painted in lively colours.

▶ Turn left down avenue Eugène-Dumez enter the Excentric neighbourhood, between rue André-Chenier and rue Martin-Luther-King.

Quartier Excentric – This small, U-shaped neighbourhood was the brainchild of mason, decorative artist and inventor François Reynaert. Born in Rosendaël in 1887, Reynaert decided to turn his hand to architecture in 1927. He bought a plot of marshland on which he built three streets, house by house. Each home was inspired by the name given to it by its owner. Starting with L'Escargot (The Snail), he was eventually commissioned to build a total of 35 houses, including Le Baldaquin (The Canapy), Les Volutes (The Scrolls), and the Excentric Moulin dancehall, now abandoned. Although privately owned and therefore not open to the public, they're worth admiring from the outside.

▶ Continue along avenue Eugène-Dumez, then turn left down avenue Rosendaël.

Villa Myosotis – This villa was built entirely out of wood in 1894 to get around a ban on building on army land. Its Scandinavian style is highly representative of the light, elegant architecture found in the neighbourhood before 1945. Its technical ingenuity was rewarded with the Paris Architecture Prize in 1900.

▶ Return to the belfry by crossing the pont de Rosendaël, then head down rue du Président-Poincaré.

Musée des Beaux-Arts★ (Fine Arts Museum)

Pl. du Gén.-de-Gaulle. ◷*Open Wed–Mon 10am–12.15pm, 2–6pm.* ❧*Guided tours (1hr 30min).* ◷*Closed 1 Jan, 1 May, 15 Aug, 24, 25 and 31 Dec (afternoons).* ✆*4.50€ (child 1.50€), no charge 1st Sun of the month.* ♿*℘03 28 59 21 65. www.ville-dunkerque.fr.*
This museum (rebuilt in 1973) houses a rich collection of paintings from the 16C to the 20C and exhibits exploring Dunkerque's history. A panel of 540 Delft tiles depicting the bombardment of the port in 1695 offers a dramatic introduction to a fine selection of works including 16C and 17C Dutch and Flemish masters (Snyders, Pourbus, Schoubroeck, Van Dyck, Van Cleef and Van der Poel), 18C Italian painters – Giordano and Magnasco – and French art from the 17C to 19C, including works by Rigaud, Lesueur, Hubert Robert and Vernet, along with the Plage de Tourville by Boudin. Don't miss the room dedicated to the privateer Jean Bart.

ADDITIONAL SIGHTS
Lieu d'Art et Action Contemporaine (LAAC)★

◷*Open Apr–Oct Tue–Sun 10am–12.15pm, 2–6pm.* ◷*Closed Mon, the week of Mardi Gras and the week following Heritage Days, 1 Jan, 1 May, 1 Nov, 24, 25 and 31 Dec (afternoons).* ✆*4.50€ (under 18 yrs – no charge).* ♿ *℘03 28 29 56 00.*
Architect Jean Willerval bore in mind the existing garden when he built his modern concrete building sheathed in white ceramic. The museum is devoted to con-

temporary earthenware and glassware from 1950–1980, including CoBrA, César, Soulages, Warhol and Télémaque. Based on the theme of **"Dialogues in ceramics"**, the museum aims to increase public awareness of this art form.

The Museum of Contemporary Art stands in the middle of a **sculpture park★** designed by landscape gardener Gilbert Samel. The paths climb outcrops lined with impressive sculptures set against the backdrop of the North Sea.

Mémorial du souvenir

R. des Chantiers-de-France. ○*Open Apr–Sep 10am–noon, 2–5pm; rest of the year: contact tourist office (groups only).* ○*4€ (under 12s no charge).* ✆*03 28 66 79 21. www.dynamo-dunkerque.com.* Housed in the casemate where French and Allied forces established their headquarters during the Battle of Dunkerque and Operation Dynamo, this exhibition explores the events of May–June 1940.

Fort-Mardyck Zoological Park

R. des Droits-de-l'Homme. ○*Open Feb–Mar & Oct–Dec: 10am–5pm (last admission 4.15pm); Apr–Sep: 10am–6pm (last admission 5.15pm).* ○*Closed Dec–Jan.* ○*4€ (under 7s 2€).* ら ✆*03 28 27 26 24. www.parc-zoologique.fr.* Brown bears, seals, beavers, otters and lynx cats are among more than 170 animals and 40 species found in this zoological park. Get close up and personal with pelicans and storks in the avaries or brush up your animal knowledge in the educational farm.

🚗 DRIVING TOUR

TOWARDS BELGIUM

62km/38mi tour marked on the microregion map (p356). Allow 3hr.

◐ Leave Dunkerque by the pont Carnot.

Start your tour at the pleasant seaside resort of **Malo-les-Bains**. Founded in 1870 by a Dunkerque shipowner named Malo, this residential neighbourhood of Dunkerque is renowned for its original and imaginative **Art nouveau houses**. To the east of the port, follow the sea-wall walk overlooking the fine sandy **beach** to the casino.

👥 **Aquarium municipal** – *45 av. du Casino.* ○*Open Wed–Mon 10am–noon, 2–6pm.* ○*Closed Jan 1, May 1, Dec 25.* ○*2€ (under 16s free), Sun and public holidays no charge.* ら ✆*03 28 59 19 18.* Get the full nautical experience by exploring 20 tanks containing 150 different species of fish from the North Sea, South America, Africa and Oceania.

Eglise Saint-Jean-Baptiste – ○*Open Sep–Jun. 9.30am–11.30am, 2.30–5.30pm (Fri 5pm); Jul–Aug 9.30am–11.30am.* ✆*03 28 63 52 19.* This prow-shaped brick church (1962) has a steeple in the form of a mast.

Heading east, take time to explore the 👥**"Dunes de Flandre"**: a 15km/9mi beach and 700 ha/1 730 acre of dunes, now a nature reserve, which stretches all the way to La Panne in Belgium. Try your hand at storm sailing, boat sailing, wind surfing, sand yachting and the latest Dunkerque craze, sea paddling.

The area of **Zuydcoote** shot to literary fame following the publication of Robert Merle's 1949 novel *Weekend in Zuydcoote,* set during the evacuation of 1940.

Bray-Dunes – 🚏 *Pl. Jérôme-Rubben, 59123 Bray-Dunes.* ✆*03 28 26 61 09. www.bray-dunes.fr.* A memorial on the **seawall walk** commemorates the 12th French motorised infantry division, which fought until 4 June 1940. 🚶 Discover the dunes by foot on the Marchand dune tour *(8.5km/5mi – 3hr),* the Ghyvelde fossil dune*(8km/5mi – 2hr40min)* or the Perroquet dune tour *(5km/3mi – 1hr40min). Visit www.tourisme-nord.fr or www. ot-dunkerque.fr for more information.* 👥 Ask the tourist office for the "Family Walks in Northern France" guide. These child-friendly tours explore the dunes, wildlife and local landmarks.

◐ Return to the D 601.

Bommelaers-Wall Ecomuseum and Farm★ – ◔Open Apr–Oct 10am–6pm; Sat, Sun, public holidays by request; Nov-Mar 10am–5.30pm, Sun and public holidays by request. ◔Closed 25 Dec and 1 Jan. ▨5€ (under 15yrs 3€). ℘03 28 20 11 03. www.ecomusee-flandres.com. Step back in time to the beginning of the 20C and explore the region's rural customs, from chicory roasting to witchcraft (including torture instruments) at this typical Flemish eco-farm. No tours in English.

▶ Continue along D 601 (N 39 in Belgium). Turn left (N 34).

Although the countryside looks exactly the same, the local language is Dutch. The road runs alongside the tramway and the ever-present sea.

The seaside resort of **De Panne** is popular with French tourists and sand yachting enthusiasts for its breakwater-free **beach**, where the sea rolls back up to 250m/155mi at low tide.

Continue west to **Westhoek**, a protected nature reserve and its 340km/211mi of dunes bristling with lyme grass, creeping willow and sea buckthorn. Or head southeast to the **Oosthoek** municipal nature reserve and explore its 61ha/150 acres of dunes and woodland criss-crossed by signposted trails.

🚶🚶Hop over to the **Plopsaland** theme park in Adinkerke (3km/2mi to the south).

Despite its modest size, **Koksijde** boasts two seaside resorts, Koksijde-Bad and Saint-Idesbald, and the highest coastline in Belgium, towering 33m/108ft above the sea.

Duinenabdij (Abbaye des Dunes) – Koninklijke Prinslaan 8. Founded by the Benedictine order in 1107, Duinenabdij grew to be one of the biggest abbeys in Western Europe before its destruction at the hands of Calvinists in 1566. Archaeologists began excavating its impressive remains in 1949. Their finds are showcased in a **museum**. Don't miss

the wooden post windmill built in 1773, on leaving the site.

Museum Paul-Delvaux – Delvauxlaan 42, Saint-Idesbald. A collection of paintings, watercolours, drawings, prints and sketches exploring the artist's journey from post-impressionism and expressionism through to surrealism.

Upstaging sand yachters and flysurfers at low tide, the shrimp fishermen of **Oostduinkerke** wade their horses breast-deep into the sea to trawl their catch.

Nationaal Visserijmuseum (National fisheries museum) – Pastoor Schmitzstraat 5. Discover a collection of model boats and maritime instruments.

Folklore Museum – Koksijdesteenweg 24. Explore the inside of a regional interior, workshops, stores and a small school in this intriguing ecomuseum.

▶ Turn right down N 330, then right along N 396. Take N 34 before joining N 39 at La Panne. Return to Dunkerque along D 601.

ADDRESSES

🛏 STAY

🍽🍽**Hôtel Ibis** – 13 r. du Leughenaer. ℘03 28 66 29 07. www.ibishotel.com. ♿. Wi-fi. 110rooms. ⊏8€. Restaurant🍽. Fully renovated building dating from the 1970s. Comfortable bedrooms, extensive store, contemporary-style bar and breakfast buffet presented on a fishing boat.

🍽🍽**L'Escale Malouine** – 38 av. Faidherbe. ℘06 35 97 44 08. http://lescalemalouine.com. 4rooms. ⊏8.50€. Close to the beach, this hotel with a typical early 20C seaside design has a children's play area and light-filled breakfast room. Friendly owners.

🍽🍽🍽**Hôtel Borel** – 6 r. L'Hermite. ℘0328665180. www.hotelborel.fr. ♿. Wifi. 48 rooms. ⊏10€. Smart brick-built hotel close to the marina. Well-kept, fully-equipped renovated rooms. Cosy lounge and continental breakfast buffet.

🍴 EAT

🍽🍽 **Entre Ciel et Mer** – 16 r. de Flandre. ℘03 28 59 39 00. Closed Sun eve, Mon. A short walk from Malo beach, in a street powdered with sand from the beach, this nautical-themed restaurant serves dishes made with fresh fish.

⊜⊜ **Soubise** – *49 rte de Bergues. 59210 Coudekerque-Branche. ℘03 28 64 66 00. Closed 1–13 Apr, 22 Jul–17 Aug, 21 Dec– 7 Jan, Sat and Sun.* 🅿. This 18C posthouse bordering the canal now houses a warm and welcoming restaurant. Traditional, well-prepared and generously portioned dishes. The respected chef celebrated 50 years of culinary excellence in 2010.

⊜⊜ **La Cambuse** – *25 r. du Gouvernement. ℘03 28 66 43 30. http:// la-cambuse.com. Closed Sun.* 🅿. Located in a former boat shed, this trendy restaurant has an industrial design and cast iron pillars. Brasserie style menu made from local produce.

⊜⊜ **L'Estaminet** – *6 r. des Fusiliers-Marins. ℘0328669835. www.estaminetflamand-dk.fr. Mon–Fri 11am–3pm, 6.30pm–11pm; Sat 6.30pm–midnight. Closed 2 weeks end Jul–early Aug, 1 week in Dec, Sun and Mon Jul–Aug.* A bona-fide Flemish witch-themed eatery decorated with second-hand store curios. Sip on a flambéed beer as you try your hand at board games.

GOING OUT

Bommel Bar – *57 r. de l'Amiral Ronarc'h. ℘0328210778. Tue–Sat 6pm–2am, Sun 6pm–midnight.* A friendly pub serving 25 different types of beer, including seven home-brewed draught beers.

ACTIVITIES

Mer et Rencontre – *4 digue Nicolas-II. ℘03 28 29 13 80. www.meretrencontres. com. Activities by appointment and according to tides. Closed 17 Dec– 3 Jan.* ⊜ *27€ 2hr-sand yachting introduction.* Fancy a spot of sea kayaking, all-terrain biking or kite flying? This accredited French sea yachting school runs a 2-hour introduction followed by a spin on the sand. Don't forget your waterproofs, old trainers and a change of clothes.

Loisirs – A magnet for boardsport buffs, the Dunes de Flandre offer sailing, storm sailing, flysurfing, windsurfing, sea kayaking, sand yachting and more.

Greeters - *www.tourisme-nord.fr.* Greeters offers visitors the opportunity to enjoy a free tour in the company of an English-speaking local. Contact the tourist office.

EVENTS

Carnival – Every Sunday before Mardi Gras, the inhabitants of Dunkerque dance through town singing carnival songs.

World Folklore Festival – *Contact tourist office. www.bray-dunes.fr.* First half of July in Bray-Dunes. Artists from 12 countries perform at this annual festival of traditional music, song and dance.

Gravelines

Laid out with military precision, the red-tiled houses of Gravelines lie hidden behind an impressive chain of walls, moats, bastions and gates. The town is also home to a marina.

VISIT
Ramparts, counterguards and half-moons

Gravelines' well-preserved ramparts are dominated by Charles V's arsenal towards the River Aa in the west. Each angle bastion is protected by a system of half-moons, moats and counterguards designed to slow the enemy's advance. Start by walking along rue de Calais, across the moat and down boulevard Salomé. On the left, after the bridge, join

▶ **Population:** 12 421

🜂 **Michelin Map:**
p356 A1; 302 A2.

🛈 **Info:** Tourist Office, 11 r. de la République, 59820 Gravelines, ℘03 28 51 94 00, www.tourisme-gravelines.fr.

◉ **Don't Miss:** The ramparts

◗ **Location:** Located 2 km/ 1mi from the sea, half-way between Calais and Dunkerque, Gravelines is the outer harbour of Saint-Omer. Access via A 16/E 40, D 940 or D 601.

🕐 **Timing:** Allow a full day.

the pathway and cross the bridge. Head left towards the counterguard before reaching a wooded half-moon on the right. Cross the bridge on the right, towards the second counterguard and continue to the bridge leading to Varenne barracks.

☞ WALKING TOUR

Musée du Dessin et de l'Estampe originale

Chateau de l'Arsenal. ◷*Open Jul–Aug Mon, Wed–Thu 2–6pm, Sat, Sun, public holidays 10am–noon, 3–6pm; Sep-Jun Mon, Wed, Thurs, Fri 2–5pm, Sat, Sun, public holidays 3–6pm.* ◷*Closed 20 Dec–3 Jan, 1 May, 1 Nov.* ⌨*2€ (under 18yrs no charge), no charge 1st Sun of the month.* ℘*03 28 51 81 04.*

Built in 1742, this former **gunpowder store**, explores the history and techniques of printing and engraving through the works of Dürer and Léger. The museum continues in the underground casemate (1693) bringing the 18C fortified town back to life.

Musée des Jeux Traditionnels

645 r. Gaston Dereudre, 59279, Loon-Plage. ◷*Opening times vary. Call for information.* ℘*03 28 61 52 45.*
A display of traditional wooden toys.

Gravelines Port-Royal

Rte de Calais. ◷*Open Apr–Oct Mon 2–5pm, Tue–Fri 10am–noon, 2–5pm, Sat 10am–noon; Nov–Mar Wed–Fri 10am–noon, 2–5pm, Sat 10am–noon. Guided tour (1hr).* ⌨*7€ (under 12yrs 3.50€).* ℘*03 28 21 22 40. www.tourville.asso.fr.*
Explore the history of Jean Bart and 17C privateering in the arsenal before crossing the Pont Vauban to admire a reproduction of the corsair's ship at the **Espace Tourville**.

Eglise Saint-Willibrord

◷*Open Fri 9.30–11.30am, guided tour by request.* ℘*03 28 23 00 15.*
A flamboyant gothic church housing the tomb of one of Louis XIV's greatest generals, Claude Berbier du Metz.

Moulin du Polder

Rte. de Petit-Fort-Philippe.
Don't miss this post mill made from American pitch pine in 1925.

EXCURSIONS
Petit-Fort-Philippe

▷ *2 km/1mi via D 11.*
This fishing port and resort owes its name to King Phillip II of Spain. If you're feeling fit, climb the 104 steps of the 35m/114ft **lighthouse** (◷*open Jul–Aug 10am–12.30pm 2–6.30pm Mon 2–6.30pm, Apr–Sep Wed–Sun 2–6pm;* ◷*closed 1 May;* ⌨*1.50€ (under 18s 1€);* ℘*03 28 51 94 00).*

Grand-Fort-Philippe

▷ *2km/1.25mi via the D 11G.*
◷*Open Apr–Sep Mon–Sun 3–6pm.*
Discover the history of this fishing port at the **Musée de la Mer** (28 bd. Carnot), and the **Musée du Sauvetage** (bd. de la République) coastguard museum.
⌨*Joint ticket 2€.*

Platier d'Oye nature reserve

▷ *W of Grand-Fort-Philippe.*
400ha/988 acres of grey and white dunes.

Chœur de lumière à Bourbourg★

▷ *9km/5.6mi SW via D 11. 29 pl. du Gén.-de-Gaulle, 59630 Bourbourg. Centre interprétation Art et Culture, 1 r. Pasteur, 59630, Bourbourg.* ◷*Open Sun–Mon 2–6pm, Tue–Sat 9am–noon, 2–6pm.* ℘*03 28 22 01 42.*
Housed in the former choir of the Eglise Saint-Jean-Baptiste, damaged during World War II and walled up until the 1990s, the chœur is the backdrop for sculptures by Anthony Caro.

ADDRESSES

☝/ EAT

⌷⌷ **Le Turbot** – *26 r. de Dunkerque.* ℘*03 28 23 08 54, www.leturbot.com. Closed Sun eve, Mon.* A simply decorated restaurant specialising in locally caught scallops prepared to traditional recipes.

Bergues★★

The historic ramparts of Bergues overlook scenic pastureland famous for their butter, cheese and wool. The yellow-ochre tones of the buildings are reflected in the waters of the moat and canals which partly surround the town. Despite wartime damage, Bergues has retained its historic character with winding streets, large squares and silent quays skirting the River Colme.

> ▶ **Population:** 4 207
> ⚓ **Michelin Map:** p356 B1/2; 302: C2.
> ℹ **Info:** Pl. de la République, Bergues. ℘03 28 68 71 06. www.bergues-tourisme.fr.

A BIT OF HISTORY
The Walled Town – The walls, pierced by four gateways and surrounded by a deep moat, date partly from the Middle Ages (Bierne Gate, Beckerstor, curtain wall east of Cassel Gate) and partly from the 17C.
The fortifications were used by French troops during the defence of Dunkerque, forcing the Germans to use Stukas and flames to breach them.

⚐ WALKING TOUR
Allow approx. 2hr 30mins.

Belfry
🕐*Open Mon–Sat 10am–11.30am, 2–5.30pm; Sun, public holidays 10am–12.30pm, 3–5.30pm.* 🕐*Closed 1 Jan, 1 May, 1 Nov & 25 Dec.* ⬤*2.60€.* ℘*03 28 68 71 06.*
Erected during the 14C, remodelled in the 16C and dynamited by the Germans in 1944, the belfry (54m/ 177ft high) was rebuilt by Paul Gélis who sought to preserve the main structure of the former edifice while simplifying the exterior decoration. It is made of yellow bricks known as "sand bricks" and is surmounted by the lion of Flanders; the **carillon** comprises 50 bells *(contact tourist office for information on recitals).*

Porte de Cassel
This 17C gateway has a **drawbridge** and a triangular pediment featuring a carved sun, Louis XIV's emblem.
From the gateway, note the unique perspective on the **medieval curtain wall** as it rises towards the Saint-Winoc towers on the right.

Rempart Ouest
The western rampart was built in 1635. Beyond the **Poudrière du Moulin** stands the **Tour Nekestor** and the **Porte de Bierne** (16C) with its drawbridge, offering views of the **ruins of a medieval tower** and several **historic locks**.

Rempart Nord
The northern rampart links the **Porte de Dunkerque**, which overlooks the start of the inner canal, the **Tour Guy-de-Dampierre** (1286) and the first **Porte d'Hondschoote**.

Couronne d'Hondschoote★
On the north side of the walls, Vauban used the branches of the River Colme to build an extensive system of bastions completely surrounded by large moats which serve as a bird sanctuary today.

Couronne and Abbaye de St-Winoc
The Couronne was designed to protect the abbey of the same name. It comprises three mighty **bastions** (1672–92): the St-Winoc bastion, the King's bastion and the St-Pierre bastion. Most of the buildings of the Benedictine **abbey** were destroyed during the Revolution; all that survives is the 18C marble front door, the Tour Pointue (rebuilt in 1815) and the 12C–13C tower of the transept, supported by reinforced buttresses.

Rempart Sud
Follow the southern rampart past three small 13C round towers, the Faux-Monnayeurs and Couleuvriniers towers, to return to the Porte de Cassel.

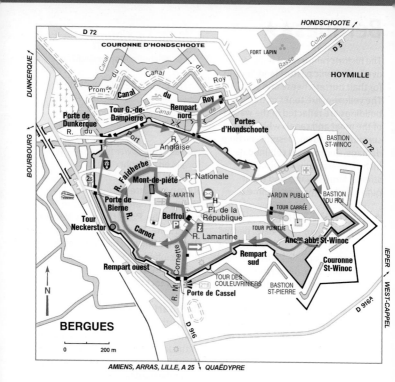

BERGUES

AMIENS, ARRAS, LILLE, A 25 \ QUAÊDYPRE

Rues Carnot and Faidherbe

These streets are lined with lovely 18C buildings including the **Hôtel de Hau de Staplande**, 22 rue Carnot.

Mont-de-piété

This elegant building with a Baroque gable is built from brick and white stone. It was designed by **Wenceslas Coebergher** (1561–1634), a painter, architect, economist and engineer who introduced the first pawnshops (monts-de-piété). It was opened in 1633 and today houses the **Musée du Mont-de-piété** (○open Wed–Sat Jul–Aug: 2–6pm, Sun and public holidays 10am–12pm, 2–6pm; Sep–Jun 2–5pm, Sun and public holidays 10am–noon, 2–5pm; ∞3.60€. ℘03 28 68 13 30; www.bergues-tourisme. fr). An outstanding painting, Hurdy-Gurdy Player, a vast canvas by **Georges de la Tour** (1593–1652), is displayed on the first floor. There are also works by several 16C–17C Flemish artists including a sketch by Rubens, and portraits by Van Dyck, Cossiers and Simon de Vox.

EXCURSIONS
Quaëdypre

▶ 5km/3mi SW via D 916 and D 37.
Perched on a gentle slope, this village boasts a **hall-church** with three naves. Take a moment to admire the 17C wood carvings and the painting by Antwerp artist Goubau, master of Largillière, on the main altar. The communion table, pulpit and confessionals come from the dominican church in Bergues (℘03 28 68 66 03, guided tour by reservation at the tourist office; 1st Sun of Jul afternoon, Heritage Days).

West-Cappel

▶ 10km/6mi to SE via D 110 then D 4.
The **Saint-Sylvestre church** (visit by reservation ℘03 28 68 39 47) was rebuilt in "sand bricks" in the 16C.

Moulin Den Leeuw

▶ 8km/5mi to S via D 916 then, to the right, the D 110. Guided tours in French (30 min) mid-Apr–Sept. ○Open Sun 2.30–6pm. ○Closed public holidays.

No charge. ℰ03 28 62 10 90.
This recently-restored post flour mill in the village of **Pitgam** dates from 1776.

Esquelbecq

8km/5mi to S then right along D 916 and D 417. Maison du Westhoek, (pl. Bergerot, 59470 Esquelbecq; ℰ03 28 62 88 57; www.esquelbecq.com) – permanent exhibition exploring the history of Westhoek and Flanders (guided tour in French) and temporary exhibitions on typical Flemish themes.
Esquelbecq has a typical Flemish **Grand'Place★** lined with 17C and 18C houses, a restored 16C church and 17C **château★**. A memorial at La Plaine au Bois commemorates the massacre of 70 British soldiers by Hitler's body guard on 28 May 1940 in a grange just outside the town (rue des Dunkirk-Vétérans).
Explore the countryside by foot (picnic tables and information panels). *Allow 2hr for the short circuit (7km/4mi) and 3hr 40min for the figure-of-eight circuit (11km/7mi). Topoguide available from the Maison du Westhoek.*

Hondschoote

A Flemish-speaking country town boasting two mills and several gabled houses.
Town hall – *Free access to marriage room and hall. Open 9am–noon, 2–5.30pm, Fri 9am–noon, 2–4.30pm.*

Closed Sat–Sun and public holidays. No charge. ℰ03 28 62 53 00. Giving onto the Grand'Place, the town hall's gothic Renaissance (1558) stone façade is adorned with tall mullioned windows and fine mouldings. The upper floor features 17C paintings.

Église Saint-Vaast – Only the 16C tower (82 m/89 yd) of this maritime Flemish hall-church survived the fire of Hondschoote in 1582.

Moulin Noord-Meulen – *500m/600yds to the N.* Although its sails last turned in 1959, this is one of the oldest windmills in Europe, dating from 1127.

Leave Hondschoote via D 947 and turn left down D 3 towards Bergues; turn right along D 79 and the road leading to the moeres.

Moeres – This term, which means marshland, refers to a former lagoon drained by Coebergher in the 17C using a system of dykes, canals and 20 windmills equipped with screwpumps.
They stretch into Belgium as far as Furnes. Admire the belfry of Dunkerque in the distance.

Return via D 947.

Cassel★

Boasting an enormous cobbled main square (Grand' Place), narrow, winding streets and low whitewashed houses, the small town of Cassel is Flemish both in its customs and appearance. The town is perched on top of Cassel Hill, the green slopes of which, formerly dotted with windmills, overlook the flat Flanders region. Traditional parades, archery events, a lively carnival, and the procession of the Reuze giants feature among the local celebrations.

▶ **Population:** 2 298
Michelin Local Map:
p356: B2; 302: C-3.

A BIT OF HISTORY
"Cassel Hill"

The highest point in the region (176m/577ft high) and a link in the Flemish hill-range, Cassel hill looks surprisingly large rising up in the middle of the Flemish plain; although about 30km/18mi from the coast, it is used as a landmark by sailors. Its peak is covered with a very hard ferruginous layer. To the east, **Mont des Récollets** (159m/ 521ft high) owes its name to a convent of Recollect nuns that stood here from 1615 to 1870.

From October 1914 to April 1915 General **Marshall Foch** had his headquarters at Cassel (*see Historic battles, p372*).

In May 1940 members of the British expeditionary corps retreating towards Yser and Dunkerque fought fiercely at Cassel, which enabled the allied forces to leave from Dunkerque.

SIGHTS
Grand'Place
The main square, irregularly shaped and cobbled, extends along the hillside near the church. Among the attractive group of 16C–18C houses on its south side features the Hôtel de la Noble Cour.

🏛 Cassel Horizons
20 Grand'Place. ◷*Open Mar–Nov: 8.30am–noon, 1.30–7.45pm, Sun and public holidays 2–6pm; Dec–Feb: Mon–Fri 8.30am–noon, 1.30pm– 5.30pm, Sat 8.30am–noon.* ◷*Closed public holidays.* ✆*2.20€ (under 14yrs 1.80€).* ☎*03 28 40 52 55. www.cassel-horizons.com.*

Housed in a former 18C townhouse overlooking the Grand'Place, this museum explores the history of Cassel, its beer, carnival and windmills. Its animated models, traditional games and interactive displays provide an ideal introduction to Flemish culture before setting off on a tour of the hills.

Musée de Flandre
26 Grand Place. ◷*Open Tue–Sat 10am– 12.30pm, 2–6pm; Sun 10am–6pm.* ◷*Closed public holidays.* ♿ ☎*03 59 73 45 60. museedeflandre.lenord.fr.*

Admire the stone façade of the 16C **Hôtel de la Noble-Cour** (a rarity in the north) before exploring this museum dedicated to the history, art and culture of Flanders. The displays offer a particularly true-to-life vision of the **Flemish identity**, including a taste for the grotesque. Bringing face-to-face the ancient and the modern, the religious and the profane, the popular and the

intellectual, the collection is divided into four sections.

The Battle of Cassel,1677, after a painting by Van der Meulen, and a rare primitive work, *The Virgin* and *The Donor Joos Van den Damme* (15C) are well worth lingering over. Other highlights include recent works by **Léo Copers** and Jan Fabre. Cassel's two giants complete the visit. Only visible on the Sunday before Mardi Gras and Easter Monday, as tradition dictates, their profiles are sihouetted onto a wall instead.

Collégiale Notre-Dame
Foch often came here to pray and meditate in this Gothic Flemish church with three gables, three aisles, three apses and square tower over the transept.

Ancienne chapelle des Jésuites
This church boasts a harmonious 17C brick and stone façade.

Castel-Meulen (Moulin)
🚶*Guided visits (1hr) Apr–Sep 10am–12.30pm, 2–6pm; Oct–Mar Sat 2–6pm, Sun, public holidays 10am– noon, 2–6pm.* ◷*Closed 25 Dec, 1 Jan.* ✆*3€. Arrange visits through the tourist office on* ☎*03 28 40 52 55. www.cassel-horizons.com.*

This 18C wooden **windmill** from Arneke was re-erected here to replace the castle's original windmill which burnt down in 1911. It produces flour (there is a bakery on the premises) and linseed oil. Celebrations take place on 14 July.

Public Gardens
The gardens at the top of the hill occupy the site of a medieval castle which once incorporated a collegiate church, the crypt of which remains. An equestrian statue of General Foch stands in the middle of the garden.

A tour of the terrace offers an excellent **panorama**★ (*viewing platforms*) over the picturesque jumble of Cassel's old rooftops, and beyond to the hills of Flanders and the plain, as far as the North Sea and the belfry of Bruges.

Mont des Récollets Farm

© Philippe Houze/hemis.fr

Mont des Récollets Farm-Wouwenberghof

1936 rte de Steenvoorde. Tickets from the Kasteelhof estaminet. ◷*Open 10 Apr–10 Nov Thu–Sun 10am–7pm.* ◷*Closed 1st week of Jul and 2nd week of Oct.* ◉*5€ (under 15s no charge). Estaminet in the garden in the afternoon.* ☎*03 28 40 59 29.*

The best time to visit the garden is 15–25 Apr for the bulb season, late June for the rose garden and the Jardin bleu and 15 Oct–10 Nov for an autumnal display of colour.

Landscape artist Emmanuel de Quill-acq invites you to discover this **garden** inspired by Flemish art and culture. Laid out around traditional a red-brick **farm-house** with traditional corbie-stepped gables surrounded by a jungle of local wild flowers, the garden combines the strict squareness of a traditional Flemish garden with a hint of whimsy.

EXCURSIONS
STEENVOORDE

◗*8km/5mi E by D 948.*
This typical small Flemish town with painted houses under red-tiled roofs is renowned for its large dairy. The town celebrates the legend of its giant, Yan den Houtkapper, a woodcutter who made a pair of everlasting boots for Charlemagne.

Windmills – Three well-preserved windmills can be seen near the town.

Two of them are wooden post mills: the **Drievemeulen** *(on D 948 west; Jul and Aug 1hr guided tours Sun 3–6pm, rest of year by reservation; 2€; ☎03 28 48 19 90; www.pays-des-geants.com)*, dating from 1776, is a typical oil mill; the **Noordmeulen** *(same hours as for Drievenmeulen)*, dating from 1576 with 18C working parts, is a wheat mill. The third, the **Steenmeulen** *(guided tours (90min) by reservation (closed last Sun and Mon of month and Nov) 9am–noon, 2–6pm; 5€; ☎06 78 18 15 73; www.steenmeulen.com)* at Terdeghem *(on D 947 south)*, is a truncated brick mill, still in working order (1864).

Wormhout

◗*10km/6mi N via D 218 and D 916.*
🏢*60 pl. Gén-de-Gaulle, 59470 Wormhout.* ☎*0328628123. http://wormhout.pagesperso-orange.fr.*
Moulin Deschodt – *Guided visits (1h) 1st and 3rd Sun Jun, 2nd Sun Jul, 1st and 2nd Sun Aug 3–6pm.* ◉*2€. By reservation the rest of the year* ☎*03 28 62 81 23.* This wooden post mill is the last of 11 windmills dating 1780.

Musée Jeanne-Devos – ◷*Open Apr–Oct Thu–Tue 2–5pm, 1st two Sundays in the month 3–6pm; Nov–Mar Mon, Tue, Sat 2–5pm.* ◉*€2.* ☎*03 28 62 81 23.* This charming Flemish house, flanked by a dovecote and set within lovely gardens at the end of a cul-de-sac, is the old Wormhout presbytery (18C). This is the former home of Jeanne Devos who collected, until her death in 1989, a multitude of objects from daily life. A photographer by profession, she left thousands of photographs portraying the ordinary and extraordinary lives of the villagers nearby.

Maison Guillaume de Rubrouck

◗*11km/7mi NW via D 11, D 211.*
◷*Open Apr–Sept Sat & Sun 2.30–5.30pm.* *Guided tour by reservation.* ◉*4€ (under 18s no charge).* ☎*06 84 68 09 81, www.guillaumederubrouck.fr.*
This small exhibition recounts the adventures of Guillaume de Rubrouck, a 13C Franciscan monk. On the orders

Historic battles

Countless battles were fought over Cassel before the town and Maritime Flanders were finally annexed by France under the Nimengen Treaty in 1678.

From October 1914 to April 1915, General Foch established his headquarters in Cassel, from where he monitored the battles of Yser and Ypres. He lodged in the Hôtel de Schœbecque, at no. 32 of what is now rue du Maréchal-Foch.

In May 1940, a section of the British Expeditionary Force held out against German troops at Cassel for three days (Operation "Dynamo"), allowing the Allied forces to evacuate from Dunkerque.

of Louis IX, between 1252 and 1255, Roubrouck embarked on a 10 000km/ 6 000mi journey from France to the outer reaches of the Mongol Empire, which then stretched from the Black Sea to the Pacific Ocean. His mission was to convert the Mongols to Christianity and establish diplomatic ties with the successors of Ghengis Khan who, after reaching Vienna in 1241, were knocking at the gates of Europe. Several decades before Marco Polo, he wrote a vivid account of his travels, which survives to this day. A room is also devoted to daily life in Mongolia (Rubrouck is twinned with a town in Mongolia).

The village also has an interesting 11C Romanesque **hall-church** complete with a 16C tower and 18C **retables** dedicated to the Virgin Mary, Saint Arnould and Saint Sylvestre, patron saint.

Millam and the Merckeghem viewpoint

⟳ *12km/7.5mi to the NW via D 226.*

As you drive along the ridge, look out for the views over the hills of Flanders *(right)* and the Flanders coastline *(left)*. Passing through the valley town of Millam, stop off at the **Chapelle Sainte-Mildrède** (18C). The yellow brick houses and red-tiled roofs of **Millam** are well-worth a detour. Just before Merckeghem, admire

the **view** over the rolling Flemish plain with Dunkerque and the sea beyond.

ADDRESSES

🏠 STAY

⊜⊜ **Chambre d'hôte Les Sources**– *326 r. d'Aire.* ✆*03 28 48 26 26. www. schoebeque.com.* ♿🅿. *5 rooms* ⌑.
Nestled amid the fields of Flanders, this bed and breakfast with bright, clean bedrooms affords panoramic views. Breakfast is served in your room or at the nearby Châtellerie de Schoebeque run by the same owners.

⊜⊜⊜⊜ **Châtellerie de Schoebeque**– *32 r. Foch.* ✆*03 28 42 42 67. www. schoebeque.com. 14 rooms.* ⌑*15€.*
A beautiful 18C Cassel residence affording countryside views to the rear. This family-run hotel gives guests a warm welcome. For an added personal touch, each of the bedrooms sports a different theme. A wagon in the garden offers the ultimate hideout for Bohemian travellers.

🍽 EAT

⊜ **La Taverne Flamande** – *34 Grand'Place.* ✆*03 28 42 42 59. Closed Feb holidays, end Aug and end Oct, Tue and Wed eves.*
After paying your respects to giant hero Reuze Papa, try the Flemish specialities served in this tavern with a terrace over the valley.

⊜⊜ **Au Roi du Potje Vleesch** – *31 r. du Mont-des-Cats, 59270 Godewaersvelde. 12km/7mi to the E of Cassel via D 948 and D 18.* ✆*03 28 42 52 56. Closed Jan, Mon, weekends by reservation.* Visitors need to pass through the delicatessen to find this tavern. Try the *potjevleesch* (a meat stew) and Henri le Douanier beer.

ACTIVITIES

🐎 **Les écuries du pays de Cassel** – *r. de l'Abesse, 59670 Bavinchave.* ✆*06 63 85 43 21. 10am–6pm. www.lesecuriesdu paysdecassel.fr.* Discover the countryside around Cassel on horseback. Special pony tours for children.

EVENTS

Carnivals– Reuze-Papa paradest each Sunday before Mardi Gras, and again on Easter Monday to celebrate the end of winter in the company of Reuze-Maman.

Bailleul

Situated in the hilly area known as Monts de Flandre, the town of Bailleul was damaged in 1918 during the last German onslaught in this region and rebuilt in authentic Flemish style.
During the Mardi Gras Carnival, headed by the giant Gargantua, a tipsy Dr. Picolissimo throws tripe to the crowds. The drive through the Monts de Flandre provides an opportunity to explore the landscape of Flanders, which is less flat than often thought.

- ▶ **Population:** 14 136
- **Michelin Local Map:** p357:C3; 302: E-3.
- **Info:** 3 Grand'Place, 59270 Bailleul. ℘03 28 43 81 00, www.montsdeflandre.fr
- ▶ **Location:** Almost on the border with Belgium, and 240km/150mi N of Paris via the A 1.
- **Don't Miss:** Don't miss the view from the belfry.
- **Timing:** Spend half a day here.

SIGHTS
Grand'Place

Despite being destroyed eight times, Bailleul and its Grand'Place have always regained their typically Flemish appearance. Before settling down in a local tavern with a glass of "3 Monts" beer, take a closer look at the town hall and its neo-Flemish belfry. The brick façade decorated with corner stones features a proclamation balcony.

Rue du Musée

This street is lined with fine houses, in particular no. 3, the town's cultural centre with its Marguerite-Yourcenar hall.

Belfry

Belfry

© Brigitte Merle/Photononstop

Guided tours Jul–Aug Sat–Sun 11am, Wed 3.30pm; May–Jun & Sep Sat–Sun 11am–12.15pm; Mar–Apr, Oct Sun 11am. ◷3.50€. ℘03 28 43 81 00. www.montsdeflandre.fr.
The belfry towering over the town hall housed the cloth market in medieval times. There is a 13C Gothic room at ground level and from the watch-path at the top, the vast **panorama★** includes the plain and Monts de Flandre to the north and the slag heaps of the mining area to the south. The city of Lille is visible on a clear day. The peal of bells chimes well-known Flemish tunes.

Musée Benoît-Depuydt

24 rue du musée. ◷Open Wed–Mon 2–5.30pm Aug. ◷3.90€, no charge 1st Sun in the month. ℘03 28 49 12 70. www.ville-bailleul.fr.
Founded in 1859, this elegant museum displays glazed earthenware from Delft and Northern France, porcelain from China and Japan, 16C to 18C furniture and carved wood as well as paintings from the Flemish, French and Dutch schools. Note in particular an Adoration of the Magi by Pieter Brueghel. Don't miss the large 18C Flemish tapestry.

Maison de la Dentelle

6 r. du Collège. ◷Open Tue–Fri, Sat (odd months) 1.30–5pm. ◷1.50€. ℘03 28 41 25 72.
This school occupies a Flemish-style house; the pediment is decorated with

a lace-maker and her spinning wheel. Some 100 students come here to learn about bobbin lace-making every year.

Conservatoire Botanique National de Bailleul

Hameau de Haendries. Open Mon–Thu 8.30am–noon, 1.30–6pm (Fri 5pm). 3€. (guided tours, 5€). 03 28 49 00 83. www.cbnbl.org.
Housed on the 30ha-/74-acre estate of a restored Flemish farm, this national botanical conservatory specialises in vegetation from Northern France. The medicinal garden contains some 700 plants and the botanical gardens are dedicated to the preservation of more than 600 **endangered species**. The GR 128 footpath, which crosses the Monts de Flandre, passes through the estate. Picnic tables, a viewing table and nature trails are available for visitors.

🚗 DRIVING TOUR

NORTHERN HEIGHTS

Allow half a day.

This itinerary will take you through the Flemish countryside into Belgium. On the way, you will see hills, mills, typical local taverns and taste "speciality" beer and soft cheeses.

▷ Follow D 23 N, then turn left along the D 223.

On your right (Belgium) is **Mont Kemmel** with **Mont Rouge** (Rodeberg) in the foreground.

▷ Turn left again onto D 318.

Straddling the border between France and Belgium, **Mont Noir** (Black Hill), with its dark wooded slopes, is part of the Monts de Flandres range (altitude 170m/558ft). A path leads to the artificial grotto (1875).
The village of **Saint-Jans-Cappel** lies at the foot of Mont Noir, immortalised in *Archives du Nord (How Many Years),* the autobiographical work of writer **Marguerite Yourcenar** (1903–87) who spent her childhood years here.
From the **Parc Marguerite-Yourcenar★**, the view extends towards Ypres, Mont Rouge and Mont des Cats, surmounted by its monastery. The sea and Artois hills are visible in clear weather. *Le sentier des jacinthes,* a marked trail (2hr 30min), runs along the slopes of Mont Noir.
The **Musée Marguerite-Yourcenar** explores the writer's life. (Guided visits in English for groups only, 45min; open Wed–Fri 10am–noon & 2–4.30pm, Sun 3.30–5.30pm; 3€; 03 28 42 20 20; www.museeyourcenar.fr).

▷ Follow D 10 north to Berthen and turn left.

Mont des Cats (altitude 158m/514ft) is part of the Monts de Flandres range. Gourmets know this area for its wonderful cheeses. On top of the hill are the neo-Gothic buildings of a Trappist monastery – **Abbaye Notre-Damedu-Mont** – founded in 1826. The **centre Charles-Grimminck** sells monastic products.

Godewaersvelde

A Flemish village served by several "estaminets" (some closed weekends). **Border Museum** – Apr–Sept: Wed–Mon 2–5pm. 3€. 03 28 42 08 52. www.musee-godewaersvelde.fr. This exhibition explores the lives of cross-border smugglers. Testimonies and belongings bring the bootleggers back to life.

▷ Head N via D 139, turn back and follow D 10 to Boeschepe.

The village of **Boeschepe** at the foot of Mont des Cats has a restored windmill, the **Ondankmeulen** (currently closed to the public for renovation 03 28 42 50 70), next to a delightful bar *(estaminet).* *For more details on estaminets, see INTRODUCTION: Where to Eat, p45.*

▷ Follow D 139 over the Belgian border and continue to Poperingue.

The residents of **Poperinge** are known as **Kei-koppen**, "Tough Heads". On the Grand'Place, a stone weighing 1 650kg/3 638lb helps explain why. The Cathédrale St-Bertinus, a Flemish hall-church, is an example of the Romano-Gothic style.

▶ Leave Poperinge via N 308 towards Dunkerque and turn left to Watou, also in Belgium.

The village of **Watou** is ideal for anyone wishing to sample the authentic atmosphere of an *estaminet*.

▶ Return to Bailleul along D 10.

EXCURSIONS
Armentières
▶ *12km/7mi to SE via A 25 or D 933.*
🛈 *33 r. de Lille, 59280 Armentières. ☎03 20 44 18 19. www.armentieres.fr/tourisme.*
Rebuilt after World War I, the **town hall and belfry** offer views over the Monts de Flanders and Lille. *☎03 20 44 18 19. www.armentieres.fr/tourisme.* ⟟Guided tour (1hr 30min) by request (7 days before). ⏱Open Apr–Oct 1st and 3rd Sat of the month 2.30pm. ⏱Closed public holidays. ⏳3.50€ (under 12s 1€) children admitted over 6yrs.
Try your hand at sail-boating and bird watching at the Prés du Hem park.

Hazebrouck
▶ *11km/7mi to the W via D 642, halfway between Bailleul and Saint-Omer.*
🛈 *Pl. du Gén.-de-Gaulle, town hall, 59190 Hazebrouck.* ⏱Open Mon–Fri 10am–noon, 2–6pm, Sat 10.30am–12.30pm, 2–5pm⚓ *☎03 28 43 44 37. www.tourisme-hazebrouck.fr.*
A typically Flemish town renowned for its summer carnival and giant parade.
Musée municipal – Pl. Georges-Degroote. ⏱Open Wed, Thu, Sat 10am–noon, 2–5pm, Sun 10am–noon, 3–6pm. ⏱Closed public holidays. ⏳3€ (under 18s no charge), no charge 1st Sun of the month. *☎03 28 43 44 46.* This former Augustinian convent (17C) is home to the town's **giants** and a collection of 16C

and 17C Dutch paintings by Rubens, Van Dyck and Teniers.
Église Saint-Éloi – A brick and stone church containing fine 17C carvings.

ADDRESSES

🛏 STAY

⊟ **Hôtel Le Gambrinus** – 2 r. Nationale, 59190 Hazebrouck. *☎03 28 41 98 79. http://hoteldugambrinus.fr. Closed 3–23 Aug. Wifi. 16 rooms.* ⟟. This central hotel's trademark is the King of Beer, a key figure in Flemish culture. Each of room has a different theme.

⊟ **Hôtel Station Bac St-Maur** – 77 r. de la Gare, 62840 Sailly-sur-la-Lys, 7km SW of Armentières. *☎03 21 02 68 20. www.lagaredesanneesfolles.fr. 7 rooms.* ♿. A former station converted into a hotel. Sleep in one of six railway carriages from the 1930s.

🍴 EAT

⊟ **Estaminet De Vierpot** – 125 Complexe Joséph-Decanter 59299 Boeschepe, 12 km N of Bailleul on D 10. *☎03 28 49 46 37.* Traditional café located at the foot of a windmill. Typical decor dating from the 1900s, complete with stove and wooden benches.

ACTIVITIES

👥 **Club Montgolfière Passion** – 253 r. d'Haire, 59190 Hazebrouck. *☎03 28 41 65 59. 150€/1hr flight. Children from 12yrs.* This hot air balloon club organises two balloon rides a day.

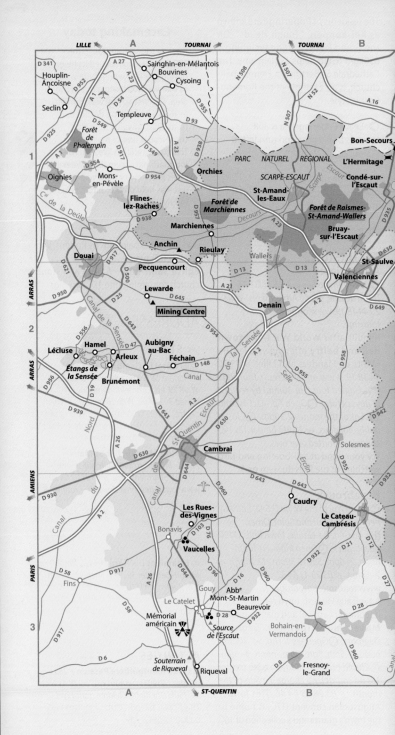

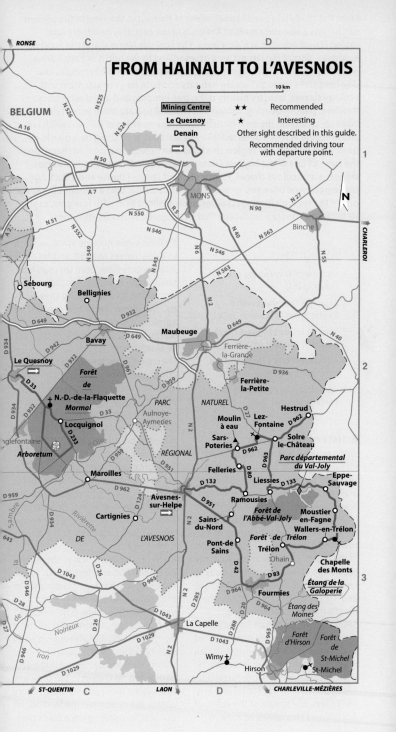

FROM HAINAUT TO L'AVESNOIS

0   10 km

Mining Centre   ★★   Recommended
Le Quesnoy   ★   Interesting
Denain   →   Other sight described in this guide.
Recommended driving tour with departure point.

BELGIUM

RONSE

N 525
N 526
N 524
A 16
N 50
A 7
MONS
N 27
CHARLEROI
N
N 51
N 550
N 546
N 90
N 563
Binche
N 552
N 549
N 546
N 55
N 543
R 5
N 6
N 563
Sebourg
Bellignies
D 932
D 649
Maubeuge
D 649
N 40
Bavay
D 942
D 649
Ferrière-la-Grande
Le Quesnoy
Forêt de Mormal
D 961
D 959
Ferrière-la-Petite
D 936
Hestrud
N.-D.-de-la-Flaquette
PARC
NATUREL
Moulin à eau
Lez-Fontaine
D 962
Locquignol
D 333
Aulnoye-Aymeries
Sars-Poteries
Solre le-Château
anglefontaine
l'Oise
D 959
RÉGIONAL
D 962
D 963
Parc départemental du Val-Joly
Arboretum
D 951
Felleries
D 80
Eppe-Sauvage
Maroilles
D 962
D 133
Liessies
D 133
D 124
Avesnes-sur-Helpe
D 951
Ramousies
Moustier-en-Fagne
Cartignies
D 934
DE
L'AVESNOIS
N 2
Sains-du-Nord
Forêt de l'Abbé-Val-Joly
Wallers-en-Trélon
Forêt de Trélon
la Sambre
Rivierette
Pont-de-Sains
D 42
Trélon
Ohain
D 83
Chapelle des Monts
D 1043
D 26
Noirieux
D 965
N 2
D 285
D 964
Fourmies
Étang de la Galoperie
D 946
D 28
Iron
D 1043
D 288
La Capelle
D 20
D 964
Étang des Moines
D 27
D 946
D 1029
N 2
D 1043
Wimy
D 963
Forêt d'Hirson
Forêt de St-Michel
St-Michel
D 1029
Hirson

ST-QUENTIN   LAON   CHARLEVILLE-MÉZIÈRES

377

HAINAUT TO L'AVESNOIS

From the shady lakes and former mines of Hainaut in the west to the ancient oak forests and nature trails of Avesnois in the east, this decidedly rural region is best enjoyed at a slow pace. The Forêt de Mormal and the Forêt de Raismes – part of the largest area of woodland to the north of Paris – are a walker's paradise where signed trails, flora tours, wildlife adventures and day-long treks through nesting habitats compete for your attention with ecology classes, forestry history talks, tree jumping and aerial acrobatics. If sailing, paddle-boating, fishing and water-skiing are more your style, the lakes created from the now-transformed mine quarries of Hainaut will have you breezing across a deserted lake in a sail boat or pitching up a pike in no time. Back on land, the region also boasts an exceptional rural heritage, from the ruins of one of the biggest Cistercian abbeys in Europe to a real Roman village, a miraculous chapel, France's largest chapter house and a Dark Age settlement. And once you've worked up an appetite, take a moment to savour one of the region's local specialities, such as sliced beef with foie gras, as you sit back and admire a landscape that has inspired artists for centuries.

Highlights

1 Dance with **Gayant the giant** in Douai (p381)

2 Explore a **coal shaft** with a former miner in Lewarde (p384)

3 Stand in France's **biggest chapter house** in Cambrai (p387)

4 Admire **Matisse's last painting** in Le Cateau-Cambrésis (p390)

5 Hike along the **Druid path** in Forêt de Mormal (p397)

Artists of the Region

When Honoré de Balzac began writing his tale of Flemish aristocratic intrigue, *The Quest of the Absolute*, in 1834 he naturally turned to the 18C bourgeois townhouses and Gothic riverside courthouse of Douai for inspiration. Dominated by a fairytale belfry that towers over its narrow medieval streets, Douai is typical of the region's genteel towns, from the sedate spa of Saint-Amand-les-Eaux to Le Quesnoy's dishevelled fortifications and the 19C gardens of Cambrai, where life still moves at a stately pace.

Several centuries before Balzac's time, the region's artists were more inspired by its pastoral scenes than its Palladian mansions: painter Jean Bellegambe, born in Douai in 1470, produced dozens of portraits of the Scarpe and Sensée valleys, the towers of the abbey of Anchin and the woods of Fline in his lifetime, while Antoine Watteau, born in Valenciennes in 1684, and his pupil Jean Baptiste Pater, born ten years later, painted the same bucolic scenes, this time suffused with rococo theatricality. This same landscape can still be admired today in the Parc Régional Scarpe-Escaut, for example, or the Forêt de Marchiennes.

The region's most famous painter, on the other hand, was more inspired by its carnivals and acrobats than its landscapes, at least during his early years. Born in Le Cateau-Cambrésis in 1869, Matisse, the son of a grain merchant, was determined to become a clown after a visit to the local circus. In 1952, after spending eighty years pursuing a very different career, he donated 52 works to his home town, which now displays these masterpieces in a former archiepiscopal palace, the town's Musée Matisse – the third largest collection of the artist's work in France.

Matisse's contemporary, the novelist Émile Zola, was less drawn to the region's countryside or clowns than to the coalmining town of Denain, near Valenciennes, on which he modelled his famous tale of working-class strife, *Germinal* (1885). But although it's still possible to visit the homes where the miners lived and descend into the dark depths of a mine shaft in the company of a miner at the Lewarde mining history centre, the region has gladly changed out of all recognition since Zola's time.

Valenciennes

A major centre for 17C and 18C French art, Valenciennes is the perfect starting point for a tour of the region's mining heritage.

A BIT OF HISTORY
Athens of the North

As its nickname suggests, Valenciennes is the birthplace of dozens of artists including sculptors André Beauneveu (14C); the "image-maker" of Charles V, Antoine Pater (1670–1747); Saly (1717–76), who worked for the court of Denmark; and **Carpeaux** (1827–75), who breathed new life into French sculpture. Famous local painters include **Antoine Watteau** (1684–1721) and Jean-Baptiste Pater (1695–1736) who both specialised in genre painting in the *fête galante* style; Louis and François Watteau, grand-nephew and great-nephew of Antoine; and landscape painter Henri Harpignies (1819–1916).

SIGHTS
Maison espagnole

This 16C half-timbered, corbelled house built during the Spanish occupation now houses the tourist office.

Musée des Beaux-Arts★

ⓝ*Open Wed–Sun 10am–6pm, Thu 10am–8pm (Thu 8pm).* ◉4€. &
☏*03 27 22 57 20. www.valenciennes.fr.*
This early-20C museum has an extensive collection of works from the 15C–17C Flemish School (Rubens), 18C French works and 19C sculptures (Carpeaux).

EXCURSIONS
St-Saulve

ⓒ*2km/1.25mi NE. Leave Valenciennes by av. de Liège, N 30.*
Chapelle du Carmel – *1 r. Henri-Barbusse.* ⓝ*Open 9–11.30am & 1–5pm.* ☏*03 27 46 24 98.* Designed by the architect Guislain, whose designs play on the effects of volume and simple materials, this Carmelite chapel (1966) is bathed in light from the geometric stained-glass windows above the altar.

▶ **Population:** 357 395
ⓘ **Michelin Local Map:** p376: B2.
ⓘ **Info:** Office du tourisme 1 r. Askievre, 59300 Valenciennes ☏03 27 28 89 10. www.tourisme valenciennois.fr.
ⓒ **Location:** Close to the Belgian border, SW of Lille (56km/35mi) and linked by the A 23.
ⓟ **Parking:** There are mostly one-way streets, but plenty of small car parks.
ⓞ **Timing:** A half day for the Musée des Beaux-Arts.
👪 **Kids:** The Parc d'attractions Le Fleury.

Bruay-sur-l'Escaut

ⓒ *5 km/3mi N by D 935 and D 75.*
The **church** houses a **cenotaph** dedicated to Sainte Pharaïlde. ⓝ*Open Mon and Thu 10am–noon.*

Sebourg

ⓒ *9km/5.5mi E. Leave town via D 934, take D 59 on the left, right along D 350.*
For centuries, a 12C-hermit with a miraculous ability to cure hernias, attracted thousands of pilgrims to the remains of a 12C–16C **church** (👁‍🗨*guided visits 9am–noon, 2–6.30pm; ☏03 27 26 52 78*) on the slopes of the Aunelle Valley. The 14C effigies of Henri of Hainault, Lord of Sebourg and his wife are a must.

Denain

ⓒ *10km/6mi SW by N 30.*
A former coalmining town, Denain was the inspiration for Émile Zola's novel *Germinal*. Although the last mine closed in 1948, its slag heap dominates the town. The Academy of Music (1852) on avenue Villars was once home to the poet-miner Jules Mousseron (1868–1943). Walk up the alleyway between nos. 138 and 140 Ludovic-Trarieux to admire the **Cité Ernestine**, semi-detached miners' houses and, to the north, the **Cité Bellevue** a row of foremen's houses.

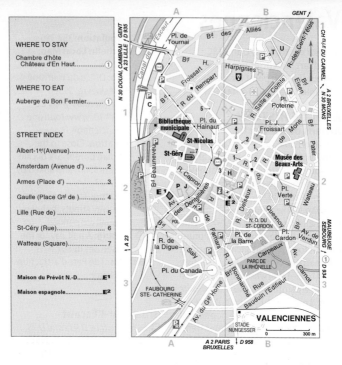

WHERE TO STAY

Chambre d'hôte
Château d'En Haut............①

WHERE TO EAT

Auberge du Bon Fermier........①

STREET INDEX

Albert-1er (Avenue)................1

Amsterdam (Avenue d')..........2

Armes (Place d')....................3

Gaulle (Place G al de)..............4

Lille (Rue de)........................5

St-Céry (Rue).......................6

Watteau (Square)..................7

Maison du Prévôt N.-D.............E¹

Maison espagnole...................E²

ADDRESSES

🖛 STAY / 🍴 EAT

**⊜⊜ Chambre d'hôte Château
d'En Haut**– *Château d'en Haut.* 59144
Jenlain. 6 km/4mi SE by D 934 and D649.
℘03 27 49 71 80. http://chateaudenhaut.
free.fr. 🅿 🍴. 5 rooms. 🛏. A remarkable
18C chateau decorated with antiques
and fine marquetry. Furnished with four-
poster beds, there is a rambling estate.

⊜⊜⊜ Auberge du Bon Fermier–
64r. Famars. ℘03 27 46 68 25. www.
bonfermier.com. Wi-fi.16 rooms. 🛏10€.
Restaurant ⊜⊜⊜. An authentic 17C inn
with an historic brick and stone façade.
The stable block houses a restaurant.

ACTIVITIES

♟♟ Parc d'attractions Le Fleury –
5 r. Bouchain. 59111 Wavrechain-sous-
Faulx. ℘03 27 35 71 16. www.lefleury.fr.
Open May–Sept. 🎫11€. A 23ha/56 acre
amusement park.

Douai★

The inspiration for Honoré de
Balzac's tale of spendthrift Flemish
nobles, *The Quest of the Absolute*,
Douai's aristocratic charms are still
to be found in its remarkable Gothic
and Renaissance architecture and
refined townhouses.

A BIT OF HISTORY

Renowned for the quality of its cloth
in the Middle Ages, the town became
a major centre of learning in the 16C,

▸ **Population:** 518 727
🕭 **Michelin Local Map:**
p376: A1/2.
🛈 **Info:** 70 pl. d'Armes 59500,
Douai. ℘0327 88 26 79.
www.ville-douai.fr.

following the founding of its university
by Phillip II of Spain in 1562, attracting
students from as far away as England
and the Netherlands. Annexed by France
in 1667, Douai was chosen as the site of a

Jean Bellegambe (1470–1534)

This artist, who seems to have spent his entire life in Douai, mastered the transition from the Gothic tradition (religious subjects treated with realistic detail and harmonious colours) to the Renaissance (works decorated with columns, pilasters, shells and garlands), combining the objective, intimate realism of the Flemish School with the intellectualism of the French School. Douai can be recognised in his works: the belfry and town gates and the River Scarpe.

regional court of justice, the Parliament of Flanders, in 1714, whose richest members commissioned the construction of elaborate townhouses, many of which survive to this day. From the mid-19C, the arrival of the industrial revolution allowed Douai to exploit its rich seams of coal, increasing its wealth.

Gayant is born – When Douai narrowly escaped falling into French hands on 16 June 1479, a procession was organised to thank the patron saint of the town. Over the years, this annual event became more colourful, with each corporation supplying a float decorated with symbolic characters.

Gayant the survivor – In 1770, the bishop of Arras forbade the procession, which celebrated a French defeat, and replaced it with another one on 6 July, to celebrate the arrival of French troops in Douai in 1667. The giants were given another lease of life in 1778, only to be wiped out again by the Revolution. They reappeared in 1801 and were given their present costumes 20 years later.

WALKING TOUR

Start from **Porte de Valenciennes**, which is Gothic on one side (15C) and Classical on the other (18C) and walk to the place d'Armes and its outdoor cafés.

▶ Walk along r. de la Mairie.

Town Hall and Belfry★

◷Open Jul and Aug. Guided tours (1hr), 10–11am, 2–6pm; rest of year daily 11am (except Mon), 3–5pm. ◷4.50€. ☏03 27 88 26 79. www.ville-douai.fr.
The construction of this Gothic ensemble began in 1380 and was resumed several times between 1471 and 1873.

Inside the **town hall** (Hôtel de Ville), the Gothic Council Chamber (15C), the old chapel and the White Salon with its 18C wood panelling are open to visitors. The 64m/210ft **belfry** dates from 1410.

▶ Follow the vaulted passageway and cross the courtyard to r. de l'Université.

Rue de la Comédie

To the right stands the Louis XV-style **Hôtel d'Aoust** with a Rococo door.

▶ Continue along r. de la Comédie and turn right onto r. des Foulons.

Rue des Foulons

Once occupied by "foulons", or linen-drapers, in the Middle Ages, this street is lined with the 18C houses on the left-hand side. Don't miss the Louis XIII-style **Hôtel de la Tramerie** at no. 132.

▶ Follow r. de la Mairie on the right then r. Gambetta to rue Bellegambe.

Rue Bellegambe

The Modern Style boutique in rue Bellegambe (opposite the church) features a shop front decorated with sunflowers.

▶ Walk back and turn left towards the town hall.

SIGHTS
Musée de la Chartreuse★★

◷Open Wed–Mon 10am–noon, 2–6pm. Guided tours (1hr) ◷4.40€, no charge 1st Sunday of the month. ☏03 27 71 38 80. www.museedelachartreuse.fr.
The museum is housed in an interesting group of 16C, 17C and 18C buildings, once the old charter house. On the left

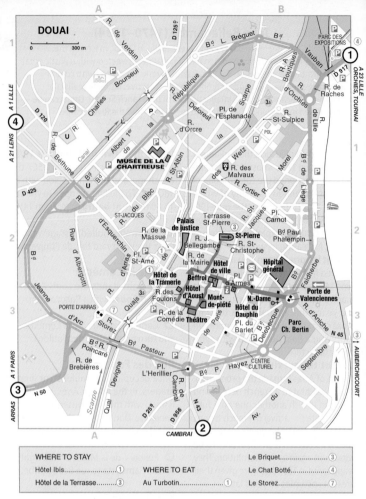

is the Hôtel d'Abancourt; on the right, beneath a huge square tower, is a Flemish Renaissance-style building. This is where the first Carthusian monks settled in the 17C. They built the small cloisters, the refectory, the chapter-house and the chapel, which was completed in 1722. The great cloisters and the monks' cells were destroyed in the 19C. The museum is divided into two parts: the Fine Arts Section and the Archaeology and Natural History Section.

Fine Arts

The collections consist principally of fine early paintings.

Rooms 1 – 3 – Early Flemish, Dutch (the *Master of Manne*, the *Master of Flemalle*) and Italian paintings. Large 16C altarpieces from other abbeys are also on display here.

Don't miss **Anchin Polyptych★** by Bellegambe (*room 2*) portraying the Adoration of the Cross or the Adoration of the Holy Trinity, and the Marchiennes Polyptych by Van Scorel (Utrecht School, 16C). Two masterpieces of the Italian Renaissance, Veronese's *Portrait of a Venetian Woman* and Carracci's *Scourging of Christ*, a work of rare intensity, are on display in room 3. The bronze *Venus of Castello* recalls the work of the sculptor and architect Giambologna. Although he spent most of his career in Italy, he was born in Douai in 1529 and trained in Flanders.

Rooms 4–6 – Start with the relief map of Douai (1709) before exploring the collection of 16C Flemish and Dutch Mannerists.

Rooms 7–8 – Don't miss the works by Rubens (*Céres and Pan*) and Jordaens (*Study of a head*), landscapes by Momper and Govaerts, and a witchcraft scene by David Teniers.

Rooms 11–12 – The French School (17C–19C) is well represented here by portrait painters Le Brun (*Louis XIV on Horseback*), Vivien, Largillière, Boilly and David (*Mme Tallien*). Works by Impressionist painters are also on show, including Renoir, Sisley and Pissaro, and Post-Impressionists.

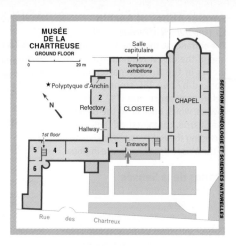

MUSÉE DE LA CHARTREUSE
GROUND FLOOR
0   20 m
★ Polyptyque d'Anchin
N
Salle capitulaire
Temporary exhibitions
2 Refectory
CLOISTER
CHAPEL
1st floor
Hallway
5   4   3   1   Entrance
6
Rue   des   Chartreux
SECTION ARCHÉOLOGIE ET SCIENCES NATURELLES

▶ Return to the ground floor.

Cloisters

The cloister vaults are pointed despite having been built in 1663, in the middle of the Classical period. The red brickwork contrasts pleasantly with the white stone of the ribs and the framing.

Chapter-house

This was also built in 1663 in the same style; it now has temporary exhibitions.

Archaeology and Natural History

The evolution of man is traced from the Palaeolithic Age to AD 400 based on excavations in the north of France (*first floor*). The collection includes a cast of the skull of Biache Man, who is thought to have lived about 250,000 years ago; discovered at Biache-St-Vaast.

The Gallo-Roman period is explored through artefacts found at Bavay (statuettes) and Lewarde (busts). The models of the Merovingian village of Brebières and the necropolis at Hordain are worth lingering over.

Palais de Justice

27 pl. Charles-de-Pollinchove
🔊Guided tour of the Parliament Chamber, Jul–Aug Sat 3.30pm; rest of year public holidays 3.30pm. ⊛4.50€. www.ville-douai.fr.

Once home to the monks of Marchiennes Abbey, the law courts were built in the early 16C and almost entirely rebuilt in the 18C before becoming the seat of the Flanders Parliament in 1714. The old prison, from which Vidocq, a famous 18C French adventurer, escaped has been turned into an **exhibition centre** (*enter from the riverside*). The items on show explore the history of Douai and the law courts.

The first-floor courtroom, the **Grande Salle du Parlement** (1762), is furnished with a vast marble fireplace, carved Louis XV woodwork, a portrait of Louis XIV and allegorical paintings by Nicolas Brenet (1769).

EXCURSIONS
Flines-les-Raches

▶ *11km/7mi NE by D 917 and D 938.*
The village has a curious **church**, which is entered through a very old brick and sandstone belfry-porch (some say dating back to AD 800). The narrow nave opens onto chapels from various periods. In the first two chapels on the right, the roof beams are decorated with historiated corbels and bear the arms of the Abbess of Flines (1561–1571).

Former Abbey of Anchin

◐ *1km/1/2mi N of Pecquencourt.*

The entrance to this Benedictine abbey, one of the oldest religious establishments in the Nord département, is flanked by two 18C stone pavilions. Before its destruction in 1792, its church towers, which once lined the banks of the Scarpe, contained valuable items including the *Polyptyque d'Anchin* now in the Musée de la Chartreuse in Douai.

Étangs de la Sensée

◐ *12km/8mi to the S by D 643 and D 47 or D 14E4.*

This tributary of the Escaut marks the border between Cambrésis and Flanders. From Lécluse to Wasnes-au-Bac, further to the west, the river feeds into a series of attractive lakes fringed with high grasses and poplar trees.

The most popular spots are **Lécluse** (a lake), **Hamel** (equestrian centre), **Féchain**, **Arleux** (garlic growing), **Brunémont** (a beautiful view over the lake and sailing base) and **Aubigny-au-Bac**, which has an 👥 **activities centre** (*r. de la Plage, 59265;* ◷*open May–Jun 11am–6pm, Jul–Aug 10am–7pm, 1st and 2nd weekend of Sept 11am–6pm;* ☏*03 27 89 24 24;* ✆*contact for charges;* ♿*)* where you can try your hand at fishing, pedal boating, sailing, water skiing or karting.

Mining History Centre in Lewarde★★

◷*Open Mar–14 Nov 9am–5.30pm, 15 Nov–29 Feb 1–5pm, Sun 10am–5pm.* ☛ *Guided tours (1hr 30min). Audioguides in English.* ✆*11.50€ (5–18 yrs 5.90€).* ☏*03 27 95 82 82. www.chm-lewarde.com.*

Plunge deep into the earth and explore 450 m/492 yd of coal galleries at France's biggest mining museum. The museum explores 345 million years of coal history and 300 years of mining techniques. Start with the temporary exhibition in the former storehouse (1927) before moving on to a selection of photographs and personal belongings that reveal the harsh reality of life in a mining town.

ADDRESSES

🛏 STAY

🍽🛏 **Hôtel Ibis** – *Pl.Saint-Amé.* ☏ *03 27 87 27 27.* 🅿. *42 rooms* 🛏. The standards of Ibis hotels in a historic buildings dating back to the 16C and 18C. Rooms on the 3rd floor have exposed ceiling beams.

🍽🛏 **Hôtel de la Terrasse** – *36 Terrasse St-Pierre.* ☏*03 27 88 70 04. www.laterrasse.fr. 24 rooms* 🛏, *half board possible. Restaurant* 🍽🛏🍽🛏. The perfect starting point for a stroll along the nearby banks of the Scarpe. The functional but rather small soundproofed rooms housed in three separate buildings were last decorated in the 1980s. The popular restaurant serves traditional cuisine. Excellent wine list.

🍴 EAT

🍽 **Le Storez** – *116 r. Storez.* ☏*03 27 98 88 80. Closed Sun evening and Mon.* Opposite the Porte d'Arras, a remnant of the city's old ramparts, this brick house has been serving customers since 1896. Fare consists of dishes with a maritime accent, with a retro-style decor.

🍽🛏 **Au Turbotin** – *9 r. Massue.* ☏*03 27 87 04 16. www.au-turbotin.net. Closed Aug 1–21, Sat lunch, Sun and Mon eve.* This former seed merchant's shop is bright and popular with people in the legal profession. Seafood menus.

🍽🛏 **Le Briquet** – *Mine centre, 59287 Lewarde. 8km/5mi from Douai by D 645.* ☏*03 27 95 82 82. www.chm-lewarde.com. Closed Jan, May 1, Dec 25.* ♿🅿. The traditional "briquet" sandwich has been replaced by fine fare served under the watchful eye of St Barbe, the patron saint of miners in this former sawmill.

🍽🛏 **Le Chat Botté** – *Château de Bernicourt, 59286 Roost-Warendin.* ☏*03 27 80 24 44. www.restaurantlechatbotte.com. Closed 1st half of Aug, Sun eve and Mon.* 🅿. A moment of quietude in a shady park of the Château de Bernicourt. The restaurant, set up in the outbuildings, has a dining room decorated with coloured rattan chairs. Excellent selection of wines (Bordeaux).

EVENTS

Fête des Gayants – The whole giant family parades through the streets the Sun following 5 July.

Garlic festival – 1st weekend of Sept in Arleux.

St-Amand-les-Eaux

Once home to one of the region's richest abbeys, the historic spa town of St-Amand-les-Eaux is surrounded by thousands of acres of former mining land, now converted into forests, parkland and lakes.

SIGHTS
Abbey

Although the abbey was largely destroyed between 1797 and 1820, its impressive tower offers a glimpse of its former magnificence.

Abbey Tower – Museum★

◔Open May–Sept Wed–Mon 2–5pm, Sat & Sun 10am–12.30pm & 2–6pm (Oct–Apr 2–5pm) ◶No charge. ℘03 27 22 24 55.
This colossal 17C tower (82m/269ft high) is divided into five floors. From bottom to top, each is decorated in a different classical style: Tuscan, Doric, Ionic, Corinthian and composite. The tower's dome contains a **large bell** (4,560kg/718st).

Établissement thermal

◔4km/2.5mi E by D 954 and D 151.
The Fontaine-Bouillon spa was known to the Romans for its curative powers and was brought back into use in the 17C by Vauban. The waters and mud, bubbling up at a temperature of 26°C/82°F, are used to treat rheumatism.
The **Établissement thermal** (1303 rte. de la Fontaine Bouillon; ◔open Mar–Nov ℘03 27 48 25 00; www.chainethermale. fr) was rebuilt after WWII and houses a hotel and casino; its park (8ha/20 acres) extends into the forest along the Drève du Prince driveway, created for the future Napoléon III in 1805.

PARC NATUREL RÉGIONAL SCARPE-ESCAUT

This 43 240ha-/107 000 acre-nature park is divided into farmland to the north, forestry, wetlands and wildlife corridors in the centre and former mining areas to the south.

- ▶ **Population:** 17 175
- ◷ **Michelin Local Map:** p376: B1.
- ▯ **Info:** 89 Grand'Place, 59230 St-Amand-Les-Eaux. ℘03 27 22 24 47. www.tourisme-porteduhainaut.fr.
- ◖ **Location:** Close to the border with Belgium, 30km/18mi from Lille via the D 955.
- ◎ **Don't Miss:** Culinary specialities including acorn tarts, hazelnut-flavoured flat cake and the local "abbey beer".

CONDÉ-SUR-L'ESCAUT

◖ 13km/8mi E by D 917
▯26 pl. Pierre-Delcourt, 59163 Condé-sur-l'Escaut. ◔Open Jun–Sept Tue–Sat 10am–1pm, 2–6pm, Sun 3–6pm; Oct–May Mon–Sat 9.30am–12.30pm, 1.30–5.30pm. ℘03 27 28 89 10. www.tourismevalenciennois.fr.
Lying at the confluence between the Escaut and Haine rivers, this former stronghold was fortified by Vauban in the 17C. The **Hôtel de Bailleul,** an austere 15C sandstone building flanked by four corbelled towers on pl. Verte and the 18C **Hôtel de Ville** on pl. Delcourt are worth a detour.

Château de l'Hermitage

◖ 16km/10mi to the NE by D 954, then D 75 bearing left to Vieux-Condé.
Garden and park only.
The 18C gardens and parkland of this Palladian château (1789) are open to visitors. Contact the tourist office ℘03 27 28 89 10. ◶5€.

Forêt de Raismes-St-Amand-Wallers★

Dotted with marshland and small lakes, this former mining site has been transformed into a 4 600ha-/11 370-acre forest of oak, beech and poplar groves. After a spot of sailing, mini-golf or mountain biking at the ▮▮ **Etang d'Amaury** head over to the

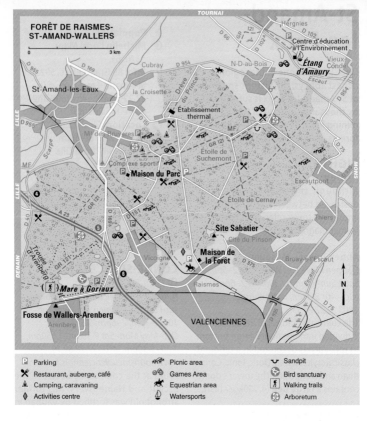

FORÊT DE RAISMES-ST-AMAND-WALLERS

0   3 km

Parking	Picnic area	Sandpit
Restaurant, auberge, café	Games Area	Bird sanctuary
Camping, caravaning	Equestrian area	Walking trails
Activities centre	Watersports	Arboretum

centre d'éducation à l'environment (℘ 03 27 25 28 85; www.adepse.pnr-scarpe-escaut.fr) for an introduction to the forest's plants and animals.

The **Maison de la Forêt** (Étoile de la Princesse; ◔open Apr–Nov Wed 2–6pm, Sun and public holidays, 3–6pm; ✎contact for charges; ♿ ℘03 27 36 72 72) explores the history of the forest, its fauna and flora and former mining activities. Amenities include recreation and picnic areas, trails, water sports and a bird sanctuary. ⚐Hike over the **Site Sabatier** (Etoile-la-Princesse) and the **Fosse de Wallers-Arenberg** (guided tours; ℘03 27 24 02 67), two former slag heaps, now teeming with silver birches, before walking the ⚐**bird watching trail** (2hr) at the 112ha/280-acre **Mare à Goriaux** lake, home to great-crested grebes, coots and osprey.

You can learn more about how one town converted its slag heap into a nature reserve at the **Maison du terril** at **Rieulay** (◔open Mon–Fri 9am–noon, 2–5pm, Sat & Sun by reservation; ✎no charge; ♿ ℘03 27 86 03 64). Alternatively, the monumental 18C entrance of a former Benedictine monastry in nearby **Marchienne** now houses a small museum exploring abbey life (◔open Apr–Sept Wed–Sat 2–5pm; rest of year: contact for details; ✎3€; ℘03 27 90 58 54). The nearby 800ha-/2000-acre **Forêt de Marchiennes** (♿see map, above) has four nature paths which cross at the Croix-au-Pile.

MAISON LEROUX IN ORCHIES

◉ NW by the D 957. Maison Leroux, 25 r. Jules-Rocht. ◔Open Tue–Fri 10am–12pm, 2–5.30pm, Sat 2.30–5.30pm. ✎6€. ♿ ℘03 20 64 83 70. www.lamaisonleroux.org.

A cutting-edge museum exploring the history of chicory.

Cambrai★

Overlooked by the three towers of the belfry, the cathedral and St Géry's Church, this former military stronghold on the eastern bank of the River Escaut (or Scheldt) is set around a Grand'Place where the giants Martin and Martine make an appearance every 15 August. A good excuse to sample Cambrai's small chitterling sausages (andouillettes) and its mint-flavoured sweets (bêtises de Cambrai).

▶ **Population:** 33 738
⌚ **Michelin Local Map:** p376: A2.
▯ **Info:** Office de tourisme, 48 r. de Noyon, Cambrai. ℰ03 27 78 36 15. www. tourisme-cambresis.com.

A BIT OF HISTORY
"Swan of Cambrai"
François de Salignac de La Mothe-Fénelon (1651–1715), a powerful lord and famous writer, was made archbishop of Cambrai in 1695. **Fénelon,** nicknamed the "Swan of Cambrai", was venerated for his gentleness and charity, which was often called upon during the War of the Spanish Succession, when starving peasants from the surrounding region poured into the archdiocese.

 WALKING TOUR

OLD TOWN
Allow 2hr.

The town gate, **Porte de Paris**, a vestige of the medieval fortifications, is flanked by two round towers dating from 1390.

▶ Follow av. de la Victoire towards the town hall, visible at the end of the street, to pl. du St-Sépulcre on the left.

Cathédrale Notre-Dame
⌚*Open Mon–Thu & Sat, 8am–12pm, 2–7pm; Fri, 2–7pm; Sun, 9am–12.30pm, 3–6pm.* ⌚*Closed Sun 3–6pm Oct–April.*
Originally dedicated to the Holy Sepulchre, the abbey church was elevated to the rank of cathedral after the Revolution. It was built in the 18C and has been altered several times since. The rounded chapels terminating the transept are decorated with *trompe-l'œil grisailles*, painted in 1760 by the Antwerp artist

Martin Geeraerts. Fénelon's tomb was sculpted by David d'Angers in 1826. The **Maison Espagnole** (*Tourist office*) is housed in a wooden house, its gables sheathed in slate, dating from the late 16C. You can see the medieval cellars and, on the first floor, the oak carvings which once adorned the façade. Don't miss the 17C and 18C private mansions along r. du Grand-Séminaire, r. de l'Epée and r. de Vaucelette, one of which houses the fine arts museum.

As you walk across pl. Jean-Moulin, note the rounded east end of the chapel of the former St-Julien hospital.

Église St-Géry
⌚*Closed for renovation works until 2013.* ℰ*03 27 78 36 15*
A classical construction (1698–1745) dominated by a tower (76m/249ft tall), the old church of St Aubert's Abbey replaced an older temple dedicated to Jupiter Capitolinus.

The beautiful **rood screen** (1632) is a fine example of the Baroque style with its contrasting red and black marble and its carved decoration which create an impression of movement. The monumental pulpit, installed in 1850, was the work of Cambrai craftsmen.

The north transept houses Rubens' enormous painting, **The Entombment★★**, while the southern transept features a 14C statue of an archbishop discovered in 1982 in the crypt.

▶ Cross pl. du 9-Octobre to reach pl. Aristide-Briand.

Entirely rebuilt after World War I, the **Place Aristide-Briand** is dominated by the **hôtel de ville**, which has a 19C-style façade and Louis XVI peristyle. The hall is

Bêtises de Cambrai

These oblong mint-flavoured sweets with a yellow stripe on the side are, according to legend, the result of a fortunate error made by a 19C apprentice. His mother complained that he had made a mistake (*bêtise*), hence the name given to these mint humbugs which were nevertheless appreciated for their digestive and refreshing qualities. Another legend tells how farming folk would visit Cambrai's market to sell their wares, only to spend half of their profits on these sweets!

surmounted by a columned bell-tower, flanked by the town's two jack-o'-the-clocks, Martin and Martine. Legend has it that these two individuals were 14C blacksmiths who rid the region of a tyrannical lord by felling him with hammer blows. The bronze figures (2m/6.5ft tall), dressed as turbaned Moors, date from 1512. Walk to the southwest corner of the square for views of a 15C–18C **belfry** (70m/230ft tall).

Part of the Baroque fortifications, the early-17C **Porte Notre-Dame** owes its name to the statue of the Virgin Mary on its outer façade. Featuring unusual diamond-shaped stones and grooved columns, it is topped by a sun representing Louis XIV, added to the pediment after the town was captured from the Spanish by the French.

ADDITIONAL SIGHTS
Musée des Beaux-Arts

⏰*Open Wed–Sun 10am–12pm, 2–6pm.* ⬤*3.50€, no charge 1st Sun in the month.* ♿ ☎*03 27 82 27 90.* *www.tourisme-cambresis.com.*

The town museum is housed in a mansion built for the Comte de Francqueville c. 1720. It has been restored and extended with two new buildings.

The **archaeology** department occupies the vaulted 18C cellars. The Gallo-Roman display explores ancient ceramics, housing and funeral practices, while the exhibits from the Merovingian

period include funerary artefacts from sites near Cambrai.

Don't miss the fine 16C **rood screen★** originally from the chapel of St-Julien Hospital among the artefacts exploring the **heritage of Cambrai**. The **Fine Arts** section features late-16C and 17C Dutch works. The 18C French School is represented by Berthelemy, de Lajoue, and Wille, while a display of works explore the 19C and 20C. The museum's sculpture collection includes works by Rodin, Bourdelle, Zadkine and Guyot.

Quartier de la Citadelle

Citadelle – The Porte Royale and barracks are the only vestiges of the citadel built by Charles V, later extended by Vauban. All of the countermine galleries have been preserved intact.

Public gardens – For a breath of fresh air, head for the late-19C gardens (1862-1867) created on the esplanade of the **citadel** by Paris-based architect Barillet Deschamps. Extended following the demolition of the fortifications, the park is scattered with statues of classical gods and Cambrai's famous citizens.

The **Jardin aux Fleurs** features a remarkable patchwork of plants, while the ♟**Jardin Monstrelet** (named after a medieval chronicler) boasts a bandstand and play areas. Don't miss artificial grottoes and a swan lake in the **Jardin des Grottes**.

EXCURSIONS
Abbaye de Vaucelles

▶*12km/7mi to the S of Cambrai by D 644 and D 96 or D 76 and D 103, between Bantouzelle and Les Rues-des-Vignes.* ⏰ *Open Mid-Mar–mid-Nov, Tue–Sat 10am–noon, 2–5.30pm, Sun and public holidays 3–6.30pm. Open Mon Jul–Aug.* ⏰*Closed 1st Sun of Sept.* ⬤*6.50€ Audioguide available. Allow 1hr.* ☎*03 27 78 50 65. www.vaucelles.com.*

Now mostly in ruins, the **former Abbaye de Vaucelles**, once Europe's biggest Cistercian abbey, still boasts Europe's largest chapter house. Start with the early Gothic **scriptorium**, formerly one of the biggest libraries in France with 40 000 works (most of which

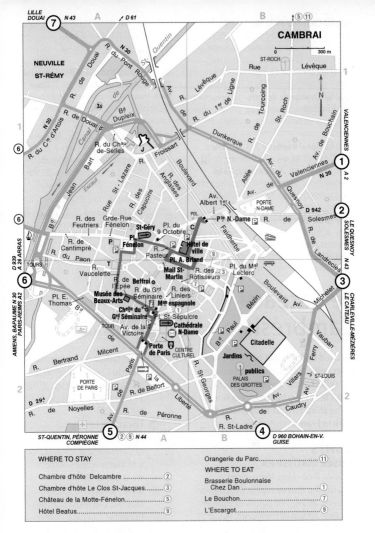

were destroyed in the two world wars), before visiting the only room where the monks were allowed to talk, the **auditorium.** Move on to the **chapter house★**(1175) where the monks met daily to read a chapter of the monastic rule, then walk down the **sacred passage** with its scale model of the original abbey.

Les Rues-des-Vignes

🕐 *4km/2mi to N by D 103.*

Descend into a Gallo-Roman cellar or walk through a Carolingian village at the **Archéo'site** (🕐 *open Mar–mid-Nov, Tues–Fri 9am–noon, 2–6pm, Sat,* *Sun 2–6pm;* ⬙*5.50€ (children 4.50€);* ℘*03 27 78 99 42; http://archeo.ruesdes-vignes.free.fr).*

ADDRESSES

🍴 STAY

⊜⊜ **Delcambre (B&B)** – *Ferme de Bonavis, 59266 Banteux.11km/6.8mi S of Cambrai by D 644.* ℘*03 27 78 55 08. www. bonavis.fr.* ♿🅿⊟. *4 rooms.* This former coach inn with a pleasantly roomy interior was converted to a farm (still working) after WW II; sober rooms with high ceilings and parquet floors.

⊝⊜🍴 **Château de la Motte-Fénelon** – *Pl. du château, par allée St-Roch. ℘03 27 83 61 38. www.cambrai-chateau-motte-fenelon.com. 10 rooms ⊡.* Set in leafy parkland, this 1850 château has stylish rooms with white-leaded furniture.

⊝⊜🍴 **Orangerie du Parc**– *Same contact details as château. 30 rooms ⊡.* Comfortable bungalow accommodation in an 8ha-/19 acre-park, close to the château.

⊝⊜🍴 **Hôtel Beatus** – *718 av. de Paris. ℘03 27 81 45 70. www.hotelbeatus.fr.* ☐. *Wi-fi. 32 rooms ⊡. Restaurant ⊝⊜🍴.* Shaded by large trees, this spacious hotel has contemporary rooms, some with a Provençal decor.

⊝⊜🍴 **Le Clos Saint-Jacques (B&B)** – *9 r. St-Jacques. ℘03 27 74 37 61. www.leclos stjacques.com. Closed 12–23 Aug, 21 Dec–4 Jan. Wi-fi. 5 rooms. ⊡10€.* An historic

residence in the town centre. Restaurant serving regional specialities.

🍴 EAT

⊝ **'Chez Dan' Brasserie Boulonnaise** – *18 r. des Liniers. ℘03 27 81 39 77. Open Wed–Mon.* This brasserie with a maritime decor offers traditional northern hospitality and a warm ambience.

⊝⊜ **Le Bouchon** – *31 r. des Rôtisseurs. ℘03 27 78 44 55. Closed 3 wks in Aug, Mon, Tues, Wed eve and Sun.* An affordable eatery serving ample portions. Bistro-style cooking and regional menu.

⊝⊜ **L'Escargot**– *10 r. du Gén.-de-Gaulle. ℘03 27 81 24 54. Closed 15–31 Jul, 21–26 Dec, Fri eve and Wed.* A warm rustic inn serving quality cuisine and regional dishes including andouilette.

Le Cateau-Cambrésis

Perched on the right bank of the River Selle, between Cambrésis and the rolling pastures of Thiérache, Henri Matisse's birthplace is home to the third largest collection of his work in France.

SIGHTS
Musée Matisse★★
🕐*Open Wed–Mon 10am–6pm.* 💬*Guided tour available. Reservation required.* ⊛≤*5€. Temporary exhibition 7€. Free 1st Sun of the month.* ♿. *℘03 59 73 38 00. http://museematisse.lenord.fr.* Housed in the **former palace of the archbishops of Cambrai** (18C) over-looking a stunning park designed by Louis XIV's landscape gardener, Le Nôtre, the Musée Matisse begins its exploration of Matisse's career with an overview of his **early years** in Le Cateau-Cambrésis, his studies in Paris and his apprenticeship in **Gustave Moreau's studio** where he produced his first Rodin-inspired sculptures. Three major works go on to explore the **invention of Fauvism** (*Première nature morte à l'orange*), Matisse's adoption of pure colour (*Rue du Soleil à Collioure*) and his

▸ **Population:** 7 453
♿ **Michelin Map:** p376: B3; 302 J7.
🅸 **Info: Office de tourisme**, 9 pl. du Com.-Richez, 59360 Le Cateau-Cambrésis. ℘03 27 84 10 94. www.tourisme-lecateau.fr
▶ **Location:** Le Cateau-Cambrésis is 22km/14mi SE of Cambrai and 35km/22mi S of Valenciennes. Access via D 643 or D 932.
👁 **Don't miss:** The Musée Matisse; the historic abbey brewery.
🕐 **Timings:** Allow at least 2 hours to visit the museum.

liberation from design and realism (*Portrait de Marguerite* – an example of A 1 600 ft/182m lavender trail in the organic **eco-gardens** traces the outline of the ruined church, once bigger than Notre Dame in Paris.Matisse's recognition of the expressive value of African art).

The emergence of Matisse's mature style (1918–1939) forms the subject of the next section, **From Nice to Tahiti,** which includes some of his finest still lives and female portraits: the *Fenêtre à*

Tahiti★★★, *Autoportrait*, *Le Buffet vert*, the *Grand nu assis* and the remarkable series of heads of his model Henriette. Moving onto the **1940s**, the high point in the artist's career, the museum presents works produced in Matisse's studio in Vence: bouquets of flowers, sunny interiors and sensual women with sleek forms, each with a remarkable unity of line and colour. The section ends with **Matisse's ceiling** (1950), a portrait of Matisse's three grandchildren, drawn by the 80-year old artist on the ceiling above his bed in Nice using a stick of charcoal tied to the end of a fishing rod, and his last painting, **Femme à la gandoura bleue★★★** (1951).

As his eyesight failed, during the last ten years of his life (1944–54) the artist made ingenious use of paper **gouache-painted cutouts** to achieve a unity of colour and design. The **Océanie, le ciel ★★★** and **Océanie, la mer★★★** are typical of the way Matisse challenges our vision of the horizon by combining the sky and the sea in a single whole.

The museum also explores different mediums, starting with the original plaster casts of four **bas reliefs** sculpted by the artist in 1909, 1913, 1916/1917 and 1930 of a women from behind. The studies Matisse produced between 1948 and 1951 for his decoration of a **chapel in Vence** can also be seen here, including the *Tête de saint Dominique*.

Lastly, the **drawings room★★★** houses the largest collection of drawings and engravings by Matisse in France, arranged according to the artist's wishes. Spanning 100 works, they reveal Matisse's breathtaking graphic diversity. Don't miss the charcoal *Autoportrait* (1900), the *Odalisque à la culotte de satin rouge* and his *Nu accroupi*.

The **Alice Tériade collection★★** is one of the largest donations of major artworks made to a French museum in the last twenty years. It includes books by the world's greatest modern artists, the *Grande femme* by Giacometti, *Le Roi de carte* by F. Léger and *Tête de femme couronnée de fleurs* by Picasso. Leave time at the end of your visit for the **dining room** of the Villa Natacha

in Saint-Jean-Cap-Ferrat, where Alice Tériade and her publisher husband Stratis entertained their artist friends. It includes a stained-glass window and ceramic wall by Matisse.

Photographs by **Henri Cartier-Bresson★** of Alice and Stratis Tériade and Henri Matisse end the exhibition.

🚶‍♀️Drawing pads for kids are available at the entrance to the museum.

👣 WALKING TOUR

In **Place Anatole-France**, the statue of Maréchal Mortier by Douai sculptor Théophile Bra, whose work also appears on the Arc de Triomphe in Paris, looks out over the long, sloping Grand'Place, which runs down to the 16C **hôtel de ville** and its 18C **belfry**. The symmetry of the former abbey-church **Église Saint-Martin** (1634) contrasts with its elaborate Baroque stonework by Cambrai sculptor Gaspar Marsy. Burgundian emblems – the cross of Saint Andrew – recall a time when the town was a Spanish possession inherited through the Duchy of Burgundy.

EXCURSIONS
Caudry-en-Cambrésis
◗ *8km/5mi to the W by D 643.*
🏢*Pl. du Gén-de-Gaulle, 59540, Caudry.*
📞*03 27 70 09 67.*
Caudry is famed for lacemaking, an industry explored in the **Musée de la Dentelle de Caudry** (*Pl. des Mantilles;* 🕐 *open Wed–Fri 9am–noon, 2–5pm, Sat, Sun 2.30–6pm.* 👓*3€.* ♿ 📞*03 27 76 29 77. www.museedentellecaudry.fr*).

Maison Forestière - Wilfred Owen Tribute
◗ *8km/5mi to the E by D 959*
🏢*Across Bois-L'évêque, 59360 Ors.*
🕐*Open Wed–Mon 9.30am–12.30pm, 2–6pm.* 🕐*Closed Sun after., 15 Dec–31 Jan.* 👓*No charge.* 📞*03 27 77 62 10.*
The cellar where World War I poet Wilfred Owen wrote his last letter to his mother has been transformed into a work of art.

Avesnes-sur-Helpe

An ideal starting point for a drive through the patchwork of meadows and slate-roofed hamlets of the Avesnois region or a hike in the Parc naturel régional de l'Avesnois, Avesnes-sur-Helpe is an architectural gem in its own right.

WALKING TOUR

The town's narrow **Grand'Place** is surrounded by slate-roofed houses. A double staircase with wrought-iron balustrades fronts the 18C **Hôtel de Ville** built in blue Tournai stone.

▶ Follow r. d'Albret.

Located on top of one of the bastions, the **Square de la Madeleine** offers a bird's-eye view of the Helpe Valley.

EXCURSIONS
Cartignies
▶ 6km/3.7mi SW along D 424.
Some 40 **blue-stone oratories.**

Maroilles
▶ 12km/7.5mi W along D 962.
Explore the history of Maroilles cheese at the **Parcours des Sens** (Rte de Noyelles, 59550 Maroilles; open Tue–Sun; 5€; 03 27 07 03 34). Price includes tasting session.
The **Maison du Parc Naturel Régional de l'Avesnois** (4 cour de l'Abbaye, 59550 Maroilles; open May–Sept Mon–Fri 9am–noon & 2–5pm, Sun 3–7pm; Oct–Apr Mon–Fri 9am–noon, 2–5pm; 03 27 77 51 60; www.parc-naturel-avesnois. fr) provides useful information about hiking and local heritage sites.

DRIVING TOUR

AVESNOIS REGION★★
Round-trip of 100km/62mi.
Allow 2hr 30mins.

▶ **Population:** 5 003
▶ **Michelin Local Map:** p377: CD3.
▶ **Info:** 41 pl. du Gén.-Leclerc, 59440 Avesnes-Sur-Helpe. 03 27 56 57 20. www.avesnes-sur-helpe.com
▶ **Location:** On the south bank of the River Helpe-Majeure close to the Belgian border, and closer to Brussels than to Paris.
▶ **Parking:** On street parking (limited).
▶ **Don't Miss:** Taste the local cheeses, Maroilles and Dauphin.

This region, which lies south of Maubeuge and extends along the Belgian border, is known for its orchards, woodlands and pastures, through which meander the Helpe-Majeure and Helpe-Mineure rivers, and for its pretty villages of brick, slate and stone. The vast forests and the cluster of lakes around Liessies and Trélon recall a time when great abbeys – Maroilles, Liessies and St-Michel – dominated the region, constructing mills and forges on every river. Many small industries developed in the 18C and 19C: glassmaking at Sars-Poteries, Trélon and Anor, wood turning at Felleries, spinning at Fourmies and marble quarrying at Cousoire.

▶ Leave Avesnes by D 133 (east) towards Liessies.

The 16C **church** at **Ramousies** contains two beautiful Renaissance altarpieces from Antwerp workshops that once belonged to Liessies Abbey.

▶ Continue along D 80 to Felleries.

Since the 17C, **Felleries** inhabitants have specialised in bois-joli: turned wood and cooperage. These workshops developed at the same time as the textile industry, the former making bobbins and spindles for the latter.

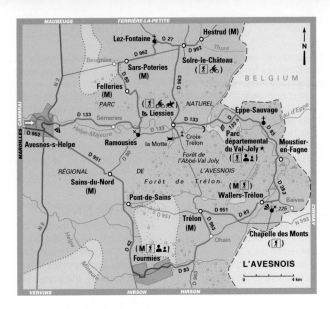

The Moulin des Bois-Jolis Museum
(🕐 *open Apr–Oct Mon–Fri 2–6pm, weekends and public holidays 2.30–6.30pm;* �#*3.50€;* 🚻 ✆*03 27 60 66 11*), housed in a 16C watermill, showcases a wide variety of treen (wooden) items made in Felleries: butter moulds, salt boxes, spindles, tops, etc.

Since the 15C the earth around **Sars** has been used by potters and many small pottery workshops exist locally. In the 19C, two glassworks were set up specialising in dinner services and bottles, employing a workforce of 800.

The **Musée-Atelier du Verre★** *(1 r. du Général de Gaulle;* 🕐 *open Wed–Mon 10am–12.30pm, 1.30–6pm;* 🚍*3€;* ✆*03 59 73 16 16; http://museeduverre.lenord. fr)*, housed in the former home of the glassworks manager, boasts an unusual collection of popular glassware made by the workers for their own use. The pieces enabled the workers to make full use of their talent, artistry and imagination.

A menhir, known as the **Pierre de Dessus-Bise**, stands on place du Vieux Marché. In folklore, infertile women who sit on it become able to bear children.

The **watermill** north of the village was built in 1780 and still contains its great wheel and workings.

▷ Take D 962 east, then turn left 3km/1.9mi further on.

The wooden vaults of the 15C **church** at **Lez-Fontaine** are decorated with paintings dating from 1531.

▷ Follow D 27 to Solre-le-Château.

The seigniorial château at **Solre-le-Château** no longer exists but there are still many 17C and 18C houses. The sober Renaissance **town hall** (late 16C) has an austere bell-tower. A covered market was held on the ground floor.

▷ Walk through the archway leading to pl. Verte.

The 16C Gothic **church** is made of local blue stone. The **belfry** was part of the fortifications. The mauve spire (1612) is crowned by a large bulb with openings. 17C–18C houses surround the square *(if the church is closed, ask at the town hall).*

▷ Take D 962 towards Grandrieu.

The Musée de la Douane et des Frontières (🕐 *open Oct–Aug Wed–Sun 10am–7pm, Mon 10am–noon;* 🚍 *2€;*

Blue-stone Oratories

Blue-stone oratories have been built in the Avesnois and Thiérache regions since 1550. They are mostly located at roadsides, but also in fields, along ancient footpaths and even in woods or set in walls. These characteristic constructions consist of a narrow shaft surmounted by a fine recess, closed off by wire mesh as in Le Favril or Dimont, and a larger crowning piece. Each recess was intended to hold one or several polychrome statues carved by the clog makers of Mormal Forest. The oratories were erected for various reasons: in thanksgiving for a cure (as in Bérelles), to ask for a favour, to assert a certain social status, or to abide by a family tradition. The Avesnois region is said to possess more than 700 blue-stone oratories including some 40 of them in the village of Cartignies alone.

℘03 27 59 28 48), at **Hestrud** is housed in the former customs building, illustrates the history of the borders of the Avesnois region since 1659.
🏃 You could discover the surrounding villages on the *Halte à la douane* walking trail *(www.circuits-de-france.com)*.

▶ Return to Soire and follow D 963.

The village of **Liessies** was founded by 8C Benedictine monks who had exclusive use of the surrounding woods. The abbey prospered and from 17C until the Revolution the they were powerful lords. The **Église St-Jean-et-Ste-Hiltrude** (👣 *Tours of abbey park and glasshouses;* 🕐*open Apr–Jun & Oct Mon–Sat 9am–noon & 2–7pm, Sun 9.30am–1pm, 3–7pm; rest of the year Mon–Sat 9am–noon, 2–7pm, Sun 9.30am–1pm; ℘03 27 61 81 66)* stands near the site of the old abbey.
Starting from the village, walk to the 18C **Château de la Motte**, built of red brick, and the **Abbé-Val Joly Forest**. The 18C **Calvaire de la Croix-Trélon** stands to the east of the intersection of the Trélon road (D 963) and the Château de la Motte access road.

▶ From Liessies follow D 133 along the Helpe Valley.

The road becomes more winding and the slopes heavily wooded in this area.

Parc du Val-Joly★

The construction of the dam at Eppe-Sauvage on the Helpe-Majeure created a magnificent reservoir surrounded by the wooded banks of the River Helpe and its tributary, the Voyon. The park has many leisure facilities and includes a campsite with bungalows.

Located on a plain where the River Helpe and River Eau d'Eppe meet, the village of **Eppe Sauvage** is home to the **Église St-Ursmar**, containing two remarkable 16C painted wood triptychs. After Eppe-Sauvage, the valley opens out and becomes less wooded; the marshes here are called *fagnes*.

The village of **Moustier-en-Fagne** derives its name from a 16C priory or *moustier*. Olivetan Benedictines, who devote themselves to painting icons, live in the monks' quarters. A handsome 1520 **manor house** is visible (left) on entering the village.

▶ Continue S and, 2km/1mi beyond Moustier, fork left onto D 283, then right.

The top of a knoll (225m/738ft high) affords a clear **view** of **Trélon Forest**.

The **Chapelle des Monts** *(15min on foot)* is an 18C chapel surrounded by lime trees.

Built entirely in blue stone, the beautiful **Wallers-Trélon** owes its unique appearance to the numerous quarries nearby.

Hike along one of the nature trails – the **Pierre bleue** trail starting at the Maison de la fagne (4.5km/2mi, 1h 10min) or the **Monts de Baive** trail from Baive church (2.5km/1mi, 50min) – to discover the unusual flora of the Monts de Baive.

▶ Take D 83 S; turn right onto D 951.

Formerly known for its glass industry, **Trélon** is today the location of the **Musée du verre** (r. Clavon; ◷ open Apr–Oct Mon–Fri 9am–noon & 2–6pm, Sat & Sun 2.30–6.30pm; ◉5.50€; ♿ ✆03 27 59 71 02; www.ecomusee-avesnois.fr), housed in a 19C glassworks, containing kilns from 1850 and 1920.

▶ Follow D 963 then D 83 to Fourmies.

Fourmies

🛈20A r. Jean-Jaurès, 59610 Fourmies. ✆03 27 59 69 97. http://fourmies.canalblog.com. A centre for worsted wool production, Fourmies is fringed by forests and lakes created by the monks of Liessies.

Musée du Textile et de la Vie sociale ★★ – Pl. Maria-Blondeau. ◷ Open Feb–Nov 9am–noon, 2–6pm, Sat & Sun 2.30–6.30pm. Guided tours (2hr). ◉5.50€. ♿ ✆03 27 60 66 11. www.ecomusee-avesnois.fr. Explore a 19C bonnet workshop and discover how looms have developed.

Étangs des Moines

▶ To the SE of Fourmies.
👥 Try a spot of rowing, fishing or swimming in this former mill reservoir.

Étang de la Galoperie★

▶ 9km/14mi E of Fourmies.
Fed by the Anorelles stream, this lake reaches far into a neighbouring forest. 🚶(45min on foot AR) Running along the northwest bank of the river, this pathway leads to a WWII pillbox.

▶ Take D 42, then D 951.

The village of **Pont-de-Sains** is home to a château once belonging to early-19C politician Talleyrand.

▶ Return to D 951 in opposite direction.

In **Sains-du-Nord**, The **Maison du Bocage** (rue J.B. Lebas; ◷open Apr–Dec Mon–Fri 2–6pm, Sat, Sun, public holidays 2.30–6.30pm; ◉3.50€; ✆03 27 59 82 24; www.ecomusee-avesnois.fr), explores life in the woodlands and pastures of the Avesnois (stock farming, cheese-making, etc.) in a converted 19C farmhouse.

ADDRESSES

🛏 STAY

⊜⊜ **Les Prés de la Fagne (B&B)** – 5 r. Principale. 59132 Baives.1km/0.5mi E of Wallers-Trelon. ✆03 27 57 02 69. www.lespresdelafagne.new.fr. 🅿. 5 rooms. ⌖. This tastefully restored 17C barn successfully blends different eras – some guest rooms even have a bathtub at the foot of the bed!

🍴 EAT

⊜⊜ **Auberge des Etangs des Moines**– 97 r. des Etangs 59610 Fourmies. ✆03 27 60 02 62. www.restaurant-les-etangs-desmoines.com. Closed 1–21 Aug, Sat midday, Sun eve., Mon. Traditional dishes with a rustic edge served next to a roaring fire.

SHOPPING

Le Verger Pilote – 1810 rte. de Landrecies, 59550 Maroilles. ✆03 27 84 71 10. www.levergerpilote.fr. Open Mon–Sat 9am–6pm. This boutique sells a complete range of regional specialities, including Maroilles, beers, pear cider, and home made flamiches.

ACTIVITIES

Sentiers pédestres – 59610 Fourmies. ✆03 27 60 66 11. www.ecomusee-avesnois.fr. Walking tours departing from the Wignehies village hall. Contact the Ecomusée de l'Avesnois.

EVENTS

Fête du Maroilles et de la flamiche – ✆03 27 84 80 80. Celebrate the region's famous cheese on the 2nd Sun in Aug.

Féron'art – ✆03 27 60 10 46. Around 15 Aug, Féron is transformed into an artists' village with music, cinema, painting and theatre topping the agenda.

Le Quesnoy★

Nestled deep in the countryside close to the lakes of Mormal Forest, this peaceful town of whitewashed houses is home to one of France's best preserved forts.

Built from coarse stone, flint and lime mortar covered with bricks, Le Quesnoy's perfectly preserved **fortifications★** form a polygon of defensive curtain walls with projecting bastions. Although similar to the fortifications built by Vauban in the region, these defences, particularly its bastions and projecting towers, date in part from the time of Emperor Charles V (16C). Various all-season paths offer pleasant walks.

▶ Leave from pl. du Général-Leclerc and head for the postern gate by avenue d'Honneur des Néo-Zélandais.

The gateway leads to the moat where the men of the New Zealand Rifle Brigade scaled the walls in November 1918. The Monument des Néo-Zélandais commemorates their exploits. Contact the tourist office for a walking guide.

▶ **Population:** 4 917
▶ **Michelin Local Map:** p377: C2.
▶ **Info:** 1 r. du Mar.-Joffre, 59530 Le Quesnoy. ✆03 27 20 54 70. www.tourisme-lequesnoy.com.
▶ **Location:** Between the Oise and the Cambrésis, via Valenciennes or Bavay by the N 49 and D 934, and from Cambrai by the D 942.
▶ **Parking:** Limited parking within the fortifications (fee); park near the Étang du Pont Rouge.
▶ **Don't Miss:** The ramparts.
▶ **Timing:** Allow 90 min to 2hrs for the ramparts.

▶ Follow the moat around the south front of the ramparts.

From **Étang du Pont Rouge** continue to **Lac Vauban** which lies at the foot of the ramparts to each side of the Porte Fauroeulx. The bridge provides a lovely view of the red-brick walls and bastions.

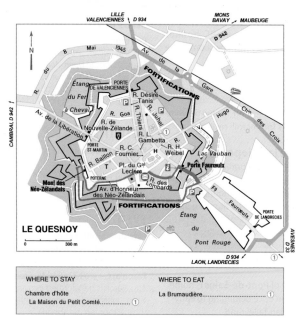

WHERE TO STAY	WHERE TO EAT
Chambre d'hôte	La Brumaudière.....................①
La Maison du Petit Comté...............①	

🚗 DRIVING TOUR

LA FORÊT DE MORMAL★

26km/16mi shown in green on the map on page 376. Allow 90min. 🚌 *La Place, 59530 Locquignol* ✆*03 27 35 05 05.*

The biggest forest in the Nord-Pas-de-Calais region (9 100ha/22 000 acres), **Mormal** is home to a large number of tree species and teems with local wildlife, including boars. 🚶 The forest is crossed by pathways, many of which are hard surfaced.

The long hiking trail GR 122 (21km/13mi), walking trails (Nerviens, Étoquies, Druides and Sabotiers), horse trails (81km/50mi) and several recreational areas *(the arboretum next to the Étang David, the Haisne pasture and its educational trail. ✆03 20 74 66 10, www.tourisme-avesnois.com)* are options.

▶ Leave Le Quesnoy by D 33. Cross Potelle then Jolimetz. Cross the D 932, which runs along the edge of the forest from the northeast to the southwest.

The small chapel **Notre-Dame-de-la-Flaquette** is dedicated to the Virgin May. An historic centre for clog-making,

Locquignol is the largest village in the *département.*

▶ Continue along the D 233 to the Ermitage crossroads. Turn right, then right again at the Pont-Routier crossroads.

Located opposite the Étang David, on the other side of the road, don't miss the **arboretum**, where you can learn more about the many tree species.

ADDRESSES

🏨 STAY / 🍴EAT

🛏️**Chambre d'hôte La Maison du Petit Comté**– *3 r. de la Couronne.* ✆*03 27 41 36 36. Closed 2 wks in summer and in winter.* ▣🍴 *2 rooms* 🛏️. This house at the heart of the village has artfully furnished rooms. Given the lack of accommodation in the area, this guest house is surprisingly elegant.

🛏️🛏️**La Brumaudière** – *3 rte. du Quesnoy. 59530 Locquignol.* ✆*03 27 44 53 39. www.la-brumaudiere.com. Closed 2nd half of Aug, Sun eve, Mon–Fri.* ♿▣. Located in a former farmhouse, this bar-restaurant overlooks a small lake at the entrance to the village. Rustic decor with a fireplace and traditional French cuisine.

Maubeuge

Established around a 7C nunnery, Maubeuge was fortified by Vauban in the 17C. Although its town centre was rebuilt after World War II, the Porte de Mons and its drawbridge provide a vivid picture of the Sun King's once mighty ramparts.

SIGHTS
👥 Parc zoologique

Av. du Parc. 🕐 *Open Apr–Jun and Sept 10am–6pm, Oct–6 Nov 1–5.30pm.* 👁️*9€ (under 6s 5€).* ✆*03 27 53 75 84. www.zoodemaubeuge.fr.* Discover deer, lamas, sea lions, hippopotamuses and lions in this extensive zoo. A top destination for families.

▶ **Population:** 33 561
🗺️ **Michelin Map:** p377: D2; 302 L6.
🚌 **Info: Office de tourisme** – Pl. Vauban, porte de Mons, 59600 Maubeuge. ✆03 27 62 11 93. www.ville-maubeuge.fr.
▶ **Location:** At the intersection between N 2 and D 649 in the Vallée de la Sambre.
👁️ **Don't Miss:** The peal of bells in the Église Saint-Pierre-Saint-Paul.
🕐 **Timing:** Allow 2hrs to explore the town.
👥 **Kids**: The zoo; the pottery museum in Ferrière-la-Petite.

Porte de Mons

© Hervé Gyssels/Photononstop

Porte de Mons

Built in 1682, this gateway was the linchpin in Vauban's ramparts and is one of the best preserved parts of the fortifications. It was once flanked by an arsenal and a series of external redoutes. The square was large enough to accommodate 40 000 men.

From inside the ramparts, the gate forms a pedimented pavilion with a garret roof. The guardroom has heavy wooden doors and a drawbridge winch. Take the curved bridge across the moat and head towards the demi-lune, which features a gateway with sentry lodges. Cross back over the moat to the northern façade of the ramparts.

Église Saint-Pierre-Saint-Paul

Rebuilt in 1955 to plans drawn up by Lurçat, the church is surmounted by a glass-tiled bell tower housing a **peal of bells**. Don't miss the reliquary containing the veil of Saint Aldegonde (late 15C).

Chapitre des chanoinesses

Walk to the bottom of place Verte to admire the late-17C brick and stone building once housing the Dames de Maubeuge, the secular canonesses who succeeded the cloistered nuns of Sainte-Aldegonde.

Ancien collège des Jésuites

A harmonious Baroque building (17C) by architect Du Blocq.

EXCURSIONS
♣♣ Ferrière-la-Petite Pottery Museum

▶ *10km/6mi S by the D 936 then D 27. Bear left towards Ferrière-la-Petite.* ⏱ *Open 9am–noon, 1.30–5pm, Sat, Sun, public holidays 3–6pm, guided tours available (90min).* ⏱ *Closed 1 Jan, 1 May, 25 Dec.* ✦*3€ (under 18s no charge).* ✆ *03 27 62 79 60. www.musee-poterie-ferrierelapetite.fr.*

Housed in one of Ferrière-la-Petite's twelve original 19C workshops, this

From St Aldegonde to the Metal Crisis

Founded by Saint Aldegonde in the 7C, Malbodium (from the low Latin malboden, a meeting point for regional courts presided over by local dignatories) was initially a cloth-making centre before the growth of its metalworking industries in the 12C. Known as Maubeuge after 1293, it was the birthplace of painters Jean Gossart or "Mabuse" (c. 1478-1532) and Nicolas Régnier, also known as Niccolo Renieri (c. 1590-1667). From 1637 to 1667, Spain and France fought for control over the town before it was annexed by France under the Treaty of Nijmegen in 1678 and fortified by Vauban. In 1940, 90 percent of the town was destroyed in a series of bombing raids. Its current design is the work of architect André Lurçat.

museum is set around an impressive 1880 brick "bottle kiln" (5m/16ft in diameter). Exploring 300 years of ceramics in Avesnois, it features a display of faience and blue stoneware. A pottery demonstration given by local craftspeople rounds out the visit. All pottery for sale.

Bavay★

▶ 14.6km/9.07mi west by D649.

This small town is famous for its natural mint-flavoured candies called "Chiques de Bavay". At the time of Caesar Augustus, Bagacum was an important town in Roman Belgium, situated at the junction of seven important roads.

Grand' Place

The 17C belfry sits next to an 18C town hall, built of granite. A fluted column in the square supports a statue of Brunhilda, Queen of Austrasia, who legend says built the seven roads of Bavay in just three days and three nights.

Remains of the Roman City

In 1942 Canon Biévelet began excavating a site cleared by bombing in 1940. The excavations revealed the remains of a large group of monumental buildings: a civil basilica, a forum, a portico above a horseshoe-shaped underground gallery (*cryptoporticus*) and a room over a deep cellar stand along an east-west axis.

Forum Antique de Bavay

Open 9am–noon & 1–6pm.
Guided tours Wed, Sat & Sun 2pm.
Closed Wed & Sat morning, 2nd half of Jan, 1st half of Sept; 4.50€.
6.50€. 03 59 73 15 50.

Discover a hoard of fine **bronze figurines★** hidden by a Bavay craftsman, along with hundreds of other archaeological finds in this large modern museum exploring everyday life in Bagacum (Roman Bavay).

A 3D film challenges kids to solve a series of puzzles in 3C Bagacum.

Bellignies

▶ 3km/3mi to the N by D24.

From the 19C to 1940, this small town in the Hogneau valley was famous for its marble which was cut and shaped by the men and polished by the women. The **Musée du Marbre et de la Pierre bleue** (open mid-Jan–mid-Dec Sat & Sun 2–6pm; 2.50€; 03 27 66 89 90) provides an insight into traditional marble-working tools and the objects once produced in the town's workshops.

ADDRESSES

🛏 STAY

Le Grand Hôtel – 1 pte. de Paris. 03 27 64 63 16. www.grandhotel-maubeuge.fr. 30 rooms. Although this hotel fronts onto a busy road, it has recently been fully soundproofed. The light, spacious rooms have well-appointed bathrooms.

🍽 EAT

Restaurant Côté Jardin – 55 av. de France, Maubeuge. 03 27 64 34 47. Closed Sun and Mon eves. Located in a busy shopping street, this restaurant with a large picture window is perfect for a post-shopping pick-me-up. Pleasant contemporary decor and hearty traditional cuisine.

SHOPPING

La Romaine – 30 pl. Charles-de-Gaulle, Bavay. 03 27 63 10 06. Daily (except Mon) 7am–7pm. Closed 15 Jul–15 Aug. This establishment guards the secret of the renowned 'Chiques de Bavay' – sweets flavoured with apple, cherry or coffee.

ON THE TOWN

Le Manège – R. de la Croix. 03 27 65 93 83. www.lemanege.com. 10am–1pm, 2–6pm, Sat 9am–noon, Mon 2–6pm, closed Jul–Aug and Sun. Le Manège doubles as a theatre and live performance venue for dance, circus and musical events.

ACTIVITIES

Union aérienne Sambre et Helpe – Aérodrome de la Salmagne. 03 27 68 40 25. http://uash.free.fr. 130€ 30min flight for 3 persons max. Learn to fly or discover the Val de Sambre and the Avesnois region from the air on a customized flight.

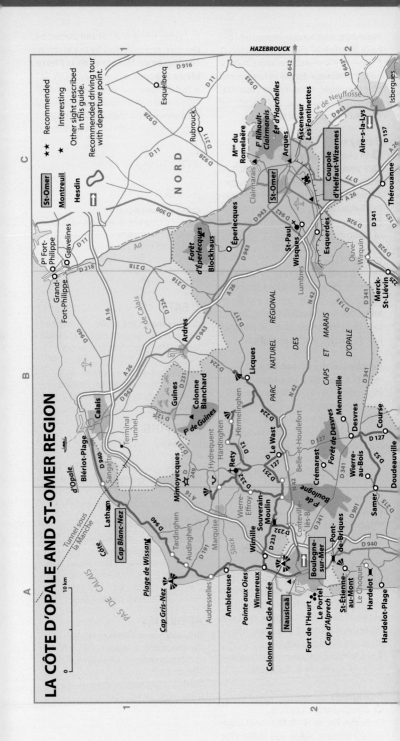

LA CÔTE D'OPALE AND ST-OMER REGION

Recommended
★★ **Recommended**
★ **Interesting**

Other sight described in this guide.

Recommended driving tour with departure point.

St-Omer
Montreuil
Hesdin

HAZEBROUCK

NORD

PAS DE CALAIS

Esquelbecq
Rubrouck
Mon du Romelaëre
Fᵗ Rihoult-Clairmarais
Éᵗ d'Harchelles
Ascenseur Les Fontinettes
Aire-s-la-Lys
Arques
Clairmarais
St-Omer
Coupole d'Helfaut-Wizernes
Thérouanne
Éperlecques
St-Paul
Wisques
Esquerdes
Ouve
Wirquin
Merck-St-Liévin
Pᵗ Fort-Philippe
Gravelines
Grand-Fort-Philippe
Forêt d'Éperlecques
Blockhaus
Ardres
Lumbres
Licques
Calais
Terminal Tunnel
Blériot-Plage
Guînes
Colonne Blanchard
Fᵗ de Guînes
Hardinghen
Hermelinghen
Le Wast
Belle-et-Houllefort
PARC
NATUREL
RÉGIONAL
DES
CAPS
ET
MARAIS
D'OPALE
Menneville
Desvres
Forêt de Desvres
Course
Côte d'Opale
Latham
Sangatte
Tunnel sous la Manche
Cap Blanc-Nez
Plage de Wissant
Tardinghen
Audinghen
Cap Gris-Nez
Mimoyecques
Rety
Marquise
Wierre-Effroy
Souverain-Moulin
Wimille
Conteville-lès-B.
Crémarest
Wierre-au-Bois
Samer
Doudeauville
Ambleteuse
Pointe aux Oies
Wimereux
Colonne de la Gde Armée
Audresselles
Slack
Nausicaá
Fort de l'Heurt
Le Portel
Cap d'Alprech
Boulogne-sur-Mer
Fᵗ de Boulogne
St-Étienne-au-Mont
Pont-de-Briques
Le Choquel
Hardelot
Hardelot-Plage

0   10 km

400

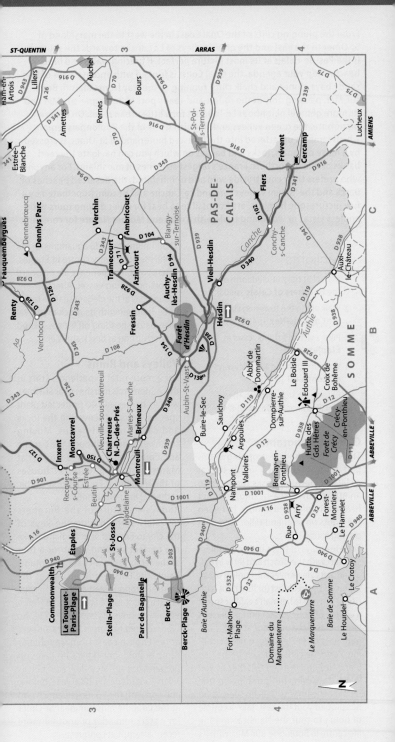

From the plunging cliffs of the Opal Coast in the west to the marshland of St-Omer to the east and the green valleys of La Canche towards the south, this is the Pas-de-Calais at its most picture perfect. If bracing walks and breezy beaches top your agenda, the Opal Coast is fringed with endless acres of fine sandy bays, dunes and chalk cliffs running all the way from Calais to Berck-sur-Mer, pausing only at the rough-and-ready port of Boulogne-sur-Mer and its more genteel neighbour Le Touquet for a little urban relief. On a more rustic note, the green valleys and sluggish rivers of the Boulonnais region, which rambles unfettered into the forested hinterland of St-Omer, is crossed by a maze of canals, locks and barges on which you can navigate the reed banks of one of northern France's largest stretches of marshland. For anyone who prefers their countryside wild and uninhabited, the deserted beaches of Berck and the "seven valleys" around La Canche and Hesdin, punctuated by a few picturesque hamlets, are impossible to beat for quiet driving tours with endless vistas or woodland trails with a map and Mother Nature for company.

Highlights

1 Marvel at the muscled form of the **Burghers of Calais** (p403)

2 Walk along the towering cliffs of the **Cap Gris-Nez** (p408)

3 Pilot a virtual fishing vessel in **Étaples** (p417)

4 Walk through the 17C alleyways of **Montreuil** (p420)

5 Ride on a barge through the marshes near **St-Omer** (p424)

Cliff-top Panoramas

The views are so jaw-dropping in this part of the world that a simple stop at a cliffside viewpoint risks turning into an afternoon of sea-gazing, so don't hesitate to pick and choose between the sights on offer and tailor your own driving tour.

For a few days of sea, sand and endless sky start with the beach and jetty in Calais, with its views over the English coast, followed by breakfast (or lunch for late-risers) at a real fisherman's café or spend a couple of hours discovering the city's world-class lace industry at Cité Internationale de la Dentelle, before strolling along the cliffs and bays of the Cap Blanc-Nez and the Cap Gris-Nez as you watch the world's busiest shipping lane unfold beneath you. If all this sea-gazing has piqued your interest, take a couple of hours to tour the Nausicaä marine life centre in Boulogne-sur-Mer, with its 11 000 animals and 36 aquariums, or the Maréis sea discovery centre in Étaples, where you can experience life on board a working fishing vessel. Alternatively, spend a day at the elegant seaside resort of Le Touquet with its mock medieval villas before heading off for a weekend of windsurfing at Berck-sur-Mer.

Valleys and Ruins

For a more rural experience, start at the Audomarois marshes near St-Omer, with its barges and 40 protected plant species, before discovering the locks and canals of Fontinettes. Moving southwest, motor through the Canche and Course valleys with a stop off at Montreuil to admire its 17C houses or the remains of France's first Gothic cathedral in Thérouanne.

Rodin's sculpture of the Burghers of Calais surrendering the keys of the city to Edward III of England make the perfect starting point for a tour of the region's cross-channel heritage. Relive the Battle of Agincourt at the Centre Historique Médiéval near Hesdin, retrace the steps of Francis I and Henry VIII as you drive along the Field of the Cloth of Gold tour near Guînes, or peer at the English coast from Napoleon's camp at Boulogne where his invasion preparations suffered the same fate as Julius Caesar's nearly 2000 years before, and end with the V3 rocket launch pad at the Coupole museum near St-Omer for a stark reminder of another more recent attempt at conquest.

Calais

The ideal starting point for excursions along the Opal Coast to Le Touquet, Calais is France's busiest passenger port, serving 20 million travellers a year. Its proximity to England – the white cliffs of Dover are just 38km/23.5mi away and often clearly visible from the promenade – has had a major impact on the port's history.

A BIT OF HISTORY
The Channel Tunnel

The first man to suggest building a tunnel between Britain and France was an engineer called Nicolas Desmaret in 1751.

First attempts – In 1880, 1 840m/1mi of galleries were tunnelled at a site called the "Puits des Anciens" along with 2 000m/1.25mi on the English side before the work was stopped. A fresh approach was tried in 1922. Technical progress in the 1960s gave the project a boost but a 400m/433yd gallery was abandoned once again.

Birth of Eurotunnel – During a Franco-British summit conference in September 1981, the idea of building a fixed link was again mooted by British Prime Minister Margaret Thatcher and French President François Mitterrand. The first link was established on 1 December 1990 and the official opening of the tunnel took place on 6 May, 1994.

Facts and figures – Most of the tunnel lies at a depth of 40m/130ft below the seabed, in a layer of blue chalk. Enormous tunnel-digging machines bored their way through the rock at a rate of 800 to 1 000m/867 to 1 083yd a month. The **trans-Channel link** consists, in fact, of two railway tunnels 7.60m/25ft in diameter connected every 375m/406yd to a central service gallery 4.80m/16ft in diameter built for the purposes of ventilation, security and system maintenance.

The Burghers of Calais – After his success at Crécy, **Edward III** of England needed to create a power-base in France. He began the siege of Calais on 3 September 1346, but eight months later had not been able to breach its defence.

▶ **Population:** 104 852
🔽 **Michelin Local Map:** p400: B1.
🅱 **Info:** 12 bd. Clemenceau, 62100 Calais. ☏03 21 96 62 40. www.ot-calais.fr.

As starvation began to bite, six burghers, led by **Eustache de Saint-Pierre**, prepared to sacrifice themselves to spare the lives of the other citizens of Calais. In thin robes, "barefoot, bareheaded, halters about their necks and the keys to the town in their hands," they presented themselves before the king to be delivered to the executioner. They were saved by the intercession of Edward's wife, Queen Philippa of Hainault.

Calais was in the hands of the English for over two centuries and was liberated only in 1558, by the Duke of Guise. This was a mortal blow to **Mary Tudor**, Queen of England, who said: "If my heart were laid open, the word "Calais" would be engraved on it."

Calais Lace

Together with Caudry-en-Cambrésis, Calais is the main centre of machine-made lace, employing about 2 000 workers using over 350 looms. Englishmen from Nottingham introduced the industry at the beginning of the 19C; quality was improved around 1830 when the first Jacquard looms were introduced. Three quarters of the lace made in Calais is exported.

 WALKING TOUR

Monument des Bourgeois de Calais★★

This famous work by **Rodin**, *The Burghers of Calais* (1895), is located between the Hôtel de Ville and Parc St-Pierre. With their exaggerated veins and muscles, they express the heroic nobility of the men obliged to humiliate themselves before the King of England.

The Burghers of Calais *by Rodin*

Hôtel de Ville

The early-19C town hall is built of brick and stone in 15C Flemish style. The **belfry** (75m/246ft) can be seen for miles in all directions. A **stained-glass window** recalls the departure of the English.

Musée de la Guerre

Parc Saint-Pierre, opposite the town hall. ⓒ*Open May–Sept 10am–6pm; Feb–Apr and Oct–Nov 11am–5pm.* ⊙*6€ (under 14s 5€).* ⓹ ℘*03 21 34 21 57.*
Used by the German army as a telephone exchange 1940–1945, this bunker now houses a display of memorabilia exploring the occupation of Calais, the Battle of Britain and the Resistance.
⚏Discover hundreds of species of sea and freshwater fish at the **Parc Saint-Pierre** aquarium (ⓒ*open Wed, Sat, Sun 3–6pm;* ⊙*2.50€, child 1.50€;* ⓹ ℘*06 03 59 81 86; www.cac.asso.fr).*

▶ Walk along bd. Jacquard. After the bridge, continue straight on. Walk past the tourist office and Parc Richelieu on bd. Clemenceau, turn right and continue until you reach the Musée des Beaux-Arts.

Musée des Beaux-Arts et de la Dentelle★

ⓒ*Open Apr–Oct Tue–Sat 10am–noon & 2–6pm, Sun 2–6pm; Nov–Mar Tue–Sat 10am–noon & 2–5pm, Sun 2–5pm.* ⊙*4€.* ⓹ ℘*03 21 46 48 40. www.calais.fr.*
The **19C and 20C sculpture** collection features works by Rodin and the stud-

ies he made for *The Burghers of Calais*, before exploring Rodin's predecessors, including Carrière-Belleuse, Carpeaux and Barye. The museum also has a selection of **paintings from the 17C to the 20C** by the Flemish and North European schools, alongside works by modern and contemporary artists such as Jean Dubuffet, Félix Del Marle, Picasso and Fautrier. Housed in a former tulle-making factory, the **lace section** explores machine-made and hand-made lace.

Église Notre-Dame

From the 14C to the 16C, this church came under the authority of the Archbishop of Canterbury. The influence of English and Tudor design can be seen in the tower, choir and transept.

▶ Walk down r. de la Paix. On the right: the Tour du Guet and the place d'Armes.

Place d'Armes

Before its destruction in WW II, this was the heart of medieval Calais. Only the 13C **watchtower** has survived. To the left is the Bassin Ouest; to the right is the Bassin du Paradis and the rear harbour used as a marina.

⚏ Beach and western jetty

Skirting a fine sandy beach, this seawall promenade is a perfect spot to enjoy an ice-cream and watch the ferries glide in and out of the port. The view from the western jetty is particularly interesting.

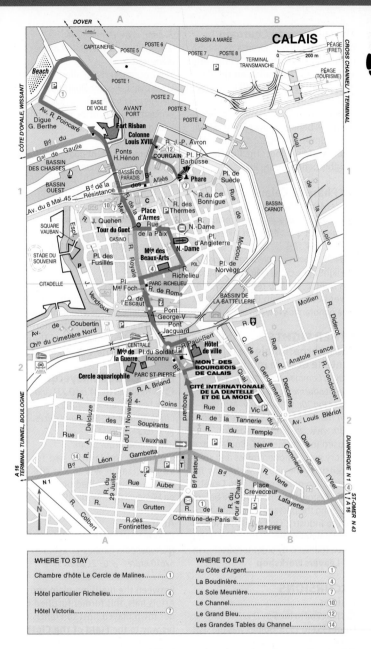

WHERE TO STAY

Chambre d'hôte Le Cercle de Malines...........①

Hôtel particulier Richelieu............④

Hôtel Victoria............⑦

WHERE TO EAT

Au Côte d'Argent............①

La Boudinière............④

La Sole Meunière............⑦

Le Channel............⑩

Le Grand Bleu............⑫

Les Grandes Tables du Channel............⑭

Spot the Cap Blanc-Nez and the cliffs of England in the distance.

◖ From the jetty, return to the inner harbour via the raised walkway that run around the dock and the Fort Risban.

Built in the 16C on the site of an English tower, the **Fort Risban** protected the entrance to the port.

◖ Cross the new H.-Hénon bridges, then turn left along the quay and continue towards Courgain.

The Quartier du Courgain

Rebuilt after WW II, Courgain is home to the city's fishing folk. Get up early and head to the stands on the Quai de la **Colonne-Louis-XVIII** to buy fish fresh from the trawlers. The fleet – a dozen or so boats – is moored below the quay, behind a row of huts. Finish with a drink at the Café du Minck, the haunt of old seadogs. The **lighthouse** is visible behind Courgain.

👤👥 Phare de Calais

Bd. des Alliés. 🔍*Guided tour (1hr).*
🕐*Open Feb–Dec Sun & public holidays 10am–noon, 2–5.30pm, Sat & Wed 2–5.30pm.* 🎫*4.50€ (5–15yrs 2€).* 📞*03 21 34 33 34. www.pharedecalais.com.*
The lighthouse (53m/174ft tall; 271 steps) was built in 1848 to replace a watch-tower beacon. Climb the steep stairs for a panoramic **view★★**.

OTHER SIGHTS
Cité internationale de la dentelle et de la mode★★

Quai du Commerce, car park of the quai de la Gendarmerie. 🕐*Open Apr–Oct Wed–Mon 10am–6pm; Nov–Mar Wed–Mon 10am–5pm.* 🎫*8€.* ♿ 📞*03 21 00 42 30. www.citedentelle.calais.fr.*
Housed in a former 19C Boulart lace factory with a modern glass and steel extension, the museum begins its exploration of lacemaking on **Level 1** with a history of handmade lace before exploring the passage from craftsmanship to industry. On **Level 2**, discover five Leavers looms, still in working order, followed by a demonstration in the **Leavers workshop**.

EXCURSIONS
Guînes

▶*11km/7mi to the S by D 127.*
From 1352 to 1558, Guînes was the seat of a powerful count, a vassal of the English crown. Surrounded by forests, the town makes an ideal starting point for tours of the Trois Pays area.

👤👥 Tour de l'Horloge★

🕐*Open Jul–Aug 10.30am–6.30pm; Apr–Jun, first half of Sept Sun–Mon*

2–6pm. 🎫*6€ (family ticket 19€).*
📞*03 21 19 59 00. www.tour-horloge-guines.com.*
This clocktower (1763) offers panoramic views over Calais, the Opal Coast and the Flanders plains. An interactive museum evokes the history of the town, from the Vikings to Thomas Becket.

👤👥 Écomusée Saint-Joseph-Village

🕐*Open Apr–Sept 10am–7pm; mid-Feb–Mar Tues–Thurs, Sun 10am–6pm; Oct–mid-Nov Tues–Thurs, Sun, public holidays 10am–6pm.* 🎫*10€.*
📞*03 21 35 64 05. www.st-joseph-village.com.*
Explore a village from 1900–1950, including a school, bakery and mill.

Forêt de Guînes

▶The road to the south of Guînes enters a hilly area of woodland extending 785ha/1 940 acres to the northern edge of the Boulonnais region. The road ends at the **Clairière du Ballon**.

Fortresse de Mimoyecques

▶*10km/6mi to the W by D 231 and, after Landrethun-le-Nord, D 249. Check for opening times and prices.* ♿ 📞*03 21 87 10 34. www.mimoyecques.com.*
Chosen as the launch pad for the V3 Howitzer in WW II, the site was destroyed by an Allied bombing raid on Mimoyecques in July 1944.

Ardres

▶*8 km/5mi to the E by D 231.*
🛈 *Chapelle des Carmes- pl. d'Armes, 62610 Ardres.* 📞*03 21 35 28 51. www.ardres-tourisme.fr.*
Between the maritime plain and the Artois hills, this former fortified border town played host to Francis I on his way to the **Field of the Cloth of Gold**. *(Follow in the footsteps of Francis I by taking the "Field of the Cloth of Gold" driving tour – ask at the Guînes Office du tourisme).*
The triangular **Grand'Place** is lined with historic pitched-roof houses. Don't miss the 17C Carmelite chapel.

ADDRESSES

🛏 STAY

🛏 **Hôtel Victoria** – 8 r. du Cdt-Bonningue, at pied du phare. ✆03 21 34 38 32. http://hotel-victoria-calais.active hotels.com. 14 rooms. ⌂6€. Well situated a short walk from the Channel Tunnel station, this small hotel is nothing fancy but impeccably maintained.

🛏 **Hôtel particulier Richelieu** – 17 r. Richelieu. ✆0321346160. www.hotel richelieu-calais.com. 🅿. Wi-fi. 5 rooms⌂. Behind an austere façade and worse-for-wear common areas, the cosy, modern bedrooms have been completely renovated. Large bathrooms with hip baths. Ask for a park view. Free Wi-fi.

🛏 **Chambre d'hôte Le Cercle de Malines** – 12 r. des Malines. ✆03 21 96 80 65. www.lecercledemalines.com. 🅿. 5 rooms⌂. Once the home of a Calais lacemaker, this elegant townhouse has four bedrooms decorated in a mix of classic and contemporary styles.

🍴 EAT

🍴 **La Boudinière** – 2691 rte de Waldam, 62215 Oye-Plage.14km/9mi E of Calais by D119. ✆03 21 85 93 14. www.laboudiniere. com. Oct–May Thu–Tue midday, Fri and Sat eves; Jun-Sept daily. ♿🅿. Lost in the Calais countryside, this quiet little restaurant serves meat chosen by the owner-chef himself. Friendly reception.

🍴 **La Sole Meunière** – 1 bd. de la Résistance. ✆03 21 34 43 01. www.solemeuniere.com. 🅿. 18 rooms⌂. The house speciality is sole, cooked five different ways. Opt for a table by the bay windows for a view of the port.

🍴 **Au Côte d'Argent** – 1 digue G.-Berthe. ✆03 21 34 68 07. www.cotedargent.com. Closed 17 Aug–7 Sep, Wed eve (Sep–Mar), Sun eve and Mon. Dine in a setting that looks like a boat, as you watch the ferries come and go.

🍴 **Le Channel** – 3 bd. de la Résistance. ✆03 21 34 42 30. www.restaurant-lechannel.com. Closed 2–7 Jan, Sun eve. and Tue. A last chance to sample French cuisine before heading for England! Try the French twist on 'steak pie'.

🍴 **Les Grandes Tables du Channel** – 173 bd Gambetta. ✆03 21 35 30 11. www.lechannel.fr. ♿🅿. Lunch menu 16€. Quirky cuisine served in the industrial-chic restaurant of the Calais national theatre. Not to be confused with the Le Channel restaurant.

🍴 **Le Grand Bleu**– Quai de la Colonne. ✆03 21 97 97 98. www.legrandbleu-calais. com. Closed 17–26 Feb, 26 Aug–10 Sept, Tue eve and Wed. Contemporary maritime cuisine to match the modern décor.

La Côte d'Opale★

The Opal Coast extends from the Baie de Somme to the Belgian border at the western end of the **Parc naturel régional des Caps et Marais d'Opale**. A local painter, Édouard Lévêque, first used the term in 1911 to describe the coast's opal-like waves, although its landscapes inspired painters and writers such as Corot and Victor Hugo long before the 20C. The most spectacular part of the coastline lies between Boulogne and Calais, where the cliffs, worn away by the strong north-south current, skirt the Boulonnais hills.

- 🕑 **Michelin Local Map:** 301; p400: AB1.
- ℹ **Info:** Office du tourisme de la Terre des Deux Caps, pl. de la Mairie, 62179 Wissant ✆03 21 82 48 00; www.terredes2caps.fr.
- ▶ **Location:** The Opal coast borders the English Channel and the North Sea from Mers-les-Bains to Bray-Dune. Use the D 940 to explore.
- 🕑 **Don't Miss:** Enjoy moules et frites and other seafood at Mers-les-Bains.
- 👥 **Kids:** Make the most of the beach as Wissant.

🚗 DRIVING TOUR

50km/30mi. Approx. 2hr 30min.

Boulogne-sur-Mer★

🚗 *See BOULOGNE-SUR-MER.*

▶ Leave Boulogne by D 940.

A winding coastal road offering glimpses of the sea, the ports and the beaches, D 940 leads across hill crests which are intermittently bare or covered with close-cropped meadows.

To the north the road arrives at the Escalles cran, resembling a mountain pass but at an altitude of less than 100m/328ft. Car parks flank the road, allowing access to the sea or walks among the dunes.

Swimming Beaches

Pay attention to the colour of the flag flying near the lifeguard station:

- **Green** – *Lifeguards in attendance. Swimming authorised and not considered dangerous.*
- **Orange** – *Lifeguards in attendance. Swimming considered dangerous.*
- **Red** – *Swimming prohibited.*

Wimereux★

The Wimereux Valley (🚗 *see Le BOU-LOGNE-SUR-MER, Driving Tour*) opens onto a large seaside resort popular with families. Walk along the promenade skirting the sand-and-pebble beach for views of the Straits of Dover, the Grande Armée Column and Boulogne, where the promenade narrows to a path leading to **Pointe aux Oies**, where Napoléon III landed on 6 August 1840 before attempting to win over the garrison stationed there.

▶ Between Wimereux and Ambleteuse, the road runs beside tall dunes.

Ambleteuse

Formerly a naval base protected by **Fort d'Ambleteuse** (🕐 *open Jul–Aug Sat & Sun 3–6pm, May–Jun & Sept–Oct, Sun 3–6pm, last admission 30min before closing;* ⊜*3€;* ℘*06 75 52 73 57*), built by Vauban between 1685 and 1690, this picturesque village stands above the mouth of the River Slack, where James II of England landed after fleeing his kingdom in 1689. Napoleon based part of his flotilla here while planning his invasion of England (🚗 *see BOULOGNE-SUR-MER*). The **Musée Historique de la Seconde Guerre Mondiale** (🕐 *open daily Apr–Oct, 10am–6pm, Jul–Aug 7pm, Nov & Mar Sat & Sun 10am–6pm;* ⊜*7.80€;* ♿*, ℘03 21 87 33 01; www.musee3945.com*) on the outskirts of Ambleteuse retraces the history of World War II, from the conquest of Poland in 1939 to the Liberation.

▶ 3km/2mi after Audresselles, turn left onto D 191.

Cap Gris-Nez★★

This "grey-nose cape" looks out to the English coast less than 30km/19mi away. The gently sloping cliffs rise to 45m/148ft. The lighthouse (28m/92ft tall) with beams visible 45km/28mi away, was rebuilt after the war at the tip of a bare, windswept peninsula dotted with the remains of ruined German pillboxes. The underground base of the Gris-Nez CROSS, the organisation responsible for supervising the busiest shipping lane in the world, is located here. A plaque commemorates the sacrifice made by Captain Ducuing and his sailors who died defending the semphore against a German tank regiment commanded by General Guderian on May 25, 1940.

Straight ahead, the **view★** extends to the white cliffs of England. On the French side you can see Cap Blanc-Nez and Boulogne along the coast.

The **Musée du Mur de l'Atlantique** (🕐 *open daily Jul–Aug 9am–7pm; Apr, May–Jun & Sept–Oct 10am–6pm; Feb, Mar, Nov 2–5.30pm;* ⊜*8€;* ℘*03 21 32 97 33; www.batterietodt.com*) is housed in the former Todt battery, a World War II pillbox which served as a German launch pad for 2m/6ft-long missiles fired towards England. There are collections of arms and uniforms, and a naval gun on rails (280 bore, made by Krupp in 1943), which is 35m/115ft long, could fire 15 times per hour and had a range of 62–86km/38.5–53.4mi.

👤👥 Wissant ⌂

This splendid beach of fine, firm sand is sheltered from the eastern winds and currents. It forms a vast curve between Cap Gris-Nez and Cap Blanc-Nez. Villas stand among the dunes.

The **Musée du Moulin** (🕐open 2–6pm by reservation. 📷3€. 📞03 21 35 91 87, www.lemoulin-wissant.com) is housed in a former flour mill driven by hydraulic power. It features pinewood parts, cast-iron waterwheels and a conveyor belt.

Cap Blanc-Nez★★

The "white-nose cape" is a vertical mass of chalk cliffs rising 134m/440ft above the waves, offering extensive **views**★★ of the English cliffs and the French coast from Calais to Cap Gris-Nez. This view has inspired many a figure in history: Nicolas Desmarets was the first person to consider linking France to England in 1751, followed by Aimé Thomé de Gamond, who suggested a variety of options: a tunnel constructed of metal tubes, a concrete undersea vault, a pontoon, an artificial isthmus, a mobile bridge and a viaduct-bridge. Crossings were eventually achieved by balloon (Blanchard), plane (Blériot), steamboat (the first regular line was established in 1816), by raft and on skis, to mention just a few.

▶ Retrace your steps to Mont d'Hubert.

Lower down the hill is the monument to **Latham** (1883–1912), the pilot who attempted, unsuccessfully, to cross the Channel at the same time as Blériot. Between **Sangatte** and Blériot-Plage, the chalets are built directly on the sea-washed dunes.

Blériot-Plage

This beautiful beach extends along to Cap Blanc-Nez. At Baraques (500m/550yd west of the resort), near D 940, a monument commemorates the first aerial crossing of the Channel, by **Louis Blériot** (1872–1936). On 25 July 1909 he landed his aeroplane on the Dover cliffs, following a flight lasting half an hour.

Calais 👤see CALAIS.

🥾 HIKE

Cap Blanc-Nez to Cap Gris-Nez

🚶 22km/13mi round trip (seasoned walkers only), fully signposted.
Allow one day (with a hearty picnic).
For a shorter walk simply complete part of the route then retrace your steps.
Depart from one of the two capes or Wissant town hall. Pick up a recommended walking guide (no charge), from the Terre des Deux Caps tourist office (at Wissant, Marquise or Ambleteuse), information on www.tourisme.terredes2caps.fr.
One of the most beautiful walks along the coast, following the GR 121 (on foot or mountain bike), this tour promises breathtaking views over the dunes, beaches, heaths and cliffs.

ADDRESSES

🛏 STAY

⊝⊝ **La Grande Maison** – Hameau de la Haute-Escalles 62179 Escalles. 📞03 21 85 27 75. lagrandemaison.chezalice.fr. 5 rooms. 🍽. Located between the two caps, ideal for hikers. Gîtes also available.

🍴 EAT

⊝⊝ **La Sirène** – 62179 Audinghen. 📞03 21 32 95 97. Closed 1 Dec–25 Jan, eves (except May–Aug), Sun eve., Mon. 🅿. Situated on the Cap Gris-Nez beach, this restaurant commands fantastic views. Choose a table in one of the two large dining rooms with wide bay windows for a meal of grilled lobster.

EVENTS

Festival de la Côte d'Opale – 📞03 21 30 40 33. www.festival-cotedopale.fr. 3 weeks Jul. Different towns along the Côte d'Opale (Berck, Boulogne-sur-Mer, Calais, Desvres, Dunkerque, Étaples, Hardelot, Le Portel, Le Touquet-Paris-Plage and Wimereux) team up for a festival of music with rock, jazz, commercial and classical. In November, the **Tendances Côte d'Opale** sets the stage for jazz players and local designers.

Boulogne-sur-Mer★★

Founded by the Romans, Boulogne is a brash but loveable city with busy, crowded streets. Europe's largest fish processing and trading centre, Boulogne counts the literary historian **St Beuve,** (1804–69), the engineer **Frédéric Sauvage** (1786–1857), the inventor of the propeller used in steam navigation, and the Egyptologist **Auguste Mariette,** among its illustrious citizens.

A BIT OF HISTORY

Chosen by Julius Caesar as the base for his ill-starred invasion of England in 55 BC, and a major port connecting Britain with the rest of the Empire after Emperor Claudius finally conquered the island in AD 43, Boulogne was an obvious choice of location for the **Boulogne Camp,** where Napoléon Bonaparte kept his troops mustered from 1803 to 1805 in readiness for his invasion of England. On 26 August 1805, a year after being crowned emperor, Napoléon finally abandoned his project when he turned against the Austrians instead.

In August 1840 the future Napoléon III tried to raise the town against Louis-Philippe, but the attempt floundered and he was imprisoned in Ham Fort.

The Father of Egyptology – Boulogne-born Egyptologist **Auguste Mariette** (1821–81) made one of archaeology's greatest finds - Memphis, the ancient capital of the Pharaohs in 1850. He directed numerous excavations in Egypt and founded the Boulaq Museum, now Cairo's Egyptian Museum.

SIGHTS
👪 Nausicaä★★★

Centre National de la Mer. 🕐*Open Jul–Aug, 9.30am–7.30pm; Sept–Jun 9.30am–6.30pm.* 🕐*Closed 3 weeks in Jan, 25 Dec.* 👓*18€ (children 11.70€).* ♿.📞*03 21 30 99 99. www.nausicaa.fr.* The largest sea-life centre in Europe. **Nausicaä** contains 36 aquariums and more than 10 000 marine animals.

▶ **Population:** 135 116
🗺 **Michelin Local Map:** p400: A2.
🛈 **Info:** 24 quai Gambetta, 62203 Boulogne-Sur-Mer. 📞03 21 10 88 10. www.tourisme-boulognesurmer.com.
▶ **Location:** Accessible from the A 16. Amid the newer shopping streets of the ville basse are some of the best food shops in the whole region.
👁 **Don't Miss:** Nausicaä; the ville haute.
🕐 **Timing:** Nausicaä takes around two hours (best visited in the afternoon). Allow a half day to tour the town.
👪 **Kids:** Nausicaä and its aquariums; the beach at Portel.

Diver and sand tiger shark, Nausicaä
© C/A. ROSENFELD-NAUSICAA

Journey through the World's Seas – Start your tour with a giant jellyfish "test tube" and a series of North Sea and Mediterranean aquariums before admiring the swirling shoals of tuna in the **Espace Diamant des Thons**, an inverted pyramid-shaped aquarium.

Man and the Sea – The visit continues with a circular corridor exploring this long relationship before taking a closer look at sea resource management in the **celestial dome**.

Tropical Lagoon Village – The museum takes a tropical turn here, with a display of colourful fish in a greenish-blue lagoon, followed by a little theatrical light relief in the **Underwater Observatory**, where Californian sealions dive through the waves or stretch on the rocks in the **aerial observatory**. An escalator leads to the next area, a **hands-on basin** teeming with cod and turbot, where children can stroke thornback rays, followed by a small fish farm. The visit ends with the spectacular **Anneau des sélaciens**, a panoramic circular tank filled with sharks. The museum also offers a cinema (130 seats), shops, restaurant, bar and cafeteria.

La Ville Basse

The **outer harbour** is protected by two jetties, of which the Digue Carnot is 3 250m/over 2mi long.

The **inner harbour** consists of a tidal dock reserved for ferries, small trawlers and yachts and the Napoléon and Loubet docks for the big fishing boats.

Quai Gambetta is busiest when the trawlers unload their catch.

Beach – Already well-known in the 18C, the fine, white-sand beach became fashionable from the mid-19C onwards. The town is extremely popular with families and sailing, land-sailing and speed-sailing enthusiasts.

Église St-Nicolas – Standing in pl. Dalton, *(market Wednesdays and Saturdays)*, this is the oldest church in Boulogne. It was built from 1220 to 1250 and altered in the 16C (apse, transept, chancel vaults, chapels) and in the 18C, when the nave was rebuilt. The 17C high altar features a fine painting of *The Flagellation* by Lehmann.

WALKING TOUR

La Ville Haute★★

The upper town, enclosed by ramparts, stands on the site of the old Roman *castrum*. It is overlooked by the dome of the Notre-Dame basilica and is popular for its pleasant strolls along the ramparts and the town's historic buildings.

Ramparts – The fortifications were built in the early 13C on the foundations of the Gallo-Roman walls and were strengthened in the 16C to 17C.

They form a rectangle reinforced by the **castle** to the east, and accessed by four gates flanked by two towers. The parapet walkway is accessible from each gateway and offers **views★** of the town and port.

Pilâtre de Rozier and Pierre Romain took off in a balloon from the **tour Gayette**, a former jail at the western corner, in the very first attempt to cross the Channel by air in 1785; they crashed just north of Boulogne.

A pyramid-shaped monument in the garden between Boulevard Auguste-Mariette and the ramparts is dedicated to **Mariette** the Egyptologist.

▶ Walk through the western Pte. des Dunes to place de la Résistance and pl. Godefroy-de-Bouillon.

Library – The library is located in the old Annonciades Convent. The 17C buildings and cloisters house study and exhibition rooms. The main reading room occupies the 18C chapel with its superb coffered ceiling.

Belfry – *Tours (contact tourist office) Mon–Fri 8am–6pm, Sat & Sun 8am –noon. No charge. 03 21 87 80 80.* The 13C Gothic belfry *(access through the Hôtel de Ville)*, has a 12C base (the former keep from the castle of the counts of Boulogne) and an 18C octagonal section at the top. It houses Gallo-Roman statues and regional antique furniture. The top of the belfry (183 steps) offers an extensive **view★** of Boulogne.

▶ pl. de la Résistance leads into pl. Godefroy-de-Bouillon located at the junction of the four main streets.

Hôtel de Ville – The 18C façade of red brick with stone dressings contrasts sharply with the primitive Gothic belfry.

Hôtel Desandrouin – To the right as you come out of the town hall stands this Louis XVI mansion where Napoleon stayed several times from 1803 to 1811.

▶ Follow r. de Puits-d'Amour alongside Hôtel Desandrouin and turn right.

Rue Guyale – This street is home to the merchants' guildhall, the back of the Annonciades Convent and the rough-stone façades of historic houses.

▶ From pl. Godefroy-de-Bouillon take r. de Lille.

Head to no. 58 to see the oldest **house** in Boulogne (12C). The Basilique Notre-Dame stands on the left. Rue du Château on the right leads to the former residence of the counts of Boulogne.

Basilique Notre-Dame

Access via the south transept in r. de Lille.
◷*Open Apr–Aug 9am–noon, 2–6pm; Sept–Mar 10am–noon & 2–5pm.*
The basilica (1827–1866), built on the site of the old cathedral destroyed after the Revolution has preserved its Romanesque crypt. The superb, soaring **dome★** with its circle of large statues rises behind the chancel.
Crypt – *Closed for renovation until end of 2013.* ✆*03 21 30 22 70.* Under the basilica, a labyrinth of underground passages links 14 chambers. One of them houses the **Treasury★** which contains the relic of the Holy Blood offered by Philip the Fair to Our Lady of Boulogne. Don't miss the **crypt of the painted pillars** dating from the 11C.

▶ Take r. du Château opposite.

Château-musée★

r. de Bernet. ◷*Open Wed–Sun 10am–12.30pm & 2–5.30pm, Sun and public holidays 10am–12.30pm, 2.30–6pm.* ◉*4.50€. No charge 1st Sun of month.* ✆*03 21 10 02 20.*
www.tourisme-boulognesurmer.fr.
Formerly the residence of the counts of Boulogne, this polygonal building was the first in western Europe to abandon the traditional keep.
Mediterranean archaeology is represented by an Egyptian section (sarcophagi and funerary objects gifted by Mariette the Egyptologist) and a group of **Greek vases★★** dating from 5–6C BC, including a black-figure jug depicting the suicide of Ajax.

Beyond this are rooms containing porcelain, ceramics and earthenware from French and foreign manufacturers.
The ethnographic collection includes the **Eskimo and Aleutian masks★★** brought back from a voyage to North America by the anthropologist Pinart, and a Maori battle canoe from New Zealand. The guard-room displays collections from the Middle Ages and the Renaissance: copper and brassware, sculptures, paintings and coins.

Maison de la Beurière★

◷*Open mid-Jun to mid-Sept Tue–Sun 10am–1pm, 3–6pm; mid-Sept–mid-Jun Wed & Sat 10am–noon, 2–5pm.* ◉*2.50€.* ✆*03 21 30 14 52.*
www.tourisme-boulognesurmer.com.
A third of the Boulonnais population lived in this ancient seafaring quarter, known as "la Beurière". Mostly destroyed during WW II, only one narrow, stepped street of five or six houses now remains. A small museum illustrates the life of a seafaring family around 1900.

EXCURSIONS
Colonne de la Grande Armée★★

▶*3km/2mi N by N 1 and turn left on a small road.* ◷*Open mid-Jun–Sept Wed–Sun 10am–12.30pm & 2.30–6.30pm; Sept–May Fri–Sun 10am–noon & 2–4pm.* ◷*Closed 1 Jan, 1 May, 1 and 11 Nov, 25 Dec.* ◉*3€.* ✆*03 21 80 43 69.*
http://wimille.monuments-nationaux.fr.
Designed by architect **Eloi Labarre** (1764–1833) to commemorate the Boulogne Camp, the column is made from Marquise marble. It rises 54m/177ft high. A staircase (*263 steps*) leads to the square platform (190m/623ft above sea level) from where the **panorama★★** extends over Boulogne.

Légion d'honneur monument

▶*2km/1.25mi N by D 940 and a path to the right.*
This obelisk marks the site of the throne on which Napoléon I sat on 16 August 1804 for the second distribution of the Legion of Honour decorations.

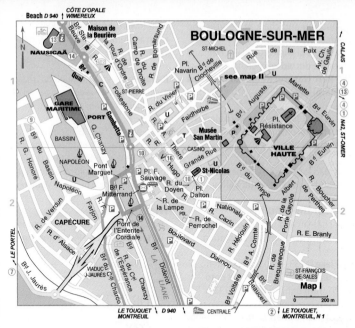

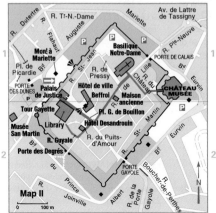

WHERE TO STAY	
Ferme-auberge du Blaisel............................	①
Chambre d'hôte Le Clos d'Esch.................	②
Hôtel La Ferme du Vert......	④
Hôtel de la Plage..............	⑦
Hôtel Faidherbe................	⑩
Chambre d'hôte Le Beaucamp.................	⑬
Hôtel La Matelote.............	⑭
Hôtel Métropole................	⑯

WHERE TO EAT	
Chez Jules.......................	①
Ferme-auberge de la Raterie.................	④
Le Châtillon....................	⑨
Le Doyen........................	⑩
Restaurant de Nausicaä......	⑬

St-Étienne-au-Mont view★

⬥ *5km/3mi along D 52 then right up a steep hill (13 percent gradient).*
From the cemetery adjacent to the hilltop church (altitude 124m/407ft), there is a **view★** of the Liane Valley and Boulogne downstream.

Hardelot-Plage ⚲⚲

⬥ *15km/9mi S by D 940 and D 113E.*
A seaside resort with a gently sloping sandy beach: walking, riding and cycling paths and golf, sailing and kite-flying

facilities. The 13C **château** north of the village was rebuilt in the 19C by an Englishman in the style of Windsor Castle.

🚗 DRIVING TOUR

LE BOULONNAIS★

75km/46mi round-trip. About 3hr.

The complex relief of the countryside is due to differing geological formations: marble in Marquise, sandstone in Outreau and chalk in Desvres and Neufchâtel.

The valleys of Wimereux, Liane, Hem and Slack are dotted with orchards. Part of the **Parc Naturel Régional des Caps et Marais d'Opale**.

⊙ Leave Boulogne eastward along N 42; 3km/2mi on, over the roundabout, turn onto D 232.

This road, edged with beeches and elms, descends into **Wimereux Valley**.

Souverain-Moulin

The château and its outbuildings look very attractive in their leafy setting.

⊙ Take D 233 (east) to Belle, then turn left onto D 238 and right onto D 251. Turn right again onto D 127.

The **Maison du Parc National Régional des Caps et Marais d'Opale** is situated in the **manoir du Huisbois** (⊙open Mon–Fri 9am-noon & 2–5pm; ℘03 21 87 90 90; www.parc-opale.fr) a 17C house of local grey stone. Information and exhibitions on Boulonnais.

⊙ From N 42 to Saint-Omer, turn left on D 224 to Licques.

Licques

Licques is famous for its turkeys, introduced in the 17C by the local monks.

⊙ From Licques, follow D191 towards Hermelinghen.

After Le Ventus, the road rises to reveal **views★** over the Boulonnais valleys.

⊙ At Hardinghen, take D127 and D127E5 towards Rety.

Rety

This small Flamboyant **church** dates from the late 15C, with a 12C tower. ⊙Open 9.30–11.30am, 2–5pm. Contact town hall on ℘03 21 92 89 75.

⊙ On exiting Rety, turn left onto D 232 then, after crossing D 127E5,

right towards Hydrequent. Exit the town and turn left down D 243 to the viewpoint.

Panorama over the "Napoléon" marble quarry in the foreground and the aggregate quarry behind.

⊙ Return to D 232. Don't miss the mill on the Slack River, immediately on the left. At Wierre-Effroy, take D 234 to Conteville-lès-Boulogne, then right along D 233, which hugs the Wimereux.

Wimille

The **cemetery** contains the tombs of Pilâtre de Rozier and Pierre Romain.

⊙ Return to Boulogne.

ADDRESSES

🛏 STAY

⊙ **Le Clos d'Esch (B&B)** – 126 r. de l'Église. 62360 Echinghen. 4km/2.5mi E by D 940 towards St-Léonard and D 234 towards Échingen. ℘03 21 91 14 34. www.leclosdesch.fr. 🅿🅿. 4 rooms ⌷. Located at the centre of a small village, this renovated farm is a pleasant stop-over.

⊙⊜🍽 **Hôtel Faidherbe** – 12 r. Faidherbe. ℘0321316093. www.hotelfaidherbe.fr. Closed 20 Dec–10 Jan. 🅰🅿. 33 rooms ⌷. Between the town centre and the port. Cheerful welcome from Victor the mynah bird.

⊙⊜🍽 **Hôtel Métropole** – 51 r. Thiers. ℘03 21 31 54 30. www.hotel-metropole-boulogne.com. Closed 20 Dec–12 Jan. Wi-fi. 25 rooms. ⌷11€. Comfortable modern or rustic bedrooms. Dapper breakfast room opening onto a garden.

⊙⊜ **Hôtel de la Plage** – 168 bd. Ste-Beuve. ℘03 21 32 15 15. www.hotelboulogne plage.com. Wi-fi. 42 rooms. ⌷7€. Functional rooms facing the back are quiet, those facing the front have views of the sea from the 3rd floor.

⊙⊜🍽 **Hôtel Le Beaucamp** – 62720 Wierre-Effroy.13km/8mi NE of Boulogne-sur-Mer by D 942, rte. de St-Omer, D232 and D 242E1. ℘03 21 30 56 13. www.lebeaucamp.com. Closed 20 Dec–20 Jan. 🅿. 5 rooms ⌷.This woodland manor has been in the same family since the 19C. Comfortable rooms.

⊜⊜ **Hôtel de la Ferme du Vert** –
R. du Vert. 62720 Wierre-Effroy. ℰ03 21
87 67 00. www.fermeduvert.com. Closed
17–25 Mar, 19 Dec–20 Jan, Sun (except
Jul–Aug). �𝗣. 16 rooms. ⊡12€, half-
board possible. Restaurant⊜⊜⊜. 19C
farmstead with simple, elegant rooms.
Restaurant and cheese shop.

⊜⊜⊜ **Ferme-auberge du Blaisel** –
Ch. de la Lombarderie, 62240 Wirwignes.
12km/7mi SE of Boulogne-sur-Mer by D 341
towards Desvres. ℰ03 21 32 91 98. www.
fermeaubergedublaisel.com. Closed 23
Dec–5 Jan, Sun eve and Wed. ⟨𝗣⟩3 rooms ⊡.
Restaurant⊜⊜. Fresh, seasonal fare.
Cosy guest rooms upstairs.

⊜⊜⊜⊜ **Hôtel La Matelote**– 70 bd.
Ste-Beuve. ℰ03 21 30 33 33. www.la-
matelote.com. Wi-fi. 35 rooms. ⊡15€. On
the seafront opposite Nausicaä. Friendly
atmosphere and comfortable rooms.

⟨𝗬⟩ EAT

⊜ **Le Doyen** – 11 r. du Doyen.
ℰ03 21 30 13 08. Closed 2 wks in Jan,
Sun (except public holidays). A small eatery,
nattily decorated in pastel hues, serving
traditional seafood.

⊜ **Le Châtillon** – 6 r. C.-Tellier. ℰ03 21 31
43 95. www.le-chatillon.com. ⟨⟩. Open
4.30am to 4pm to cater for dockers and
fishermen. Fish straight from the sea.
Chef's speciality: stuffed squid.

⊜⊜ **Chez Jules** 8-10 pl. Dalton.
ℰ03 21 31 54 12. www.chez-jules.fr.
Closed 2 wks (end Sept), 23 Dec–15 Jan,
Sun eve (except Jul–Aug). ⟨⟩. A brasserie
serving hearty dishes: moules-frites,
crêpes and wood-fired pizzas.

⊜⊜⊜ **Restaurant de Nausicaä** –
Bd. Ste-Beuve. ℰ03 21 33 24 24. Closed
Mon (low season). This split-level seafood
eatery commands panoramic sea views.

SHOPPING

Le Craquelin – ℰ03 21 10 13 40. 7am–
12.30pm, 3–7.30pm, Sun 7am–1pm. Closed
Mon. Head to "Fred" the bakers on 30 pl.
Dalton for this brioche delight.

Le Touquet-Paris-Plage★★

Cushioned between the Canche
estuary, the Channel and vast
swathes of woodland, Le Touquet
has the quaint charm of an
elegant seaside resort. Its villas
and bungalows, surrounded by
impeccable lawns, flowerbeds and
pine trees, have a certain old-world
flavour that make it easy to forget
the glass-and-steel blocks along the
seafront. Offering a varied line-up
of exhibitions, activities, concerts
and horse-racing events, Le Touquet
attracts tourists year-round.

VISIT
Digue-promenade
The **promenade** is edged by gardens
and car parks. The south end leads to a
sand-yachting club and therapy centre.

The beach and port
The sea recedes at low tide, revealing
a gently-sloping beach that stretches

▶ **Population:** 5 299
⟨⟩ **Michelin Local Map:**
p401: A3.
⟨⟩ **Info:** Palais de l'Europe,
Pl. de l'Hermitage, 62520
Le Touquet-Paris-Plage.
ℰ03 21 06 72 00.
www.letouquet.com.
⟨⟩ **Location:** On the coast,
68km/43mi S of Calais, and
accessible by the A 16
(Junction 26 and then the
N 39 to Étaples.
⟨𝗣⟩ **Parking:** There is plenty
of paid parking along the
Digue-promenade, but in
good weather you will need
to be there early.
⟨⟩ **Don't Miss:** The maritime
forest of the 'Jardins de
la Manche'.
⟨⟩ **Timing:** The walk will take
around half a day.

as far as the mouth of the River Authie.
The **coastal road** follows to the marina

and the water sports club, sheltered by Pointe du Touquet headland.

Sports and leisure activities

Near the attractive shopping galleries of the Hermitage district are the **Sports Centre**, the select **Casino du Palais** and the **Palais de l'Europe,** a venue for conferences and cultural events. The **Museum** (Qopen Jul–Aug 10am– 12.30pm & 2–6pm, Sept–Jun Wed–Fri & Mon 2–5pm Sat & Sun 10am–noon & 2.30–6pm; 3.50€; 03 21 05 62 62) displays works by the Étaples School (1880–1914) along with paintings by Le Sidaner and a modern art section.

"Jardins de la Manche"

This forest (800ha/1 900 acres) was planted in 1855; its maritime pine, birch, alder, poplar and acacia trees protect about 2 000 luxury villas – either Anglo-Norman in style or resolutely modern – from the wind, with 45km/28mi of bridlepaths and 50km/31mi of forest tracks reserved for hikers.

Four walks start from place de l'Hermitage: **La Pomme de Pin** for "amateurs", **Le Daphné** for serious hikers, **La Feuille de chêne** for keen "explorers" and **L'Argousier** for really "experienced" hikers.

Three golf courses extend south of the forest. Along the River Canche are the **racecourse**, the **equestrian centre**, the **shooting range** (*archery*) and the **airport**.

WALKING TOUR

From pl. de l'Hermitage, take av. du Verger.

This is Le Touquet's most fashionable avenue, lined with flowerbeds and white-painted boutiques (1927) recalling the Art Deco style. Further on the **Hôtel Westminster** is one of the resort's most prestigious establishments with its red-brick façade and protruding windows.

Bear left and walk along rue St-Jean.

The turreted **Village Suisse** (1905) is in mock medieval style. The shopping arcades have terraces upstairs.

Return to the hotel and follow av. des Phares.

Behind the hotel, the red-brick **lighthouse** was rebuilt by Quételart in 1949 with a hexagonal design.

Cross av. des Phares and follow r. J.-Duboc to boulevard Daloz.

Villa Cendrillon (1923) on the corner of the boulevard has a pretty loggia and an unusual overlapping roof. At no. 44, the **Villa La Wallonne** marks the beginning of a lively shopping area. Note the façade of **Villa des Mutins** (1925) at no. 78 with its two gables overlooking rue de Lens. Opposite, **Villa Le Roy d'Ys** at no. 45 looks like a traditional Normandy dwelling with its timber-framed walls. The **Hôtel de Ville** was built from local stone in 1931 in Anglo-Norman style with cemented timber-framing; it is flanked by a belfry (38m/125ft tall).

Take r. Jean-Monnet to the beach.

Villa Le Castel (1904) at no. 50 combines the neo-Gothic and Art Nouveau styles. Rue Jean-Monnet continues through the arch of the **covered market** (1927–32), a half-moon-shaped ensemble, and leads to boulevard Pouget on the seafront lined with other holiday houses.

Take av. du Verger which leads back to pl. de l'Hermitage.

EXCURSIONS
Stella-Plage

Leave Le Touquet along Ave F.-Godin for 5km/3mi, turn right onto D 144.
Behind the dunes that fringe the beach, the woods, which extend all the way from Le Touquet, are dotted with villas.

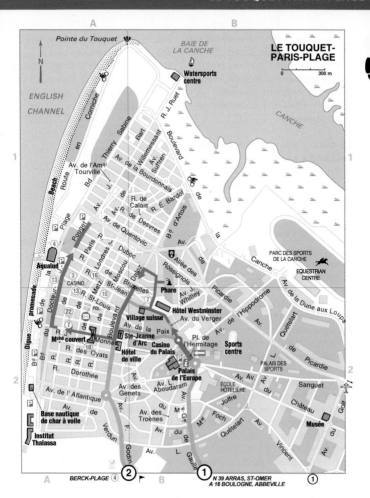

LE TOUQUET-
PARIS-PLAGE

0   300 m

WHERE TO STAY		WHERE TO EAT	
Hôtel des Pelouses	(4)	Le Café des Arts	(3)
Hôtel Le Chalet	(7)	Le Nemo	(4)
Hôtel Le Nouveau Caddy	(10)	Le Village Suisse	(7)
Hôtel Les Embruns	(13)	Pérard	(10)
Hôtel Red Fox	(16)	Côté Sud	(13)
Hôtel Windsor	(22)		

St-Josse

▶ 10km/6mi SE on N 39, D 143 and
D 144 (views of Étaples).

The hill-top village of St-Josse was
once home to an abbey founded by
Charlemagne in memory of St Josse, a
7C pilgrim and hermit whose reliquary
is venerated in the church's early-16C
chancel. About 500m/550yd east, in
the middle of a wooded close, stands
St Josse's Chapel, a place of pilgrimage.

Étaples

▶ 10km/6mi to the E by N 39. La
Corderie, bd. Bigot-Descelers, 62630
Étaples-sur-Mer. ⏰Apr–Sept 10am–1pm,
2–6.30pm; Oct–Mar 10am-12.30pm,
2–6pm, Sun 2–6pm. ☎03 21 09 56 94.
www.etaples-tourisme.com.

At the meeting point between the Channel and the North Sea, Étaples is a deep-
sea and coastal fishing port. Although
its gigantic trawlers now operate out

of Boulogne-sur-Mer (the sandbanks of the Canche estuary put Étaples off-limits to modern vessels), the crews remain attached to their port of origin, as you'll discover in the town's museums.
Visit the fish market for the full Étaples experience.

♿♟ Maréis - Centre de découverte de la pêche en mer★

La-Corderie Bd Bigot-Descelers.
Apr–Sept: 10am–1pm, 2–6.30pm; Oct–Mar: 10am–12.30pm, 2–6pm, Sun 2–6pm. Guided tours (90min). Closed 1st wk Jan, 25 Dec. 6€ (child 4.50€), 17€ family ticket. "Pass-Port" combined ticket 7.50€, entry to three museums: Maréis, Musée de la Marine, Musée Quentovic. ℘03 21 09 04 00. www.mareis.fr.

Pilot a virtual fishing boat, clamber "on board" a high-tech trawler (24m/79ft) equipped with radars, navigational aids and depth sounders, and learn how to tie a sailor's knot in this modern marine museum.

Housed in a former rope factory, the Maréis – "things of the sea" in Latin – museum takes an inventive and hands-on approach to modern fishing with 3D films, interactive terminals and touch tanks. Plumb the depths in seven specially designed aquariums offering a fish-eye view of how shoals of fish interact in the sea.

Musée de la Marine

Bd de l'Impératrice. Open May–Sept 10am–noon, 3–7pm, Sun 2–7pm; Oct–Apr 10am–noon, 3–6pm, Sun 3–6pm. 3.50€ (under-12s 1.50€). ℘03 21 09 77 21. www.2p2m.org.

This traditional museum explores the history of fishing boats from construction and net tanning to safety at sea.

Musée Quentovic

8 pl. du Gén.-de-Gaulle. Jul–Aug Wed–Mon 10am–noon, 2–6pm, Sun 10am–noon, 2.30–5.30pm; Sept–Jun 2–5pm, Sun 2.30–5.30pm. Closed early Oct. 23€ (6–12s 1€), no charge 1st Sun of the month. ℘03 21 94 02 47. www.2p2m.org.

Etaple and Le Touquet stand on the site of the Merovingian port of Quentovic, once one of the largest ports in Europe, where Anglo-Saxons, Vikings, Romans and Gaulish hoards each left their mark. Housed in two 18C buildings, this museum explores this archaeological "melting pot".

Commonwealth Military Cemetery

1km/0.5mi N of Etaples (D 940).
Over 10 000 soldiers are buried here in the largest Commonwealth cemetery in France.

♿♟ Berck-sur-Mer

Take the D 940 or A 16 then D 303. Between the Baie d'Authie and Côte d'Opale.

A paradise for sand yachters, kite-flyers and kite-surfers. This health and seaside resort on the Opal Coast boasts 12km/7mi fine sandy beaches stretching as far as the mouth of the Canche estuary. Guaranteed fun for kids.

Berck offers countless activities for kids along its 1 400 ha/6 mi sq of fine sandy **beaches**: wave pool, toboggans, billiards and bowling on the seafront esplanade. *Try a sea-shore horse trek.*

Musée

60 r. de l'Impératrice. Open Jul–Aug Wed–Sun 10am–12.30pm, 2–6pm, Mon–Tue 2–6pm; Sep–Jun: 10am–noon, 3–6pm, Mon–Tue 3–6pm. Closed 1 Jan, 1 May. 3.50€ (under 18s no charge). ℘03 21 84 07 80. www.opale-sud.com.

Housed in a former police station, this fully-renovated museum sets the stage for a collection of paintings by local artists from 1860-1914, a reconstruction of a traditional Berck interior, model boats and fishing equipment. Don't miss the northern marine archaeology exhibition upstairs, where you'll find 6C jewellery and Merovingian weapons.

Église Notre-Dame-des-Sables

R. du Dr-Cazin.
This church (1882) has its original pitch pine frame crafted by local carpenters.

♣♣ Parc d'attractions de Bagatelle★

▶ *5km/3mi by D 940 towards Le Touquet.* ◷ *Open Apr–Sept Sat & Sun 10.30am–7.30pm and some weekdays (contact for details).* ◉ *21.50€ (3–11yrs 18.50€).* ♿ ℘ *03 21 89 09 91. www.parcbagatelle.com.*

France's oldest amusement park offers 26ha/64 acres of fun: big top shows, fairground attractions and a big wheel

ADDRESSES

☞ STAY

◔◔ **Le Chalet** – *15 r. de la Paix.* ℘ *03 21 05 87 65. 15 rooms* ▭. Although only 50m/55yds from the beach, this hotel looks like it migrated here from the Alps. Spruce bedrooms decorated along a seaside or mountain theme.

◔◔ **Hôtel Red Fox** – *60 r. de Metz.* ℘ *03 21 05 27 58. www.hotelredfox.com. Wi-fi. 71 rooms* ▭. Comfortable, modern rooms in the centre of town, those on the top floor have a mansard roof.

◔◔ **Hôtel Windsor** – *7r. St-Georges.* ℘ *03 21 05 05 44. Closed 4–28 Jan. 28 rooms* ▭. This beach front hotel offers comfortable rooms accommodating from one to four persons. Pleasant lounge; breakfast room decorated with ceiling mouldings.

◔◔ **Les Embruns** – *89 r. de Paris.* ℘ *03 21 05 87 61. www.letouquet-hotel-les-embruns.com. Closed 15 Dec–14 Jan. 20 rooms* ▭. Located near the water, this attractive hotel has stylish rooms, some with balconies or overlooking the garden. Small sitting room and library.

◔◔ **Hôtel des Pelouses** – *BdEdmond-Labrasse. 62520 Cucq.* ℘ *03 21 94 60 86. www.lespelouses.com. Closed 20 Dec–16 Jan.* ▣. *26 rooms* ▭, *half-board possible. Restaurant* ◔◔. Just 1.8km/1mi from the beaches, with modern and spacious rooms. Restaurant specialises in seafood. Children's menu.

◔◔◔ **Hôtel Le Nouveau Caddy** – *130 r. de Metz. pl. du Marché-Couvert.* ℘ *03 21 05 83 95. www.lenouveaucaddy.com. Closed 3 wks in Jan.* ▣ *20 rooms* ▭. Over-looking the market square, close to the beach and shops, this welcoming hotel has simple rooms with a seasonal theme.

♥/ EAT

◔ **Le Nemo** – *Bd. de la Mer.* ℘ *03 21 90 07 08. www.lenemo.com. Closed Dec–Jan.* ♿ Enter this restaurant inspired by Jules Verne and dive 20 000 leagues under the sea. You'll find deep-sea diving suits, mariners' charts, woodwork, pewter pieces, marine curios. Pleasant terrace on the ocean side.

◔ **Restaurant Côté Sud** – *187 bd. du Dr-Pouget.* ℘ *03 21 05 41 24. www.le-touquet-cote-sud.com. Closed 8 Mar–1 Apr, 14 Jun–20 Jun, 22 Nov–9 Dec, Sun eve (low season), Mon midday and Wed.* An attractive restaurant decorated in the colours of the south of France with sun-drenched food to match: rabbit in rosemary sauce, and spicy red mullet, for example. Amazing sea views.

◔◔ **La Café des Arts** – *80 r. de Paris.* ℘ *03 21 05 21 55. www.restaurant-lecafedesarts.com. Closed Tue and Wed.* ♿. A popular establishment with locals serving a modern take on traditional French dishes and a good-value four-course menu.

◔◔ **Pérard- Restaurant-Poissonnerie-Traiteur** – *67 r. de Metz.* ℘ *03 21 05 13 33. www.restaurantperard.com.* ♿. Connoisseurs take note – fish soup is this restaurant's pride and joy! As with other seafood dishes, the ingredients come directly from their own fishmonger's shop next door.

◔◔◔ **Le Village Suisse** – *52 av. St-Jean.* ℘ *03 21 05 69 93. www.levillagesuisse.fr. Closed 3–15 Jan, 24 Nov–8 Dec, Sun eve (Oct–Apr), Tue midday and Mon (Sep–Jun).* Situated directly over the "village" shops, this elegant restaurant resembles a Swiss chalet. A comfortable, inviting dining room, courteous staff and delicious seasonal dishes.

SPORT AND LEISURE

Golf du Touquet – *Av. du Golf. A 16, exit 26.* ℘ *03 21 06 28 00. www.opengolf-club.com. Summer: 7am–8pm; Winter: 8am–6pm.* ◉ *85€ (under 25yrs 60€).* Two 18-hole courses, one through the forest and the other along the sand dunes of the shore, plus a 9-hole learning course.

Boobaloo – *38 r. St-Louis.* ℘ *03 21 05 66 47. Closed Jan.* Cycle hire.

Sea cruises - *62630 Étaples.* ℘ *03 21 09 56 94. www.etaples-tourisme.com. Apr–Sep according to tides.* ◉ *6.50€ (child 4.50€).* Discover the baie de Canche, the Canche estuary and its wildlife on a 45-minute boat ride.

Montreuil★

Perched on the edge of a plateau overlooking the Canche Valley, this picturesque **town★** protected by a citadel and ramparts enjoys a nostalgic charm. Close to the coast and Le Touquet, Montreuil is the perfect starting point for tours of the region.

A BIT OF HISTORY
Royal patronage

Montreuil developed around two buildings: the monastery founded in the 7C by the Bishop of Amiens, and the fortress built in 900 by the Count of Ponthieu. In 1537 Emperor Charles V's troops forcibly seized the town, almost completely destroying it in the process. The ramparts were rebuilt by the engineers of François I, Henri IV and Louis XIII. In 1804, at the time of the Boulogne Camp, Napoleon stayed in Montreuil, and in 1916 British commander Douglas Haig made it his headquarters.

SIGHTS
Citadelle★

⊙*Open Mid-Apr–mid-Oct 10am–noon, 2–5pm; May–Mar Wed–Mon 2–5pm.* ⊙*4€. ℘03 21 06 10 83.*

Montreuil citadel was built in the second half of the 16C, but contains elements of an 11C and 13C structure. It was completely remodelled in the 17C.

Start by visiting the two 13C round towers which flank the royal château before moving on to the Tour de la Reine Berthe (14C). Inside you'll find the emblems of the lords killed at Agincourt in 1415; the sentry walk offers attractive **views★★**

Citadelle

© S. Sauvignier/MICHELIN

▶ **Population:** 2 428

⚇ **Michelin Local Map:** p401: B3.

⧉ **Info:** 21 r. Carnot, 62170 Montreuil, ℘03 21 06 04 27. www.tourisme-montreuillois.com.

◉ **Location:** Just 11 mi/ 17.7 km inland from Le Touquet via the N 39, and 30mi/48km N of Abbeville along the N1.

⊞ **Parking:** Limited roadside parking.

⊛ **Don't Miss:** A tour of the ramparts, and the cobbled Rue Clape-en-Bas.

⊙ **Timing:** Keep a relaxed half day to explore the citadelle and the ramparts.

over the Canche Valley: the former Carthusian monastery of N.-D.-des-Près and the Vallée de la Course as it opens out into the plain (right); and the Canche estuary and Le Touquet with its lighthouse (left). End your tour by exploring the casemates (1840) and the 18C chapel.

Remparts★ (Ramparts)

⚇The red-brick and white-stone walls with bastions date largely from the 16C-17C, 13C elements have remained.

◉ Leave the citadel over the bridge and turn right onto the path that runs alongside the walls; continue for 300m/330yd towards the Porte de France gate.

From the sentry walk there is a lovely perspective of the 16C curtain walls with their series of 13C towers.

⟡ It is possible to walk right round the ramparts (*1hr*) along a shaded path offering views over the countryside.

Rue du Clape-en-Bas

This charming cobbled street is lined with low, whitewashed houses with mossy tiled roofs, typical of dwellings in the Canche Valley.

Chapelle de l'Hôtel-Dieu
⏱*Open Jul–mid-Sept 3–6pm.* 👛*1.50€.* Rebuilt in 1874 by a pupil of Viollet-le-Duc, the chapel retains its 15C gate.

Église Saint-Saulve★
This former 11C Benedictine abbey church was rebuilt in the 13C and 16C. Don't miss the capital friezes to the right of the nave and two 18C paintings: the *Vision de saint Dominique* by Jouvenet on the main altar; to the left, in the Chapelle Notre-Dame, the *Prise de voile de sainte Austreberthe,* by Restout.

🚗 DRIVING TOURS

VALLÉE DE LA COURSE
From Montreuil to Samer

38km/24mi marked in green on the regional map. Allow 1hr.

▶ Leave Montreuil by D 901 on the right then D 150 on the left towards Estrée. D 150 follows the Vallée de la Course.

Montcavrel
The village's Gothic Flamboyant-style church contains three early 16C capitals displaying historiated friezes (*☎03 21 81 58 92 – key available at the corner of the church from Mme Davenne).*

▶ Follow D 149 to Recques-sur-Course, then D 127 to the N. This road winds through the Vallée de la Course.

Desvres
📍*41 rte. des Potiers, 62240 Desvres. ☎03 21 92 09 09. www.tourisme-desvres-samer.fr.*
The **Maison de la faience** (⏱*open Apr–Sept 10am–12.30pm, 2–6.30pm, Sun 2–6.30, Oct–Mar Tue–Sun 2–5.30pm; 👛5€; ♿ ☎03 21 83 23 23; www.desvres museum.org)* explores the history of faience.

Forêt de Desvres
🌲*Crossed by the D 253, D 127 and D 238 to the north of the town, for fine views over the Vallée de la Liane.*

Samer
This market town features a cobbled Grand'Place lined with 18C houses.

Wierre-au-Bois
This is the native village of the writer Sainte-Beuve (1804–1869).

▶ Return to Montreuil.

VALLÉE DE LA CANCHE
From Montreuil to Hesdin

25km/15mi tour marked in green on the regional map. Allow 1hr.

▶ Leave Montreuil towards Neuville, cross La Canche and take D 113 on the right.

The valley opens onto gentle slopes dotted with long whitewashed cottages, meadows, woodland and villages.

Chartreuse Notre-Dame-des-Près
Founded in the 14C, this Carthusian monastery was rebuilt in 1872 and converted into a hospice in 1903. Stop between Neuville and Marles for views over the ramparts of Montreuil.

Brimeux
A popular spot for fishing and hunting close to a vast lake. Follow D 349 to Aubin-Saint-Vaast, then turn right up the sloped D 136 E2. Stop at the summit for views over the valley surmounted by Hesdin forest.

▶ On the left, take D 138 to admire the views over the forest and Hesdin.

VALLÉE DE LA COURSE
From Hesdin to Frévent

38km/24mi marked in green on the regional map. Allow 1hr.

▶ Leave Hesdin E by D 110.

Set off from **Vieil-Hesdin** along the left bank of the Canche and the "villages in bloom" route (D 340). At Conchy-sur-Canche, turn left down D 102 to the 18C **Château de Flers** before returning to D 340. Join D 941 at Boubers-sur Canche to **Frévent**, where the **Musée Wintenberger** (pl. du Château) explores local agricultural life. Finish at the 18C **Château de Cercamp**, built on the site of an 12C Cistercian monastery.

ADDRESSES

🏠 STAY

⊜⊜ **Hôtel Ferme du Moulin aux Draps**– Rte. Crémarest. 62240 Desvres. 1.5km/1mi by D 254 E. 𝒫03 21 10 69 59. http://hotel-moulinauxdraps.com. Closed 22 Dec–18 Jan, Sun eve (Oct–Mar). 🄿. Wi-fi. 20 rooms ⌸. A peaceful vintage farmstead set in acres of pasture and woodland. Pleasant rooms.

⊜⊜⊜ **Haute Chambre (B&B)** – 124 rte. d'Hucqueliers, 62170 Beussent. 10km/6mi N of Montreuil by D 901 then D127. 𝒫03 21 90 91 92. Closed 1st half of Sep and mid-Dec–mid-Jan. 🄿🍴. 5 rooms ⌸. Rather difficult to find, this 1858 manor has been marvellously restored by the owners. Plush bedrooms and an idyllic park.

🍴 EAT

⊜⊜ **L'Auberge d'Inxent** – 318 r. de la Vallée-de-la-Course, 62170 Inxent. 𝒫03 21 90 71 19. Closed 22 Jun–10 Jul,

15 Nov–4 Feb, Tue and Wed. 🄿. 5 rooms. ⌸10€. This 1765 house has always been an inn. Tasty Artois cuisine.

⊜⊜⊜ **Auberge La Grenouillère** – 62170 Madelaine-sous-Montreuil. 𝒫03 21 06 07 22. www.lagrenouillere.fr. Closed 20 Dec– 4 Feb Tue and Wed (except Jul–Aug). 🄿. 4 rooms ⌸. A country inn with a frog theme serving quality fare. A few guest rooms.

SHOPPING

M. et Mme Leviel – Fond des Communes, 62170 Montcravel. Closed Sun. 𝒫03 21 06 21 73. Sales of dairy products. Speciality: apérichèvres, goat's cheese hors-d'œuvres.

Desvres Tradition– 1 r.du Louvre, 62240 Desvres. 𝒫03 21 92 39 43. 8am–12.30pm, 1.30–7pm, Sun 10am–12.30pm. Handmade faience ware.

EVENTS

Festival "Les Malins Plaisirs"– Théâtre de Montreuil. pl. du Gén.-de-Gaulle. 𝒫03 21 98 12 26. www.lesmalinsplaisirs.com. Opera, comedies, ballet, walks tastings in Aug.

Strawberry festival– Celebrate strawberries in **Samer** third week in June.

Artisanales gourmandes– exhibition of Desvres faïence in the park of the Maison de la faïence in **Desvres** (every 2yrs one weekend in Sep).

Hesdin

Cradled in the hollow of a valley forged by the union of the rivers Canche and Ternoise, Hesdin is a charming country town. Founded by Emperor Charles V, it offers an ideal base from which to explore the Sept Vallées region, nourished by the rivers Lys, Authie, Canche and its four tributaries.

👣 WALKING TOUR

Hôtel de ville

𝒫03 21 86 84 76. www.tourisme7vallees. com (check for times).Formerly the palace (16C) of Mary of Hungary, sister of Emperor Charles V, this building became Hesdin's town hall in 1629. Entered via a gateway decorated with escutcheons,

▸ **Population:** 2 684

🐾 **Michelin Map:** p401: B4.

🚩 **Info:** Office de tourisme – Pl. d'Armes, 62140 Hesdin. 𝒫03 21 86 19 19. www. tourisme7vallees.com.

◖ **Location:** La Canche, spanned by seven bridges, flows through the town. Access: north-south by D 928, west by D 439, and east by D 939.

◉ **Don't Miss:** Entrance to the Église Notre-Dame.

👫 **Kids:** The Centre historique médiéval for hands-on fun with chainmail and swords.

the building contains an outstanding tapestry room (18C) and ballroom.

▶ Take r. de la Paroisse and cross the Canche.

Église Notre-Dame

Enter through a typical late-Renaissance gateway, surmounted by a round-headed arch featuring sculpted caissons and fluted Corinthian pilasters to explore the hall-church, which benefits from 18C Baroque furnishings.

▶ Walk around the left of the church to the chevet.

Stand on the bridge spanning the Canche for **views** over the river banks lined with brick houses with tiled roofs.

▶ Return by r. Daniel-Lereuil.

Don't miss the birthplace of **Abbé Prévost** (1697–1763) writer, at no. 11.

EXCURSION
Forêt d'Hesdin

▶ *By D 928 to the N.*
This 1 020ha/2 520acre forest of oak and beech trees carpets the plateau running along the north of the River Canche and its small, secluded valleys.

🚗 DRIVING TOUR

TERNOISE AND PLANQUETTE

44km/27mi tour marked in green on the regional map. Allow 1hr.

▶ Leave Hesdin by D 939 to the E and turn left down D 94. The road winds through a lush, green landscape dotted with typical whitewashed country cottages.

Following their defeat at the Battle of Agincourt, the French nobility were buried at **Auchy-lès-Hesdin** in the **Saint-Georges abbey** church (13C–17C).

▶ Continue along D 94. At Blangy, turn left along D 104, then right to Ambricourt.

Ambricourt inspired *The Diary of a Country Priest*, a novel by **Georges Bernanos** (1888–1948).
The church in **Verchin** is worth a visit. Beneath its twisted spire, caused by the use of unseasoned wood, the early-17C **Église Saint-Omer** (🕐*open Sat and Sun, school holidays 8.30am–6pm; ✆03 21 47 37 07*), built in Flamboyant Gothic style, features lierne vaults and tiercerons. Visit the village church at **Tramecourt** adjacent to a brick château with stone dressings (17C).

Azincourt

🛈 *24 r. Charles-VI, 62310 Azincourt. ✆03 21 47 27 53. www.azincourt-medieval.fr.*
Azincourt is famous as the site of the Battle of Agincourt, fought here on 25 October 1415 by an army of 9 000 men led by Henry V against a French army almost twice its size.

👥 Centre historique médiéval

R. Charles-VI. 🕐*Open Apr–Sept 10am –6pm; Nov–Mar Wed–Mon 10am–5pm.* 🎫*7.50€ (under 6s free).* &. ✆*03 21 47 27 53. www.azincourt-medieval.com.*
The museum starts with a 40-panel introduction to the One Hundred Years War before wading into the thick of the fighting with an animated model of the battle itself, followed by a collection of chainmail, bows and crossbows, arrows, swords, daggers and pikes.
Battle site – A map guide is provided at the start of your visit *(4km/2mi tour by car)*. Displays and orientation panels pin point the position of the two armies.

▶ Turn left down D 928 and right down D 155 to Fressin.

Fressin

🛈 *9 r. de la Lombardie, 62140 Fressin. ✆03 21 86 56 11.*
Explore life in this 15C **château ruins** built by Jean V de Créquy, chamberlain to Philippe le Bon *(audio tour guide;* 🕐*open Apr–Sept Tue–Sun 11am–6pm;* 🎫*5.50€; ✆03 21 86 56 11; www.chateaudefressin.fr)*. The Flamboyant **Gothic church** (13C–16C) contains a seigniorial chapel with flame-like window tracery.

St-Omer★★

St-Omer's quiet, aristocratic streets lined with pilastered mansions clustered around a cathedral contrast pleasantly with its down-to-earth northern suburbs where low Flemish houses line the quays of the River Aa.

CATHEDRAL DISTRICT★★
Cathédrale Notre-Dame★★

○Open Apr–Sept 8.30am–6pm (Oct–Mar 5pm). ◉No charge. &. ℘03 21 98 08 51. www.tourisme-saint-omer.com.
The majestic cathedral stands in the heart of the former "Notre-Dame cloister". The **chancel** dates from 1200, the transept from the 13C, and the nave from the 14C and 15C. The pier of the large south door is ornamented with a 14C Virgin Mary and a tympanum depicting the Last Judgment. In a corner of the chancel stands an octagonal Romanesque tower.

Works of Art★★

Works of particular interest include:
+ the 13C cenotaph (1) of St-Omer;
+ the 16C mausoleum (2) of Eustache de Croy, Provost of the St-Omer Chapter and Bishop of Arras.
+ the 13C statue of Notre-Dame-des-Miracles (3), an object of pilgrimage;
+ a 13C low-relief Nativity (4); the 8C tomb of St Erkembode (5), Abbot of St Bertin's;
+ the Astronomical Clock with a mechanism dating from 1588 and the Flamboyant rose window above.

The **rue des Tribunaux** runs behind the east end of Notre-Dame and in front of the 17C **palais épiscopal**, which now houses the law courts, leading to place Victor-Hugo. The square is the busy centre of St-Omer and features a fountain celebrating the birth of the Count of Artois, the future Charles X.

Hôtel Sandelin and Museum★

○Open Wed–Sun 10am–noon & 2–6pm. ◉5.50€. &. ℘03 21 38 00 94. www.tourisme-saint-omer.com.

▸ **Population:** 15 747
⌖ **Michelin Local Map:** p400: C4.
▤ **Info:** 4 r. du Lion d'Or, 62500 St-Omer. ℘03 21 98 08 51. www.tourisme-saint-omer.com.
◖ **Location:** Close to the channel port of Calais and 257km/160mi N of Paris.
▣ **Parking:** Limited town centre parking; find a place (*charged*) near the cathedral, or the tourist information centre.
⊛ **Don't Miss:** A trip on the flat-bottomed boats.
○ **Timing:** Leave at least 2 hrs for the cathedral. Take 2 or 3 days to discover the region.
▲▴ **Kids:** The Fontinettes Barge Lift at Arques is fascinating.

Built in 1777 for the Viscountess of Fruges, the house has a large gateway and elegant Louis XV railings.
Ground Floor – The drawing rooms overlooking the gardens form a suite of *salons* with finely carved wainscoting, 18C fireplaces and Louis XV furnishings. The paintings include a portrait of *Mme de Pompadour as Diana the Huntress* by Nattier and four works by Boilly.
The woodcarving room and the Salle Henri Dupuis, containing Antwerp ebony cabinets, lead to the **Salle du Trésor** where exhibits include the famous gilt and enamelled **base of the St Bertin Cross★** (12C).
First and Second Floors ★– Collection of local ceramics and an outstanding series of **Delftware**.

●✦● WALKING TOUR

Jardin public★

A vast park (20ha/48 acres) on part of the 17C ramparts, with formal French and English gardens and views of the bastion, rooftops and cathedral tower.

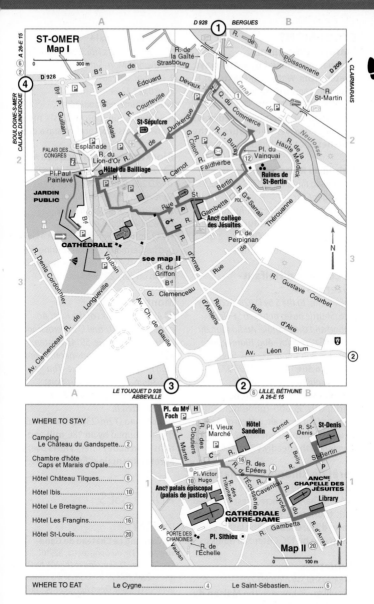

WHERE TO STAY	
Camping Le Château du Gandspette...	(2)
Chambre d'hôte Caps et Marais d'Opale...	(1)
Hôtel Château Tilques...	(6)
Hôtel Ibis...	(10)
Hôtel Le Bretagne...	(12)
Hôtel Les Frangins...	(16)
Hôtel St-Louis...	(20)

WHERE TO EAT			
	Le Cygne...	(4)	Le Saint-Sébastien... (6)

Place du Maréchal-Foch

The town hall (1834–1841) was built using stone from the former abbey.

◯ Follow r. L.-Martel, place Victor-Hugo, r. des Epeers and r. St-Bertin.

St-Bertin & Faubourg Nord

All that remains of the abbey are a few arches and the lower part of the tower

(1460). Via place du Vanquai, stroll through the Faubourg Nord along quai des Salines lined with Flemish houses.

◯ At the end of quai des Salines, turn left on r. de Dunkerque then right on r. St-Sépulcre.

Église St-Sépulchre

Consecrated in 1387.

EXCURSIONS
Marais Audomarois
The marshes, linked by **waterways**, stretch from Watten in the north to Arques just south of St-Omer, and from Clairmarais Forest to the Tilques watercress beds. Large flat-bottomed boats known as *bacôves* offer **tours of the marshes** or can be hired.

Maison du Romelaëre
Ⓘ *Opening times vary.* ℘ *03 21 38 52 95.* *www.eden62.fr.*
The visitor centre for the Audomarois marshes in the **Parc Naturel Régional des Caps et Marais d'Opale** is a good starting point for footpaths.

La Coupole d'Helfaut-Wizernes★★
Ⓓ *5km/3mi to the S by D 928. Access by A 26. Shuttle buses between St-Omer station and the coupole. Audio tour 2hr 30min.* Ⓘ *Open Jul–Aug 10am–7pm; Sept–Jun 9am–6pm.* ⚥. *9.50€ (6–16yrs 6.50€)* ℘ *03 21 12 27 27.* *www.lecoupole-france.com.*
The oldest rocket launch pad in the world, this 55 000-tonne dome (the same weight as an aircraft carrier) hides an underground town where the Nazis developed the deadly V2 rocket.

Forêt de Rihoult-Clairmarais
Ⓓ *4.5km/2.5mi E of St-Omer.*
🚶 A 1 167ha/2 884 acre forest managed with tourists in mind (*picnic tables*). **Étang d'Harchelles** is the last of seven ponds dug by 12C Cistercian monks.

Esquerdes
Ⓓ *8km/5mi SW along D 211.*
This village is home to the **Maison du papier** (Ⓘ *open daily Jul–Aug 2–6pm; Apr–Jun Tue–Fri & Sun 2–6pm;* *4€;* ⚥ *℘ 03 21 95 45 25*) which explores papermaking from early China to today.

Arques
Ⓓ *4km/2.5mi SE on N 42.*
Arques is a major port at the junction of the canalised Aa and the Neuffossé Canal, linking the Aa and Lys rivers.

Arc International★
🔸 *Guided tours (1hr30min) by request in advance, Mon–Sat 9am–12.30pm & 1.30–5pm.* *6.50€. Min. age 8 years.* ⚥ *℘ 03 21 12 74 74.* *www.arc-international.com.*
Arc International produce six million items in glass, opal and crystal a day.

Blockhaus d'Éperlecques★
Ⓓ *15 km/9mi NW by D 943, then D 300 and D 205.* Ⓘ *Open Mar & Nov 2.15–5pm, Apr & Oct 10am–6pm; May–Sept 10am–7pm.* ℘ *03 21 88 44 22.* *www.leblockhaus.com.*
This 22m/72ft-high bunker was a launch pad for German V2 rockets during WW II. It was knocked out of action by a Tallboy bomb on July 25 1944.

Mont de Watten
Ⓓ *Along the banks of the River Aa, close to the D 207 and D 213 crossroads.*
🛈 *12 r. de Dunkerque, 59143 Watten.* Ⓘ *Open Jun–Sep 10am–noon, 2–6pm, Mon 2–6pm; Oct–May Tue–Thu 2–5.30pm, Fri–Sat 10am–noon, 2–5.30pm.* ℘ *03 21 88 27 78.* *www.watten.fr.*
Dominating (72m/236ft) the Aa valley, this hill topped by an 18C **mill** and the ruins of an abbey offers **views** over the **Forêt domaniale d'Éperlecques**.

ADDRESSES

🛏 STAY
🛌 **Camping Le Château du Gand-spette**– 133r. du Gandspette, 62910 Éperlecques. 11.5km/7mi to the NW by D 943 and D 207. ℘ *03 21 93 43 93. www.chateau-gandspette.com. Open Apr–Sept.* ⚥. *167 pitches.* At the foot of a château, this campsite also hires out mobile homes. Sports facilities.

🛌🛌 **Caps et Marais d'Opale (B&B)** – 11 quai du Commerce. ℘ *03 21 93 89 82.* *www.bb-opale.fr.st.* 🛏 *3 rooms* 🍴.
An elegant manor house on the canal, with carved wood panelling and a pretty garden veranda.

🛌🛌🛌 **Hôtel Les Frangins** – 5 r. Carnot-℘ *03 21 38 12 47. www.frangins.fr.* ⚥ 🅿. *26 rooms* 🍴. Located in the historical centre of St-Omer, 'Les frangins' offers practical, quiet renovated rooms.

🛏️🛏️🛏️ **Ibis** – 2-4 r. Henri-Dupuis. ✆03 21 93 11 11. www.ibishotel.com. 🅿️ 65 rooms ⬜. Centrally located in an historic building. Modern, comfortable rooms and efficient, friendly service.

🛏️🛏️🛏️ **Hôtel Saint-Louis** – 25 r. d'Arras. ✆03 21 38 35 21 www.hotel-saintlouis.com. Closed 18 Dec-5 Jan. Wi-fi. 30 rooms ⬜. A former post office in the cathedral district, a restaurant serves local specialities.

🛏️🛏️🛏️ **Hôtel Le Bretagne** – 2 pl. du Vainquai. ✆03 21 38 25 78. www.hotelle bretagne.com. 🅿️ Wi-fi. 69 rooms ⬜, half-board possible. A central, modern building with smart rooms and brasserie.

🛏️🛏️🛏️🛏️ **Château Tilques** – 62500 Tilques. ✆03 21 88 99 99. www.chateau tilques.com. 🅿️. 53 rooms ⬜. A 19C red brick castle. Château rooms and contemporary annex.

🍽️ EAT

🍴🍴 **Le Cygne** – 8 r. Caventou. ✆03 21 98 20 52. www.restaurantlecygne. fr. Closed Feb holidays, Aug, Sun eve and Mon (except public holidays). Close to the cathedral, this is the main eatery in town, serving fresh, traditional French cuisine.

🍴🍴🍴 **Le Saint-Charles** – 10r. Sainte-Croix. ✆03 21 11 26 08. www.cheztante fauvette.com. An intimate brasserie near the Cathedral. Good value menu.

🍴🍴 **Le Saint-Sébastien**–2pl. de la Libération. 62500 Blendecques. ✆03 21 38 13 05. Closed 22–30 Dec, Sun. A family-friendly traditional restaurant in the centre of a tiny town just outside St-Omer.

Aire-sur-la-Lys

Aire is dominated by the high towers of its belfry and collegiate church.

SIGHTS

The **Grand'Place** is lined with a Flemish **hôtel de ville**, an 18C arcaded belfry and late Renaissance **bailiwick★**. The **Collégiale Saint-Pierre★** (🕐open May–Oct 8am–6pm; Nov–Apr 8am–5pm; ♿ ✆03 21 39 65 66) is a fine example of Flamboyant Gothic and Renaissance architecture with a 62m/203ft **tower★** and oak **organ case** from Clairmarais abbey church. The **Eglise Saint-Jacques** (🕐open Jul–Aug Tue–Sun 3–6pm; ✆03 21 39 65 66) has a 17C façade.

🚗 DRIVING TOUR

AA VALLEY TO DENNLYS PARC

50km/31mi tour marked in green on the map (p400). Allow 1hr15min.

▶ Leave Aire to the west by D 157.

Thérouanne (🏛️Grand-Rue, 62129 Thér-ouanne; ✆03 21 93 81 22) is home to the ruins of one of the first Gothic cathe-drals in France. Head through the valley

▶ **Population:** 9 655
♿ **Michelin Map:** p401 C2; 301 H4.
🏛️ **Info:** Office de tourisme – Le Bailliage, Grand Place, 62120 Aire-sur-la-Lys. ✆03 21 39 65 66. www.ot-airesurlalys.fr.
▶ **Location:** On the Lys, between Béthune and St-Omer. From A 26 head towards Lillers, then D 943 or D 188.
🕐 **Timing:** Allow half a day to tour the town and Aa valley.

towards **Merck-Saint-Liévan,** the site of a 16C–17C **church** with a star-vaulted ceiling. Continue towards **Fauquem-bergues** (🏛️Av. Roland-Huguet; ✆03 21 38 38 51) where there is a 13C **church** with a fortified tower and machicolated gatehouse. **Renty** has an old mill and peaceful lake.

🎠 Dennlys Parc

🕐Open Jul–Aug 10am–7pm; rest of year call for times. ⬜14€ (3–12yrs 12€). ♿ ✆03 21 95 11 39. www.dennlys-parc.com. Haunted house, big wheel, rollercoast-ers and countless other rides.

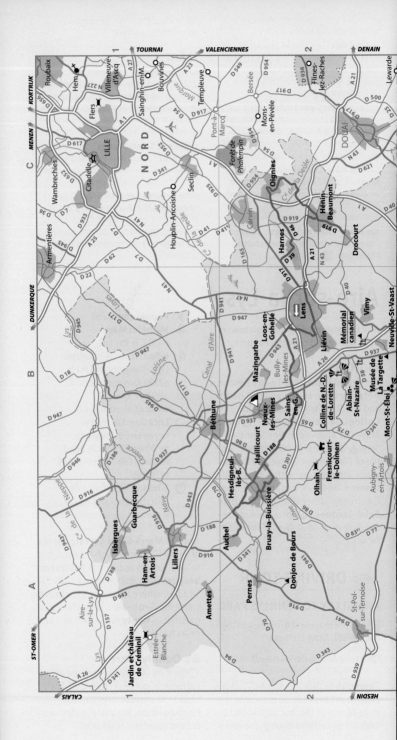

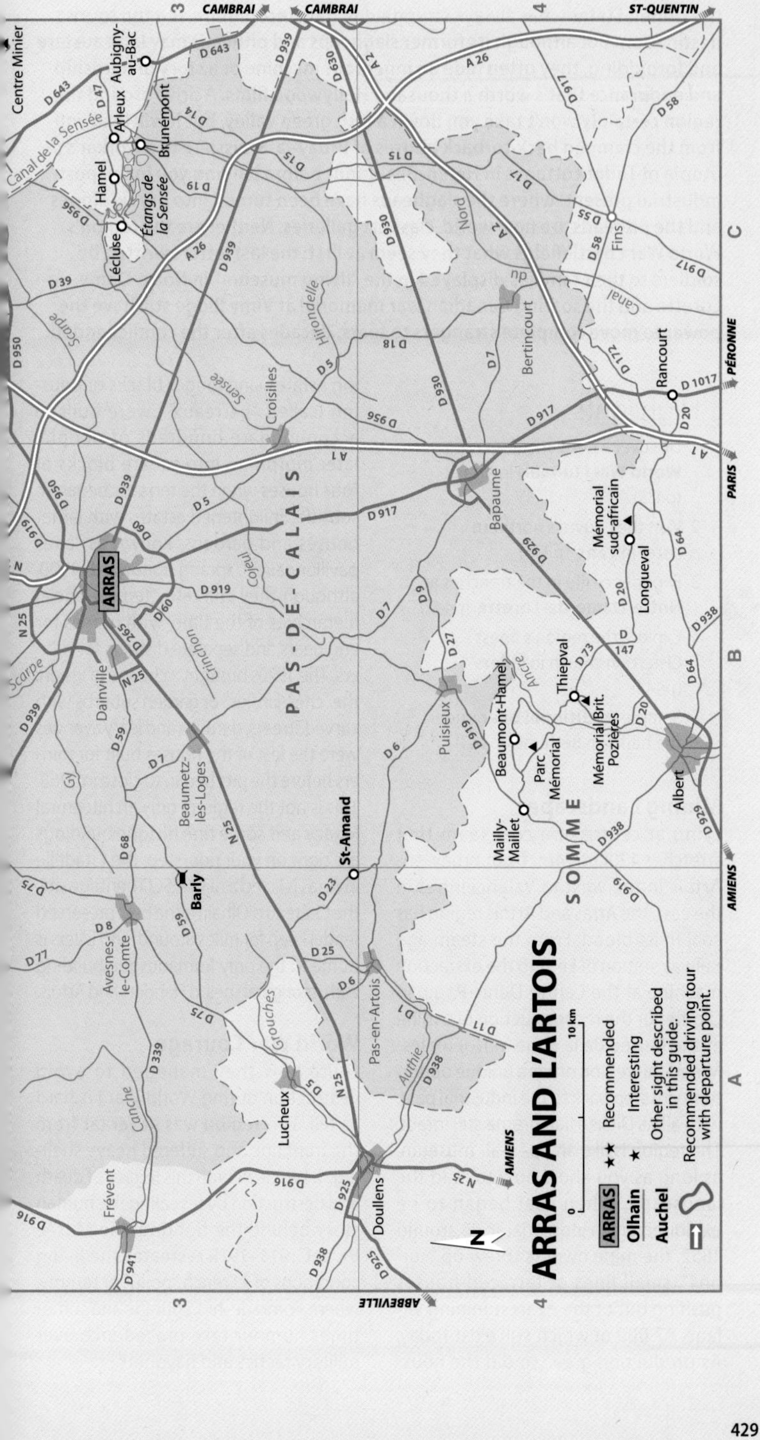
ARRAS AND L'ARTOIS
ARRAS ★★ Recommended
Olhain ★ Interesting
Auchel Other sight described in this guide.
Recommended driving tour with departure point.
0 10 km
N
PAS-DE-CALAIS
SOMME
Nord
ARRAS
Centre Minier
Arleux
Aubigny-au-Bac
Hamel
Brunémont
Lécluse
Étangs de la Sensée
Canal de la Sensée
Scarpe
Sensée
Croisilles
Hirondelle
Bertincourt
Fins
Rancourt
Canal du Nord
Bapaume
Mémorial sud-africain
Longueval
Thiepval
Mémorial Brit. Pozières
Beaumont-Hamel
Parc Mémorial
Mailly-Maillet
Albert
Ancre
Puisieux
Cojeul
Crinchon
Dainville
Beaumetz-lès-Loges
Gy
St-Amand
Barly
Avesnes-le-Comte
Grouches
Lucheux
Pas-en-Artois
Authie
Canche
Frévent
Doullens
CAMBRAI
CAMBRAI
ST-QUENTIN
PÉRONNE
PARIS
AMIENS
AMIENS
ABBEVILLE
A 1
A 2
A 26
N 25
D 939
D 917
D 930
D 929
D 919
D 938
D 925
D 916
D 941
D 950
D 956
D 643
D 630
D 1017
3
4
A
B
C

ARRAS AND L'ARTOIS

The region around Arras and Artois – once home to one of France's biggest coal fields, the equivalent of Leeds in England or the Powder River Basin in the United States – has always struggled to gain recognition as a top tourist destination. But although its former slagheaps and pitheads may look austere and forbidding, they often hide an ingenious machine or a story of hardship and endurance that's worth a thousand Hollywood films. A drive around the region certainly won't take you down a lush green valley, but it will lead you from the cramped back-to-back houses of Bruay-la-Bruissière to a worker's utopia of Tudor cottages in Hénin-Beaumont before landing you in the post-industrial present, where the slagheaps have been turned into dry ski slopes and the pitheads are now world-class art galleries. Neither are the region's World War I battlefields what they seem at first: the last letters written by soldiers to their families displayed in the "living museum" in Notre-Dame-de-Lorette and the soaring Canadian war memorial at Vimy Ridge still have the power to move complete strangers to tears, decades after the conflict ended.

Highlights

1 Discover a network of secret **World War I tunnels** in Arras (p435)

2 Visit the Louvre's northern sister in **Lens** (p438)

3 Experience life in the trenches at **Notre-Dame-de-Lorette** (p442)

4 Explore the region's finest Cistercian church in **Lillers** (p443)

5 Sample **traditional beer** under the belfry in Béthune (p443)

Mining Landscape

Lying at centre of a coal seam that stretches 120km/74mi from Bruay-en-Artois in the west to Valenciennes in the east, the Arras and Artois region has coal in its blood. From the steam age railway station of Lens to the extraction machine at the Centre Denis-Papin in Oignies or the reconstruction of a mine at the Musée de la Mine in Noeux-les-Mines, this region offers a unique opportunity to step back to the industrial past, with all its Dickensian drama still intact. The region is like an open-air museum, as long as you know how to read the landscape. When coal began to be exploited on an industrial scale around 1852, the mine owners threw up "corons", small lines of terraced houses pushing out of the nearest mining village, 67 000 of which still exist today. As production grew, so did the hous-ing estates, and longer blocks of housing (called "barreaux") were built to accommodate hundreds of people, later morphing into square blocks of four houses when the terraces began to subside. Enlightened estates with larger houses and gardens, known as "cités pavillonnaires", sprang up towards 1900, although they still reflected the social hierarchies of the time, with homes for engineers and separate districts for miners. The 1920s brought a change of vision: the "cités-jardins" or garden suburbs with curved streets, gardens and leafy avenues were the last of the houses built for miners before the pits began to close in 1968. This is not the region's only architectural legacy and some fine historic buildings are right on your doorstep: the Citadelle in Arras is listed as a UNESCO heritage site, the Château d'Olhain is the best preserved feudal keep for miles around, and Lillers is home to the only Romanesque building with its original shell in Flanders and Artois.

World War Courage

Quite how they managed to avoid destruction during World War I is hard to tell. This region was never far from the front line and suffered heavy shelling. It has dealt with this legacy of death and destruction by revealing the human story behind the fighting: the Musée Vivant 1914–1918 recreates the living conditions of a French "poilu" or tommy, where comradeship, courage and sometimes humour take precedence over military tactics and bayonets.

Arras★★

Centred around the Grand'Place and the Place des Héros, the capital of the Artois region is renowned for its chitterling sausages (*andouillettes*), Atrébate beer and heart-shaped gingerbread cakes.

A BIT OF HISTORY

Medieval wealth – The Roman town of Nemetacum was founded on the slopes of Baudimont hill, known today as La Cité. In the Middle Ages the town developed from a grain market around the Benedictine abbey of St Vaast into a centre of woollen cloth manufacture and later became a centre for art, patronised by bankers and rich Arras burghers.

The town is famous for its troubadours (*trouvères*) such as **Gautier d'Arras, Jean Bodel**, author of *Le Jeu de saint Nicolas*, and above all the 13C **Adam de la Halle** who brought dramatic art to Arras with his play **Le Jeu de la Feuillée**.

From 1384 the manufacture of high-warp tapestries, under the patronage of the dukes of Burgundy, brought Arras widespread fame – and the word *arras* passed into English to indicate a tapestry wall-hanging. After the Renaissance, this activity decreased as Beauvais and Antwerp took over.

Youth of "The Incorruptible" – **Maximilien de Robespierre**, whose father was an Artois Council barrister, was born in Arras in 1758. Orphaned at an early age, the young man became the protégé of the bishop and received a scholarship to attend school in Paris. Robespierre became a barrister on his return to Arras and was affiliated with the **Rosati** (an anagram of "Artois") poetic society. During this period the pale young man, later the spirited leader of the Revolution, courted young ladies with verse.

An acquaintance of Robespierre, **Joseph Lebon** (1765–95), a former priest, was mayor of the town during the Reign of Terror and presided over the destruction of many churches and regularly sent aristocrats and rich farmers to the guil-

▶ **Population:** 40 535
◔ **Michelin Local Map:** p429: B3.
🛈 **Info:** Hôtel de ville, pl. des Héros, 62000 Arras. ☎03 21 51 26 95. www.ot-arras.fr.
◖ **Location:** The centre of the town is marked by three large squares, the Grande Place, the Place des Héros, and the Petite Place, surrounded by many buildings restored to their pre-war WW I conditions, notably the Gothic town hall and the 19C cathedral.
🅿 **Parking:** There are (paid) parking areas in and around the centre of Arras. Try the one near the tourist information office.
◉ **Don't Miss:** La Grande Place and the Place des Héros.
◔ **Timing:** Start with a walk around the centre of town, which will give you a feel for the place. Allow about 1 hr.
👥 **Kids:** Cité Nature is a popular attraction.

lotine set up in place du Théâtre. Lebon himself was later guillotined.

Arras and the Battles of Artois – During the First World War, the front was close to Arras until 1917, so much of the area suffered heavy shelling. The most violent conflicts took place in the strategically important hills north of the town. After the Battle of the Marne, the retreating Germans fought to hold the hills, clinging to Vimy Ridge and the slopes of Notre-Dame-de-Lorette Hill. In 1914 they attacked Arras, but were headed off at the battles of Ablain-St-Nazaire, Carency and La Targette.

In May and June 1915 **General Foch**, in command of the northern French forces, attempted to pierce the German ranks; his troops took Neuville St-Vaast and

Notre-Dame-de-Lorette. The attack failed at Vimy however, which was won only in 1917 by the Canadians.

🐾 WALKING TOUR

MAIN SQUARES
Grand'Place and Place des Héros★★★

The two main squares in Arras, the theatrical Grand'Place and Place des Héros, joined by the short rue de la Taillerie, are fairly impressive. They existed as early as the 11C, but have undergone countless transformations over the centuries.

Their magnificent façades are fine examples of 17C and 18C Flemish architecture. The council of the period was careful to control the town's development, permitting construction "in stone or brick, with no projecting architectural elements." The façades – formerly embellished with carved shop signs, of which a few remain – rest on monolith-columned arcades which protected market stallholders and customers alike from inclement weather. The squares take on a different charm at night when the floodlit gables stand out against the night sky.

The smaller and livelier of the two squares, **Place des Héros**, is surrounded by shops and overlooked by the belfry.

▷ Stand facing the town hall and take r. D.-Delansorne, which starts in the left-hand corner of pl. des Héros and leads to r. Paul-Doumer.

On the corner of rue Doumer stands the **Palais de Justice** (Law Courts), the former seat of the Artois government (1701), embellished with Corinthian pilasters and its side entrance (1724) decorated with Regency shells.

▷ From r. Doumer, follow the second or third side street on the left.

During the Revolution, the guillotine stood in the lively **Place du Théâtre**. The **theatre** dates from 1784 (its façade has been restored). It was built where the fish market stood; it faces the **Ostel des Poissonniers** (1710), a narrow Baroque house carved with sea gods and mermaids. In rue des Jongleurs, note the majestic 18C Hôtel de Guines; at no. 9 rue stands the former residence of the famous revolutionary Robespierre (**Maison Robespierre** ⊙*open May–Sep 2–5pm Sat & Sun 2.30–6.30pm, Oct–Apr Tue–Thu 2–5.30pm, Sat & Sun 3.30–6.30pm; ⊗2€; ☎03 21 51 26 95)*, who lived in this house from 1787 to 1789. It has been turned into a **Musée du Compagnonnage** (crafts guild), which displays masterpieces by the best craftspeople in France.

▷ Walk across the square and take r. St-Aubert on your right; pl. du Wetz-d'Amain is a little farther on the left.

Grand'Place

© Y. Tierny/MICHELIN

The **Place du Wetz-d'Amain** is graced by a pretty Renaissance house, to which a Classical stone porch was later added. It served as a refuge for the monks of Mont St-Éloi.

 Turn back, follow r. du Gén.-Barbot which crosses r. St-Aubert; turn left on r. A.-Briand; Église Notre-Dame-des-Ardents is on your left. One of the streets on the right leads to place V.-Hugo and the lower town.

Fragments of the Holy Taper, a supposedly miraculous candle entrusted by the Virgin Mary to two minstrels to cure ergotic poisoning in the 12C are kept at the **Église Notre-Dame-des-Ardents** The silver reliquary is to the left of the high altar, in a latticed recess (*lighting below, to the right*).

 Follow one of the streets on the right to reach pl. Victor-Hugo and the lower town.

Basse-ville

This district lies between the town and the citadel. It is arranged around the lovely, octagonal **place Victor-Hugo**, built in 1756, where the cattle market used to be held.

Follow rue des Promenades towards the **Jardins du Gouverneur** and **Jardin des Allées**: a **stele** erected in honour of the Rosati depicts a marquess and a 20C man watching a procession of muses.

The **Citadel** (🕐 *open May–Aug 6am–10pm; Sept–Apr 6am–8pm; closed mid-Jun–mid-Jul;* 🎫*no charge;* 👣*2hr-guided tours by reservation 7 days in advance;* 🎫 *6.40€;* 📞*03 27 20 54 70; www.explorearras.com)*, a UNESCO World Heritage site, stands just across boulevard du Général-de-Gaulle; the octagonal stronghold designed by Vauban was built between 1668 and 1672.

It is composed of five bastions. A model of the fortifications is displayed in the entrance hall. The tour includes the arsenal and the Baroque Chapelle St-Louis. Avenue du Mémorial des Fusillés leads to the **Mur des Fusillés** where 217 members of the Resistance were executed during the Second World War.

 Return to pl. V.-Hugo and walk to the Cité district via r. Victor-Hugo. Then take the cours de Verdun on the right; cross pl. du 33e and continue along rue de Châteaudun leading to r. d'Amiens.

Cité

Place de la Préfecture was once the heart of medieval Arras. Today the *préfecture* (county council) occupies the former bishop's palace (1780).

Opposite, the Église St-Nicolas-en-Cité (1839) stands on the site of Notre-Dame-de-la-Cité Cathedral, which was destroyed between 1798 and 1804. It houses a triptych depicting the *Climb to Calvary*, painted in 1577 by P Claessens of Bruges. Follow rue Baudimont on the right for 135m/150yd to reach **place du Pont-de-Cité**. The name recalls the bridge on the River Crinchon (flowing underground), which linked the Cité to the town when each had its own fortifications.

 From the square, follow r. de Turenne which skirts the Jardin Minelle (on the left) and leads to quai du Rivage.

The **Jardin Minelle**, which replaced the town's fortifications, is a haven of peace. **Place de l'Ancien-Rivage** is set back from the pleasant *quai du Rivage*. The square-turreted house was once the St-Éloi hospice, founded in 1635 by one of the town's goldsmiths. Until the 19C, the square formed a dock that was linked to the old harbour.

 Return to the Grand'Place along r. du Mont-de-Piété, pl. G.-Mollet and r. Ste-Croix.

ADDITIONAL SIGHTS
Ancienne Abbaye St-Vaast★★

The old abbey was founded in the 7C by St Aubert on the hill overlooking a tributary of the River Scarpe, and was entrusted

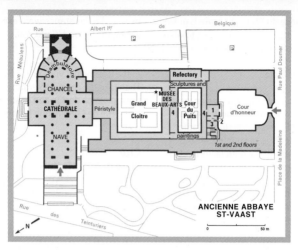

with the relics of the first bishop of Arras, St Vaast. **Cardinal de Rohan** began rebuilding the abbey buildings in 1746; they were deconsecrated during the Revolution and restored after 1918.

Musée des Beaux-Arts★

22 r. Paul Doumer. ◷*Open Mon & Wed–Fri 11am–6, Sat & Sun 9.30am–6pm.* ◷*Closed 1 Jan, 1–8 May, 14 Jul, 1–11 Nov, 25 Dec.* ◉*7€ no charge 1st Wed and 1st Sun in the month.* ℘*03 21 71 26 43.*

The museum offers an account of the town's history: The **Italian Room** (**1**), decorated with the original lion from the belfry (1554) in Arras, is used as a reception area. The tour begins in a series of small rooms on the left (**2** and **3**) containing the Gallo-Roman archaeology collection. The **galleries around the small cloister** (**4**), known as the Cour du Puits, contain some fine medieval sculptures and paintings, including tapestries made in Arras (legend of St Vaast); don't miss the 13C **Anges de Saudémont★** with their delicately rendered curly hair, almond-shaped eyes and faint smile. The 16C is illustrated by triptychs by **Bellegambe** (Adoration of the Christ Child) and an Entombment by Vermeyen.

Refectory – A tapestry bearing the arms of Cardinal de Rohan hangs above the great marble fireplace.

Grand cloître – The main cloister, which used to lead into the minster, contains capitals carved with garlands. The **staircase**, decorated with a fine series of paintings by Giovanni Baglioni (1571–1644), leads to the **first floor** dedicated to paintings from the 16C to 18C by the French School (Vignon, Nicolas de Largillière, Vien, Bouliar, Doncre) and the Dutch School (Brueghel the Younger, Adriaen Van Utrecht and Rubens).

The **Salle des Mays de Notre-Dame** owes its name to the works given to Notre-Dame Church in Paris every springtime between 1603 and 1707 by the guild of gold- and silversmiths. It contains huge works by La Hyre, Sébastien Bourdon, Louis de Boullongne, Philippe de Champaigne, Joseph Barrocel and Jouvenet. On the **2nd floor**, Italian and glazed earthenware are display alongside Arras and Tournai porcelain decorated with light, delicate motifs (note the "**Buffon bird dinner service**" commissioned by the Duc d'Orléans).

Around the small cloister are works by various schools of early-19C French landscape artists including Corot and Dutilleux. One spacious room is given over to large 19C works (**Delacroix, Chassériau**). Next to this room is the Salle Louise-Weiss containing 19C paintings by Monticelli, Ribot and Ravier.

Cathédrale

Entrance in r. des Teinturiers. ◷*Open May–Oct, Tue–Sat 10.30am–12.30pm & 2–6pm; Nov–Apr 2.30–5.30pm.* ♿℘*03 21 21 40 49.*

The building of the abbey church of St Vaast was only completed in 1833. The Classical façade is graced by a monumental flight of steps. 19C statues of saints adorn the side aisles.

Hôtel de Ville and Belfry

The City Pass Or gives admission to sites including the Hotel de Ville, Cité Nature, the Belfry, the Musée des Beaux-Arts and the underground Circuit des Souterrains. Available from the Office de Tourisme. ⊗19€ *(child, 10€). ℘03 21 51 26 95. www.ot-arras.fr.* **Hotel de Ville:** ⚫ *Guided visits (30min) Jul–Aug: Sun–Fri 2.30–3pm.* ⊗4€. **Belfry★:** ⏱*Opening times vary.* ⊗2.70€.

The town hall was destroyed in 1914 and rebuilt in the Flamboyant style. The front, with its uneven arches, stands on the western side of place des Héros, and the 75m/246ft belfry, with its 40-bell peal, rises over the more severe-looking Renaissance wings.

Circuit des souterrains

⚫*Guided tours 45min. Apr–Sept 9am–6.30pm, Sun 10am–1pm, 2.30–6.30pm; Oct–Mar: 9am–noon, 2–6pm, Sun 10am–12.30pm, 2.30–6.30pm, Mon 10am–noon, 2–6pm.* ⏱*Closed 1, 4–22 Jan and 25 Dec.* ⊗5.20€.

The 10C galleries, or *boves*, cut into the limestone bank on which the town stands, served as a refuge in wartime (during WW I the British set up a field hospital here for 24 000 troops) and above all as an enormous wine cellar.

👥 Cité Nature

25 bd. Schuman. ⏱*Open Tue–Fri 9am–5pm, Sat–Sun 2–6pm.* ⊗7€. ♿ ℘*03 21 21 59 59. www.citenature.com.* This former warehouse houses an exhibition on ecology and agriculture.

Carrière Wellington★

R. Delétoile. ⏱*Open 10am–12.30pm, 1.30–6pm.* ⊗6.60€. ♿ ℘*03 21 51 26 95. www.carriere-wellington.com.* This network of secret tunnels dug by the Allies during World War I was linked to the quarries of Arras to accommodate

24 000 men in preparation for an attack on the German lines.

EXCURSIONS
Saint-Amand

▶ *18km/11mi SW by N25 then D23.* The cemetery chapel houses a late-13C stone **Virgin with Child**. ℘*03 21 48 25 66. Ask for Gérard Bray.*

Château de Barly

▶*20km/12mi to the W of Arras by D59.* ⚫*Guided tour (1hr) Jul–mid-Aug: Tue–Sun 1–7pm.* ⊗6€ *(under 10s no charge).* ℘*03 21 48 41 20.*

This Louis XVI-style neoclassical château is a typical example of rural Artois architecture: the farmyard gives onto a main courtyard, pigeon coop, chapel and a small rear park. Don't miss the **wood panelling★** and carvings (1784) by Arras master César-Auguste Lepage.

ADDRESSES

🛏 STAY

⊟⊟ **Château de Saulty (B&B)** – *82 r. de la Gare, 62158 Saulty. 19km/12mi SW of Arras towards Doullens by N 25.* ℘*03 21 48 24 76. Closed Jan.* ⊟. *4 rooms* ⊇. Built in 1835, this château is set in a 45ha/112 acre park. Smart, spacious guest rooms. Breakfast includes home-made jams and fresh juice.

⊟⊟ **Le Clos Grincourt (B&B)** – *18 r. du Château, 62161 Duisans. 7km/4mi to the W of Arras by D 939 then D 56.* ℘*03 21 48 68 33. www.leclosgrincourt.com.* ⊟. *3 rooms* ⊇. A lovely bourgeois house (17C–19C) with apartment-like rooms. Attentive service.

⊟⊟ **Les Volets Bleus (B&B)**– *47 r. Briquet-Taillandier, 62223 Anzin-St-Aubin.* ℘*03 21 23 39 90. www.voletsbleus.com.* ♿⊟. *3 rooms* ⊇. A pretty residence in a flowered garden facing the Arras golf club. The the gourmet meals and buffet breakfasts are extraordinary.

⊟⊟⊟ **Hôtel Diamant** –*5 pl. des Héros.* ℘*03 21 71 23 23. www.arras-hotel-diamant.com. 12 rooms* ⊇. A choice location on the Place des Héros. Pleasant reception and small rooms, impeccably maintained.

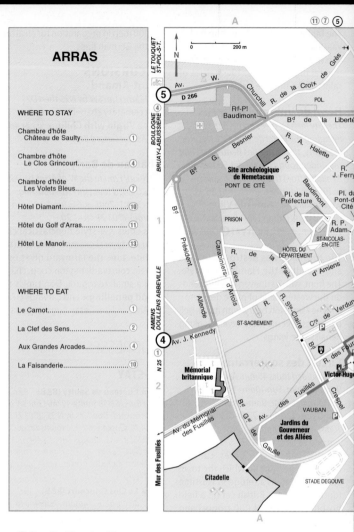

Hotel Le Manoir – *35 rte. Nationale. 62580 Gavrelle. 11km/7mi NE of Arras by D 950 towards Douai.* ℘*03 21 58 68 58. www.lemanoir62.com. Closed 1st half of Aug, 25–31 Dec.* ᵼ. *19 rooms*. This bourgeois manor opens onto verdant countryside. Simple, clean rooms housed in the former stables. Traditional French cuisine.

Hôtel du Golf d'Arras– *R.Briquet-Tallandier. 62223 Anzin-St-Aubin.* ℘*03 21 50 45 04. www.golf-arras.com. Wi-fi. 64 rooms. Restaurant.* At the entrance to the Arras golf club, this Louisiana-inspired hotel has well-appointed rooms and a bright gourmet restaurant and bar with a daily menu.

¶/ EAT

Aux Grandes Arcades – *8–12 Grand'Place.* ℘*03 21 23 30 89. Closed Sun eve (in winter).* ᵼ. *19 rooms*. This restaurant on the Grand'Place offers a brasserie menu and a restaurant menu of local specialities to enjoy on the summer terrace. 15C vaulted cellar.

Le Carnot – *12 pl. Foch.* ℘*03 21 71 08 14. www.hotelcarnot.com. 29 rooms.* Traditional regional specialities to enjoy on the terrace or in the cosy dining room.

La Clef des Sens – *60 pl. des Héros.* ℘*03 21 51 00 50. www.laclefdessens.com. Closed 24 Dec–11 Jan.* ᵼ. *Restaurant.* This restaurant overlooking the place des

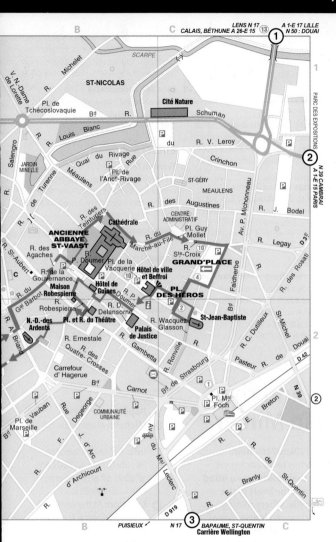

Héros has an eclectic menu and decor (banquettes, red wood panneling and a lobster tank). Views over the belfry from the upper floor and terrace.

🍽🍽🍽 **La Faisanderie** – *45 Grand'Place. ℘03 21 48 20 76. www.restaurant-la-faisanderie.com. Closed 3–24 Aug, Thu lunch, Sun eve, Mon.* Giving onto the Grand'Place, this 17C residence has a brick-vaulted cellar. Modern cuisine.

TAKING A BREAK

Pâtisserie Sébastien Thibaut – *50 pl. des Héros. ℘03 21 71 53 20. 8am–7.30pm. Closed Mon.* For the past 100 years, this pastry shop has been delighting locals

with its *Cœur d'Arras* (a ginger-bread confection). Enjoy a home-made ice-cream on the summer terrace.

SHOPPING

Marché – *℘03 21 51 26 95.* Traditional Wed morning market on the place des Héros; Sat morning on the Grand'Place, place des Héros and place de la Vacquerie.

Andouillette – Available at all delicatessens across the region. Made from calf's caul, seasoned with parsley, shallots, spices, herbs and juniper.

Charcuterie A l'Andouillette d'Arras – *3r. du marché-au-Filé. ℘03 21 22 69 96 Mon–Sat 8am–7pm.* This small store not far from the town hall has been selling local chitterling sausages for over a century. It sells over one tonne of this tripe-based delicacy every month.

ON THE TOWN

Irish Pub – *7 pl. des Héros.*
✆03 21 71 46 08. Tue–Sat 11am–1am; Sun & Mon 3pm–1am. The name tells the game: wooden tables, a waxed parquet, a good choice of beer and music with a Celtic accent.

Théâtre d'Arras – *r. Paul Doumer.*
✆03 21 71 66 16. Box office open Tue–Sat, 2–7.15pm. Closed Jul–Aug. This is a listed pretty 400-seat *théâtre à l'italienne*. The line-up features music and drama.

ACTIVITIES

Stade d'eau vive (fresh water stadium) **– Base nautique Robert-Pecqueur** – *R.Laurent-Gers. 62223 St-Laurent-Blangy. 2km/1mi NE of Arras. ✆03 21 73 74 93. www.eauxvivesslb.fr.st.* Originally designed for the 2004 Olympic Games, this 300m/985ft long, 12mi/40ft wide

artificial torrent was excavated between the Scarpe lock and one of its overflow branches. Kayaks, rafts and canoes may be rented here at very reasonable prices.

Fête de l'andouillette – The city centre is transformed into a giant inn on the last Sun of August. Street shows, parades and tastings.

EVENTS

Terre en fête– Every two years on the 2nd weekend in June, Arras organises one of the biggest agricultural shows in France:farm machinery, breeding stock and tasting sessions.

Water jousting– In July, try your hand at water jousting on the Scarpe river.

Andouillette festival– The city centre transforms itself into an open-air inn on the last Sunday in August: street theatre, orchestras, parades and tasting sessions.

Embrasement du beffroi– In late Aug/early Sept at 10.30pm, a light and sound show is organised at the foot of the belfry.

Lens and the Bassin Minier

Stretching 120km/74mi from Bruay-en-Artois to Valenciennes, this former coal field is now a listed heritage site at the heart of the Pays de Gohelle. Where mining offices and cramped houses once stood, there are now universities, museums, thriving modern neighbourhoods and, of course, the Louvre-Lens art gallery, built on the site of a former pithead!

SIGHTS

If you're arriving by train into Lens, take a moment to admire the Art Deco **station** (1926), a tribute to the golden age of steam. In the mine's heyday, all coal produced in the nearby pit was transported via Lens. A sandstone mosaic in the hall depicts local mining techniques.
Nearby, the **former offices of the mine company,** designed by Lille architect Cordonnier and now the Université

- ▸ **Population:** 36 192
- ⚲ **Michelin Map:** p428: B2; 301 J5.
- ▤ **Info:** Office de tourisme – 26 r. de la Paix, 62300 Lens. ✆03 21 67 66 66. www.tourisme-lenslievin.fr.
- ◖ **Location:** At the centre of the quadrilateral formed by Lille, Douai, Arras and Béthune. From Béthune, access by D 943; from Arras, N 17; from Lille, N 41-N 47; from Douai, A 21.
- ✿ **Don't miss:** The tourism office guided tour – discover the Lens-Liévin region, the Louvre-Lens, the former offices of the Compagnie minière, Art Deco Lens Art deco and the Félix-Bollaert stadium.
- ◷ **Timing:** Allow 1 day.
- ♙ **Kids***:* The Musée de l'École et de la Mine at Harnes.

d'Artois *(r. de l'Artisanat)*, are built in the same style. Note the sloping roofs with skylights and decorative brickwork.

Musée Louvre-Lens★★

Maison du projet. R. Georges-Bernanos. ⓞ*Open Wed–Sun 10am–6pm.* ⌀*No charge until end of 2013. Temporary exhibitions* ⌀*9€.* ℘*03 21 18 62 62. www.louvrelens.fr.*

A satellite of the Louvre in Paris, this 20ha/50acre museum and park is located on the site of a former pithead. The **Galerie du Temps** displays 250 works in chronological order, like a book on the history of art. It is also possible to explore "behind the scenes" at the museum by visiting its repositories. The **Pavillon de verre** provides a showcase for works from the Nord-Pas-de-Calais region. Two major **temporary exhibitions** are organised every year.

EXCURSION
Mémorial canadien de Vimy★

▶*6km/4mi S of Lens by N 17. Follow the pylons. Allow 2hrs.* ⓞ*Open Mar–Oct 10am–6pm; Nov–Feb 9am–5pm.* ⓞ*Closed mid-Dec–mid-Jan.*

This gigantic memorial soars from the peak of "Hill 145", the highest point on the 14km/9mi-long Vimy Ridge. The ridge was held by the Germans until 9 April, 1917 when four divisions of the Canadian army captured it at the cost of 10 062 lives.

Austere and colossal in scale, the **Memorial** (1936) is built on land given to Canada after the war. Walter Seymour Allward spent 11 years building this monument, which pays tribute to the 66 655 Canadians killed during World War I. Sitting on an 11 000 tonne concrete base, it is sculpted from 6 000 tonnes of limestone imported from a Roman quarry on the Adriatic coast. The female figure at the front of the monument represents Canada crying for her lost children. The two groups of sculpted figures on either side of the front wall, at the bottom of the steps, represent the "Breaking of the Sword" and the "Sympathy of the Canadians for the Helpless". The perimeter wall is engraved with the names of 11 285 Canadians killed in France with no known grave.

At the summit of the twin pylons, which symbolise the sacrifices of Canada and France, stand Justice and Peace, with Truth, Knowledge, Galantry and Sympathy arranged below.

A network of Canadian and German **trenches** have been restored on the side of the hill, along with part of the **Grange tunnel,** once measuring 750m/2500ft long. The ground is still littered with explosives and shellholes. ▸*Guided tours of tunnels (50min) by reservation Mar–Oct 10am–6pm; Nov–Feb 9am–5pm; guided tour of the battlefield (1hr) by reservation: May–Nov 10am, 11.30am, 1.45pm and 3.15pm; year-round open access to the Centre d'interprétation historique, cemeteries and trenches.* ⌀*No charge.* ℘*03 21 50 68 68 and 03 22 76 70 86.*

To the south, **Neuville-Saint-Vaast** was taken from the Germans by the 5th DI of General Mangin in June 1915, after eight days of fierce fighting.

🚗 DRIVING TOUR

Les GUEULES NOIRES

115km/71mi marked in green on the regional map (♿*p428) . Allow 1 day.*

▶ Leave Lens to the SW.

Liévin

On the outskirts of Liévin, turn right down D58 towards Béthune, then right again at the roundabout, towards the pithead frame.

The square is dominated by the **pithead frame** of no.3b (1923), closed in 1978. The **National miners' memorial** commemorates the mining accident of 27 December 1974 when a firedamp explosion killed 42 men.

▶ Drive around the pithead frame then turn right at the lights towards Loos-en-Gohelle.

The twin **slagheaps** (130m/426ft) rise over pit no.11.

Loos-en-Gohelle

Closed in 1986, **pit no.11/19** is now a listed monument. The 184m/600ft slagheap is the highest in Europe *(guided tours)*. The renovated buildings are home to several theatre companies.

▶ Return to the main road, turn right and cross bridge. At the lights, turn left along D943 towards Béthune and left down D165 towards Grenay. Pass Bully-les-Mines to Sains-en-Gohelle (D166E).

Sains-en-Gohelle

At the roundabout, turn left along D937 towards Hersin-Bruay, then first on the right.
The orthogonal **Cité no.10** is a housing estate built between 1905 and 1914. *Take the 3rd street on the left, then turn right.* Continue along the tree-lined street to the church, surrounded by schools, a teacher's house and a presbytery.

▶ Return towards Sains-en-Gohelle. Before the church, turn right then left at the stop sign. Take the D75E, then D188 to Hersin-Coupigny.

Hersin-Coupigny

On leaving the town, to the left is the **Longue-Pierre mining village**. In reality, these are terraced houses divided into groups of 10 units, arranged to resemble a traditional mining village.

▶ Follow D188 towards Barlin, then Haillicourt. Once you reach Haillicourt turn left towards Houdain after the lights.

The twin **slagheaps** of pit no.6 in Bruay-la-Buissière rise to the left.

▶ At the roundabout, turn right towards Bruay-la-Buissière.

Bruay-la-Buissière

The Cité no.16 extends into Bruay. Drive around the church to the right.
Austere semi-detached houses line rue de Mauritanie and rue du Cap-Vert.

▶ At the end, turn left then right at the lights.

On the left, the **barreaux** (1899) a series of thirty homes adjoining early-20C outbuildings were transformed by a regeneration project in 1990.

▶ Turn right then left towards the town centre. Opposite the Lycée Carnot, turn right towards the "hôtel de ville", then "parking Wery". Follows the signs to the Écomusée de la Mine on the left.

Écomusée de la Mine (*by reservation; ℘06 63 04 72 90; www.bruaylabuissiere. fr.*) Commentaries and sound effects recreate the harsh working lives of miners in this former **mine training school**.

▶ Retrace your route. At the stop sign, turn left. Take D188 to Marles-les-Mines then D70 towards Auchel. In front of Marles town hall, turn right towards the Cité de Marles; follow the signs for "Auchel centre". At the waste ground, turn right towards the housing estate.

Auchel

🖸 61r. Laënnec, 62260 Auchel.
℘03 21 61 51 80. www.artoiscom.fr.
Dominated by slagheaps, the **Cité d'Auchel** is a typical example of this region's spaced terrace housing.

▶ Return towards Marles and take D188 to Bruay-la-Buissière. At Barlin, turn left along D179.

Nœux-les-Mines

The **Musée de la Mine** (*Av. Guillon;* 🕒*open 9am–11, 2–4.30pm;* ↝*guided tours by request;* 🕒 *closed Sat and Sun;* ⊕*5€ (under 12yrs 2€); ℘03 21 25 98 58*), a former training centre for "galibots" (young miners) explores the development of mining techniques, including a reconstruction of a mine gallery.

▶ Return to D937, turn right towards towards Loisinord.

The newly renovated "**coron**" no. 3 is now home to dozens of families.

▶ Return to the roundabout, turn right to Mazingarbe.

Mazingarbe
The bd. des Platanes, lined with engineers' houses *(left)*, runs alongside the organic chemistry plant.

▶ Turn right, drive along the main plant entrance and turn left after the level crossing. Take D943 towards Lens, then A21 around the town, towards Arras-Douai. Exit at Loison. D917 towards Lille then, near Annay, D39 left to Harnes.

👥 Musée de l'École et de la Mine at Harnes
24 r. de Montceau-les-Mines. Open *Tue–Thu 2–6pm. Contact for holiday times.* No charge. *03 21 75 38 97. www.museedelamine.org.*
Run by a retired teacher and a former porion, this museum features a 1900 classroom and a "mini Lewarde" mine.

▶ Leave Harnes to the SW, then take D46 left to Courrières until Oignies.

Mining in Pas-de-Calais began in **Oignies** with the discovery of a coal seam in 1842 and ended when pit no.9 became the last mine to close in 1990. The 👥**Centre Denis-Papin** *(R. Émile-Zola;* open *Apr–Oct 2nd and 4th Sun of the month, 2–6pm; 2hr30min guided tours;* 4.60€; *03 21 74 80 50)* is home to a powerful extraction machine. Ride on a 1:8 scale steam railway with miniature carriages.

▶ Continue along the same road; turn right, then left (1km/0.6mi) at the second roundabout to pit no.9/9bis.

The buildings, pithead frames and slagheap of **pit no.9/9bis**, were used for the filming of *Germinal* in 1992.

▶ Return to the main road, take D160 right to Dourges.

Hénin-Beaumont
A major advance in workers' housing, the **Cité Foch** (1922) is one of the finest garden suburbs in France. Its curved streets lead to mock Tudor houses.

▶ Return in the direction you came and head for the town centre and Drocourt.

in **Drocourt**, St Barbe, the patron saint of miners, stands at the centre of the **Cité de la Parisienne**, once home to miners' families.

▶ Return towards Hénin-Beaumont then Lens by A21.

ADDRESSES

🛏 STAY

Hôtel Espace Bollaert – *13 C rte de Béthune.* *03 21 78 30 30. www.espace-bollaert.fr.* *54 rooms.* Opposite the legendary Lens football stadium, this recently-built hotel offers functional rooms. Take advantage of the "match/meal/mattress" deals on match nights.

🍴 EAT

Restaurant Lyonnais – *Parc de la Glissoire. 62210 Avion. 3km/2mi S of Lens.* *03 21 70 04 03. http://restaurantlyonnais. com. Closed Sun eve and Mon.* Housed in a former mining school, surrounded by a vast park and lakes, this restaurant serves Lyon-inspired dishes.

TAKING A BREAK
Brasserie d'Annoeullin– *4 Grand'Place. 59112 Annœullin.* *03 20 86 83 60. www.brasserie-dannoeullin.com. Mon–Fri 8am–noon, 1–5pm. Closed 1 wk in Jul, 1 wk in Aug, and 1 wk in Dec.* This traditional brasserie has been serving its speciality beers, Angélus, Pastor'Ale and Bock 4, to the region's beer lovers since 1905.

ACTIVITIES
👥 **Loisinord** – *R. Léon-Blum. 62290 Nœux-les-Mines.* *03 21 26 84 84. Mon, Tue, Thu–Sat 2–8pm, Wed 10am–noon, 2–8pm, Sun 10am–8pm (last admission 6.45pm).* An artificial ski slope and a water sports centre for skiing and pedal-boating in a lake formed in a mining hollow.

Colline de
Notre-Dame-de-Lorette★

The culminating point of the Artois hill range, Notre-Dame-de-Lorette (166m/544ft high) was the target of countless offensives during World War I. Between October 1914 and September 1915, 188 000 soldiers lost their lives on this hill. The lantern tower sweeps the Artois plain with a ray of light, paying tribute to them.

A BIT OF HISTORY

Notre-Dame-de-Lorette features in numerous dispatches during the First World War, especially during the Battle of Artois from May to September 1915.

SIGHTS

The **cemetery**, the main ossuary with its 52m/170ft high **lantern tower** (◐open Jul–Aug 9am–7pm, Jun 9am–6pm, May 9am–5.30pm, Sept 9am–5pm, Aug & Oct–Apr 9am–4pm; ◐closed 1 Jan and 25 Dec; ◎no charge; ✆03 21 45 15 80) and seven other ossuaries house the remains of 20 000 unknown soldiers. From the top floor, there is a vast **panorama★** of the mining basin (*north*), the Vimy Memorial (*east*), the ruined church of Ablain St-Nazaire, the towers of Mont-St-Éloi and Arras (*south*). The **musée vivant 1914–1918** (◐same as the lantern tower; ◎5€) features photographs and shells.

- ⚲ **Michelin Local Map:** p428: B2; 301: J-5.
- ⊞ **Info:** 100 Rue Pasteur, 62153 Souchez. ✆03 21 72 66 55.
- ◖ **Location:** 11km/ 7mi SW of Lens by the D 58E, and from Béthune or Arras by the D 937 then D 58E.

⊙ A computer is available to search for the names of soldiers buried here.

EXCURSIONS
Dolmen de Fresnicourt
◗ 3km/2mi by D57.
This ridge is carpeted by a sacred forest and its legendary stone "fairy's table".

Musée de la Targette
◗ 7km/4mi SE by D937 at Neuville-Saint-Vaast. 48 rte Nationale. ◐Open Thu–Sun 9am–5pm. ◎4€.
This display of over 2 000 artefacts explores the battles of Artois.

⚇ Château d'Olhain★
◗ 19km/12mi to the W by D57. ◐Open Jul–Aug 3–6.30pm, Apr–Jun & Sept–Oct Sun 3–6.30pm. ◎4€. ✆01 39 18 33 14. www.chateau-olhain.com.
One of the best-preserved medieval castles in the region (1200), the Château d'Olhain is entered by a drawbridge leading to a courtyard, watchtower (*100 steps*), guardroom, cellars and chapel.

Lillers

Once famous for the watercress that grows in abundance around its artesian wells, Lillers is now better known for its Romanesque collegiate church.

Lillers and the surrounding area sit on a layer of impermeable clay covering a strata of chalk that acts like a groundwater sponge. The clay exerts so much pressure on the water that if a hole is

- ▸ **Population:** 9 768
- ⚲ **Michelin Map:** p428: A1; 301 H4.
- ⊞ **Info:** 4 pl. Roger-Salengro, BP 44, 62192 Lillers Cedex. ✆03 21 25 26 71. www.tourismepaysdelalysromane.fr.
- ◖ **Location:** Access by A 26. From Saint-Omer follow D 943; from Hazebrouck follow D 916.

drilled in the ground, the water spurts out without the need for a pump.

This local phenomenon (there were once 500 artesian wells in Lillers) is the reason why watercress thrives here.

SIGHTS

👁 Don't miss the "urban" watercress bed at 51 rue de la Cantrainne. The 18C chapel on Place Roger-Salengro (town centre) is also well worth a visit.

Collégiale Saint-Omer

🕐 Open May–Sept Mon–Sat 9am–noon, 2–6pm, Sun 10am–12.30pm, 2.30–5pm. ☎03 21 25 26 71.

The only Romanesque building (12C) in Flanders and Artois to retain its original shell, this church has a restored façade and transept gable.

The interior is divided into three levels: an arcade of broken arches with double arch moulding (Cistercian design), a triforium and Roman arch windows under a wooden ceiling. Note the Romaneque water lily carvings in the ambulatory and the Christ du Saint Sang du miracle (12C) in the apsidal chapel: the filled-in hole on his right thigh marks the spot where an iconoclast landed a blow that is said to have produced a miraculous flow of bright-red blood.

EXCURSIONS
Amettes

🕐 7km/4mi to the SW by D 69.

A popular place of pilgrimage, this small town nestled in a valley is the birthplace of **Saint Benoît Labre** (1748–1783) who visited the great sanctuaries of Europe and died destitute in Rome.

Créminil garden and château

🕐 15km/10mi NE by D 943 then D 94 and D 341. ⊶ Not open to the public.

Next to the elegant 15C castle surrounded by moats, a local association has planted a series of **medieval gardens** (identical to a typical garden of the late 15C) where they grow beans and peas, medicinal plants and flowers.

Bours

🕐 15km/9mi S (D 916); left after Pernes.

The **keep** (🕐 open Late-Mar–late-Oct Sun 3–6pm, Mon–Sat by request. Guided tour possible (1hr); ⊗no charge; ♿☎03 21 04 76 76; www.donjondebours.sitew.com) flanked by six corbelled turrets, stands in the middle of a field. Built by the lords of Bours at the end of the 14C on the ruins of a fortress, it is decorated with sculptures of crude human heads.

Guarbecque

🕐 8km/5mi NE by D 916 then D 187.

Dominated by a sturdy 12C bell tower, with an eight-faced spire cornered by pinnacles, the **church** is graced with twin windows under arches decorated with billets and diamond shapes.

Béthune

🕐 12km/7.5mi to the E by D 182 then D 943.

Béthune, a lively and welcoming town, despite its reputation as a cold former mining town. Once surrounded by Vauban-style fortifications and located on a fertile plain, it is now home to a major river port linked to the Lys and the Deûle by the Aire canal.

Grand'Place and belfry – Lined with delightful houses dating from after World War I, the Grand'Place is built in the purest Flemish style. The sandstone **belfry** (30 m) with corner bartizans dates from the 14C. One of its many functions was to provide a watch tower to spot the approach of the town's potential enemies. Take the rue du Carillon, to visit the **Église Saint-Vaast**, dominated by its brick tower (68m/223ft). Destroyed in 1916, it was rebuilt in 1924. The debris was used to restore the belfry between the two world wars. Don't miss the Chapelle Sainte-Marie with its large organs and the **mosaics** decorating the gateway and pulpit.

Hesdigneul-lès-Béthune

🕐 4km SW of Béthune.

The **church**, dominated by a bell tower and porch, sports highly original star-vaulting (15C) in the chancel.

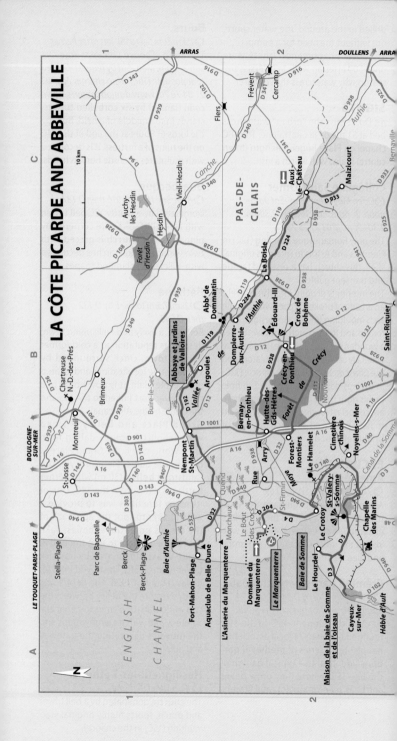

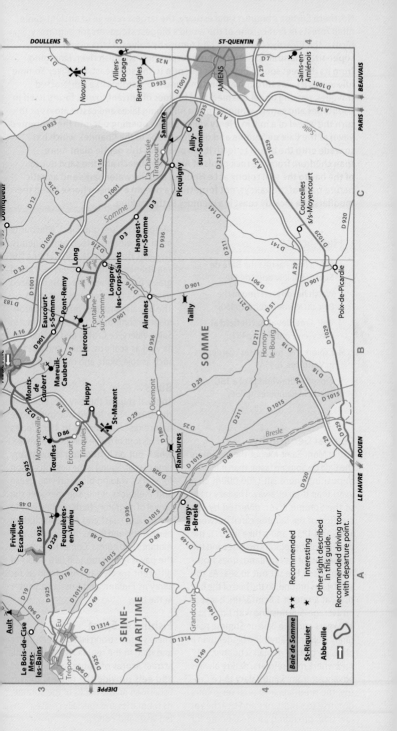

DOULLENS 3 **ST-QUENTIN** 4

Villers-Bocage
Bertangles
Naours
AMIENS
Sains-en-Amiénois

D 17
D 933
N 25
D 933
D 1001
A 16
N 25
A 29
D 7
D 1001
BEAUVAIS
PARIS

Dompierre
D 12
D 933
A 16
D 216
D 1001
Somme
Long
Pont-Remy
Eaucourt-s-Somme
D 901
D 32
D 183
A 16
D 1001
La Chaussée-Tirancourt
Samara
Ailly-sur-Somme
Picquigny
Selle
A 16
D 3
Hangest-sur-Somme
Longpré-les-Corps-Saints
Fontaine-sur-Somme
Liercourt
D 3
D 216
D 936
D 211
Courcelles-s/s-Moyencourt
D 1029
A 29
C

Mareuil-Caubert
Monts-de-Caubert
Huppy
St-Maxent
Airaines
Tailly
SOMME
Hornoy-le-Bourg
Poix-de-Picardie
D 901
D 901
D 936
D 211
D 211
D 51
D 18
D 1029
D 920
B

Tœufles
Moyenneville
Ercourt
Trinquies
D 925
D 22
A 28
D 86
Rambures
Oisemont
D 29
D 180
D 25
D 928
Bresle
D 211
D 1015
A 29
D 929
ROUEN
LE HAVRE

Friville-Escarbotin
Feuquières-en-Vimeu
Blangy-s-Bresle
D 925
D 29
D 48
D 936
D 1015
D 49
D 928
D 1015
A 28
D 149
D 920
A

Ault
Le Bois-de-Cise
Mers-les-Bains
Eu
Le Tréport
Grandcourt
SEINE-MARITIME
D 19
D 940
D 925
D 2
D 49
D 1015
D 1314
D 149
D 14
3
DIEPPE
4

Baie de Somme
St-Riquier
Abbeville

★★ Recommended
★ Interesting

Other sight described
in this guide.

Recommended driving tour
with departure point.

445

LA CÔTE PICARDE *and Abbeville*

Northern Europe's biggest tidal estuary, the largest reserve of ancient game-filled forests in France, one of the world's biggest stopovers for migratory birds... the Picardy coast doesn't do nature by halves. At the origin of this super-sized natural environment is a surprisingly sluggish river. Emerging from its discreet source beyond St Quentin to the southeast, the River Somme idly winds its way through arboretums and eco-gardens like a distracted traveller, passing under the medieval bridges of ancient towns, losing itself in tributaries and canals, stopping off to fill fishing lakes and castle moats or to turn the wheel of a mill in a leafy valley before opening out into the contented yawn of the Baie de Somme and dipping its toe in the Channel, which has to wade onto the beach to fetch it. No one loves this gentle giant more than children: from the rock pools of Ault's tiny beach and the sand dunes of the bay to the seal colony at Le Hourdel and the water parks and aquatic nature trails of the valleys, not forgetting a ride on a Henson horse along the mudflats, the Picardy coast is a memory in the making.

Highlights

1 Ride a horse across the **Baie de Somme** at low tide (p449)

2 Watch **herons nesting** in the Parc du Marquenterre (p450)

3 Visit a **medieval battlefield** at Crécy-en-Ponthieu (p452)

4 Explore the "five senses" garden in **Valloires** (p454)

5 Cross the drawbridge of a **15C castle** in Rambures (p459)

Coastal Geography

Like at Mont-Saint-Michel, the sea enters the Baie de Somme faster than it leaves, depositing more silt (700 000m cu a year) than it takes away. The lazy pace of the Somme River, diverted by the creation of the Somme canal between 1786 and 1835, and a dike in 1911, the draining of the region's marshes and the expansion of its farmland, does nothing to wash the silt out to sea. As the sand gains ground, so the bed of the bay rises, at a rate of 1.8cm/3/4inch a year on average. Still bustling with boats just 150 years ago, the Baie de Somme now rarely welcomes anything bigger than a pleasure boat or a small schooner.

And where man retreats, nature always advances: from Saint-Valery to Le Crotoy, the mudflats and tidal reservoirs give rise to sandbanks and beaches at low tide, providing an ideal home for samphire or "sea gherkins", a favourite meal for wintering teals and wigeons. Towards the coast, the silt fattens the sandbanks to form *mollières* (raised grassy banks) where the grass is grazed by region's delicious *prés-salé* lamb. The bay also provides an ideal environment for shrimps or "sauterelle" fished in Saint-Valéry, Le Crotoy and Le Hourdel, as well as scallops, squid and flat fish such as sole, skate and monkfish.

Birds

The real stars of this bay are, however, the birds. The listed Marquenterre nature reserve is home to 350 species of birds (out of 650 in Europe as a whole), which put on a stunning show at any time of year. Spring is the nesting season for storks, wading birds, greylag geese and shelducks, while summer sees the arrival of migratory birds on their way to the Iberian coast and Africa, including black storks and flocks of spoonbills, cormorants and egrets. Come the autumn, the bay is filled around 6 000 ducks of different species arriving from as far away as Finland and Russia to winter in the bay.

Fishing as Sport

There's also a strong link between water and man in the region. Waterfowl still attract scores of hunters, while trout and eels provide the main sport for fishermen on the banks of the Somme, its tributaries and specially created fishing lakes and ponds.

Saint-Valery-sur-Somme★

Capital of the Vimeu region, St-Valery is a pleasant marina and fishing port with a small beach, timber-framed houses and ramparts overlooking the Baie de Somme, the inspiration of artists including Boudin, Degas and Seurat.

> ▸ **Population:** 2 686
> ◔ **Michelin Local Map:** p444: A2.
> 🆘 **Info:** Office du tourisme de St-Valery-sur-Somme, 2 pl. Guillaume-le-Conquérant, 80230. ☏03 22 60 93 50. www.saint-valery-sur-somme.fr.

A BIT OF HISTORY

St-Valery (pronounced "Val'ry") grew up around a 7C abbey housing the remains of the evangelising Gaulish monk Gualaric (later known as "Valery"). **William the Conqueror** launched his invasion of England from here in 1066. During the Hundred Years War, the town passed through the hands of the French, the English (who demolished the cloister and abbey towers to strengthen the castle) and the Burgundians. In 1431, Joan of Arc was led through the town on her way to Rouen, where she was burnt at the stake. The population survived the French Revolution relatively unscathed, although the abbey and château were confiscated and sold as building material. After a long period of peace, it became a major supply centre for the British during World War I.

VILLE BASSE

The lower town extends 2km/1.25mi to the mouth of the Somme River, where the port is located. The port is a mooring point for coastal fishing boats known as "sauterelliers" after the shrimps or "sauterelles" that form the bulk of the local fishing trade.

Start you tour along the **Digue-promenade★** to the sheltered beach which affords **views** over the Bay to Le Crotoy.

Beyond the Relais Guillaume de Normandy are the ramparts of the upper town. The 🏠🚶**Ecomusée Picarvie★** (🕐open Wed, Sat–Sun 10am–12.30pm, 1.30–6pm; ⊚5.90€; ☏03 22 26 94 90)

recreates regional life before the 19C, including wickerworking, shoe-repairing, locksmithing and barrel-making.

VILLE HAUTE

The upper town still retains some of its original fortifications. Start with the **Porte de Nevers**, built in the 14C and heightened in the 16C, which owes its name to the dukes of Nevers who possessed St-Valery in the 17C. Next, head to the **Porte Guillaume**, a 12C gate between two towers offering a majestic **view** over the Baie de Somme.

The **Herbarium des Ramparts** (36 r. Brandt; 🕐open May–Oct Tue–Fri 10am–6pm, Sat & Sun 10am–12.30pm, 3–6pm; ⊚5€; ☏03 22 26 69 37; www.jardin-herbarium.fr) is a garden once belonging to the nuns who ran the local hospital. It contains over 1 000 plant species.

Beyond the Porte Guillaume, take rue de l'Abbaye: **St-Valery's Abbey** used to lie in the vale to your left. Its brick and stone **Bishop's castle** survives, with a carved 18C pediment.

▷ From pl. de l'Ermitage, take the path up to the chapel (30min round trip).

The chequered sandstone and flint **chapelle des Marins** houses the tomb of St Valery. Overlooking the Baie de Somme, the chapel offers extensive **views★** over the salt meadows, the estuary and the Marquenterre reserve in the distance.

Ault★

A "balcony onto the sea", the chalk cliffs of Ault are swept by sea breezes and carpeted with lush green meadows.

VISIT
Beaches

Almost completely covered at high tide, Ault's small beach reveals its mirrored rock pools at low tide. Two more beaches are found opposite Onival to the north.

SIGHTS
Église Saint-Pierre

Tour by request at the tourist office.
The 14C–15C Gothic church has a flint and stone chequered façade.

Villas

Ault and **Onival** were among France's first 19C seaside resorts. A number of fine villas decorated with **ceramic tiles** remain from this period. *Contact the tourist office for walks.*

Ault Lighthouse

The lighthouse on the last escarpment of Ault's ancient cliffs is decorated with white and red ceramic tiles. Walk along rue Degauchy and boulevard du Phare for stunning views over the Baie de Somme, Picardy and the Channel.

Hâble d'Ault

North of Onival. Until the 18C, the Hâble d'Ault was used as a safe haven during storms. Gradually sealed off by pebbles from the Ault cliffs, the Hâble is now a stretch of lagoon and marshland that is home to some 200 bird species. Although a coastal nature reserve, a 62ha/153acre section of the park is reserved for hunting. In June and July, the Hâble is covered in a mauve and yellow carpet of sea kale and wild thyme.

▸ **Population:** 2 072
⚐ **Michelin Map:** p445: A3; 301 B7.
🛈 **Info:** Office de tourisme – Pl. du Mar.-Foch, 80460 Ault. ℰ03 22 60 57 15. www.ot-ault.fr.
◖ **Location:** Ault stretches from the floor of a **valleuse** (a dry vale suspended above the shore) to a terrace with fine views over Le Tréport, to the south-southwest. Access by D 940.
⊛ **Don't Miss:** Dramatic views down to the sea from the village; beaches; Hâble d'Ault nature reserve; Belle Époque villas in Mers-les-Bains.
👪 **Kids**: Rock pools on Ault beach at low tide.

EXCURSIONS
Le Bois-de-Cise

◖*4km/2mi SW. The access road to Bois-de-Cise forks off to D 940.*
500m/550yds after entering this Belle Epoque resort nestled in woodland between Ault and Mers-les-Bains, turn right down the "route panoramique" which follows the northern slopes of a wooded valley. Past the chapel, a slope leads down to several Art Nouveau villas. The pebble beach below boasts a rocky "platin" (reef).

Mers-les-Bains★

◖*9 km/6mi to the SW.* 🛈 *43 r. Jules-Barni, 80350 Mers-les-Bains.* ⊙*Open 10am–noon, 2.30–5.30pm, Apr–Sept Sun 10am–noon, 3–5pm, Oct–Mar Mon, Wed–Sat.* ℰ*02 27 28 06 46. www.ville-merslesbains.fr.*
Opposite Tréport, this seaside resort became fashionable after the opening of the railway in 1872. The cosy seafront Belle Époque **villas★** are an eclectic mix of Art Nouveau turrets, steeples, oriels, loggias, wrought-iron balconies and ceramic tiling.

Baie de
Somme★★

Stretching 5km/3mi between the Pointe du Hourdel and the Pointe de St-Quentin, the arch of the Somme estuary is bathed in luminous hues of pink, opal, grey and gold.

A BIT OF HISTORY

A natural silting process has created **mollières** or salt-pastures all along the bay where lambs now graze. The bay's three **fishing ports** (St-Valery-sur-Somme, Le Crotoy and Le Hourdel) specialise in **shellfish**.

🚗 DRIVING TOUR

AROUND THE BAY

Restored trains pulled by steam or diesel engines operate on the **Chemin de fer de la Baie de Somme** *(for a timetable and charges:* 📞03 22 26 96 96; www.chemin-fer-baie-somme.asso.fr *or the tourist office) between Le Crotoy and Cayeux-sur-Mer.*

◐ Take D 940 towards Saint-Valery then left along D 111.

Parc du Marquenterre★★
&See PARC DU MARQUENTERRE.

Continue to **Le Crotoy**, a popular seaside resort affording beautiful **views★** of the bay. The local **beach** lends itself to peedsailing, kite-flying and landsailing.
Further along the road from Sailly-Flibeaucourt to the hamlet of Nolette, stop off at the **Chinese Cemetery in Noyelles**, home to more than 800 tombstones of Chinese nationals hired by the British between 1917 and 1919 to help with the war effort. Most of these men died of Spanish Influenza.

◐ Return to D 940.

& **Michelin Local Map:** p444: A2.

🛈 **Info:** Office du tourisme du Crotoy, 1 r. Carnot, 80550 📞03 22 27 05 25. www.tourisme-crotoy.com.

Saint-Valery-sur-Somme★
&See SAINT-VALERY-SUR-SOMME.

👥 Maison de la baie de Somme et de l'Oiseau★
🕐*Open daily 10am–5pm; times vary according to season.* 🕐*Closed 1 Jan and 25 Dec.* 💶6.90€. & 📞03 22 26 93 93. www.maisondeloiseau.com.
A superb collection of **naturalised birds** displayed in reconstructions of their natural habitats (cliffs, sand and mudflats, dunes and gravel pits).

Le Hourdel
The typical Picardy houses of this small fishing harbour stand at the tip of an offshore bar running all the way from Onival. With binoculars, you may spot **harbour seals** on the estuary sands.

Cayeux-sur-Mer
This resort is bordered by a promenade and a 2km-/1mi-long path lined with 400 cabins. The long beach extends from the Hâble d'Ault to the Pointe de Hourde. Footpaths crisscross the woods.

ADDRESSES

🛏 STAY

😐😐 **Logis Auberge de la Dune** – *1352 r. de la Dune, 80550 Le Crotoy.* 📞03 22 25 01 88. www.auberge-de-la-dune.com. *11 rooms. Restaurant*😐😐. A small, friendly country inn with cosy rooms serving regional specialities.

🍽 EAT

😐😐 **La Clé des Champs** – *Pl. des Frères-Caudron, 80120 Favières.* 📞03 22 27 88 00. www.restaurant-lacledeschamps.fr. *Wed–Sun. Closed 2 wks in Jan, 1 wk in Feb, 1 wk in early Sept.* 🅿. This simple country inn serves traditional fare.

Parc du
Marquenterre★★

The Marquenterre nature park is an alluvial plain reclaimed from the sea between the Authie and Somme estuaries. Its name derives from *mer qui entre en terre* ("sea that enters the land"). Made up of briny marshes, salt-pastures and sand dunes, today this reserve is home to 344 species of birds (the continent of Europe has 650 species in all), 265 species of plants and 27 species of mammals living on land and in the sea, including a large colony of seals.

A BIT OF HISTORY

Reclaimed from the sea – The process of reclaiming the land was started in the 12C by monks from **St-Riquier** and **Valloires** who erected the first dikes and attempted to canalise the rivers. Perched on a hill, **Rue**, the future capital of the Marquenterre area, ceased to be an island in the 18C. During the 19C, dikes and beaches were strengthened, which allowed the development of vegetable and cereal growing. In 1923, the industrialist **Henri Jeanson** bought an area of marshland along the coast, which his successors drained and diked using Dutch methods, so that it was eventually possible to grow bulbs. The plans failed and gave rise to the idea of a bird sanctuary.

The birth of the bird sanctuary – The Marquenterre has always been an important habitat for migratory and sedentary birds. To prevent over-hunting, the Hunting Commission created a reserve on this site in 1968 along a 5km/3mi stretch of coastline. The owners of the Marquenterre estate later created a bird sanctuary to allow the public to watch the birds in their natural habitat. In 1994, it was granted "protected nature reserve" status.

👥 THE BIRD SANCTUARY

🕐 *Open daily Jan 10am–5pm, Feb–Mar 10am–6pm, Apr–Sep 10am–7.30pm, Oct–Nov 10am–6pm, Nov–Dec*

- 🛈 **Michelin Local Map:** p444: A2.
- **Info:** Comité Départemental du Tourisme de La Somme, 21 r. Ernest-Cauvin, 80000 Amiens. ✆03 22 71 22 71. www.somme-tourisme.com.
- **Location:** The park is accessible from Abbeville via the D 940, direction Crotoy.
- **Don't Miss:** The pleasure of moving silently across dunes, forests and marshes to observe migratory birds, concealed behind observation blinds.
- 🕐 **Timing:** There are three different paths around the park that will take you from 45min for the shortest one to 2hrs for a more in-depth tour.
- 👥 **Kids:** The red discovery trail is just perfect for kids!

10am–5pm. 🕐*Closed 1 Jan, 25 Dec.* 🌐*10.50€.* ✆*03 22 25 68 99. www.parcdumarquenterre.com.* 🕐 *It is advisable to visit on a rising tide when the birds leave the stretches of the Baie de Somme or during the spring and autumn migration periods.*

The Bird Sanctuary covers 250ha/618 acres on the edge of the reserve and houses numerous species of birds, including the red-beaked shelduck, geese, tern, avocet, gulls, herons, sandpipers and spoonbill. Three marked **trails** and trained guides will help you discover the riches of the park at your own pace.

🚶 **Red discovery trail** – *1.5km/0.9mi.* This introductory tour of the park will offer you a close-up view of the birds that live here permanently: ducks, seagulls, geese and herons. Their calls attract wild birds of the same species. A few familiar mammals can be seen on the way: Henson horses, weasels and

MAKING THE MOST OF THE PARK

WHEN TO GO

The park is interesting whatever the season and there are always different species of birds to watch. **Spring** is the nesting season for many species such as storks, small waders (avocets, oystercatchers, plovers), grey lag geese, shelducks. The herons' nesting place is particularly spectacular since five species of large waders, including spoonbills, nest high in the pine trees. **Summer** is the migrating season for black storks; it is also the time when small waders gather at high tide and when large gatherings of spoonbills, cormorants and egrets can be seen. **Autumn** sees the mass arrival of many species of ducks coming to spend the winter in the park (up to 6 000 birds, some of them arriving from Russia and Finland, can be observed). The park is the most important wader ringing centre in France, and studies on migration are carried out in co-operation with the Natural History Museum in Paris.

WHAT TO TAKE WITH YOU

Solid walking shoes, a wind-waterproof coat, and a pair of binoculars *(also available for hire at the park)*.

RIDING TOURS

Espaces Equestres Henson – *34 ch. des Garennes, 80120 St-Quentin-en-Tourmont. ☏03 22 25 03 06. www.henson.fr.* The Henson horse riding centre organises guided riding tours for all levels of ability, including beginners and children.

hares, as well as amphibians and insects (toads, dragonflies, etc).

Blue observation trail – *4km/2.5mi.* This walk follows a path through the dunes to various observation hides.

Green extended observation trail – *5km/3.1mi.* An additional path shows the reserve from a completely different angle, allowing an in-depth look at its fauna and flora.

EXCURSIONS

L'Asinerie du Marquenterre

La Ferme-la-Bonne-Dame, 80120 Quend. ⏲ Open Apr–mid-Sep Sun–Fri 10am–6pm. ⊚ 5€, farm tours; 30€ half-day hike. ☏06 21 26 02 94. www.asineriedumarquenterre.fr.
Almost nowhere is out of bounds for kids on this farm where chickens, cockerels, ducks, geese, goats, rabbits, pigs and donkeys wander around in total freedom. Watch chicks hatch in the hen house, hold ducklings in your hands, visit the guinea pig corner or pet a lamb, foal or baby rabbit. Events, picnic area and a rest area are also available.

The Henson horse breed

This small robust horse is a cross between a French saddle horse and a Norwegian Fjord pony. Its coat varies from light yellow to brown, and its mane is a mixture of black and gold. This breed was developed in 1978 in a small village of the Baie de Somme area, thanks to the determination of **Doctor Berquin**. Hensons show remarkable endurance; they can remain out in the fields all year round and cover great distances without getting tired. Their docile and affectionate behaviour make them ideal companions for children and long-distance riders. They also fare very well in team competitions and horse shows generally.

Rue★

A sea port in the early Middle Ages, Rue is now an ideal spot for hunting, fishing and hiking.

SIGHTS
Chapelle du Saint-Esprit★

℘03 22 25 69 94. ⊙ Narthex open to visitors. Guided tours (90min) by request (7 days in advance). ⊙Closed Jan 1, Nov 11, Dec 25. ☜ No charge.
The **outside** of this 15C–16C Flamboyant Gothic church housing a miraculous crucifix (washed up on the shore in 1101) is decorated with life-size statues. The **interior★★** features a narthex with high vaulting and a pendentive keystone.

BEFFROI

☜Guided tour (90min) by request (7 days in advance) Tue, Fri and 1st and 3rd Sun of month 11am. ☜3.50€. ℘03 22 25 69 94. The shell of this tower dates from the 15C. The **Musée des Frères Caudron** *(10 pl. Anatole-France; ⊙Mon 2–6pm, Tue–Sat 9.30am–12.30pm, 2–6pm, Jul–Aug Sun 9.30am–12.30pm, by request at the tourist office; ☜3€; ℘03 22 25 69 94; www.ville.rue.fr)* is devoted to aviation.

Chapelle de l'Hospice

⊙Open 10am–7pm; guided tours by students Jul–Aug. ℘03 22 25 69 94.
The chapel's frame, taken from a ship's hull (16C), rests on beams carved with hunting scenes.

▸ **Population:** 3 076
⚲ **Michelin Map:** p444: B2.
ℹ **Info:** 10 pl. Anatole-Gossellin, 80120 Rue. ℘03 22 25 69 94. www.ville-rue.fr. The tourist office runs guided tours in English (1 or 2 sites) for 3.50€, min. 6 pers. In Jul–Aug students guide you around the chapels and the Musée des Frères Caudon (3.50€).
▶ **Location:** Between the Baie de Authie and the Baie de Somme, Rue is accessed via the A 16; at exit 24, take D 32.
👥 **Kids:** The aviation museum is perfect for budding pilots.

Église Saint-Wulfy
Built in neoclassical style in 1820, this church contains rich **furnishings**.

EXCURSIONS
Château d'Arry
▶ *4km/2mi to the E by D 938.*
This residence built by Louis XV in 1761 is visible from the road.

Chapelle du Hamelet
▶ *8km/5mi to the S by D 940 then D 140 to the left; cross Favières.*
This small chapel has a vault shaped like a ship's hull.

Crécy-en-Ponthieu

Crécy is an ideal starting point for a historical tour of the region. King Edward III of England and his army of 3 900 knights, 11 000 longbow men and 5 000 armed Welshmen defeated a French army of 1 200 knights, 6 000 Genoese archers and 20 000 men-at-arms here in 1346.

SIGHTS
Start with the 14C–15C **Saint-Séverin church**, containing paintings thought

▸ **Population:** 1 611
⚲ **Michelin Local Map:** p444: B2.
ℹ **Info:** Office du tourisme, 32 r. Mar. Leclerc-de-Hauteclocque, 80150. ℘03 22 23 93 84. www.crecyenponthieu.com. Check website for guided tours of the battlefield.

to be by pupils of Poussin, before admiring the 13C **Croix de Bourg**, probably built by Edward I in memory of Eleanor of Castille. Next, head to the **Edward III Mill** *(1km/0.5mi north on D 111)* from where the king commanded his army, followed by the **Croix de Bohême** *(on D 56 southeast of Crécy)* where **John the Blind**, King of Bohemia, was killed.

🚗 DRIVING TOUR

29km/18mi round trip. About 1hr.

The **Forêt de Crécy** (4 300ha/10 625 acres) is crossed by ten footpaths and 47km/29mi of bridle paths.

▷ From Crécy, take D 111 to the Le Monument crossroads, then right onto the Forest-Montiers road.

The road runs past some superb beech and oak copses.

▷ Head to Le Poteau de Nouvion, then right onto Le Chevreuil forest road to La Hutte-des-Grands-Hêtres crossroads.

Walks along the Sentier des Deux-Huttes are highly recommended.

▷ Return to Poteau de Nouvion and turn right towards N 1 and Forêt-Montiers.

Francis I's son, Charles, died of plague here at the age of 23.

▷ Take N 1 in a northerly direction.

Bernay-en-Ponthieu still has an old **posting house** opposite the church. The façade of the former **coaching inn** dates from the 15C.

▷ Turn right onto D 938 and return to Crécy-en-Ponthieu.

Vallée de l'Authie★

At the frontier between Artois and Picardy, the Authie valley is famed for its charming villages.

🚗 DRIVING TOUR

AUXI-LE-CHÂTEAU TO FORT MAHON-PLAGE

38km/34mi tour marked in green on the map (⚙ p444). Allow 1hr.

Start with the remains of Auxi castle in Auxi-le-Château, nestled in the hollow of the Authie valley, before exploring the village's 16C **church** and **town hall**. Exit Auxi to the left down D 933 to Maizicourt with its early-18C **château** *(not open to the public)*. The 10ha/24acre **gardens** (⚙ *open May–Oct Mon–Fri 2–6pm, Sat and Sun Jun–Sept;* ⚙ *10€;* ⚙ ⚙ *03 22 32 69 64; www.jardinsdemaizicourt.com)* combine French and English style.

> ⚙ **Michelin Map:** p444: B112; 301 C/H 5/7.
> ⚙ **Info:** Office du tourisme – 1000 av. de la Plage, 80120 Fort-Mahon-Plage. ⚙ 03 22 23 36 00. www.tourisme-fortmahonplage.com.
> ⚙ **Location:** From Gennes-Ivergny to the coast, the river marks the boundary between the Somme and Pas-de-Calais.

👪 Maze for children

Return to Auxi-le-Château then D 224 along the left bank of the Authie to Le Boisle, a traditional basket-weaving village, before heading to Dompierre-sur-Authie with its 15C Flamboyant Saint-Pierre church (⚙ *03 22 23 52 59 by request)*. Cross the Authie to D 119, which passes in front of the monumental gateway to a ruined 12C Premonstrant Abbaye de Dommartin. At Sauichoy return to the south bank by

D 137 to Argoules with its manor, small 16C church and 400-year old lime tree. Continue to the **Abbaye et jardins de Valloires**★★ (&see below) before motoring through Nampont-Saint-Martin where the tides still reached until the 18C. Below the D 485, note the small 15C–16C moated castle. Continue west by D 485 and D32. At Fort-Mahon, before turning left to Fort-Mahon-Plage, continue north (4km/2km) towards the **Baie d'Authie**, the natural frontier between the Somme and Pas-de-Calais. An ideal spot for walking. For walking tours, contact the Fort-Mahon-Plage tourist office.

Fort-Mahon-Plage

This long sandy beach is skirted by a seawall promenade.

Aquaclub de Belle Dune – Promenade du Marquenterre. Open Mid-June–early Sept 11am–7pm; Dec 19–31 2–7pm; late Sept–May 2–7pm, Thu, Sat & Sun 11am–7pm. Times may vary. 13€ (low season 10€). 03 22 23 73 00. A water sports centre with indoor and outdoor pools, slides and golf.

Abbaye et Jardins de
Valloires★★

Located in a remote spot in the the Authie Valley, this abbey is a unique example of 18C Cistercian architecture. The "Jardin des Îles" forms an ocean of greenery dotted with islands; the rose garden is filled with sweet-smelling flowers.

A BIT OF HISTORY

The abbey of Valloires was founded in the 12C by **Guy II**, count of Ponthieu. In 1346, the bodies of knights killed at Crécy were transported here. Ravaged by several fires in the 17C, the abbey was rebuilt in the 18C based on plans by **Raoul Coignard**. The decoration is the work of Austrian sculptor **Simon Pfaff von Pfaffenhoffen** (1715–84). Run by a charity since 1922, the abbey still opens its 18C rooms (&see Addresses).

ADDRESSES

STAY

Chambre d'hôte Le Prieuré – Imp. de l'Église. 62180 Tigny-Noyelle. D 901 Nempont-St-Firmin and D 940 towards Tigny-Noyelle. 03 21 86 04 38. 5 rooms. Restaurant. Four rooms and a suite in a delightful house set in parkland. Picardy fireplace.

EAT

Le Moulin de Maintenay – 25 r. du Moulin. 62870 Maintenay. 3km/1.8mi from l'abbaye de Valloires by D 192. 03 21 90 43 74. Closed Jan–Feb. This restored 12C mill houses a museum and serves light snacks. Try the pancakes!

SHOPPING

Vannerie Candas – 53 rte. Nationale, 80150 Le Boisle. 03 22 29 65 66. www.vannerie-candas.fr. Open 10am–12.30pm, 2–7pm, Sun 2.30–7pm. Rattan and wicker furniture. Great for decorating ideas.

Michelin Map: 301: D-5

Info: www.abbaye-valloires.com and www.jardinsdevalloires.com.

Location: Argoules is in the north of the department of the Somme, 35km/22mi north of Abbevile.

ABBEY★

Guided tour only (1hr). Apr–Nov 10.30am–6.30pm (times may vary). 8€. 03 22 29 62 33. www.abbaye-valloires.com.

A curious mix of austere simplicity and exuberant Baroque and Rococo flamboyance would best describe the architecture at Valloires. Upon entering the vast courtyard, you will note a 16C **dovecote** to your left, and to your right, the **abbot's loggings**. The reception hall, decorated with remarkable **wood pan-**

elling★, portraits and a Louis XIV chandelier, is a fine example of 18C classic elegance, and a complete departure from the sober lines of the **cloister**, with its plain groined vaults. The east wing housed the old chapterhouse and the refectory on the ground floor, while the monk's cells were upstairs. Adjoining the church, the **vestry** boasts finely decorated wood panels by Pfaffenhoffen and paintings by Parrocel.

Church★ – Inside, note the **organ** (1), supported by a **gallery★** carved by Pfaffenhoffen with musical instruments. The statues on each side symbolise Religion. The balustrade and small organ case are decorated with *putti* and cherub musicians. The graceful **wrought-iron gates★★** (2) which enclose the choir are attributed to Jean-Baptiste Veyren (1704–1788) who also provided metal work for Amiens Cathedral. The central part is surmounted by the Valloires arms and Moses' serpent (prefiguration of the Crucifixion), framed by baskets of flowers.

Two angels in gilded lead by Pfaffenhoffen are located around the **high altar** (3). The south transept houses **recumbent effigies** (4) of a count and countess of Ponthieu. In the north transept, you can still see the window through which sick monks could follow services.

Carved religious emblems adorn the **stalls** (5). Those reserved for the abbot and the prior stand on either side of the entrance to the apsidal chapel, which is decorated with wood panels by Pfaffenhoffen.

GARDENS★★

ⓘ Open 11 Mar–30 Apr 10am–6pm; 1 May–31 Aug 10am–7pm; 1 Sept– 11 Nov 10am–6pm. ⌖6.50€.
🕐 1hr30min. ☎03 22 23 53 55. www.jardinsdevalloires.com.

Landscaped by **Gilles Clément** in 1987, this 8ha/19.7acre park contains 5 000 species of plants and trees, mostly from the northern hemisphere and Asia.

Jardin à la française – Laid out in the formal French style, this garden is somewhat reminiscent of Cistercian rigour. Yew trees evoking the pillars of the church surround the "plant cloister".

Jardin des îles – The colours of these island gardens, set on high ground within an English-style park, change with the seasons. The **winter** island displays the subtle hues of maple and birch tree. The **gold** island is home to elder and hazelnut bushes. The **shadow** island contains plants which do not favour sunlight. The **cherry-tree** grove, near the **lilac** island, showcases flowering varieties of prunus. The **silver** island, located next to the **viburnum** island, displays velvety white flowers. Other areas with evocative names include the **crimson-foliage** island, the **autumn** grove, the **butterfly** island and the island of **decorative fruit**, beautiful but sometimes poisonous, as well as the "**bizarretum**" where oddly shaped plants are gathered.

Espace Lamarck – Dedicated to the evolution of species, this garden was named after botanist **Jean-Baptiste Lamarck** (1744–1829) who outlined a

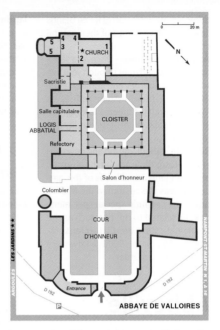

ABBAYE DE VALLOIRES

theory of the evolution of living beings linked to the variations of their natural environment.

♣♣Jardin des 5 sens – Discover a selection of plants and trees through your five senses: strawberries and apples (taste), thorny plants (touch), aspens with leaves that rustle with the breeze (hearing), colourful petunias (sight), jasmine, lily and mint (smell).

Roseraie – About 200 old and new varieties of roses grow among the aromatic plants and medicinal herbs of this garden, as was the custom in the Middle Ages. They include special specimens directly related to the site, such as the emblematic **Rose des Cisterciens** created in 1998 for the 900th anniversary of the Cistercian Order.

Abbeville

Abbeville (pronounced Abb'ville) is the capital of the Ponthieu region and borders the River Somme, about 20km/12mi from the sea.

A BIT OF HISTORY

Abbeville (from the Latin *Abbatis Villa*) originally developed around the country house of the abbot of St-Riquier.
From the 13C to the 15C, the town became the property of the English, the Burgundians and the French as they fought for possession of the Somme Valley. It finally became French under Louis XI in the 15C.

SIGHTS
Collégiale St-Vulfran

1 pl. de l'Amiral-Courbet. ◯ *Open mid-Apr–Sep Tue–Sat 10am–6pm, Sun–Mon 2–6pm; Oct–Apr daily 2–5pm.* ♿ *✆03 22 24 27 92.*
This collegiate church is a fine example of the Flamboyant Gothic style. Its construction began in 1488, but was interrupted in 1539 owing to lack of funds. The neo-Gothic chancel was not completed until the 17C. Note the soaring twin towers, over 55m/180ft high. The Renaissance panels of the **central**

Jardin bleu – In this part of the gardens, trees and shrubs such as the evergreen oak, the indigo or the Hibiscus, add a subtle touch of blue.

Jardin de marais – The wilder Marsh Garden with its artificial canal is reminiscent of the arm of the Authie River which used to flow across the estate.

ADDRESSES

🛏 STAY

🍽 🍽 **Hostellerie de l'Abbaye de Valloires** – *A 16 exit 24 and D 1001 and Vron D 175.* ✆*03 22 29 62 33. www.abbaye-valloires.com.* ♿ 🅿. *18 rooms* 🍽. Located at the very heart of the Cistercian abbey, this hostel is a fine setting for a contemplative retreat.

▸ **Population:** 24 567
👣 **Michelin Local Map:** p445: B3.
🛈 **Info: Office du tourisme** 1 pl. Amiral-Courbet, 80100. ✆03 22 24 27 92. www.abbeville-tourisme.fr.

doorway harmoniously blend with the elegant **façade★**.

Musée Boucher-de-Perthes★

24 r. Gontier Patin. ◯ *Open Wed–Mon, 2–6pm.* ◯ *Closed 1 Jan, 1 May, 14 Jul, 1 Nov, 25 Dec.* 🎫*1€.* ✆*03 22 24 08 49.*
This museum is divided into three buildings: one of the oldest belfries in France (13C), the former Mint (15C), and a modern building at the back. Of particular interest, its **archaeology section** showcases the Boucher de Perthes prehistoric collections (including paleolithic and neolithic tools), a mammoth tooth discovered on Ault beach, and Gallic, Gallo-Roman and Merovingian findings. Medieval sculpture, ceramics and tapestries, paintings from the 16C to the 18C and 17C furniture from Picardy are also on display. Do not miss a sculpture by Camille Claudel (1864–1943).

Église du St-Sépulcre

pl. St-Sépulcre. ◷*Open mid-Apr–Sept 10am–6pm (Sun, Mon 2–6pm); mid-Oct–mid-Apr Sun, Mon 2–5pm; 1–15 Oct 2–5pm.*

After extensive Flamboyant Gothic remodelling in the 19C and partial destruction in 1940, little remains of the original 15C building.

Its outstanding contemporary **stained-glass windows★★** by Alfred Manessier (1911–1993), a major non-figurative painter, represent *The Passion* and the *Resurrection of Christ*.

SURROUNDS
Château de Bagatelle★

133 rte. de Paris. ◷*Open mid-Jul–mid-Aug Wed–Mon, 2–6pm; mid-May–mid-Jul, Sep–mid-Oct Sat & Sun 2–6pm. Interior guided tour only. Self-guided tour of the grounds.* ◠*8€ (combination ticket).*

Restored in 2000, this elegant 'Folly' was originally built c. 1740 as a country home for textile industrialist Abraham Van Robais. In spite of successive additions, it has kept its harmonious proportions and a unity of style.

Interior – Reception rooms: Rococo decoration, 18C furniture, delicately painted panelling. A graceful double staircase with a wrought-iron balustrade was ingeniously adapted to fit the hall.
Grounds★ – French garden adorned with statues and **English-style park**.

The Vimeu Region

Between the River Somme and River Bresle, the Vimeu region of Picardy, gets its name from a tributary of the latter. This farming country also contains several châteaux and villages hidden among the trees. Locksmiths and wrought-ironsmiths have worked here since the 17C.

🚗 **DRIVING TOUR**

FROM ABBEVILLE TO AMIENS

58km/36mi . Approx. 3hr.

▶ Exit Abbeville to SE via D3.

The road runs past Monts de Caubert and along the bottom of the hillside, skirting ponds and meadows.

▶ Turn left along D 901 to Pont-Remy.

Château de Pont-Remy was built on an island near Pont-Remy in the 15C, but it was rebuilt in 1837 in the Gothic Troubadour style.

▶ Return south along the D 901, across the Paris-Calais railway line.

The charming **Église de Liercourt** of Flamboyant Gothic style, with its gable tower has a fine basket-handled doorway.

▶ Continue along D3 to Le Catelet and cross the Somme River to the left.

The great Gothic **church** in the hillside village of **Long** was rebuilt in the 19C, but retained its original 16C spire. The Louis XV **château** (⌁ *not open to the public*) is elegant.

▶ Return over the Somme to Le Catelet then left onto D3 and right into Longpré.

Longpré-les-Corps-Saints derives its name from the relics which the **church** founder, Aléaume de Fontaine, sent from the Crusades. A small British military cemetery is located roughly 1km/0.5mi to the south of the village.

▶ Head SE along D 32.

Hangest-sur-Somme's 12C–16C **church** contains 18C furniture from the Abbaye du Gard. In 1940 the German 7th Tank Division commanded by **Rommel** crossed the River Somme between Hangest and **Condé-Folie** using the only railway bridge that had not been blown up. Condé-Folie is also the site of a major French cemetery.

▶ Take D 3 SE to Picquigny then north to La Chaussée-Tirancourt.

♣▲ Parc Samara★

⏱*Open Mar–Jun and Sept–Nov 9.30am–5.30pm (Sat & Sun 6pm), Jul–Aug 10am–6.30pm.* ⬮*9€.* ✆*03 22 51 82 83. www.samara.fr.* This park (25ha/62acres) lies at the foot of a Celtic settlement overlooking the River Somme. Footpaths lead to an **arboretum**, a **botanical garden** and **reconstructions** of dwellings from the Neolithic, Bronze and Iron Ages.

▶ Cross back to the south of the Somme and left towards Ailly.

The market town of **Ailly-sur-Somme** is overlooked by the sober lines of its modern church whose unusual design comprises a great slanting roof.

▶ Follow the road parallel to the Paris-Calais railway line (D 1235) to Amiens.

Saint-Riquier★

This fortified town sprang up around a powerful Benedictine abbey.

A BIT OF HISTORY

Formerly called Centule, the town owes its name to **Saint Riquier**, evangeliser of the Ponthieu region who died in 645. His body was transported to Centule and a Benedictine monastery was erected around his tomb. In 790, Charlemagne gave it to his son-in-law, the poet **Angilbert**, who extended the abbey.

SIGHTS
Abbey church★★

⏱*Open Apr–Oct Tue–Sat, Sun 10am–12pm & 2–5pm.* ⏱*Closed end Jun–mid-Jul, Nov–Mar.* ⬮*Guided tours.* ⬮*3€.* ♿✆*03 22 28 20 20.* Destroyed and re-built several times, the present, largely Flamboyant (15C–16C) church still retains some of its 13C architectural features.

Exterior – The west front is essentially made up of a large square tower (50m/164ft high) flanked by stair towers and covered in abundant ornamentation.

Interior★★ – The beauty, size and simplicity of the architecture are worth admiring. The two storeys of the large central nave (13m/42ft wide, 24m/78ft high, 96m/314ft long) are separated by a frieze and a balustrade. The chancel still has its 17C decoration and furniture: wrought-iron **gates★**, lectern and monks' stalls, and a marble screen surmounted by a large wooden Cruci-

▶ **Population:** 1 186
◈ **Michelin Local Map:** p444: B2.
🛈 **Info:** Office du tourisme de St-Riquier, Le Beffroi, 80135. ✆03 22 28 91 72. www.saint-riquier.com.

fix by Girardon. The **south transept** is unusual: its end is cut off by the sacristy and the treasury above it which occupy three bays of the cloister gallery. The **Lady Chapel** contains stellar vaulting with ribs running down to historiated corbels (Life of the Virgin Mary); at the entrance, *The Apparition of the Virgin to St Philomena* (1847) is by Ducornet, an armless artist who painted with his feet. In **Saint Angilbert's Chapel**, the five polychrome statues of saints are typical of 16C Picardy sculpture: Veronica, Helen, Benedict, Vigor and Riquier. **Treasury** – This was the abbot's private chapel. The walls of the beautiful early-16C vaulted chamber are decorated with murals from the same period. The treasury contains a 12C Byzantine Crucifix, 13C reliquaries, and a 16C hand-warmer.

Abbey buildings

Rebuilt in the 17C, the abbey now houses the **Musée départemental de la Vie rurale en Picardie**, entirely dedicated to rural life and crafts in Picardy. ⏱*Open Jul-Aug 10am–6pm; May–Jun & Sep 10am–noon, 2–6pm; mid-Mar–Apr & Oct-Nov 2–6pm, Sat–Sun 10am–noon, 2–6pm.* ✆*03 22 28 20 20.*

Airaines

Ancestral home of the dukes of Luynes, whose ruined château can still be seen on the hillside, this small industrial town was heavily damaged during the Battle of the Somme in June 1940. General Leclerc was born and lived a few miles south of Airaines.

SIGHTS
Notre-Dame church and priory

This former chapel (12C and 13C) of a Cluniac priory attached to Saint-Martin-des-Champs in Paris has a clean, simple Romanesque façade. To the left of the entrance, note the Romanesque immersion **baptismal font**. The sides of the font are sculpted with catechumens, one of which is being tempted by the devil in the form of a dragon.The priory building (16C) houses a **Centre d'art et de culture** exhibition centre.

EXCURSIONS
Château-Fort de Rambures★

🕐*Open Jan–mid-Feb Sun 2.30–4pm; Feb holidays Thu–Tue 2–5pm; Mar Thu–Tue 2–6pm; Apr–mid-Jul Thu–Tue 10am–noon, 2–6pm; mid-Jul–Aug Thu–Tue 10am–6pm; late Aug–Sept Thu–Tue 10am–noon, 2–6pm; Oct Thu–Tue 2–6pm; Nov–Dec Sun 2.30–4pm.*
Visit of the château by guided tour only (1hr). 🕐*Closed 1 Jan, 25 Dec.* ✆*7€ (castle and grounds), 5.50€ (grounds only).* ✆*03 22 25 10 93. www.chateaufort-rambures.com.*
Rambures Castle is a fine example of 15C military architecture. During the Hundred Years War, it played a significant role as a French enclave in the middle of the English-occupied territories and came to be called "the key to the Vimeu," a strategic region between Picardy and Normandy.
E**xterior** – In the 18C, Rambures was converted into a country residence, and the courtyard façade pierced with huge windows. However, with its enormous machicolated round towers and rounded curtain walls, its deep moat

⚙ **Michelin Map:** p444: B3; 301 E8.

🗊 **Info:** Syndicat d'initiatives – Pl. du 53e, RICMS. 80270 Airaines. ✆03 22 29 34 07.

◖ **Location:** Halfway between Abbeville and Amiens, Airaines rises up from the banks of the river of the same name, which runs into the Somme. The D901 crosses the town from N to S and the D936 from E to W.

and tall watchtower, and its amazing brick walls (3–7m/10–23ft thick), the old fortress is still a powerful example of medieval architecture.
Interior –For many of the rooms, the only source of daylight is still through loopholes. The alterations begun in the 18C did allow for some level of comfort and the reception rooms are decorated with woodwork and marble chimney-pieces. Don't miss the 15C watch-path; the library-billiards room with its collection of portraits; the kitchen, located in the old guard-room above the dungeons; and the cellars, used to shelter the villagers during invasions.

Park and gardens

Designed in the 18C, Rambures' English-style park (40ha/99acres) is planted with some rare trees. The **rose garden** (with 400 different species), the **garden of simples**, and the **fern collection** are a real treat.

Musée de la Verrerie at Blangy-sur-Bresle

▶*7km/4km to SW by D 180 then D 928. Manoir de la Fontaine.* 🕐*Open mid-Mar–mid-Nov Wed–Fri 10am–noon, 2–6pm, Sat, Sun, Mon 2–6pm. Guided tours (45min, 4 pers min) 10.30am, 2.30pm, 3.30pm and 4.30pm.* ✆*4.70€ (6yrs 1.90€).* ✆*02 35 94 44 79.*
Retrace the history of glassmaking and perfume bottle design in this museum housed in a 16C manor house.

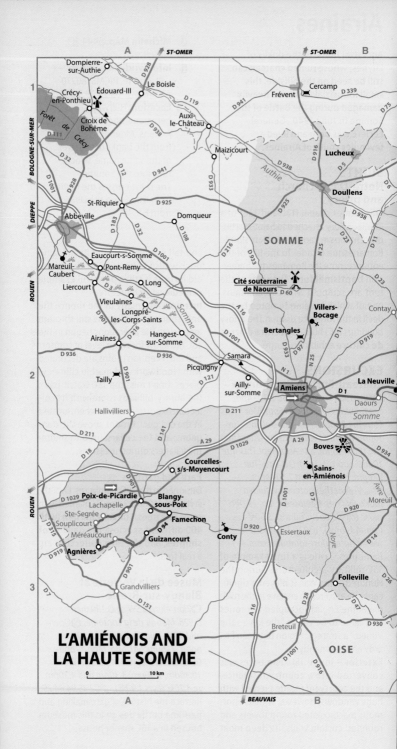

L'AMIÉNOIS AND
LA HAUTE SOMME

0   10 km

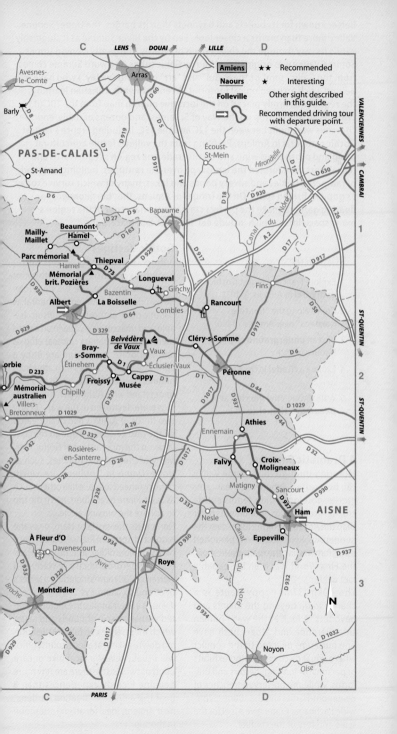

Better known for its bullets and bayonets than its barges, the Upper Somme Valley more than merits a closer look. Fed by the River Somme as it sluggishly winds its way through the chalky plain of Picardy, the gently sloping Upper Somme Valley was originally settled by Gallic tribes (the word Somme comes from the Gallic "som" or "peaceful" and "arr" meaning "valley") who have left behind a rich archaeological footprint. A centre of early Christian learning, the region was firmly placed on the lucrative pilgrim map from the 10C (it remains an official stop on the Way of St James) and dozens of richly-endowed churches were built between the 12C and the 15C, including France's largest Gothic cathedral in Amiens. Profiting from the valley's fertile agricultural basin and prosperous wine and textile trade, the region's feudal lords and rich abbots transformed the landscape over the centuries, building a myriad of ramparts, castles and silvery ponds and lakes, many of which survive today as popular fishing spots. On the fringes of Amiens, the "hortillonages" or floating gardens make the perfect start to a culinary tour of the region's many specialities, which include eel, foie gras and macaroons.

Highlights

1 Explore France's biggest **Gothic cathedral** in Amiens (p463)

2 Cruise along the **"floating gardens"** near Amiens (p466)

3 Visit an **underground city** in Naours (p472)

4 Explore a **citadel** in Doullens (p472)

5 Walk through the trenches at **Beaumont-Hamel** (p475)

A Dramatic Setting

Motoring through the Somme Valley can be a surreal experience: neat cemeteries no bigger than tennis courts crop up in corn fields, monuments taller than the Arc de Triomphe loom over the hedgerows, and spent shells ploughed up by up farmers line the roadside. In short, the First World War is an inescapable fact of life.

The 60km/37mi Poppy Route is a chance to go beyond the bullets and bayonets to look at the war's human side. Péronne and Albert both have fine museums devoted to the conflict where you'll discover moving exhibits of personal belongings, letters and uniforms, while the preserved trenches of Beaumont-Hamel and the 100m-/328ft-wide Lochnagar Crater give a feel for the scale and fury of the conflict.

Gothic Vestiges

Before 1914, this region was better known as a centre for Flamboyant Gothic architecture. The 19C poet John Ruskin described Amiens cathedral as "Gothic pure, authoritative, unsurpassable, and unaccusable ..." Seen on a summer evening, when its colossal effigies and elaborate tympanum are lit by a light show that recreates the cathedral's original painted façade, you'll begin to understand why. Although many buildings were destroyed in the war – nearly two thirds of Amiens had disappeared by the end of 1945 – enough remains for even the most ardent of Gothic fans. Many of the smaller churches, such as Notre-Dame in Doullens are worth booking ahead to see, while others, such as Saint-Pierre near Albert, merit the trip to admire the outside alone.

Don't miss the castle at Ham, once the biggest in northern France, the Art Deco belfry of Montdidier, and the unforgettable underground city of Naours, a warren of 300 rooms including a baker's oven and six chimneys.

If you're a keen angler, the region is dotted with a mosaic of ponds and lakes, which themselves can take a little hunting down. Asking at a local tourist office will usually reveal a local pike or carp pond or two. Lastly, there are few more genuine Picardy experiences than a boat trip along the "floating gardens" near Amiens, ideal for an idle afternoon in the sun.

Amiens★★

The historic capital of Picardy, Amiens is home to France's largest Gothic cathedral. From the canals of St-Leu in the north to the narrow medieval streets of rue Bélu and the post-war city centre, Amiens is a must for architectural explorers.

A BIT OF HISTORY

In Gallo-Roman times Amiens was the capital of a Belgian tribe, the Ambiani. In the 4C the town was converted to Christianity by Firmin and his companions. When the town's Romanesque church was destroyed by fire in 1218, Bishop Evrard de Fouilloy and the people of Amiens decided to build a replacement worthy of the "head of John the Baptist," a precious albeit fragmentary relic brought back in 1206 from the fourth crusade by Wallon de Sarton, canon of Picquigny.

Natural target – Standing at the bridgehead of the valleys of the River Somme and River Aisne -major obstacles to invaders from the north – Amiens is no stranger to war. In 1918, the city was attacked by German General Ludendorff, who bombarded its streets with 12 000 shells. It was next set ablaze in 1940 and in 1944 its prison was the target of an aerial attack aimed at releasing its Resistance prisoners.

Local heroes – After playing an important role in the life of **Saint Martin**, patron saint of France, the city has also set the scene for famous writers such as **Choderlos de Laclos** (1741–1803), **Jules Verne** (1828–1905), **Paul Bourget** (1852–1925), **Roland Dorgelès** (1885–1973) and the physicist **Edouard Branly** (1844–1940).

CATHÉDRALE NOTRE-DAME★★★

🕐 *Open daily Apr–Sept 8.30am–6.15pm; Oct–Mar 8.30am–5.15pm.* 🚶 *Guided tours.* ✆5.50€. ☎03 22 71 60 50.

A UNESCO World Heritage Site, Amiens Cathedral is the largest Gothic building in France (145m/475ft long with

▶ **Population:** 136 000

⏱ **Michelin Map:** p460: B2.

ℹ **Info:** Office de tourisme d'Amiens Métropole. 40 pl. Notre-Dame, 80000. ✆03 22 71 60 50. www.amiens-tourisme.com.

▷ **Location:** The majority of the city's attractions sit on the south bank of the Somme River, some clustered around the cathedral, others a little farther west and southwest. Consider taking an art and history tour for an overview of the city. Good shopping areas are rue du Hocquet and place du Don. Cross the River Somme to explore the Quartier St-Leu.

ℙ **Parking:** There are several parking areas near the cathedral and on the perimeter roads enclosing the cathedral district.

🕭 **Don't Miss:** The cathedral, the Picardy Museum, the Hortillonnages (gardens), the flea market.

🕐 **Timing:** Allow 1–2hrs to see the cathedral. The walking tour requires 1hr, as does the Picardy Museum.

👪 **Kids:** The house of Jules Vernes; the Christmas market

⏱ **Also See:** Corbie, the Parc Samara, and the Cité souterraine de Naours.

vaults 42.5m/139ft high). Its design was entrusted to **Robert de Luzarches** who was succeeded by Thomas de Cormont and his son Renaud. The cathedral was begun in 1220 and the speed with which it was built explains the remarkable unity of style.

Restored by Viollet-le-Duc in the 19C, the cathedral was unscathed by the bombing of the city in 1944.

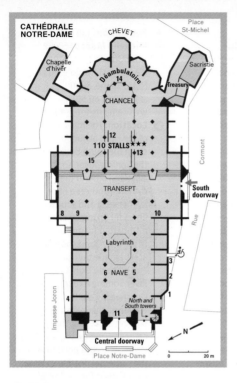

CATHÉDRALE NOTRE-DAME

On the north side, note the statue of Charles V (**4**) on the 14th buttress supporting the tower.

Go round the cathedral to the right, passing a giant St Christopher (**1**), an Annunciation (**2**) and, between the 3rd and 4th chapels, a pair of woad merchants with their sack (**3**).

▷ Follow r. Cormont to place St-Michel.

Admire the view of the **east end** with its pierced flying buttresses and the soaring lead-covered chestnut **spire** (112.70m/370ft high).

▷ Retrace your steps and enter the cathedral through the south doorway.

The **south doorway**, known as the Golden Virgin Doorway because of the statue which used to adorn the pier, is dedicated to St Honoré who was bishop of Amiens. Visitors can mount the 307 steps to the top of the **north tower** *(via the South tower and Rose gallery)*.

Exterior

The superbly restored **west front** has three doorways; the **Kings' Gallery** supporting colossal effigies; the great Flamboyant rose-window (16C) framed by twinned open bays; and the small **Bell-ringers' Gallery** topped by light arcading between the towers.

The **central doorway** is framed by the Wise and Foolish Virgins who, together with the Apostles and the Prophets on the piers, escort from a respectable distance the famous **Beau Dieu**, a noble and serene Christ. The tympanum portrays the Last Judgment presided over by a more archaic and severe God. The **left doorway** is dedicated to **St Firmin**, the evangelist of Amiens. The quatrefoils on the base enclose representations of a **Calendar** symbolised by the signs of the Zodiac and the Labours of the Months.

▷ Walk along impasse Voron.

Interior

The cathedral's **nave** is the highest in France, reaching 42.50m/139ft. Its elevation consists of exceptionally high arcades surmounted by a band of detailed foliage, a blind triforium and a clerestory; 13C recumbent **bronze effigies★** of the cathedral's founding bishops lie in the third bay: Evrard de Fouilloy (**5**) and Geoffroy d'Eu (**6**); the latter faces towards St-Saulve Chapel which contains a figure of Christ in a long gold robe.

In the center of the nave, note the striking black and white pattern of the **labyrinth**, a 19C replica of the original, built in 1288 and damaged during the French Revolution.

The **north transept** is adorned with a 14C rose-window with star-shaped central tracery. The font (**8**), to the left of the door, dates from 1180 and was originally used to wash the dead. On the west wall, a painted sculpture in four parts represents Christ and the money lenders in the Temple (**9**) (1520). The **south transept**, which is illuminated through a Flamboyant rose-window, bears on its west wall four scenes in relief (**10**) portraying the conversion of the magician Hermogene by St James the Great (1511).

The perspective back down the nave reveals its elegance and the boldness of the organ loft supporting the **great organ** (**11**) (1442) with its delicate golden arabesques.

The chancel is enclosed within a beautiful 18C choir screen, wrought by Jean Veyren. Stunning works of art, the 110 Flamboyant **stalls★★★** (**12**) were created between 1508 and 1519 by master cabinet-makers Arnould Boulin, Antoine Avernier and Alexandre Huet. They are arranged in two rows and surmounted by wooden tracery, and are presided over by two master-stalls destined for the king and the dean of the chapter. Over 4 000 figures evoke Genesis and Exodus, the life of the Virgin Mary, and scenes of 16C life in Amiens.

In the **ambulatory** on the right, on the choir screen above two recumbent effigies, eight remarkable carved and coloured stone groups (1488) under delicate Gothic canopies evoke the life of **St Firmin** (**13**), his martyrdom and his exhumation by St Saul three centuries later. Behind the main altar, facing the central chapel containing a 19C gilded statue of the Virgin Mary, are the tombs of Cardinal de la Grange (1402) and Canon Guislan Lucas, famous for its **Weeping Angel** (**14**), carved by Nicolas Blasset in 1628 (the angel became a popular postcard for allied soldiers during World War I).

The choir screen north of the chancel bears scenes from the **life of St John** (**15**) (1531) *(read from right to left)*.

WALKING TOUR

Start near the cathedral and cross the river via the Dodane bridge.

Quartier St-Leu★

Several arms of the Somme flow through this district, which has undergone wide-scale renovation in an effort to preserve its special charm. Craft and antique shops, trendy cafés and restaurants now occupy the spaces where tanners, millers, weavers and dyers once worked. From the bridge known as **Pont de la Dodane**, there is a fine **view** of the cathedral. Rue Bélu, rue des Majots, rue Motte and rue d'Engoulvent are lined with small colourful half-timbered houses. Don't miss the **église-halle St-Leu**, a 15C hall-church with three aisles and a 16C Flamboyant Gothic bell-tower, the nearby **Théâtre des Marionnettes** or Jean-Pierre Facquier's puppet workshop *(see Addresses)*. if you have time, take a spin in a horse-drawn carriage or a boat ride from Saint-Leu (contact the tourist office)

▶ Return to pl. Notre-Dame and walk along the south side of the cathedral, best viewed from the pedestrian street leading to pl. Aguesseau.

Quartier St-Leu

© SommeTourisme-AB/FLeonardi

On the corner of the law courts, a low-relief sculpture by J. Samson (1830) depicts the story of St Martin's Cloak.

Maison du Sagittaire et Logis du Roi

The **Sagittarius House** (1593), with its Renaissance front, owes its name to the sign of the Zodiac embellishing its two arches. The adjacent **King's Lodging** (1565), featuring a pointed-arch door decorated with a Virgin with a Rose, is the seat of the **Rosati** of Picardy.

Old Theatre

The Louis XVI façade was designed by Rousseau in 1780; three large windows are framed by low-relief sculptures of garlands, medallions, muses and lyres.

Bailliage

The restored front is all that remains of the bailiff's residence built under François I in 1541, presenting mullioned windows, Flamboyant gables and Renaissance medallions. On the right, note the "fool" wearing a hood with bells.

Bell-tower

Guided tours. ✆03 22 22 58 97.
Located on place au Fil, this enormous bell-tower consists of a square 15C base and an 18C belfry surmounted by a dome. Looking down rue Chapeaux-des-Violettes, note the 15C **Église St-Germain**, built in Flamboyant Gothic style, with its leaning tower. On your way back to the cathedral, stop by the Dewailly clock and the statue of *Marie sans chemise*, a nymph symbolising spring by Albert Roze (1861–1952).

👥 Hortillonnages★

Maison des Hortillonnages, 54 bd. Beauvillé. ⓞ*Guided boat tours (45min) Apr–Oct daily 2pm.* ⬤*5.70€.*
ⓞ*Closed 1 Jan.* ✆*03 22 92 12 18. www.hortillonnages-amiens.fr.*
Emblematic of Amiens, these "floating gardens" are exclusively accessible by boat. They are small vegetable gardens known as *aires* which have been cultivated since the Middle Ages by market gardeners or *hortillons* (from the Latin *hortus* meaning garden) who supplied the local population with fruits and vegetables. The gardens stretch over an area of 300ha/740 acres amid a network of canals or *rieux* fed by the many arms of the River Somme and River Arve.

ADDITIONAL SIGHTS
Musée de Picardie★★

48 r. de la République. ⓞ*Open Tue, Fri–Sat 10am–noon, 2–6pm, Wed 2–6pm, Thu 10am–noon, 2–9pm, Sun 2–7pm.*
ⓞ *Closed, 1 Jan, 1 and 8 May, 14 Jul, 1 Nov, 25 Dec.* ⬤*5€ (no charge 1st Sun in the month).* ♿✆*03 22 97 14 00.*
The museum's significant collections of archaeology, medieval art and fine arts are housed in a Napoleon III building constructed between 1855 and 1867.

Archaeology – *Lower level.* The collection is dedicated to regional prehistory and protohistory, including one of Belgian Gaul's most important cities **Samarobriva** (Amiens).

Medieval Art – *Ground level.* This remarkable collection showcases 9C–13Cpieces of **religious statuary** which formerly adorned Amiens cathedral and local churches and abbeys. It also presents 14C religious statues and finely ciseled medieval pieces made of ivory, enamel or silver. Finally, 15C and 16C examples of votive sculpture and funerary statuary from Picardy give an insight into the late Gothic period.

Fine Arts – *Ground and upper levels.* The museum's **sculpture** collection includes 17C and 18C classic and baroque pieces, as well 19C Romantic and Realist works. Note *Christ Triumphant* by Nicolas Blasset (1600–1659) and the *Head of an Old Woman from Picardy* from another local artist Albert Roze (1861–1952).
Painting definitely holds a place of choice in this museum. The Grand Salon contains huge historical paintings (18C–19C) by Van Loo and Vernet. Enormous murals by **Puvis de Chavannes** (1824–1898) adorn the main stairway and first-floor rooms.

The Notre-Dame du Puy Gallery and part of the following room house the works of art of the **Confrérie du Puy Notre-Dame d'Amiens**. Spot François I in the Renaissance panel (1518) entitled *Au juste poids, véritable balance* ("For just weight, true scales"), and Henri IV under the Gothic canopy bearing the poem entitled *Terre d'où prit la vérité naissance* ("Land where Truth was born") (1601).

The Nieuwerkerke Gallery presents 17C paintings from the Spanish School (Ribera and El Greco), the Dutch School (Frans Hals) and the French School (Simon Vouet).

The following rooms are devoted to 18C French painting including works by Oudry, Chardin, Fragonard and Quentin de La Tour, as well as the nine *Chasses en pays étrangers* ("Hunts in Foreign Lands") by Parrocel, Pater, Boucher, Lancret, Van Loo and De Troy for Louis XV's small apartments at Versailles. Italian masters (Guardi, Tiepolo) express the charm of Venetian painting.

The Charles-Dufour gallery is dedicated to 19C French landscape painters and in particular to the Barbizon School (Millet, Isabey, Corot, Rousseau). Modern art is represented by Balthus, Masson, Fautrier, Dubuffet, Picasso and Picabia.

Maison de Jules Verne

2 r. Charles Dubois. Open Mid-Apr–mid-Oct Mon, Wed–Fri 10am–12.30pm, 2–6.30pm, Sat–Sun 11am–6.30pm. Mid-Oct–mid-Apr (except Tue) 10am–12.30pm, 2–6pm, Sat–Sun, 2–6pm. Closed 1 Jan, 1 May, 25 Dec. 7.50€. 03 22 45 45 75.

Jules Verne (1828–1905) was born in Nantes but spent much of his life in Amiens where he wrote masterpieces such as *Around the World in Eighty Days* and *Michel Strogoff*. He played an active part in local life and was a town councillor. With more than 20 000 documents and various personal effects, this house, where he lived from 1882 to 1900, provides information about the writer and his works. Don't miss the smallest room in the house, a replica of his study where he used to write his novels.

Jardin archéologique de St-Acheul

10 r. Raymond Gourdain. Open daily 9am–12.30pm, 2–7pm. Closed 1 Jan, 25 Dec. No charge but guided tour by reservation. 03 22 97 10 61.

In 1859, the geologist Albert Gaudry performed the first excavations in the Friville quarry, near the old cemetery of St-Acheul, to the east of the town. SInce 1872, it has given its name to a Lower Palaeolithic civilisation, the **Acheulian**, who were the first group of humans to use **biface** stone tools. A long alleyway, the **Fil du temps** (time line) takes you on an evolutionary journey back in time and space to 450 000 BC and leads to the entrance of the garden where a **geological cross section** shows the successive layers of sediment accumulated since that time.

A footbridge leads to an **observation tower** (19m/62ft) revealing a **panoramic view** of the site, the Somme Valley and Amiens.

Parc zoologique d'Amiens

Allé du zoo, Esplanade de la Hotoie. Open Mon–Sat Apr–Sept 10am–6pm (Sun and holidays 10am–7pm). Oct–Mar Wed, Sat, Sun and holidays 2–5pm. Closed 1 Jan, 24–25 and 31 Dec. 5.80€/3.80€. 03 22 69 61 12. www.amiens.com/zoo.

Bordering the Promenade de la Hotoie (18C) and its lake, the zoo is committed

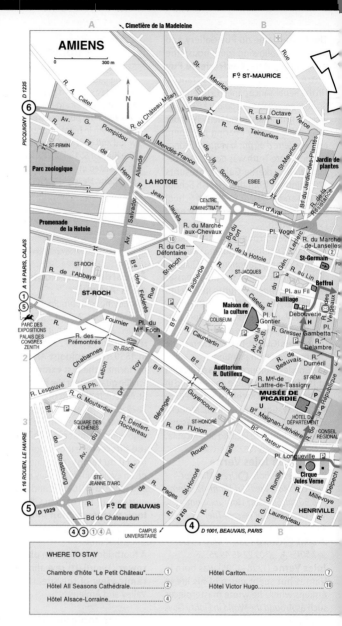

AMIENS

to protecting endangered species such as the red panda and maned wolf.

🚗 DRIVING TOURS

A natural geographical barrier, the **Somme River** gave its name to two major battles, one in 1916, the other in 1940. Its source is upstream of St-Quentin, at an altitude of 97m/318ft; from there it flows 245km/152mi westward. The gentleness of this descent, together with the absorbent quality of the peat through which the river meanders, largely explains the lazy pace of its

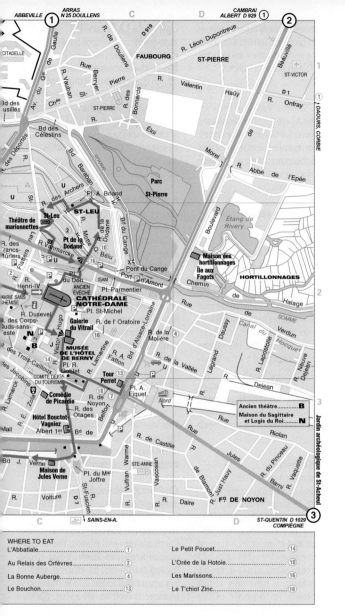

WHERE TO EAT

waters. which have formed the wide, lush **Somme Valley** in Picardy's chalky plateau.

FROM AMIENS TO PÉRONNE

63km/38mi. About 1h 30min.

◗ Take D 1 (east) out of Amiens.

Views over Amiens, dominated by its world-famous cathedral and by the 26-storeys of the **Perret Tower**, a symbol of the city's reconstruction after WW II.

◗ At Daours, turn left at the traffic lights then right towards La Neuville.

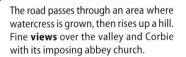

The road passes through an area where watercress is grown, then rises up a hill. Fine **views** over the valley and Corbie with its imposing abbey church.

Corbie

Lying in the Somme Valley, at the confluence of the Ancre River. It developed around a powerful Benedictine abbey, renowned for its library and scriptorium, whose influence spread across Europe and which was granted the rare privilege of minting coins.

Musée des Amis du vieux Corbie

◔*Open Tue–Sat mid-Jun–mid-Sept 2.30–5.30pm. Guided tour (1hr) by reservation.* ✆*03 22 96 43 37.*
Essentially dedicated to the history of the abbey, the museum contains pieces from the Merovingian (7C), Carolingian (8C), Viking (9C–10C) and Romanesque (11C–13C) periods: statues and various stone carvings, pottery, seals, coins etc. Also note a relief map of the 1636 **siege of Corbie** (then occupied by the Spanish) by the army of Louis XIII.
From the vast place de la République, enter the 18C **monumental gateway** to the abbey. The cloisters and convent buildings were razed during the French Revolution.

Abbatiale St-Pierre

👓*2.50€ (guided tours), 0.50€ (unaccompanied). Call tourist office* ✆*03 22 96 95 76 for more details.*
The construction of the former abbey church lasted from the 16C to the 18C. The transept and chancel, in a state of collapse, were demolished in 1815. The **interior**, which used to be 117m/384ft long, is now only about 36m/118ft long. To the right of the altar, the sculpture of **Saint Bathild** is an example of majestic 14C statuary. On a pillar in the north aisle is a 13C head of **St Peter**.

Chapelle Ste-Colette

The chapel was built in 1959 on the site of the house in which St Colette was born and contains a 16C statue of the saint kneeling.

Église de La Neuville

2km/1mi W, on the right bank of the River Ancre.
Above the doorway of the early-16C church is a large, interesting **high-relief carving**★ showing Christ's entry into Jerusalem on Palm Sunday. The relief is remarkable for its clarity and wealth of detail: spectators are perched in the trees and, in the background, a miller wearing a cotton bonnet stands at the window of his mill.

Australian Memorial

3km/2mi S. Leave Corbie by D 1 (toward Amiens) and in Fouilloy, turn left onto D 23 toward Villers-Bretonneux.
In spring 1918, the hills around **Villers-Bretonneux** were at the centre of a fierce battle between the Germans and the Australians, following the German offensive into Picardy. More than 10 000 Australian men lost their lives. A memorial and a cemetery recall their sacrifice. Extended **views** over the Somme River and Amiens.

▶ From Corbie to Chipilly, follow the banks of the Somme River.

This stretch of the tour winds around the region's lakes and ponds Don't miss the **views** over the towers of Corbie on the horizon at certain bends in the road.

▶ From Etinehem, follow D 1F to Bray-sur-Somme.

Spanning the Somme River, the Somme Canal and several ponds, the ancient port of **Bray-sur-Somme** has strong fishing traditions. Its **church**, with its big square bell tower and Romanesque chancel, is well worth a visit. ◔*Open Mon–Tue, Thu–Sat 9.30am–5pm (Wed and Sun afternoon only).* ◀*Guided tours available by request.* ✆*03 22 76 11 38.*

▶ Take D 329 (south) until you reach Froissy on the Somme Canal.

From the hamlet of **Froissy**, visitors can ride to Dompierre *(7km/4.3mi)* on board the **P'tit train de la Haute Somme** which used to supply the trenches during the World War I.

Froissy's old covered market houses the 👥**Musée des Chemins de fer militaires et industriels** (🕐*for the museum's opening hours and train timetable (Jul–Aug Tue–Sat; May–mid-Jul and Sept Sun) check www.appeva.org or call ☏03 22 83 11 89;* 🎟*9.80€ (museum and train ride)*, which showcases an interesting collection of renovated locomotives and wagons.

▶ Drive back to Bray-sur-Somme, then take D 1 towards Cappy.

A former river port, **Cappy** is now an attractive marina. The 12C Romanesque **Église St-Nicolas**, remodelled in the 16C, has a massive square tower surmounted by a turreted steeple.

▶ Take the road to Éclusier-Vaux, on your left. It crosses the Somme River and the village of Vaux, then winds up towards the plateau.

Belvédère de Vaux★ is a good place to enjoy the **panorama★** over the River Curlu and the red rooftops of the hamlet of Vaux. On a clear day, you can see Péronne in the distance.

▶ Upon entering the village of Maricourt, turn right onto D 938.

As you drive along the plateau, admire the valley below. The road crosses the motorway, passing the **Étangs de la Haute-Somme** near **Cléry**, then the Canal du Nord.

Péronne

An old fortified town of the Upper Somme Valley that stretches between fish-filled ponds and "hardines", cultivated marshlands similar to Amiens' famous water gardens. It was marked by centuries of territorial power struggles, then largely destroyed by German troops during WW I. Today, the area around Péronne has become popular for eel, carp and pike fishing, as reflected in the local gastronomy which includes specialities such as smoked eel, stuffed pike and Colvert beer.

In 1468, **Charles the Bold** (Duke of Burgundy) imprisoned by his rival **Louis XI** (King of France) for a few days in Péronne, then under Burgundian control. Louis, who had supported the uprising of the town of **Liège** against Charles, was forced to sign a humiliating treaty in which he agreed to help quell the revolt in Liège. Louis XI, who never forgot this affront, ended up bringing Péronne under French control after Charles the Bold's death in 1477.

In 1536, the Spanish army of **Charles V** undertook the siege of Péronne, but was forced to retire after the town put up a valiant fight, galvanised by its heroine, **Marie Fouré**. A procession is organised every year in July to commemorate the event. In 1870, the town was besieged by the **Prussians** who bombarded the town for 13 days. During **World War I**, Péronne was occupied by the Germans and virtually destroyed.

Historial de la Grande Guerre▲▲

pl. André-Oudinot. 🕐*Open daily Apr–Nov 10am–6pm; Dec–Mar 9.30am–5pm.* 🕐*Closed mid-Dec–28 Feb.* 🎟*7.50€.* ♿ ☏*03 22 83 14 18. www.historial.org.*

Entered through a 13C **castle**, the Museum of the Great War is housed in a Le Corbusier-inspired structure (Henri-Edouard Ciriani, 1992) built on stilts by a pond. It offers an international view of a conflict which involved combatants and civilians from over 20 nations and provides keys for understanding the roots of the war. A series of 50 etchings by German artist Otto Dix invites visitors to reflect on the horror of war. Displayed in shallow **marble pits** evoking the trenches, weapons, military gear and personal belongings illustrate life on the front. Video monitors and a 30-minute film entitled *En Somme* also feature archival footage of the period.

Hôtel de Ville

Place du Cdt-Daudré. ◷*Open Tue–Fri 2–5.30pm, Sat 9am–noon, 2–4.30pm.* ◷*Closed public holidays.* ℘*03 22 73 31 10. www.ville-peronne.fr.*

Behind the distinctive Neo-Renaissance façade of the town hall (looted and destroyed during WWI, then rebuilt in the 1920s), stands the **Musée Alfred-Danicourt**. Particularly renowned for its collection of **Gallic coins**, it also exhibits several prehistoric tools as well as Greco-Roman, Merovingian and Carolingians artefacts.

Porte de Bretagne

Off r. St-Sauveur.

Marking the frontier between the kingdom of France and Flanders, this gateway (1602) was one of two entrances giving access through the town walls (destroyed before World War I). It is now a free-standing brick pavilion with a slate roof, adorned with the emblem of Péronne. Beyond the moat, walk through the gate of the demi-lune and follow the old brick **ramparts** with stone courses (16–17C) for an attractive **view** over the lakes.

EXCURSIONS
Cité souterraine de Naours★

◗ *20km/12mi N by N25.* ◷*Open May–Aug 10am–6.30pm; Feb–Apr, Sept–Nov 10am–noon, 2–5pm.* ◷*Closed mid-Dec–mid-Jan.* ⊚*11€. Audioguides in English.* ℘*03 22 93 71 78. www.grottesdenaours.com.*

Large enough to accommodate 3 000 people and their cattle, the ancient underground city of Naours has 2km/1mi of streets, several town squares, 300 rooms, three chapels, stables and a bakery. These "muches" or shelters, found across Picardy, are carved out of the soft limestone plateau and date back to the 9C Norman invasions. They were used frequently during the Wars of Religion and the Hundred Years War.

Doullens

◗ *30km/18mi N by N25.* ◱*Le Belfroi, r. du Bourg, 80600 Doullens.* ℘*03 22 32 54 52. www.doullens-tourisme.com.*

Straddling the Authie river, this peaceful town lined with typical brick houses with raised dormer windows is dominated by a 16C **citadel** ringed by a pleasant moat walk graced with five intact demi-lunes. Maréchal Foch was made Supreme Allied Commander in 1918 in the **town hall**, which commemorates the event with a small exhibition. Housed in the former Dames de Louvencourt convent, the **Musée Lombart** has an interesting collection of local archaeological finds.

Lucheux

◗ *37km/18mi N by N25 then D5.*

Once home to the powerful Counts of Saint-Pol, this pleasant village nestled in a leafy valley is home to a ruined castle (12–16C). Entered via two round pepper-box towers, the castle has a 13C hall with twin bays topped by triangular arches and a curious three-headed console, adjacent to a mound with a square Romanesque keep. The town's **belfry** – the former town gate – dates from the 12C to 14C. Don't miss the historiated capitals in the 12C church.

Église de Sains-en-Amiénois

◗ *8km/5mi to the south by D 7.*
◗ *Guided tour Sat Easter–early Nov, 10am–noon.* ⊚ *No charge.* ℘*03 22 09 50 63.*

Admire the recumbent statues of 4C martyrs St Fuscien and his companions below a bas-relief of their beheading.

Boves

◗ *9km/5mi SE by D 116.*

This small village, the seat of a marquisate from 1630, is overlooked by the **ruins** of a 12C castle. Enter the grassy farmyard dominated by a mound with two imposing keep walls and climb to the top for **views** over the lakes of Fouencamps and Amiens.

Château de Bertangles

◗ *10km/6mi to the N by N25.*
◷*Guided tour (45min) by request (7 days in advance) mid-Jul–mid-Aug 5.30pm (every 30min).* ⊚ *4€. Allow 1hr.* ♿ ℘*03 22 93 68 36. www.chateaubertangles.com.*

Sitting at the centre of the invasion route, Bertangles has been destroyed many times. The Regency château was built by Louis-Joseph de Clermont-Tonnerre (1730–1734).

The **gate of honour**★, dedicated to hunting, is by Jean Veyren, an ironsmith of Corbie. Behind the gate, the main court affords views over five arc-shaped gardens around a lawn. The façade of a freestone building with projecting wings is decorated with sculptures symbolising peace: the Three Graces, the Four Seasons, "comédie italienne" masks and musical instruments.

The **staircase** is a fine example of stereotomy (sizing and shaping of stone). The rooms are lined with oak panneling. An Aubusson tapestry in the dining room features the triumph of Alexander in Babylon.

Note the pigeon coop (1 800 pigeonholes) and **a water sprinkler**, a replica of a Spanish noria, used to source water 60m/196ft below the ground.

Villers-Bocage

▶ *4km/2mi N of Bertrangles by D97.*
The **church** (13C–16C) contains a 16C *Entombment of Christ*. Note the expressive figures and the clothes of the women with rich fittings, typical of the Renaissance. ℘*03 22 93 70 24. Guided tours Mon–Fri 2–5pm.*

ADDRESSES

🛏 STAY

⊜**Hôtel Victor Hugo** – *2 r. de l'Oratoire.* ℘*03 22 91 57 91. www.hotel-a-amiens.com. Wi-fi. 10 rooms. ⊡6.50€.* Small family hotel a stone's throw from the cathedral. A lovely wooden staircase leads up to simple and well-kept rooms.

⊜⊜**Hôtel Alsace-Lorraine** – *18 r. de la Morlière. ℘03 22 91 35 71. www. hotelalsacelorraine.fr. 14 rooms ⊡. 8.50€.* This comfortable little hotel behind an imposing carriage entrance is a five-minute walk from the train station. Bedrooms give onto the inner courtyard.

⊜⊜**Chambre d'hôte Le Petit Château** *–2 r. Grimaux. 80480 Dury.*

℘*03 22 95 29 52. lepetitchateau-dury.fr.* 🅿 🛏. *5 room ⊡.* Just 10 mins. from central Amiens, this massive 19C rural residence offers comfortable guest rooms in an outbuilding.

⊜⊜🏨**All Seasons Cathédrale** – *17 pl. au Feurre. ℘03 22 22 00 20. www. allseasons.com. Wi-fi. 47 rooms ⊡.* This central hotel is set in a magnificent 18C post house. Well-appointed rooms, some ideal for families.

⊜⊜🏨**Hôtel Carlton** – *442 r. Noyon. ℘03 22 97 72 22. www.lecarlton.fr. Wi-fi. 24 rooms. ⊡10€. Restaurant ⊜⊜.* Behind the attractive 19C façade, discover a modern interior. Every room features waxed furniture. The restaurant, Le Bistrot, serves grilled meats.

🍽 EAT

⊜**Le Petit Poucet** –*52 r. des Trois-Cailloux. ℘03 22 91 42 32. Closed Mon, 9 Jul–9 Aug.* 🅰. This establishment is popular with locals who come for a slice of quiche, a *ficelle picarde* (baked crepes, stuffed and rolled), a mixed salad or a box of takeout pastries.

⊜**Le T'chiot Zinc**– *18 r. de Noyon. ℘03 22 91 43 79. Closed Mon (Jul–Aug), Sun and public holidays (rest of the year).* A short walk from the Perret tower, in a central pedestrian street, this typical bistro serves leek pie, suckling pig and other Picardy specialities.

⊜⊜**Le Bouchon** – *10 r. Alexandre-Fatton. ℘03 22 92 14 32. www.lebouchon.fr. Closed Sun eve.* 🅰. A Parisian-style bistro near the railway station specialising in typically Lyonnais dishes; a "no fuss" atmosphere.

⊜⊜**Au Relais des Orfèvres** – *14 r. des Orfèvres. ℘03 22 92 36 01. Closed 3 wks in Aug, 2 wks in Feb, Sat, Sun, Mon noon.* An attractive blue dining room serving reasonably priced, modern cuisine.

⊜⊜**L' Orée de la Hotoie**– *17 r. Jean-Jaurès. ℘03 22 91 37 05. Closed 25 Jul–20 Aug, 22–28 Dec, Sat eve, Sun eve and Mon.* A small, quiet house opposite the park offering traditional cuisine prepared by a talented chef.

⊜⊜**La Bonne Auberge** – *63 rte. Nationale, 80480 Dury. ℘03 22 95 03 33. Closed 12 Jul–11 Aug, Sun eve, Mon and Tue.* The smart regional façade is covered with flowers in summer. The recently decorated dining room offers contemporary cuisine.

⊜⊜🍽 **Les Marissons** – *Pont de la Dodane. ☎03 22 92 96 66. www.les-marissons.fr. Closed Wed noon, Sat noon and Sun.* The place to be in the Saint-Leu quarter: this former marine workshop boasts a pleasant décor of beams and round tables.

⊜⊜ **L'Abbatiale**– *11 pl. Jean-Catelas-80800 Corbie. ☎03 22 48 40 48. Closed 25 Dec-1 Jan, Sun. ♿. 7 rooms ⊡6€.* Opposite the Église St-Pierre, this unpretentious inn offers guests a warm welcome. Choose from a brasserie menu or classic dishes.

SHOWTIME AND ART

Maison de la Culture d'Amiens– *pl. Léon-Gontier. ☎03 22 97 79 79. www.maisondelaculture-amiens.com.* Two halls (1 070 and 300 seats), a movie theatre devoted to art and experimental films and two exhibition rooms. An interesting and eclectic selection of events.

👥 **Théâtre de Marionnettes** – *Chés Cabotans d'Amiens, 31 r. Édouard-David, quartier St-Leu. ☎03 22 22 30 90. www.ches-cabotans-damiens.com.* This fascinating family-orientated show, established in 1933, is given in a veritable miniature theatre with a beautifully designed set.

La Lune des Pirates– *17 quai Bélu. ☎03 22 97 88 01. www.lalune.net. 8.30pm. 1hr concert eves.Closed Jul-Aug. ⊜10€.* A former café now home to a contemporary music, cultural and exhibition space.

SHOPPING

Atelier de Jean-Pierre Facquier – *67 r. du Don. ☎03 22 92 49 52.* Monsieur Facquier carves life into pieces of wood before your eyes, transforming them into traditional Picardy puppets.

Jean Trogneux – *1 r. Delambre & 2nd branch at Parvis de la Cathédrale. ☎03 22 71 17 17. www.trogneux.fr.* The Trogneux family, confectioners for five generations, sell more than two million Amiens macaroons a every year!

Marché des Hortillons – Saturday mornings at **Place Parmentier**.

ACTIVITIES

👥 **Chés barboteux d'Amiens**– *Île Ste-Aragone. ☎03 22 44 40 57. Wed & Sat 2–5pm,Sun–Tue, Thu–Fri by reservation.*

Closed Jul. 5€ initiation 2hr canoë or kayak. Canoë and kayak hire and initiation; supervised excursions.

👥 **Le Picardie** – *Port d'Amont. ☎0322 921640. www.picroisi.c.la. mid-Apr–mid-Oct: by reservation (3hr cruise) 12.30–3.30pm,eve. (2hr cruise) 7–9pm. 40€ (under 12 yrs 20€).* Several cruise options, lunch or dinner on board this boat and restaurant.

👥 **Les bateaux de Saint-Leu**– *Quai Bélu. ☎0322716020. Mid-May–Sep Wed–Sun 1–5.30pm, Sat & Sun 11am–5.30pm; Oct Sat & Sun 11am–5.30pm. 5€ (under 12yrs 3€)* 35 min with boatman guide. Cruise along the neighbourhood's many picturesque canals and discover the shimmering houses and pleasant atmosphere of Saint-Leu.

EVENTS

"Amiens, cathedral in colour"– A multicoloured light installation by designer Skertzò projected onto the western entrance of Amiens cathedral recreates its medieval appearance, based on scientific data. June to September at nightfall, and 1 Dec to 1 Jan at 7pm.

Parfums d'hiver– *www.marchedenoel.fr.* Every year in December. the city hosts the biggest Christmas market in the north. There are 125 chalets throughout the city.

Festival d'Amiens, musiques de jazz et d'ailleurs – *☎0322 91 0486. www. amiensjazzfestival.com.* The city welcomes the world's biggest names in jazz every March, all styles (Afro, electro, classic and more) in auditoriums, bars and the street.

"Le souffle de la terre" light and sound show – *Ch. d'Haineville, 80250 Ailly-sur-Noye. ☎03 22 41 06 90. www.aillysurnoye.com. Aug–Sept, Fri & Sat 9.30pm. 16€ (5–12s 9€). Restaurant under the big top from 7pm.* A larger-than-life show performed on a 4ha/10 acre site around a lake. Retraces the history of the inhabitants of Picardy over the last 2 000 years.

Flea market – France's second biggest flea market after Lille is held the first weekend in October in 51 streets, attracting people from around the world.

Albert

Close to the frontline during the Battle of the Somme in 1916, and again during the Battle of Picardie in 1918, Albert was almost totally destroyed during WW I. Today it is a well-planned, modern town boasting 250 Art Deco façades. It is an ideal starting point for the Poppy Route WW I battlefield tour.

▶ **Population:** 10 065
⚲ **Michelin Local Map:** p461: C2.
▦ **Info:** Office du tourisme, 9 r. Gambetta, 80300. ☎03 22 75 16 42. www. paysducoquelicot.com.

🚗 DRIVING TOUR

POPPY ROUTE

Round trip of 34km/21mi. 1hr. www.somme-battlefields.com.

East and north of Albert, the **Poppy Route** (Circuit du Souvenir) commemorates the soldiers who fell during the Allied attack of the summer of 1916 (Battle of the Somme). For more details, visit the Historial de la Grande Guerre in Péronne (⚲see PÉRONNE).

Musée des Abris 'Somme 1916' is housed in a 13C underground tunnel turned into an air-raid shelter in 1938. It is a moving exhibition of wartime memorabilia, and the evolution of weaponry. ⏱Open Apr–Sept 9am–6pm; Feb–Mar, Oct–Nov 9am–noon, 2–6pm (Dec 5pm). ☞5.50€ ☎03 22 75 16 17. www.musee-somme-1916.eu.

▷ Exit Albert and head NE by D 292 towards Bapaume. On the right, note the first British cemetery.

The gaping **Lochnagar Crater** at **La Boisselle**, saved from being turned into farmland by Englishman Richard Dunning, was detonated under the German lines at the start of the Battle of the Somme.

▷ Take the D 20 W, then D 151

Overlooking the Ancre Valley, the 45m/147ft-high **Mémorial de Thiepval** is engraved with the names of the 73 367 Allied soldiers killed during the battle who have no known grave. The village

of Thiepval was turned into an underground fortress by the Germans during the summer of 1916 and was besieged by the British for 116 days.

The **Ulster Tower** (⏱open daily Wed–Sun 2–5pm; ⏱closed last Sun of month; ☞no charge; ☎03 22 75 60 47) commemorates the men of the 36th Irish division.

▷ Take D 73 on the left across the Ancre.

Parc-mémorial de Beaumont-Hamel★ (⏱open daily May–Oct 10am–6pm. Nov–Apr 9am–5pm; ⏱closed Christmas holidays; ☜guided tours in French and English; ☎03 22 76 70 86) was the site of a bloody battle fought by the Royal Newfoundland Regiment in July 1916, on the opening day of the Battle of the Somme. Topped by a bronze caribou, the memorial includes a platform affording impressive **views** over the battlefield which can be explored on foot.

▷ Return to D 73, cross Thiepval and continue to Pozières.

The **Mémorial de Pozières** marks where the village of Pozières barred the way to Thiepval hill. Because of its strategic importance, Australian and Canadian forces were assigned to take the village in the opening stages of the Battle of the Somme. The names of some 14 690 fallen men are engraved on the Australian memorial.

▷ Take D 147 then, in Bazentin, D20 on the left.

In July 1916, the Germans dropped shells containing tear gas on the South African positions signalling the start of a fierce five-day battle to regain control over "Devil's Wood". Out of the 3 153 men who engaged in combat, only 780 survived. The **Mémorial de Longueval** (🕐 *open Feb–Apr, mid-Oct–Nov 10am–6pm; Apr–mid-Oct 10am–5.45pm;* 🕐 *closed Mon and Tue morning;* 📞 *03 22 85 02 17*) and the museum commemorate South African soldiers who lost their lives during both World Wars.

▶ Continue E along D 20.

Three war cemeteries (French, British and German) are located at **Rancourt**. The sole and only memorial to French soldiers killed during the Battle of the Somme bears some 8 566 names.

▶ Return to Albert by D 20 to Ginchy, then D 64.

Ham

Nestled in the marshy Upper Somme Valley between Santerre and Vermandois, Ham is a busy river port linking the Somme and Saint-Quentin canals.

SIGHTS
Église Notre-Dame
Close to the town hall, this former abbey church is built in Romano-Gothic style (12C–13C) and sports a Romanesque gateway. On the right are the **former abbey** buildings (1701). The Notre-Dame **crypt** can be visited by request at the Office de Tourisme.

Train station frescoes
Destroyed by the Germans in 1917, Ham station was rebuilt in 1929. The **interior** features four large frescoes by Marie-Fernande van Driesten-Parys, born in Lille in 1874.

🚗 DRIVING TOUR

LE PAYS HAMOIS

EXCURSION
Mailly-Maillet
▶ *12km/7mi to the N of Albert by D 938 then D 919 on the right.*
This small rural town was once a powerful fief whose lords took part in several crusades. One of them died with his son at the Battle of Crécy.

Eglise Saint-Pierre – 🕐 *Open Tue and Thu 2–6pm, Fri–Sun and Wed by reservation.* 🕐 *Closed public holidays.* ♿ 📞 *03 22 76 27 97.* Built in the 16C under the patronage of Isabeau d'Ailly, wife of Jean III de Mailly. The Flamboyant Gothic **gateway**★ was begun in 1509. The pier depicts the Christ of Pity.

Chapelle Madame – 📞 *03 22 76 21 25. By reservation only.* This sepulchral chapel is located at the end of a tree-lined drive. Its Baroque Jesuit architecture is fairly rare in this region.

▶ **Population:** 5 400
🚗 **Michelin Map:** p461: D3.
ℹ **Info:** 📞 03 23 81 30 00 or www.hautesomme-tourisme.com
▶ **Location:** E of Amiens and 18km SW of Saint-Quentin. Access by D 930 from Saint-Quentin or D 943 then D 930 from Amiens.

35km/21mi tour marked in green on the map (*see p461*). Allow 2hr.

▶ Leave Ham by D937, towards Péronne. Cross Sancourt and Matigny before arriving in Croix-Moligneaux.

At the centre of **Croix-Moligneaux**, the Saint-Médard **church** was built in the 13C and presents a Renaissance porch. *Visit by request at the town hall.* 📞 *03 23 88 90 64.*

▶ Continue along D937 to Athies.

The king of the Francs Clotairel owned a palace in **Athies** where Radegonde, his future wife, was raised. The **church** has a 13C gate with a tympanum depicting the Nativity and Flight from Egypt.

◆ At the entrance to Athies, turn left along D45. At Ennemain, drive down towards the Somme. Take D103 to Falvy.

The village of **Falvy**'s rustic 12C **church** combines Romanesque and early-Gothic features, alternating Roman and Gothic arches. Don't miss the **views** over the Somme Valley from the steps.

◆ Head towards Y.

Y is the village with the shortest name in France.

◆ Take D615 towards Ham then D17 to Offoy.

Offoy is surrounded by marshes and lakes irrigated by the Somme.

◆ Return to D930 on the left.

The industrial town of **Eppeville** is home to one of the largest sugar refineries in the north of France.

◆ Continue straight on to Ham.

Montdidier

Built on the side of a chalky hill, at the extreme southwest of the Santerre plateau, Montdidier suffered heavy damage during World War I. It rose from the ashes in 1931, when its town hall and church were rebuilt.

 WALKING TOUR

Hôtel de ville
The interior of this Art Deco building is decorated with frescoes by Maurice Picaud, illustrating the history of the town. The wrought iron chandelier in the entrance weighs more than a tonne.

Église du Saint-Sépulcre
Open by request at the Office de Tourisme. Destroyed in 1918, this Flamboyant Gothic church, rebuilt in 1930, is identical to the 16C original. Besides a 16C Entombment of Christ, the interior contains rare examples of stained glass by Nancy School artist Jacques Grüber on religious themes: the history of the Hebrew people, the discovery of the True Cross, and the Crusades. The six Brussels tapestries displayed in the nave were woven in the 17C and illustrate several scenes from Exodus.

- ▶ **Population:** 6 333
- ♿ **Michelin Local Map:** p461: C3; 301 i10.
- 🛈 **Info:** Office de tourisme – 5 pl. du Gén.-de-Gaulle, 80500 Montdidier. ℘03 22 78 92 00. www.montdidier-tourisme.com.
- ◐ **Location:** At the intersection between D 930 and D 935, Montdidier is halfway between Compiègne and Amiens.
- ◷ **Timing:** Don't miss the Folleville medieval festival in September
- 👪 **Kids:** St Nicolas Market 1st weekend in Dec.

Église Saint-Pierre
Visits by request at the Office de Tourisme. Built between the 14C and the 16C, Saint-Pierre suffered the same fate as the town's other church. Its gateway is the work of Chappion, the master mason of Beauvais cathedral. Don't miss the Entombment of Christ (16C), the Romano-Byzantine baptismal fonts (11C) and the Romanesque Christ (12C).

Prieuré

Built in the 14C using stones from a former keep, the priory was used to dispense justice to the local area, firstly as a royal audience chamber then as a law court. Damaged in World War I, it was rebuilt in neo-Gothic style. Walk to the end of the priory promenade for **views** over the Vallée des Trois Doms.

EXCURSIONS
Church and remains of the Château de Folleville★

▶ 18km/11mi to the W by D 26 then D 190. ◐ Open May–Sept Wed–Sat 10am–noon, 2–5.30pm. ◐ Closed Oct–Apr, groups by reservation only. ◉3€. ℘03 22 41 49 52. http://folleville.c.la.

Perched on a hillock overlooking the Noye Valley, this was once the fief of Raoul de Lannoy, chamberlain and counsellor to Louis XI, Charles VIII and Louis XII. After displaying outstanding bravery at the siege of Quesnoy in 1477, he was presented with a chain by Louis XI.

This chain can be found carved on a Renaissance Carrare marble baptismal font near the entrance to the rural Gothic nave of the 15C–16C **church★**. Explore the Flamboyant Gothic **chancel★** with its Renaissance decorative elements before admiring the first **tomb★** on the left. The foot of the tomb is decorated with garlands of pea blossoms or "fleurs de pois", a reference to the name of the lady of the manor. The second **tomb★** reveals the evolution of the funerary arts from recumbant to kneeling representations of the defunct.

The castle ruins – The only vestige of the castle (13C–16C) is a 25m/82ft watch tower. Cylindrical at the base, it becomes hexagonal towards the machicolated battlements and dodecagonal towards the top.

Ravenel

▶ 18km/11mi to the south by D 329, D 929 to Crèvecoeur-le-Petit, then D 47. This peaceful village derives its name from "ravenelle", part of the wild radish family. In the 16C, the land between Ravenel and Rollot formed the Duchy of Halluin. The Halluin family built a number of remarkable churches on their estates, including the church in Ravenel.

Its **tower★** features Flamboyant motifs (blind elements) and openwork Renaissance designs. The upper platform is surmounted by a dome. The rounded oriel windows "furnishing" the re-entrant angle of the buttresses feature among the most original details.

Saint-Martin-aux-Bois

▶ 6km/4mi by D 47 then D 73 at Maingnelay-Montigny. ◐ Open Jul–Aug Sun 2–7pm; Sept–Jun by request (7 days in advance) 2–7pm. ◆ Guided tour 90 min. ◉No charge. ℘03 44 51 03 55.

Overlooking the plain of Picardy, the Saint-Martin abbey-church stands alone at the far end of the village (access via the former fortified gateway), to which it gave its name. The church's slender 13C nave, damaged during the Hundred Years War, is as high (27m/89ft) as it is wide (31m/101ft). The pillars of the nave meet the springing of the vaults at a very high level. The chevet – a masterpiece of High Gothic architecture – has an openwork design. The superb late-15C **stalls** are a fine example of Flamboyant art. The stall misericords depict scenes from daily life and local sayings.

A Fleur d'O

▶ 9km/6mi to the N by D 41. 23 r. de la Chaussée, 80500 Davenescourt. ◐ Open mid-Jun–Sept daily 2.30–6.30pm. ◉6€. ℘03 22 78 09 83. www.jardinafleurdo.com.

Three gardens (2ha/5acre) arranged harmoniously around a 3 500 sq m/37 000 sq ft lake fed by the gentle River Avre.

Roye

▶ 20km/12mi NW by D 934. Steeped on the northern slope of the Avre valley, rich in beetroot and wheat, Roye is the headquarters of a sugar refinery and a grain market. It is also an industrial centre. The town was rebuilt after World War I, including the church which still features its 16C chancel.

Poix-de-Picardie

A small country town perched on the banks of the River Selle, Poix was once the stronghold of the de Noailles family.

VISIT
Église Saint-Denis
⊙*Open Jul–Aug 3–6pm.* ↝*Guided tours by request, contact* ℘*03 22 90 09 98.*

This 16C Flamboyant Gothic church once stood within the walls of a castle. Enter through a gateway surmounted by an ogee arch to admire the lierne, tierceron and hanging keystone vaulting.

EXCURSIONS
Château de Courcelles-sous-Moyencourt
▷*7km/4mi NE by D 1029 then left by D 258.* ⊙*Open Jul and Sept 2–6pm.* ⊜*5€ (child 2.50€).* ℘*03 22 90 82 51.*

This 18C **château**, built in stone with brick panneling, is reached through a French-style park, preceded by a monumental gateway.

Église Saint-Antoine de Conty
▷*17km/10mi to the E by D 920.*

Walk to the right side of this church, built in a harmonious 15C and 16C Flamboyant style, for a strange perspective of its projecting gargoyles. Crowned with pyramidal roof trussing, the tower bears the scars of shrapnal from canonballs fired at Conty during a siege in 1589.

🚗 DRIVING TOUR

LES ÉVOISSONS

30km/18mi tour marked in green on the map (⊙*p460*). Allow 2hr.

This tour winds through the countryside, along valleys planted with poplar trees.

▷ From Poix take D 920 E to Conty.

The road fringes **Blangy-sous-Poix**, dominated by a 12C Romanesque church with a polygonal bell tower.

▶ **Population:** 2 285
⚲ **Michelin Map:** p460: A3; 301 E9.
🛈 **Info:** Office de tourisme – Salle des fêtes, pl. de la République, 80290 Poix-de-Picardie. ℘03 22 41 06 05. www.ville-poix-de-picardie.fr.
▶ **Location:** The village was rebuilt after being destroyed in June 1940. The viaduct of the Amiens-Rouen train line rises up before you reach the town, which is 24km/14mi to the SW of Amiens by D 1029/E 44 and 20km/12mi to the S of Airaines by D 901.
⊛ **Don't miss:** Évoissons tour; Saint-Antoine church in Conty.
👪 **Kids:** Nature tours with picnic spots.

Continue to **Famechon** and its 16C Flamboyant Gothic church.

▷ Turn right down D 94.

Guizancourt
Stradling the Évoissons river, this hillside village has a walking trail (30min) offering **views** over the valley.

▷ Cut across D 901 and take the "chemin de Baudets" which follows the valley to Méréaucourt; continue on to Agnières.

Agnières
The **church** stands alone at the foot of a feudal mound under a 13C castle. Take a historic walk *(2km)* around the site.

▷ Cross Souplicourt then Sainte-Segrée. Drive through a shady forest before reaching Saulchoy-sous-Poix. At Lachapelle, take D 919 to return to Poix.

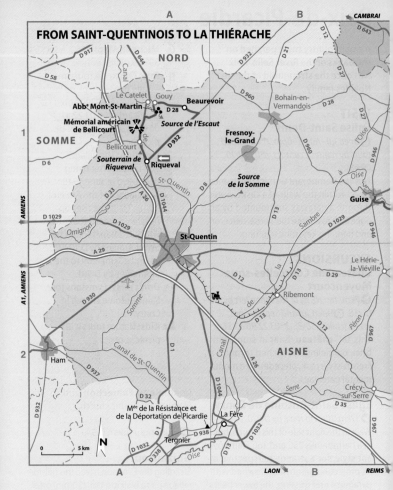

FROM SAINT-QUENTINOIS TO LA THIÉRACHE

Few landscapes lend themselves to walking and hiking tours as well as the region to the east of Saint-Quentin. A brief interlude of hedgerows, copses, orchards and dairy farms between the open fields of Picardy to the east, the Avesnois nature reserve to the north and the dense woodland of the Massif Ardennais to the south, this region is the source of two rivers and home to one of France's longest canals, all of which offer ideal walking paths. Part of a continuous band of flora and fauna stretching deep into nearby Belgium, the region is easiest to explore along one of its many nature trails, including the "Axe Vert", a 30km/17mi stretch of pathways along the gently sloping Serre and Oise valleys. Ranging from one hour to one day, many walks end with a welcoming coaching inn offering a very affordable bed for the night.

Touring the Area

If walking is not top of your agenda, there are many other ways to explore the local countryside. You can take a driving tour around La Thiérache's sixty "fortress-churches" and discover the source of the Somme in Fonsommes or the Escaut at Mont-Saint-Martin, or admire the dizzyingly high vaulting of the Abbaye de Saint-Michel near Hirson. Alternatively, a slow cruise along the Saint-Quentin canal, which links the

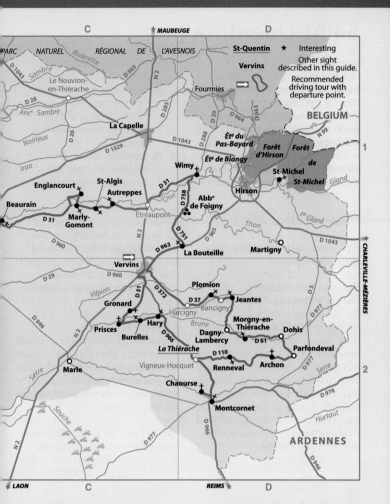

Somme and Oise basins to the River Escaut, takes you on a diagonal tour through some of the region's finest meadows and villages. Linking Chauny to Cambrai, this 100km-/62mi-long canal, complete with a 5 670m-/3.5mi-tunnel at Riqueval, was considered by Napoléon I as one of the greatest achievements of his time.

Local Tours and Exhibitions

For a beginner's guide to local wildlife, take a few minutes to visit the exhibitions organised at Parc de l'Isle, at the very heart of Saint-Quentin, where you can also take a tour of some of its 3 000 Art Deco façades and buildings. For more architectural adventures, don't

Highlights

1 Discover the **Art Deco** streets of Saint-Quentin (p482)

2 Watch Riqueval's **tug boat** (p485)

3 Tour the **fortified churches** of La Thiérache (p486)

4 Enjoy a **lakeside walk** in Hirson (p489)

5 Explore **Marle**'s archaeology museum (p489)

miss the basilica in Saint-Quentin and the 19C Familistère workers' housing complex in Guise.

Saint-Quentin★

Dominated by its vast Grand'Place and magnificent basilica, built to house the remains of St Quentin, this city is prized for its fine arts museum, its large collection of works by Maurice Quentin de la Tour, official portrait painter to Louis XV and its Art Deco heritage, the style adopted to rebuild the city following its devastation during World War I.

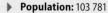

- ▶ **Population:** 103 781
- **Michelin Local Map:** p480: A2.
- **Info:** Office du tourisme du St-Quentinois, 27 r. Victor-Basch, 02100. ℘03 23 67 05 00. www.saint-quentin-tourisme.fr.
- **Location:** 161km/100mi N of Paris, and mid-way between Cambrai and Laon.

WALKING TOUR

Walk from place de l'Hôtel-de-Ville to rue des Canonniers.

Rue des Canonniers

The 18C **Hôtel Joly-de-Bammeville** (no. 9), which featuring a staircase with 18C wrought-iron banisters, houses the town library. Founded in 1697, it was moved here in 1934, the last of many homes. The former collection included over 20 000 volumes. A 17C western façade and 18C southern façade with sculpted arcades give onto a glazed courtyard. The entrance to the old **Hôtel des Canonniers** (no. 21) has military trophies carved in low relief.

The Art Deco Trail

St-Quentin suffered extensive damage during WW I and was partially rebuilt in the 1920s by architect **Louis Guindez** (1890–1978). A walk through the town's streets reveals numerous house fronts decorated with bow windows, projecting balconies, floral or geometric motifs, coloured mosaics and wrought-iron work. Among the most outstanding buildings are the **Carillon cinema** (r. des Toiles), the **music school** (47 r. d'Isle), the **buffet** in the railway station and, next to it, the **bridge** flanked by lantern towers.

▶ Return to pl. de l'Hôtel-de-Ville and follow r. des Toiles. Walk round the basilica, cross r. du Gouvernement near the east end of the basilica. r. E.-Ovres leads to the Champs-Élysées Park.

Champs-Élysées

The site of the original fortifications was turned into a pleasant **park** (10ha/24 acres) during the Restoration period: playgrounds, sports field, flower garden. The surrounding avenues are lined with fine Art Deco buildings.

▶ The Parc d'Isle Jacques-Braconnier is accessible via bd. Gambetta and pl du 8-Octobre leading to the quai Gayant bridge. Turn left after the bridge.

Parc d'Isle Jacques-Braconnier

The **Marais d'Isle** covers over 100ha/247 acres. It features fishing and water sports facilities, and also a **wetlands reserve** which lies along the route taken by migratory birds from Northern and Eastern Europe.

You will be able to see rare plant species and also to observe numerous birds, particularly nest-building species (crested grebes) and overwintering species (ducks). Near the entrance to the park (av. Léo-Lagrange), the **Maison de l'environnement** (&open Mon–Fri 10am–noon, 2–5p;. no charge; ℘03 23 05 06 50) features a permanent exhibition on renewable energies and the greenhouse effect.

ADDITIONAL SIGHTS
Hôtel de Ville★

Guided tours by prior arrangement with the tourist office. Open Mon–Sat 8am–noon, 1.30–5pm. *No charge.* &. $03 23 06 90 00.

This is a gem of Late Gothic architecture (early 16C). The vigorous design of the façade includes ogival arches topped with pinnacles, mullioned windows and a traceried gallery beneath three gables. It is decorated with picturesque carvings in the Flamboyant Gothic style. The guardrail enclosing one of the porch arches once served as a yardstick for cloth merchants (the "yard" in Saint Quentin measured around 1.25m/4ft). The bell tower, completely rebuilt in the 18C, contains a peal of 37 bells. Inside, the **wedding hall,** a mixture of medieval and Renaissance styles, still sports its original beams. The beautiful Art Deco **council chamber,** stairway and landing are noteworthy. On the square in front of the town hall, the house at the corner of rue Saint-André has an Art Deco façade.

Rue de la Sellerie

Note the series of Art Deco buildings either side of the neo-Gothic Espace St-Jacques and, opposite *(no. 23)*, the bow window and devil's chimney roofing.

Espace St-Jacques

14 r. de la Sellerie.

Built on the ruins of a 13C church, this gallery proposes temporary art exhibits and houses the **Musée des Papillons** (*open Feb–Dec Wed–Mon 2–6pm;* *closed 1 Jan, 1 May, Whitsun, 14 Jul, 1 Nov, 25 Dec;* 2.60€; $03 23 06 93 93), with the largest collection of butterflies and other insects in Europe.

Rue de la Sous-Préfecture

This street is lined with fine Art Deco shops and houses displaying remarkable ironwork: nos. 13, 19/21, 25 (a former garage) and 47 (mosaic façade).

▶ Opposite the préfecture, take the rue de l'Official.

Hôtel des postes

Built in 1936 on the site of the birthplace of Maurice-Quentin de La Tour. Note the wrought iron door, monumental Art Deco chandelier and entrance hall decorated with six Cubist **mosaics** depicting the different modes of modern communication.

Opposite, on rues des Toiles, note to the right, the façade of the **Le Carillon cinema** with its beautiful coloured sign.

Basilica★

Guided tours available, 1hr (by reservation 2 days in advance). Open 10am–4pm. Closed Mon morning. *No charge.* &. $03 23 67 05 00.

A masterpiece of Gothic architecture, St-Quentin Basilica began as a collegiate church dedicated to Saint Quentin, who worked as a missionary in the region and was martyred at the end of the 3C. It only became a basilica in 1876, and barely escaped destruction in 1918.

Exterior – The west front incorporates a massive belfry-porch; its lower part dates from the late 12C whereas the upper storeys were rebuilt in the 17C and the top after 1918. The spire dates from 1976 and reaches the height of the original one (82m/269ft).

Interior – The 15C nave (34m/111ft high) has a long maze (260m/284yd) traced on its floor, which the faithful followed on their knees. The impressively large

Hôtel de Ville, Saint-Quentin

© Hervé Gyssels/Photononstop

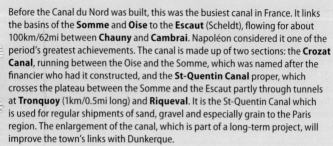

St-Quentin Canal

Before the Canal du Nord was built, this was the busiest canal in France. It links the basins of the **Somme** and **Oise** to the **Escaut** (Scheldt), flowing for about 100km/62mi between **Chauny** and **Cambrai**. Napoléon considered it one of the period's greatest achievements. The canal is made up of two sections: the **Crozat Canal**, running between the Oise and the Somme, which was named after the financier who had it constructed, and the **St-Quentin Canal** proper, which crosses the plateau between the Somme and the Escaut partly through tunnels at **Tronquoy** (1km/0.5mi long) and **Riqueval**. It is the St-Quentin Canal which is used for regular shipments of sand, gravel and especially grain to the Paris region. The enlargement of the canal, which is part of a long-term project, will improve the town's links with Dunkerque.

13C **chancel**★★ consists of a double transept, double aisles, an ambulatory and radiating chapels. The vaulting of the chapels right of the ambulatory rests on two columns, following the elegant arrangement of the Champagne region.

Musée Antoine-Lécuyer★

🕐*Open Wed–Fri 10am–noon, 2–5pm (Sat & Sun 6pm).* 🕐*Closed Sun morning, 1 Jan, 1 May, Whitsun, 14 Jul, 1 Nov, 25 Dec.* ∞*2.60€.* 🖉*03 23 06 93 98. www.museeantoinelecuyer.fr.*

The pride of the museum is its collection of 78 magnificent **pastel portraits**★★ by **Quentin de La Tour** (1704–88), who was born and died in St-Quentin. La Tour painted the leading lights of 18C French society, including Voltaire, Rousseau and the Marquise de Pompadour.

The groundfloor features a collection of 17C and 18C Italian and French paintings and works from the Northern School.

EXCURSIONS
Maison du textile
at Fresnoy-le-Grand

▶ *16km/10mi to the NE by D 8. 54 r. Roger-Salengro.* 🕐*Open Apr–Sept Tue–Fri 10am–1pm & 2–6pm, Sat 2–6pm; Oct–Mar Tue–Fri 10am–1pm, 1st Sun of month 2–6pm.* 🕐*Closed 1 Jan, 1 May, 1 and 11 Nov, 25 Dec.* ∞*5€ (under 8yrs no charge), 10€ family.* ♿ 🖉*03 23 09 02 74. www.la-maison-du-textile.com.*

Explore the history of cloth production in Picardy in this former textile factory in Fresnoy, once a major mill town. Displays include several weaving looms (28 of which are listed as historic monuments) and a room dedicated to cutwork embroidery.

👥 Discovery tours, games and hands-on workshops.

Source de la Somme

▶ *12km/7mi to the NE by D 67.*

The Somme spring from this unassuming source in Fonsommes, next to the former abbey of Fervaques. After a 245km-/152mi-journey, the river spills into the Channel.

ADDRESSES

GUIDED TOURS

The tourist officer organises a range of visits to industrial sites (textile, energy, food processing, etc.). *By reservation. Pick up a guide for the dates and conditions of visits to each company.*

TRANSPORT

Chemin de fer touristique du Vermandois – *www.cftv.fr. Information and reservations: Laure Peillon, CFTV, 02100 St-Quentin.* 🖉*03 23 64 88 38. Every Sun in Jul and Aug and once a month Sep–Dec and Feb–Jun.* Enjoy a meal in the dining car of the Vermandois Express (1928-1930) pulled by a steam engine and relive the charm of a local train journey as you travel 22km/13.6mi from Saint-Quentin to Origny-Sainte-Benoîte via Ribemont along the lush green Sambre to Oise canal.

Riqueval

The Grand Souterrain de Riqueval is a 5 670m/3.5mi-long underground passage carrying the Saint-Quentin canal across the plateau dividing the Somme and Escaut basins. The highlight of the visit is the arrival of the tug that pulls the boats through the tunnel… at a speed of 2.5km/1.5mi an hour.

VISIT
Underground entrance

Barge tugs: departing from Riqueval (southern end) 7.10am and 3.10pm, departing from Vendhuile (northern end) 9.30am and 5.30pm. Closed 1 Jan, Easter Sun, 1 May, 14 Jul, 11 Nov, 25 Dec. A pathway called the "Grand souterrain du canal de Saint-Quentin" descends through the woods to the tunnel entrance where you can watch the barge **tugs** at work.

Musée du Touage

Hameau de Riqueval (next to the D 1044), 02420 Bellicourt. ⏱**Open daily Apr–Sept: 10am–1pm, 2–6pm (closed Sat & Sun morning); Jan–Mar & Oct–Dec: Tue–Fri 10am–1pm, 2–6pm.* 👥*Guided tour 1st Sat of the month, 2.30pm in front of the tourist office.* ⏱*Closed 1 Jan, 1 May, 1 and 11 Nov, 25 Dec.*💶*5€ (8-12yrs 2€).* 📞*03 23 09 37 28. www.cc-vermandois.com.*

- 🖋 **Michelin Map:** p481: A4.
- 📄 **Info:** 📞03 23 67 05 00. www.saint-quentin-tourisme.fr.
- ▶ **Location:** 12km/7mi N of Saint-Quentin and 28km/17mi S of Cambrai by D 644. From Péronne, to the W, take D 6, D 331, then D 1044 on the right.
- 🕐 **Timing:** The tug boat operates twice a day. Allow 2hrs for the tour.

The tourist office (Maison de pays du Vermandois) is housed in an electric tug dating from 1910. Learn about tugging techniques and the history of the Grand Souterrain: information panels and videos. Regional produce.

🚗 DRIVING TOUR

SOURCE OF THE ESCAUT RIVER

24km/15mi tour marked in green on the map (p480). Allow 45min.

▶ Leave Riqueval to the north by D 1044.

The **Bellicourt American Memorial** is a white stone cenotaph to commemorate

---

The Grand Souterrain

Built on the order of Napoléon Bonaparte in 1801, the tunnel was constructed between 1802 and 1810 under the direction of the engineer A.-N. Gayant. It was opened in 1810 by Napoléon I and the Empress Marie-Louise, who sailed along it on a gondola. During the 1914-1918 war, it served as a German shelter.

Tugs – The poor ventilation in the tunnel means that boats need to be pulled through by a chain-hauled tug: the barge's engines are switched off and a chain is attached to the front of the boat. An electric chain-hauled tug (25m-/82ft-long, 5m-/16ft-wide and weighing 90 tonnes) is pulled through the tunnel by a chain hoist. The chain is 8km-/5mi-long and fixed to the end of the canal. It is wound around drums located at the centre of the boat. Until 1863, 7 to 8 men pulled the boats through and the crossing took 12 to 14 hours. It was replaced by a tug called a "rougaillou", driven by horsepower. A steam tug took its place in 1874, followed by an electric tug in 1910.

Joan of Arc tower, Beaurevoir

© Daniel Thierry/Photononstop

Hidden in a wooded hollow, the mysterious **Source of the Escaut River** was once a place of pilgrimage. This is where the Escaut river begins its 400km/250mi journey across France, Belgium and the Netherlands.
Walk along the 100m-/328ft-river bank trail fringed by aspen and ash trees.

▶ Pass in front of Mont-Saint-Martin again and continue to Gouy then turn right into Beaurevoir.

At **Beaurevoir**, note the tower of the castle where Joan of Arc was held captive from August to November 1430, by the Comte de Luxembourg, who handed her over to the English.

▶ Return to Riqueval by D 932.

the sacrifices of the 90 000 American troops who served in battle with the British army between 1917 and 1918. The area around the memorial offers **panoramic views** over the plateau that cut acroos the German trenches.

▶ Continue on D 1044 towards Le Catelet and after 2km/1mi, turn right twards Mont-Saint-Martin.

Mont-Saint-Martin is the ruins of a former Premonstratensian abbey.

▶ Turn right down D 71 to reach the path leading to the source (car park).

ADDRESSES

🍴 STAY/ 🍽 EAT

🛏🍴 **Ferme-auberge du Vieux Puits** – *5 r. de l'Abbaye, 02420 Bony. ℘03 23 66 22 33. www.isasite.net/ferme-du-vieux-puits. Closed 25 Dec–1 Jan, Thu lunch.* ♿🅿. *Restaurant🛏🍴.* This farm has comfortable, simply furnished rooms. Head to the inn for a meal prepared using fresh farm produce. Heated swimming pool in season, tennis and mountain biking. Sauna available to guests.

La Thiérache★

Famous for its unusual fortified churches, La Thiérache is a hilly and heavily wooded region dotted with typical brick and stone houses with pitched slate roofs. One of the most fertile areas of northern France, it is coveted for its maroilles and cider.

🚗 **DRIVING TOURS**

FORTIFIED CHURCHES★ ▶

La Thiérache was invaded repeatedly between the Hundred Years War in the

- 🎫 **Michelin Local Map:** p481: CD2.
- ℹ **Info:** Office du tourisme de Vervins et du Vervinois, 1 pl. du Général- de- Gaulle, 02140. ℘03 23 98 11 98. www.ot-vervins.com.

14C and 15C to the conflicts between the Spain and France in the 16C and 17C. Rather than sheltering behind castles and ramparts, the local population took refuge in their existing 12C and 13C churches, which they fortified with **watch-turrets**, **round towers** and square keeps pierced with **arrow slits**, resulting in an unusual **architectural mix** of **brick and stone**. Other fortress-churches date entirely from the turn of the 17C. The two following driving tours will help you discover some of this fascinating architectural heritage.

FROM VERVINS AND BACK

79km/49mi. About 3hr.

The charm of the region's capital **Vervins** lies in its ramparts, cobbled streets and houses with steeply pitched slate roofs and brick chimneys. **Notre-Dame Church** features a 13C chancel, 16C nave and an imposing brick tower (34m-/111ft-tall).
Inside, 16C mural paintings adorn the piers and a composition by Jouvenet (1699) portrays *Supper in the House of Simon*. Also note an 18C organ case and pulpit.

▶ Leave Vervins by D 372 SE.
At Harcigny take D 37 E.

The 16C **church** at **Plomion** features a west front flanked by two towers and a square keep with a great hall leading up to a garret. A picturesque, large covered market stands in front of the church.

▶ Take D 747 E toward Bancigny and Jeantes.

The façade of the **church** at **Jeantes** is flanked by two towers. Inside, expressionist frescoes by Charles Van Eyck (1962) represent scenes from the *Life of Christ*, and a 12C font.

The ancient village of **Dagny-Lambercy** has preserved its cob houses and half-timbered houses with brick courses.

At **Morgny-en-Thiérache**, the chancel and nave of the **church** date from the 13C. The chancel was raised by a storey to create an room for refugees.

There are many half-timbered and cob houses at **Dohis**. The **church** has a 12C nave and a porch-keep from 17C.

▶ From the village, follow the road to Parfondeval.

Perched on a hill, the lovely village of **Parfondeval** was awarded the title of one of the "Most Beautiful Villages in France", and has a 16C Renaissance-style **church** standing like an impenetrable fortress behind the rampart of neighboring houses.

▶ Back at the entrance to the village take D 520 W to Archon.

The road offers a **view** over Archon and its undulating countryside.

At **Archon**, Cob-walled and brick houses surround the **church** guarded by two massive towers. Between the towers, the footbridge served as a look-out.
The D 110 runs through **Renneval** (fortified church) and Vigneux-Hocquet.

▶ Head for Montcornet along D 966.

Montcornet has a Gothic **St-Martin Church**, thought to have been built by the Knights Templars in the 13C, with a chancel ending in a flat east end, which is almost as long as the nave. 16C additions include a Renaissance porch and eight bartizans with defensive loopholes.

▶ Continue along D 966 toward Vigneux-Hocquet. Turn left onto D 58.

A prestigious medieval *bourg*, **Chaourse** gradually declined to the benefit of Montcornet. The 13C **church** (nave and tower) was fortified in the 16C. Interesting **view** of the Serre Valley.

▶ Turn around and return by D 966 toward Hary.

At **Hary**, a 16C brick keep rises above the chancel and nave of this 12C **church**.

▶ D 61 follows the Brune Valley.

Burelles' 16–17C village **church** features a number of defences: arrow slits, a reinforced keep with watch-turret, barbicans and watch-turrets above the north transept, the chancel flanked by a turret. The upper floor of the transept was turned into a vast fortified room.

The 12C chancel and nave of the **church** at **Prisces** were given an enormous, square brick keep (25m/82ft tall) with two turrets on opposing corners.
The four floors inside allowed soldiers to take shelter.

▷ Cross the Brune River and follow D 613 to Gronard.

The **church** here, partially hidden behind lime trees, has a keep flanked by two round towers.

▷ Return to Vervins along D 613 and D 966.

The route offers a picturesque **view** of Vervins and its surrounding area.

FROM VERVINS TO GUISE

51km/32mi. About 2hr.

This tour largely follows the **Oise Valley** which also features a number of fortified churches.

Vervins ⓖ See above.

▷ From Vervins, follow D 963 to La Bouteille.

The church here has thick walls (over 1m/3ft) and is flanked by four turrets. It was built by Cistercians from the nearby **Abbaye de Foigny**, now in ruins.

▷ D 751 and VC 10 lead to Foigny. Cross D 38 and take the little road which runs beside the abbey ruins, to Wimy.

The keep of the fortified church at **Wimy** is flanked by two cylindrical towers. Inside, note fireplaces, a bread oven and, upstairs, a room for those seeking refuge. D 31 crosses Etréaupont and continues through **Autreppes**. The road runs by

its fortified church and continues past the village of **St-Algis.**
Two great watch-turrets were added to the portal of the 13C–14C sandstone church at **Marly-Gomont**. The large arrow slits near the base allowed cross-bows to be used.

▷ Take D 774 N to Englancourt.

Overlooking the Oise River, the forti-fied **church** has a west front flanked by watch-turrets, a square keep in brick and a chancel with a flat east end reinforced by two round towers.

▷ Return to D 31 via D 26.

The **fortress-church** (16C) at Beaurain stands isolated on a hill that rises from lush surroundings. Its great square keep is flanked by towers, as is the chancel.

▷ Continue on to Guis e by D 960

Guise

🛈 2 r. Chantraine. ℘03 23 60 45 71.
Set in dense woodland, this peaceful town lined with red and white brick houses is home to the 🏚👤 **Familistère Godin**★ (ⓞ open Jul–Aug 10am–6pm; Sept–Jun 10am–noon, 2–6pm; 1hr30min guided tours in English; ≋8.50€; ℘03 23 61 35 36; www.familistere.com), a hous-ing complex built by Jean-Baptiste Godin (1817–1888) for the employees of his stove factory. Centred around airy glazed courtyards, its three main blocks contained 500 spacious apartments with all modern comforts (running water and toilets) served by a school, theatre and debating hall.
Guise is also famous for the **Château des ducs de Guise**★ (ⓞ open daily Jul–Aug 10am–noon 2–6pm; Feb–Nov Tue–Sun 10am–noon 2-6pm (5pm winter), 2-5pm; 👣 guided tours 1hr15min; ≋6€; ℘03 23 61 11 76; http://chateaudeguise.fr) where you can explore the dungeons, cellars, vaulted passageways and keep of France's first bastioned castle. Don't miss the display of 16C weaponry and armour.

Hirson

Lying between the Thiérache and Avesnois regions, Hirson makes the perfect starting point for excursions.

LES ÉTANGS

Linked by the Oise, each lake in Hirson forest once had its own forge with a water-powered hammer to work iron from Féron, Glageon and Trélon.

Étang de Blangy

▷ *2km/1mi to the N by D 1043. Opposite the cemetery, turn right across the Oise, then down a track on the left.*
After the railway viaduct in this steep wooded valley, stop at the lake.

Étang du Pas-Bayard

▷ *6 km/4mi N by D 1043. Turn right down D 963, then along the chemin du Pas-Bayard.*
The "Route Verte" leads through **Hirson oak forest** (private property).

EXCURSIONS
Abbaye de Saint-Michel
▷*4km/3mi to the E by D 31.*

▸ **Population:** 10 327
Michelin Map: p481: D1.
Info: ℰ03 23 58 03 91. www.evasion-aisne.com.
Location: On a bend of the River Oise, in the NE of Aisne. Access via D 1043/E 44 or D 1050/D 963.
Kids: A nature walk in the Forêt Saint-Michel.

◷*Open Apr–Oct Mon–Fri 2–6pm, Sat 2.30–6.30pm; Nov–Mar daily 2–6pm (90min).* ⊜*4.30€.* ℰ*03 23 58 87 20. www.abbaye-saintmichel.com.*
Founded in 945, the Abbaye de Saint-Michel has a 12C–13C Gothic chancel, cloister and transept lit by a 12-column **rose window★**. Don't miss the 16C gallery **mural paintings**.

Forêt de Saint-Michel
This 3 000ha-/7 400acre-beech and oak forest is popular with fishermen and birdspotters for its trout and nesting black storks.

Marle

High in the hills of the Pays de la Serre, Marle's picturesque houses, coaching inns and beautiful Gothic church hide a "barbaric" Merovingian past, as a visit to the town museum reveals!

WALKING TOUR

Start your tour in a street lined with ancient houses leading to the old château courtyard on place de la Motte, affording **views** over the Vallée de la Somme. Admire the brick and stone **coaching house** (1753) at no.26 Fauberg Saint-Nicolas decorated with sculpted low reliefs.
Stop off at the **Gothic church** (◷*open by request Mar–Oct Wed–Mon 9am–6pm;* ℰ*03 23 20 02 09*) to admire a statue of

▸ **Population:** 2 524
Michelin Map: p481: C2.
Info: ℰ03 23 27 76 76. www.evasion-aisne.com.
Location: 25km/15mi to the N of Laon. From Paris, Soissons, Laon and Brussels, take N 2.
Kids: Merovingian farm at the archaeology museum.

Enguerrand de Bournonville (15C). Next, head to the **Musée des Temps barbares** (◷ *open Mar–Oct 2–7pm;* ⊜*5.50€;* ℰ*03 23 24 01 33; www.musee destempsbarbares.fr*) where you're invited to explore life in the region in the 6C through a display of jewellery, glassware, ceramics, furniture and everyday objects discovered in a Merovingian necropolis 8km/5mi from Marle.

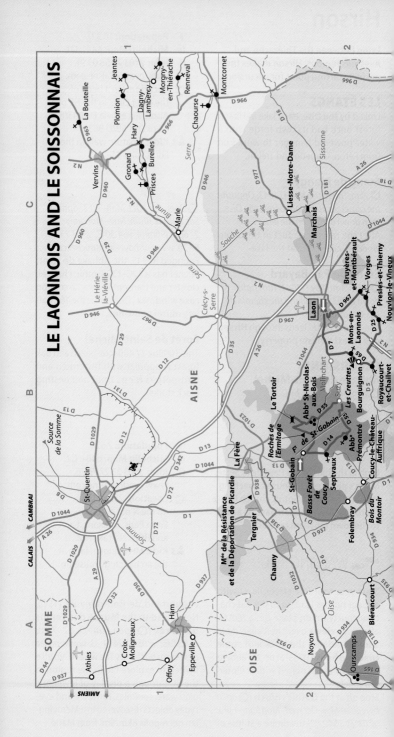

LE LAONNOIS AND LE SOISSONNAIS

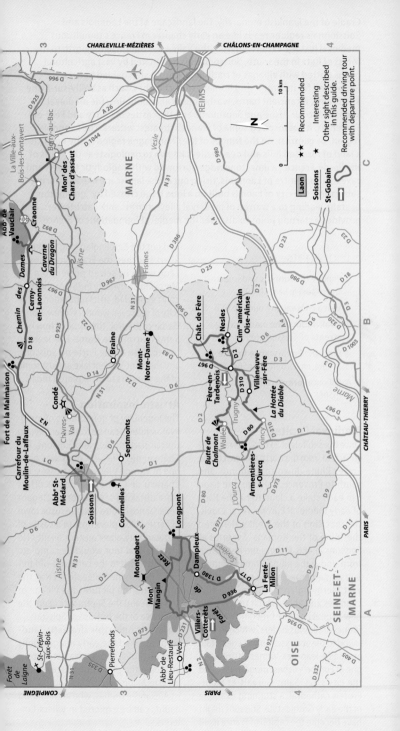

CHARLEVILLE-MÉZIÈRES
CHÂLONS-EN-CHAMPAGNE

REIMS

MARNE

★★ Recommended
★ Interesting Other sight described in this guide.
● Other sight described in this guide.
★ Recommended driving tour with departure point.

Laon
Soissons
St-Gobain

10 km

Berry-au-Bac
La Ville-aux-Bois-les-Pontavert
D 996
D 925
A 26
D 1044
D 980
D 386
N 31
Vesle
Tismes
D 967
Aisne

Abbᵉ de Vauclair
Craonne
Monᵗ des Chars d'assaut
Caverne du Dragon
Chemin des Dames
Cerny-en-Laonnois
D 18
D 925
D 967
D 22
D 967

Braine
Mont-Notre-Dame
D 14
N 31
D 22
D 6

Chât. de Fère
Nesles
Cimᵗⁱᵉ américain Oise-Aisne
D 2
Fère-en-Tardenois
D 310
Villeneuve-sur-Fère
La Hottée du Diable
D 80
Trugny
Coincy
D 310
D 1
D 967

Fort de la Malmaison
Condé
N 2
Chivres-Val
D 6
D 1

Carrefour du Moulin-de-Laffaux
Abbᵉ St-Médard
Soissons
Septmonts
D 1
Butte de Chalmont
Vallée
Armentières-s-Ourcq
D 973

Courmelles
Longpont
D 80
l'Ourcq
D 973
D 4
D 11
D 9

Montgobert
Retz
Dampleux
D 1380
D 77
La Ferté-Milon
D 936
l'Ourcq
Savières

Monᵗ Mangin
Forêt de
Villers-Cotterêts

Forêt de Laigue
St-Crépin-aux-Bois
Pierrefonds
D 973
D 335
Abbᵉ de Lieu-Restauré
Vez
N 2
D 922
D 932

COMPIÈGNE
PARIS
PARIS
CHÂTEAU-THIERRY

SEINE-ET-MARNE
OISE

491

LE LAONNOIS *and Le Soissonnais*

Cradle of the Frankish monarchy, the landscape of the Laonnois and Soissionnais regions reads like an early chapter in France's tumultuous medieval history. Extending from the Vallée de l'Ailette in the north to the forest of Retz in the south, Soissonnais is dominated by vast agricultural plains dotted with villages of traditional Corbie-step gabled houses. Renowned for its Gothic and Romanesque churches, such as Vailly-sur-Aisne and Braine, its ancient barns, wash-houses and fountains, the medieval keeps of Vic-sur-Aisne and Septmonts and the castles of Coucy and Fère-en-Tardenois, it has inspired some of France's greatest writers. The Laonnois region, by contrast, on the fringes of the Champagne region to the north, is a land of forested hills and deep valleys known to geologists as the "cliffs of the Île-de-France", a limestone ridge burrowed with troglodytic tunnels and caves. At the centre of Laonnois, rising out of the landscape like a surfacing submarine, the city of Laon is built on a long ridge crossed by "grimpettes" or stairs leading to a warren of medieval alleys, turrets and watchtowers, and provides a starting point to discover the medieval foundations of France.

Highlights

1 Explore the **tunnels** underneath the citadel in Laon (p493)

2 Visit a **château** in Coucy (p500)

3 Stroll through the **medieval streets** of Soissons (p501)

4 Cross the **Renaissance bridge** in Fère-en-Tardenois (p504)

5 Follow a **forest trail** in Retz (p506)

Medieval Capitals

Once the capitals of a Frankish state that stretched from the north and east of the Lower Rhine down to Burgundy and south to Provence, Soissons and Laon can each stake a claim to be the Paris of early medieval Europe. After Clovis, the first King of the Franks, defeated the "King of the Romans" Syagrius at Soissons in 486, kicking the last crutch from under the ailing Roman Empire, Soissons emerged as the capital of the vast Merovingian kingdom. The fine churches and abbeys built to serve the new capital became breeding grounds for new religious orders, which in turn founded the abbeys of Saint-Léger (1139) and Saint-Jean-des-Vignes (1076), once one of Europe's richest monasteries, and the city's 12C Saint-Gervais-et-Saint-Protais cathedral, a stunning example of the early Gothic style. Soissons might have become the capital of France itself had not the Carolingian king Pepin the Short switched the Frankish capital to Laon when he seized power from the Merovingian dynasty in 751. As the royal court expanded, so its reputation as the "city of the seven wonders" grew. Notre-Dame cathedral, the abbey church of Saint-Martin, the Dame Eve leaning tower, close to the Porte de Soissons, and the Saint-Vincent lake are just some of the wonders to be explored today.

Artistic Inspiration

The ingenuity of generations of medieval architects can be found far beyond the ramparts of Laon and Soissons. The Château des Sires in Coucy was once one of Europe's largest fortresses; the Château de Fère-en-Tardenois offers a breathtaking setting for an elegant Renaissance bridge, and the rustic town of Ferté-Milon plays host to a castle of extraordinary, albeit austere, beauty. No architectural tour would be complete without a visit to the centuries-old forest of Retz in the Vallée de la Crise, the setting for the picturesque village of Longpon and the Septmonts keep, the residence of the bishops of Soissons. Unsurprisingly, this dramatic landscape sparked the early imaginations of several of France's greatest writers, including the playwright Racine, born in Ferté-Milon, and the historical novelist Alexandre Dumas, whose childhood haunts can be explored in Villers-Cotterêts.

Laon★★

Former capital of France under the Carolingian dynasty, Laon occupies a dramatic site★★ along a narrow, hilly ridge (100m/328ft high) overlooking wide plains. Located on the borders of Picardy, the Paris Basin and the Champagne region, Laon is renowned for its Gothic cathedral, picturesque houses and alleyways, a mysterious network of underground galleries and its medieval ramparts.

- ▶ **Population:** 26 265
- **Michelin Local Map:** p490 B2.
- **Info:** Office du tourisme de Laon, pl. du Parvis-Gautier-de-Mortagne, 02000. ℰ03 23 20 28 62. www.tourisme-paysdelaon.com.
- **Location:** Laon is 130km/mi from Paris via the N 2, and 50km/mi from Reims by the N 44.
- **Don't Miss:** The nave of Cathédrale Notre-Dame, reaching to an amazing height; the collections of the Musée d'Art et d'Archéologie.

A BIT OF HISTORY

Carolingian Capital – Ancient **Laudunum** was the capital of France during the Carolingian period (9C–10C). Berthe au Grand Pied, Charlemagne's mother, was born northeast of Laon, while Charles the Bald, Charles the Simple, Louis IV d'Outremer, Lothar and Louis all lived on "Mount Laon" in a palace near the Ardon Gate. The reign of the Carolingians was brought to an end in 987 when **Hugues Capet** seized power and took Laon by treachery. Charlemagne's descendants were driven out and Capet established his capital in Paris.

From the Carolingian period on, Laon became a renowned religious and intellectual centre under the impetus of **Scot Erigène** and **Martin Scot** (9C); **Anselme** and **Raoul de Laon** (11C); and Bishop **Gautier de Mortagne** (12C), who commissioned the building of the cathedral. In the 13C the town's ramparts were rebuilt, and from the 16C Laon was a powerful military stronghold, besieged on several occasions, including once by Henri IV in 1594. In 1870 the munitions magazine exploded, killing or injuring over 500 people.

 WALKING TOUR

VILLE-HAUTE

Laon is divided into two sectors. The Upper Town or **Ville-Haute** is Laon's historical centre. The Lower Town or **Ville-Basse**, was severely damaged during both world wars, and does not particularly lend itself to tourism. Driving can be very tricky in the Upper Town, and parking is extremely limited, so visitors are advised to leave their car in the Lower Town and travel to the Upper Town on the cable-drawn railway called the **Poma** (open Mon–Sat 7am–8pm, Jul–Aug Sun 2.30pm; closed holidays; 1.10€ for round trip; ℰ03 23 79 07 59 SNCF train station; www.tul-laon.net).

Palais épiscopal

Adjacent to the cathedral, the former Bishop's Palace now houses the local court house. It is preceded by a courtyard offering a view of the east end of the cathedral.

The 13C building on the left rests on a gallery of pointed arches, its capitals decorated with plant motifs.

Upstairs, the **Grande Salle du Duché** (over 30m-/98ft-long) houses the Assize Court. In the building at the far end (17C) were the bishop's apartments which lead directly to the two-storey 12C chapel. The lower chapel was reserved for servants while the upper chapel, in the form of a Greek cross, served for religious ceremonies in the bishop's presence.

Facing the palace, the **Maison des Arts et Loisirs** stands on the site of the third hospital founded in the 13C. The hall

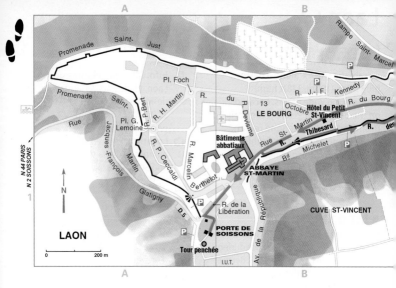

of this municipal theatre houses contemporary art exhibits. ⓞOpen Tue–Fri 1–7pm, Sat 1–6pm. ⓞClosed from mid-Jul–Aug and holidays. ℘03 23 22 86 86.

In **rue Sérurier**, no. 53 has a 15C entrance and no. 33 bis incorporates the 18C door of the old town hall. The 16C–17C Dauphin Inn, at no. 7–11 **rue au Change**, has its original wooden gallery.

Cathédrale Notre-Dame★★

ⓞOpen daily 9am–6.30pm. Audio guide (4€) from the Office de Tourisme. ℘03 23 20 28 62.

This is one of the oldest Gothic cathedrals in France. Its construction began in the 12C and was completed around 1230. The cathedral originally had seven towers: two on the west front, one over the transept crossing and four on the transept arms, two of which lost their spire during the Revolution.

The unusual **west front**, which boasts three finely decorated porches (rehandled in the 19C), is framed by two famous towers (56m/184ft tall), attributed to **Villard de Honnecourt**. Imposing yet harmonious, these are pierced by large bays and framed by slender turrets, and they bear great oxen on their corners. Built on the same model, the two towers of the transept arms reach

a height of 60m/196ft and 75m/246ft. **Interior** – Its dimensions are amazing: 110m/360ft long, 30m/98ft wide and 24m/78ft high (Notre-Dame de Paris: 130m/426ft, 45m/147ft, 35m/114ft). Roofed with sexpartite vaulting, the **nave★★★** rises to a magnificent height through four levels: great arches, galleries, a blind triforium and a clerestory. Beyond the nave, the wide chancel terminates in a flat east end, as in Cistercian churches. The transept crossing offers a good view of the nave, chancel, transept arms and the Norman-style lantern tower (40m-/131ft-high).

Beautiful 13C **stained-glass windows** grace the apse's lancet bays and rose window. The rose window in the north transept also contains 13C stained glass representing the Liberal Arts. Note the chancel railings and 17C organ.

▶ Leave the cathedral by the south transept and follow the outer wall of the cloisters, decorated with a frieze of sculpted foliage. On the corner is an Angel with a sundial.

Hôtel-Dieu

One of the few surviving medieval hospitals in France, this 12C–13C building used to open onto the street, but its bays and wide tierce-point arches have

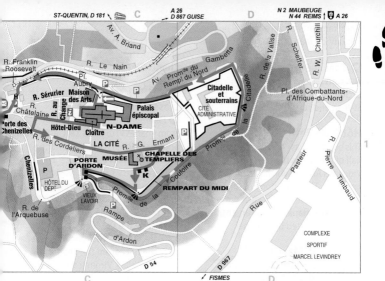

been walled up. On the lower level, the **Salle gothique Bernard de Clairvaux** *(open to the public)* attended to the needs of pilgrims and passers-by. Now occupied by the tourist office, the great **Hall of the Sick**, on the upper level, has retained some interesting elements, including mural paintings from the 15C.

◗ Follow r. Châtelaine, then one of the two lanes on the left leading to r. des Cordeliers. Cross place des Frères-Le Nain and continue along r. G.-Ermant.

Musée d'Art et d'Archéologie de Laon★

32 r. Georges-Ermant. ◷*Open Tue–Sun Jan–May, Oct–Dec 2–6pm; Jun–Sept 11am–6pm.* ◷*Closed 1 Jan, 1 May, 14 Jul, 25 Dec.* ◉*4€.* ℰ*03 23 22 87 00.*
Part of the museum's Mediterranean archaeology section, the **Greek art** collection consists of some 17 000 pieces: vases, terracotta, figurines and sculptures, including a striking head of Alexander the Great (3C BC).
The section on regional archaeology displays local finds such as tools, jewellery, weapons, figurines and pottery from the Gallo-Roman and Merovingian periods. Finally, the Beaux-Arts section includes paintings by the Master of the Rohan

Hours (15C), the **Le Nain** brothers (17C), Desportes (17C) and Berthélemy (18C).

Chapelle des Templiers★

32 r. Georges-Ermant. ◷*See museum.* ◉*No charge.* ℰ*03 23 22 87 00.*
Halfway between the cathedral and Laon's first medieval castle, the Temple commandery founded here in the 12C was a recruiting centre for the warrior-monks. After the order was suppressed, the building passed on to the Knights of St John of Jerusalem.
The porch and the gallery were added in the 13C and 14C. The interior houses two remarkable **statue-columns** of prophets removed from the west front of the cathedral.

◗ On leaving, turn right onto r. G.- Ermant, then follow r. Vinchon.

The street is lined with historic houses: no. 44 was the 13C Val des Écoliers Priory (15C chapel and 18C portal) and no. 40 the Val-St-Pierre Abbey refuge (15C–16C).

Rempart du Midi and Porte d'Ardon★

The 13C Porte d'Ardon stands at the end of the southern ramparts, flanked by watchtowers with pepper-pot roofs. The south ramparts end in a **citadel** built for Henri IV by Jean Errard.

▶ Continue to the St-Rémi rampart, and turn left toward pl. du Général-Leclerc. Walk along r. du Bourg, r. St-Jean and rue St-Martin.

Hôtel du Petit St-Vincent

This building was constructed in the first half of the 16C as the town refuge for St Vincent's Abbey, which was outside the ramparts. The main body of the Gothic building by the road is surrounded by turrets and flanked with an entrance vault surmounted by a chapel.

Abbaye St-Martin★

Open Tue–Sat. Guided tours (30min). 03 23 20 28 62.
Restored after a fire in 1944, this 12C–13C former Premonstratensian abbey church is an example of the Early Gothic style. The **west front** is pierced by a great bay; its gable is decorated with a high-relief carving of Saint Martin. The tympana over the side doors depict the Decapitation of John the Baptist (*right*) and the Martyrdom of Saint Lawrence, who was roasted alive (*left*).
Interior – The chancel and the transept chapels have flat east ends, following Cistercian custom. Recumbent figures lie near the entrance: Raoul de Coucy, a Laon Knight (late 12C) and Jeanne de Flandre, his sister-in-law, abbess of Sauvoir-sous-Laon (14C). The wooden panels in the nave are in the Louis XV style and those in the chancel Louis XIII. A 16C Christ of Compassion stands to the right of the Chapelle St-Eloi, separated from the church by a Renaissance stone screen.

Porte de Soissons★

The gate was built in the 13C from quarried stone and reinforced with round towers. A curtain wall links the gate to the **Tour Penchée** or leaning tower, so-named following subsidence.
Rue Thibesard follows the sentry path along the ramparts, offering unusual **views★** of the cathedral. Its towers rise above the old slate roofs with their

red-brick chimneys. Continue along the ramparts and **rue des Chenizelles**, a cobbled street, to the 13C **Porte de Chenizelles**.

EXCURSIONS
Liesse-Notre-Dame

▶ *15km/9mi NE. Access by D 977.*
From Charles VI to Louis XV, Liesse was a popular place of royal pilgrimage.
Basilique Notre-Dame – *2 r. Abbé Duploye.* 03 23 22 20 21. www.notreda-medeliesse.com. Built by three knights in fulfilment of their promise, the church was rebuilt in 1384 and expanded in 1480. Note the spiralled slate spire and 15C gate. Inside, a 16C rood screen separates the nave from the chancel which features a black Virgin (copy).

Château de Marchais

▶ *3km/2mi to the S of Liesse N.-D. by D 24.* Not open to the public.
This Renaissance château featuring dormer windows with sculpted pediments and pinnacles played host to the Kings of France when on pilgrimage to Liesse.

🚗 DRIVING TOUR

LE LAONNOIS

31km/19mi driving tour marked in green on the map (p491). Allow 2hrs.

The small town of **Mons-en-Laonnois** has a Greek cross **church** with a 13C chancel and 14C nave. *For tours contact the town hall on* 03 23 24 12 93.
Follow the signs for the "panorama des Creuttes", which takes you to the "crowned mountain" of Laon (180m/590ft) for a fine **view★**.
Note the "**creuttes**" or troglodyte caves on the journey up. The tour continues through to **Bourguignon**, a listed village with beautiful stone houses, and to **Royaucourt-et-Chailvet, Nouvion-le-Vineuz, Presles-et Thierny, Vorges** and **Bruyères-et-Montérault**: all villages with superb Medieval churches ranging from 12–13C.

Chemin des Dames

⚓ **Michelin Regional Map:**
p491 B3.

The Chemin des Dames is a roadway running along a ridge separating the Aisne from the Ailette River. It owes its name to the daughters of Louis XV, known as "Mesdames", who followed this route on their way to the Château de La Bove. It still bears the scars of the bitter fighting which took place here during World War I.

A BIT OF HISTORY
Nivelle Offensive
In 1914, after the first Battle of the Marne, the retreating Germans stopped at this excellent defensive spot which they fortified by making use of the quarries (*boves* or *creuttes*) hollowed out of the ridge. On 16 April 1917, the French commander **General Nivelle** sent an army under **General Mangin** to attack the German positions. Terrible French losses ensued, sparking a mutiny in the French ranks.

🚗 DRIVING TOUR

FROM SOISSONS TO BERRY AU-BAC

▶ From Soissons, take N 2 toward Laon, then turn right onto D 18.

The **Carrefour du Moulin de Laffaux** marks the western extremity of the Chemin des Dames. Signs along the itinerary below lead you through eight major historic sites, each of them indicated by informative panels explaining their military significance:

Fort de la Malmaison (1), the site of a major German cemetery; **Royère viewpoint (2)**, overlooking the Ailette valley, recalls the Malmaison offensive of October 1917; **Cerny-en-Laonnois (3)**, the Chemin des Dames memorial, French and German military cemeteries, and the memorial lantern, which can be seen from the cathedrals of Soissons, Laon and Reims; **Caverne du Dragon (4)**, see below; **Monument des Basques (5)**, commemorating the sacrifices made by Basque soldiers during WW I; **Plateau de Californie (6)** a 45min walk on the edge of a forest with panels and sculptures providing an insight into life as a soldier; **Craonne (7)**, the site of a victory won by Napoleon in 1814; **Berry-au-Bac (8)**, site of the first use of tanks in military history (16 April, 1917).

If you only have time to visit one sight, head for the memorial museum in the **Caverne du Dragon★** (🕐open Feb–Apr Tue–Sun 10am–6pm (Apr Sat & Sun 7pm); May, Jun, Sept 10am–6pm (May & Jun Sat & Sun 7pm); Jul–Aug 10am–7pm; Oct–Dec Tue–Sun 10am–6pm; ⊕5€ (1hr 30min guided tour only); ℘03 23 25 14 18; www.caverne-du-dragon.fr) exploring the lives of German and French soldiers in these underground galleries.

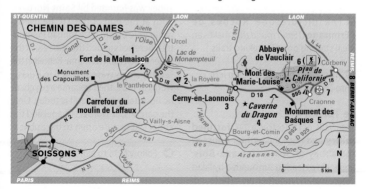

Forêt de
Saint-Gobain★

Spread over 6 000ha/14 000 acres between the Oise and the Ailette rivers, this beautiful forest covers a plateau of quarries, vales and lakes. Deer-hunting, a tradition here since the time of Louis XV, continues today.

🚗 DRIVING TOUR

SAINT-GOBAIN ROUTE

23km/14.3mi. About 2hr.

This itinerary takes you along roads winding through the forest, with several interesting stops along the way, from the birthplace of the Royal Glassworks to a series of historic religious buildings nestled in lush green valleys.

Saint-Gobain

This small town lies on the edge of a limestone ridge. It owes its name to an Irish hermit called **Goban** who settled in a nearby forest in the 7C. St-Gobain is best-known for its **Manufacture royale des grandes glaces**, a prestigious mirror glass factory founded in 1692 by Louis XIV at the request of his senior minister Colbert. It was the first to use a casting method which allowed the production of large mirrors.

▶ Take D 7 towards Laon. At the La Croix-des-Tables crossroads turn left onto D 730.

🚶 The picturesque **Roches de l'Ermitage** (*15min round trip*) makes an ideal starting point for hiking trails.

▶ Turn right onto D 55 , then left onto D 556.

Le Tortoir★

The walls of Le Tortoir, a 14C **fortified priory** and once a daughter-house of the abbey of **St-Nicolas-aux-Bois**, appear in a clearing surrounded by lakes where teal and moorhen are to be found.

♿ **Michelin Local Map:** p490 B2.

ℹ **Info:** Office du tourisme de Chauny, pl. du Marché-Couvert, 02300. ℘03 23 52 20 79. www.officede tourismedechauny.com.

▶ Return to D 55 and continue S.

The ruins of an abbey appear soon after the village of St-Nicolas-aux-Bois.

Abbaye St-Nicolas-aux-Bois★

⊶ *Not open to the public.*
The Benedictine abbey occupied a delightful setting here on the floor of a valley. The road first skirts the moat which protected the abbey walls and then two ponds encircled by greenery, beyond which the 15C abbey buildings appear.

Croix Seizine

▶ *400m/440yd from D 55 on your right.*
This expiatory monument was erected by Enguerrand V, Lord of Coucy, who was castigated in 1256 by Saint-Louis for having executed students from St-Nicolas-aux-Bois who were caught hunting on his land.

▶ In Suzy, turn right onto D 552.

Abbaye de Prémontré★

🕐*Open Apr–Oct 9am–7pm. Nov–Mar 9am–5pm. ℘03 23 23 66 66.*
Nestled in a wooded valley, this former abbey was founded by **Saint Norbert**. Born at the end of the 11C he lived a worldly life before retreating to Prémontré where he founded the abbey and the order which took its name. Rebuilt in the 18C, the abbey was converted to a glassworks in 1802, then became a psychiatric hospital, which it still is today. Only the gardens, St-Norbert Chapel and the abbot's house are open to the public.

▶ Follow D 14 to Septvaux.

Septvaux

This Romanesque church with its two belfries stands on a rise overlooking a lovely 12C wash-house *(on the road to Coucy).*

▶ D 13 returns to St-Gobain.

EXCURSIONS
La Fère

🛈 *R. du Gén.-de-Gaulle, 02800 La Fère.* ℘*03 23 56 71 91.*

Musée Jeanne-d'Aboville★

🕐*Open Wed–Mon 2–6pm.* 🎫*No charge.* ℘*03 23 56 71 91. www.ville-lafere.fr.*

This museum has a fine collection of works from the Northern school, including 16C mannerists Jean Massys, Simon and Martin De Vos, and 17C Dutch painters including Emmanuel De Witte (church interiors), Heem (still life) and Peeters (marine studies). The French school is represented by *Combat de cavalerie* by Deruet, *Panier de prunes* by Pierre Dupuis (17C), *Déjeuner de campagne* by Étienne Jeaurat and *Portrait de Madame Adélaïde* by Élisabeth Vigée-Lebrun (18C). A number of interesting Gallo-Roman finds from Versigny are on display in the archaeology section.

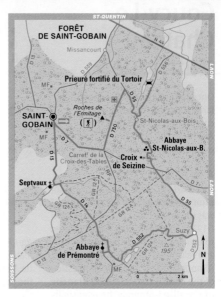

Tergnier

▶ *11km/7mi to the NW of Saint-Gobain by D 13, D 1032 and D 424.*

Musée de la Résistance et de la Déportation de Picardie

1 pl. Carnégie, Fargniers, near to Tergnier. 🕐*Open Tue–Sat 10am–noon, 2–6pm, Sun and public holidays 2.30–6.30pm* 🕐*Closed 22 Dec–2 Jan, 1 May, 1 Nov.* 🎫*4€ (under 25yrs no charge).* ℘*03 23 57 93 77. www.resistance-deportation-picardie.com.*

Goering's briefcase and a Citroën Traction, the car favoured by the Gestapo in France, feature among the exhibits in this museum exploring Nazi terror techniques and the sabotage methods used by the French Resistance.

A reconstruction of a prisoner's cell and a selection of moving recordings in the basement recall the deportation of French Jews.

Chauny

▶ *14km/9mi to the W of Saint-Gobain by D 7 then D 937.*

Like Saint-Quentin, Chauny was rebuilt in the Art Deco style following extensive damage during WW I. Don't miss the 1920s **market hall**.

ADDRESSES

♿ *See also the addresses in Laon.*

🍴 EAT

Toque Blanche – *24 av. Victor-Hugo, 02300 Chauny.* ℘*03 23 39 98 98. www.toque-blanche.fr. Closed 2–4 Jan, 16–21 Feb, 3–23 Aug, Sat lunch, Sun eve and Mon.* 🅿. *8 rooms* 🛏. A 1920 residence surrounded by parkland. Tasty contemporary cuisine served in a Romantic decor. It is also a lovely spot for a late afternoon drink.

Le Lautrec – *15 r. Luce de Lancival 02410 Saint Gobain.* ℘*03 23 56 83 64. Closed Mon eve and Wed midday.* 🅿. *8 rooms* 🛏. This small brick-built restaurant on the edge of a main road is the only restaurant in the area. But that doesn't mean the owner compromises on quality.

Coucy-Le-Château-Auffrique★

Once home to one of Europe's largest castles, Coucy enjoys commanding views over the Ailette Valley from the walls of its medieval fortifications★.

A BIT OF HISTORY

The Lord of Coucy – "Neither king nor prince am I: I am the Lord of Coucy!" was the proud boast of **Enguerrand III** (1192–1242), the castle's owner. Related to Louis IX of France, he fought loyally and valiantly at the **Battle of Bouvines.** Although he sought to take possession of the French throne during **Blanche of Castille**'s regency, he eventually returned to royal favour.

SIGHTS
Château

◷Open daily May–Sep 10am–1pm, 2–6.30pm. Oct–Apr 10am–1pm, 2–5.30pm. ◷Closed 1 Jan, 1 May, 25 Dec. ⊕5.50€. ℘03 23 52 71 28.
Enter the **bailey** before the castle proper. To the right of the entrance, the **Guardroom** (Salle des Gardes) contains a model and documents relating to Coucy. The foundations of a Romanesque **chapel** are visible on the approach to the castle, an irregular quadrilateral at the end of the headland. The great round **towers** were over 30m-/98ft-high and the **keep**, destroyed in 1917, reached a height of 54m/177ft. The dwellings were rebuilt by Enguerrand VII (late 14C), then completed by Louis of Orléans (late 15C). The remains of two large **chambers** still exist, with a **cellar** beneath. **Views** over the Ailette and Oise valleys from the west tower.

Porte de Soissons

This gate, which was built in the 13C, is reinforced by the Coucy tower and now houses the **Tour musée** (◷open Wed–Fri 10am–1pm & 2–6pm, Sat 10am–noon & 2–6pm, Sun 1–6pm; for more details call

▶ **Population:** 995
⬦ **Michelin Map:** p490 B2.
🛈 **Info:** Office du tourisme de Coucy-le-Château, 8 r. des Vivants, 02380. ℘03 23 52 44 55. www.coucy.com.
⊙ **Location:** 12mi/19km N of Soissons, and reached by the D 1, D 934 or the D 13.
⊗ **Don't Miss:** Soissons port.
◷ **Timing:** Two hours to explore the ramparts, and one for the museum.

the tourist office; ℘03 23 52 22 22) which features models of the town and its castle. **Views** over the Ailette Valley from the upper part of the tower.

Église St-Sauveur

This church with a Romanesque façade and Gothic naves (12C–14C) was almost entirely rebuilt after World War I.

Porte de Laon

Located at the base of the headland, this gate (13C) played a major defensive role. Guarded by two huge round towers, the walls are 8m-/26ft-thick at their base.

Domaine de la Grangère

This garden was once part of the Governor's estate where the legitimised son of Henri IV and Gabrielle d'Estrées, **César, Duke of Vendôme,** was born in 1594.

EXCURSIONS

After admiring the **Château de Folembray**, a regular haunt of Francis I and his official mistress Françoise de Foix, continue to **Blérancourt**, where the château (1612–1619) built by Saloman de Brosse, architect of the Palais de Luxembourg in Paris, houses the **Franco-American Museum** (℘03 23 39 60 16; www.museefrancoamericain.fr) exploring Franco-American relations. Don't miss the house of **Saint-Just** (2 r. de la Chouette; ℘03 23 39 72 17), nicknamed the "archangel of the Reign of Terror".

Soissons★

Surrounded by a rich agricultural plain, the capital of the first Merovingian kings is dominated by the tall spires of one of medieval Europe's most powerful monasteries. Largely rebuilt after World War I, the city has retained its magnificent abbey and Gothic cathedral.

A BIT OF HISTORY

Soissons played an important role under the first Frankish monarchs. After Clovis defeated the Romans outside the city gates, he demanded that his booty include a vase which had been stolen from a church in Reims. A soldier angrily opposed him, broke the vase and cried "You will have nothing, O King, but that which Destiny gives you!" The following year, while Clovis was reviewing his troops, he stopped before the same soldier, raised his sword and split the soldier's skull, saying "Thus you did with the Soissons vase".

SIGHTS
Ancienne Abbaye de St-Jean-des-Vignes ★★

🕐 *Open Apr–Sept 9am–7pm; Oct–Mar 9am–6pm (Sat & Sun open 10am).*
🕐 *Closed 1 Jan and 25 Dec.* 🚫No charge. 📞03 23 53 42 40. www.musee-soissons. org. 🚶 Guided tours: 📞03 23 53 17 37.
The old Abbey of St John of the Vines (1076) was one of the richest monasteries of the Middle Ages. In the 13C–14C, the generosity of the Kings of France, bishops, great lords and burghers allowed the Augustinian monks to build a great abbey church. In 1805, however, an imperial decree approved by the Bishop of Soissons ordered its demolition, so that its materials could be used to repair the cathedral. The resulting outcry led to the preservation of the west front, one of the city's iconic architectural landmarks.

West front – The cusped portals are delicately cut and surmounted with late-13C gables. The rest of the front dates from the 14C, except for the two Flamboyant bell towers (15C), the **north**

Population: 29 453
Michelin Local Map: p491 A3; 306: B-6.
Info: Office du tourisme de Soissons, 16 pl. Fernand-Marquigny, 02200. 📞03 23 53 17 37. www.tourisme-soissons.fr.
Location: 100km/62mi from Paris by N 2. Accessed from St-Quentin and Coucy-le-Château-Auffrique by the D1, and from Rouen, Beauvais or Reims by the N 31/E 46.

tower being larger and more ornate. An elegant openwork gallery separates the central portal from the great rose window, which has lost its tracery.

Refectory★ – Built into the extension of the west front, at the back of the great cloister, this 13C construction has two naves with pointed vaulting. The transverse arches and ribs rest on seven slender columns with foliate capitals. Eight great lobed rose windows pierce the east and south walls.

Cloisters – All that remains of the **great cloister★** are two 14C galleries. The pointed arches separated by buttresses had a blind arcade, the remains of which can be seen in the south bays. The **small cloister** features two beautiful Renaissance bays.

Cathédrale St-Gervais-et-St-Protais ★★

🕐 *Open daily Jul–Aug 9.30am–noon, 2–6.30pm; Sept–Jun 9.30am–noon, 2–4.30pm.* 🚶Guided tours available. 📞03 23 53 17 37.
The purity of its lines and the simplicity of its design make this cathedral one of the most beautiful examples of Gothic art. Its construction began in the 12C with the south transept. The chancel, nave and side aisles date from the 13C. The north transept and the upper part of the façade were not completed until the early 14C.

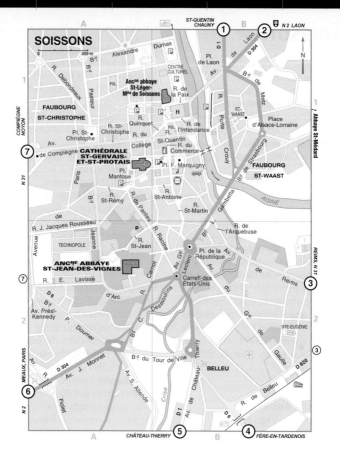

The Hundred Years War brought work to a halt before the north bell tower, inspired by the towers of Notre-Dame in Paris, was completely built. It was never finished. The **interior★** is totally symmetrical, with no extraneous detail breaking the harmony of this vast vault. Divided into four levels, the wonderfully graceful **south transept★★** ends in an apse. Note the 13C–14C stained-glass windows in the **chancel** and, hung in the **north transept**, Ruben's *Adoration of the Shepherds*.

ADDITIONAL SIGHT
Ancienne Abbaye de St-Léger – Musée de Soissons

Open Apr–Sept Mon–Fri 9am–noon, 2–6pm, Sat–Sun 2–6pm; Oct–Mar Mon–Fri 9am–noon, 2–5pm, Sat–Sun 2–6pm. ℘03 23 55 94 73. www.musee-soissons.org.

Guided tours: ℘03 23 53 17 37. Founded in 1139, St Leger's Abbey was devastated in 1567 by Protestants who also demolished the nave of the church. Today, the old monastery buildings house the collections of the museum. The **archaeology** section is dedicated to the development of the Aisne Valley from the Neolithic period to the High Middle Ages. A skilful chronological presentation traces the **history** of Soissons from Gallo-Roman times to the post-war era.

Don't miss the museum's **fine arts** with a collection of Flemish, French and Italian paintings from the 16C–19C.

EXCURSIONS
Courmelles

4km/7mi S by D 1.
The 12C **church** with its short bell tower has retained its Romanesque chevet.

Cathédrale St-Gervais-et-St-Protais

© Christophe Lehenaff/Photononstop

Septmonts

▶ 6km/7mi S by D 1 then D 95 on the left.
Lined with houses decorated with
Corbie-step gables, typical of the Soissonnais region, this village in the Crise
valley is dominated by a 14C **keep★**
(open mid-Mar–mid-Sept 9am–noon
& 1–7pm; mid-Sep–mid-Mar 9am–noon
& 1–5.30pm; no charge; 03 23 74 91
36; www.septmonts-village.fr). Built by
bishop Simon de Bucy, its high watchtower surmounted by tall chimneys
enjoys views over the village and the
Soissonnais region. The park is planted
with over one hundred species of trees.
Erected in the 15C, the **church** has a bell-
tower-porch decorated with openwork
bays. Inside, the multi-coloured beam of
glory is sculpted with medallions representing the apostles.

Fort de Condé at Chivres-Val

▶ 12km/7mi E by D 925. Open Jun–
Aug 9.30am–6.30pm; Apr–May, Sept–
Nov 9.30am–5.30pm. 5€. 03 23 54
40 00. www.fortdeconde.com.
Built by Vauban, this fort was part of the
second line of defence protecting Paris
from eastern invaders. Built in dressed
stone in the shape of a pentagon, the
fortifications were almost totally rebuilt
after suffering damage in 1870. A fine
example of 19C military architecture, it
was designed to bombard the enemy
approaching from the Aisne and Vesle
valleys and could house 658 men.

Braine

▶ 17km/10.5mi to the E (N 31).
A former staging post on the road from
Soissons to Reims, Braine developed
around a bridge over the Vesle leading to a castle. A 16C timber-framed
house with a small turret protecting a
carriage entrance has survived on Pl.
Gén-de-Gaulle. On the outskirts of Vesle,
the **Saint-Yved** church, a former Premonstratensian abbey church founded
by the Comte de Braine at the end of
the 12C, has retained its nave and two
bays, a transept and a chancel with High
Gothic chapels. On the reverse side of
the façade, two 13C sculptures depict
Christ and the Virgin surrounded by 24
statutes on a Jesse tree. Inside, the vast
chancel sports a triforium and a lantern
tower similar to that of Laon cathedral.

Mont-Notre-Dame

▶ 24km/15mi to SE (N 31). Take D 14
on the right to Braine. 34 pl. Gén-de-
Gaulle, 02220 Braine. 03 23 55 94 73.
www.tourisme-soissons.fr.
The hill dominating the Vesle valley is
surmounted by a church dedicated to St
Mary Magdelene. This Art Deco building
replaced a collegiate church destroyed
by the Germans in 1918. Its 60m/200ft
high belltower is topped by a statue.

ADDRESSES

⊜ STAY / ⊮ EAT

⊜⊜⊜ **Chambre d'hôte Domaine de
Montaigu** – 16 r.de Montaigu, 02290
Ambleny, 10km/6mi to the W of Soissons.
03 23 74 06 62. www.domainedemon
taigu.com. P 5 rooms. This luxurious residence offers peace and quiet.
Chic bedrooms and a prestigious
dining room.

⊜ **Hostellerie du Lion d'Or** – 1 pl. du
Gén.-de-Gaulle, 02290 Vic-sur-Aisne, 12km/
7.5mi to the W of Soissons. 03 23 55 50 20.
www.liondor.fr. Closed 2 wks in Feb, 1 wk
in May, 2 wks in Aug, Sun eve, Tue eve and
Mon. Dating back to 1580, this warm and
friendly restaurant serves market fresh
food around an open fire.

Fère-en-Tardenois

Renowned for its château and Renaissance galleried bridge, the capital of the Tardenois region straddles the River Ourcq. At the centre of the second Battle of the Marne in 1918, it plays host to a major American cemetery.

▶ **Population:** 3 355
◔ **Michelin Map:** p491 B4.
🖥 **Info:** ✆03 23 82 31 57 or www.fere-en-tardenois-tourisme.com.
▶ **Location:** Halfway between Soissons and Château-Thierry on the A4 .
👨‍👦 **Kids:** A walk over the magical Hottée du Diable.

SIGHTS
Halles
Built in 1540 by Anne de Montmorency, this former wheat market has a chestnut frame supported by wide cylindrical stone pillars.

Église Sainte-Macre
Contact the presbytery for details.
✆03 23 82 24 58.
Rebuilt in the 16C.The apse is lit by modern stained glass by Simon. A reliquary in the left-hand aisle houses the remains of St Macre, a virgin martyred in 303. The main altar features a painting by Vignon depicting the Adoration of the Magi.

🚗 DRIVING TOURS

EAST OF THE TARDENOIS
16km/10mi tour marked in green on the map (◔p491). Allow 2hrs.

▶ Leave Fère-en-Tardenois to the N by D 967, crossing through the forest of Saponay.

This tour begins at the 13C **Château de Fère**, built in the 13C on land belonging to a junior branch of the French royal family. The Renaissance **galleried bridge★★** leading to the castle, thought to have been designed by Jean Buliant, rests on five Roman arches. Note the seven round towers built from dressed stoned, the bases of which are decorated with a curious dog-tooth design. The tour continues to **Château de Nesles**, (☛*currently closed for renovation, contact for details; ✆03 23 82 90 93; www.chateaude-nesles.com)*, a 15C castle surrounded by a curtain wall guarded by eight towers.
Oise-Aisne American Cemetery

(🕐*open 9am–5pm;* ☛*40min free guided tours; ✆03 23 82 21 81; www. abmc.gov)* is the second largest WW I American cemetery in France. The cemetery is built on the site of a fierce battle fought between the 42nd "Rainbow" Division and the 4th Division of the Prussian Guard in October 1918.

WEST OF FÈRE-EN-TARDENOIS
25km/15mi tour marked in green on the map (◔*p490)*. Allow 3hrs.

▶ Leave to the S by D 967 towards Beuvardes. At Villemoyenne, turn right down D 79 towards Villeneuve.

The French writer Paul Claudel (1868-1955) was born in the presbytery adjoining the chevet of Saint-Georges Church at **Villeneuve-dur-Fère**, the first stop on this tour of the region.
🔼 Deep in the forest of Coincy, a sandy pathway leads to a large uneven surface of sandstone rocks sculpted by the elements, called **La Hottée du Diable**. Walk through the furrowed plateaux of the Tardenois to Coincy. The ruins of the 13C **Château d'Armentières-sur-Ourcq** are completed by a 15C postern tower and several Renaissance additions. Erected in 1934 to commemorate the second Battle of the Marne, the granite **Monument de la butte de Chalmont** overlooking the Tardenois plain features Les Fantômes, a sculpture representing eight soldiers with different weapons. Return to Wallée. Take the road on the left to the troglodytic caves, inhabited since prehistoric times.

La Ferté-Milon★

A pleasant rural town guarded by a late Middle Age castle, La Ferté-Milon is the birthplace of French dramatist Jean Racine. Jean de La Fontaine, famous for his fables, was also a frequent visitor to the town.

🐾 WALKING TOUR

▶ From the car park on the Ile de l'Ourcq. Allow 2hrs. Cross the arm of the mill, graced by a large wheel, into the old town around Notre-Dame church. Turn left after the bridge down rue de Reims.

Musée Jean-Racine

🕐 Open Apr–Oct Sat, Sun and public holidays 10am–12.30pm, 3–5.30pm. 🎫4.50€. ♿ 📞03 23 96 77 42.

Racine spent his childhood in this house, which belonged to his grandmother. A small display explores the playwright's life, his work and the history of the town. Turn right down rue Racine, an ancient cobbled alleyway. At no. 1 is a beautiful house where Marie Rivière, Racine's sister, lived.

Église Notre-Dame

Open during mass (May–Oct 2nd and 4th Sun of the month).

This is where 26-year old **Jean de La Fontaine** (born in Château-Thierry), married Marie Héricart, aged only 14. This church (12C), modified several times, has a semi-circular chevet built and decorated by Philibert Delorme at the request of Catherine de Médicis.

Château★

The rectangular esplanade running up to a terrace overlooking the valley was once the castle's interior courtyard. On entering the interior "shell" of the château, note the debris dating from the demolition of the castle in 1594, dwarfed by toothing stones designed to support an extension that was never built. Pass through the de-crowned porte de Bourneville and take a few steps back

▶ **Population:** 2 108
♿ **Michelin Local Map:** p491 A4; 306: A7.
ℹ️ **Info:** Office de tourisme – 31 r. de la Chaussée. 02460 La Ferté-Milon. 📞03 23 96 77 42; www.laferte milon.fr. The tourist office runs a discovery tour between Ferté-Milon and Villers-Cotterêts.
▶ **Location:** On the edge of the Oise and Seine-et-Marne, 35km/22mi from Soissons and Compiègne. The town overlooks the River Ourcq and canal.
🕐 **Timing:** Allow 2hrs. Don't forget your binoculars to admire the château façade.

onto the grass to admire the façade. Pierced with windows on three levels and topped by a machicolated cornice, the castle has three large towers joined by a lancet arch with almond-shaped bases. At the top of the towers, don't miss the magnificent 15C **low-reliefs★**, decapitated effigies of "gallant knights", sculpted into niches under an arch. One of the low-reliefs is decorated with a **Crowning of the Virgin★** *(between the two central towers of the entrance)*.

▶ Take the r. des Bouchers and r. de Reims, and turn right into pl. du Port-au-Blé. Cross over the footbridge.

Bords de l'Ourcq

Downstream, note the tower of the outer wall and the garden of Héricart, where La Fontaine courted his fiancée. Upstream, the "corn loft on the water" features a projecting building that once housed the pulleys of the crane that lowered the sacks of wheat into "flûtes" or store ships on the Ourcq.

Église Saint-Nicolas

R. de la Chaussée. This 15C church houses a beautiful ensemble of **stained glass** dating from the 16C.

Villers-Cotterêts

Once a favourite hunting ground of Francis I, Villers-Cotterêts is a peaceful town fringed by the forest of Retz. It is also the birthplace of Alexandre Dumas, a prolific 19C writer of historic adventure novels.

▶ **Population:** 9 839
◔ **Michelin Local Map:** p491 A4; 306: A7.
🛈 **Info:** Office de tourisme, pl. A.-Briand, Villers-Cotterêts 02600. ℘03 23 96 55 10. http://tourisme.cc-villers-cotterets.fr.

🥾 WALKING TOUR

Several generations of Dumas have left their mark on the streets of Villers-Cotterêts. **Place du Docteur-Mouflier** (formerly place de la Fontaine) is mentioned in Dumas Senior's memoirs. His grandfather's **hotel** stood on the square, as did the **lawyer's office** where he was employed, and Madame Dumas' **tobacconist's shop**. The writer's **birthplace** is at 46 rue A.-Dumas.

Walk to the square, then take rue de Bapaume to the cemetery where the **Dumas' family grave** is located. A **statue** of Dumas by **Bourret** stands in the small public garden, on rue L.-Lagrange.

Musée Alexandre-Dumas

24 r. Demoustier. ◔*Open Wed–Mon 2–5pm (Sun 6pm).* ◔*Closed last Sun of the month.* ◷*3.40€.* ℘*03 23 96 23 30.* Three small rooms are dedicated to the famous "Three Dumas": letters, manuscripts, novels, paintings, satirical cartoons, busts and various objects.

ADDITIONAL SIGHT
Château François I

◔ 🥾 *May– Oct: guided tours Tue–Sun at 11am and 3pm. Nov–Apr: guided tours daily Mon–Sat at 11am and 3pm.* ◷*4.50€.* ℘*03 23 96 55 10.*
Enter the courtyard to see the east and west wings bordered by buildings decorated with Renaissance elements. The **main staircase**★ has a spectacular double flight of stairs (1535). The carvings on the ceiling are from the school of **Jean Goujon**. The **King's staircase**, contemporary with the main staircase, has its original decoration of carved mythological scenes from *The Dream of Polyphyle*.

Outside, all that remains of **Le Nôtre's park** are the outlines of the parterre and the perspective of the Allée Royale.

🚗 DRIVING TOUR

FORÊT DE RETZ

45km/28mi tour marked in green on the map opposite. Allow 2hr 30min.

▶ Leave Villers-Cotterêts by D 973 towards Pierrefonds; after 1km/0.5mi, turn right and park at Malva lake.

⊘ Picnic and recreational areas are available around Malva, the Grande-Ramée lake, La Fontaine du Prince, Rond-Capitaine and La Fontaine Gosset (Fleury).
A topographical guide to the forest of Retz is available for sale (3€) in bookshops and tourist offices.

The three Dumas

Grandfather: Thomas-Alexandre Dumas (1762–1806), general in Napoléon's army.

Father: Alexandre Dumas Senior (1802–1870), famous writer best known for his historical novels such as *The Three Musketeers,* 1844.

Son: Alexandre Dumas Junior (1824–1895), also author and dramatist, best known for *The Lady of the Camelia,* 1848.

The Forest of Retz

The forest consists mainly of beechwood copses and smaller numbers of oak, hornbeam, ash, cherry, maple, silver birch and chestnut trees. The sandy soil is planted primarily with conifer trees. There are also some fifteen remarkable trees to discover, including Saut-du-Cerf, Pré-Gueux and Amours beeches, and the Crapaudières and Roi du Rome oaks. The forest is also teeming with wildlife.

Ermitage Saint-Hubert

15min round trip by foot through the forest clearing. The path cuts halfway along the drive leading to the château, the Allée Royale. The small building, restored in 1970 and decorated with salamanders, the symbol of Francis I, was home to a hermit until 1693.

▶ At the "Passant, arrête-toi" monument, turn right along the Faîte road. After 2km/1.2mi, park on a bend. Walk through the forest on foot.

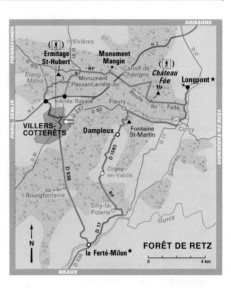

A granite stele marks the location of a lookout tower **Monument Mangin** used as a command post by French general Mangin on 18 and 19 of July, 1918.

Château-Fée

🥾 *30min along a forest trail, returning to the Château Fée.*
It may sound like a château, but this is actually a hill in a reforested area.

Abbaye de Longpont★

🕐 *Open Sat, Sun and public holidays, 11am–noon, 2.30–6.30pm.* ≈7€.
Allow 1hr. *Guided tour (45min).*
♿ ℘06 19 98 58 86.
www.longpont.com.
Located in a wide valley bordering the forest of Retz, the peaceful **village** of Longpont is accessible by D 804 or N 2. It is dominated by the imposing ruins of a church and several buildings once belonging to a Cistercian abbey founded

by Saint Bernard in the 12C. The abbey is heralded by the four large conical turrets of a 14C fortified gate, a vestige of an earlier wall, as you leave the forest.
Ruins of the abbey church – The church, designed in pure Gothic style, was consecrated in 1227 in the presence of Saint Louis and his mother, Blanche de Castille. The main façade remains standing, although the tracery of the rose window has disappeared.

Dampleux

The **Fontaine Saint-Martin** is an abundant spring, the harnessing of which (inspection holes, lake and overflow) is one of the symbols of the Forest of Retz, the reservoir of the Paris region.
The road crosses through the Oigny-Dampleux clearing. From the top, drive down into the Ourcq valley.

▶ D 17 leads to La Ferté-Milon. Take D 936 to Villers-Cotterêts.

L'OISE

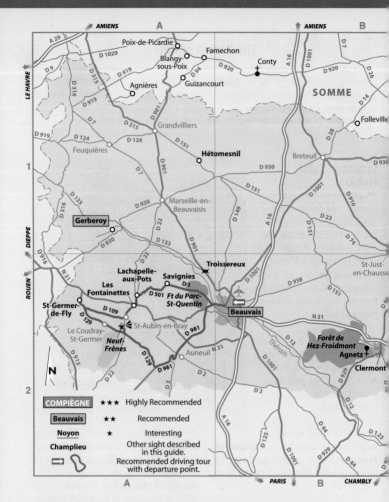

COMPIÈGNE	★★★	Highly Recommended
Beauvais	★★	Recommended
Noyon	★	Interesting
Champlieu		Other sight described in this guide.

Recommended driving tour with departure point.

For centuries, Oise was the bucolic back garden of the Paris elite. Dotted with rambling palaces, fountains, fairytale castles and hunting forests, it has seduced and ruined its fair share of dynasties. Marking the transition from Picardy to the Île-de-France, Oise is conveniently located just 45km/28 mi from Paris, but a world away from its clamour and commotion. With its damp clay soil, eastern Oise is oak tree country, a species that begrudgingly shares the forest of Compiègne with 14 500ha/35 000 acres of beeches and pine trees, vales, lakes and villages that open onto the valleys of the Oise and Aisne. To the north, east and south of Compiègne, a series of knolls and headlands form a steep-sided crescent, plunging 80m/262ft in certain areas, offering an ideal terrain for the commanding castles of Compiègne and Pierrefonds, tiny timber-framed houses and sky-hungry abbey churches. Oise's chalky western cattle-grazing plains, on the other hand, have an earthier feel, where pottery chimneys compete for attention with the spires of Beauvais cathedral and the Oise canal strikes out on its sluggish journey through 34km/21mi of ingenious locks fringed by peaceful towpath walks.

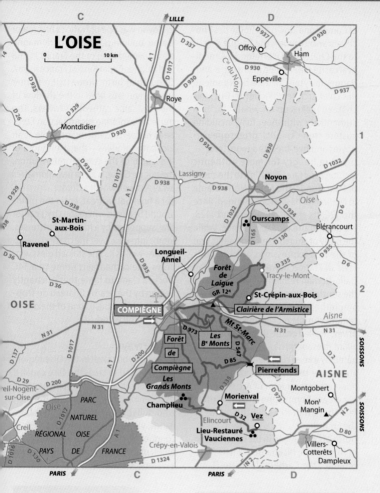

L'OISE

Royal Reputation

Standing in front of the Louis XV façade of the Château de Compiègne, it's not difficult to understand the pull this region had on its royal residents. Hidden behind a dense curtain of forest and crammed with an exquisite mixture of furniture from the 17C to the 19C, its rooms read like a history of Bourbon excess and Napoleonic megalomania.

A short drive away to the west, near Rethondes, there lies a railway carriage that had as great an impact on European history as the salons of Compiègne. It was here that the armistices of 1918 and 1940 were signed, in the simple, functional surroundings of converted dining car.

Highlights

1 Explore a **royal château** in Compiègne (p512)

2 Learn about life on **Oise canal** in Longueil-Annel (p517)

3 Discover Napoleon III's **mock medieval castle** in Pierrefonds (p521)

4 Admire the soaring vaults of **Noyon cathedral** (p527)

5 Get an insight into Oise's pottery traditions in **Beauvais** (p532)

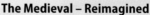

The Medieval – Reimagined

Just when you thought one large palace was enough for anyone, head west out of Compiègne, down the Route des Princesses and through the Laigue massif to the Château de Pierrefonds. A medieval castle remodelled into a cape-and-dagger fairytale fortress by Napoléon III's chief architect, Viollet-le-Duc, this château makes up for what it lacks in authenticity with sheer folly, including austere stone knights, grotesque gargoyles and five-breasted monsters.

If you're hungry for more authentic architectural fare, 8km/5mi to the south of Pierrefonds, the Eglise Notre-Dame in Morienval has hardly changed since the 12C. Its arches, build around 1123, are among the oldest in France, while the body of church itself represents one of the first expressions of the Gothic style in France. More ancient still, the Gallo-Roman remains of Champlieu to the south feature a romantically ruined amphitheatre within a neat bath and temple complex. Even the tiny village of Vez, nestled on the slope of a hill a few kilometres south, has a 14C castle dominated by a keep commanding stunning views over the Automne valley where none other than Joan of Arc stayed on her way to Compiègne and the terrible fate that awaited her at the hands of the English.

North of Compiègne in the hillier terrain of Noyonnais, nicknamed "Little Switzerland", the Cathédrale Notre-Dame in Noyon was one of France's first major Gothic buildings, where Charlemagne was crowned King of the Franks in 768 and Hughes Capet King of France in 987. Of humbler birth, protestant reformer Jean Calvin was born in the shadow of the very same cathedral's towers. The museum exploring his impact on European history and the region's role as an incubator of ideas – the stronghold of the leader of the counter-reformation, the duc de Guise, is just a few kilometres away – is well worth a detour.

For a final Gothic treat, enter the plains around Beauvais where the city's cathedral, supported by a forest of buttresses, looms into view over the grazing meadows. As well as its fine stained glass windows, the cathedral is home to a 14C clock, a claim to fame that's instantly beaten by the nearby Château de Troissereux, which houses one of the oldest clocks in the world.

Waterways

Wherever you travel in the Oise region, you're bound to cross the Oise canal. If you're curious about who built the canal, its ingenious lock system and the men who pulled its barges with their bare hands, visit the Maison des Bateliers in Longueil-Annel, where a towpath exhibition makes the ideal starting point for a waterside walk.

Étangs de St-Pierre, Forêt de Compiègne

© Stéphane Ouzounoff/Photononstop

Compiègne★★★

A genteel provincial town, Compiègne was a royal residence long before it hosted the brilliant parties of the Second Empire. Discover its sumptuous château or walk through its vast forests and discover the clearing where the armistices of 11 November 1918 and 22 June 1940 were signed.

A BIT OF HISTORY

Origins – The city of Compiègne developed around the 9C palace of **Charles the Bald** and the abbey he founded to house the relics of Saint Cornelius. This abbey preceded Saint-Denis (& see SEINE-ST-DENIS) as the royal necropolis.

Joan of Arc imprisoned – In May 1430, the Burgundians and the English camped beneath Compiègne's town walls, on the north side of the River Oise. Joan of Arc came to survey the enemy position and returned on the 23rd, entering the town from the south. That same evening, she attempted an assault, crossing the river and chasing the Burgundian vanguard. However, reinforcements came to the aid of the Burgundians, while the English attacked from the rear. The 'Maid of Orléans' covered the retreat with a handful of men. She reached the moat just as the commanding officer in Compiègne gave the order to raise the drawbridge, fearing the enemy would slip inside with the last of the French soldiers. A short skirmish ensued. A Picardy archer toppled Joan of Arc from her horse and she was taken prisoner. Frémiet's **equestrian statue** of Joan of Arc stands on the spot where she was captured near place du 54e-Régiment-d'Infanterie.

A castle of many owners – Compiègne was a favourite haunt of French kings. Originally consisting of four main buildings haphazardly arranged around a central courtyard, the château was not always an obvious royal residence, as **Louis XIV** pointed out in his famous remark about the château: "At Versailles, I am lodged like a king; at Fontainebleau, like a prince; and at Compiègne,

▶ **Population:** 108 234

⌖ **Michelin Local Map:** p509: CD2 H-4; map 106 fold 10.

🛈 **Info:** Office du tourisme de Compègne, pl. de l'Hôtel-de-Ville, 60200. ✆03 44 40 01 00. www.compiegne-tourisme.fr.

▶ **Location:** Most of the city occupies the left bank of the Oise River. The château dominates Place du General de Gaulle. Three blocks south of the town centre stands the town hall which houses the tourist office.

🅿 **Parking:** Parking places around the château, near St-Jacques Church, on Cours Guynemer, and at at the train station (on the opposite side of the river).

😊 **Don't Miss:** The château, with its royal and imperial private apartments, and two outstanding museums; the forest surrounding the town and the famous Clairière de l'Armistice.

🕐 **Timing:** Allow at least 2hrs for the château, more if you'd like to explore the grounds. And if you want to discover the highlights of the forêt de Compiègne, note that the driving tours we suggest require 1hr to 1hr30min each.

👥 **Kids:** Kids should find a visit to the Cité des Bateliers, in Longueil-Annel, quite interesting, as they will get to take a look at a barge hold, walk along a canal and learn how a lock works.

like a peasant." He had new apartments built facing the forest. His 75 visits here were marked by sumptuous feasts and military camps.

Louis XV ordered the complete rebuilding of the palace in 1738, although a master plan of 1751 was brought to a halt by the Seven Years War. **Louis XVI** continued the project but left the palace unfinished. He was only able to occupy the royal apartments in 1785. A great terrace was built in front of the palace's façade, overlooking a park. It was connected to the gardens by a monumental central flight of steps, replacing the old moat. After the Revolution, the palace served first as a military school, then as an engineering college. In 1806, **Napoléon I** had the château entirely restored by the architect Berthaut, the painter Girodet and the decorators Redouté and the Dubois brothers.

A wedding palace – It was in the Compiègne Forest that, on 14 May 1770, the future Louis XVI was introduced to **Marie-Antoinette of Austria** for the first time. On 27 March 1810, the great-niece of Marie-Antoinette, **Marie-Louise of Austria**, was also scheduled to arrive in Compiègne. She had married Napoléon I by proxy and the Emperor couldn't wait to meet his bride. A dinner planned in Soissons was cancelled and instead the couple had supper at Compiègne.

The Second Empire "Series" – Compiègne was the favourite residence of **Napoléon III** and **Empress Eugénie**. They came every autumn for several weeks to hunt. They also entertained the celebrities of the time, arranged in five "series" of about 80 people grouped by "affinities". Lodging the guests was often difficult and many distinguished individuals slept under the eaves. The war of 1870 interrupted this joyous life and the work on the new theatre. During the Emperor's long periods of residence at Compiègne most of the First Empire furniture was replaced.

The World Wars – From 1917 to 1918 the palace was the headquarters of General **Nivelle** and then **Pétain**. The armistice of 11 November 1918 (between the Allies and Germany) was signed in the Compiègne forest. On 22 June 1940, another treaty (between Germany and France) would be signed on the same spot (*see p518*).

Compiègne suffered heavy bombing during World War II. **Royallieu**, a district south of the town, served from 1941 to 1944 as a centre from which prisoners were sent to various Nazi concentration camps (note the memorial at the entrance to the military camp as well as in Compiègne railway station).

PALACE★★★

⚲*Open Wed–Mon 10am–6pm.* ✎*Guided tours.* ⚲*Closed 1 Jan, 1 May, 25 Dec.* ✎*7€ (for all permanent exhibits).* ✆*03 44 38 47 02. www.musee-chateau-compiegne.fr.*

Viewed from the square, the palace is paradoxically a Louis XV château built almost entirely from 1751 to 1789. An austerely Classical château, it covers a vast triangular area (3ha/7.5 acres). The decoration inside and the collection of 18C and First Empire tapestries and furnishings are, however, exceptional.

Among the many details unifying the various apartments are fine *trompe-l'œil* paintings by Sauvage (1744–1818) over the doors. Work on the new **Théâtre Impérial**, which began in 1867 during the reign of Napoléon III, was interrupted by the Franco-Prussian War in 1870. Today, its interior layout has become popular as a venue for concerts and operettas.

Appartements Historiques★★

The Historic Apartments of the palace begin with an exhibition on the château's history; beyond them rises the Queen's Grand Staircase (or Apollo Staircase), which led directly to the Queen's apartment. Beyond the stairs is the entrance hall or Gallery of Columns which precedes the **Grand Staircase** (1).

Climb the staircase with its beautiful 18C wrought-iron balustrade to the landing which provides the setting for a great Gallo-Roman sarcophagus; it once served as a font in the abbey church of St Cornelius and is a relic of very early Compiègne.

The first-floor **Guardroom** (1785) (2) leads into the antechamber or **Ushers' Salon** (3), which gave access to both the King's apartment (*left*) and the Queen's (*right*).

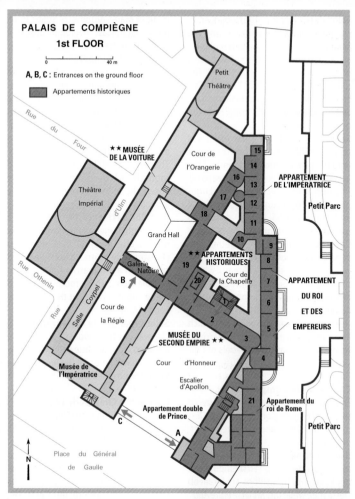

PALAIS DE COMPIÈGNE
1st FLOOR

0 _____ 40 m

A, B, C : Entrances on the ground floor

Appartements historiques

Rue du Four

★★ MUSÉE
DE LA VOITURE

Théâtre
Impérial

d'Ulm

Petit
Théâtre

Cour de
l'Orangerie

15
14
16   13
17   12
11
18   10
9
Grand Hall
★★ APPARTEMENTS
HISTORIQUES
Galerie
Natoire   19
Cour de
la Chapelle   8
B   20   7
Cour de   6
la Régie   5
MUSÉE DU
SECOND EMPIRE ★★   3
Cour   d'Honneur   4
Musée de
l'Impératrice   2
Escalier
d'Apollon   21
Appartement double
de Prince   Appartement du
roi de Rome
C   Petit Parc
A
Place du Général
de Gaulle

APPARTEMENT
DE L'IMPÉRATRICE

Petit Parc

APPARTEMENT

DU ROI

ET DES

EMPEREURS

Rue Othenin

Rue

Salle
Coypel

N

Appartement du Roi et des Empereurs

The King's and Emperors' apartment houses exceptional groups of objects, works and memorabilia.

Salle à manger de l'Empereur (4)– It was here that on 1 May 1814, Louis XVIII entertained Czar Alexander. The dining room's decor and furnishings are First Empire. Pilasters and doors, surmounted by *grisaille* paintings by Sauvage, stand out against the fake rose-pink onyx. Note a striking *trompe-l'œil,* also by Sauvage, representing Anacreon. During the Second Empire, a private theatre was set up here, with those close to the empress taking part in charades and revues.

Palace of Compiègne

© Yann Guichaoua/age fotostock

513

Salon des Cartes (5) – The Nobles' Antechamber under Louis XVI became the Senior Officers' Salon under Napoléon I, and ended up as the Aide-de-Camp Salon or the Card Salon under Napoléon III. The room contains furnishings from the First Empire (chairs covered in Beauvais tapestry) and the Second Empire. Note the quoits and pin table.

Salon de Famille (6) – This room was once Louis XVI's bedchamber. The **view**★ onto the park extends the length of the avenue to the Beaux Monts (&see p519). The furnishings recall Empress Eugénie's taste for mixing styles: Louis XV armchairs, unusual little seats for two (*confidents*) or for three (*indiscrets*) etc.

Cabinet du Conseil (7) – Together with Versailles and Fontainebleau, Compiègne was one of the three châteaux where the king held counsel. Representatives of the Republics of Genoa and of the Kingdom of France signed two successive treaties here (1756 and 1764) which accorded France the right to garrison troops in the maritime citadels of Corsica. An immense tapestry illustrates the Crossing of the Rhine by Louis XIV.

Chambre de l'Empereur (8) – The Emperor's bedchamber has been restored to its First Empire glory, with Jacob-Desmalter furnishings and friezes representing eagles.

Bibliothèque (9) – This room was used as a library during the First Empire. The bookcase and furnishings are by Jacob Desmalter, while the *Minerve entre Apollon et Mercure* painted on the ceiling is the work of Girodet. A secret door used to lead to the Empress's apartment.

Appartement de l'Impératrice

These rooms comprised the queen's principal apartments, the only ones in which Marie-Antoinette ever stayed. Later, they were particularly favoured by Empresses Marie-Louise and Eugénie.

Salon du Déjeuner (10) – The delightful breakfast room, with pale blue and yellow silk hangings, was prepared for Marie-Louise in 1809.

Salon de Musique (11) – This was one of Empress Eugénie's favourite rooms. The Louis XVI pieces, from the apartment of Marie-Antoinette at St-Cloud, recall that the last sovereign consort of France kept the queen's memory alive.

Chambre de l'Impératrice (12) – The majestic tester bed is enclosed by white silk curtains and gold-embroidered muslin. Paintings by Girodet represent the seasons, and the Morning Star appears in the centre of the ceiling. The round boudoir leading to the bedchamber served as a dressing-room and for taking baths. The last three of these interconnecting rooms form a decorative First Empire ensemble. Seats are arranged formally around a couch in the **Grand Salon** (13); the **Salon des Fleurs** (14) owes its name to the eight panels painted with lily-like flowers, after Redouté; the **Salon Bleu** (15) strikingly contrasts blue walls and seats with a red marble fireplace and console tables. These rooms belonged to the imperial prince at the end of the Second Empire.

Salle à manger de l'Impératrice (16) The walls of this modestly sized room are lined with "antique yellow" stuccomarble. It was here that the Archduchess Marie-Louise dined with the Emperor for the first time.

Galerie des Chasses de Louis XV (17) The room is hung with Gobelins tapestries, which were woven as early as 1735 based on sketches by Oudry. One represents a hunt along the River Oise and includes the silhouettes of Compiègne and the old Royallieu Abbey. The series continues in the **Galerie des Cerfs** (18), formerly the Queen's Guardroom, then the Empress' Guardroom.

Galerie du Bal (19)– The room (39×13m/ 128×43ft) was constructed within a few months for Marie-Louise's arrival by gutting two floors of small apartments. The ceiling paintings glorify the Emperor's victories; the mythological scenes at the end of the room are by Girodet. Throughout the Second Empire the gallery served as a dining room furnished with an immense table.

Galerie Natoire and Salle Coypel – These were built by Napoléon III to lead to the imperial theatre. Their decoration illustrates the Story of Don Quixote. **Tapestry drawings**★ by Natoire (1700–77).

Chapel (20)– The First Empire chapel is surprisingly small for such a vast château, as the great chapel planned by Gabriel was never built. It was here, on 9 August 1832, that the marriage took place between Princess Louise-Marie, eldest daughter of Louis-Philippe, and Leopold I, King of Belgium. Princess Marie of Orléans, the French king's second daughter, designed the stained-glass window.

Appartement double de Prince – Napoléon I had this apartment arranged to receive a foreign sovereign and his or her consort. This excellent group of Empire rooms comprises a dining room, four salons and a great bedchamber.

Appartement du roi de Rome – This apartment has been restored to its appearance in 1811, when Napoléon I's son (five months old at the time) stayed in it for one month. All the original furnishings adorn the salon-boudoir, bathroom, boudoir, bedchamber and main drawing room. In the middle of the apartment, a room (**21**) has been restored to appear as it did at the end of the 18C, when it was used as Queen Marie-Antoinette's games room.

Musée du Second Empire★★

The museum is located in a series of small, quiet drawing rooms and presents life at Court during the Second Empire. Beyond the first room, displaying **Daumier**'s humorous drawings, a space is devoted to the "beauties" of the period. **Princess Mathilde** (1820–1904), one of the reign's great figures, has pride of place here. She was for a brief time the fiancée of Louis Napoléon, her close cousin.

The museum is home to the famous painting *The Empress with her Ladies-in-Waiting* by **Winterhalter** (1855). Among the many sculptures by **Carpeaux** in the last rooms, note the bust of **Napoléon**, aged by the fall of the Empire.

Musée de l'Impératrice – This collection includes memorabilia of official life and life in exile, as well as popular objects associated with Empress Eugénie.

Musée de la voiture et du tourisme★★

Created in 1927 on the initiative of the Touring Club of France, this museum is dedicated to the history of locomotion, from the origins of horse-drawn vehicles to the early years of the automobile. Its fascinating collection includes 18C–19C carriages, cycles, early electric and steam vehicles and cars up to World War I.

Grand Hall – Antique carriages are on display in what was formerly the kitchen courtyard: the oldest, a travelling berlin coach, which belonged to the kings of Spain, dating from c. 1740; the berlin coach in which Bonaparte made his entrance to the town in 1796. Also on show are 18C and 19C travelling carriages, a mail-coach, charabancs, a Madeleine-Bastille omnibus and Orsay broughams, and the imperial train carriage used by Napoléon III for his trips between Paris and Compiègne.

Kitchens and Outbuildings – This section explores the evolution of the two-wheeler, starting with the heavy ancestors of the bicycle, hobbies (1817). Around 1880, the penny-farthing, built out of iron tubing, was introduced with an unusually large front wheel to increase its speed. Developments such as the invention of the chain belt rendered large wheels unnecessary.

First Floor – These rooms are devoted to foreign vehicles and their accessories: Dutch and Italian cabriolets, a Sicilian cart, palanquin, sleighs, etc.

Petit Parc

The "Petit Parc" refers to the gardens (the "Grand Parc" surrounding the gardens covers part of the forest).

The Emperor's guiding idea was *"to link the château as soon as possible to the forest, which is the true garden and the real beauty of this residence"*. The enclosing wall which blocked the view of the woods was taken down and replaced by iron railings. Beyond, the openness of avenue des Beaux-Monts creates a magnificent linear perspective (4km/6mi long).

Impatient to reach the forest without having to go through the town,

Napoléon I had a central ramp built for carriages between the terrace and the park over a glorious flight of steps by Gabriel.

The Petit Parc was redesigned as a formal English garden by **Berthault**. The present layout dates from the Second Empire.

ADDITIONAL SIGHTS
Hôtel de ville

This remarkable building was constructed under Louis XII in the late-Gothic style. It was restored during the 19C and the façade statues date from this period. They represent, from left to right around the central equestrian statue of Louis XII: Saint Denis, Saint-Louis, Charles the Bald, Joan of Arc, Cardinal Pierre d'Ailly and Charlemagne. The belfry, which consists of two floors and a slate-covered spire flanked by four pinnacled turrets, houses a communal bell melted and reshaped in 1303. At the base of the spire, three figures, called **picantins** and dressed as Swiss foot-soldiers from the period of Francis I, ring the hours and the quarter-hours.

▲▲ Musée de la Figurine historique★

In the Hôtel de la Cloche. ⏰*Open Tue–Sun 10am–noon, 2–6pm.* ⏰*Closed 1 Jan, 1 May, 14 Jul, 1 Nov, 25 Dec.* ✺*3€ (no charge 1st Sun of the month).* ♿ *℘03 44 20 26 04.*
www.musee-figurine.fr.

This museum houses a collection of over 100 000 model figures in tin, lead, wood, plastic, paper and cardboard, sculpted wholly or partly in the round or flat.

Église St-Jacques

The church features a 15C tower, the highest in the town, at one of the corners of its west front. This was the parish church of the king and the court, so funds were readily available for the chancel to be reworked in marble in the 18C and for the addition of carved-wood panels at the base of the nave's pillars. The harmony of the Gothic style at the time of Saint-Louis is particularly evident in the chancel with its narrow, clerestory lit triforium and the 13C transept.

An ambulatory was added in the 16C. The chapel in the north aisle houses three 15C painted wooden statues.

Vieille Cassine

From place St-Jacques, cross r. Magenta to reach r. des Lombards. This half-timbered house (no. 10) dates from the 15C. This is where the "Maîtres du Pont" used to live. They controlled the boat traffic on the Oise River, especially dangerous around the Saint-Louis bridge.

Musée Antoine-Vivenel

⏰*Open Tue–Sun 10am–1pm, 2–6pm.* ⏰*Closed 1 Jan, 1 May, 14 Jul, 1 Nov, 25 Dec.* ✺*3€ (no charge 1st Sun of month).* *℘03 44 20 26 04.*
www.museevivenel.fr.

Housed in the **Hôtel de Songeons** (late 18C), the gardens of which were turned into a public park, the museum focuses on antiquities from Picardy and the Mediterranean with artefacts and art pieces from Prehistory to the end of the Gallo-Roman period. Note three bronze helmets dating from c.600 BC, as well as Greek and Roman marbles

---

The Motorcar's "first steps"

Vehicles of note include the **Panhard** No 2, the first car equipped with a four-stroke **Daimler** engine; the 1895 **vis-à-vis** by **Bollée & Son** which was one of the entrants in the race from Paris to Marseille-en-Beauvaisis (north of Beauvais); the **De Dion-Bouton** series, the large 1897 break belonging to the Duchess of Uzès, the first woman driver; the 1899 **Never-satisfied** on **Michelin** tyres, which was the first car to attain speeds of 100kph/62mph; and the 1900 4-CV **Renault**, the first saloon car. Steam, combustion and electric motors are also exhibited, showing the various ideas of the researchers and creators of the automobile industry.

and bronzes. Don't miss the remarkable **Greek vases★★** from Etruria and Southern Italy.

The first-floor rooms have preserved their Directoire wainscoting. They house a collection of paintings, including a large altarpiece representing the Passion by Wolgemut (Dürer's teacher), ceramics (pitchers in "Flemish stoneware"), ivories and Limousin enamels.

EXCURSION
Longueil-Annel

◯ *6km/3.7mi NE along N 32.*

This village lies on the banks of the River Oise and the canal running alongside it. The **▲▲Cité des Bateliers** (◯ *open mid-Apr–Mid-Oct Tue–Sun 10am–7pm; mid-Oct–Mid-Apr Tue– Fri 1pm–6pm, Sat–Sun 10am– 6pm; ◯ closed Jan and 25 Dec; ◯5.30€; ℘03 44 96 05 55; www. citedesbateliers.com*), a museum exploring the history of inland waterways, includes a visit to a former boatmen's café, now a small museum, the hold of the *Freycinet* barge, a stroll along the banks of the canal and a tour of the Janville lock.

🚗 DRIVING TOURS

FORÊT DE COMPIÈGNE★★

The State forest of Compiègne (14 500ha/35 800 acres) is a remnant of the immense **Cuise Forest** which extended from the edge of the Île-de-France to the Ardennes. Dotted with beech groves, avenues, valleys, ponds and villages, it occupies a hollow with the valleys of the River Oise and River Aisne. A series of hills and promontories sketch a crescent to the north, east and south. These peaks rise on average 80m/262ft above the sandy base of the hollow, which is grooved with numerous rivulets. The largest of these, the **Ru de Berne**, links a series of ponds.

🚶The forest is criss-crossed by 1 500km/ 930mi of roads and footpaths. Francis I first cut rides through the trees, while Louis XIV and Louis XV extended the network.

1 BEAUX MONTS★★

18km/11mi. About 1hr.

◯ Leave Compiègne by avenue Royale. At carrefour Royal, turn left onto rte. Tournante. At carrefour du Renard, take a right onto rte. Eugénie.

Some of the forest's oldest **oak trees★** stand around the **Carrefour d'Eugénie** junction, some dating from the time of Francis I.

◯ Take the winding road on the left which climbs to the Beaux Monts.

Stop at the summit, near the **Beaux Monts★★** viewpoint. From here, the **view★** stretches along the straight line of the avenue des Beaux-Monts through the forest all the way to the palace, barely visible 4km/2.5mi away. This magnificent linear perspective had been drawn to remind the Emperor's bride of the castle of Schönbrunn near Vienna.

◯ Continue past the "Cèdre Marie-Louise" and park your car as you come across a dirt road on your right.

The **Point de vue du Précipice** offers an extensive **view★** over the woody stretches of the Berne River valley and Mont St-Marc.

◯ Return to your car and keep going.

The road runs through a magnificent grove of oak and beech to a junction.

◯ Take a right, cross route Eugénie and park your car as you come across the first dirt road to your right.

The **Chapelle St-Corneille-aux-Bois**, attached to the abbey of St-Corneille in Compiègne, was originally built here in 1164 to welcome pilgrims and travellers. It now has a 13C Gothic structure and a 15C roof frame shaped like a ship's hull. The 16C **pavilion** built next to the chapel for Francis I's hunting staff has suffered from a 19C renovation.

▶ Return to your car. Continue to D 14 and turn right toward Compiègne.

② CLAIRIÈRE DE L'ARMISTICE★★

6km/3.5mi NE.

▶ Leave Compiègne by N 31 (east). Go straight across carrefour d'Aumont and carry straight on (D 546) to carrefour du Francport and the car park.

The **First Armistice** was signed by the Allies and the Germans on 11 November 1918 in a clearing of the Compiègne Forest, near the village of **Rethondes**. A site where a network of tracks existed for heavy artillery installations was cleared to make room for the **private train** of the Supreme Allied Commander, Field-Marshal Foch, and for that of the German plenipotentiaries. Twenty two years later, on 22 June 1940, Nazi Germany would force the French to sign, in the very same Pullman, the **Second Armistice** which established a German occupation zone in Northern France. Today, rails and flagstones, marking the site of the former railway carriages, surround a memorial.

Wagon du maréchal Foch

ⓘ*Open daily mid-Oct–Mar 9am–noon, 2–5.30pm; Apr–mid-Oct 9am–12.30pm, 2–6pm.* ⊙4€. ☎03 44 85 14 18.
The original dining-car, which was converted into an office for Field Marshal Foch, was exhibited in the courtyard of the Invalides in Paris from 1921 to 1927, then returned to the forest clearing. Transported to Berlin as a trophy in 1940, it was destroyed in the Thuringia Forest in April 1945. In 1950, it was replaced by a similar railway car. Housed in a little museum, this replica showcases artefacts used by the delegates during the meeting.

③ MONT SAINT-MARC AND PONDS★

26km/16mi. About 1hr 30min.

▶ Leave Compiègne by N 31 E.

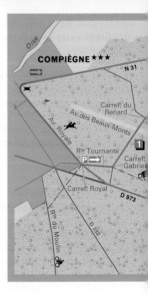

Pont de Berne is where the Dauphin, the future Louis XVI, met Marie-Antoinette for the first time.

▶ Turn right toward Pierrefonds (D 547). At Vivier-Frère-Robert, turn left onto rte. du Geai.

The slopes of **Mont St-Marc★** are covered with beeches. On reaching the plateau, turn left onto the forest road that follows the edge; there are good views of the valleys of the Berne and Aisne Rivers, Rethondes and Laigue Forest. The road follows the northern promontory of the hill. Some 2.5km/1.5mi farther along, **Carrefour Lambin** offers a particularly fine **view** of the Aisne Valley.

▶ Return by the same road and fork left onto the first road suitable for vehicles. Drive down rte. du Geai and continue toward Pierrefonds. Turn right and continue along the main street in Vieux-Moulin.

Vieux-Moulin, a former woodcutters' village later became a wealthy holiday resort. The church was rebuilt in 1860 at Napoléon III's expense.

▶ Turn left at the junction take rte. Eugénie to Étang de l'Étot.

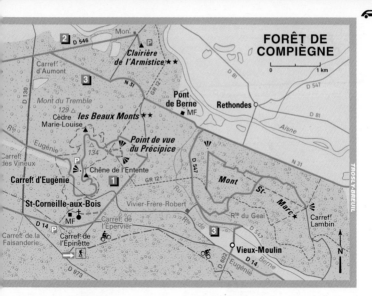

FORÊT DE COMPIÈGNE

The **Étangs de St-Pierre** ponds were created to stock fish; they were dug by members of the Celestine community from the priory of Mont-St-Pierre, to the west. Empress Eugénie's former chalet is now a forest warden's house.

⊙ About 1km/0.5mi beyond the last pond, at a fork near the edge of the forest, take the small road on the left that climbs up to the hilltop districts of Pierrefonds.

④ GRANDS MONTS★

27km/17mi. About 1hr 30min.

Tour starts in Château de Pierrefonds (⊙ See CHÂTEAU-DE-PIERREFONDS).

⊙ Leave Pierrefonds by D 85, W.

The road first rises to a wooded plateau, where the beautiful beech groves were largely destroyed during storms in 1984; it then descends into St-Jean-aux-Bois. The charming village of **St-Jean-aux-Bois** was appropriately renamed "Solitude" in 1794.

⑤ FORÊT DE LAIGUE

Tour ⑤ (31km/19.2mi) marked in green on map on ⊙p520. Allow 90min.

Separated from Compiègne by the Aisne river, the Laigue forest is four times smaller (3 800ha/9 390acres) than the **Compiègne** forest. The clayey subsoil and brooks create a humid environment suitable for oak trees.

⊙ Leave Compiègne by route de la Clairière-de-l'Armistice. Continue across the Aisne to the carrefour du Francport. Turn right.

The Armistice was signed near **Rethondes** on 11 November, 1918. On Sunday 10 November, Foch and Weygand attended mass in the small **church**, an event commemorated by the stained glass window in the apse.

⊙ Continue NE by D 547.

The **Saint-Crépin-aux-Bois** parish **church**, which benefited from the generosity of the lords of Offémont, marks the transition from the Gothic style (architecture) to the Renaissance (decoration). The **furnishings**★ include items from Sainte-Croix priory (chancel retable, two Virgins). Note the epitaph dedicated to Madeleine de Thou (17C) by her husband on the right wall.

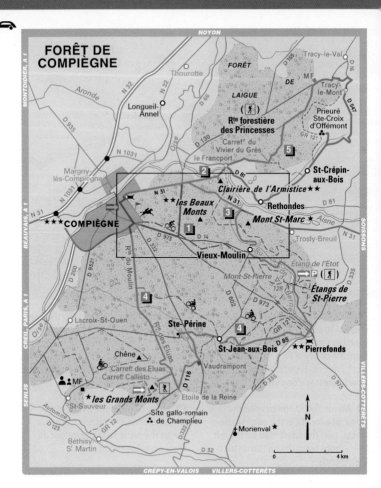

FORÊT DE COMPIÈGNE

○ Continue NE along D 547.
2km/1.2mi after Saint-Crépin, turn left.

The ruins of the priory and abbey of **Sainte-Croix d'Offémont** (16C) are set in the park of the medieval castle of Offémont.

○ Return by D 547 to Tracy-le-Mont. At Tracy-le-Val, turn left towards Ollencourt; follow D 130 which crosses the Forêt de Laigue. After the forester's house in Ollencourt, turn left along the route des Princesses (unpaved).

Route forestière des Princesses leads to the Massif de Laigue: walking tours leave from the "zone de silence du mont des Singes".

ADDRESSES

🛏 STAY

🍽🍽 **Auberge de la Vieille Ferme** – *58 r. de la République, 60880 Meux. ℘03 44 41 58 54. www.hotel-restaurant-oise. com. Closed 3 wks Aug and 25 Dec–1 Jan. Wifi. 14 rooms ⬒, half-board possible.* A venerable red-brick farm in the Vallée de l'Oise. The well-appointed rooms are located on two interior courtyards.

🍽 EAT

🍽 **Le Palais Gourmand** – *8 r. du Dahomey. ℘03 44 40 13 13. Closed 2 wks Aug, Sun eve and Mon.* This beautiful house (1890) contains a warren of rooms decorated with engravings of old Compiègne. Traditional menu.

Château de
Pierrefonds★★

Complete with its crenellated towers, soaring walls, drawbridge and walkways, this impressive fairy-tale castle dominates the pretty lakeside village of Pierrefonds. In the 19C, the original 15C fortress was altered and transformed into an imperial residence for Napoléon III. It is the crowning achievement of architect Viollet-le-Duc, whose idealised vision of a medieval court can still be admired today.

- **Michelin Local Map:** p509 D2: I-4. Also see map under Forêt de Compègne (left).
- **Info:** Office du tourisme de Pierrefonds, pl. de l'Hôtel-de-Ville, 60350. ℘03 44 42 81 44. www.pierrefonds-tourisme.net.
- **Location:** SE of Compiègne, reached by the D 973.
- **Parking:** Free parking on rue Sabatier, a 10min walk from the castle.

A BIT OF HISTORY

Louis of Orléans' Castle – In 1406, King **Charles VI** elevated to a duchy the **Valois Earldom** which he had bestowed on his younger brother, **Louis I of Orléans.** It consisted of Béthisy, Crépy and La Ferté-Milon, together with **Pierrefonds** where a castle had stood since the 12C. Louis of Orléans assumed the regency during the episodic fits of madness of his brother, but was assassinated in 1407 by his cousin John the Fearless, Duke of Burgundy. However, before his death, he constructed a **chain of fortresses** on his Valois lands, of which Pierrefonds was the linchpin. He had the original castle rebuilt by Charles VI's architect, and Pierrefonds triumphantly withstood sieges by the English, the Burgundians and the royal troops.

In the 16C, the castle passed to Antoine d'Estrées, Marquess of Coeuvres and father of **Gabrielle d'Estrées**, mistress of Henri IV. On the death of the King, the Marquess took sides with the Prince of Condé against the young Louis XIII. Besieged once again by the royal forces, Pierrefonds castle was finally seized and dismantled.

Viollet-le-Duc's Castle – In 1813 Napoléon I bought the castle ruins for a little under 3 000 francs. Napoléon III, an enthusiastic archaeologist, entrusted its restoration in 1857 to **Viollet-le-Duc**. It was only a matter of returning parts of it (the keep and annexes) to a habitable condition, leaving the curtain walls and towers as "picturesque ruins". At the end of 1861, however, the programme of works took on an altogether different, larger dimension; Pierrefonds was to be transformed into an imperial residence. Fascinated by medieval life and Gothic architecture in particular, Viollet-le-Duc set about a complete, much criticized reconstruction of the castle, following the basic shapes that were already outlined by the numerous walls and fragments remaining at the time, embellished with a number of highly imaginative additions. The castle was completed in 1884, long after both the emperor and the architect were dead.

VISIT

Open May–Sept daily 9.30am–6pm. Sept–end Apr Tue–Sun 10am–1pm, 2–5.30pm. Last admission 45min before closing. 1hr guided tours available. Closed 1 Jan, 1 May, 25 Dec. 7€. ℘03 44 42 72 72. http://pierrefonds. monuments-nationaux.fr.

Exterior

The quadrangular castle (103m/337ft long, 88m/288ft wide) has a large defensive tower at each corner and in the middle of the walls. On three sides, it overlooks the village, almost vertically; to the south a deep moat separates the castle from the plateau.

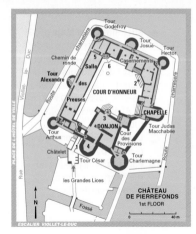

Tour Godefroy
Tour Josué
Tour Hector
Chemin de ronde
Caservements
5
6
Salle
Tour Alexandre
des
2
COUR D'HONNEUR
Preuses
CHAPELLE
3
DONJON
Tour Judas Macchabée
Cour des Provisions
Tour Arthus
1
4
Châtelet
Tour César
Tour Charlemagne
les Grandes Lices
Fossé
N

CHÂTEAU DE PIERREFONDS
1st FLOOR

0   40 m

ESCALIER VIOLLET-LE-DUC

The walls have two **sentry walks**, one above the other: the covered lower one is dressed with machicolations. The **towers** (38m/124ft-high with 5–6m/16–20ft-thick walls) are crowned with two storeys of defences; from the cart track (*route charretière*), they are a formidable sight. Eight statues of named military heroes adorn them, indicating the building's political significance.

Walk along the esplanade and cross the first moat to the forecourt known as Les Grandes Lices. A double **drawbridge (1)** – one lane for pedestrians, the other for vehicles – leads to the castle doorway which opens into the **main courtyard**.

Interior

A permanent exhibition in the barracks celebrates Viollet-le-Duc and his work (engravings, paintings, photographs

of the ruins, history of the castle etc). Another exhibition, devoted to the **Monduit workshops**, displays a collection of works of art in lead, including the lion weathervane of the Arras belfry. The exhibits were made in the Monduit workshops at the same time as the commissioned items. They were used to illustrate the workshops' skills at world exhibitions. The **main front** appears with its basket-handled arcading forming a covered shelter, surmounted by a gallery. Neither of these existed in the original castle, but were created by Viollet-le-Duc, freely inspired by the courtyard at the Château de Blois. The **equestrian statue** of Louis of Orléans (**2**) by Frémiet (1868) stands before the monumental stairway.

The inside of the **chapel**, heightened by Viollet-le-Duc, presents a bold elevation with a vaulted gallery above the apse, which was another of the architect's inventions. The doorway pier incorporates a figure of St James the Great with Viollet-le-Duc's features.

The **keep**, where the lord had his living quarters, stands between the chapel and the entrance. Viollet-le-Duc accentuated its residential function by giving it an elegant open stairway. It is flanked by three towers. The two on the outside are round whereas the one on the inside is square.

The **provisions courtyard**, between the keep and the chapel, communicates with the main courtyard by means of a

Château de Pierrefonds

© arenysam/Fotolia.com

postern gate and with the outside world by another postern, 10m/30ft above the foot of the castle walls.
To introduce food and other supplies into the fortress, a steeply inclined wooden ramp was lowered, and provisions dragged up.

Logis au donjon

Reaching the first floor of the keep, the tour leads through the **Imperial couple's rooms**: the **salle des Blasons** or Grande Salle (3), with woodwork and a few, rare pieces of furniture designed by Viollet-le-Duc. Among the symbolic decorative motifs, notice the Napoleonic eagle, the thistle (Empress Eugénie's emblem) and on the chimney-piece the heraldic arms of Louis of Orléans (the "broken" arms of France) and another family emblem, a knotted staff.
Beyond the **Emperor's bedroom** (4), which enjoys a view down over the fortified entrance, the tour leads to the Salle des Preuses, leaving the keep.

Salle des Preuses

Dedicated to the Worthies, this timber-ceilinged former courtroom (52×9m/170×29ft) was created by Viollet-le-Duc. The roof is shaped like an upturned ship. The mantelpiece of the double **fireplace** (5) is decorated with statues of nine worthy women, heroines from tales of chivalry. The central figure of Semiramis has the features of the Empress whereas the others are portraits of ladies of the court.

Tour d'Alexandre and Chemin de Ronde Nord

The original walls on this side of the ruins still stand 22m/72ft high; note the different colour of the stones. Along the **sentry walk**, Viollet-le-Duc highlighted the last step forward in defence systems before the arrival of the cannon: level walkways without steps or narrow doorways, which allowed the defenders (housed in nearby barracks) to muster quickly at critical points without blundering into obstacles. The view extends over Pierrefonds Valley.

Salle des Gardes

A double spiral **staircase** (6) leads down to this **guard-room** (also called **Salle des Mercenaires**) which now houses lapidary fragments: remains of the original 15C statues of the heroic figures on each tower.

ADDRESSES

STAY

Camping La Croix du Vieux Pont – *R. de la Fabrique, 02290 Berny-Rivière.18km/11mi to NE by D 335 and N 31, at the entrance to Vic-sur-Aisne, on the banks of the Aisne. ℘03 23 55 50 02. www.la-croix-du-vieux-pont.com. 520 pitches.* A well-equipped campsite offering lake and river fishing, pony rides, paddle boats and swimming pools.

Domaine du Bois d'Aucourt – *1.1km/0.7mi W of Pierrefonds via D 85, dir. St-Jean-aux-Bois. ℘03 44 42 80 34. www.boisdaucourt.com. 12 rooms. 12€.* No two rooms are alike in this 19C manor house in the heart of the Compiègne forest. Choose from Scotland, Seville, or a Zen meditation chamber.

Chambre d'hôte L'Ermitage – *74 r. de l'Impératrice-Eugénie. exit NE by D 335, rte de Soissons and 1km/2.4mi by road on left. ℘03 44 42 85 64. 5 rooms.* Renovated 1860 residence oozing restrained refinement. Period slate floor and stunning rooms. Free use of bikes and stables.

EAT

Ouradon– *8 r. du Beaudon. ℘03 44 42 86 62.* Opposite the lake, this contemporary crêperie with lemon yellow walls serves buckwheat pancakes, crêpes made with slightly salty butter, and mixed salads.

Aux Blés d'Or – *8 r. Jules-Michelet. ℘03 44 42 85 91. Closed 3–6 Jan, 19–27 Feb, 29 Nov–12 Dec, Tue and Wed.* This inn is a pleasant, family-friendly stopover with recently fitted-out rooms that are simple, comfortable and well maintained. The impressive silhouette of the medieval château can be admired from the restaurant's terrace. Good choice of fixed-price menus with an accent on traditional fare.

Morienval★

Nestled on the edge of a forest in the peaceful Automne valley, this small village is home to one of the earliest expressions of Gothic architecture in France, Notre-Dame de Morienval. Rebuilt over the centuries, this abbey church is a fine illustration of the transition from the Romanesque style to Gothic design.

▶ **Population:** 1 048
◉ **Michelin Local Map:**
   p509: D2; map 106 fold 11.
▷ **Location:** 72.4km/45mi northeast of Paris.

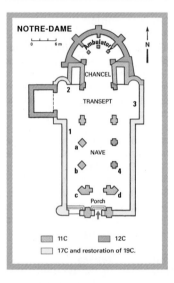

ÉGLISE NOTRE-DAME★

◷*Open 9am–7pm by prior arrangement only.* ✆*03 44 88 66 36.*
Notre-Dame church depended on a nunnery said to have been founded by **King Dagobert** in the 7C, and which was destroyed in 885 by the Vikings. The reconstruction of the nunnery and its church started in the 11C. Little has changed since the 12C, except for the reconstruction of the clerestory in the chancel. The narrow bays visible today date from the last restoration project (1878–1912).

Exterior – The abbey church has a distinctive silhouette, with its three towers, one adjoining the west front and two flanking the chancel; the north tower is marginally shorter and slimmer than the south tower. Go northward around the church to the apse; note the ambulatory

which was squeezed onto the semicircle of the chancel at the beginning of the 12C, to give it extra strength.

Interior – The extremely narrow ambulatory is the most unusual part of the church. Its arches, dating from about 1125, are some of the oldest in France. This is one of the first known uses of ogee arches in the curved part of a building; they are an integral part of the vaulting they support. The transition from groined vaulting to quadripartite vaulting is also visible.

A large number of memorial stones stand along the wall of the north aisle; one commemorates the great abbess Anne II Foucault (1596–1635). Farther along the same wall, past the northern arm of the transept, is a statue of **Our Lady of Morienval** (17C).

On the wall of the opposite aisle, 19C engravings show the church as it was before the last restoration. In the southern arm of the transept stands a 16C Crucifixion group once mounted on a rood

Église Notre-Dame

© S. Sauvignier/MICHELIN

beam, and a large 17C terracotta Saint Christopher stands on the same side in the nave near the main doorway.

🚗 DRIVING TOUR

VALLÉE DE L'AUTOMNE

41km/25.4mi tour marked in green on the map (🕮 p509). Allow 2hrs (without visits).

▶ Leave Morienval to the S by D 335 towards Crépy-en-Valois.

The road crosses Crépy-en-V from east to west.

▶ At Élincourt, turn right down D123 and right again at Orrouy.

Champlieu

The remains of the Romanesque church recall this hamlet's prestigious past, close to the forest of Compiègne. Revealed in the last century, the **Gallo-Roman ruins** are crossed by an ancient Roman road that ran from Senlis to Soissons, the "chaussée Brunehaut". The **theatre,** 70m/229ft in diameter, could seat 3 000 people. Only the first three rows of the tiers remain visible; the rest of the amphitheatre is covered in grass. The base of the stage and backstage are visible opposite the tiers; the six public entrances can be seen above the site.

The **baths** are small for a public building (53m/173ft by 23m/75ft). You can still make out the *atrium*, the square entrance court, the *frigidarium*, the *tepidarium* and the *caldarium*.

The **temple** *(on the other side of the road)* consists of an initial *fanum*-type sanctuary (1C) onto which a second, larger square temple has been built (20m/65ft on each side). A stone gutter runs around the temple site.

▶ Return to D 32 for 10km/6.2mi; Lieu-Restauré is on the right.

Abbaye de Lieu-Restauré

Currently closed for renovation. Call for re-opening dates. 📞 03 44 87 01 55.

Built in the 12C to replace a small chapel – hence its name, the "Restored Place" – this Premonstratensian abbey was rebuilt in the 16C.

Walk down the church, decorated with a **rose window**★ with Flemish tracery before entering the nave on the left-hand side, then walk round the ruins of the abbey church. To the south, excavations have revealed the cloister and refectory, indicated by the bases of several columns and a chimney. The guest quarters and storeroom (18C) have been restored. Items found during the excavations (pottery, capitals, etc.) are on display in the museum.

▶ Continue along D32; after 1km/0.5mi turn left; 50m/55yd after a tower on the side of the road, park at the entrance.

Vez★

This hillside village gave its name to the Valois. Vez comes from the Latin *vadum*, "the ford". In 1918, General Mangin was based here before the French offensive in July.

The **château**★ (🕐 *open Jul–8 Sep daily 2–6pm;* ⬤6€; ♿ 📞03 44 88 55 18; www. donjondevez.com) was built in the 14C on the site of a much earlier castle. The square wall is dominated by the **keep**. At the middle of the courtyard, the chapel houses Gallo-Roman objects and prehistoric artifacts from Valois, as well as marble recumbent statues sculpted by Frémiet. The 1995 **Wall Drawing** on the ground floor of the keep is by American artist Sol LeWitt. Climb to the top of the chapel for **views** over the Vallée de l'Automne. On the right corner of the curtain wall, a plaque commemorates Joan of Arc's stay here in 1430. Behind the chapel are the ruins of the living quarters of the lord of the manor (13C). The minimalist landscaped garden sometimes showcases contemporary sculpture. *The Vallée de l'Automne continues along the Aisne towards Villers-Cotterêt and the Forêt de Retz (🕮 see VILLERS-COTTERÊT).*

Longueil-Annel

A red-brick village crossed by barges as they slide gently along the Oise canal and through its many locks, Longueuil-Annel is best enjoyed at a slow pace.

SIGHTS
Cité des Bateliers ★
59 av. de la Canonnière. ○*Open mid-Apr–mid-Oct Tue–Sun 10am–7pm; mid-Oct–mid-Apr Tue–Fri 1–6pm, Sat & Sun 10am–6pm.* ○*Closed Jan, 25 Dec.* ○*5.30€ (5–12 yrs 3.10€).* ℘*03 44 96 05 55. www.citedesbateliers.com.*
The multi-media "Cité des bateliers" explores the life of boatmen and developments in canal technology.

Maison des bateliers
This former boatmen's café has been turned into a small museum where you can explore the history of Longueil-Annel, the navigational innovations that enable barges to travel over hilly terrains, and the switch from towed to motorised barges. Don't miss the harness that the haulers passed around their chest to pull the boats along the towpath at a steady speed of 900m/1 000yd an hour. Haulers could still be seen working on the canal until 1970.

Péniche Freycinet
Moored opposite the house, this barge is named after Charles Louis de Freycinet, French minister of public works from 1877 to 1879. He set the standard size for waterways, which in turn restricted barges to a maximum dimension of 38.50m/126.3ft long by 5.05m/16.5ft wide. Discover the wheelhouse and an exhibition on the "three in a marrage" relationship between a boatman, his wife and their barge.

☙WALKING TOUR

Canal towpath
○*Departing from the barge, head towards the lock.*
Sound booths along the canal bank

- **Population:** 2 346
- **Michelin Map:** p509: D2; 305 I4.
- **Info:** ℘ www.ville-longueil annel.fr.
- **Location:** 6km/3.7mi NE of Compiègne, runs along the banks of the Oise and its lateral canal. Access by A 1, exit 10, then D 1032 towards Noyon.
- **Timing:** Allow half a day for the boat museum and towpath.
- **Kids:** A visit to the Freycinet barge.

recall the meetings between boatmen and "land lovers" in the boatmen's café and the boat workshop.

The **Janville lock** has two separate lock mechanisms. Spot barges coming upstream or going downstream and watch as the lock keeper opens the gates from his control cabin.

Don't miss the **view** over the canal banks lined with brick houses. The walk continues along the old towpath (1.6km/1mi), where panel posts recall the boatmen's "ten commandments".

ADDRESSES

⌂ STAY
○○ **Chambre d'hôte de M. et Mme Benattar** – *3 r. de la Mairie.* ℘*03 44 76 16 28.* P ⊠. *3 rooms* ⊠. This former 18C farmstead has three bedrooms and a suite spread over the ground and upper floors, plus a small living room.

AGENDA
The 1st Sun of July, the **pardon des bateliers** draws crowds to Longueil-Annel: mass on a boat chapel, fireworks and regional produce stalls.
L'Oise en guinguette – In mid-May, the banks of the Oise canal come to life between Longueil-Annel, Pont-l'Évêque and Noyon. Events along the canal banks, concerts and street shows *(contact the Cité des bateliers).*

Noyon★

A city of art and history, Noyon witnessed the coronation of two early French monarchs and the birth of Protestant reformer, Jean Calvin.

A BIT OF HISTORY

Originally Gallo-Roman, Noyon was elevated by **Saint Medard** to a bishopric linked in 581. The town witnessed two coronations, **Charlemagne**'s in 768 as King of the Franks, and **Hugues Capet**'s in 987 as King of France. Noyon was one of the first French cities to obtain its own charter, in 1108.

CATHEDRAL★★

◔ *Open 9am–6pm.* ✆ *Possibility of guided tour by reservation at the Tourist Office:* ✆ *03 44 44 21 88. www.noyon-tourisme.com*

Noyon's cathedral is a remarkable example of the **Early Gothic style,** skilfully combining the typically sober, solid appearance of Romanesque architecture with the breadth and harmony of the Gothic Style. Four buildings preceded the present cathedral, whose construction began with the chancel in 1145, and ended with the west front in 1235. It was restored after WW I.

Exterior – The sparse front is preceded by an early-13C porch with three bays. It was reinforced in the 14C with two flying buttresses decorated with small gables. The 14C **north tower** is discreetly decorated with fine mouldings and twists of foliage on the gallery arcades, and foliate friezes under the upper shoulders of the buttresses. Compare it with the older (1220), more austere south tower. The square in front of the cathedral, called the **Place du Parvis**, is edged with a semicircle of canons' residences. To the north stands the old **chapter library** (only open in the summer), a fine 16C timbered building. One of the library rooms containing blacklisted works was known as "Hell."

Interior★★ – The nave has five double bays. The elevation rises through four storeys: great arches, large and elegant galleries with double arcading which are

particularly striking when viewed from the transept crossing, shallow triforium and clerestory. The chancel vault is as high as the nave's. The eight ribs of the apse radiate from a central keystone and develop into a cluster of small columns. Nine chapels open onto the ambulatory. Among the furnishings is the Louis XVI high altar shaped liked a temple and some large 18C wrought-iron gates enclosing the chancel and the chapels. Today only a single gallery remains of the **old cloisters** (*north aisle*); the bays with beautiful radiating tracery overlook the garden. The opposite wall is pierced with pointed arch windows and a door giving onto the 13C **chapter-house**.

▸ **Population:** 14 471

◔ **Michelin Local Map:** p509: D1.

🛈 **Info:** Office du tourisme de Noyon, 1 pl. Bertrand-Labarre, 60400. ✆03 44 44 21 88. www.noyon-tourisme.com.

▸ **Location:** 24km/15mi NE of Compiègne by the N 32.

◉ **Don't Miss:** The early Gothic cathedral; the Musée du Noyonnais.

◔ **Timing:** A good time to visit is the first weekend of July for the fruit festival.

Red-Fruit Festival

The area around Noyon is the main red-fruit producing region in France, 90% of the production being destined for the manufacture of **sorbets**. In July, when the **Marché aux Fruits Rouges** is on *(first Sunday of the month)*, the square in front of the cathedral is dotted with punnets of mouth-watering strawberries, redcurrants, cherries and blackcurrants. Activities include pastry tasting and competitions of fruit-stone throwing.

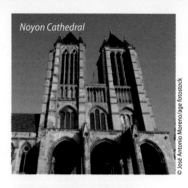

Noyon Cathedral

© José Antonio Moreno/age fotostock

ADDITIONAL SIGHTS
Musée du Noyonnais

⊙*Open Apr–Oct Tue–Sun 10am–noon, 2–6pm (Nov–Mar 5pm).* ⊙*Closed 1 Jan, 14 Jul, 11 Nov, 25 Dec.* ⚭*3.50€.* ℘*03 44 09 43 41.*

This local history museum's collections are housed in a brick and stone Renaissance building (the old bishop's palace) and a 17C wing, rebuilt after WW I. Artefacts from excavations in Noyon and the surrounding area (Cuts and Béhéricourt) include 12C chess pieces, a cache of Gallo-Roman coins and ceramics.

Musée Jean-Calvin

⊙*Open Apr–Oct Tue–Sun 10am–noon, 2–6pm (Nov–Mar 5pm).* ⊙*Closed 1 Jan, 14 Jul, 11 Nov, 25 Dec.* ⚭*3.50€.* ℘*03 44 44 03 59.*

Located on the site of **Jean Calvin**'s birth house (destroyed during WW I), this museum is dedicated to the French Protestant reformer (1509–1564). Portraits, engravings and documents give visitors an overview of the religious movement that swept 16C Europe.

Abbaye d'Ourscamps ★

▷ *6km/3.7mi to the south by D 165 then D 48.* ⊙*Open daily 9am–noon, 2–6pm.* ⟲*Guided tour by request (4 days adv.) May–Sept: 10.30am and 3pm, Sun 3pm.* ⚭*2.50€.* ℘*03 44 75 72 00.*

Founded in 1129, the monastery expanded rapidly in the 17C and 18C. A former gatehouse to the left of the **main gate** (1784) leads to an 18C building on either side of a central pavilion with doric columns, built to hide the unfashionable Gothic façade of the abbey church. The 18C monks' living quarters are on the left; the building on the right, devastated in 1915, was never restored. *Pass under the archway.*

Church ruins – At the end of the pathway once occupied by the nave (demolished in the 19C) stands the skeleton of the Gothic church (13C). The ambulatory, double on the right and single in the chevet, served five absidioles.

Chapel – A former infirmary, this 13C chapel has two rows of thin pillars and oculus windows. The perspective is broken by the high 17C chancel stalls.

ADDRESSES

🛏 STAY

⊜⊜ **Le Cèdre** – *8 r. de l'Évêché.* ℘*03 44 44 23 24. www.hotel-lecedre.com. 35 rooms.* ⊇*8.50€.* A red brick hotel offering smart rooms with cathedral views.

🍽/EAT

⊜⊜ **Dame Journe** – *2 bd Mony.* ℘*03 44 44 01 33. www.damejourne.fr. Closed 7–20 Sept, 5–12 Jan. Closed Mon and Sun, Tue, Wed and Thu eves.* This restaurant with a regular clientele has Louis XVI-style armchairs and wood panelling. Good choice of menus.

⊜⊜⊜ **Saint Éloi** – *81 bd. Carnot.* ℘*03 44 44 01 49. www.hotelsainteloi.fr. Closed 1st half of Aug, Sat lunch and Sun eve. 8 rooms* ⊇. An elegant restaurant in a 19C residence.Louis XV-style chairs.

AGENDA

Red fruit market – On the 1st Sun of month, the square and streets around the cathedral are covered with punnets of strawberries, redcurrant, blackcurrant, and raspberries grown by local producers.

Beauvais★★

The approach to Beauvais from the Pont de Paris is dominated by its magnificent cathedral, an architectural masterpiece almost defying the laws of gravity.

A BIT OF HISTORY

Bishops and Burghers – Beauvais, the capital of the Belgian tribe the **Bellovaci**, became a Gallo-Roman city enclosed by walls during the 3C. From the 11C the city had as its lord a bishop, who was often in conflict with the town's wealthy merchants and jealous of their franchises. One of the bishops, **Pierre Cauchon**, has a dubious claim to fame: while the town wanted to surrender to Charles VII, Cauchon rallied to the English. Chased out of Beauvais in 1429 by the burghers, he took refuge in Rouen where, on 30 May 1431, he sent **Joan of Arc** to the stake.

Jeanne Hachette – On 27 June 1472, Beauvais was besieged by Charles the Bold, Duke of Burgundy, who was marching on Paris with 80 000 men. The town had no troops so men and women ran to the ramparts and watched in horror as ladders were laid against the fortifications. **Jeanne Laîné**, the daughter of a humble craftsman, saw an assailant appear at the top of the wall, a standard in hand. She threw herself on him and struck him with a hatchet, sending him flying into the moat below. This example fired the courage of the others; the resistance gained momentum, giving time for reinforcements to arrive. Charles lifted the siege on 22 July. Each year, at the end of June, Beauvais honours Jeanne "Hachette".

Tapestries – In 1664, Louis XIV founded the **Manufacture Royale de Tapisserie**. The artisans worked on horizontal looms producing low-warp tapestries in wool and silk which are noted for being extremely fine; they were usually used as upholstery. The Manufacture Royale changed its name to Manufacture Nationale in 1804. Evacuated to Aubusson in 1939, the workshops were unable to return to Beauvais

after the buildings were destroyed in 1940. The looms were relocated to the Gobelins Works in Paris and returned to Beauvais in 1989.

Ceramics and stained glass – Glazed earthenware and stoneware, manufactured locally since the 15C, have turned Beauvais into one of the great ceramic centres of France. Around 1850, pottery workshops were replaced by ceramic and tile factories.

 WALKING TOUR

BISHOP'S PALACE AND SURROUNDS

Place Jeanne-Hachette

There is a fine **statue** of the local heroine opposite the town hall with its beautifully restored 18C façade.

▷ Take r. de la Frette. Turn right on r. Beauregard, then left on r. St-Pierre.

Ruins

On the corner, you will see traces of the **Collégiale St-Barthélémy** and, opposite, behind the Galerie Nationale de la Tapisserie, the ruins of **Gallo-Roman town walls**.

▷ Turn right on r. du Musée, then follow the r. de l'Abbé-Gelée.

Ancien Palais Épiscopal

The former bishop's palace was restored in 2000. Flanked by two large **towers** with pepper-pot roofs, the 14C **fortified doorway** was built by Bishop Simon de Clermont de Nesle with the large fines that the town had to pay after a riot in 1306 during which the bishopric was pil-

▶ **Population:** 59 003
◉ **Michelin Local Map:** p509: B2.
▤ **Info:** Office du tourisme de Beauvais, 1 r. Beauregard, 60000. ℘03 44 15 30 30. www.beauvaistourisme.fr.

laged. At the far end of the courtyard stands the main body of the palace; set ablaze in 1472 by the Burgundians, it was rebuilt around 1500 and retains an elegant Renaissance façade. It now houses the Oise Museum.

Musée Départemental de l'Oise★

1 r. du Musée, in the Ancien Palais Episcopal. Some collections may not be visible due to renovation works. ◐*Open Wed–Mon 10am–noon, 2–6pm (Jul–Sept 10am–6pm).* ◐*Closed 1 Jan, Easter, 1 May, Whit Mon and 25 Dec.* ℰ*03 44 11 43 83. www.oise.fr.*

The museum houses a rich collection of medieval **woodcarvings** from churches and abbeys and **sculpted fragments** from some of old Beauvais' timber-framed houses. The **Fine Arts** collection spans the 16C French School (*Résurrection du Christ* by Antoine Caron) and 17C and 18C Italian and French Schools. The 19C and 20C section includes works by Paul Huet (*Le Retour du Grognard*), Thomas Couture and Ingres, to name a few. Don't miss the **Art Nouveau furniture** by Gustave Serrurier-Bovy and **ceramics** by Auguste Delaherche.

15C House

The oldest house in Beauvais (15C) was dismantled from rue Oudry to be rebuilt rue de l'Abbé-Gelée (no. 16). An association called **Maisons paysannes de l'Oise** proposes temporary exhibits on rural habitats. ◐*Open Mon 2–6pm, Tue–Sat 10am–6pm.* ℰ*03 44 48 77 74.*

▷ To return to pl. J.-Hachette, turn right on r. J.-Racine then right down r. Carnot.

SIGHTS
Cathédrale St-Pierre★★★

R. St-Pierre. ◐*Open daily Nov–Apr 9am–12.15pm, 2–5.30pm. May–Jun and Sept–Oct 9am–12.15pm, 2–6.15pm. Jul–Aug 9am–6.15pm.* ℰ*03 44 48 11 60. www.cathedrale-beauvais.fr.*

During the Carolingian period (751–987), a small cathedral, known as the **Basse-Œuvre**, was erected. In 949, another cathedral was begun, but it was destroyed by two fires.

Subsequently, in 1225, the bishop and chapter decided to erect the biggest church of its day, a **Nouvel-Œuvre** (New Work) dedicated to Saint Peter. Started in 1238, the construction of the chancel proved to be a real challenge for the architects. The height to the vault's keystone was to be slightly above 48m/158ft, making the roof (68m/223ft high) about the height of the towers of Notre-Dame in Paris. But the pillars were too widely spaced and the buttresses on the piers too weak. In 1284, the chancel collapsed: 40 more years of work went into saving it. The three large arches of the chancel's right bays were reinforced by the addition of intermediary piers, the flying buttresses multiplied, the abutments strengthened.

The Hundred Years War interrupted the project. In 1500, work resumed on the cathedral. The construction of the transept was entrusted to **Martin Chambiges** (c.1460–1532), and in 1550, the transept was finally completed. Unfortunately, instead of building the nave next, it was decided to erect an open-work tower over the transept crossing, surmounted by a spire. The cross at the top of the spire was positioned in 1569, at a height of 153m/502ft. But as there was no nave to counterbalance the thrusts, the piers

Map — Cathédrale St-Pierre

Rue de l'Abbé Gelée · Place Vérité · CATHÉDRALE ST-PIERRE · Rue du Musée · CLOISTER · St-Paul Entrance · Astronomical clock ★ · Treasury · BASSE-ŒUVRE · Orgue · TRANSEPT · CHANCEL · Ambulatory · CHEVET ★ · N · Rue St-Pierre · St-Pierre Entrance · 0 · 20 m gave way on Ascension Day in 1573, just as the procession had left the church. The spire was never rebuilt.

Chevet★ – *See illustration in the Introduction.*

The chancel dates from the 13C. Like the Flamboyant transept arms, it is shored up by flying buttresses with high piers which rise up to the roof. The transept arms were to have been very long and framed by towers.

South transept façade – Richly decorated, it bears two high turrets flanking the **Portail de St-Pierre** (St Peter's Doorway), the embrasures, tympanum and arching of which are adorned with niches beneath openwork canopies. The doorway is surmounted by a rose-window with delicate tracery.

Interior★★★ – The dizzying height of the vaults (almost 48m/157ft high) is immediately apparent. The generous transept is almost 58m/190ft long. There is an open triforium and the clerestory is 18m/59ft high. Seven chapels open off the ambulatory. Most of the 16C **stained-glass windows★★** are to be found in the transept, including the **Roncherolles** stained glass (1) dating 1522. Also admire the rose-window (1551) featuring the Eternal Father in the central medallion. Underneath, 10 Prophets and 10 Apostles or Doctors stand in two rows. In a side chapel to the right of the chancel, note a 16C polychrome **altarpiece** (3).

Set in a Roman Byzantine style case, the monumental **Astronomical Clock★** (display at 40min past the hour 10.40am, 11.40am, 2.40pm, 3.40pm, 4.40pm; 4€; 03 44 48 11 60) was made by engineer Louis-Auguste Vérité from 1865 to 1868. In the glazed openings, 52 dials show the positions of the planets, the seasons, etc. Several times a day, 68 automats re-enact the Last Judgement.

To the right of the astronomical clock is possibly the world's oldest surviving **chiming clock** (14C) (2). Don't miss the chapter house (4) in the east wing of the **cloister**.

Église St-Étienne★

The nave and the transept of the church dedicated to St Stephen are Romanesque. Their restraint, softened by the "Beauvais-style" bracketed cornices, contrasts with the architectural richness of the chancel, rebuilt a little after 1500 in a refined Flamboyant style. The chancel, higher than the nave, is encircled by chapels. The tower flanking the west front served as the town belfry. The left aisle gives on to a Romanesque doorway with a carved tympanum and arching. The chancel's Renaissance **stained-glass windows★★** are by Engrand, including the **Tree of Jesse★★★**.

Manufacture nationale de la tapisserie

24 r. Henri Brispot. Guided tours only available for groups. 03 44 14 41 90.
The national tapestry works have, since 1989, been housed in the former slaughterhouses. Today the factory contains about a dozen looms.

Galerie nationale de la Tapisserie

22 rue Saint-Pierre. Open Tue–Sun 10.30am–5.30pm. Closed 1 Jan, 1 May, 25 Dec. No charge. 03 44 15 39 10.
Housed in a low-roofed building beyond the cathedral's east end, the gallery stages **temporary exhibits** showcasing 400 years of French tapestry.

EXCURSIONS
Église de Marissel

1.5km/1mi to the E. R. Aimé-Besnard. Closed Sun during mass and heritage days. 03 44 48 61 37.
Immortalised by Corot in 1866, the church's 16C façade features a Flamboyant Gothic gateway leading to a chevet with a Romanesque apsidiole.

Château de Troissereux

8km/5mi to the NW by D 901. Guided tour (45min). Open Apr–11 Nov: 2-5pm; 12 Nov–30 Nov & Feb–Mar: Sat & Sun 2–5pm. Medieval clock tour: 2.15pm (40min). 8€ park and château, 12€' clock tour. ☏*03 44 79 00 00. www.chateau-troissereux.com.* Set in a park, this 15C–16C Renaissance château houses one of the oldest clocks in France.

Forêt de Hez-Froidmont

◉ *16km/10mi to the E by N 31.* This hilly massif carpeted with trees runs north to the plain of Picardy and south to the Vallée du Thérain.

Agnetz

◉ *20km/12.5mi to the E, on a right turn before Clermont.* The **church**'s soaring 14C bell tower is relieved on each side by three twin Gothic bays. The Flamboyant apse was added in the 16C. Contact the town hall for visits: ☏*03 44 68 23 00.*

Clermont

◉ *22km/13.6mi to the E by N 31, after Agnetz. Leave your car in r. du Châtellier and walk down to r. de la Porte-de-Nointel passing under an arch.* ▮ *19 pl. de l'Hôtel de Ville, 0600 Clermon-de-l'Oise.* ◷ *Open Tue–Sat 9am–noon, 1.30–5pm.* ☏*03 44 50 40 25.* A slender belfry rises from the gable of the **former hôtel de ville**. Three statues (St Louis, Robert de Clermont and Charles IV) provide a reminder of the town's royal connections.

⬗ DRIVING TOUR

LE PAYS DE BRAY

58km/36mi. Allow 2hr.

Carved liked a buttonhole into the chalk of the Paris basin, the landscape of the Bray is one of wide panoramas, farmland and gently curving valleys.

◉ Leave Beauvais along av. J.-Mermoz. Turn left towards Gisors (D 981). 5km/3mi beyond Auneuil, turn right (D 129). Cross Le Vauroux. At Lalandelle, follow signs for "Table d'orientation" offering fine views over the countryside. Turn right onto D 22 when you descend.

Note a hollow where the strata of the underlying chalk is clearly visible.

◉ Retrace your route to the crossroads and continue along the D 574.

Pass through the village of Coudray-St-Germer, then down into the valley, with **views★** over Gournay.

St-Germer-de-Fly

Saint Germer founded an abbey here in the 7C. Its huge **church★** was built between 1150 and 1175. *Ongoing renovations. Contact tourist office for information* ☏*03 44 82 62 74.*

◉ Take D 109 towards Cuigy-en-Bray and Espaubourg, and the narrow road along the foot of the steep slopes of the Bray. At St-Aubin-en-Bray, turn left. Cross the RN to Fontainettes.

Cradle of the Beauvais pottery industry, **Les Fontainettes** specialises in garden pottery and sandstone piping. The **Musée de la Poterie** at **Lachapelle-aux-Pots** exhibits work by local potters such as Delaherche and Klingsor. ◷ *Open Apr–Oct daily (except Mon), 2–6pm, Sat–Sun and holidays, 2.30–6.30pm.* ◷ *Closed Nov–Mar and Mon during holidays.* ⬰*2€.* ☏*03 44 04 50 72.*

Savignies

Once famous for its pottery, this village has retained many original chimneys.

ADDRESSES

🖂 STAY / ⅄ EAT

⊝⬕⬔ **Hostellerie St-Vincent** – *241 r. de Clermont.* ☏*03 44 05 49 99. 79 rooms* ⌑*11€. Restaurant* ⊝⬕. A recently-built hotel near main roads and the motorway slip road offering redecorated, functional rooms. Traditional menu.

⊝⬕⬔⬕ **Hôtel Mercure** – *21 av. Montaigne.* ☏*03 44 02 80 80. www. accorhotels.com. Wi-fi. 60 rooms* ⌑. *Restaurant* ⊝⬕⬔⬕. A 1970s building with spacious, renovated rooms. Pool terrace in summer. Traditional menu.

Gerberoy★★

A former medieval stronghold and one of the most beautiful villages in France, Gerberoy is filled with the scent of a thousand roses. Lined with 17C and 18C wood-framed brick houses with beams painted in pastel colours, the village's steep cobbled alleyways are just as lively now as they were when they inspired the French 19C Intimist painter Le Sidaner.

👣WALKING TOUR

Filled with enchanting scents, the narrow alleyways of this delightful village lend themselves perfectly to lazy afternoon strolls. Flowers are king in Gerberoy where roses, daffodils and hydrangeas fill the streets with an irresistible charm. Although the houses are well preserved, Gerberoy manages to avoid looking like a chocolate box cliché. With its carvings and timber-framed houses shimmering with colour, it's easy to lose track of time as you climb through the streets to the ramparts.

Remparts – From the top of the water tower, admire the **Henri Le Sidaner gardens** (*www.lesjardinshenrilesidaner.fr*) landscaped by the gardener on the ruins of the village fort. Enter through the former castle gateway and climb to the collegiate church, passing in front of the houses formerly belonging to the resident canons.

Collégiale Saint-Pierre – This 15C church features stalls decorated with sculpted misericords (1460) and Aubusson tapestries (17C).

Behind the church, in rue du Château, enjoy the view over the Maison bleue, at the corner (1691): a postern overlooks the walls overgrowth with plants. Take a walk around the former moat, now lined with trees.

Musée municipal – Located on the upper floor of the town hall (18C), this museum explores the history of the district and includes ceramics, antique books, statuettes, engravings and paint-

▶ **Population:** 111
⚲ **Michelin Map:** p508: A1 305 C3.
▤ **Info:** Tourist Information Office – 20 r. du Logis-du-Roy. ☎03 44 82 54 86. www.gerberoy.fr
◐ **Location:** Fortified village on a natural mound 20km/12.4mi NE of Beauvais. Access by D901 then D 133 after Troissereux.
⊘ **Don't miss:** Municipal museum; rose festival.
◐ **Timing:** Picnic on the ramparts.
👨‍👦 **Kids:** Wood crafts in Hétomesnil.

Nature painter

The village was rediscovered by the painter Henri Le Sidaner (1862–1939). In 1903, he bought a country house where he spent his summers with his family until the end of this life. The village inspired 200 of his paintings, including *La Tonnelle* and *La Table au soleil*.

ings by **Henri Le Sidaner**. Temporary exhibitions by local artists on the ground floor. ◐*Open Apr–Sept: Sat, Sun, public holidays 2.30–6pm.* 👣*Guided tour available (1hr 45min) by request (1 mth adv.).* ✎*No charge.* ☎*03 44 46 32 20. www.gerberoy.fr.*

ADDRESSES

EVENTS

Fête des roses – If there's one annual festival not to miss, it's the rose festival, which honours the queen of flowers, the rose, every third Sunday in June (except on election days).

Les Moments musicaux de Gerberoy – Held on the 2nd weekend in June, classical and world music concerts are performed in the collegiate church (*www.momentsmusicauxdegerberoy.org*).

INDEX

INDEX

INDEX

INDEX

INDEX

W

Y

Z

INDEX

STAY

¶/ EAT

MAPS AND PLANS

THEMATIC MAPS

MAPS AND PLANS

MAP LEGEND

	Sight	Seaside resort	Winter sports resort	Spa
Highly recommended	★★★	≗≗≗	✳✳✳	‡‡‡
Recommended	★★	≗≗	✳✳	‡‡
Interesting	★	≗	✳	‡

Selected monuments and sights

◉ ⇨	Tour - Departure point
⛪ ✝	Catholic church
⛪ ✝	Protestant church, other temple
✡ ☗ ☪	Synagogue - Mosque
▨▨	Building
■	Statue, small building
✝	Calvary, wayside cross
◎	Fountain
⊶•▪▪	Rampart - Tower - Gate
⋈	Château, castle, historic house
⸬	Ruins
∪	Dam
✿	Factory, power plant
☆	Fort
∩	Cave
⌑	Troglodyte dwelling
⊓	Prehistoric site
▼	Viewing table
Ѱ	Viewpoint
▲	Other place of interest

Abbreviations

A	Agricultural office (Chambre d'agriculture)
C	Chamber of Commerce (Chambre de commerce)
H	Town hall (Hôtel de ville)
J	Law courts (Palais de justice)
M	Museum (Musée)
P	Local authority offices (Préfecture, sous-préfecture)
POL.	Police station (Police)
▣	Police station (Gendarmerie)
T	Theatre (Théâtre)
U	University (Université)

Sports and recreation

⤜	Racecourse
⛸	Skating rink
≋ ▨	Outdoor, indoor swimming pool
▦	Multiplex Cinema
⚓	Marina, sailing centre
⌂	Trail refuge hut
▫▪▫▪▫	Cable cars, gondolas
▫++++++	Funicular, rack railway
🚂	Tourist train
◈	Recreation area, park
🎡	Theme, amusement park
⚕	Wildlife park, zoo
⊛	Gardens, park, arboretum
◔	Bird sanctuary, aviary
🏃	Walking tour, footpath
☺	Of special interest to children

Special symbol

🏖	Beach

Additional symbols

🛈	Tourist information
═══ ═══	Motorway or other primary route
❶ ➊	Junction: complete, limited
▭▭ ═══	Pedestrian street
ɪ════ɪ	Unsuitable for traffic, street subject to restrictions
▭▭▭▭ ----	Steps – Footpath
▦ ▦	Train station – Auto-train station
🚌 🚌	Coach (bus) station
▬▬	Tram
Ⓜ	Metro, underground
🅿	Park-and-Ride
♿	Access for the disabled
⊗	Post office
⊚	Telephone
⊠	Covered market
⚔	Barracks
△	Drawbridge
∪	Quarry
✕	Mine
Ⓑ Ⓕ	Car ferry (river or lake)
⛴	Ferry service: cars and passengers
⛴	Foot passengers only
③	Access route number common to Michelin maps and town plans
Bert (R.)...	Main shopping street
AZ B	Map co-ordinates

547

COMPANION PUBLICATIONS

REGIONAL AND LOCAL MAPS

To make the most of your journey, travel with Michelin maps at a scale of 1:200 000: **Regional maps nos 511** and **514** and the new Local maps, which are illustrated on the map of France opposite.

And remember to travel with the latest edition of the **map of France no 721 (1:1 000 000)**, also available in atlas format: spiral bound, hard back, and the new mini-atlas – perfect for your glove compartment.

INTERNET

Michelin is pleased to offer a route-planning service on the Internet: **www.travel.viamichelin.com www.viamichelin.com**

Choose the shortest route, a route without tolls, or the Michelin recommended route to your destination; you can also access information about hotels and restaurants from *The Red Guide*, and tourist sites from *The Green Guide*.

The Michelin Adventure

It all started with rubber balls! This was the product made by a small company based in Clermont-Ferrand that André and Edouard Michelin inherited, back in 1880. The brothers quickly saw the potential for a new means of transport and their first success was the invention of detachable pneumatic tires for bicycles. However, the automobile was to provide the greatest scope for their creative talents. Throughout the 20th century, Michelin never ceased developing and creating ever more reliable and high-performance tires, not only for vehicles ranging from trucks to F1 but also for underground transit systems and airplanes.

From early on, Michelin provided its customers with tools and services to facilitate mobility and make traveling a more pleasurable and more frequent experience. As early as 1900, the Michelin Guide supplied motorists with a host of useful information related to vehicle maintenance, accommodation and restaurants, and was to become a benchmark for good food. At the same time, the Travel Information Bureau offered travelers personalised tips and itineraries.

The publication of the first collection of roadmaps, in 1910, was an instant hit! In 1926, the first regional guide to France was published, devoted to the principal sites of Brittany, and before long each region of France had its own Green Guide. The collection was later extended to more far-flung destinations, including New York in 1968 and Taiwan in 2011.

In the 21st century, with the growth of digital technology, the challenge for Michelin maps and guides is to continue to develop alongside the company's tire activities. Now, as before, Michelin is committed to improving the mobility of travelers.

MICHELIN TODAY

WORLD NUMBER ONE TIRE MANUFACTURER

- 70 production sites in 18 countries
- 111,000 employees from all cultures and on every continent
- 6,000 people employed in research and development

Moving
for a world

Moving forward means developing tires with better road grip and shorter braking distances, whatever the state of the road.

CORRECT TIRE PRESSURE

RIGHT PRESSURE

- Safety
- Longevity
- Optimum fuel consumption

-0,5 bar

- Durability reduced by 20% (- 8,000 km)

-1 bar

- Risk of blowouts
- Increased fuel consumption
- Longer braking distances on wet surfaces

forward together
where mobility is safer

It also involves helping motorists take care of their safety and their tires. To do so, Michelin organises "Fill Up With Air" campaigns all over the world to remind us that correct tire pressure is vital.

WEAR

DETECTING TIRE WEAR

The legal minimum depth of tire tread is 1.6mm.
Tire manufacturers equip their tires with tread wear indicators, which are small blocks of rubber moulded into the base of the main grooves at a depth of 1.6mm.

Tires are the only point of contact between the vehicle and road.

The photo below shows the actual contact zone.

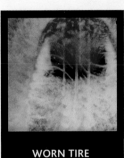

If the tread depth is less than 1.6mm, tires are considered to be worn and dangerous on wet surfaces.

NEW TIRE

WORN TIRE
(1,6 mm tread)

Moving forward
means sustainable mobility

By 2050, Michelin aims to cut the quantity of raw materials used in its tire manufacturing process by half and to have developed renewable energy in its facilities. The design of MICHELIN tires has already saved billions of litres of fuel and, by extension, billions of tons of CO2.

Similarly, Michelin prints its maps and guides on paper produced from sustainably managed forests and is diversifying its publishing media by offering digital solutions to make traveling easier, more fuel efficient and more enjoyable!

The group's whole-hearted commitment to eco-design on a daily basis is demonstrated by ISO 14001 certification.

Like you, Michelin is committed to preserving our planet.

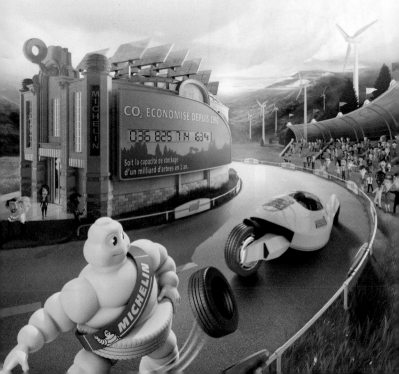

Chat with Bibendum

Go to
www.michelin.com/corporate/en
Find out more about
Michelin's history and the
latest news.

Michelin develops tires for all types of vehicles.
See if you can match the right tire with the right vehicle…

Solution : A-6 / B-4 / C-2 / D-1 / E-3 / F-7 / G-5

NOTES

NOTES

NOTES

Michelin Travel Partner

Société par actions simplifiées au capital de 11 288 880 EUR
27 cours de l'Ile Seguin - 92100 Boulogne Billancourt (France)
R.C.S. Nanterre 433 677 721

No part of this publication may be reproduced in any form
without the prior permission of the publisher.

© Michelin Travel Partner
ISBN 978-2-067190-38-2
Printed: February 2014
Printed and bound in France : Imprimerie CHIRAT, 42540 Saint-Just-la-Pendue - N° 201402.0254

Although the information in this guide was believed by the authors and publisher to be accurate
and current at the time of publication, they cannot accept responsibility for any inconvenience,
loss, or injury sustained by any person relying on information or advice contained in this guide.
Things change over time and travellers should take steps to verify and confirm information,
especially time-sensitive information related to prices, hours of operation, and availability.